MANAGEMENT SCIENCE/ OPERATIONS RESEARCH

MANAGEMENT SCIENCE/ OPERATIONS RESEARCH

ELWOOD S. BUFFA
University of California, Los Angeles

SECOND EDITION

Model Formulation and Solution Methods

JAMES S. DYER
University of Texas, Austin

JOHN WILEY & SONS

New York
Chichester
Brisbane
Toronto

Designer: Judith Fletcher Getman
Production: Ellen P. O'Neill
Cover: John Hite
Copy editor: Rosemary Wellner

Library of Congress Cataloging in Publication Data:

Buffa, Elwood Spencer, 1923–
    Management science/operations research.

    Includes index.
    1. Operations research.   2. Management.   I. Dyer,
James S., joint author.   II. Title.
T57.6.B83   1981   658.4'034   80-18082
ISBN 0-471-05851-3

Printed in the United States of America

10 9 8 7 6 5 4 3 2 1

Elwood S. Buffa is Professor of Management Science and Operations Management at the Graduate School of Management at the University of California, Los Angeles. He received B.S. and M.B.A. degrees at the University of Wisconsin, and a Ph.D. degree from UCLA. He worked as an Operations Analyst at the Eastman Kodak Company in Rochester, New York, before entering the teaching profession, and has served as a consultant in a wide variety of enterprises in situations involving management science analyses. He currently serves on the Board of Directors of Planmetrics, Inc., a planning decision group that develops and installs computer based planning models. He has published many research papers and books in the field of Management Science and Operations Management. Professor Buffa has also held administrative posts as Associate Dean of the Graduate School of Management and Chairman of the Academic Senate at UCLA.

James S. Dyer is Professor of Management at the Graduate School of Business, University of Texas, Austin, where he received his B.A. degree in physics and his Ph.D. degree in business administration. Prior to returning to The University of Texas, he was a member of the faculty of the Graduate School of Management, University of California, Los Angeles.

Dr. Dyer has consulted for such organizations as the RAND Corporation, the Jet Propulsion Laboratory, the Western Interstate Commission on Higher Education (WICHE), Los Alamos Scientific Laboratories, and Standard Oil Company (Indiana). His experience with the Jet Propulsion Laboratory included the use of utility and game theoretic concepts to structure a group decision-making process for the Voyager Project. His articles have appeared in various professional journals, including *Management Science* and *Operations Research,* and he is an associate editor of *Management Science.* He is a member of The Institute of Management Science and of the Operations Research Society of America.

Management Science/Operations Research is intended for use in introductory, undergraduate survey courses in Management Science/Operations Research (MS/OR). It may also be appropriate for similar courses required during the first year of many MBA programs. We presume that the user of the book *does not* intend to specialize in MS/OR; consequently, these students will never be involved in the details of formulating sophisticated mathematical models and obtaining solutions through the use of special purpose algorithms. At one extreme, they may be users of the results of large-scale MS/OR studies. Operating in this role, they must have the following skills:

1. The ability to recognize situations in which MS/OR might be used effectively.
2. The ability to conduct two-way communication with a technical specialist; that is, they must be able to
   a. explain the nature of problems to specialists in a meaningful way, and
   b. understand the specialist's product sufficiently well to verify its appropriateness and potential usefulness.
3. The ability to understand the results of MS/OR studies so that they can obtain full value from the information available from such studies.

At the other extreme, we have students who plan to work in small businesses, where the size of the operations would make it unlikely that a formal MS/OR analysis would ever be performed. For these students, we can provide a way of thinking and organizing information that should aid their "intuitive" decisions. The general concept of model building as an integral part of problem solving is stressed throughout the book. We are convinced that the process of problem definition associated with MS/OR (bound the problem and identify the decision variables, the objective function, and the constraints) can provide a useful conceptual framework for any manager if it is presented properly. We devote considerable attention to this point.

Somewhere between these two extremes are individuals who occasionally encounter relatively small straightforward problems that can be analyzed using MS/OR techniques. Examples are simple inventory problems, project scheduling problems, and even simple resource allocation problems. We would expect the users of this book to be able to formulate models appropriate for analyzing these problems, utilize canned computer programs (perhaps in time-share) to obtain solutions, and evaluate results.

Recognizing the needs of the users of this book is important, since these needs should determine both the content and the level of presentation of materials. For example, such needs seem to stress the importance of model building and formulation skills. At the same time, there is less justification for devoting much space to technical details of algorithms or computer codes. The only apparent reason for introducing such materials would be to remove some of the mystery from the solution strategies and to provide a basis for understanding the limitations of the various approaches.

Thus, we emphasize model building and formulation, and interpretation and use of the results from an analysis. To implement these objectives, transfer to reality is emphasized by giving examples of the use of quantitative methodology in real organizations. Although relatively less emphasis is placed on algorithms, when they are presented an effort is made to provide an intuitively appealing description of the solution process. The mathematical treatment has been kept very light, and no mention is made of theorems or mathematical derivations without a significant pedagogical justification.

Another unique feature of this book is an attempt to provide numerous examples from the public and not-for-profit sectors of the economy. There are several arguments for including these examples. The student can be impressed with the generality of both the techniques and mathematical models by avoiding a series of "maximize profit" or "minimize costs" objective functions. In addition, more and more students entering schools of business administration or management plan to work in the public and not-for-profit sectors. Finally, it is conceivable that the book might be appropriate for use in similar introductory courses that are now evolving in schools of education, public administration, and public health.

We have attempted to organize the materials in a manner that will assist the manager in relating the various models and methods by defining a relationship among evaluation, predictive, and optimization models. We are aware that many instructors will not use the full range of topics provided because of time limitations, the desire for a special focus, or simple personal preference and emphasis of favorite topics. Nevertheless, several scenarios for the use of this book benefit from our organization of the materials and we have isolated four: a basic coverage of MS/OR, a focus on optimizing models, a model-building focus, and a public sector and not-for-profit focus.

For a *basic coverage,* we recommend Chapters 1 and 2 that set the basic rationale for the whole book, and the framework for the model building process; Part II (Optimization Models), Chapters 3, 4, 7, 8, and 10,; Part III (Predicting the Effects of Risk), Chapters 11 through 13; and Part IV (Evaluation Models), Chapter 14.

For a focus on *optimizing models,* we recommend Chapters 1 and 2 plus the entire Part II section, which deals with optimizing models.

For a *model-building focus* that minimizes the exposure to the mathematical details of the techniques of MS/OR, we recommend Chapters 1 and 2; Part II (Optimization Models), Chapters 3, 4, 7, 8, and 9; Part III (Predicting the Effects of Risk), and Chapters 11 and 12, with Chapter 13 optional.

Finally, for a *public and not-for-profit focus,* the issue of the evaluation model becomes critical, and the optimizing models may be relatively less useful. Therefore, we recommend Chapters 1 and 2; Part II (Optimization Models), Chapters 3, 4, and 8; all of Part III (Predicting the Effects of Risk); and all of Part IV (Evaluation Models).

Naturally, other combinations and orderings of the chapters are possible. However, we do recommend that Chapters 1 and 2 always be read first because they present the organizational and conceptual framework for the book and describe the model-building process. We also recommend that the brief introduction to each part of the book be read before assigning any chapters within that part.

MAJOR CHANGES IN THE SECOND EDITION

The primary focus of the book on model formulation and managerial use, and on interpretation of results is as evident in the second edition as it was in the original edition. Nevertheless, there are many major changes in the second edition that are based on our own use of the book, reviewers' comments, and on feedback from adopters of the first edition. We have reorganized the sequence of materials, placing optimization models very early in the outline, made very important additions and changes in the chapters dealing with linear optimization models, improved the presentation in almost all chapters, added short cases to the end-of-chapter materials where appropriate, and deleted chapters where it seemed that the previous materials were not deemed useful by adopters.

Additions and changes to Part II, optimization models We have made major changes and additions to the materials dealing with linear optimization models and linear programming. The initial chapter now has a variety of formulations of linear optimization models of production problems so that students will be exposed to several formulation situations before attempting to apply the process in the problems and short cases. An important new chapter on Applications of Linear Optimization Models (Chapter 4) has been added. This chapter provides a wide range of illustrative model formulations in financial decisions, marketing, personnel planning, and the public and not-for-profit sector. It is our presumption that instructors will wish to be selective in assigning materials to students from among the large number of applications in Chapter 4, depending on the particular emphasis desired. The explanations of the algebraic, Gaussian elimination, and tableau techniques of the simplex method have been unified in Chapter 5. We feel that this unification will be very helpful to students in understanding the simplex algorithm. Finally, Chapter 6, Linear Programming: Special Situations, Sensitivity Analysis, and Duality, is an important new chapter that presents additional technical details. ´

The remaining chapters, 7 through 10, have been edited to improve and clarify the explanations and the managerial emphasis.

Changes in Part III, predicting the effects of risk The materials in Chapter 11, Waiting Line Models, have been edited to provide more intuitive explanations for the waiting time and system time effects of changes in the parameters of queuing systems. Also, the number of problems available at the end of the chapter has been expanded, and a large number of short cases have been added that reflect real-life situations with which students should be able to identify.

The materials in Chapter 12, Monte Carlo Simulation, have been generalized and expanded to include risk analysis and network simulation as well as the simulation of waiting lines. Again, the number of problems and short cases have been expanded. Chapter 13, Markov Chains, has been edited to clarify the basic concepts, but is otherwise unchanged.

Additions and changes to Part IV, evaluation models A new chapter, Chapter 16 has been created to emphasize the importance of the concept of the value of information. This new chapter covers both perfect information and imperfect information, and contains several new examples and situations. To provide space for this new material, the previous chapters on utility theory and multiple criteria have been combined into a single chapter that we feel will be more satisfying to a majority of instructors.

Addition of short cases The text emphasizes the manager's role in model formulation and the interpretation of results. In many problems in the first edition, we emphasized managerial situations with a somewhat fuller managerial setting than might have been necessary for a standard problem. In the second edition, we have expanded these managerial situations into short cases that should help business and management students to identify with the application of management science to real management situations. These short cases are particularly well adapted to classroom use. While they do not present all the background details of the usual case approach, they are efficient. There is so much material that must be presented in MS/OR courses that the longer cases may require too much preparation and classroom time if used to a substantial degree.

Materials deleted We have relunctantly dropped three of the chapters that were included in the first edition: Forecasting Models, Dynamic Structural Models, and Dynamic Programming Models. These decisions were made based on the frequency of use of the materials by adopters in relation to the competition for limited space in the book. The materials are important, but they may be covered in other courses, as if often true of forecasting, or are regarded as somewhat specialized, and therefore reserved for advanced courses.

Elwood S. Buffa
James S. Dyer

ACKNOWLEDGMENTS

The book draws heavily on the literature of Management Science and Operations Research; where specific materials have been used, they are cited. We have benefited greatly from reviews and comments for the first edition by well-known professors such as Linus Schrage, University of Chicago; Steven C. Wheelwright, Stanford University; Robert Winkler, Indiana University; Edwin Shapiro, University of San Francisco; Norman R. Baker, University of Cincinnati; David Goodman, Southern Methodist University; and Ross E. Lanser, San José State University.

The manuscript for the second edition has benefited enormously by feedback from users and by careful reviews at several stages by Professors Thomas W. Bolland, Ohio University; William R. King, University of Pittsburgh; Art Kraft, University of Nebraska–Lincoln; R. Warran Langley, University of Colorado; and Marc Posner, University of Wisconsin–Milwaukee.

January 1981   E.S.B.
                                                                                               J.S.D.

CONTENTS

PART I

Introduction

CHAPTER 1

An Introduction to Management Science

Whether in a private, nonprofit, or public organization, the most important and the distinguishing function of a manager is problem solving. The field of management science is dedicated to aiding managers in their problem-solving efforts. This is accomplished through the use of mathematical models to analyze the problems. We will provide some perspective for understanding the importance of mathematical model building by first considering the problem-solving process.

Much has been written about problem solving and various authors have provided their own descriptions of the problem-solving process. These descriptions tend to be influenced by the experiences and concerns of the individual authors, but they do contain common elements.

Problem solving defined

Just what is problem solving? Certainly it is an activity in which you are successful, or you would not be in a position to read this book. You have solved the basic problems of survival and of education in the modern world, but perhaps you have never explicitly considered what problem solving is all about. Jackson [1974] defines problem solving very simply as "the business of *purposefully* inventing and choosing among ways to get you where you want to go." Perhaps the simplest description of the problem-solving process was provided by John Dewey [1910]:

1. Define the problem
2. Identify the alternatives
3. Select the best alternative

This description seems straightforward enough. The key, of course, is to go through this process in such a manner that the "best" alternative is actually identified and selected. In a similar spirit, Jackson suggests that the most crucial tasks of a problem solver are identifying "things that might be done," determining "ways to anticipate results," and developing "ways to evaluate results." While other authors have elaborated on certain aspects of the problem-solving process and provided suggestions regarding how these tasks might be accomplished, the basic statements are common to most descriptions of the problem-solving process.

The problem-solving process

At this point, it may be helpful to provide some additional detail regarding the problem-solving process. One extended view of this process is provided in Figure 1-1.

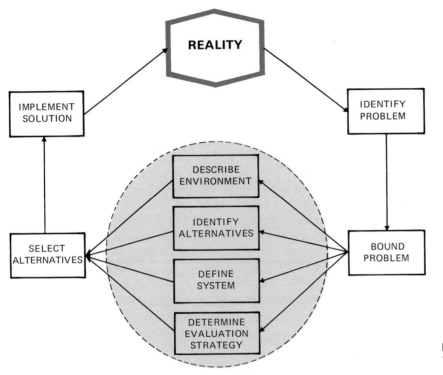

FIGURE 1-1
The problem-solving process

First, the existence of a problem must be recognized. That is, one must observe reality and note that one's perception is not consistent with one's conception of how things ought to be. This recognition may occur because of changes in reality (we choose to ignore the philosophical issues related to the notion of *reality*), because of changes in the individual's perception, or because of changes in his or her notion of what ought to be. This perceived problem may be actually occurring, or the observer may be forecasting a potential problem that will occur unless some action is taken. The individual may also be recognizing an opportunity for improvement.

The reason for this recognition of a problem or of an opportunity for improvement need not concern us here, although we do suggest that the management problem solver take an active role in identifying problems before they become so serious as to create a crisis. Instead, we are more concerned with what to do once a problem or opportunity has been identified.

A problem solver's first task is "bounding" the problem. In essence, you must think about what to think about. The event that created your awareness of a problem may be only a symptom of the actual problem. For example, the event that caused your concern may have been an unusually large number of items out-of-stock in inventory. If you decide to "solve" the problem by focusing your attention on inventory policies, you may overlook the "real problem," which may lie in production scheduling.

As a second example, a problem solver may consider the de facto racial segregation of public schools to be undesirable. While busing or redistricting may provide some racial balance in the schools, the real problem may lie in the housing patterns of individuals and in the concept of the neighborhood school. The long-term solution of this difficult problem may require a strategy focused on issues quite different from the transportation of students.

Certainly the task of bounding a problem is not a trivial one. It may be the most important step in the problem-solving process, since asking the right questions may be the most significant determinant of a successful solution. One way of getting started is the use of an exploratory scenario as suggested by Jackson. The problem solver begins by letting the mind "run loose" and talking about or writing down ideas concerning possible alternatives, their potential effects, obstacles that might be encountered, and so on. In essence, this process is simply an active way of "mulling things over," and clearly requires insight and judgment on the part of the problem solver.

After the problem has been recognized and bounded, the problem solver can begin the other required tasks. Alternative means of dealing with the problem must be devised. There must be an understanding, or definition, of the system and its environment so that the problem solver can predict the effects of implementing alternate solutions. Finally, the problem solver must determine the criteria used to evaluate these different effects.

In some instances, the search for alternate solutions may require a great deal of creativity. New ways of dealing with problems may be sought. In other cases, it may be relatively easy to identify the alternatives because constraints eliminate many courses of action.

The system definition is an attempt to specify how the implementation of an alternative will actually affect the system. That is, if you take a particular action, your system definition should provide the means of predicting the results. In some cases, this system definition may remain implicit and never be verbalized by the problem solver. Managers may indicate that they cannot describe how a particular system behaves, and yet they comfortably predict the effects of different alternatives based on intuition. Unless their intuition is equivalent to a wild guess, they must at least have some gross hypothesis about how things work in their system.

The behavior of the system may also be influenced by some aspects of its environment that cannot be controlled by the problem solver. For example, the profitability of a manufacturer will be influenced by the demand for the product. In order to predict the effects of implementing alternate production plans, the manufacturer must be able to describe the environment in sufficient detail to obtain forecasts of future demand.

Finally, the problem solver must determine a strategy for evaluating the effects of the alternatives. In some cases this strategy will be obvious. If the only effect of the selection of an alternative is on the profits of an organization, the evaluation strategy may be to rank one alternative higher than another if it generates more profit. In other cases involving uncertain or risky effects from the alternatives, or involving multiple effects that must be considered, the determination of the evaluation strategy may not be so straightforward. For example, how would you evaluate alternate plans for deploying ambulances, even if the results from the different alternatives could be forecasted with complete certainty? How would you trade off the cost of the alternative versus the number of lives saved? What is it worth to save another human life? Is your answer different if you know that the person whose life you save will be a rich person or a poor one? A young woman or an old man? A member of your family or a stranger? You? These are difficult questions that have no simple answers acceptable to everyone.

After forecasting the effects of implementing each alternative and determining the evaluation strategy, the problem solver should be in a position to select an alternative. This alternative becomes the solution to the problem that has been identified. One final step remains — the implementation of the solution in the real world.

By now it should be clear why organizations are not being run by the models of management science. Time and again we saw the need for human judgment during our discussion of the problem-solving process. It seems unlikely that machines will ever be created that are sufficiently sensitive to detect all the problems of an organization. Mechanical sensors might very well note changes in the real world or even improve our perception of it. However, the concept of the way the world ought to be is purely artificial and dependent on human judgment. Once a problem has been identified, judgment is required in thinking about what to think about. Obviously, creating alternatives, defining the system, and determining an evaluation strategy all require judgmental inputs. Finally, after an alternative has been selected, only a trivial technological change can be implemented in an organization without involving the manager in the role of change agent.

Where do the models of management science fit into the problem-solving process? The use of these models generally falls into the area within the dashed circle in Figure 1-1. That is, management science models can be used to help forecast what the environment will be like, identify alternatives, provide a system definition that predicts outcomes, and implement an evaluation strategy. The intent of these models is to aid the problem solver in performing these vital tasks in the problem-solving process. Seldom, if ever, do these models actually solve the problem.

MANAGEMENT SCIENCE MODELS

Models and problem solving

As we have seen, the management problem solver has an interest in being able to predict "how things work." One important role of the model is to increase an individual's *understanding* of how things work. This potential for increased understanding should motivate a manager to learn more about model building as an aid to problem solving.

Broadly defined, a model is a device for aiding rational thinking. More specifically, the models we are interested in provide a simplified representation of a complex system or phenomenon. To be helpful in problem solving, a model must include the essential, relevant features of the system being studied.

In order to deal with the complexity of the world, all individuals use models to aid their understanding of the surrounding environment. For example, we have models of certain shapes within our heads that help us to recognize important traffic signs, such as stop signs, from among the multitude of other shapes we perceive in our environment. A model is an economizing device that reduces the infinite number of possibilities to a much smaller, finite number of categories. It ignores much information potentially available to the problem solver and uses categories to collect together many other bits of information that may be considered similar for the process of problem solving. While all stop signs differ at some level of detail, they may all be placed in the same category when determining a driver's behavior.

If a model simplifies a problem solver's view of a problem by leaving out much information and by creating categories, what features must it retain to be useful?

Ideally, a model used for problem solving will include the important features, or elements, of the system under study, as well as the interrelationships among these elements that determine causes and effects. If such a model exists, the problem solver may actually manipulate the elements of the system within the model and observe their effects. Either by trial and error or by using more sophisticated approaches, the problem solver will determine how to adjust these elements so that the resulting impact on the system is consistent with the objectives.

Thus, the managerial problem solver can use such a model, if it exists, to perform experiments and test hypotheses much as a natural scientist uses the laboratory. Because of this similarity, the area of management concerned with model building is often referred to as management science.

Examples of models

Let us now consider three examples of models that have been used in problem solving. Figure 1-2 shows a model of an aircraft in a wind tunnel. The problem being studied is the determination of the appropriate external shape of the aircraft. This model captures the central features of shape very well. However, it does not include important elements of the aircraft, such as the internal workings, that are largely irrelevant to this problem.

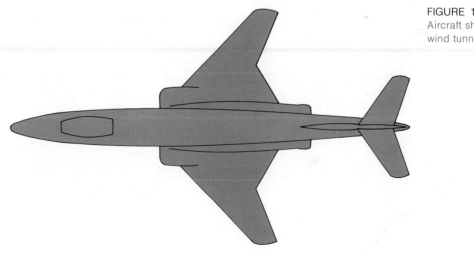

FIGURE 1-2
Aircraft shape in a wind tunnel

Figure 1-3 illustrates a dummy under observation during a staged automobile accident. This model gives the essential features of the behavior of a human body involved in an accident, but detailed physical appearance, skin coloring, and internal workings are omitted because they are irrelevant to the problem being studied.

A third example of a model is provided by the diagram of the problem-solving process shown in Figure 1-1. The problem-solving process is exceedingly complex and may vary from individual to individual according to the person's own unique style. Nevertheless, in Figure 1-1, we have attempted to capture the essential elements of this process in order to solve the problem of organizing our discussion. In so doing we have omitted certain details. For example, the steps in the process are all interdependent. The task of defining the system may affect the range of alternatives that are considered, and vice versa. Similarly, there may be interactions between the

FIGURE 1-3
Automobile-testing
dummy

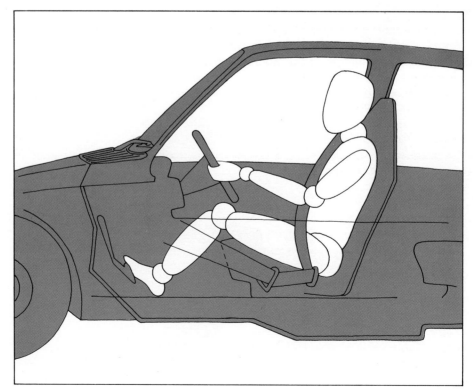

evaluation strategies and the alternatives considered. Thus, this model would be more realistic if arrows were drawn in both directions between all pairs of blocks. However, such arrows would make the drawing extremely messy and would perhaps defeat our purpose of presenting a simplified view of a complex process. In addition, it is important to note that this is not the only model of the problem-solving process that could be drawn. (Try to construct your own.) Nevertheless, this model will have been useful if it aided your understanding of the important aspects of the process.

This same feature of nonuniqueness is common to almost any model of a complex process. Other models, perhaps very different ones, may also be useful in enhancing a problem solver's understanding of a complex process. The danger of model building is that the problem solver will come to regard the model as the problem and forget that it is only one way (generally very limited) of looking at the problem.

Mathematical models

We have been describing models in general. Although any form of a model may be useful to the problem solver, and thus should be encouraged, the field of management science is generally concerned with mathematical models. Why, you may ask, is this so? You may feel that the world is complex enough without hiding it behind a screen of mathematical symbols and notation. However, those who have mastered the language of mathematics (even to a limited extent) find that they can benefit significantly from mathematical models. A mathematical model forces the model builder to make explicit assumptions about the important elements of the problem and the cause-effect relationships that exist within a particular system. Using the logical rules of mathematical analysis, the model builder can check these assumptions and relationships to ensure their internal consistency. The logic of mathematics also provides a means of exploring the consequences of these assumptions. Further, the results of these analyses can be independently verified by others.

Successful applications

Can the mathematical models of management science be applied successfully to real-world problems? The answer is a definite yes. Mathematical models of various kinds are in widespread use, and often provide impressive bottom-line results for managers. Table 1-1 contains a list of some specific applications and a brief summary of their bottom-line impacts. This list is presented here to motivate your interest in the use of mathematical models and to illustrate their wide versatility. Many of the appli-

TABLE 1-1   Illustrative Applications of Management Science Models

Type of Application Company [Ref.]*	Bottom-line Benefits
Integrated profit planning and analysis *British Airways European Division* [1]	Profits up more than 10 million British pounds per year
Integrated materials management *Booth Fisheries* [2]	Finished inventories down 55%, transportation costs down 9%, production costs down 8%, and order fill rate up from 89% to 97%
Production planning (primary metals) *Cerro de Pasco* [3]	Multimillion dollar profit improvement
Debottlenecking a bulk chemical plant *Dart Industries* [4]	$375,000/yr savings with no capital investment
Ingredient blending (stainless steel) *Fagersta AB* [5]	Raw materials savings of $200,000/yr
Inventory policies and deployment *Florida Power & Light Company* [6]	Annual savings approaching $3,300,000
Flight crew scheduling *Flying Tiger Line* [7]	$300,000/yr savings
Financial planning and analysis *Getty Oil Company* [8]	Benefits in the millions
Fleet management *Hertz Rent-A-Car* [9]	Fleet productivity up more than 10%

Source: From A. M. Geoffrion and R. F. Powers, "Management Support Systems," Working Paper No. 287, Western Management Science Institute, UCLA, March 1979; used by permission.

* These reference numbers correspond to the numbered Applications References at the end of this chapter.

cations listed in Table 1-1 are discussed in more detail in subsequent chapters, or appear in the list of "applications references" at the end of the chapter describing the type of model actually applied.

THE MODERN MANAGER AND MANAGEMENT SCIENCE

We have argued that problem solving is the most important function of a manager, that model building is an aid to problem solving, and that the mathematical models of management science are an important special class of models. We hope that you are

Illustrative Applications of Management Science Models	TABLE 1-1 (CONT'D)

Type of Application *Company* [Ref.]*	Bottom-line Benefits
Distribution planning *Hunt-Wesson Foods, Inc.* [10]	Annual savings in the low seven figures
Project selection *Market Compilation Europe* [11]	Major turnaround in profitability
Fuel management and allocation *National Airlines* [12]	Multimillion dollar fuel savings
Resource utilization and allocation *Scott Paper Company* *Packaged Products Division* [13]	Production of 2 million cases per year above the previously understood "maximum"
Production, logistics, and marketing *Swift Chemical Company* [14]	Annual profits up several million dollars
Production and distribution planning *Union Carbide (Chemicals and Plastics)* [15]	Multimillion dollar savings
Sales force management *United Airlines* [16]	Sales agents' productivity up 8%
Distribution operations planning and management *Whirlpool Corporation* [17]	Annual savings "in the millions"
Marketing and production policy analysis *Anonymous manufacturing firm* [18]	Canceled plans to build a new plant, reduced the product line

Source: From A. M. Geoffrion and R. F. Powers, "Management Support Systems," Working Paper No. 287, Western Management Science Institute, UCLA, March 1979; used by permission.

* These reference numbers correspond to the numbered Applications References at the end of this chapter.

persuaded that you should learn something about the field of management science. Yet we do not feel that you should be subjected to a detailed discussion of mathematical techniques and theories, but believe that you should learn enough about the field so that you will be in a position to use effectively the models and techniques that are available in real-world situations.

We will presume that the typical reader of this book does not intend to specialize in management science and become a professional in this field. Thus, it seems unlikely that you will ever be involved in the details of formulating sophisticated mathematical models and obtaining solutions through the use of special-purpose computer programs. At one extreme, you may be the user of the results of large-scale management science studies. Operating in this role, you should have the following skills:

1. The ability to recognize situations in which management science might be used effectively.

2. The ability to conduct two-way communication with a technical specialist; that is, you must be able to
   a. explain the nature of your problem to a specialist in a meaningful way and
   b. understand the specialist's product sufficiently well to verify its appropriateness and potential usefulness.

3. The ability to understand the results of management science studies so that you can obtain full value from the information available.

At the other extreme, you may find yourself working in a small business. The size of the operation would make it unlikely that a formal management science analysis would ever be performed. Nevertheless, the models of management science provide a way of thinking and of organizing information that should aid your intuitive decision making. One of the most powerful aids in problem solving is the use of analogies. A justification for the case method in management education is the expectation that the graduate, when faced with a real-world problem, will be able to say, "Aha, this problem is similar to the problem faced by the company in the XYZ case. With only a few modifications, the analysis and solution for that case may apply here." Similarly, by gaining an exposure to the models of management science, managers may be able to recognize a problem as being similar to those analyzed using a particular management science technique. This recognition should be helpful in identifying the data needed and in exploring possible alternate solutions.

Somewhere between these two extremes, managers may be in a position in which relatively small, straightforward problems are encountered that can be solved by management science techniques. The manager should be able to formulate models appropriate for analyzing these problems, utilize standard computer programs written by others to obtain solutions, and interpret the results.

In each of these contexts, the manager should have the ability to recognize problems that can be analyzed by using management science models and should have some model formulation skills. Therefore, we will present numerous examples of models throughout this book and attempt to explain the process of thought that developed these formulations. To avoid extraneous details, the initial presentations of these example formulations will be in the context of "toy" problems that we have created to illustrate certain points. We then will discuss examples of real-world implementations of management science models and techniques and attempt to examine their significance critically. At the same time, we will emphasize the interpretation of the results obtained from these models and attempt to point out where managerial discretion and judgment must be used to provide a meaningful interpretation in the real world.

We will avoid devoting a great deal of time to the technical details of the mathematical analyses associated with the different management science models. Nevertheless, managers should have some idea how these analyses are performed. This knowledge is important to understanding both the power and the potential limitations of these techniques. Further, such understanding will help remove the mystique often associated with the "black box" known as the computer, and should increase the manager's self-confidence in challenging and analyzing the results that pour from it. In order to obtain this understanding, it will be necessary for you to work through some small examples by hand. Please keep in mind while you are pushing the pencil that these exercises are not suggested because they are "good for you" per se, or because we expect that you will actually be performing similar analyses by hand in your position as a manager. You should concentrate on understanding what each technique is doing in a substantive sense. What kinds of results are being generated, and how do these results follow from your formulations of the problem? Although we will attempt to help you in gaining this insight, it will require careful reflection on your part.

PLAN OF THE BOOK

We have seen that management science is primarily concerned with those aspects of problem solving related to identifying alternatives, understanding "how things work," and evaluating the predicted effects of implementing alternatives. Each different mathematical model of management science may focus on one or more of these aspects. Therefore, it is helpful to categorize these models according to their primary functions.

Figure 1-4 provides more detail regarding the items in the circle in Figure 1-1. There are several kinds of models represented in Figure 1-4. First, we may wish to predict, or forecast, the status of the environment. These forecasts are generally concerned with the demand on the system for its product and they are based on models that are usually statistical in nature. Forecasting models are a specialty in themselves

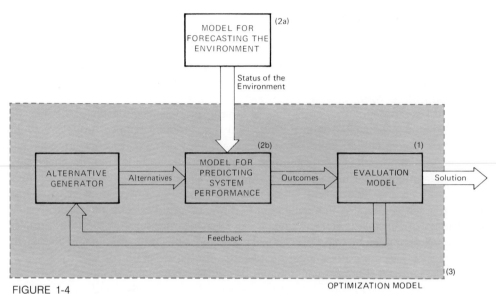

FIGURE 1-4
Models of management science

and are not covered in this book; however, discussions of these important models are available in Benton [1972], or Makridakis and Wheelwright [1978]. The forecasting model is shown as being outside the system in Figure 1-4. The system under study is enclosed by a dashed line.

Given the forecast, we need a model that predicts how the system reacts to changes in the environment and to changes in the alternate decisions being considered by a manager. Essentially, this is a model of how the system works when it transforms alternate decisions into outputs when given a specific forecast of the environment. This predictive model is represented by Box 1 in Figure 1-4.

In Chapter 2 we will discuss the basic concepts of mathematical model building and illustrate these concepts by creating predictive models of how systems work. We will make the notion and definition of a *system* more precise, and see how a mathematical model may be used to provide this system definition and become a model for predicting system performance. We will illustrate how the familiar break-even model may be viewed as a predictive model. We then provide several real-world examples of the actual use of predictive models in the form of large-scale corporate planning models in private, public, and not-for-profit organizations.

When an outcome is predicted by the model represented by Box 1, how is it evaluated? This may actually require another model, as indicated by Box 2 in Figure 1-4. When the outcome from each alternative is known with complete certainty and it involves only a single criterion, such as profit, the manager's evaluation may be simple and direct. For example, the manager may be seeking the alternative that maximizes profit, or perhaps the alternative that minimizes costs.

The predictive model in Box 1 transforms the forecasts of the environment and the statement of an alternative into a predicted outcome. This outcome is then evaluated by the model in Box 2. But how are the alternatives generated? They may be simply the specific ones that the manager wishes to compare, based on experience with the particular system and the particular situation that raises the current issues. Also, the manager may draw on technical specialists to suggest reasonable alternatives that should be analyzed.

In some situations, however, we can systematically consider all possible alternatives and choose the optimal or "best" alternative in terms of the evaluation model. Such a modeling system considers alternative 1, predicts its outcome in Box 1, and evaluates the outcome in Box 2 as before. The difference is in the *feedback* of information about the evaluation of the alternative shown in Figure 1-4. With the information feedback, the alternative generator automatically generates a new alternative by the rules of mathematical analysis, repeating the prediction and evaluation steps. The cycle is repeated in a way that scans the entire set of feasible alternatives. When all of these submodels are combined in this manner we have an *optimization* model, indicated by the dashed line that encloses the alternative generator, predictive model, and evaluation model, and labeled Box 3 in Figure 1-4.

The optimization models of management science are the most powerful and exciting models available to the manager. These models are surveyed in Part II of this book, and build on the modeling concepts presented in Chapter 2. We cover several types of optimization models: linear optimization models and linear programming in Chapters 3 through 6, network models in Chapters 7 and 8, optimization models that may restrict some variables to integer values in Chapter 9, and inventory models in Chapter 10. It will be important for you to understand the characteristics of problems that can be analyzed using these methods, the manner in which these models are formulated, and the way the associated mathematical analysis produces a solution.

As you will see, the optimization models of management science are primarily suited for applications where the outcomes from alternate decisions can be predicted with certainty. When risk and uncertainty are introduced into a problem it may be impossible or impractical to formulate an optimization model to analyze it. In these more complicated cases, managers may be satisfied if they can simply *predict* the effects of risk on the outcomes associated with their alternatives, and even these predictions may be expressed in terms of probabilities. In Part III we consider predictive models that explicitly include risk and uncertainty. These models are generally required when we are unable to control the effects of the environment on our system or forecast them with certainty. Many of the predictive models incorporating risk are based on the fields of waiting line theory, Monte Carlo simulation, and Markov chains as described in Chapters 11, 12, and 13.

When risks are associated with the outcomes, the problem of evaluating these outcomes becomes more difficult as well. Similarly, the introduction of multiple criteria such as profit and market share, or cost and social responsibility, may require a more elaborate analysis focused on the evaluation of alternatives. Evaluation models can be developed based on a field of management science known as decision theory. An understanding of decision theory can be a very practical aid to a manager, even when the required mathematical calculations are made on the back of an envelope rather than on a computer.

Part IV is devoted to the development of the appropriate evaluation models for risky decisions and for decisions with multiple criteria. In Chapter 14 we examine how the "expected value" of outcomes may be used effectively in making risky decisions, and we construct decision trees to represent risky alternatives and to evaluate them. In Chapter 15 we show how to take into account the manager's attitude toward risky decisions by constructing utility functions. These same ideas can also be applied to the problem of reconciling multiple criteria. Finally, in Chapter 16 we consider how to place a monetary value on new information that might be used to reduce or eliminate the risk in a problem.

Most of the book deals with the formulation, solution methods, and managerial interpretation of the kinds of models we have just discussed. But when should management science be used? What are its benefits versus costs, its conceptual value, and how does one choose an appropriate model? We synthesize these issues in Chapter 17.

Appendixes A and B present the rudiments of probability theory and statistics that are necessary to understand the materials included in the text. These appendixes provide a convenient review and reference. Readers who seek a "refresher" in these topics should study them carefully before proceeding. Others may prefer to consult some basic programmed textbooks such as those offered by Martin [1969a, 1969b], and Mason [1970, 1971].

CHECK YOUR UNDERSTANDING

1. Consider each of the following hypothetical situations:
   a. Suppose you are an urban planner who has been involved in the study of a large-scale, sociotechnical system, such as a rapid transit system. What would you consider to be the most important phase of the problem-solving process (refer to Figure 1-1)?
   b. Suppose you are an architect who must design a new building. Again referring to Figure 1-1, what do you consider to be the most important phase of the design process?

2. Are there fundamental differences in the problem-solving processes followed by an urban planner and an architect, or are there only different emphases on phases of the process? Discuss.

3. Select a problem of personal interest to you, such as the choice of a career, the purchase of a new car, or the travel plans for your vacation. Create an exploratory scenario by listing possible alternatives, potential effects of alternatives, obstacles that might be encountered, and so on. Intermix these items while letting your mind "run loose." Did you gain any additional insights into the problem?

4. Although you will be able to sharpen the definition of the following terms as you proceed through the book, on the basis of the discussion in this chapter, define:
   a. predictive model
   b. evaluation model
   c. optimization model
   What are the relationships among them?

5. Are the models of the aircraft in Figure 1-2 and of the dummy in Figure 1-3 examples of evaluation, predictive, or optimization models? Explain.

6. List three examples of problems you may be required to solve in following your own career plans. For each example, discuss how a model might be a potential aid. What do you need to know about the models of management science?

GENERAL REFERENCES

Benton, W. K., *Forecasting for Management*, Addison-Wesley Publishing Co., Reading, Mass., 1972.
Dewey, J., *How We Think*, D. C. Heath, 1910.

Geoffrion, A. M., and R. F. Powers, "Management Support Systems," Working Paper No. 287, Western Management Science Institute, UCLA, Los Angeles, Calif., 1979.

Jackson, J. R., "Coping with Complexity," mimeographed, Graduate School of Management, University of California, Los Angeles, 1974.

Martin, E. W., *Mathematics for Decision Making: A Programmed Basic Text,* Vols. 1 and 2, Richard D. Irwin, Inc., Homewood, Ill., 1969a.

———, *Programmed Learning Aid for Basic Algebra,* Learning Systems Company, Homewood, Ill., 1969b.

Makridakis, S., and S. C. Wheelwright, *Forecasting Methods and Applications,* John Wiley & Sons, New York, 1978.

Mason, R. D., *Programmed Learning Aid for Business and Economic Statistics,* Learning Systems Company, Homewood, Ill., 1970.

———, *Programmed Learning Aid for College Mathematics,* Learning Systems Company, Homewood, Ill., 1971.

APPLICATIONS REFERENCES

Loughran, B., and P. Cocks, "Airline Programme Planning in British Airways European Division," *Interfaces,* Vol. 7, No. 2, February 1977.

Jaikumar, R., and U. Rau, "An On-Line Integrated Materials Management System," *Interfaces,* Vol. 7, No. 1, November 1976. Also private communication from K. Molenkamp (VP), October 1978.

Lietaer, B., "A Corporate Short Term Planning Model: A Case Study in the Non-Ferrous Metal Industry," Chap. 2 in H. Salkin and J. Saha (eds.), *Studies in Linear Programming,* North-Holland, 1975.

Personal communication from J. Del Favero (President of the Chemical Plastics Group) and O. K. Smith (Director of Operations Research) of Dart Industries, October 1978.

Westerberg, C., B. Bjorklund, and E. Hultman, "An Application of Mixed Integer Programming in a Swedish Steel Mill," *Interfaces,* Vol. 7, No. 2, February 1977.

Spechler, J., and F. Swendeman, "Applications of a Computerized Materials Distribution Planning Model to a Major Electric Utility," *1977 NCPDM Conference Proceedings.* Also personal communication from F. Swendeman, October 1978.

Marsten, R., M. Muller, and C. Killion, "Crew Planning at Flying Tiger: A Successful Application of Integer Programming," *Management Science,* Vol. 25, No. 12, December 1979, pp. 1175–1183. Also personal communication from M. Muller, September 1978.

Cooper, D. O., L. B. Davidson, and W. K. Denison, "A Tool for More Effective Financial Analysis," *Interfaces,* Vol. 5, No. 2, February 1975.

Edelstein, M., and M. Melnyk, "The Pool Control System," *Interfaces,* Vol. 8, No. 1, November 1977.

Geoffrion, A., "Better Distribution Planning with Computer Models," *Harvard Business Review,* July–August 1976.

Kalvaitis, R., and A. G. Posgay, "An Application of Mixed Integer Programming in the Direct Mail Industry," *Management Science,* Vol. 20, No. 5, January 1974.

Darnell, D. W., and C. Loflin, "National Airlines Fuel Management and Allocation Model," *Interfaces,* Vol. 7, No. 2, February 1977.

Cramer, R., "Modern Approaches to Distribution Planning/Management," 1978 NCPDM Annual Conference presentation. See also page 7 of Scott Paper Company's Annual Report of 1974.

Reddy, J., "A Model to Schedule Sales Optimally Blended from Scarce Resources," *Interfaces,* Vol. 6, No. 1, November 1975.

"Production and Distribution Planning System," IBM Application Brief GK20-0898-0, Data Processing Division, 1133 Westchester Ave., White Plains, N.Y. 10604.

Fudge, W., and L. Lodish, "Evaluation of the Effectiveness of a Model-Based Salesman's Planning System by Field Experimentation," *Interfaces,* Vol. 8, No. 1, November 1977. Also personal communication from L. Lodish, October 1978.

Sterling, J., "What If . . . ?," *Distribution Worldwide,* May 1976. Also personal communication from J. Crouse (VP), October 1978.

Byrd, Jr., J., and L. T. Moore, "The Application of a Product Mix Linear Programming Model in Corporate Policy Making," *Management Science,* Vol. 24, No. 13, September 1978.

CHAPTER 2

Mathematical
Model
Building

FIGURE 2-1
Input-transformation-output module as a basis for predictive models

Mathematical models are commonly used to analyze the behavior of a system. These models are designed to predict the outcomes of alternate courses of action. The alternatives may be generated in some systematic manner that attempts to exhaust the feasible alternatives, or they may be hypotheses for what a manager thinks could be a good strategy. The alternatives may be viewed as inputs being transformed by the predictive model into a set of outcomes. This transformation of alternatives into outcomes may be influenced by the nature of the environment.

Predicting system performance

We can view the problem of predicting system performance in the context of any productive process as indicated in Figure 2-1. We have input, process or transformation, and output in the general format of systems theory. Figure 2-1 simply says that, given an input to a process, that input will be transformed in some way to produce an output.

First, let us take a physical process such as steel making with an electric furnace. As shown in Figure 2-2(a), the inputs are basically iron ore, coke, limestone, and labor, and the output is steel. Between input and output there was a transformation process that we have called an electric furnace. We could replace "electric furnace" with a mathematical transformation function in order to compute output for given inputs. Suppose we are interested in output *quantity*. The transformation function would then be a simple mathematical statement of the tons of steel output for given quantities of the inputs. The mathematical transformation is a predictive model for output, given stated inputs. Now suppose you are a metallurgist, and your interest is in the transformation of the inputs into certain *qualities* of steel alloys. In this case, the metallurgist's transformation function is in terms of the recipe and timing necessary to obtain the output of a specific alloy, rather than the quantity of output. Your predictive model has a different purpose and is expressed in different units, but it is still a model that indicates how a system works.

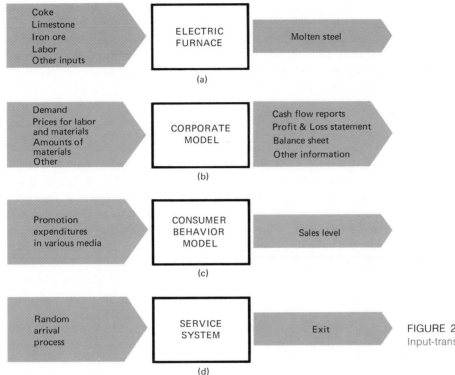

FIGURE 2-2
Input-transformation-output modules

Now let us expand our thinking to include a more highly aggregated system. The system is now an economic enterprise with inputs of consumer demand, labor, materials, and other costs, and the outputs are predictions of cash flow, profit and loss, balance sheet, and other information of interest. The transformation of input to output is accomplished by the enterprise itself, but we will substitute a model for the enterprise, which gives the equivalent transformations. We show the corporate model as a predictive model in Figure 2-2(b). Such corporate models are now in common use in industry and in some service and government operations as mechanisms for predicting performance, given stated inputs. Managers can use such models to test the effects of possible changes in demand, prices, wages, market structures, new equipment, and so on.

Obviously, we can now see that predictive models can be of any type. In Figure 2-2(c), we show a model of consumer behavior that might be developed to indicate the effect on sales of expenditures for promotion in various media. In Figure 2-2(d), we show a service system model in which people arrive at the service window of a bank or post office, probably randomly. Since the time for service is itself variable, depending on many factors, there may be some interacting effects on the size of the waiting line and waiting time that will result. These examples indicate the variety of the systems that can be analyzed with mathematical models.

Components of a model for predicting system performance

Variables We often speak of the *variables* within a mathematical model. These are the elements of the model that can take on different values. An *alternative* is expressed as a particular set of values for these variables. For example, suppose we model a physical process such as steel making with an electric furnace [Figure 2-2(a)]. The variables in this model would be the quantities of ore, coke, limestone, and labor that are used. An alternative would consist of specific values for these variables. That is, we would identify an alternative by specifying the exact quantities of ore, coke, limestone, and labor to be used. These variables are often called *decision variables* or *controllable variables,* since their values can be determined by the decision maker.

Parameters The *parameters* of a model are the known entities not directly controllable by the decision maker. Some parameters may be determined by the nature of the environment. For a specific set of assumptions regarding the environment, these parameters are constants. However, they may vary as the environment changes. These parameters are often called *uncontrollable variables* to indicate that they do vary with the environment but are not controlled by the decision maker. The values of some of these uncontrollable variables are determined from forecasting models.

Other parameters are known and are not affected by the environment. They may be determined by physical laws and always maintain constant values in the model no matter how the environment may change.

The corporate model discussed in connection with Figure 2-2(b) included costs of labor and materials as essential elements. These parameters would be considered uncontrollable variables, since the company cannot directly manipulate their values. For a given set of assumptions regarding the environment, these values will be determined within the model.

In the steel-making example, the number of pounds of steel produced from quantities of iron ore and scrap is determined by the physical laws of a specific technology.

It does not change at the discretion of the decision maker, and it is not influenced by the environment. Thus, parameters reflecting these physical laws would be included in the model.

Logical relationships The logical relationships in a mathematical model are explicit statements regarding how the system actually functions. They are cause-effect relationships among the variables and parameters of the model. For example, we might write

$$I_t = I_{t-1} + P_t - D_t$$

to indicate that the inventory of a product at the end of time period t, I_t, equals the inventory at the end of period $t-1$, I_{t-1}, plus the production of the product in period t, P_t, minus the demand for the product in period t, D_t. This is a mathematical statement of a simple accounting relationship.

Other logical relationships place upper and lower limits on the values of variables or on mathematical expressions involving several variables. For example, we might write

$$P_{t-1} + P_t \geq 100$$

to indicate that the production in time period $t-1$ plus the production in time period t must be greater than or equal to 100. The production levels are variables in this expression, while the number 100 is a particular value for the two-period production level parameter. Other logical relationships may involve probabilistic statements.

In some mathematical models, most notably the optimization models to be discussed in Part II, these logical relationships are called *constraints*.

The purpose of a model for predicting system performance

Commonly, the manager will play the role of alternative generator for a model for predicting system performance. In this role, the manager will specify values of the decision variables in the model. In addition, the manager will specify some scenario regarding the nature of the environment in which the system will be operating. The specification of this scenario must be sufficiently detailed to provide information to any forecasting models used to determine the parameters of the model for predicting system performance. In some cases, values may be assigned to these parameters subjectively based on the manager's implicit forecasting model for the environment.

Given this information, the model should predict the outputs of the system that would be created if the same alternative were actually chosen under identical environmental conditions in the real world. These outcomes would then be evaluated by the manager, perhaps using one of the evaluation models discussed in Part IV.

Notice that the manager has the option of analyzing many different alternatives under the same environmental assumptions or of analyzing the same alternative under many environmental assumptions. If the logical relationships are computerized, the process of making these analyses can be greatly simplified.

CREATING A MODEL FOR PREDICTING SYSTEM PERFORMANCE

Creating a useful mathematical model for predicting system performance is not a trivial task in a complex, real-world environment. Nevertheless, the investment of time and effort, especially by the manager who will eventually use the model, can lead to significant benefits. We now consider how such a model might be constructed. In order to provide a concrete reference for this discussion, we illustrate the concepts by developing a simple model for break-even analysis. It is important to emphasize that our interest here is on the model-building procedure rather than on the break-even analysis per se.

Initial formulation

Getting started Suppose a manager recognizes a problem and believes that a model for predicting system performance might be useful. The first task is to *bound* the problem by identifying as specifically as possible those questions to be answered by the model.

For example, suppose the manager of a small manufacturing firm that produces one item is having difficulty determining a proper pricing strategy and in forecasting profits or losses. A mathematical model might be useful in dealing with this task. The problem could be bounded by identifying the following set of initial questions that the manager would like to have assistance in answering:

1. For a given set of costs, production, and price figures, what will my profit or loss be?

2. What will be the effect on profits (or losses) if I change my price, given that costs and demand remain constant?

3. How will my profit or loss be affected if demand changes?

4. What if my variable costs of production increase? How will my profit or loss change?

Notice that such a list of questions should be provided by the manager who will actually be *using* the system. It should not be generated by a professional analyst on the basis of what he or she thinks the manager should want. The responsibility for such a list falls on the manager, and developing the list is most important in ensuring that a mathematical model created for the manager will actually be used. Thus, the manager needs to have the proper expectations regarding the types of questions on which legitimate help can be expected from a mathematical model.

Identifying the important elements The model builder must now abstract from the real world those essential elements of the system relevant to answering the questions posed by the manager. As illustrated in Figure 2-3, this process is one of *simplification* of the complexity of the real world.

The circles in Figure 2-3 indicate elements in the real world to be represented by

FIGURE 2-3
Modeling as a simplification of the real world

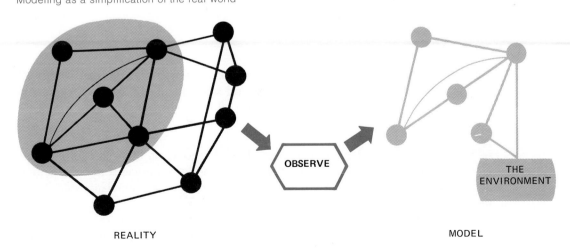

REALITY   MODEL

variables and parameters in the model. The lines between the circles suggest that the connected elements are interdependent in some fashion, and this interdependence could be specified using logical relationships. Finally, the shaded area places bounds on the problem in the real world. It is the task of the model builder to observe this reality and to abstract a simplified model.

In our example, it is clear that the questions posed by the manager can be answered by considering the internal workings of one company, and then only its financial aspects. The linkage of this company to its environment will be through the demand for the product produced by the company. From studying the questions, it seems that the profit (or loss) of a company is determined by the relationship between revenues and costs.

Determine logical relationships Next, the model builder must hypothesize the logical relationships among these elements to create the model. In some cases, these relationships may be based on empirical data, while in other cases we can only appeal to the criterion of "reasonableness." In our example, we know that

Profit (loss) = revenues − costs

which is a mathematical statement of the logical relationship among these elements.

This simple mathematical relation serves as our initial formulation of a model for predicting system performance. What have we learned from this model? It is clear from an analysis of this model that

1. if revenues increase, so do profits, or
2. if costs decrease, profits increase.

Further, this interpretation of the results seems reasonable in the real world. Although these statements may seem trivial and self-evident, the basic concepts employed in the more elaborate model building efforts in the real world are essentially the same.

Adding more detail We have begun with a simple model as our initial formulation. However, we do not have sufficient detail in this model to answer some of the questions posed by the manager. For example, we do not have logical relationships in the model that determine the effects of price, demand, and variable costs on revenues and total costs. Therefore, we must add more detail to the model.

First, let us consider the revenues in the model. Revenues are generated by selling items at a particular price. Therefore, the sales price and the number of items sold must be important elements in our model. The specific relationship among revenues, price, and items sold is

Revenues = (price)(items sold)

We can use some simple mathematical notation to condense this model, defining p as the price per unit of our product and x as the number of units produced and sold. Now, we have the expression

Revenues = px

to summarize this relationship. This expression is a logical relationship written in algebraic form.

The costs are a bit more complicated. First we have the costs of being in business, the fixed costs. These include rent or lease payments, license fees, and other costs that must be met even if we do not produce a single item. Next, there are the costs of doing business, the variable costs. These costs include expenditures for labor and raw materials and are influenced by the number of units we produce. Mathematically, the logical relationship dealing with costs is written

Total costs = fixed costs + (variable costs per unit)(number of units sold)

This logical relationship adds the fixed costs to the variable costs, which are determined by the product of the variable costs per unit produced times the number of units produced and sold. Now, let us simplify this expression by defining f as the fixed costs and c as the variable costs per unit sold. Then, the total costs equal $f + cx$.

We can now replace the elements of revenues and costs in our original model and obtain a new model with additional detail:

Profit (loss) = $px - (f + cx)$

Now, do we have sufficient detail in the model shown in Figure 2-4? Perhaps so. The manager may substitute values for the elements of this model and determine profit or loss. Simultaneously, the manager may answer the other questions that are posed.

Bootstrapping We use the term *bootstrapping* to refer to a strategy of model formulation based on beginning with a simple model and adding detail. We have illustrated

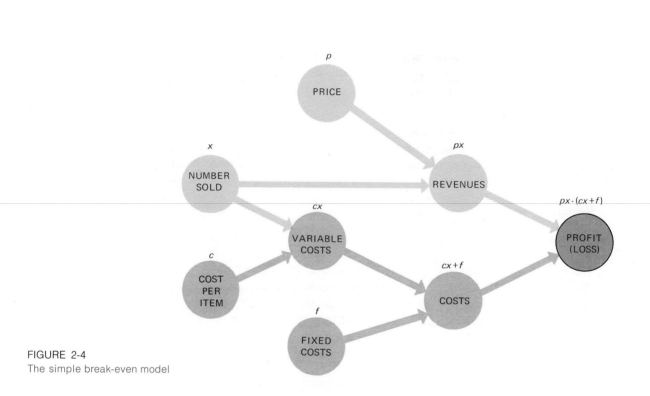

FIGURE 2-4
The simple break-even model

this strategy with the simple break-even model, and it is a most important strategy in real-world applications.

Specialists in management science and operations research are often tempted to study a problem, then go off in isolation to develop an elaborate mathematical model for use by the manager. Unfortunately, the manager may not understand this model and may either use it blindly or reject it entirely. The specialist may feel that the manager is too ignorant and unsophisticated to appreciate the model, while the manager may feel that the specialist lives in a dream world of unrealistic assumptions and irrelevant mathematics.

Such difficulty can be avoided if the manager works with the specialist to develop first a simple model that provides a crude but understandable analysis. After the manager has built up confidence in this model, additional detail and sophistication can be added, perhaps only a bit at a time. This process requires an investment of time on the part of the manager and sincere interest on the part of the specialist in solving the manager's real problem, rather than in playing with sophisticated models.

However, a bootstrapping approach to model building seems to be one of the most important factors in determining the successful implementation of a mathematical model. This approach also simplifies the difficult task of validating the model.

The appropriate level of detail The creation of a mathematical model is still very much an art instead of a science. Although there are a number of generally accepted rules of thumb, there is no simple list of steps that will lead automatically to a successful model. The objective of modeling is to obtain the benefits of a mathematical model at a relatively low cost. Naturally, the benefits from a model will increase, other things being equal, as the level of detail in the model increases to provide an improved representation of reality. Unfortunately, the costs of modeling also increase, since more detail requires more information and a heavier computation burden. The art of modeling requires trading off the benefits of an increased level of detail against their associated increases in the costs of information and computation.

Since the technology will be available to construct and use more detailed models, the greatest bottleneck may be the ability of the manager to understand these more sophisticated models. On the one hand, this emphasizes the importance of boot-strapping as an approach to model development. On the other hand, it emphasizes the need for managers to study and understand the basic concepts of management science so that they will be able to use the powerful decision-making aids that are available to them.

Validation of the model

The next task is to validate the model. The objectives of this task are to ensure that the model accurately predicts the outcomes of alternatives and to simultaneously increase the manager's confidence in the model.

There are two potential dangers in not adequately validating a mathematical model. The first is that the manager will be so impressed by the elegance and sophistication of the mathematical model and its computer printouts that he or she will never question whether the basic assumptions on which it depends are actually sound. A mathematical model may be precisely wrong, and we often mistakenly believe that one who thinks elaborately thinks well.

At the other extreme, the manager may not have sufficient confidence in the mathematical model to actually rely on it. Most individuals prefer a simple, crude analysis they can understand to a sophisticated analysis they cannot comprehend.

Reasonableness criterion The validation should consider the internal logic of the model as determined by the logical relationships. All the assumptions on which these relationships were based should be specified and made known to the manager. The logic of the model should reflect the manager's view of the real world and not the analyst's view. For example, analysts often assume that the variables in the model are related by linear rather than nonlinear relationships. Although this assumption is valid in many real-world situations, in others it may seriously distort the model.

A second issue is the validity of the data used in the model. Forecasting models may be required to provide values for some of the parameters. These data sources should also be scrutinized.

Finally, the model must be run several times to ensure that the logical relationships and the mathematical analysis were correctly programmed in the computer. The model may be restricted by fixing many of the decision variables and logical relationships so that the appropriate answer will be obvious, or at least can be calculated by an experienced staff analyst. Then the results of the model can be compared against those obtained by hand. The source of any discrepancies should then be identified, whether it be errors in the basic assumptions, the logical relationships, the input data, or a bug in the computer program.

Predictive criterion A second approach is to match the model against past history. The actual data used in prior time periods in the real-world system that the model is to represent can be put into the model, and the outcomes can be compared. Again, it should be possible to justify any discrepancies that occur.

Thus, validation requires that we manipulate the model and compare the results with what has happened (or what we would expect to happen) in the real world. This process may cause us to revise the model until we are satisfied with the results.

Figure 2-5 illustrates that the initial model formulation is compared against the real world. In this example, additional logical relationships are identified in the revised model in order to represent reality more closely.

The break-even analysis model should be validated by questioning whether the basic assumptions are appropriate. For example, we have assumed that costs consist of a variable component, and a fixed component that remains constant no matter what the level of production actually is. In a real-world situation, a more elaborate cost model would probably be required.

Analysis

A model for predicting system performance is analyzed by exploring the structure and behavior of the model as a consequence of the initial assumptions and the logical

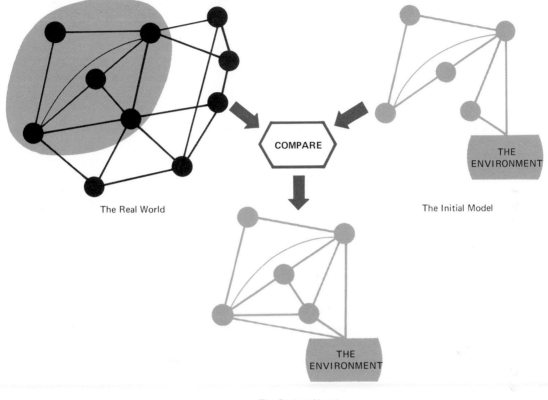

The Real World

The Initial Model

COMPARE

THE ENVIRONMENT

THE ENVIRONMENT

The Revised Model

FIGURE 2-5
Revision of a model

relationships. This analysis is "objective" in the sense that it can be verified or repudiated on the basis of logical arguments alone.

Let us consider an example of analysis based on the break-even model. The manager may ask, "What if my fixed costs are $2000 per week, my price is $30 per unit, my variable costs are $15 per unit, and I sell 300 units per week? What will my profit or loss be?" We can use the break-even model to calculate the profit or loss using the logic of mathematical analysis. Substituting for the decision variables and parameters, we have

$$f = 2000 \qquad c = 15$$
$$p = 30 \qquad x = 300$$

Using the logical relationship, we obtain

$$\text{Profit (loss)} = (30)(300) - (15)(300) - 2000$$
$$= 9000 - 4500 - 2000 = 2500$$

Thus the profit in this situation would be $2500 per week.

In addition to the probationary exercises to validate a model, Geoffrion [1976] suggests a series of computer runs. These include the following:

1. *Base case runs.* The model should be run with several future scenarios for the organization.

2. *Sensitivity analysis.* Additional runs should be made to test the sensitivity of the model to any questionable assumptions made in the model. The objective is to learn if these assumptions have significantly affected the results from the model. Other runs can be made to test the sensitivity of the results to the values of key parameters.

3. *"What if" questions.* Managers may wish to explore basic questions of interest to them such as, "What if a new competitor enters the market?" or "What if we suffer a strike that lasts for *n* weeks?" or "What if fuel shortages reduce our effective trucking capacity by 10 percent?"

Interpretation

Once the model has been analyzed and the results have been obtained, the manager must *interpret* their meaning back in the real world. In the few cases where the model captures the problem perfectly, interpretation may be a straightforward task. More commonly, the model is not a perfect fit, so the results of the analysis may require careful scrutiny, since the best solution for the model may not be the best solution for the real-world problem.

Formulation is a process of simplification or extraction from the real world. During interpretation, the manager must reconsider the results from the mathematical anal-

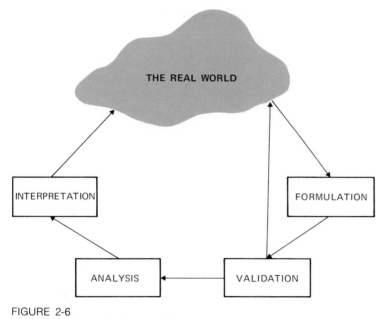

FIGURE 2-6
The steps of mathematical modeling

ysis in the context of the complexities omitted or ignored during formulation because of intangibility or technical difficulties. The results may need to be modified to allow for other considerations. Returning to the break-even model, the manager finds from the analysis that a weekly profit of $2500 could be realized if 300 units per week are sold at a price of $30. Can 300 units per week actually be sold at this price, since the model provides the profit calculation only for successful sale of these units? Could more than 300 units be sold at this price, or could 300 units be sold at an even higher price? These issues must be confronted before the results of the analysis are implemented in the real world.

The basic steps of model building are illustrated in Figure 2-6. Model formulation and interpretation of the results of analysis require skill and insight on the part of a manager. Once the relatively straightforward tools of mathematical analysis are understood and available to a manager, formulation and interpretation become the intellectually challenging activities.

COMPUTER-BASED CORPORATE SIMULATION MODELS

Computer-based corporate simulation models are a particular kind of predictive model. These models have been well received by practicing managers, partly because *the model itself makes no pretense of making managerial decisions.* Instead, these models represent the financial or other flows of an enterprise and can therefore be queried with *what if* questions by managers. Since the models simulate the enterprise, a range of hypotheses concerning prices, volume, various costs, and so on can be tested to form a sound planning base. The models provide answers to questions asked, but the manager retains the traditional role as decision maker.

Computer-based corporate models have commonly been developed in computer interactive mode to facilitate a "manager active" situation in which results from one query may stimulate new questions. We have then an extremely powerful combination of decision maker and predictive model in a loop. Very complex computations reflecting assumptions about volume, price, costs, or the effects of a labor dispute, can be handled in a short turnaround time as low as a few minutes, including data input, computing, and output.

Basically, the mathematical relationships are as simple as the accounting flows discussed earlier in the chapter in connection with the break-even analysis example of model building. We summarized those relationships in Figure 2-4, which showed eight elements that enter break-even models. Previously, we used the simple break-even model as a vehicle for developing the concepts of model building. We now build on those ideas to develop a more sophisticated model. It will be more sophisticated because it will more closely represent the complexities of an enterprise and because we assume the power of a computing system. However, the relationships are no more sophisticated than those used to construct the simple break-even model.

PLYWOOD MANUFACTURING AS AN EXAMPLE

The physical flow of material for a plywood manufacturing operation is shown in Figure 2-7 where we see that the material inputs are company-owned logs together with purchased logs (if required). These materials are processed through the veneer manufacturing phase that involves cutting a thin sheet of veneer from the surface of the log (peeling) and drying it to a specified moisture content. By-products of the peel-dry process are green lumber cores and chips, which are sold at transfer prices to other divisions of the enterprise. Plywood is then glued and pressed with veneer produced in the previous operation or (if required) purchased veneer.

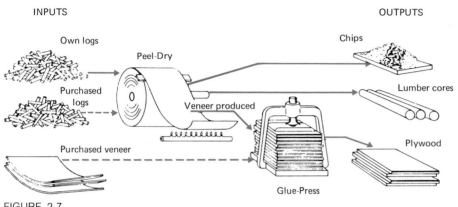

FIGURE 2-7
Overall flow of plywood operations
Figures 2-7, and 2-10 through 2-15 are from J. B. Boulden and E. S. Buffa, "Corporate Models: On-Line Real-Time Systems," Harvard Business Review, *July–August 1970. Used by permission.*

Although this description of the process is simplified, it serves as an adequate basis for our discussion. The capacity of the glue-press operation in relation to the available company-produced veneer determines the amount of purchased veneer required. Similarly, the capacity of the peel-dry operation in relation to desired veneer output determines the amount of purchased logs required.

Model formulation

We begin with simple relationship diagrams that describe the profit or loss of the plywood company.

Revenue The three outputs that produce revenue are chips, lumber cores, and plywood, as shown in Figure 2-8(a). For plywood, revenue is simply the quantity produced and sold multiplied by the price as indicated in Figure 2-8(b). The price is an estimate or an actual market price; however, the quantity is the lesser of two figures — the plant capacity or the desired production level determined by forecasts coupled with a planning process — as indicated by Figure 2-8(c). Now, if we enter into our model the specific numbers for plywood price, desired quantity, and capacity, we can obtain the total revenue generated by plywood sales through the simple mathematical relationship

Plywood revenue = price × minimum of (desired quantity, capacity)

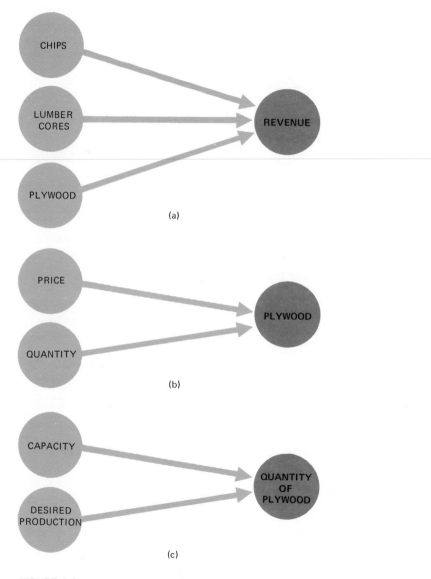

FIGURE 2-8
Plywood company revenue model formulation

A similar analysis could be used to determine revenue from chips and lumber cores; we could then specify a model to estimate total revenues as the sum of the three components of revenue.

Costs Now we consider the cost model. In an actual application we may wish to include very detailed cost breakdowns of the marketing costs, variable production costs, fixed costs, and miscellaneous costs shown as components in Figure 2-9(a). Each of these separate components of the total cost must be analyzed to develop the appropriate relationships. For example, the marketing costs might be generated from subcomponents of discounts and allowances, sales commissions, and freight charges, as shown in Figure 2-9(b).

Each of these costs might be estimated as a percentage of the total plywood sales revenues, for example. Therefore, our model would use the plywood sales revenue generated and apply specific percentages to determine marketing costs. Similar analyses would be required to develop models representing the behavior of the other costs.

We see now that the process of *formulating* a profit (loss) model is quite straightforward. The logic consists primarily of simple arithmetic operations, though the number of calculations will be large as we try to represent a real organization, since there will be various sizes, types, and grades of plywood. Because of the complexity, we program such models on a computer in order to retain the logic for repetitive use and to achieve rapid turnaround time for computing the effects of alternatives that reflect price and cost changes. To use such a profit (loss) model we must specify the inputs or values of the elements of the model. These values include the *parameters* that define specific conditions as we discussed previously, and the *decision variables* that may be changed at the discretion of the manager.

Use of computer version of the plywood model

We now assume the power of the computer and see how the plywood model can be of managerial use. We also assume now that the plywood operation is really only a division of a larger concern. The inputs and outputs of the plywood model are shown in Figure 2-10. We have added the product and overhead relationships to the forecasts of production volume and prices.

Depending on our needs, we can structure outputs in various ways, such as profit and loss statements, materials and sales analyses, personnel planning schedules, and so on. The computer will not provide the necessary inputs for the model or the

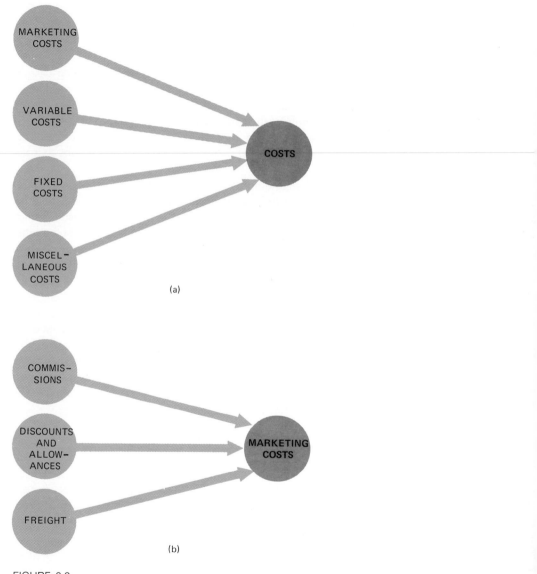

FIGURE 2-9
Plywood company cost model formulation

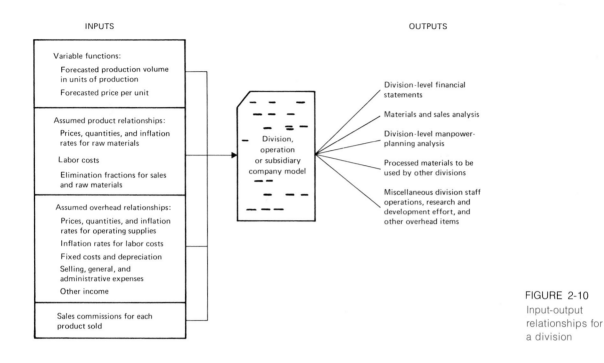

INPUTS

OUTPUTS

FIGURE 2-10
Input-output
relationships for
a division

logical relationships—that is our function. *The computer's function is to carry out the computations defined by the logic we provide.*

Using a system of precoded commands we can call for model output in various forms. For example, in Figure 2-11 we have called for the profit and loss statement based on a set of parameters. Note that the model provides summary ratios such as gross and net profit to sales. Also, the output could have been called for by quarters or in some other format.

The problem-solving value of such a model lies in our ability to ask meaningful questions that may involve changing the values of the decision variables. Each set of values for the decision variables represents a different alternative. In addition, we may wish to determine the outcomes associated with each alternative, given several future scenarios. These scenarios are described by modifying the parameter values. For example, we can ask for a profit and loss report for a given profit objective and specific assumptions regarding the state of the environment. Also, using that concept we

```
YEAR 76

    LINE ITEMS        YRT
SALES PLY         138550.0
SALES CHIPS         7051.5
SALES LUMBER        4545.0
SALES ELIM
TOTAL SALES       150146.5
D&A PLYWOOD         2771.0
COM PLY             8313.0
FREIGHT PLY         1122.0
TOT COM            12206.0
NET SALES         137940.5
RAW MATERIAL       25570.0
VENEER PURCH       32356.5
OP SUPPLIES        14101.2
LABOR              33860.4
COST ELIMIN
COST OF SALE      105888.1
GROSS PROFIT       32052.4
FIXED COSTS         5000.0
SELLING EXP         3000.0
G&A EXPENSE         3000.0
OTHER EXPENSE        500.0
TOT IND EXP        11500.0
NET PROFIT         20552.4
GP/NS                  .23
TIE/NS                 .08
NP/NS                  .15
```

FIGURE 2-11
Computation of profit and loss statement from predictive model

```
        DESIRED YEARLY PROFIT = 0/

        TOT SALES       PROFIT        FRAC 1
        150146.50     20552.36        1.0000
         53870.76          .00         .3588
```

FIGURE 2-12
Computation of break even sales and fraction from predictive model

can perform a break-even analysis by specifying a profit objective of zero in response to the system's query as shown in Figure 2-12. The system responds by computing the sales and percentage of current forecasted sales necessary for break-even operation.

Now suppose we wish to assess the impact on profits of a labor cost increase. By reference to a parameter list, we know that labor cost is coded as P24. We call for "parameter sensitivity," and the system responds by asking which parameter we wish to test as well as the minimum-maximum limits of the test and the increments of variation. We respond by typing 24 for parameter 24, a minimum of $5, a maximum of $6, in increments of 0.25; that is, 24/5/6/.25, as shown in Figure 2-13. The system then computes net profit for each value of the labor cost parameter automatically generating outcomes, given four different scenarios (see Figure 2-13). Such a computation might be of great importance during a labor negotiation.

```
P-L MODE =
PARAMETER SENSITIVITY
P#/MIN/MAX/INCREMENT/ = 24/5/6/.25/

     YEAR 76                P/L

P24 = 5.000

LINE ITEMS               YRT
NET PROFIT             20552.4

P24 = 5.250

LINE ITEMS               YRT
NET PROFIT             18859.3

P24 = 5.500

LINE ITEMS               YRT
NET PROFIT             17166.3

P24 = 5.750

LINE ITEMS               YRT
NET PROFIT             15473.3

P24 = 6.000
                                    FIGURE 2-13
LINE ITEMS               YRT        Sensitivity of net profit to the parameter P24,
NET PROFIT             13781.0      labor cost per hour for the plywood case
```

Larger systems of models Now, assuming that the plywood operation is a division of a much larger corporation, a straightforward extension of the concepts we have discussed can result in the consolidation of the outputs of the plywood division model with other divisions into a "group" consolidation model as shown in Figure 2-14. This process would require the specification of similar additional relationships.

Finally, the results of several group models can be consolidated at the corporate level, also shown in Figure 2-14. Top executives are likely to be most interested in the group and corporate consolidation models. Yet, by using the kind of structure illustrated by the plywood model as a basic building block, together with the successive layers of aggregation we have indicated, the manager can ask for effects of proposed changes in prices, costs, equipment, financing, and so on, at any level within the organization. Also, managers can quickly estimate the net effects on the total enterprise.

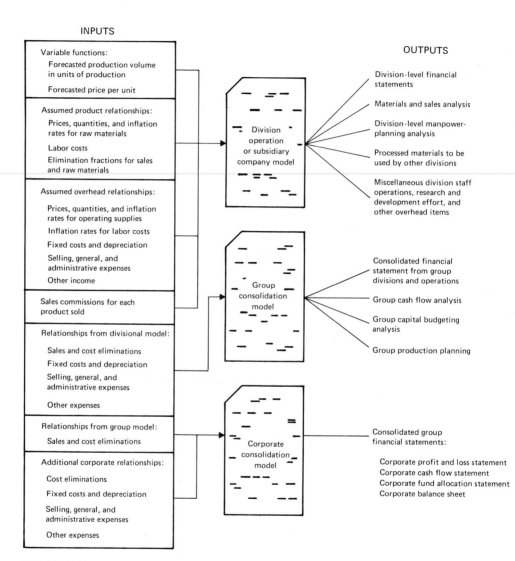

FIGURE 2-14
Input-output relationships for division
or subsidiaries, group consolidation,
and corporate consolidation

MANAGERIAL USE OF COMPUTER-BASED PREDICTIVE MODELS

Predictive models of enterprise operations of the type we have just discussed are in general use. Large-scale applications have been made at Van den Bergh & Jergens, a subsidiary of Unilever [Buffa, 1972] and for a division of Imperial Chemical Industries [Stephenson, 1970] in England. Reports have been published on the use of corporate planning models at Xerox Corporation [Seaberg and Seaberg, 1973], in financial institutions [Hamilton and Moses, 1973, 1974], and for aggregate production planning [Lee and McLaughlin, 1974]. Here we will discuss an application at the Inland Steel Company.

Inland Steel's use of predictive models focuses on the production process. The models that have been developed and their relationships are shown in Figure 2-15. Using the models, corporate planners can quickly simulate the effects of a wide variety of planning assumptions. Each model deals with a basic process in the sequence from raw materials to finished products. The models simulate the various costs incurred in converting ores to molten iron, converting molten iron to steel ingots, processing ingots, and finishing the steel to various end products.

Common questions asked by Inland Steel management using the models are the following: How much raw material is required to meet production forecasts? What are the cost effects of various hot metal to scrap ratios and the resulting yield under various assumptions of raw material costs? What are the capacity requirements for proposed levels of operation?

The first actual test of the models was in the preparation for the next year's profit plan and the related five-year profit and cash projection. For the first time, alternate strategies and assumptions were used during the planning process and during the executive review of the total corporate plan.

In approaching the profit-planning cycle for the coming year, the company management was faced with unusual uncertainties. This situation led to the use of the models to simulate operations, given four significantly different scenarios. All four were based on a basic premise that a strike in the automotive industry was a near certainty during the fourth quarter of the current year, and that if this should occur there would be a significant impact on fourth-quarter shipments for the company. However, the sales forecast for next year indicated a very strong sales demand for the first seven months of that planning period, ending with the August 1 deadline date for negotiations with the Steel Workers Union, and a possible steel strike.

The *first scenario* of this basic premise was that the sales forecast for next year would follow a normal seasonal distribution of shipments, much like what would happen in any normal year, with no impact from the actions of customers through hedge buying of steel inventories in anticipation of a possible steel strike. This assumption gave a base condition for planning.

The *second scenario* was that the historic pattern of prestrike hedge buying would occur in the first seven months of next year, as it had in all similar periods in the post-

FIGURE 2-15
Relationships in
Inland Steel model

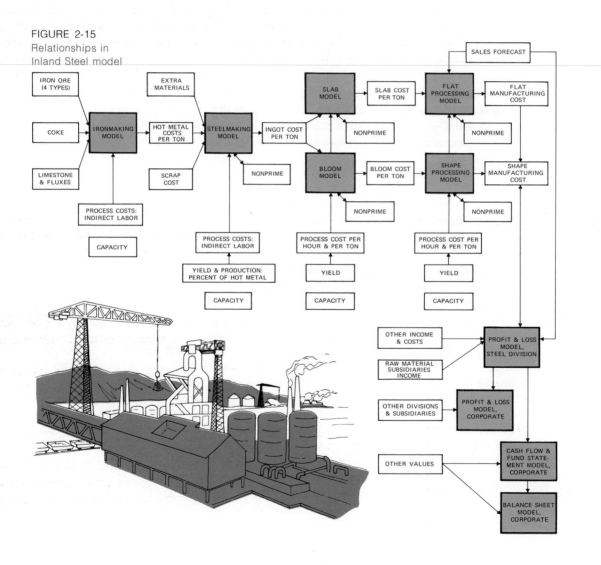

war period, and that there would be no steel strike, since agreement would be reached late on July 31. In this condition, sales demand would decline sharply in August, September, and October, with some recovery in the later months of the fourth quarter of next year.

The *third scenario* involved the previous basic premise, but assumed a 30-day strike in the steel industry, with resumption of production and shipments after 30 days.

The *fourth scenario* assumed a 90-day steel strike, with the same prestrike hedge-buying sales pattern occurring, as stated in the basic premise.

The financial model was used to simulate operations, given these four basic scenarios, all with the premise that there would be an auto strike in the fourth quarter of the current year. Management determined a formal profit plan for the coming year consistent with scenario two, which included a prestrike buildup of inventories, but no strike occurring in the steel industry. However, the other options were maintained in the profit-planning manual as alternate strategies in the event conditions should change as they approached the August 1 strike deadline.

In September, top management made a major decision to build semifinished and finished inventories to the largest level in the company's history to capitalize on the strong demand forecast for the first half of next year. The reason for this decision was that if the forecast were correct and inventories were not accumulated, the mills would not be able to produce steel fast enough to meet the customer delivery requirements, and there would be a loss of sales revenue. This plan was followed through the next year. The excess inventory was liquidated on schedule by June 1, and the company achieved an all-time record industry market share of 6.8 percent versus a normal rate of 4.8 to 5.2 percent.

In late June, it became apparent that the sales demand would not hold up through July 31 as anticipated, and that the odds for a strike on August 1 were growing. Because the preliminary sales forecast from market research for the second year indicated a very strong market, the company also evaluated similar inventory buildup strategies for both the poststrike period, should a steel strike occur, and for production over the last five months, should there be no strike.

In early July, the management requested the five-year cash projection and an accelerated updating of the annual cash forecast. Management recognized that rigorous planning of capital expenditures and long-term financing was required to meet the heavy capital needs for normal expansion and replacement, pollution control equipment, long-term bond issues scheduled for retirement, and very large requirements and opportunities for investment in new projects.

The Inland Steel Company continues to develop the use of predictive models for production scheduling, developing raw materials and mines, and planning subsidiary operations.

PREDICTING THE EFFECTS OF RISK

To this point the models in this chapter have involved variables that were assumed to be known with certainty. We call them *deterministic* because their values are assumed to be completely determined. There are many situations, however, where it is not appropriate to make such an assumption.

An understanding of the effects of variations in the value of a variable may be the most important factor in decisions involving such items as investment required, investment returns, size of markets, share of markets, the load on systems, activity or service time, costs, and so on. When we take this variability into account in models the variables are called *stochastic variables,* and we say that the variables predict the effects of risk that is created by these stochastic variables. We use stochastic variables in a model when the variability makes an important difference in the decision to be made.

An example

Suppose that we have a novelty product that we think might have an excellent potential market. The market for novelties is usually short lived so we try to estimate the total market for the product. Since there is no history of such a product to use as a guide, forecasting in the statistical sense is of no value. We do what we can in trying to assess the market through consumer tests, panels, and so on. Still, market estimation is a precarious activity and we have fairly broad limits on the predicted size of the market. The most likely size of the market is 100,000 units, but there is the possibility that the market could be as large as 140,000 units or as small as 60,000 units. In fact, our market estimates and associated probability estimates are expressed in the following schedule:

Market Size	Probability of Occurrence
60,000 units	0.15
80,000 units	0.30
100,000 units	0.40
120,000 units	0.10
140,000 units	0.05
	1.00

Price The price to charge is also a factor, with $10 being the most likely price. But if the market appears strong it may be possible to increase the price to $12. On the other hand, if the market appears weak we may have to cut the price to $8 or even $6. Again, we can express the possibilities in terms of a probability distribution:

Price	Probability of Occurrence
$ 6	0.1
$ 8	0.3
$10	0.5
$12	0.1
	1.0

Costs Finally, costs of manufacturing, distribution, and selling are estimated to be $4 per unit—leaving a handsome profit of $6 per unit if the $10 price holds. But the very nature of the product is such that we have no real experience on which to base a firm estimate of costs. The $4 estimate is not without foundation, but if everything goes just right it could conceivably be as low as $2. On the other hand, if production problems develop, the costs could easily be as high as $6 per unit. The probability of each of these possible events is estimated as follows:

Costs	Probability of Occurrence
$2	0.1
$4	0.6
$6	0.3
	1.0

Profits If we used our most likely estimates for market size, prices, and costs, the expected profits would be $10 − $4 = $6 per unit, or $600,000 for the whole program. But that combination of events can be upset rather easily. For example, if costs are $6 ($P = 0.3$) and prices only $8 ($P = 0.3$), then per unit profit is only $2. Now if the market size holds at our best estimate, we still make $200,000. But there is a reasonable probability that the market size would be only 80,000 ($P = 0.3$), in which case profits would be only $160,000.

These are just some of the possibilities. You can see even more dire possibilities in even smaller prices in combination with high costs that produce no profit at all, or a small profit margin in combination with the poorest market showing that produces only modest profits. On the other hand, the best combination of market size, price, and costs provides a profit of $1,400,000. In order to explore these possibilities more systematically, we need to use a mathematical model that is designed to predict the effects of the risks introduced by these three stochastic variables. These types of models are discussed in Part III.

WHAT SHOULD THE MANAGER KNOW?

Model formulation

The manager must play an active role in the creation and use of mathematical models. This task cannot be successfully accomplished by a technical staff or outside consultant working in isolation. The manager must be involved, and must bear the principal responsibility for recognizing problems that can be analyzed successfully by mathematical models. The manager must create the list of questions to be answered by the model as an aid in bounding the formulation. The manager's understanding of the system must be expressed in a manner that can be captured by logical relationships, and he or she must participate in the probationary exercises with the model in order to gain confidence in its validity. Finally, the manager must *use* the model in a creative way to attack and solve the particular problem.

Models only reflect what has been structured; they cannot create a new structure. The model should serve to reduce the routine, pencil-pushing work of the manager, releasing time for even more creative thought and innovation. The model can also assist by quickly computing the results of some of these innovative ideas and by helping to develop intuition regarding a particular problem area.

However, the most dramatic and creative new solutions will "break the model" in the sense that they cannot be represented with the existing structure of the model, even though a conscious effort has been made to provide sufficient flexibility to allow the manager to try a wide range of alternatives. These creative solutions are ideas that were not considered during model building because they were not a simple extension of the existing system or operations, but represent a significant innovation. Perhaps the highest compliment that could be paid to a model would be that it contributed to its own obsolescence by providing the insights to the manager that allowed a leap beyond it. Certainly, the manager should be alert for such opportunities.

Although managers may often seek the aid of specialists trained in modeling and the technology of management science, they must play the role of catalyst in guiding the model-building effort. They know the problem and its needs better than anyone else, and it is their responsibility to ensure that this information is clearly communicated to the specialist. Managerial participation may require a significant commitment of time, but without it the model-building activity may be merely an academic exercise.

The important point to remember is that the manager will still be left with the responsibility of making the decision, and this responsibility cannot be delegated to the model. The model can aid the manager by sharpening intuition and by predicting the outcomes from choosing alternate solutions. However, in the final analysis, the decision will be made by the manager. The degree to which this decision is improved as a result of the use of a mathematical model will generally be determined by the involvement of the manager in its creation.

Computer-based predictive models take a position in a manager's environment similar to that of staff. The manager calls on various staff members to perform special studies. In essence, the staff is providing the manager with answers to *what if* questions. Managers have always asked these kinds of questions to improve their own planning and decision making. By manual methods, however, the staff had to labor for many months to provide answers. Computer-based predictive models perform the same basic functions except that, because they are constructed to represent certain phases of operations, the models can provide answers to the questions very quickly.

What managers need to know about predictive models is in general what they must know about their staff. They must have faith in their staff's competence to properly evaluate the alternatives raised. Thus, for predictive models, the managers need to be close enough to the original design of the models to be sure that they will have the capabilities they want. They need to know the kinds of questions likely to be raised and be sure that the models will have the flexibility required to deal with them.

Also, managers must be interested in the model validation phase; they must be convinced that the models truly predict system performance in order to have the required faith. Given faith in the models, managers are limited only by imagination and the capability limits of the models.

Model validation

The manager should insist on initial runs of these kinds of predictive models using historical data input to test their validity. The nature of the relationships within such models should produce a high level of conformance between model and known result. If the model builder approximates some functions by using averages, the manager should determine the sensitivity of the model to changes in the averages, and whether or not an approximation is justified. For example, if product mix is fairly stable in sales, an average price could be used at higher levels of aggregation.

Formulating scenarios

The manager's greatest interest will be in formulating alternate hypotheses or scenarios for what would happen if certain events were to occur. The specific questions may become quite detailed and quite dependent on the nature of the enterprise. However, the manager can take advantage of the sensitivity analysis capability of computer-based predictive models to determine which variables are important, but by using the model these effects can be quantified.

In general, in profit-oriented organizations the manager will be interested in what happens if prices, material costs, and labor costs change. In the Van den Bergh & Jurgens Ltd. (a subsidiary of Unilever) use of computer-based predictive models, a list of seventeen typical *what if* questions are reported [Buffa, 1972], including the testing of prices and costs, marketing plans for specific products and their effects, response to competitors' price actions, alternate forecasts, and the effect on resources and profits of the acquisition of a competitor.

In a banking application, management focused on the effects of changes in discount rate, reserve requirements, banking regulations, levels of earning assets, and changes in the deposit base.

The creation of a mathematical model requires a significant investment of time and money. However, once this capital investment has been made, the actual use of the model is generally very inexpensive. Therefore, it should be used often, even at the whim of the manager.

Interpretation of results

The entire focus of computer-based predictive models seems to be on quantitative factors. On the surface it appears that such models would be useful only for problems in which we accept a quantifiable criterion such as cost or profit. In fact, however, a modern manager is likely to use them as a part of a more complex decision process that considers the quantitative effects produced by the models as well as other factors that are not quantifiable. Then the trade-offs required are made in the decision process.

The predictive models actually facilitate this trade-off process because the manager can ask for and obtain quickly and efficiently the quantitative effects of a scenario, which allows one to "price" the nonquantifiable advantages or disadvantages. In the case of Inland Steel's use of its computer-based models, management was undoubtedly using a complex set of criteria in deciding on its strategy. These criteria included the risk of inventory building in the face of market uncertainties, the impact on labor relations and the community, the reaction of stockholders, and so on. The models provided information regarding costs and profits for alternatives, and this information could then be used in the judgmental trade-off process.

In essence, the models provide input to the evaluation models discussed in Chapters 14, 15, and 16 where formal models provide mechanisms for trade-offs. For example, subjective estimates of the probabilities of the occurrence of each of the scenarios could be made and this information could be used in a decision tree as described in Chapter 14.

CHECK YOUR UNDERSTANDING

1. Consider each of the following situations:
   a. The development of a long-range plan for a large integrated forest products company
   b. The development of a production plan for a large steel manufacturing company
   c. The development of a plan for locating and dispatching ambulances

   For each situation, assume that a predictive model is to be developed to aid in its resolution and that you are the manager with the primary responsibility for the plan.

   (1) Bound the problem by listing the questions you would expect a predictive model to answer.
   (2) Identify the important elements in each problem. Indicate whether each element is a decision variable or a parameter.
   (3) Determine the important logical relationships among these elements using a diagram such as the one in Figure 2-4.

2. Explain the differences between a controllable variable, an uncontrollable variable, and a parameter determined by physical laws. Describe a problem in which you identify examples of each.

3. What is meant by the term *bootstrapping,* and why is it so important?

4. For each of the situations in Exercise 1, provide the following:
   a. At least two examples of future scenarios that you would expect to be used in base case runs of the predictive model. Be specific.
   b. At least two questionable assumptions or key parameters on which you would perform a sensitivity analysis.

5. For the break-even model described in this chapter, develop the following:
   a. Base case analyses with forecasted sales of 200 and 400 units per week.
   b. Base case analyses with variable costs of $14 and $20 per unit.

c. A sensitivity analysis of the assumption of linearity in the variable costs by supposing that the first 100 units produced per week have a variable cost of $25 per unit, the next 100 cost $15 per unit, and the remaining units cost $10 per unit. Is there a serious discrepancy with the linear model when the sales are 300 per week? 400 per week? 200 per week?

d. A *what if* analysis of a new production system that would lower unit costs to $10 but would increase fixed costs to $3000. For which levels of weekly sales would the old production system be superior, and for which levels would the new system be superior?

6. Explain why model formulation and interpretation are the intellectually challenging activities in mathematical modeling for a manager.

7. A small fiberboard company is in the process of constructing a budget model and wishes to construct the model in the general format of computer-based corporate simulation. It is decided that the model will be set up for the first and second half plus the year summary. The fixed costs are simple, $1 million per six months. The company produces only one product, and sales forecasts in units by six-month periods are 200,000 and 300,000, or 500,000 for the year. The price is $2 per unit and variable cost is $1.50 per unit.

The output of the model will have six lines, as defined in Figure 2-16 under the heading *Output Description*.

FIGURE 2-16
Work sheet for
budget model

(1) Output Line	(2) Output Description	(3) Relationship	(4) Model Logic	(5) Definitions	(6) Input Data
1	Volume (units)	Volume	V1	V1 = Volume per quarter (units)	200,000/300,000
2	Sales ($)				
3	Variable cost				
4	Gross Margin				
5	Fixed cost				
6	Profits				

a. Define the relationships required for each line of output in column (3). Output line 1 is simply listed as *volume* in column (3). Other lines of output might be the sum or product of items such as price, costs, and so on.

b. Following the relationships defined in column (3), define equivalent algebraic relationships in column (4), with the definitions of variables used in column (5). As symbols, use V for vectors of numbers, P for parameters, and D for previously computed values in a line of output. For example, D4 would represent the result of the computation in line 4 and could be used in subsequent computations. As an example, we have shown V1 for output line 1 under column (4), and defined it as the vector of volume per six months.

c. List the input data required to "drive" the budget model in column (6). For example, we have shown the volume vector previously given by six-month periods. Note that some lines will have no data input.

8. When Figure 2-16 is filled in, the budget model is complete. If the variable costs increase by $0.10 per unit, what will be the impact on annual profits? What parameters, vectors, or other input data need to be changed to run the model with the new assumption?

9. Referring to the budget model, determine the sensitivity of profit in each of the two periods, and annually, to changes in variable cost. Compute the profit for variable costs of $1.50, $1.60, and $1.70 per unit. How would this computation be accomplished in the computer model?

10. Assuming that variable costs increase by $0.10 as in Exercise 8, how many units must be sold during the first six months to break even for the first six months?

11. Why is it of value to maintain a modular concept in building large-scale computer-based corporate models?

12. In a structural sense, how can a multitude of divisions, groups, and subsidiary companies be related in large-scale corporate models?

SHORT CASES

The president of a large bank (assets of more than $2 billion) is considering the development of a computerized financial planning system to facilitate rapid analysis and comparison of short and longer term policies and performance. You are the consultant who is developing the system.

    The present system requires largely manual computation of only a few alternatives that

CASE 2-1

management feels are the most likely and promising. It is time consuming both in terms of staff-hours and overall time to evaluate an alternative. In addition, the manual system does not consider all important interrelationships of financial flows and therefore does not reflect the full financial impact of alternatives. Specifically, the manual system is not able to evaluate rapidly and accurately the full impact of changes in the discount rate, reserve requirements, earning assets, and the deposit base.

In structuring the system of planning models, you decided on six functional modules plus a composite planning model to predict overall performance. The six functional models centered on commercial loans and installment loans in the fund-using category, deposits in the fund-providing category, plus modules for noninterest income and expenses. The structure of basic inputs and outputs of the six functional models and the composite model is shown in Figure 2-17, along with the key bank variables.

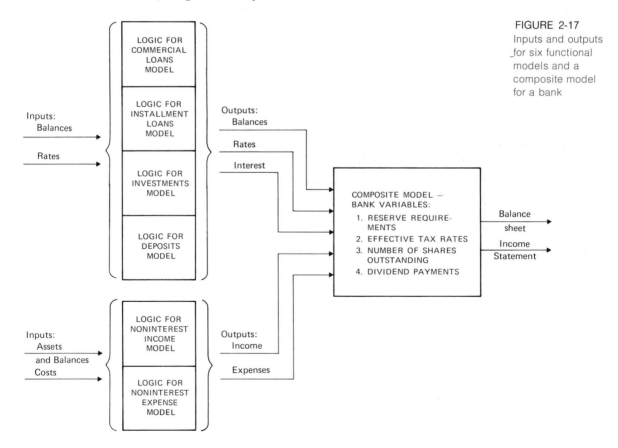

FIGURE 2-17
Inputs and outputs for six functional models and a composite model for a bank

At a meeting where the basic model structure is presented to the officers of the bank, the president asks, "Of what use would the models be to me and my staff? What questions will it answer?"

Since the meeting is an event preceding the final report, you have the opportunity to provide the answers to the president's questions. Draft that part of the report that provides the *what if* questions for which the system of models would be able to provide answers. Would the basic structure of the models need to be revised in order to provide all the answers that you envision?

Tax planning is an important reality for many individuals and most profit enterprises. Formulate the structure of a tax planning model by developing a block diagram of the basic modules, indicating the inputs, transformations (what functions performed), and outputs for each module. The blocks in the diagram need not be thought of as separate models.   CASE 2-2

Begin by listing the key factors, or *what if* questions that might be important in determining the short- and long-term impact on taxes. Who would use such a tax model? Can it reflect tax laws as well as tax rulings? How can it be made flexible enough to allow for changes in tax laws and rulings?

The NEWSprint Company is a large supplier of paper to the newspaper industry. It operates through a system of four paper mills located in the United States and has an international division that operates two Canadian plants. Paper is supplied to the United States and international markets from both the domestic and Canadian plants; however, organizationally the international division is separate.   CASE 2-3

NEWSprint is considering the development of computer-based corporate planning models, and you are a consultant. Discussions with management indicate that primary problems revolve around shifting patterns and changes in demand forecasts, demand at individual mills, distribution costs, and inventory levels. In addition, capital expenditures for the company as a whole are an important aspect of planning and affect mill output and productivity.

Propose a structure of models and their linkage to meet company needs that you might use as the basis of a presentation to company management. What kinds of *what if* questions would your system answer?

GENERAL REFERENCES

Ackoff, R. L., *A Concept of Corporate Planning,* Wiley-Interscience, New York, 1970.

Buffa, E. S., *Operations Management: Problems and Models,* third edition, John Wiley & Sons, New York, 1972, Chapter 21.

Churchman, C. W., "Reliability of Models in the Social Sciences," *Interfaces,* Vol. 4, No. 1, November 1973.

Elmaghraby, S. E., "The Role of Modeling in IE Design," *The Journal of Industrial Engineering,* Vol. 19, No. 6, June 1968.

Little, J. D. C., "Models and Managers: The Concept of a Decision Calculus," *Management Science,* Vol. 16, No. 8, April 1970.

Morris, W. T., "On the Art of Modeling," *Management Science,* Vol. 13, No. 12, August 1967.

Naylor, T. H., *Corporate Planning Models,* Addison-Wesley, Reading, Mass., 1979.

Rivett, P., *Principles of Model Building,* John Wiley & Sons, New York, 1972.

Schrieber, A. N., editor, *Corporate Simulation Models,* Graduate School of Business Administration, University of Washington, 1970.

Strauch, R. E., " 'Squishy' Problems and Quantitative Methods," The Rand Corporation, Santa Monica, Calif., P-5303, October 1974.

Urban, G. L, "Building Models for Decision Makers," *Interfaces,* Vol. 4, No. 3, May 1974.

Wheelwright, S. C., and S. G. Makridakis, *Computer-Aided Modeling for Managers,* Addison-Wesley, Reading, Mass., 1972.

Zeleny, M., "Managers without Management Science," *Interfaces,* Vol. 5, No. 4, August 1975.

APPLICATIONS REFERENCES

Barkdoll, G., "Models—New Management Decision Aid," *Industrial Engineering,* December 1970, pp. 32–40.

Boulden, J. B., *Computer Based Planning Systems,* McGraw-Hill, New York, 1975.

———, and E. S. Buffa, "Corporate Models: On-Line, Real-Time Systems," *Harvard Business Review,* July-August 1970.

———, and E. R. McLean, "An Executive's Guide to Computer-Based Planning," *California Management Review,* Vol. 17, No. 1, Fall 1974, pp. 58–67.

Cohen, R., S. Auerbach, and W. A. Wallace, "A Test of an Interactive Community Development Impacts Model in a Rural Environment," *Interfaces,* Vol. 7, No. 1, November 1976.

Cooper, D. O., L. B. Davidson, and W. K. Denison, "A Tool for More Effective Financial Analysis," *Interfaces,* Vol. 5, No. 2, Part 2, February 1975, pp. 91–103.

Dietz, R. V., and R. V. Scavullo, "Industrial Progress: A System to Develop Utility Systems Planning," *Public Utilities Fortnightly,* May 9, 1974.

Geoffrion, A., "Better Distribution Planning with Computer Models," *Harvard Business Review,* Vol. 54, No. 4, July-August 1976.

———, "Progress in Computer Assisted Distribution System Planning," Working Paper No. 219a, Western Management Science Institute, University of California, Los Angeles, revised June 1975.

Gershefsky, G. W., "Building a Corporate Financial Model," *Harvard Business Review,* January-February 1969, pp. 72–82.

———, "Corporate Models—The State of the Art," *Management Science,* Vol. 16, No. 6, February 1970.

Hamilton, W. F, and M. A. Moses, "A Computer-Based Corporate Planning System," *Management Science,* Vol. 21, No. 2, October 1974, pp. 148–59.

———, "An Optimization Model for Corporate Financial Planning," *Operations Research,* Vol. 21, No. 3, May–June 1973, pp. 677–92.

Lee, W. B., and C. P. McLaughlin, "Corporate Simulation Models for Aggregate Materials Management," *Production & Inventory Management,* 1st Quarter, 1974, pp. 56–67.

Loughran, B. P., and P. J. Cocks, "Airline Programme Planning in British Airways European Division," *Interfaces,* Vol. 7, No. 2, February 1977, pp. 21–36.

Naylor, T. H., "Why Corporate Planning Models," *Interfaces,* Vol. 8, No. 1, Part 1, November 1977, pp. 87–94.

Naylor, T. H., and H. Schauland, "A Survey of Users of Corporate Planning Models, *Management Science,* Vol. 22, No. 9, May 1976, pp. 927–37.

Ogden, J., " 'What Happens If': A Planning System for Utilities," *Public Utilities Fortnightly,* March 1972.

Rosenthal, B., and R. C. Murphy, "Instant Manpower Replanning Is Here," *State Government Administration,* February 1975.

Ruhl, G. J., "Conservation: What Is It Worth? A Quantitative Approach Using a Rate and Revenue Model," *Public Utilities Fortnightly,* December 19, 1974, pp. 33–37.

Seaberg, R. A., and C. Seaberg, "Computer Based Decision Systems in Xerox Corporate Planning," *Management Science,* Vol. 20, No. 4, December, Part II, 1973, pp. 575–84.

Stephenson, G. G., "A Hierarchy of Models for Planning in a Division of I.C.I.," *Operational Research Quarterly,* Vol. 20, 1970, pp. 221–45.

Optimization Models

The use of optimization models is the most exciting and potentially valuable contribution of management science. That is true because, given a criterion, these models combine the elements of alternative generator, predictive, and evaluation models in such a way that the *best possible* solution can be determined. Best possible means that no superior combination of the decision variables exists for the model. These are the powerful optimizing methods of management science such as mathematical programming, network optimization, inventory models, and others.

Implicit in the preceding euphoric statement about best possible solutions are the assumptions that the submodel that predicts system performance is a valid representation of how the system works and that the evaluation model reflects the preferences of the decision maker. As we will see, these are important assumptions and sometimes it may be difficult to meet them.

Let us begin by recalling the scheme of models in management science from Chapter 1, shown again in Figure II-1. Optimization models combine the alternative generator, predictive model, and evaluation model, as indicated by the highlighted area in Figure II-1. The output of the combined system is a combination of values for the decision variables that produced the best solution; we call

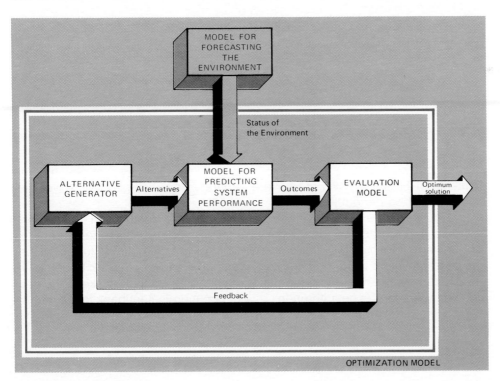

FIGURE II-1
Elements of an optimization model

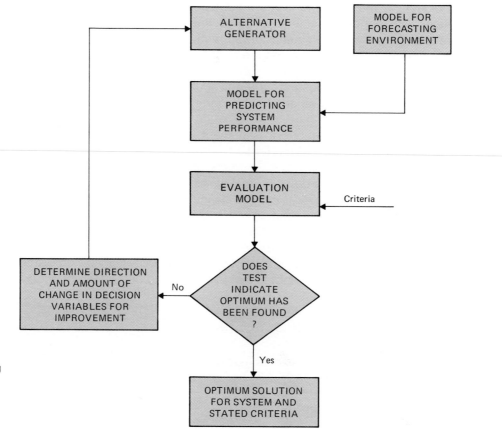

FIGURE II-2
Flow chart showing
test for optimality
and coupling to
alternative
generator

this the *optimum* solution. In the optimization models we study, the different elements of Figure II-1 will not have a separate and distinct identity, yet their functions will be performed.

In Figure II-2, we have developed a flow chart that contains all the elements of Figure II-1. In addition, below the evaluation model we have inserted a test for optimality in which we determine whether or not the solution just produced can be improved. If it can be improved, we need some mechanism to determine the direction of change and the amount of change we should make in the decision variables for the next iteration. This information is sent back to the alternative generator to produce a new alternative. System performance is predicted and evaluated, and the cycle is repeated until the test for optimality indicates that no further improvement is possible. We have diagrammed the process as an interative one. However, some of the solution techniques combine these steps and go directly to the optimum solution, while others actually do iterate in the manner we have described.

Concept of A Test for Optimality

The simplest case of a test for optimality is one in which we have a single decision criterion such as cost or profit, and the value of the criterion varies as a function of a single decision variable. Suppose, for example, that we wished to determine the least cost inventory to hold as a buffer to absorb variations in demand. The larger the buffer inventory, the greater the inventory holding cost, but the lower the cost of lost sales and back ordering. Since one component of cost is increasing and the other decreasing as buffer inventory increases, the composite cost function plotted in relation to buffer inventory size would be similar to Figure II-3. Cost decreases to a minimum and then increases

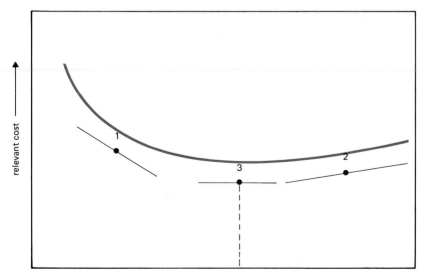

size of buffer inventory (units)

FIGURE II-3
Typical curve of relevant cost versus the size of buffer stock indicating optimum at a point where the slope of the curve is zero

again as inventory holding costs become the dominant factor.

We can see by inspection that the optimum inventory size is at point 3 in Figure II-3, the minimum point of the cost curve. Mathematically, the test for the minimum point is in terms of the slope of the curve. The minimum will be where the slope of the curve is zero. In this kind of situation the iterative process is not necessary since we can test for the minimum (or maximum) much more directly using appropriate mathematical techniques, as we will see in Chapter 10.

Plan for Part II

All the models discussed in Part II will be of the optimizing type. We begin with linear optimization models in Chapters 3 and 4, where we discuss their formulation and use. Chapters 5 and 6 describe the linear programming methods that are used to solve linear optimization models. Network models are introduced in Chapters 7 and 8. The network models of Chapter 7 are used to design and analyze alternate product distribution systems, and the network models of Chapter 8 are used to plan and schedule major projects. The optimization models of Chapter 9 include decision variables that can only assume integer values, such as 0, 1, 2, ..., instead of fractional values. These models are often applied in the analysis of large-scale capital budgeting problems. Finally, the optimization models used in inventory management are presented in Chapter 10.

CHAPTER 3

Linear Optimization Models

The optimization models of the greatest significance to managers have been linear optimization models and their associated powerful solution technique known as linear programming. Linear optimization models have been applied in a wide variety of industries and not-for-profit activities such as steel, oil refining, utilities, education, meat packing, health care, refuse collection, and many others.

The kinds of applications have included all sorts of resource allocation problems such as long-range financial planning, aggregate capacity planning, portfolio planning and selection, plant location, production planning and scheduling, political districting, corporate financial planning, warehousing and distribution, air pollution control, water pollution control, promotion and advertising decisions, and so on. Obviously, linear optimization models are not simply theoretical concepts applicable to toy problems. They are powerful, useful managerial models.

In this chapter and in Chapter 4, we emphasize formulating linear optimization models and interpreting results. In fact, we assume a computer solution technique exists so that if we learn how to formulate linear optimization problems, we can use a "black box" to provide solutions. Then we can take the manager's viewpoint and see how the results can be interpreted in the most useful way. In Chapters 5 and 6, we look inside the black box to see how the solution technique works.

THE NATURE OF LINEAR OPTIMIZATION MODELS

Linear optimization models are characterized by linear mathematical expressions. In addition, they are usually deterministic in nature; that is, they do not take account of risk and uncertainty. The parameters of the model are assumed to be known with certainty. Finally, as we will see, linear optimization models are used most often when we are attempting to allocate some limited or scarce resources in order to make decisions that use the resources in question in such a way that a stated criterion is optimized (either minimized or maximized).

THE MEANING OF LINEARITY

In linear models, we *must* use only linear mathematical expressions. Recall our use of simple break-even analysis in Chapter 2. Figure 3-1 shows the elements of the profit (loss) function that we developed there. The relationships in the profit (loss) model are linear because the decision variable, x (number sold), does not appear to any power

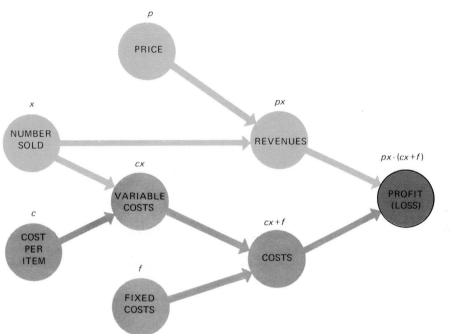

FIGURE 3-1
Elements entering
the formulation of a
profit (loss)
function

other than 1. There are no squared or higher powers of variables and there are no cross product terms where more than one variable is involved. Another way to say the same thing is to note that linear variables graph as straight lines.

In Figure 3-2 we show equations of both linear and nonlinear mathematical expressions, together with their graphs. In Figure 3-2, (a) and (b) are graphs of linear expressions and appear as straight lines, but (c) and (d) are graphs of nonlinear expressions, since (c) contains an x^2 term and (d) the cross product of $x_1 x_2$.

Figure 3-2 also illustrates the mathematical form of constraints. In Figure 3-2 (b) in the shaded portion, we see the expression $x_1 - 2x_2 \geq 4$, which states that $(x_1 - 2x_2)$ must be greater than or equal to ($\geq$) 4. When it is equal to 4, we have the straight line. Otherwise, the inequality expression constrains all combinations of x_1 and x_2 to be in the shaded portion of the graph. Conversely, all combinations of x_1 and x_2 that fall above the straight line are not admissible, since they do not satisfy the constraint $x_1 - 2x_2 \geq 4$.

Figure 3-2 (d) shows a nonlinear constraint expression in the shaded portion of

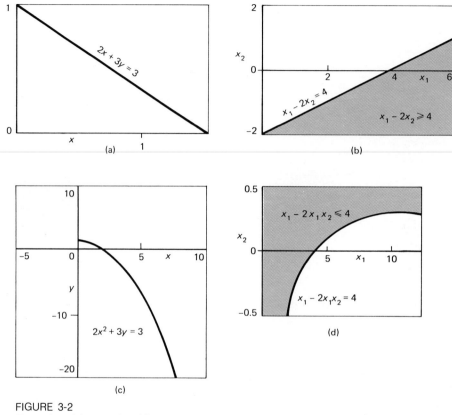

FIGURE 3-2
Examples of the graphs of linear
and nonlinear expressions

the graph. That expression constrains combinations of x_1 and x_2 to be above the curve (in the shaded portion), since the expression states that $(x_1 - 2x_1x_2)$ must be less than or equal to ($\leq$) 4. Again, when the statement on the left-hand side of the expression is equal to 4, all points fall on the curve.

Mathematical statements of constraints may be less than or equal to ($\leq$), equal to ($=$), and greater than or equal to ($\geq$). *Linear* constraints, illustrated by the expression in the shaded portion of Figure 3-2 (b), will be very important in linear optimization models.

ELEMENTS OF THE MODEL-BUILDING PROCESS

In order to develop a linear optimization model, we use the following process:

1. Define the decision variables.
2. Define the objective function, Z, a linear equation involving the decision variables that identifies our objective in the problem-solving effort. This equation predicts the effects on the objective of choosing different values for the decision variables.
3. Define the constraints—linear expressions involving the decision variables that specify the restrictions on the decisions that can be made. *Alternatives can be generated* by selecting values for the decision variables that satisfy these constraints.

Let us illustrate the process using a simple break-even analysis model, including the structure and definitions that we developed previously and shown in Figure 3-1.

Define the decision variables

In the break-even analysis model we are interested in how profits vary as a function of the number of units sold. Since we are interested in determining a value for x, the number of units produced and sold, it is the decision variable in the model.

Define the objective function

In the break-even analysis model, the manager wishes to make a profit as large as possible. Therefore the mathematical expression for predicting the effect of the choice of a production level on profits is, from Figure 3-1,

$$\text{Profit (loss)} = px - cx - f$$

Now, since the manager wishes to maximize profits, our objective function is

$$\text{maximize } Z = px - cx - f$$

The first two steps in the development of a linear break-even analysis model have been very simple. The decision variable is x, the number of units produced and sold, and the objective function is to maximize the simple mathematical statement of profit. Suppose we stop our model-building effort at this point and examine the break-even

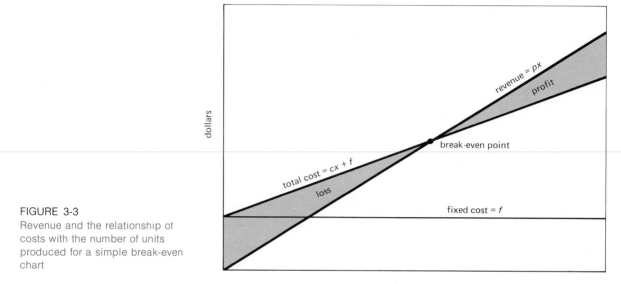

FIGURE 3-3
Revenue and the relationship of costs with the number of units produced for a simple break-even chart

chart shown in Figure 3-3. If we attempt to implement the stated objective function to find a value of the decision variable x that maximizes profits, it is obvious that we should make x very large and produce as many units as we possibly can. We see immediately, however, that we do not yet have enough information. We know that we wish to make x large, but how large can we make it? We do not know, because we have not yet defined the constraints on our decision variable x.

Define the constraints

Obviously we cannot ignore possible limitations on the size of x. We may have capacity limitations that restrict the number of units that can be produced within a given time period. If the monthly capacity of the production facility is C units—for example, 300 units per month—then we have a constraint on the decision variable x as follows:

$$x \leq C$$

Of course, we can substitute the appropriate specific capacity limitation for C.

In addition, we may not be able to sell all units produced at capacity. Perhaps the forecast for monthly demand is D units, for example 200. We have, then, an additional constraint on the decision variable,

$$x \leq D$$

To this point, the constraints define how large x can be. The linear model formulation process requires that we be very specific and also indicate how small x can be. Obviously, it cannot be negative, therefore,

$$x \geq 0$$

Thus, we can generate alternatives for our analysis by selecting any value for x that satisfies these constraints.

In summary, the linear optimization model for our break-even analysis problem is developed as follows:

1. Define the decision variables: $x =$ the number of units produced and sold.
2. Define the objective function: maximize $Z = px - cx - f$.
3. Define the constraints: $x \leq C$, $x \leq D$, $x \geq 0$.

Figure 3-4 shows the graphic relationships in the form of the well-known break-even chart to which we have added the constraints, the range of feasible solutions within the constraints, and the maximum possible profit for the model (see page 72).

For the simple break-even model, it would not have been necessary for us to go through the process in order to identify the optimum solution. The solution is obvious. What is important, however, is that the more complex linear optimization models we deal with are a straightforward extension of the process we have developed to this point.

Simplifications

While we can deal with the objective function for profit (loss) $= px - cx - f$ in break-even analysis, it can be simplified for linear models. First, let us factor out the decision variable x so that the profit function becomes

$$px - cx - f = x(p - c) - f$$

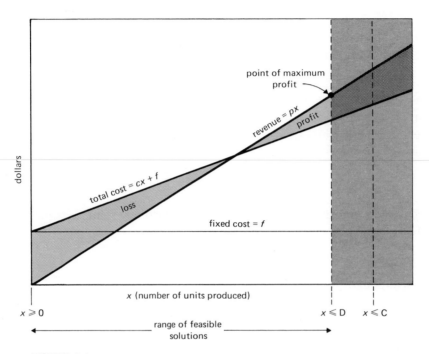

FIGURE 3-4
Relationship of revenues, costs, constraints, and range of feasible solutions for a simple
break-even analysis

Now let us define the term $(p - c)$ as the contribution to profit and overhead, r, per unit sold. The objective function is then simplified to

$$\text{maximize } Z = rx - f$$

Now let us examine the importance of the fixed cost element f in our decision problem. Note that f is not a function of the decision variable x. Therefore, our objective of making x as large as possible within the constraints is not affected by f. Thus, for decision-making purposes, we can eliminate the fixed costs, since they are irrelevant to the decision. This is an important notion in model building for managerial decision making, and we have applied it previously, for example, in the corporate planning models of the previous chapter where we considered only the costs affected by the decision. The result of this step is that the objective function is further simplified to

maximize $Z = rx$

that is, maximize the product of contribution per unit times the number of units produced and sold.

Our final linear optimization model written in the special form for linear programming is now

maximize $Z = rx$
subject to
$\quad x \leq C$
$\quad x \leq D$
$\quad x \geq 0$

A specific example

Let us now provide specific numbers for the variables and constraints. Suppose that the price per unit is $3.50, and the variable cost per unit is $2. Then r, the contribution to profit and overhead, is $p - c = \$3.50 - \$2.00 = \$1.50$. In addition, suppose that production capacity is 300 units per month and the market forecast of demand indicates that we could sell as many as 200 units per month. The specific linear optimization model is then

maximize $Z = 1.5x$
subject to
$\quad x \leq 300$
$\quad x \leq 200$
$\quad x \geq 0$

The simplified linear optimization model is shown graphically in Figure 3-5 where the objective function $Z = 1.5x$ is a straight line beginning at the origin. The constraints on capacity and demand are shown, but only the demand constraint is effective, since it is more restrictive. The feasible range of solutions is between $x = 0$ and $x = 200$ units, and we have slack (unused) plant capacity of 100 units per month.

While it is true that the break-even analysis example is so simple that the answer

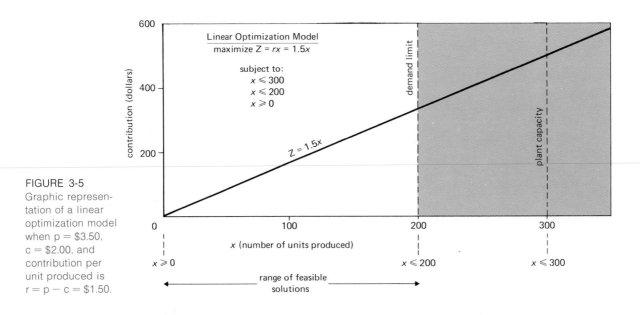

FIGURE 3-5
Graphic represen-
tation of a linear
optimization model
when p = $3.50,
c = $2.00, and
contribution per
unit produced is
r = p − c = $1.50.

is entirely obvious, it displays most of the elements of linear optimization model formulation and also introduces the important concept of a range of feasible solutions and the concept of slack in a resource.

FORMULATION OF A TWO-PRODUCT MODEL

Let us now consider a slightly more complex situation. A chemical manufacturer produces two products, which we call chemical x and chemical y. Each product is manufactured by a two-step process that involves blending and mixing in machine A and packaging on machine B. The two products complement each other, since the same production facilities can be used for both products, thus achieving better utilization of these facilities.

Definition of decision variables

Since these facilities are shared, and costs and profits from each product are different, there is the question of how to utilize the available machine time in the most profitable way. Chemical x is seemingly more profitable, but the manager once tried producing the maximum amount of chemical x within market limitations, using the balance of the capacity to produce chemical y. He found, however, that such an allocation of machine time resulted in poor profit performance. He feels now that some appropriate balance between the two products is best and he wishes to determine the production rates for each product per two-week period.

Thus, the decision variables are

x, the number of units of chemical x to be produced

y, the number of units of chemical y to be produced

Definition of the objective function

The physical plant and basic organization exists and represents the fixed costs of the organization. From the previous example, we know that these costs are irrelevant to the production scheduling decision, and they are ignored. The manager, however, has obtained price and variable cost information and has computed the contribution to profit and overhead per unit of each product sold as shown in Table 3-1. He wishes to maximize profit, and the contribution rates have a linear relationship to the objective. Therefore, the objective function that he wishes to maximize is the sum of the total contribution from chemical x, $(60x)$, plus the total contribution from chemical y, $(50y)$, or

maximize $Z = 60x + 50y$

Sales Prices, Variable Costs, and Contributions per Unit for Chemicals x and y — TABLE 3-1

	Sales Price (p)	Variable Costs (c)	Contribution to Profit and Overhead $(r = p - c)$
Chemical x	$350	$290	$60
Chemical y	450	400	50

Definition of constraints

The processing times for the two products on the mixing machine (A) and the packaging machine (B) are as follows:

Product	Machine A (hours)	Machine B (hours)
x	2	3
y	4	2

For the upcoming two-week period, machine A has available 80 hours and machine B has available 60 hours of processing time.

Machine A constraint Since we are limited by the 80 hours available on machine A, the total time spent in the manufacture of chemical x and chemical y cannot exceed the total time available. For machine A, since chemical x requires 2 hours per unit and y requires 4 hours per unit, the total time spent on the two products must be less than or equal to 80 hours, that is,

$$2x + 4y \leq 80$$

Machine B constraint Similarly, the available hours on the packaging machine are limited to 60, and since chemical x requires 3 hours per unit and y requires 2 hours per unit the total hours for the two products must be less than or equal to 60 hours, or

$$3x + 2y \leq 60$$

Marketing constraints Forecasts of the markets indicate that we can expect to sell a maximum of 16 units of chemical x and 18 units of chemical y. Therefore,

$$x \leq 16$$

$$y \leq 18$$

Minimum production constraints The minimum production for each product is zero, therefore,

$$x \geq 0$$

$$y \geq 0$$

The linear optimization model

We can now summarize a statement of the linear optimization model for the two-product chemical company in the standard format, as follows:

Maximize $Z = 60x + 50y$
subject to
$$2x + 4y \leq 80 \text{ (machine } A\text{)}$$
$$3x + 2y \leq 60 \text{ (machine } B\text{)}$$
$$x \leq 16 \qquad \text{(demand for chemical } x\text{)}$$
$$y \leq 18 \qquad \text{(demand for chemical } y\text{)}$$
$$x \geq 0 \qquad \text{(minimum production for chemical } x\text{)}$$
$$y \geq 0 \qquad \text{(minimum production for chemical } y\text{)}$$

A graphical solution

We can gain some insight into the solution of a linear optimization model by analyzing it graphically. Although this is not a practical approach to the solution of large linear optimization models of real-world problems, the basic concepts do carry over into these problems.

The constraints of the linear optimization model are shown in Figure 3-6. To see how they were plotted, suppose we consider the machine A constraint

$$2x + 4y \leq 80 \tag{1}$$

The easiest way to show the values of x and y that satisfy an inequality is to plot the straight line corresponding to the equation obtained by replacing the inequality sign with an equality sign; that is, we plot the line corresponding to the equality

$$2x + 4y = 80 \tag{2}$$

for our example. Generally, the easiest way to plot an equality is to find the x-intercept — the point on the x axis representing the value of x that satisfies this equality constraint when $y = 0$ — and the y-intercept, the value of y satisfying the equality when $x = 0$.

If $y = 0$ in Equation (2) then $2x + 4(0) = 80$, or $2x = 80$. Therefore, $x = 80/2 = 40$ is the x-intercept value for Equation (2) as shown in Figure 3-6. If $x = 0$, then $2(0)$

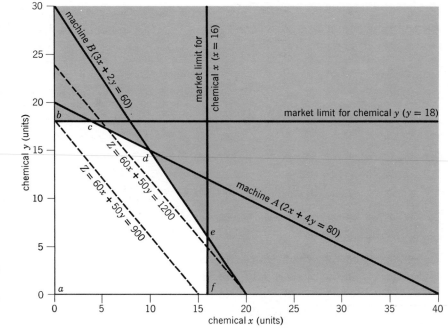

FIGURE 3-6

Graphic representation of the
limitations imposed by
machine capacity, marketing,
and minimum production
constraints

$+ 4y = 80$, so $y = 20$ is the y-intercept value. Since we know that Equation (2) passes
through the two points (40,0) and (0,20), the line can easily be plotted.

This straight line represents all the values of x and y that satisfy Equation (2), but
what about the (x,y) pairs that satisfy inequality (1)? All the points that satisfy an
inequality lie on one side of the corresponding equation, and all the points that violate
that inequality lie on the other side. On which side of the line representing Equation
(2) are the points satisfying inequality (1)? The simplest way to decide is often to consider the origin (0,0) and check to see if the values $x = 0$ and $y = 0$ satisfy the inequality. If they do, then the origin and all other points on the same side of the equality
line (2) satisfy the inequality (1). Otherwise, all points on the side of Equation (2)
away from the origin satisfy (1). In our example, $2(0) + 4(0) = 0$ and $0 \leq 80$, so the
origin satisfies inequality (1).

The solution to a linear optimization model must simultaneously satisfy *all* the
constraints of the model. Points that violate one or more of the constraints of the two
product model are in the shaded areas of Figure 3-6. For example, the values $x = 0$

and $y = 20$ satisfy the constraints $2x + 4y \leq 80$ and $3x + 2y \leq 60$, but violate the constraint $y \leq 18$. Therefore, the point $(0,20)$ is in the shaded region of Figure 3-6. The solution to our problem lies somewhere within the solution space *abcdef*. Any production schedule with a combination of amounts x and y that falls outside this solution space is not feasible since it does not simultaneously satisfy all the constraints.

We have also plotted in Figure 3-6 the linear objective function for two values of total contribution, $Z = \$900$ and $Z = \$1200$. When we set $Z = \$900$, for example,

$$60x + 50y = 900$$

Then, when $x = 0$, we must have $y = 18$ as the y-intercept since $60(0) + 50(18) = 900$, and when $y = 0$, we have $60x + 50(0) = 900$ and $x = 900/60 = 15$. The resulting straight line is very simple to plot in Figure 3-6. The "900" line within the solution space of points simultaneously satisfying all the constraints defines all the feasible solutions that would produce a contribution of $Z = \$900$. Since our objective is to maximize contribution, what happens if we increase Z to $\$1200$? Since the slope of the objective function has not changed, the line for $Z = \$1200$ is parallel to the $\$900$ line, and closer to point *d*, as we note in Figure 3-6. It is now rather obvious for this simple problem that if we substituted larger and larger values of Z in the objective function, lines parallel to the $\$900$ and $\$1200$ lines would result, and a line through point *d* would define a combination of x and y with the maximum possible contribution within the feasible solution space. Now we will see how this same solution point might be found using a computer program for solving linear optimization models.

Computer solution and interpretation of the two-product model

As we mentioned earlier, we will assume that we have a mechanism for solving linear optimization models when they are formulated in the preceding standard format. Indeed, linear programming computing codes are commonly available both in interactive mode (available from a time-share terminal) and in batch mode for large-scale linear programming problem solutions. In order to use either of these computing programs for the solution of linear optimization models, the problem must be presented to the "black box" in the precise form required. This input format is usually more user oriented in interactive time-share systems, and we use one of these programs to illustrate solutions to problems in this chapter [see Buckley et al., 1974].

Now, let us return to the chemical production problem for which we just formulated the linear optimization model in standard form. Figure 3-7 shows a portion of

```
      LPENTER
ENTER THE NAME OF THIS PROJECT CHEMICAL PRODUCTION
MAXIMIZE OR MINIMIZE:  MAXIMIZE
OBJECTIVE FUNCTION: Z=60CHEMX+50CHEMY
ENTER CONSTRAINT EQUATIONS (STRIKE JUST A CARRIAGE RETURN TO STOP INPUT)
[1] 2CHEMX+4CHEMY≤80
[2] 3CHEMX+2CHEMY≤60
[3] CHEMX≤16
[4] CHEMY≤18
```

(A)

```
      LPRUN
                    CHEMICAL PRODUCTION

THE OPTIMAL VALUE OF THE OBJECTIVE FUNCTION IS:   1350.000

                 THE VARIABLES IN THE SOLUTION ARE

VARIABLE   CHEMX   AT LEVEL    1.0000E1
           CHEMY               1.5000E1
           SLK3                6.0000E0
           SLK4                3.0000E0
```

(B)

FIGURE 3-7

The Chemical production problem

the computer output for the problem. Let us follow through the input steps as well as the solution output.

Computer input In Figure 3-7 (a) we see the input steps following the "sign on" and "call up" of the linear programming subroutine. At this point, the user types *LPENTER,* and the terminal prints *ENTER THE NAME OF THIS PROJECT.* The user responds by typing *CHEMICAL PRODUCTION.*

The terminal then asks whether this problem will have an objective of maximizing or minimizing the objective function by typing *MAXIMIZE OR MINIMIZE.* Since our problem is to maximize contribution, the user responds by typing *MAXIMIZE.*

The terminal then asks for the statement of the objective function by typing *OBJECTIVE FUNCTION.* The user simply responds by typing in the objective function, $Z = 60\ CHEMX + 50\ CHEMY$. In so doing, the user has named the variables and these names will be used for the balance of the problem. The user could have used a purely symbolic notation, but variable names that convey meaning within the context of the problem are common.

Given the objective function, the terminal then requests the constraint equations and tells us how to indicate that all the constraint equations have been entered, that is, (*STRIKE JUST A CARRIAGE RETURN TO STOP INPUT*). The user responds by typing each constraint on a separate line, using the variable names previously defined. We need not enter the last two constraints of $x \geq 0$ and $y \geq 0$, since the computer program assumes that none of the variables can take on negative values. Therefore, when the constraints have been entered, the user strikes the carriage return key as directed and the program is executed, computing the solution.

We have discussed the computer input in detail only to show how simple it is to use such programs. Many computer programs for linear programming are available; the instructions for each individual program will be unique to that program and the documentation indicates exactly how to provide input. The form of the computer output may also vary from program to program, but will be similar in content.

Computer output Figure 3-7 (b) shows the solution output. First, the terminal prints the optimum value of the objective function, $1350. In other words, it states that $Z = 1350$ in the objective function for an optimal solution.

Next, the terminal prints the values of the variables in the optimum solution. Note that scientific notation is used; that is, the value of each variable is followed by E and some number. This notation means that the number preceding the E is to be multiplied by that number of 10s. For example, $E1$ means multiply by 10, $E2$ by 100, and so on. $E0$ indicates that the multiplier is 1, or simply that the value of the variable needs no modification.

Now let us consider only the first two variables listed in the solution: *CHEMX* and *CHEMY*. The solution states that their optimal values are 10 and 15 respectively. Note that this is point d in Figure 3-6, the point where the capacity constraint lines for machines A and B intersect, as we expected, based on our graphical analysis of this problem. This is an important observation that we will use in Chapter 5 in understanding how the linear programming algorithm actually works.

Using the solution values of *CHEMX* and *CHEMY*, let us insert them in the objective function and compute Z,

$$Z = 60 \times 10 + 50 \times 15 = 1350$$

This result checks with the optimal value of Z given by the computer solution.

Checking one further bit of logic, if the solution to our problem is at the intersection of the two capacity constraint equations, then we should be able to solve the equations for the two lines simultaneously to determine the values of *CHEMX* and

CHEMY that are common to the equations. First, let us use the equation for machine *A* and solve for *x*,

$$2x + 4y = 80$$

Therefore,

$$x = 80/2 - 4y/2 = 40 - 2y$$

We then substitute this value of *x* in the constraint equation for machine *B*.

$$3(40 - 2y) + 2y = 60$$
$$120 - 6y + 2y = 60$$
$$4y = 60$$
$$y = 15$$

This value of *y* checks with our computer solution. Now, substitute $y = 15$ in the machine *A* constraint equation to determine the value of *x*,

$$2x + 4(15) = 80$$
$$x = (80 - 60)/2 = 10$$

Thus, we have verified that the solution to our problem is at point *d* of Figure 3-6 where the two constraint equations intersect. Another interpretation of this fact is that machines *A* and *B*, our two productive resources, are completely utilized in this solution—there is no residual slack capacity. This fact is important because any of the other feasible solutions in the polygon *abcdef* of Figure 3-6 would have involved some slack capacity in one or both of the two machines. If there had been slack capacity for either of the machines in the optimum solution, that fact would have been indicated in the computer output for the optimum solution. In some more complex problems, there might be slack capacity of a productive resource in an optimum solution.

Now, note that the computer output gave us the value of variables that we did not ask for explicitly, *SLK3* and *SLK4*. These are the slack values related to constraints [3] and [4], the market constraints. Constraint [3], *CHEMX* ≤ 16, was the market limit for that product. The solution simply points out to us that if we produce according to the optimum solution where $CHEMX = 10$, there will be unsatisfied demand (slack) of 6, and this fits in with the market constraint, since $CHEMX + SLK3 = 10 + 6 = 16$. Similarly, the value of $SLK4 = 3$ agrees with the market constraint, $CHEMY \leq 18$, since $CHEMY + SLK4 = 15 + 3 = 18$.

These interpretations of the optimum solution to the chemical production problem are rather simple. The important point is that equivalent interpretations of more complex problems are a straightforward extension of these ideas. The solution will state the combination of variables that optimizes the objective function. Some but not all of the constraints will be the controlling ones, and there will be slack in some of the resources; that is, they will not all be fully utilized. In our example, the slack was in the demands for the two products. Note, however, that if the demand for $CHEMY$ dropped to only 14, that is $y = 14$, it would have become one of the controlling ("tight") constraints as may be seen from Figure 3-6, and there would have been some slack capacity in machine A.

SENSITIVITY ANALYSIS AND INTERPRETATION OF RESULTS

If we wanted only the solution to the problem—the optimal combination of variables, the value of slack variables, and the optimum value of the objective function—we could stop at this point by answering *NO* to the next question typed out by the terminal. *DO YOU WISH SENSITIVITY ANALYSIS?* There is available to the decision maker, however, additional valuable information, and he or she can obtain it by simply answering the question, *YES,* as we have done in Figure 3-8 for the chemical production problem.

```
DO YOU WISH SENSITIVITY ANALYSIS? YES
                      SHADOW        LB        CURRENT        UB
CONSTRAINT      1    3.7500E0    5.6000E1    8.0000E1    8.8000E1
                2    1.7500E1    4.8000E1    6.0000E1    7.2000E1
                3    0.0000E0    1.0000E1    1.6000E1    7.2370E75
                4    0.0000E0    1.5000E1    1.8000E1    7.2370E75


PRICE        CHEMX                2.5000E1    6.0000E1    7.5000E1
             CHEMY                4.0000E1    5.0000E1    1.2000E2

-<END>-
```

FIGURE 3-8
Sensitivity analysis for the chemical production problem

While the optimum solution states what to do now, given the objective function and the constraints, the sensitivity analysis raises questions about opportunities and perhaps about what could or should be done to improve the solution to the managerial problem.

Figure 3-8 presents the sensitivity analysis in tabular form, first for each constraint and then for the prices (contributions) for each product. For each constraint there is listed a *SHADOW* (shadow price), the *LB* (lower bound of the right-hand side of the constraint), *CURRENT* (current value of the right-hand side), and *UB* (upper bound of the right-hand side). At first this appears complex, but let us define what these terms mean in our chemical production example.

Shadow prices

The shadow prices indicate the value of an additional unit in the right-hand side of the constraint. For example, recall the meaning of the first constraint for machine *A* (2 *CHEMX* + 4 *CHEMY* ≤ 80). It states that the total available capacity for machine *A* is 80 hours. What would be the marginal value (in the objective function) of one additional unit of capacity? The answer is given in Figure 3-8 as $3.75. If the capacity of machine *A* were 81 hours, the extra hour would add $3.75 to the total contribution. Conversely, if only 79 hours were available, this amount would be subtracted from total contribution.

Now observe that the shadow price for machine *B* capacity is $17.50. The marginal value of capacity for machine *B* is 17.50/3.75 = 4.7 times that for machine *A*. The shadow prices tell the manager that the opportunity provided by increasing machine *B* capacity is relatively large and allow for appraisal of expansion proposals for both machines.

The shadow prices for constraints [3] and [4] (demands) are zero because these constraints do not limit us in the current situation. If demand for *CHEMY* dropped to 14, then it would become one of the controlling constraints, as we noted previously. The optimum solution would change, but in addition, the shadow price for constraint [4] would become some positive value, indicating a marginal value to increasing demand for *CHEMY,* perhaps providing the manager with information to appraise programs to stimulate demand.

Lower, current, and upper bounds We just stated the meaning of the shadow prices, that is, the value of marginal units of resources. But for what ranges are these marginal rates valid? Can we increase capacity for machine *B* to two or three times its present capacity and expect to obtain an additional $17.50 per unit in the objective function? No, there are limits, and the bounds tell us exactly what they are. Taking the capacity of machine B as an example, it is currently 60 hours as shown in Figure 3-8 under the *CURRENT* column, but we see that the shadow price is valid in the range of 48 to 72 hours, the lower and upper bounds.

If we could increase the capacity of machine B to 72 hours, we would obtain an additional $17.5 \times 12 = \$210$ in total contribution. We would be able to increase contribution by $210 \times 100/1350 = 15.6$ percent. On the down side, if we had a breakdown of machine B, for example, and available hours fell to the lower bound of 48, we would lose $210 in total contribution. The interpretation for the bounds on the capacity of machine A is similar.

Now let us examine the significance of the bounds on the demand for the two products. Take constraint [4], the demand for *CHEMY*, for example. Its lower bound is 15. A shadow price of zero applies if demand falls to 15, that is, the constraint is ineffective in that range. But, as we have already noted, if demand falls below 15, the constraint becomes one of those controlling the solution.

Now, the upper bound for constraint [4] is listed as 7.2370E75. This is the code for infinity in this particular linear programming computer program. There is no upper bound in effect.

A graphical interpretation It may be helpful to explore the meaning of sensitivity analysis by referring to a graphical interpretation of the results. As we have explained, the sensitivity analysis shown in Figure 3-8 indicates each extra hour on machine B will be worth $17.50 as long as the total number of hours is between 48 and 72.

Suppose we assume that the manager is able to obtain an additional 6 hours on machine B, perhaps by rescheduling some other activities involving that machine. The total capacity for machine B becomes $60 + 6 = 66$ hours. Since this is within the lower and upper bounds of 48 and 72 shown in Figure 3-8 for machine B, we would expect the objective function to increase by $6 \times \$17.50 = \$105$.

This revised situation is shown graphically in Figure 3-9. The constraint line for machine B is now determined by the equality $3x + 2y = 66$, and all other constraints are unchanged. Plotting the new machine B constraint, we find an x-intercept of $66/3 = 22$ and a y-intercept of $66/2 = 33$. Notice that increasing the right-hand side of this constraint shifts it away from the origin, but the constraint line $3x + 2y = 66$ is parallel to the original constraint line $3x + 2y = 60$.

The solution to this revised problem lies somewhere within the solution space *abcd'e'f*. We use *d'* and *e'* to distinguish these points on the revised machine B con-

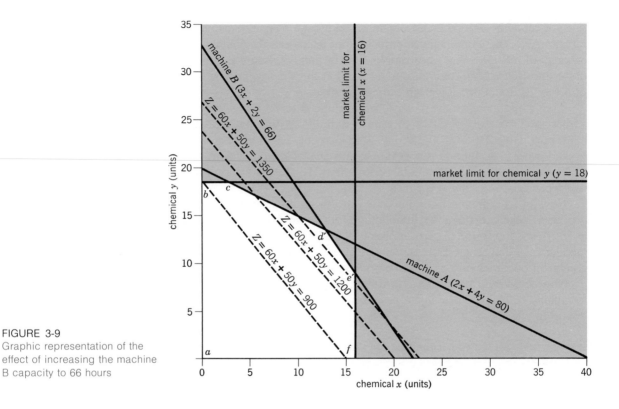

FIGURE 3-9
Graphic representation of the effect of increasing the machine B capacity to 66 hours

straint from points d and e shown in Figure 3-6.

As before, we have plotted the linear objective function for $Z = \$900$ and $Z = \$1200$. In addition, we have plotted the objective function for $Z = \$1350$, the optimal solution when only 60 hours are available on machine B! Notice that this objective function line lies partially *within* the solution space $abcd'e'f$, indicating that a larger value of Z can be found. Again, it should be obvious from Figure 3-9 that the maximum possible contribution will be found when the line corresponding to the objective function passes through point d'.

Since d' is at the intersection of the two capacity constraints, let us solve the two equations simultaneously to determine the new optimal values of *CHEMX* and *CHEMY*. We can use the machine A equation again and obtain

$$x = 40 - 2y$$

We substitute this value of X in the revised constraint equation for machine B, and obtain

$$3(40 - 2y) + 2y = 66$$
$$120 - 6y + 2y = 66$$
$$4y = 54$$
$$y = 13.5$$

Now substitute $y = 13.5$ in the machine A constraint and we find

$$x = 40 - 2(13.5) = 13$$

Therefore, the new optimal solution at d' is $x = 13$ and $y = 13.5$.
    We can now check the logic of the sensitivity analysis. When $x = 13$ and $y = 13.5$, the corresponding objective function value is

$$Z = 60(13) + 50(13.5) = 1455$$

Subtracting the optimal value of the objective function for the original problem with only 60 hours on machine B, we find that the difference is

$$\$1455 - \$1350 = \$105$$

as we expected, or an increase in the objective function of $\$105/6 = \$17.50$ for each additional hour added to the machine B constraint.
    Let us summarize the insights presented by this analysis. Adding or subtracting units to the right-hand side of a constraint shifts the constraint to another position parallel to the original constraint. In our example, the machine B constraint was shifted away from the origin by the addition of 6 hours to the original capacity of 60 hours. If this constraint was a controlling constraint in the optimal solution, the shift will change the objective function value since the optimal solution is also shifted.
    Now let us consider the lower and upper bounds on the machine B capacity of 48 and 72 hours. If the right-hand side of the machine B constraint is increased to 72 hours, the resulting graphic representation is shown in Figure 3-10. Notice that the machine B constraint is no longer necessary at this point, since the optimal solution

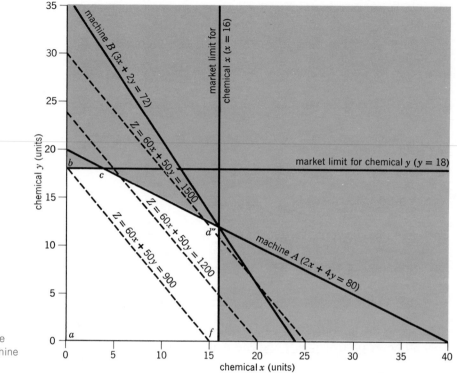

FIGURE 3-10
Graphic representation of the effect of increasing the machine B capacity to 72 hours

will occur at point d'' which is determined by the machine A constraint and the market limit constraint for chemical x. If additional hours above 72 were added to the right-hand side of the machine B constraint, there would be no further change in the optimal solution. Therefore, the "shadow price" of hours on machine B would change from \$17.50 per hour to \$0.00 per hour for each additional hour beyond the total of 72.

In general, the lower and upper bounds on right-hand constants are determined by the points at which the shift of a constraint meets a new constraint, so that the rate of change in the objective function with further shifts of the constraint is altered. The effect of reducing the right-hand side of the machine B constraint below its lower bound of 48 hours will be explored as an exercise.

Price sensitivity

The contribution rates in the objective function are termed generally *prices*. Recall that the contribution of a unit of *CHEMX* was $60 and of *CHEMY* $50, and these are shown as the *CURRENT* values in Figure 3-8. But, what if prices change? Would the changes affect the solution? The lower and upper bounds for prices shown in Figure 3-8 indicate the range of prices (contribution rates) for which the optimum solution is valid. For example, the contribution rate for *CHEMX* could be anywhere in the range of $25 to $75 and the optimum amount of *CHEMX* and *CHEMY* would still be as indicated in the present solution: produce 10 units of *CHEMX* and 15 units of *CHEMY*. Of course, the total contribution would change because of the change in the contribution rate, but the optimal *decision* would remain the same.

There is a practical significance to the price sensitivity. For example, the manager might estimate the contribution for *CHEMX* at $60, but these kinds of figures are seldom absolutely precise. Suppose that the contribution is somewhere in the $55 to $65 range. In this case, the same solution applies. The result is that the use of a rough estimate for the contribution rate is adequate, and we should not spend additional time and money to refine the estimate. Thus, the bounds help indicate how we should allocate time and money to refine cost information — if the bounds are tight it may be worthwhile to be precise, but if they are loose we would gain nothing by attempting to improve the estimates.

A graphical interpretation The lower and upper bounds for prices may also be understood by analyzing the problem graphically. The computer output shown in Figure 3-8 indicates that the upper bound on the contribution of *CHEMX* is 75. Suppose we increase the contribution of chemical x to $75. Then we would have $Z = 75x + 50y$ as the new objective function. The graphic representation is shown in Figure 3-11. As before, we have plotted the linear objective function for two values of total contribution, $Z = \$900$ and $Z = \$1200$.

The increase in the coefficient of chemical x to $75 has changed the *slope* of the objective function line. Looking carefully at Figure 3-11, we can see that the "$900" line and the "$1200" line are parallel to the constraint line for machine B. Now what happens if we increase Z? Eventually, the line corresponding to the maximum value of Z will lie *on* the constraint line for machine B, and optimal solutions will occur at *both* points d and e and at all points on the constraint line between points d and e. These points are called *alternate optimal solutions*.

To see this, recall that point d corresponds to the values $x = 10$ and $y = 15$. With

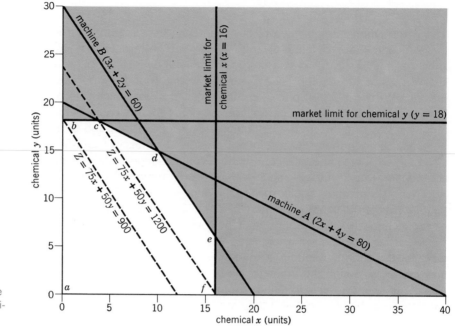

FIGURE 3-11
Graphic representation of the
effect of increasing the contribution of chemical X to $75

the new objective function,

$$Z = 75(10) + 50(15) = 1500$$

at point d. At point e, $x = 16$ and we obtain

$$y = (60 - 3(16))/2 = 6$$

from the machine B constraint. Substituting these values into the revised objective function gives

$$Z = 75(16) + 50(6) = 1500$$

at point e also.

Intuitively, a change in a "price" in the objective function changes the *slope* of the objective function. Within some range of changes in the price, the slope will not be altered enough to cause a different solution to be optimal. Outside of these upper and lower bounds, however, a new solution will be optimal.

Looking at Figure 3-11, what will be the optimal solution if the contribution rate of *CHEMX* is changed to $90, or to $10? These questions will be investigated in the "Check Your Understanding" exercises.

Summary

Let us take a moment to summarize at this point. Given a linear optimization model stated in the format we have specified, we can use a computer program to provide the optimum combination of the decision variables, the optimum value of the objective function, and the values of slack capacity or other resources in the system. In interpreting the solution, however, we can also obtain the value of a marginal unit of each resource (shadow prices) and the range over which the shadow price is valid. In addition, we can obtain the range of prices (contribution rates in our example) in the objective function for which the solution is valid.

Understanding the significance of the optimum solution and the sensitivity analysis in the context of the real problem has great value. Decision makers are in a position to appraise various proposals for changing the optimum solution. They should not look on the optimum solution as necessarily the final decision, but as a basis for asking *what if* questions. The sensitivity analysis provides them with information regarding many possible *what if* questions, and may also suggest variations of the model that may require additional computer runs.

A MODEL INVOLVING RATIO CONSTRAINTS

This example introduces the important concept of the use of *ratios* or *proportions* in the formulation of constraints, providing a bridge to the formulation of many real-world problems.

Suppose a production process is used to manufacture two products. The daily demand for the first product is 50 units, while the demand for the second is 100 units. These products can be processed either manually or by a mechanized system during a two-shift day. However, the capacity of the mechanized system is restricted to less than or equal to 40 units of product 1 per shift, or less than or equal to 75 units of product 2 per shift. Similarly, the manual system is restricted to less than or equal to 30 units of product 1 per shift, or 50 units of product 2 per shift. Suppose that, according to our accounting records, the costs of producing the products vary depend-

TABLE 3-2

Production Costs per Unit for Products 1
and 2 on Manual and Mechanized
Systems During Shifts 1 and 2

	Manual	Mechanized
Product 1		
Shift 1	10	8
Shift 2	15	11
Product 2		
Shift 1	5	4
Shift 2	6	6

ing on the system used (mechanized or manual), the type of product, and the shift, as shown in Table 3-2. The obvious question to be answered is how many units should be processed on which system during each shift, assuming that we must meet the demand.

Definition of decision variables In order to define the decision variables, it is convenient to introduce some notation that may appear complex at first, but that actually simplifies the formulation of the model. We will let M_{ij} be the number of units of product i (1 or 2) processed during shift j (1 or 2) on the manual system and let MCH_{ij} be the number of units of product i processed during shift j on the mechanized system. Thus, if we determine that $M_{11} = 20$ and $MCH_{21} = 60$, this would indicate that 20 units of product 1 are to be processed by the manual system during shift 1, and 60 units of product 2 are to be processed on the mechanized system during shift 1. Since there are two products that can be processed on either of two systems during either of two shifts, there are a total of $2 \times 2 \times 2 = 8$ decision variables.

Definition of the objective function Now we wish to let the computer determine the values of M_{ij} and MCH_{ij} that minimize the cost of meeting our daily production demand. That is, we wish to let the computer minimize the expression

$$Z = 10M_{11} + 8MCH_{11} + 15M_{12} + 11MCH_{12}$$
$$+ 5M_{21} + 4MCH_{21} + 6M_{22} + 6MCH_{22}$$

where the cost coefficients are taken directly from Table 3-2. For example, the cost of processing a unit of product 2 using the manual system during shift 1 is $5, so $5M_{21}$ appears as the fifth term in this objective function.

Definition of constraints The constraints result from the demand requirements and the capacity restrictions. To meet the demand for product 1, we must have

$$M_{11} + MCH_{11} + M_{12} + MCH_{12} = 50$$

which says that the total number of units of product 1 produced using manual labor and the mechanized system during both shifts must equal 50. Similarly, for product 2,

$$M_{21} + MCH_{21} + M_{22} + MCH_{22} = 100$$

Finally, we have capacity restrictions on both the manual and the mechanized systems during each shift. Consider the problem on the manual system during the first shift. Clearly M_{11} must be less than or equal to 30, and M_{21} must be less than or equal to 50. The temptation is to jump to the conclusion that these capacity constraints are very simple; for example, for the manual system during the first shift, we would write

$$M_{11} \le 30$$
$$M_{21} \le 50$$

and so on for the other shift and for the mechanized system.

The problem with this approach becomes apparent when we note that on shift 1 we seem to be allowing the simultaneous use of the manual system in two different ways. For example, if we use the full capacity for product 1 ($M_{11} = 30$), then M_{21} must be zero. We cannot use the same capacity more than once, and that is the key to the proper construction of the capacity constraints.

During shift 1, the total available capacity of the manual system can be used up to 100 percent. Therefore, the sum of the *fractions* or *proportions* of this capacity used by each product must be less than or equal to *one*. The fraction of the capacity used for product 1 is the number of units of product 1 processed on the manual system during shift 1, M_{11}, divided by the capacity for product 1, or $M_{11}/30$; for product 2, $M_{21}/50$. Thus, if $M_{11} = 10$, then we are using one-third of the available capacity on the manual system during shift 1 to process product 1. The capacity constraint for the manual system during shift 1 is then

$$M_{11}/30 + M_{21}/50 \le 1$$

Now, let us simplify this constraint by multiplying through by 150, the common denominator, and we obtain

$$5M_{11} + 3M_{21} \le 150$$

Following exactly the same process, we develop a similar constraint for the capacity of the manual system during the second shift. Test your understanding of this im-

FIGURE 3-12
Model with ratio constraints

```
        LPENTER
ENTER THE NAME OF THIS PROJECT:TWO PRODUCTS-RATIO CONSTRAINTS
MAXIMIZE OR MINIMIZE: MIN
OBJECTIVE FUNCTION: Z=10M11+8MCH11+15M12+11MCH12+5M21+4MCH21+6M22+6MCH22
ENTER CONSTRAINT EQUATIONS, (STRIKE JUST A CARRIAGE RETURN TO STOP INPUT)
 (1) M11+MCH11+M12+MCH12=50
 (2) M21+MCH21+M22+MCH22=100
 (3) 5M11+3M21≤150
 (4) 5M12+3M22≤150
 (5) 7.5MCH11+4MCH21≤300
 (6) 7.5MCH12+4MCH22≤300
 (7)
                           (A)
     LPRUN

                 TWO PRODUCTS-RATIO CONSTRAINTS


THE OPTIMAL VALUE OF THE OBJECTIVE FUNCTION IS:      960.000


               THE VARIABLES IN THE SOLUTION ARE


VARIABLE   MCH11              1.3333E1
           MCH12              3.6667E1
           M21                5.0000E1
           MCH21              5.0000E1
           SLK4               1.5000E2
           SLK6               2.5000E1
                           (B)
```

portant point by writing down the capacity constraints for the mechanized system, using the same reasoning.

Figure 3-12 shows the computer input and solution for the problem. The complete problem formulation is shown as the computer input in (A). According to the computer solution shown in (B), $MCH_{11} = 13.33$, $MCH_{12} = 36.67$, $M_{21} = 50$, and $MCH_{21} = 50$. The optimal values of the decision variables not listed in the computer solution are 0.0. This result indicates that we should produce 13.33 units of product 1 during the first shift and 36.67 during the second shift, all on the mechanized system. Further, we produce 50 units of product 2 on the manual system and 50 on the mechanized system, all during the first shift. Check to see that this result satisfies our constraints. The minimum total cost of this solution is 960. Finally the slack variables $SLK4$ and $SLK6$, corresponding to constraints [4] and [6] respectively, indicate that there is unused capacity on both the manual and mechanized systems during shift 2.

ANALYSIS OF A PRODUCT PLANNING DECISION

Let us now use linear optimization models to analyze some expansion problems of a company that manufactures two products, A and B, the Two-Products Company. The schedule proposed by the production manager calls for a product mix of 615 units of A, and 2600 units of B. One of the current issues is whether or not the mix is most profitable. Also, since a third product may be added to the line, a decision must be made about the possible enlargement of the four manufacturing departments.

Table 3-3 shows the labor-hour requirements for each product and the depart-

	Labor-Hours per Unit		Department Capacities (labor-hours
Department	A	B	per month)
1	3	0	6000
2	0	2.9	8000
3	2.5	2	7500
4	1.3	1.5	5000

Labor-Hour Requirements and Capacities for the Two-Product Company

TABLE 3-3

mental capacities. Also, the contribution rates are $50 per unit for product A, $35 for B, and the objective is to maximize combined contribution.

Model formulation

First, let us formulate a linear optimization model designed to indicate the best product mix for maximum contribution.

Definition of decision variables Since the objective is to determine the optimal product mix, the decision variables are the amounts of each product to produce per month. Therefore, we let A and B be the number of units per month of products A and B respectively.

Definition of the objective function We wish to

maximize $Z = 50A + 35B$

The coefficients of A and B are the contribution rates.

Definition of constraints The constraints are the expressions limiting the use of departmental labor-hours to the monthly capacities indicated in Table 3-3. Since Table 3-3 indicates labor-hours per unit for each product, the total labor-hour requirement in each department is the sum of the amounts used by each product. Department one, for example, is used only by product A, so the total is simply 3 times the number of units of product A, or $3A$, since product A requires 3 hours per unit in department one. This amount cannot be larger than the capacity of department one, so the constraint is

$3A \leq 6000$

Department two is used only by product B and its constraint expression is similar:

$2.9B \leq 8000$

Department three is used by both products. Product A requires 2.5 hours per unit, and B, 2 hours per unit. The monthly capacity is 7500 hours. Therefore, the constraint on the time requirements for the two products is

$2.5A + 2B \leq 7500$

Similarly, for department four, the capacity constraint is

$1.3A + 1.5B \leq 5000$

Assuming the nonnegativity constraints on variables, the linear optimization model is shown in the computer input in Figure 3-13 (A).

FIGURE 3-13
Two-Product Company

```
      LPENTER
ENTER THE NAME OF THIS PROJECT TWO PRODUCT COMPANY
MAXIMIZE OR MINIMIZE:  MAX
OBJECTIVE FUNCTION:Z=50A+35B
ENTER CONSTRAINT EQUATIONS (STRIKE JUST A CARRIAGE RETURN TO STOP INPUT)
 (1) 3A≤6000
 (2) 2.9B≤8000
 (3) 2.5A+2B≤7500
 (4) 1.3A+1.5B≤5000
 (5)
                              (A)
    LPRUN
                    TWO PRODUCT COMPANY


THE OPTIMAL VALUE OF THE OBJECTIVE FUNCTION IS:   143750.000


             THE VARIABLES IN THE SOLUTION ARE


VARIABLE   A      AT LEVEL      2.0000E3
           B                    1.2500E3
           SLK2                 4.3750E3
           SLK4                 5.2500E2


DO YOU WISH SENSITIVITY ANALYSIS? YES

                   SHADOW      LB        CURRENT      UB
CONSTRAINT    1   2.0833E0   3.2609E3   6.0000E3   9.0000E3
              2   0.0000E0   3.6250E3   8.0000E3   7.2370E75
              3   1.7500E1   5.0000E3   7.5000E3   8.2000E3
              4   0.0000E0   4.4750E3   5.0000E3   7.2370E75

PRICE      A             4.3750E1   5.0000E1   7.2370E75
           B             0.0000E0   3.5000E1   4.0000E1
-> END <-
                      (B)
```

Interpretation of computer solution

The optimal solution shown in Figure 3-13 (B) specifies an output of 2000 units of product A, and 1250 units of product B. The maximum contribution possible is indicated as $143,750 per month. Compare this optimal contribution with the production manager's proposed schedule, which has a contribution of

$$(50)(615) + (35)(2600) = \$121,750$$

The optimal schedule would increase contribution by $22,000, or 18.1 percent.

Now let us beware of jumping to the conclusion that the original schedule is a poor one. The optimal contribution could be obtained only if the units could be sold. Here, we observe internal controversy, for the sales manager says that she could sell 2200 units of A, and only 1500 units of B. She charges that the production manager will create a horrible inventory problem with his proposed schedule by producing 2600 units of B. Furthermore, she claims they will miss a market opportunity for product A.

Of course, we note from the optimal solution that neither of the product mixes proposed by the production manager or the sales manager seems entirely appropriate. The production manager's schedule has a relatively low contribution. The sales manager's contribution is larger [(50) (2,200) + (35) (1,500) = $162,500], but is it feasible? No, the sales manager's schedule would require 6600 hours in department one, 8500 hours in department three, and 5110 hours in department four, all exceeding capacities. Only department two's capacity would be capable of handling the sales manager's proposal. You should check these calculations to be sure you understand the implications of the sales manager's proposal.

The optimal solution indicated in Figure 3-13 shows that departments one and three would be fully utilized, and that departments two and four would have slack capacity of 4375 hours and 525 hours respectively. One of the questions to be answered is whether the slack capacity can be used by a third product.

Sensitivity analysis

Now let us examine the sensitivity analysis given for the Two-Product Company, also shown in Figure 3-13 (B). The shadow prices for the capacities of departments two and four are zero. Therefore, with the present line of products, labor-hour requirements, and contribution rates, there is no advantage in expanding these departments. However, the shadow price for department one is $2.08 per labor-hour of capacity, and this shadow price is valid in the range of 3261 to 9000 labor-hours per month. Also, the shadow price for department three is $17.50, valid in the range of 5000 to 8200 labor-hours per month.

The bounds on the contributions in the objective function indicate that for product A, the $50 contribution could increase without bounds and the optimum solution would not change. On the other hand, the $35 contribution for product B is valid for the present solution between 0 and $40, but the solution would change if the contribution rate were to increase above $40 per unit. This later contribution is therefore sensitive to increases (which may be unlikely), but not to decreases.

Introduction of a third product

After seeing the computer optimal solution and sensitivity analysis for the existing two products, both the production and sales managers wish to evaluate the potential impact of the proposed new product C, before it is introduced. They are both excited about the new product, but for different reasons. The sales manager sees the hope of added contributions. The expanded sales may be the basis for a salary increase and/or a promotion for her. The production manager sees the new product as a way of using his slack capacity. Reports on plant utilization have indicated that he has not been very effective in scheduling production, as indicated by low output per labor-hour. The optimal solution of Figure 3-13 seems to verify the report results. The production manager fears the loss of his job.

Product C has uniqueness, and market tests indicate that it can command a contribution of $75 per unit. The sales manager raises the question again of whether or not there is sufficient existing capacity. The production manager contends that existing capacities are adequate and that, indeed, a reason that product C is so attractive is that it fits in so well, using slack capacity. The analyst says, "Let's not argue, let's compute."

The labor-hour requirements for product C are: 0.15, 2.5, 3.5, and 1.5, for each of the four departments.

Three products—interpretation of computer solution

With the addition of product C, the linear optimization model becomes the computer input shown in Figure 3-14 (A). Note that the objective function and all four constraints must be altered to take product C into account. You should check to see that you understand the new linear optimization model.

The solution to the Three-Product Company case is shown in Figure 3-14 (B).

```
     LPENTER
ENTER THE NAME OF THIS PROJECT THREE PRODUCT COMPANY
MAXIMIZE OR MINIMIZE: MAX
OBJECTIVE FUNCTION: Z=50A+35B+75C
ENTER CONSTRAINT EQUATIONS (STRIKE JUST A CARRIAGE RETURN TO STOP INPUT)
  (1)  3A+0.15C≤6000
  (2)  2.9B+2.5C≤8000
  (3)  2.5A+2B+3.5C≤7500
  (4)  1.3A+1.5B+1.5C≤5000
  (5)
                               (A)
     LPRUN
                    THREE PRODUCT COMPANY


THE OPTIMAL VALUE OF THE OBJECTIVE FUNCTION IS:   160714.286


            THE VARIABLES IN THE SOLUTION ARE


VARIABLE   C       AT LEVEL      2.1429E3
           SLK1                  5.6786E3
           SLK2                  2.6429E3
           SLK4                  1.7857E3


DO YOU WISH SENSITIVITY ANALYSIS? YES

                     SHADOW        LB        CURRENT       UB
CONSTRAINT     1     0.0000E0    3.2143E2    6.0000E3    7.2370E75
               2     0.0000E0    5.3571E3    8.0000E3    7.2370E75
               3     2.1429E1    0.0000E0    7.5000E3    1.1200E4
               4     0.0000E0    3.2143E3    5.0000E3    7.2370E75

PRICE      A                    -7.2370E75   5.0000E1    5.3571E1
           B                    -7.2370E75   3.5000E1    4.2857E1
           C                     7.0000E1    7.5000E1    7.2370E75
-> END <-
                               (B)
```

FIGURE 3-14
Three-Product Company

The results are rather startling, since the optimum solution calls for production of only product C. The results are impressive in that the contribution is actually increased from $143,750 for the two-product case to $160,714 when product C is added to the line. However, it is no longer a product line, since product C dominates completely.

The production manager probably would not have generated this solution. According to his comment, he envisioned using the slack available in departments two and four from the previous solution, or the generous slack capacity available in his initially proposed schedule. Actually, however, slack is now available in three departments. The reason that product C dominates is that it is so profitable compared to the original two products. Perhaps the most important questions that need to be answered are related to the risks involved in dropping products A and B, and concentrating only on the new product C. Also, we need to be concerned about the size of the potential market for product C.

While the analysis provided by linear optimization models does not deal with risks, we can obtain some insight by looking at the bounds on the prices for the three products in the sensitivity analysis shown in Figure 3-14. In this figure, the lower bound on the attractive contribution for product C is $70, compared to the current contribution of $75. If the estimated contribution for product C decreases by $5 or more, the solution will change. Therefore, it might be worthwhile to examine the effects of a contribution for product C of less than $70 to see what the new solutions would look like and to see what would happen to the optimal value of the objective function.

The solution in Figure 3-14 is also risky because all capacity is turned over to product C. The production and sales managers both realized that their bread and butter had been in products A and B and that the market for the new product as an introduction is probably limited to 50 units. The production manager also accepted the sales manager's estimates for the markets for products A and B of 2200 and 1500 units respectively.

Three products—market constraints

The market constraints are added to the linear optimization model for the three-product case, and the new model is shown as the computer input in Figure 3-15 (a). With the market restrictions, we see that the net contribution of adding product C to the product mix is only $672, compared with the two-product case. Nevertheless, the solution calls for the maximum production of product C permitted by the market constraint, reflecting again the attractive contribution rate for product C.

Note that departments two and four still have slack capacity, and that the new solution indicates slack in constraints [5] and [6], the market constraints for A and B respectively. This means that we did not satisfy the sales manager's estimate of the market for these two products. Looking at the shadow prices in Figure 3-15(b), we see that there is still a $2.08 shadow price on the capacity for department one, a $17.50 shadow price on the capacity for department three, and that there is a $13.44

```
        LPENTER
ENTER THE NAME OF THIS PROJECT THREE PRODUCT COMPANY WITH MARKET RESTRICTIONS
MAXIMIZE OR MINIMIZE: MAX
OBJECTIVE FUNCTION:Z=50A+35B+75C
ENTER CONSTRAINT EQUATIONS (STRIKE JUST A CARRIAGE RETURN TO STOP INPUT)
  (1) 3A+0.15C≤6000
  (2) 2.9B+2.5C≤8000
  (3) 2.5A+2B+3.5C≤7500
  (4) 1.3A+1.5B+1.5C≤5000
  (5) A≤2200
  (6) B≤1500
  (7) C≤50
  (8)
```

(A)

```
        LPRUN
          THREE PRODUCT COMPANY WITH MARKET RESTRICTIONS


THE OPTIMAL VALUE OF THE OBJECTIVE FUNCTION IS:   144421.875


              THE VARIABLES IN THE SOLUTION ARE


VARIABLE   A      AT LEVEL      1.9975E3
           B                    1.1656E3
           C                    5.0000E1
           SLK2                 4.4947E3
           SLK4                 5.7981E2
           SLK5                 2.0250E2
           SLK6                 3.3438E2


DO YOU WISH SENSITIVITY ANALYSIS? YES
```

		SHADOW	LB	CURRENT	UB
CONSTRAINT	1	2.0833E0	5.1975E3	6.0000E3	6.6075E3
	2	0.0000E0	3.5053E3	8.0000E3	7.2370E75
	3	1.7500E1	5.1688E3	7.5000E3	8.1687E3
	4	0.0000E0	4.4202E3	5.0000E3	7.2370E75
	5	0.0000E0	1.9975E3	2.2000E3	7.2370E75
	6	0.0000E0	1.1656E3	1.5000E3	7.2370E75
	7	1.3438E1	0.0000E0	5.0000E1	7.4074E2
PRICE	A		4.3750E1	5.0000E1	3.1875E2
	B		0.0000E0	3.5000E1	4.0000E1
	C		6.1563E1	7.5000E1	7.2370E75

```
-> END <-
```

(B)

FIGURE 3-15
Three-Product
Company with
market restrictions

shadow price on the market constraint for product C, indicated by constraint [7]. That means that if the market can realistically be expanded for the new product, we could gain an additional $13.44 for each unit up to 741 units.

The bounds on the contribution rates (prices) are also useful in mapping strategies. Note that the lower bound for product A is only $6.25 below the current value. If the contribution drops below $43.75, the solution will change. The contribution for product B can fall to zero before the solution will change. However, we find that the contribution rate for the new product C is less sensitive than for product A. The estimated contribution rate would have to be in error by more than $-$13.44 before the solution would change.

We can see from the analysis of the Two- and Three-Product Company structures that a number of computing runs may be useful to the manager. By posing *what if* questions and scenarios for change, and by examining the sensitivity analysis, the manager can obtain a great deal of information that can help in the decision-making process. The value of linear optimization models to the manager is not simply in obtaining an optimal solution to a problem, but in interacting with the model and its variations to obtain information and insights.

FEED MIX SELECTION

To illustrate a different type of problem that can be analyzed using a linear optimization model, let us consider the selection of different grains in a feed mix. A feed and grain producer purchases and mixes three different types of grain to produce feed for cattle. The cattle feed must meet minimum standards for four basic nutritional ingredients according to current federal regulations. The percentage of each of these nutritional ingredients in each unit weight of each grain and the minimum federal regulations are shown in Table 3-4. For example, one pound of wheat contains 0.1 pounds of ingredient 1, 0.2 pounds of ingredient 2, and so on; and one pound of feed must contain 0.1 pounds of ingredient 1, 0.1 pounds of ingredient 2, and so on.

Model formulation

The current market forecast is for sales of 10,000 pounds of cattle feed during the next month. Wheat currently costs $0.10 per pound, barley costs $0.12 per pound, and rye costs $0.08 per pound. How many pounds of each grain should be purchased and mixed to meet the sales forecast at minimum cost, while meeting the federal regulations?

Nutritional Ingredients in Grains

Nutritional Ingredient	Proportion of Each Nutritional Ingredient in			Minimum Federal Regulation for Feed
	Wheat	Barley	Rye	
1	0.10	0.10	0.15	0.10
2	0.20	0.00	0.15	0.10
3	0.30	0.20	0.10	0.15
4	0.30	0.25	0.20	0.20

Decision variables The decision variables are the number of pounds of each grain — wheat (W), barley (B), or rye (R) — to include in the feed.

Objective function The objective is to minimize the total cost of the grain. The cost of wheat will be $0.1W$, barley $0.12B$, and rye $0.08R$, so we wish to

$$\text{minimize } Z = 0.1W + 0.12B + 0.08R$$

Constraints The first four constraints simply ensure that the minimum federal requirements for each ingredient are met. From Table 3-4, at least 0.1 of the total sales forecast of 10,000 pounds, or $(0.1)(10,000) = 1000$ pounds, should be nutrient 1. This constraint is imposed by

$$0.1W + 0.1B + 0.15R \geq 1000$$

Similar constraints can be written for the other three ingredients. We must also meet the sales forecast for the feed, so

$$W + B + R = 10,000$$

is the final constraint.

Figure 3-16 shows the computer input and solution for this problem. The complete formulation is shown as the computer input (A). According to the computer solution (B), we should purchase 2500 pounds of wheat (W) and 7500 pounds of rye (R) to mix for the feed. Since the variable corresponding to barley (B) does not appear in the solution, its optimal value is zero.

```
        LPENTER
ENTER THE NAME OF THIS PROJECT FEED MIX PROBLEM
MAXIMIZE OR MINIMIZE: MINIMIZE
OBJECTIVE FUNCTION:Z=.1W+.12B+.08R
ENTER CONSTRAINT EQUATIONS (STRIKE JUST A CARRIAGE RETURN TO STOP INPUT)
 (1) .1W+.1B+.15R≥1000
 (2) .2W+.15R≥1000
 (3) .3W+.2B+.1R≥1500
 (4) .3W+.25B+.2R≥2000
 (5) W+B+R=10000
 (6)
```
                          (A)
```
     LPRUN
                  FEED MIX PROBLEM


THE OPTIMAL VALUE OF THE OBJECTIVE FUNCTION IS:   850.000


          THE VARIABLES IN THE SOLUTION ARE


VARIABLE  W        AT LEVEL       2.5000E3
          R                       7.5000E3
          SUR1                    3.7500E2
          SUR2                    6.2500E2
          SUR4                    2.5000E2
```
                          (B)

FIGURE 3-16
Feed mix problem

Notice that the computer solution gives us some new variables that we did not ask for, $SUR1$, $SUR2$, and $SUR4$. These are surplus variables related to constraints [1], [2], and [4], and are similar to slack values, except that they correspond to the use of greater than or equal to ($\geq$) relationships in constraints instead of the less than or equal to ($\leq$) relationships encountered in the previous problems. Some problem formulations may include both types of constraints, so the solution may involve both slack variables and surplus variables.

For example, if $W = 2500$, $B = 0$, and $R = 7500$, then from constraint [1], there are $(0.1)(2500) + (0.1)(0.0) + (0.15)(7500) = 1375$ pounds of ingredient 1 in the feed. The difference between 1375 and the federal requirement of a minimum of 1000 pounds, or 375 pounds, is the value of the surplus variable, $SUR1$. Test your understanding of this important point by interpreting the meaning of $SUR2$ and $SUR4$. The sensitivity analysis for this problem is considered in Exercise 20.

This formulation of the feed mix problem is a simplification of an important class of applications of linear optimization models. Actual applications have been reported by Chappell [1974] and by Lyons and Dodd [1975]. Also, related models that allocate the use of food ingredients to meet nutritional requirements at minimum cost have been used by Balintfy [1975] in food management applications such as those found in university dormitories, military installations, hospitals, and other large institutions supplying food service.

WHAT SHOULD THE MANAGER KNOW?

Linear optimization models can become very complex, involving an enormous number of variables and constraints, and a manager's initial reaction could easily be one of rejection. However, managers need not be concerned with the mathematical complexities. The real value for them lies in being aware of the characteristics of problems for which linear optimization models may be useful, so that they can both suggest applications and evaluate proposals for application. In addition, a knowledge of the nature of model formulation, information requirements, and, particularly, interpretation of results is important for managers. If they so choose, they need not know the mathematical methods of the linear programming solution technique. Given the existence of linear programming computer codes similar to the one used in this chapter, the manager can assume that if the problem can be put in standard form for input, the "black box" will perform its function and provide the solution output, complete with sensitivity analysis.

On the other hand, some knowledge of what actually happens within the computer program may provide some additional insights for managers. The mathematical logic of linear programming computer codes is described in Chapters 5 and 6.

Problem characteristics

What is the nature of problems for which linear optimization methods are applicable? Linear optimization models are of value in problems that involve the allocation of limited resources to competing demands. The chemical production, product planning, and feed mix examples all had this general characteristic. In the chemical production and product planning examples, the limited resources were the productive capacities and the limited market demands; the objective was to maximize the use of the resources with respect to a criterion — maximum profits. In the feed mix example, the limited productive resources were the raw materials and limited market demands, and the objective was to optimize the use of the different ingredients in order to minimize costs.

Applications of linear optimization models in the analysis of production problems are commonplace today. In addition to the kinds of problems described here, these models have been used to analyze multiple plant location problems and scheduling problems. The problems at the end of this chapter provide examples of the analysis of production problems using linear optimization models. Examples of applications in other areas, including marketing, finance, labor and personnel management, urban planning, and education, are provided in Chapter 4.

Model formulation

Managers need to know and understand something about formulating linear models in order to use the services of staff analysts appropriately and to interpret results. They must be able to think in terms of the objective function and the constraints to their problems. If they can formulate the simpler kinds of problems we used as examples in this chapter, they can work effectively through analysts to help formulate more complex problems, for as we noted, the more complex problems are straightforward extensions of the concepts involved in the simple ones.

Interpretation of results

The heart of the managerial function is focused in the interpretation of results and in decision making. While the solution output has obvious value for the manager, the power of the results is greatly enhanced by the sensitivity analysis. Managers can put themselves in the interactive mode that we discussed in Chapter 2. They can raise intelligent *what if* questions if they understand the meaning of shadow prices and the upper and lower bounds on solutions. These questions often result in additional computing runs to evaluate alternatives that are not automatically generated within the optimization model.

CHECK YOUR UNDERSTANDING

1. Which of the following mathematical expressions are linear? Why?
   a. $x + y = 1$
   b. $x^2 + y^2 = 10$
   c. $1/x + 2x = 10$
   d. $x + xy + y = 1$
   e. $x_1 + x_2 + x_3 + x_4 = 1$

2. Graph each of the following constraints on a separate graph and shade or cross-hatch the areas of the graph that include admissible points.
   a. $x + y \leq 4$
   b. $x + y \geq 10$
   c. $2x + 3y = 15$
   d. $x \leq 10$

3. Outline the model-building process used for developing linear optimization models.

4. How are alternatives generated within the structure of the model-building process?

5. In the break-even analysis example, explain why we were able to simply drop the variable f (fixed cost) from the objective function.

6. In the break-even analysis example, there was a slack capacity of 100 units per month. Suppose that the demand constraint had been $x \leq 400$. How would the concept of slack apply?

7. In the chemical production example, the objective function that we developed was a statement of contribution to profit and overhead. Why maximize this function instead of an expression for profit? Isn't it really profit that we wish to maximize?

8. Suppose that in the chemical production problem, the availability of time on machine A is drastically reduced to only 40 hours because of a breakdown. How does this change the solution space shown in Figure 3-6? Is it likely to change the optimum number of units of each chemical to produce?

9. Explain the concept of shadow prices. How can a manager use a knowledge of shadow prices in decision making?

10. What is the interpretation of the upper and lower bounds on the shadow prices indicated in Figure 3-8? Of what value is this information to a manager?

11. Suppose that in the chemical production problem, the availability of time on machine B is increased by 1 hour to a total of 61 hours. By plotting the constraints of this revised problem, verify that the optimal solution will lie at the point of intersection of the machine A and the machine B constraints. Solve the equations for the constraint lines by substitution to find the new optimal solution. Evaluate this solution using the objective function, and compare it to the optimal solution found in Figure 3-7.

12. Suppose that in the chemical production problem the availability of time on ma-

chine B is increased by 18 hours to 78 hours. Analyze the problem graphically, as shown in Figure 3-10. What would be the impact on the optimal solution if another hour on machine B were obtained?

13. Suppose that in the chemical production problem, the availability of time on machine B is decreased by 18 hours to 42 hours. Analyze the problem graphically, as shown in Figure 3-10. What would be the impact on the optimal solution if the number of available hours on machine B was reduced by 1 hour to 41 hours? Would this decrease still cost $17.50 in contribution? Why or why not?

14. What is the interpretation of the upper and lower bounds on the "prices" given in Figure 3-8? Of what value is this information to the manager?

15. What may be the practical value of knowing that the bounds on one or more prices may be "tight"?

16. Suppose that in the chemical production problem the contribution rate of chemical x is increased to $90 per unit. Analyze the problem graphically. What would be the new optimal solution?

17. Suppose that in the chemical production problem the contribution rate of chemical x is decreased to $10 per unit. Analyze the problem graphically. What would be the new optimal solution?

18. Suppose we have a machine that is flexible and can be used to process various sizes of a product by a simple adjustment. The capacity of the machine is greater for small sizes. The capacity of the machine for three sizes is $x_1 = 500$ per month, $x_2 = 1000$ per month, and $x_3 = 2500$ per month. The monthly capacity of the machine for an average mix is stated to be 1500 per month. Write the capacity constraint expression for the machine.

19. The sensitivity analysis for the two-product model with ratio constraints (see Figure 3-12) is shown in Figure 3-17. Using this result and Figure 3-12, answer the following questions:
    a. The shadow prices for constraints [4] and [6] are 0.0. Why should you expect this result, considering the solution in Figure 3-12?
    b. Suppose the demand for product 1 increased from 50 units to 52 units. What would the total cost of production become?
    c. Suppose you can sell an additional 6 units of product 2 for a discounted price of $0.50 per unit. Should you make the sale?
    d. Your accountant announces that the costs of producing product 2 on the manual system during shift 2 have increased to $10 per 10 units. Would the optimal solution be affected? How do you know?

DO YOU WISH SENSITIVITY ANALYSIS? YES

		SHADOW	LB	CURRENT	UB
CONSTRAINT	1	1.1000E1	1.3333E0	5.0000E0	5.3333E0
	2	5.6000E0	5.0000E0	1.0000E1	1.0625E1
	3	-2.0000E-1	1.3125E1	1.5000E1	3.0000E1
	4	0.0000E0	0.0000E0	1.5000E1	7.2370E75
	5	-4.0000E-1	2.7500E1	3.0000E1	5.7500E1
	6	0.0000E0	2.7500E1	3.0000E1	7.2370E75
PRICE	M11		1.0000E1	1.0000E1	7.2370E75
	MCH11		7.2500E0	8.0000E0	8.0000E0
	M12		1.1000E1	1.5000E1	7.2370E75
	MCH12		9.8750E0	1.1000E1	1.1000E1
	M21		-7.2370E75	5.0000E0	5.0000E0
	MCH21		4.0000E0	4.0000E0	4.4000E0
	M22		5.6000E0	6.0000E0	7.2370E75
	MCH22		5.6000E0	6.0000E0	7.2370E75

FIGURE 3-17
Sensitivity analysis
for the two-product
example with ratio
constraints

-< END >-

e. What if the cost of producing product 2 on the manual system during shift 1 decreases? Would there be any effect on the solution? What if it increases slightly?

20. The sensitivity analysis for the feed mix problem is shown in Figure 3-18. Using Figure 3-18 along with the computer input and solution shown in Figure 3-16, answer the following questions:

a. Suppose that the federal requirement for ingredient 3 were lowered from 0.15 to 0.12. What would be the effect on the optimal solution? Would the cost of the feed increase or decrease? By how much?

FIGURE 3-18
Sensitivity analysis
for the feed
mix problem

DO YOU WISH SENSITIVITY ANALYSIS? YES

		SHADOW	LB	CURRENT	UB
CONSTRAINT	1	0.0000E0	-7.2370E75	1.0000E3	1.3750E3
	2	0.0000E0	-7.2370E75	1.0000E3	1.6250E3
	3	1.0000E-1	1.0000E3	1.5000E3	3.0000E3
	4	0.0000E0	-7.2370E75	2.0000E3	2.2500E3
	5	7.0000E-2	8.3333E3	1.0000E4	1.5000E4
PRICE	W		8.0000E-2	1.0000E-1	1.6000E-1
	B		9.0000E-2	1.2000E-1	7.2370E75
	R		-7.2370E75	8.0000E-2	1.0000E-1

b. Suppose that the federal regulation for ingredient 2 were lowered from 0.1 to 0.05. Would the solution change? How do you know?

c. Suppose the accountant of the firm rushes in with the news that the price of wheat has increased from $0.10 per pound to $0.12 per pound. Should the optimal mix for the feed be changed? How do you know?

SHORT CASES

CASE 3-1

The Elmore Electronics Corporation is a manufacturer of two kinds of electronic test equipment: Oscilloscopes (O) and vacuum tube voltmeters (V). The physical facilities are organized into three main departments: the circuit board department (CB), the chassis department (C) and final assembly (A). Monthly capacities for each of the two products in the three departments are given in Table 3-5, and financial data are given in Table 3-6. Current market forecasts for the two products for the coming month are for 400 oscilloscopes and 600 voltmeters.

Formulate a linear optimization model for the manager of Elmore that can be used as a basis for scheduling production for next month.

CASE 3-2

Elmore is contemplating the addition of a third product for the coming month, which it thinks will have a broad appeal to TV repairmen. It is a portable circuit board tester that can quickly check a standard circuit board by setting dials and switches to standard settings. The product has been market tested and estimates of the market and production costs have been made.

The supervisors in the chassis and circuit board departments state that they can absorb the small added load with present facilities and labor force. The assembly department supervisor, however, states that he must enlarge his labor force to a total of 3500 available hours in order to absorb the new product load.

Monthly Capacities for the Elmore Electronic Corporation			TABLE 3-5
	Time Requirements (hours/unit)		
	Oscilloscopes (O)	Voltmeters (V)	Hours Available Next Month
Chassis Department (C)	4.5	2.0	2000
Circuit Board Department (CB)	6.3	1.5	2500
Assembly Department (A)	7.0	3.0	3000

TABLE 3-6   Costs and Prices for the Elmore
Electronics Corporation

Costs and Prices (per unit)	Oscilloscopes (O)	Voltmeters (V)
Sales prices	$170	$55
Costs		
Variable labor	20	5
Material	50	10
Overhead (at current volume)	40	10

The new product is dubbed (P) for *portable* and alternate plans must be generated to include the item in next month's production schedule. The manager is delighted with the prospect that the new product may go into production, partly because overhead costs will be spread over a larger product base, making existing products more "profitable." He estimates that the per unit overhead costs will decline to $38 for oscilloscopes and $9 for voltmeters.

The portable circuit board testers (P) will sell for $400 each, and initial cost estimates indicate that variable labor will be $100, materials $125, and allocated overhead $60 per unit. Initial sales estimates are set at 50 for next month. Hours requirements in the three departments for P are estimated to be 9 per unit in the chassis department, 10 per unit in the circuit board department, and 15 per unit in assembly. Reformulate Elmore's problem as a linear optimization model.

CASE 3-3   The Goodwear Shoe Company has three plants, all of which can produce the full line of shoes: dress shoes (D), which yield a net contribution of $10 each; work shoes (W), which yield $8; and sport shoes (S), which yield $4.

A decline in the market has caused an excess capacity in all three plants amounting to 550, 650, and 300 units per day in plants 1, 2, and 3 respectively (regardless of shoe type). Even though there is excess capacity, there is an in-process inventory capacity limit because of physical layout limitations. These limitations, in turn, limit output rates. The three plants have available 1000, 850, and 400 square feet of storage space respectively. Shoe lines D, W, and S require 1.0, 1.5, and 0.8 equivalent square feet of storage. Sales forecasts are 700, 850, and 750 for shoe lines D, W, and S.

Formulate a linear optimization model that will provide management with a program of how many of each shoe type to produce in each plant. The model must meet the constraints and maximize contribution.

The Appliance Manufacturing Company produces air conditioners (*A*), refrigerators (*R*), and electric stoves (*S*). The manufacturing facility needs for the three product lines are common in certain respects, which accounts for the fact that manufacturing costs are generally low. The facilities are composed of a machine shop, which fabricates a variety of parts needed in all three products; a metal stamping department, which stamps out a variety of sheet metal parts for all three products; a unit department, which produces the refrigeration units used in *A* and *R;* and independent assembly lines for each of the three products.

CASE 3-4

Because some of the facilities are shared between the product lines, specifying their capacities posed a problem. The manufacturing manager finally resolved the difficulty by computing the limiting capacity of the machine shop if, for example, it were entirely devoted to each of the three products. He summarized these results in Table 3-7.

The contribution rates for the three products were $60, $50, and $40 per unit respectively for *A, R,* and *S.* Also, the maximums that the marketing department estimated could be sold in the coming planning period were 4000, 3000, and 2000 for *A, R,* and *S.*

Formulate a linear optimization model designed to maximize contribution within the constraints under which the company must operate.

TABLE 3-7

Capacities of Shop Facilities for Air Conditioners, Refrigerators, and Stoves

	Department Capacity for:		
	Air Conditioners	Refrigerators	Stoves
Machine shop	6000	7000	8000
Stamping department	9000	5000	4000
Unit department	7000	6000	—
A Assembly	5000	—	—
R Assembly	—	4000	—
S Assembly	—	—	3000

A refinery operating in Nebraska uses four crude oils: Oklahoma, West Texas, Wyoming, and Pennsylvania. These crudes have different delivered costs as indicated in Table 3-8. The refinery makes four basic end products: regular gas, high-test gas, diesel fuel, and fuel oil. The catalytic cracking and reforming characteristics of the refinery dictate a limited and different input mix of the crude oils, also indicated in Table 3-8. For example, 30 percent of the Oklahoma crude must be used for regular gas, 10 percent for high-test gas, 40 percent for diesel

CASE 3-5

TABLE 3-8   Refinery and Market Data

Crude	Delivered Price per Gallon (cents)	Percentage of Optimal Throughput for Each Crude			
		Regular Gas	High-Test Gas	Diesel Fuel	Fuel Oil
Oklahoma	84	30	10	40	20
West Texas	82	20	10	60	10
Wyoming	80	10	—	30	60
Pennsylvania	88	30	50	20	—
Present market requirement (gallons per hour)	—	20,000	15,000	28,000	33,000

fuel, and the remaining 20 percent for fuel oil.

The objective is to minimize crude oil costs, but meet market requirements. Let A, B, C, and D represent the number of gallons of crude oil from Oklahoma, West Texas, Wyoming, and Pennsylvania respectively that must be used per hour.

Formulate the refinery problem as a linear optimization model.

CASE 3-6   The Three Mines Company owns three different mines that produce an ore that, after being crushed, is graded into three classes: high, medium, and low grade. There is some demand for each grade of ore. The Three Mines Company has contracted to provide a smelting plant with 12 tons of high-grade, 8 tons of medium-grade, and 24 tons of low-grade ore per week. Operating costs are $180 per day for mine W, $200 per day for mine X, and $160 per day for mine Y.

The three mines have different capacities. Mine W produces 6, 3, and 4 tons per day of high-, medium-, and low-grade ores respectively. Mine X produces 3, 1, and 2 tons per day of the three ores, and Mine Y produces 1, 1, and 6 tons per day of the three ores.

How many days per week should each mine be operated to fill the orders and minimize operating costs? Let W, X, and Y represent the number of days per week each of the mines operates. Formulate the Three Mines Company's problem as a linear optimization model.

CASE 3-7   A phosphate mine in central Florida is a surface strip mine. The phosphate rock is mined and separated into two grades and stored in piles. Each month, for every ton of grade 2 rock that is mined, 1.2 tons of grade 1 rock are also mined.

The customers for the rock are fertilizer plants, and they place orders for shipments of rock over a two-month period. Because of the nature of their production processes, the customers specify a minimum monthly shipment rate in tons (their inventories allow some flexibility). The shipping requirements for January and February are as follows.

Month	Minimum Shipment in Tons
January	50
February	70

Although there is flexibility for the tonnage shipped each month, the total tonnage shipped over the two-month period *must* equal 130 tons.

On January 1, the company has 15 tons of grade 1 rock and 20 tons of grade 2 rock in inventory. The company requires that the minimum inventory level for each grade be 10 tons, so part of the shipping requirements can be met with existing inventory. Because of physical space limitations the total ending inventory for each month must be less than or equal to 50 tons for both grades combined. The revenue is $1000 per ton of grade 1 and $1200 per ton for grade 2. The strip-mining cost is the same for each grade, $900 per ton. The company wishes to determine a production and shipping schedule that will maximize contribution to profit and overhead over the two-month period.[*]

Formulate the appropriate linear optimization model. Use the following decision variables:

GRJ1, GRJ2, GRF1, GRF2 — tons of each grade of rock to produce each month

SGJ1, SGJ2, SGF1, SGF2 — tons of each grade to ship each month

EIJ1, EIJ2, EIF1, EIF2 — tons of ending inventory each month

Mesa Plastics Company is a bulk producer of sheet plastic, which they sell in three sizes (thick- CASE 3-8 nesses). They have two plants located on the same site. Plant *B* is of later design and was specifically built to produce sizes 1 and 2 economically, since these two sizes had the largest demand. However, plant *B* is less economical than *A* for size 3. Time requirements for the three products in the two plants and the variable hourly costs and time availability for plants *A* and *B* are shown in Table 3-9. Sales revenue and maximum demand for the three products are shown in Table 3-10. Management is considering how production should be allocated to the two plants for the upcoming period so as to maximize contribution.

[*] This case is a simplification of a linear programming model actually in use, as described by J. M. Reddy ("A Model to Schedule Sales Optimally Blended From Scarce Resources," *Interfaces*, Vol. 6, No. 1, Part 2, November 1975). The model has 1700 constraints and 4000 variables. An evaluation study indicated that the model is increasing profits by several million dollars per year compared to a manually prepared plan.

A computer input and output for a linear optimization model is given in Figure 3-19. How do you interpret the results?

TABLE 3-9

Time Requirements, Costs, and Capacities for the Mesa Plastics Company

	Hours per 100 Pounds	
	Plant A	Plant B
Size 1	0.25	0.20
Size 2	0.40	0.25
Size 3	0.35	0.40
Variable costs per hour	$250	$300
Maximum available hours per week	100	100

TABLE 3-10

Sales Revenue and Maximum Demand for the Mesa Plastics Company

Size	Sales Revenue per 100 Pounds	Maximum Demand per Week (100s of pounds)
1	$100	310
2	$120	300
3	$150	125

GENERAL REFERENCES

Balintfy, J. L., "A Mathematical Programming System for Food Management Applications," *Interfaces,* Vol. 6, No. 1, Part 2, November 1975.

Bierman, H., C. P. Bonini, and W. H. Hausman, *Quantitative Analysis for Business Decisions,* fifth edition, Richard D. Irwin, Inc., Homewood, Ill., 1977.

Buckley, J. W., M. R. Nagarai, D. L. Sharp, and J. W. Schenck, *Management Problem-Solving with APL,* John Wiley & Sons, New York, 1974.

```
                    MESA PLASTICS COMPANY
MAXIMIZE OR MINIMIZE:  MAX
OBJECTIVE FUNCTION:  Z=37.5A1+40B1+20A2+45B2+62.5A3+30B3
ENTER CONSTRAINT EQUATIONS (STRIKE JUST A CARRIAGE RETURN TO STOP INPUT)
[1] 0.25A1+0.4A2+0.35A3≤100
[2] 0.2B1+0.25B2+0.4B3≤100
[3] A1+B1≤310
[4] A2+B2≤300
[5] A3+B3≤125
[6]
      LPRUN
                   MESA PLASTICS COMPANY


THE OPTIMAL VALUE OF THE OBJECTIVE FUNCTION IS:   33250.000


            THE VARIABLES IN THE SOLUTION ARE


VARIABLE   A1      AT LEVEL       1.8500E2
           B1                     1.2500E2
           B2                     3.0000E2
           A3                     1.2500E2
           SLK1                   1.0000E1


DO YOU WISH SENSITIVITY ANALYSIS?  YES

                       SHADOW        LB        CURRENT        UB
CONSTRAINT      1     0.0000E0    9.0000E1    1.0000E2    7.2370E75
                2     1.2500E1    9.2000E1    1.0000E2    1.3700E2
                3     3.7500E1    1.2500E2    3.1000E2    3.5000E2
                4     4.1875E1    1.5200E2    3.0000E2    3.3200E2
                5     6.2500E1    0.0000E0    1.2500E2    1.5375E2

PRICE
           A1                     2.0000E1    3.7500E1    4.0000E1
           B1                     3.7500E1    4.0000E1    5.7500E1
           A2                    -7.2370E75   2.0000E1    4.1875E1
           B2                     2.3125E1    4.5000E1    7.2370E75
           A3                     2.5000E1    6.2500E1    7.2370E75
           B3                    -7.2370E75   3.0000E1    6.7500E1
->END<-
```

FIGURE 3-19

Computer input
and output for the
Mesa Plastics
Company

Chappell, A. C., "Linear Programming Cuts Costs in Production of Animal Feeds," *Operational Research Quarterly,* Vol. 25, No. 1, March 1974.

Charnes, A., and W. W. Cooper, *Management Models and Industrial Applications of Linear Programming,* Vols. 1 and 2, John Wiley & Sons, New York, 1961.

Cohen, R., C. McBride, R. Thornton, and T. White, *Letter Mail System Reference Design: An Analytical Method for Evaluating Candidate Mechanization,* Institute for Defense Analysis, Report R-168, 1970.

Dallenbach, H. G., and E. J. Bell, *User's Guide to Linear Programming,* Prentice-Hall, Englewood Cliffs, N.J., 1970.

Dantzig, G. B., *Linear Programming and Extensions,* Princeton University Press, Princeton, N.J., 1963.

Hillier, F. S., and G. L. Lieberman, *Introduction to Operations Research,* second edition, Holden-Day, San Francisco, 1974.

Lyons, D. F., and V. A. Dodd, "The Feed Mix Problem," *Operational Research,* North-Holland Publishing Co., Amsterdam, 1975.

McBride, C. C., "Post Office Mail Operations," in *Analysis of Public Systems,* edited by A. W. Drake, R. L. Keeney, and P. M. Morse, MIT Press, Cambridge, Mass., 1972.

Reddy, J. M., "A Model to Schedule Sales Optimally Blended from Scarce Resources," *Interfaces,* Vol. 6, No. 1, Part II, November 1975.

Thierauf, R. J., and R. Klekamp, *Decision Making Through Operations Research,* second edition, John Wiley & Sons, New York, 1975.

Wagner, H. M., *Principles of Operations Research,* second edition, Prentice-Hall, Englewood Cliffs, N.J., 1975.

CHAPTER 4

Applications of Linear Optimization Models

Chapter 3 provided numerous examples of the use of linear optimization models to analyze production problems. Now let us think more broadly about the format of this model to see the range of problems that can be analyzed through its use. Such problems occur in profit and not-for-profit enterprises and in various organization functions such as finance, marketing, and personnel planning.

In this chapter, we give examples of applications of linear optimization models in a variety of situations. In order to avoid extraneous details, these examples have necessarily been simplified. However, real-world counterparts of each of them are in routine use.

We have categorized these examples into finance, marketing, personnel, and the not-for-profit sector. In studying these examples, you should be looking for the common threads in these applications that make them capable of analysis by linear optimization models. This awareness will aid you in identifying potential applications of this powerful analytical tool in the real world.

LINEAR OPTIMIZATION
MODELS FOR FINANCIAL DECISIONS

There are many financial decisions that can be successfully analyzed using linear optimization models. The general financing mix problem has been approached by linear optimization methods at various levels in organizations. At the overall enterprise level we can raise the question of the most profitable combination of financing sources, such as equity versus debt. Or, for the shorter term use of funds, we may ask what is the most profitable allocation of funds to accounts receivable, planned payments for purchases, cash needs for operation, and cash surplus from operations? Robichek, Teichroew, and Jones [1965] formulated linear optimization models in which the objective was to minimize net interest cost while meeting cash needs. The sources of short-term funds were pledges of accounts receivable at specific interest costs, stretched payments for purchases at a cost of loss of discounts, and short-term loans. There were constraints on the amounts of all sources. Smith [1974] has collected several examples of the use of linear optimization models for the management of working capital.

Through an extension of linear programming, Hughes and Lewellen [1974] have formulated the capital rationing problem in which limited capital funds are allocated to specific capital investment projects. The objective is to select from among the complete set of investment opportunities those projects that will provide the highest possible returns without exceeding the allowed budget.

A number of other applications are reviewed in the survey *Quantitative Analysis of Financial Decisions* by Mao [1969]. The examples presented here demonstrate how financial and production decisions can be integrated, and how portfolio selection and cash management decisions can be analyzed.

Financing the production decision

In Chapter 3, we studied the linear optimization model for the chemical manufacturing firm that produces two products. This example shows how financial and production considerations for that firm can be integrated into a linear optimization model for production planning. The relevant production and financial data are summarized in Table 4-1. The firm also must pay fixed expenses of $400 in dividends and $500 on plant and equipment each month. The balance sheet for the firm at the end of December is shown in Table 4-2.

The company's two products are sold on terms of one month credit, but the variable costs of labor and materials must be paid immediately. For simplicity, we assume that the firm produces no more of each product than the monthly demand figure, so inventory is zero for both products.

The firm has a policy of maintaining a cash asset position of at least $5000 each month. In addition, the terms of the bond indenture require that the firm maintain a balance of at least $13,500 in short-term assets at all times (short-term assets are the

Data for the Chemical Manufacturing Company						TABLE 4-1
Production			Financial			
	Product				Product	
	x	*y*			*x*	*y*
Machine A (hr)	2	4	Sales price		$350	$450
Machine B (hr)	3	2	Variable costs		290	400
Monthly demand (units)	16	18	Unit contribution to profit and overhead		60	50
Total Available Time (hr per mo)			Fixed cash expenses		$900	
Machine A	80					
Machine B	60					

TABLE 4-2	Balance Sheet for Chemical Manufacturing Company (end of December)			
	Cash assets	$ 7,000	Bank loan	$ 7,000
	Accounts receivable	7,000	Long-term bonds	7,000
	Inventory	0	Equity	10,000
	Plant and equipment	10,000		$24,000
		$24,000		

sum of cash, accounts receivable, and inventory, or $14,000 at the end of December). How many units of each chemical product should the firm produce in January in order to maximize profits while observing these financial restrictions?

Decision variables As before, we let *CHEMX* be the number of units of chemical x produced in January, and *CHEMY* is the number of units of chemical y.

Objective function The objective of the production plan is to maximize the contribution to profit and overhead:

maximize $Z = 60 \ CHEMX + 50 \ CHEMY$

Constraints First, we have the same constraints on machine time and demand that were described in Chapter 3. For machine A,

$2 \ CHEMX + 4 \ CHEMY \leq 80$

and for machine B,

$3 \ CHEMX + 2 \ CHEMY \leq 60$

The demand constraints are $CHEMX \leq 16$ and $CHEMY \leq 18$.

Now let us consider the additional financial constraints on the production decision. The cash asset position at the end of January must be at least $5000. The beginning balance is $7000, and the collection of the accounts receivable will add an additional $7000, for a total of $7000 + $7000 = $14,000 of available cash. However, the fixed cash expenses of $900 per month and the variable costs of 290 *CHEMX*

+ 400 *CHEMY* must be paid in January, so we require

14,000 − 900 − 290 *CHEMX* − 400 *CHEMY* ≥ 5000

which simplifies to

290 *CHEMX* + 400 *CHEMY* ≤ 8100

The constraint on short-term assets is developed in a similar manner. In January, the short-term asset position of $14,000 is reduced by the fixed cash expenses, $900, and by the payment of the variable costs, 290 *CHEMX* + 400 *CHEMY*. The asset position is increased, however, by the revenue generated by the sales of the products, or 350 *CHEMX* + 450 *CHEMY*. In order to ensure that the short-term asset position is at least $13,500, the constraint

14,000 − 900 − 290 *CHEMX* − 400 *CHEMY* + 350 *CHEMX*
+ 450 *CHEMY* ≥ 13,500

is needed. This simplifies to

60 *CHEMX* + 50 *CHEMY* ≥ 400

The computer input and solution for this formulation are shown in Figure 4-1. The linear optimization model is the input (a) and the solution is shown as (b). Notice that the optimal solution, *CHEMX* = 12.58 and *CHEMY* = 11.13, differs from the solution determined in Chapter 3. This is because of constraint [5] on the cash position of the firm. The interpretation of this result and an examination of the sensitivity analysis are presented in Exercise 1 of "Check Your Understanding."

Formulation of a portfolio selection problem

The selection of an investment portfolio is a common problem. The objective is to maximize expected returns, but this objective is often constrained by policies that require diversification of investments. Suppose we are managing a portfolio and are dealing in four types of securities: the electronics industry, utilities, financial institutions, and the chemical industry. Data on permissible percentages of the portfolio to be invested and current expected yields are shown in Table 4-3.

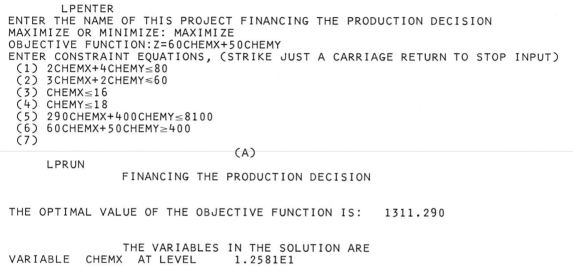

```
      LPENTER
ENTER THE NAME OF THIS PROJECT FINANCING THE PRODUCTION DECISION
MAXIMIZE OR MINIMIZE: MAXIMIZE
OBJECTIVE FUNCTION: Z=60CHEMX+50CHEMY
ENTER CONSTRAINT EQUATIONS, (STRIKE JUST A CARRIAGE RETURN TO STOP INPUT)
 (1)  2CHEMX+4CHEMY≤80
 (2)  3CHEMX+2CHEMY≤60
 (3)  CHEMX≤16
 (4)  CHEMY≤18
 (5)  290CHEMX+400CHEMY≤8100
 (6)  60CHEMX+50CHEMY≥400
 (7)
```
                              (A)
```
      LPRUN
              FINANCING THE PRODUCTION DECISION


THE OPTIMAL VALUE OF THE OBJECTIVE FUNCTION IS:    1311.290


                    THE VARIABLES IN THE SOLUTION ARE
VARIABLE    CHEMX   AT LEVEL     1.2581E1
            CHEMY                1.1129E1
            SLK1                 1.0323E1
            SLK3                 3.4194E0
            SLK4                 6.8710E0
            SUR6                 9.1129E2
```
                              (B)

FIGURE 4-1
Production problem
with financial
constraints

In addition, the electronics and financial industries are considered to be relatively high risk investments, so we require that the total percentage of the portfolio invested in both of them should be less than or equal to 40. Further, we wish to ensure that the investment in utilities should be at least 50 percent of the total investment in electronics and financial securities.

Decision variables The decision variables are the proportions of the portfolio to be invested in each of the four types of securities—E, U, F, and C.

Objective function The objective is to maximize the total yield. Therefore, we wish to maximize the proportion of the fund in electronics, E, times the yield for these securities, 0.12, plus similar terms for each of the other security types. Stated in mathematical terms, we have

$$\text{maximize } Z = 0.12E + 0.08U + 0.10F + 0.09C$$

| Permissible Investment Limits and Current Yields | | | TABLE 4-3 |
| Type of Security | Limits (%) | | Expected Yield (%) |
	Minimum	Maximum	
Electronics (E)	10	30	12
Utilities (U)	15	–	8
Financial (F)	5	20	10
Chemicals (C)	20	35	9

Constraints The decision variables represent proportions, so they should sum to 1.0. Thus, our first constraint is

$$E + U + F + C = 1.0$$

Next, we need constraints to enforce the minimum and maximum restrictions on the investment in each type of security, as shown in Table 4-3. For the electronics industry we can simply write $E \geq 0.1$ and $E \leq 0.3$ to reflect these requirements. Similar constraints can be written for the other three security types.

Also, the total investment in the electronics and financial securities must be less than or equal to 0.4, which is guaranteed by the constraint

$$E + F \leq 0.4$$

Finally, the investment in utilities must be at least 50 percent of this total. That is, we must have

$$U \geq 0.5 \, (E + F)$$

which can be written as

$$0.5E + 0.5F - U \leq 0$$

The complete formulation of this problem is shown in Table 4-4. The computer input, solution, and the sensitivity analysis are presented in Exercise 2 in "Check Your Understanding."

TABLE 4-4 — Linear Optimization Model for the Portfolio Selection Problem

Maximize $Z = 0.12E + 0.08U + 0.10F + 0.09C$

subject to

proportions	$E + U + F + C = 1.0$
minimum limit on E	$E \geq 0.1$
maximum limit on E	$E \leq 0.3$
minimum limit on U	$U \geq 0.15$
minimum limit on F	$F \geq 0.05$
maximum limit on F	$F \leq 0.2$
minimum limit on C	$C \geq 0.2$
maximum limit on C	$C \leq 0.35$
limit on sum	$E + F \leq 0.4$
limit on U	$0.5E - U + 0.5F \leq 0$
	$E, U, F, C \geq 0$

Cash management

A problem affecting many organizations is the management of their cash assets. These assets can be invested in short-term securities when excess cash is available, or the least expensive means of financing short-term debt may be sought.

Suppose that a firm is attempting to manage its cash balance so that it obtains the maximum return on its assets. It has forecasted the cash payments it can expect from its accounts receivables, and the accounts payable from its own commitments in each of the next three months as shown in Table 4-5.

TABLE 4-5 — Forecasts of Cash Receipts and Payments

Month	Forecasted Cash Inflow (in $ thousands)	Forecasted Accounts Payable (in $ thousands)
1 (Jan.)	10	40
2 (Feb.)	20	60
3 (Mar.)	40	50
	70	150

The firm can delay payment of an account by one month and pay a penalty of 2 percent. However, it cannot delay payment by more than one month.

The firm also has two marketable securities. Security A matures on March 1 with a face value of $50,000, while security B matures on February 1 with a face value of $20,000. These securities could be sold early, if necessary, to provide cash for the accounts receivable. However, if a security is sold before its maturity date, a penalty must be paid. The penalty is 0.5 percent if the security is sold one month before its maturity date, and 1.5 percent if it is sold two months before its maturity date. For example, if security A is sold in February, one month before its maturity date, the penalty cost to the firm would be $(0.005)(\$50,000) = \$250$.

In addition, the firm has a line of credit with a bank. The interest charges for borrowing are based on the assumption that the loan will be repaid on April 1.

Borrow in Month	Interest Charge (percent)
1 (Jan.)	4.0
2 (Feb.)	3.0
3 (Mar.)	2.0

This credit can be used to cover the excess cash demands over the total cash availabilities during this three-month period.

Finally, any excess cash available during one month will be invested in short-term securities that mature in 30 days or 60 days. The returns from these securities are

Maturity (days)	Yield (percent)
30	0.75
60	1.60

Assume that the firm wishes to pay all of its accounts, including those for March, prior to April 1. How should the firm manage its assets in order to maximize the net return from its financial transactions?

Decision variables The firm can obtain credit from the bank in January (J), February (F), or March (M). The amount of credit obtained in each month, in thousands of dollars, will be denoted as CRJ, CRF, and CRM, respectively. Additional monies can be obtained from the sale of securities A and B. For simplicity we assume that these sales can be divisible; that is, some proportion of each security can be sold in each month prior to its maturity. The thousands of dollars received from the sale of security A in each of the three months is SAJ, SAF, and SAM; for security B, we define SBJ and SBF.

The payments on the accounts payable can be made in the month they are due or they can be delayed one month. We let PJJ be the payment (P) in January (J) for January (J), and PFJ be the payment (P) in February (F) for January (J). Looking ahead to the constraints, we will require $PJJ + PFJ = 40$, the accounts payable in January. Similarly, we define PFF and PMF for payments in February for February and in March for February. All four of these variables are in thousands of dollars.

Finally, the excess cash in any month can be invested in short-term securities for 30 or 60 days. We define SJF as the short-term security (S) purchased in January (J) that matures in February (F), while SJM represents a 60-day short-term security that matures in March (M). Finally, SFM is a 30-day security purchased in February (F) for March (M). Again, these three variables are in thousands of dollars.

For easy reference, these decision variables are displayed in Table 4-6.

Objective function The objective of cash management is to maximize the net return from the financial decisions. The firm receives interest from the short-term investments. Using the 30- and 60-day interest rates, these interest receipts would be $0.0075SJF + 0.016SJM + 0.0075SFM$.

The costs are from the line of credit to the bank, the early sale of securities A and B, and the interest charges on late payments. In January, the costs of the cash management program would be 4 percent of the line of credit borrowing, 1.5 percent of the sale of security A, and 0.5 percent of security B, or $0.04CRJ + 0.015SAJ + 0.005SBJ$.

The costs in February and March would be similar, except that we may also incur an interest penalty for late payment of the previous month's accounts payable. In February, the cost would be $0.03CRF + 0.005SAF + 0.02PFJ$, and $0.02CRM + 0.02PMF$ in March.

Thus, to maximize the net benefits, or the interest receipts minus the interest costs, we would

maximize $0.0075SJF + 0.0075SFM + 0.016SJM$ (short-term security yields)
$- 0.04CRJ - 0.015SAJ - 0.005SBJ$ (interest and penalty payments in January)
$- 0.03CRF - 0.005SAF - 0.02PFJ$ (interest and penalty payments in February)
$- 0.02CRM - 0.02PMF$ (interest and penalty payments in March)

Constraints The first constraint says that the total amount of cash available in January must be equal to the total payments and investments made in January. When a bank extends a line of credit, the interest charge is often deducted from the loan. Since the interest rate for the line of credit is 0.04, only $1.0 - 0.04 = 0.96$ of a loan, or $0.96CRJ$,

---

Decision Variables for the Cash Management Problem   TABLE 4-6

CRJ = bank credit (CR) in January (J)

CRF = bank credit (CR) in February (F)

CRM = bank credit (CR) in March (M)

SAJ = cash from sale (S) of security A in January (J)

SAF = cash from sale (S) of security A in February (F)

SAM = cash from sale (S) of security A in March (M)

SBJ = cash from sale (S) of security B in January (J)

SBF = cash from sale (S) of security B in February (F)

PJJ = actual payment (P) in January (J) of accounts payable in January (J)

PFJ = actual payment (P) in February (F) of accounts payable in January (J)

PFF = actual payment (P) in February (F) of accounts payable in February (F)

PMF = actual payment (P) in March (M) of accounts payable in February (F)

SJF = short (S) term security purchases in January (J) held until February (F)

SJM = short (S) term security purchases in January (J) held until March (M)

SFM = short (S) term security purchases in February (F) held until March (M)

---

will be available for use by the firm. Similarly, the 1.5 percent penalty for selling security A two months prior to maturity means that only $0.985SAJ$ would be received by the firm; for the same reason, $0.995SBJ$ would be generated by the sale of security B in January. The firm also forecasts the receipt of 10 thousand dollars in January from its accounts receivable. Thus, the total cash available in January will be $0.96CRJ + 0.985SAJ + 0.995SBJ + 10$.

This cash must be used for payments in January, PJJ, or for 30-day or 60-day short-term securities, SJF and SJM. Thus, the first constraint is

$$0.96CRJ + 0.985SAJ + 0.995SBJ + 10 = PJJ + SJF + SJM$$

which simplifies to

$$PJJ + SJF + SJM - 0.96CRJ - 0.985SAJ - 0.995SBJ = 10$$

The constraint for February is similar, except that the 30-day short-term security purchases in January increased by the interest rate of 0.75 percent would provide an

---

TABLE 4-7   Linear Optimization Model of the Cash Management Problem

Maximize
$$0.0075SJF + 0.0075SFM + 0.016SJM$$
$$- 0.04CRJ - 0.015SAJ - 0.005SBJ$$
$$- 0.03CRF - 0.005SAF - 0.02PFJ$$
$$- 0.02CRM - 0.02PMF$$

Subject to
$$PJJ + SJF + SJM - 0.96CRJ - 0.985SAJ - 0.995SBJ = 10$$
$$1.02PFJ + PFF + SFM - 0.97CRF - 0.995SAF - SBF - 1.0075SJF = 20$$
$$0.98CRM + SAM + 1.016SJM + 1.0075SFM - 1.02PMF = 10$$

$$SAJ + SAF + SAM = 50$$
$$SBJ + SBF = 20$$
$$PJJ + PFJ = 40$$
$$PFF + PMF = 60$$

CRJ, CRF, CRM, SAJ, SAF, SAM, SBJ, SBF, PJJ, PFJ, PFF, PMF, SJF, SJM, SFM $\geq$ 0

---

additional source of cash, $1.0075SJF$. Also, it is possible to pay accounts receivable in January at a 2 percent interest charge. The constraint for February is

$$1.02PFJ + PFF + SFM - 0.97CRF - 0.995SAF - SBF - 1.0075SJF = 20$$

Test your understanding by writing down the appropriate constraint for March.

Finally there are four straightforward constraints for the two securities and the accounts payable in January and February. The total cash generated from the sale of security A must equal $50 thousand, or

$$SAJ + SAF + SAM = 50$$

and the cash generated from security B must equal $20 thousand, or

$$SBJ + SBF = 20$$

As mentioned earlier, the total payments for January must be equal to $40 thousand, so we let

$$PJJ + PFJ = 40$$

and similarly,

$$PFF + PMF = 60$$

The complete formulation is shown in Table 4-7, and the solution and the sensitivity analysis are the subject of Exercise 3 in "Check Your Understanding." The cash management problem has been formulated as a linear optimization problem by several authors. This example is similar to the model proposed by Robichek, Teichroew, and Jones [1965].

LINEAR OPTIMIZATION
MODELS FOR MARKETING DECISIONS

A wide range of marketing problems are candidates for analysis with linear optimization models. One classical allocation problem is selecting media for a limited promotion and advertising budget. Although the simple linear optimization model formulation of this problem has some serious limitations, it does provide a basis for bootstrapping into the more complex models that are used for analyzing these decisions today.

Retailing and sales force management models are also important for managers of the marketing function. For example, models may be used to determine the optimum size of a sales force and to divide geographical regions into equitable sales territories.

Product transportation and distribution networks are now routinely analyzed by linear optimization models and their extensions. Since applications of these distribution models are so common, we devote Chapter 7 to a review of them.

Aaker's survey [1973] of the applications of management science in marketing includes a discussion of several linear optimization models. Kotler [1971] also summarizes many of these studies. The following examples deal with the media selection problem and the determination of sales territories.

Advertising media selection

The independent party of Democrats and Republicans has a limited budget of only $600,000 to spend in promoting their candidate. They wish to maximize the exposure of their candidate within the limited budget through the media (magazines, newspapers, radio, and television). They have obtained data on the costs, exposure ratings

TABLE 4-8	Costs and Exposure Ratings for Media		
Media	Cost per Advertising Unit	No. of Voters Reached per Unit	Exposure Rating per Unit
Magazines (*M*)	$20,000	10,000	100
Newspapers (*N*)	15,000	30,000	400
Radio (*R*)	5,000	20,000	200
Television			
Prime time (*TVP*)	40,000	35,000	600
Other (*TVO*)	10,000	15,000	150

per unit, and the number of voters reached per unit for each media type, as shown in Table 4-8.

The exposure rating per unit is a subjective measure of the effectiveness of an advertising message in each media. It takes into account the profile of the voters reached by each media (age, income, political party, etc.) and the impact of the message as presented through the media.

After examining the exposure rating data, the campaign manager states: "We obviously should put the entire $600,000 into TV advertising on prime time." Campaign committee members object, however, feeling that this approach is too risky and may not reach some important kinds of voters. The committee then agrees that no more than $250,000 will be spent on any single medium, such as TV. They also feel that no more than $350,000 should be spent on the two printed media, magazines and newspapers. Further, they specify that the budget for the radio advertisement should be at least 25 percent of the total TV budget, and that the nonprime time TV budget (*TVO*) should be at least 50 percent of the prime time budget (*TVP*). They also wish to ensure that they reach at least 250,000 voters. The committee agrees that their objective is to maximize the total exposure rating of the messages.

Decision variables The decision variables are the numbers of advertising units for each of the targeted media — *M, N, R, TVP,* and *TVO*.

Objective function The stated objective is to maximize the sum of the exposure ratings per unit. The aggregate exposure rating for magazine units will be 100*M*, using the exposure rating per unit data in Table 4-8. The function that the committee wishes to maximize is the sum of the aggregate ratings for each of the media, or

$$\text{maximize } Z = 100M + 400N + 200R + 600TVP + 150TVO$$

Constraints The first constraint is on the total budget of \$600,000. From Table 4-8 we see that the total amount spent for magazine advertising would be $20M$, in thousands of dollars. The total budget constraint is then

$$20M + 15N + 5R + 40TVP + 10TVO \leq 600$$

Budget constraints on each of the media must also be formulated to ensure that no more than \$250,000 is spent on it. For example, the constraint for magazines is

$$20M \leq 250$$

The constraints for the other media are similar, except that we must aggregate the two kinds of TV time; that is, we must have

$$40TVP + 10TVO \leq 250$$

The committee wishes to ensure that no more than \$350,000 is spent on the printed media, so

$$20M + 15N \leq 350$$

Further, they also require that the radio budget be at least 25 percent of the total television budget, so

$$5R \geq 0.25(40TVP + 10TVO)$$

This constraint simplifies to

$$5R - 10TVP - 2.5TVO \geq 0$$

The nonprime time TV budget must be at least 50 percent of the prime time budget, so

$$10TVO \geq 0.5(40TVP)$$

TABLE 4-9	Formulation of the Advertising Media Selection Problem

$$\text{Maximize } Z = 100M + 400N + 200R + 600TVP + 150TVO$$

Subject to

$$20M + 15N + 5R + 40TVP + 10TVO \leq 600$$
$$20M \leq 250$$
$$15N \leq 250$$
$$5R \leq 250$$
$$40TVP + 10TVO \leq 250$$
$$20M + 15N \leq 350$$
$$5R - 10TVP - 2.5TVO \geq 0$$
$$10TVO - 20TVP \geq 0$$
$$10M + 30N + 20R + 35TVP + 15TVO \geq 250$$
$$M, N, R, TVO, TVP \geq 0$$

Finally, they wish to reach 250,000 voters, so from Table 4-8,

$$10M + 30N + 20R + 35TVP + 15TVO \geq 250$$

The complete formulation of this problem is shown in Table 4-9. The computer input and output are presented as part of Exercise 4 in "Check Your Understanding." Engle and Warshaw [1964] and Bass and Lonsdale [1966] discuss more sophisticated approaches to modeling the media selection problem for actual applications.

Determination of sales territories

A company has two salesmen, Able and Baker, who must serve customers in six different geographic sales zones. A map of the area and the six sales zones is shown in Figure 4-2. The number in parentheses in each sales zone is the number of customers or accounts in the zone. For example, there are 20 customers to be served in zone 1. Salesman Able currently lives in zone 5, and salesman Baker lives in zone 3. The company wishes to assign some proportion of the customers in each zone to each salesman. In making this assignment, the company wishes to equalize the numbers of customers assigned to each salesman and to assign a salesman districts that are close to home in order to minimize travel time.

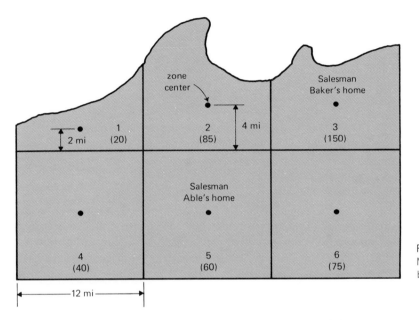

FIGURE 4-2
Map of sales area to be divided
between Able and Baker

Decision variables We can let $XA1$ be the *proportion* of the customers in zone 1 assigned to Able (A), and $XB1$ be the proportion assigned to Baker (B). Looking ahead to the constraints, we will require that $XA1 + XB1 = 1.0$, so that if $XA1 = 0.4$, then $XB1 = 0.6$. Since there are 20 customers in zone 1, *if* $XA1 = 0.4$ and $XB1 = 0.6$, then $(0.4)(20) = 8$ would be assigned to Able and $(0.6)(20) = 12$ to Baker.

Two similar decision variables would be required for each of zones 2 through 6, so that a total of twelve decision variables are needed.

Objective function The objective is to assign these customers so that the travel time is minimized. Since travel time generally depends on distance, we can focus on the distance from each salesman's home to the center of each sales zone. The center of each sales zone is approximated by a dot as shown in Figure 4-2. For simplicity, we assume that Able and Baker live in the center of zones 5 and 3 respectively.

Travel between two points is seldom in a straight line, especially in populated areas. We generally move in east-west and north-south directions according to routes determined by rectangular city blocks. Therefore, we will measure the distances in Figure 4-2 according to east-west and north-south distances. For example, to get to the center of zone 1, Able must travel 12 miles west and 8 miles north. Finally, in

TABLE 4-10	Squared Rectangular Distances in Sales Territories	
	From:	
To District	Able	Baker
1	$(12)^2 + (8)^2 = 208$	$(24)^2 + (2)^2 = 580$
2	$(0)^2 + (10)^2 = 100$	$(12)^2 + (0)^2 = 144$
3	$(12)^2 + (10)^2 = 244$	$(0)^2 + (0)^2 = 0$
4	$(12)^2 + (0)^2 = 144$	$(24)^2 + (10)^2 = 676$
5	$(0)^2 + (0)^2 = 0$	$(12)^2 + (10)^2 = 244$
6	$(12)^2 + (0)^2 = 144$	$(0)^2 + (10)^2 = 100$

order to place a severe penalty on long distances, we will square both the east-west distance and the north-south distance, and sum the result as a measure of how far each zone is from each salesman. Thus, the squared rectangular distance from Able's residence to zone 1 is $(12)^2 + (8)^2 = 208$. The squared rectangular distances from Able and Baker to the other zones are shown in Table 4-10.

For the objective function, we will minimize the sum of the squared rectangular distances multiplied by the proportion of the customers in each zone seen by each salesman. That is, we

minimize $Z =$ the squared rectangular $208XA1 + 100XA2 + 244XA3$
distances for Able $+ 144XA4 + 0XA5 + 144XA6$

plus the squared rectangular $580XB1 + 144XB2 + 0XB3$
distances for Baker $+ 676XB4 + 244XB5 + 100XB6$

Notice that minimizing the *squared* rectangular distances does not violate our requirement that the relationships be linear because these squared distances are merely coefficients in a linear expression. None of the decision variables are squared.

Constraints The constraints are very simple. As mentioned previously, since $XA1$ and $XB1$ are the proportions of the customers in zone 1 assigned to Able and Baker respectively, we require that $XA1 + XB1 = 1.0$. We need similar constraints for zones 2 through 6.

Finally, the total number of customers in the six zones is $20 + 85 + 150 + 40 + 60 + 75 = 430$. Dividing these equally, we wish to assign 215 customers to each salesman. Since the decision variables are the proportions of the customers in each zone assigned to each salesman, this constraint is written as

$$20XA1 + 85XA2 + 150XA3 + 40XA4 + 60XA5 + 75XA6 = 215$$

for salesman Able. Since exactly 215 customers are assigned to salesman Able by this constraint, then $430 - 215 = 215$ will also be assigned automatically to Baker. Therefore, we do not require a similar constraint for salesman Baker, even though including it in our formulation would do no harm.

The complete problem formulation is shown in Table 4-11. The computer solution and its interpretation are the subject of Exercise 5 in Check Your Understanding.

Hess and Samuels [1971] provide additional details regarding the sales districting model and discuss its use by a major pharmaceutical company, CIBA, to determine sales territories, and by IBM to determine service territories for typewriter servicepersonnel. More recently, Standard Oil of Indiana has used a variant of this approach to determine sales territories and it has been used to define police patrol areas in cities (see Heller, Markland, and Brockelmeyer [1971]). Also of interest is the use of this model to determine legislative districts consistent with the "one man-one vote" Supreme Court decision. This reapportionment analysis was originally made for the state of Delaware, and the model has since been used in other states and countries [Hess et al., 1965].

Linear Optimization Model for Determining Sales Territories   TABLE 4-11

Minimize $Z = 208XA1 + 100XA2 + 244XA3 + 144XA4 + 0XA5 + 144XA6$
$+ 580XB1 + 144XB2 + 0XB3 + 676XB4 + 244XB5 + 100XB6$

Subject to
$$XA1 + XB1 = 1$$
$$XA2 + XB2 = 1$$
$$XA3 + XB3 = 1$$
$$XA4 + XB4 = 1$$
$$XA5 + XB5 = 1$$
$$XA6 + XB6 = 1$$
$$20XA1 + 85XA2 + 150XA3 + 40XA4 + 60XA5 + 75XA6 = 215$$
$$XA1, XA2, XA3, XA4, XA5, XA6, XB1, XB2, XB3, XB4, XB5, XB6 \geq 0$$

LINEAR OPTIMIZATION MODELS
FOR PERSONNEL PLANNING DECISIONS

Linear optimization models can be used to schedule employee work hours on a short-term basis and to determine personnel needs over a longer planning horizon. The latter analysis provides the basis for employee recruitment and training programs. Charnes, Cooper, and Niehaus [1972] report on the extensive use of linear optimization models for personnel planning in the navy. Charnes, Cooper, Lewis, and Niehaus [1975] also describe how these models may be used to assist in meeting equal employment opportunity goals. Models for this same purpose have been developed in major corporations. Linear optimization models have also been used to determine equitable executive compensation plans (see Charnes, Cooper, and Ferguson [1955]). Here we present a simple model for scheduling work shifts and a long-term model for planning staffing activities.

Nurse scheduling

Nurses at the Good Samaritan Hospital come on duty every four hours and work eight-hour shifts. Management has found this idea of six staggered shifts to be more effective in minimizing the disruption and communication problems that occur when a shift is changed.

The hospital has also done an analysis of the work required during each of the six four-hour periods of the day. This varies from period to period as follows:

Time of Day	Period	Minimum Number of Nurses Required per Period
2 A.M. – 6 A.M.	1	25
6 A.M. –10 A.M.	2	60
10 A.M. – 2 P.M.	3	50
2 P.M. – 6 P.M.	4	35
6 P.M. –10 P.M.	5	55
10 P.M. – 2 A.M.	6	40

Each nurse works for eight consecutive hours. Nurses who begin work in periods 2, 3, and 4 are paid $40 per day, and those beginning in periods 1, 5, and 6 are paid $50 per day to compensate for the inconvenient hours. How many nurses should be scheduled to begin work each period in order to minimize the daily payroll costs?

Decision variables The decision variables are the number of nurses beginning work in each of the six periods, which we define as $N1$, $N2$, $N3$, $N4$, $N5$, and $N6$.

Objective function We wish to minimize daily payroll costs, so we

minimize $Z = 50N1 + 40N2 + 40N3 + 40N4 + 50N5 + 50N6$

Constraints The constraints for this problem simply enforce the minimum personnel requirements. The total number of nurses available during period 2 must be at least 60. This total is equal to the number of nurses beginning work in period 1 plus the number that go on duty at 6:00 A.M. in period 2. That is, we require

$N1 + N2 \geq 60$

The other constraints are similar. For example, the total number of nurses on duty during period 3, $N2 + N3$, must be at least 50, so

$N2 + N3 \geq 50$

is the second constraint. Test your understanding by writing down the other four constraints.

The complete problem formulation is shown in Table 4-12. The computer solution and the sensitivity analysis are discussed in Exercise 6 in Check Your Understanding.

Nurse Scheduling for Good Samaritan Hospital	TABLE 4-12

Minimize $Z = 50N1 + 40N2 + 40N3 + 40N4 + 50N5 + 50N6$	
Subject to	$N1 + N2 \geq 60$
	$N2 + N3 \geq 50$
	$N3 + N4 \geq 35$
	$N4 + N5 \geq 55$
	$N5 + N6 \geq 40$
	$N1 + N6 \geq 25$
$N1, N2, N3, N4, N5, N6 \geq 0$	

Personnel planning and scheduling

The employees in the manufacturing department of a major company are classified as machinists. A three-month production forecast indicates that 4000 hours of machinist time will be required in January, 4500 in February, and 4200 in March. The department has 30 machinists available on January 1, and each worker averages 150 hours of productive work each month.

Newly hired machinists must be trained for one month before being able to contribute any productive hours. This training is conducted by an experienced machinist and requires 75 worker-hours of time, so that the total productive pool of worker-hours is reduced. Each month there is a turnover rate of 10 percent among the machinists, since some quit and others are transferred to other positions in the company.

If excess worker-hours are available in a month, workers are assigned to maintenance activities rather than being laid off. A machinist makes $1200 per month, and a trainee makes $1000 during the month of training. How many trainees must be hired in January and February in order to meet the three-month personnel forecast and yet minimize the total payroll cost in the department?

Decision variables The obvious decision variables for this problem are *TRAINJ* and *TRAINF,* the number of trainees hired in January and February respectively. In addition, we need to define decision variables for the number of machinists available for work in February and March, *MACHF* and *MACHM*.

Objective function The objective is to minimize the payroll costs for the trainees hired in January and for the machinists and trainees in February and March. This objective is accomplished by

$$\text{minimize } Z = 1000TRAINJ + 1200MACHF + 1000TRAINF + 1200MACHM$$

Notice that we do not include in the objective function the cost of ($1200)(30) = $36,000 for the 30 machinists available in January because we have no control over this value. This cost may be ignored as a fixed cost, since it would not affect the solution.

Constraints Each machinist contributes, on the average, 150 productive hours per month and 4000 are required in January. However, each trainee hired in January will demand 75 productive hours in the training program. Since 30 machinists are available on January 1, we must have

$$(30)(150) - 75TRAINJ \geq 4000$$

or, after subtracting 4000 from both sides of the inequality and rearranging,

$$75TRAINJ \leq 500$$

The number of machinists available in February, $MACHF$, is equal to 90 percent of the work force in January, because of the turnover, plus the number of trainees hired in January. Therefore, we write,

$$(30)(0.9) + TRAINJ = MACHF$$

as another constraint. In order to meet the worker-hour requirement in February,

$$150MACHF - 75TRAINF \geq 4500$$

Test your understanding by writing down the two constraints needed for March.

The complete formulation for this problem is shown in Table 4-13. The interpretation of the computer solution is the subject of Exercise 7 in "Check Your Understanding."

Linear Optimization Model for Personnel Planning   TABLE 4-13

Minimize $Z = 1000TRAINJ + 1200MACHF + 1000TRAINF + 1200MACHM$	
Subject to	$75TRAINJ \leq 500$
	$MACHF - TRAINJ = 27$
	$150MACHF - 75TRAINF \geq 4500$
	$MACHM - TRAINF - 0.9MACHF = 0$
	$150MACHM \geq 4200$
	$TRAINJ, MACHF, TRAINF, MACHM \geq 0$

LINEAR OPTIMIZATION MODELS IN
THE PUBLIC AND NOT-FOR-PROFIT SECTOR

Linear optimization models have been applied to many managerial problems in the public and not-for-profit sectors. For example, in the health care field Revelle, Feldmann, and Lynn [1969] have developed a mathematical model that predicts future states of the disease tuberculosis. Controls in the form of therapy, vaccinations, or prophylaxis may be superimposed on the actual processes, thus altering the future course of the disease. Linear programming is used to select the forms of control that achieve specific reductions at minimum cost. Sensitivity analysis can then be used to determine the marginal cost of an even greater reduction in the future disease level.

Linear programming has also been applied to the problem of integrating public schools, as reported by Franklin and Koenigsberg [1973]. The objective function and constraints in their models can be modified so that the solution of each formulation provides a policy or point of view. The authors emphasize that school authorities, judges, and the public can see the logical implications of each point of view and select school assignment plans on a rational basis. Notice that there is not even a hint that the purpose of the linear programming models is to provide *the answer*. Rather its purpose is to generate the consequences in terms of costs and school assignments of different levels of desegregation and of different approaches. The selection of the best approach is still a matter for the school authorities, the judges, and the public to decide.

Problems of the environment have also been studied by using linear programming. Glassey and Gupta [1974] have developed a linear model of the production, use, and recycling of various paper and related products. The linear programming analysis indicates that if 70 percent of the potentially recoverable paper had been recycled in 1970, the annual virgin pulp consumption could have been reduced from 45 million tons to 28 million tons (or by 38 percent). The reduction in the annual cost of collecting and disposing of solid waste would have been approximately $238 million, which presumably could be used to offset the cost of collecting and processing wastepaper. In a related study, Ignall, Kolesar, and Walker [1972] used a linear optimization model to improve crew assignments for solid waste collection.

Several of our previous examples involved elements of the public and not-for-profit sector. The media selection formulation was placed in the context of "selling" a political candidate rather than a new product. The formulation of the nurse scheduling problem remains unchanged for a public, not-for-profit, or private hospital. To further demonstrate the extent of the applications of linear optimization models, we present an application in urban planning, a school desegregation model, and a budgeting model for a state agency.

Land-use allocation

Capital City is undergoing a period of rapid urban development. The new growth in the city is restricted to two planning zones, Northwest Hills (zone 2) and Town Lake (zone 3). The central city (zone 1) is overcrowded, and there is no available land for further expansion.

The three zones are linked by networks of electrical lines as illustrated in Figure 4-3. The arrows alongside the lines indicate the direction of flow of the utility. For example, electrical power can flow from the central city to Northwest Hills, but not vice versa. Also shown on Figure 4-3 is the unused capacity available on each of these lines. For example, an additional 400 units of electrical power could be transmitted from the central city (zone 1) to Northwest Hills (zone 2). The capacity in each of these utility lines can be expanded at a unit cost also shown in Figure 4-3. The additional electrical transmission capacity from zone 1 to zone 2 can be increased above

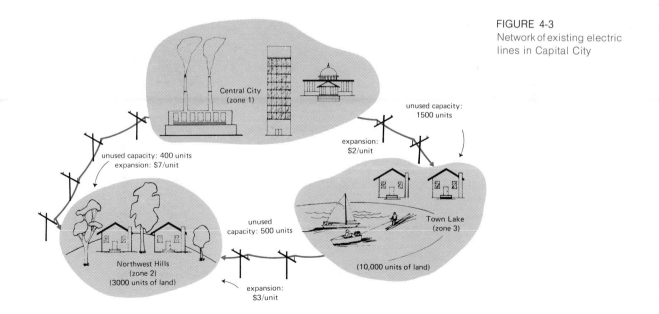

FIGURE 4-3
Network of existing electric lines in Capital City

400 units for \$7 per unit (all units have been conveniently scaled). Also, as shown in Figure 4-3, there are 3000 units of available land in Northwest Hills and 10,000 units of available land in Town Lake.

The city expects to have 600 new residential developments and 400 new industrial developments over the next ten years. Each new residential development requires 7 units of land, and 2 units of electricity. Each new industrial development requires 9 units of land and 3 units of electricity.

The city can control the growth by issuing permits for the developments in each zone. How many units of each type (residential and industrial) should the city allow to be developed in each zone (2 and 3) in order to minimize the costs of expanding the existing utility lines?

Decision variables The decisions are the numbers of developments of each type that should be allowed in each zone over the next ten years. We define $R2$ and $R3$ as the units of residential development (R) in each of zones 2 and 3. Similarly, $I2$ and $I3$ are the units of industrial development (I) in each of the respective zones.

On each of the existing utility lines there is some unused capacity. We can let $UC12$ represent the number of units of electrical power transmitted from zone 1 to zone 2 through the unused (U) capacity (C) of 400 units. In a similar manner, $UC13$ is the electrical transmission on the unused capacity from zone 1 to zone 3, and $UC32$ is the transmission on the unused capacity from zone 3 to zone 2.

We also need to define variables representing any expansions (X) of the capacities (C) of the electrical lines. Suppose we let $XC12$ represent the number of units of expansion (X) required on the electrical line from zone 1 to zone 2. In a similar manner, we define $XC13$ and $XC32$. No new utility lines are to be considered.

Objective function From the point of view of the city, the objective is to minimize any costs of expanding the existing electrical lines. Using the expansion costs from Figure 4-3, the city wishes to

$$\text{minimize } Z = 7XC12 + 2XC13 + 3XC32$$

Constraints We assume that the 600 new residential units and the 400 new industrial units will be developed. Therefore, we have

$$R2 + R3 = 600$$

and

$$I2 + I3 = 400$$

Next we must consider the available land in each zone. Since each unit of new residential development requires 7 units of land, and each new industrial development requires 9 units of land, we must have

$$7R2 + 9I2 \leq 3000$$

because there are only 3000 units of available land in zone 2. Similarily, we have

$$7R3 + 9I3 \leq 10,000$$

for zone 3.

Now let us focus on the electrical power lines. In zone 2, any new developments will generate a demand for additional units of electrical power. This power must flow into zone 2 on the line from zone 1 to zone 2, on the line from zone 3 to zone 2, or on both. Thus, we can write a constraint for zone 2 in words as follows:

$$\begin{pmatrix} \text{additional demand} \\ \text{for power in zone 2} \end{pmatrix} = \begin{pmatrix} \text{total additional flow} \\ \text{from zone 1 into zone 2} \end{pmatrix} + \begin{pmatrix} \text{total additional flow} \\ \text{from zone 3 into zone 2} \end{pmatrix}$$

Since each unit of residential development requires 2 units of electricity, and each unit of industrial development requires 3 units of electricity, the additional demand for power in zone 2 will be $2R2 + 3I2$. The number of additional units of electrical power that actually flow from zone 1 into zone 2 on the unused capacity of 400 units is $UC12$. However, the capacity on the line from zone 1 to zone 2 can be expanded by $XC12$, so the *total* additional flow on this line is given by $UC12 + XC12$. Similarly, the total additional flow of electrical power on the line from zone 3 to zone 2 is given by $UC32 + XC32$, where the unused capacity $UC32$ must be less than or equal to 500 units. The electrical power constraint for zone 2 becomes

$$2R2 + 3I2 = UC12 + XC12 + UC32 + XC32$$

and the limitations on the unused capacity shown in Figure 4-3 are enforced by

$$UC12 \leq 400$$

and

$$UC32 \leq 500$$

Notice that electrical power may flow from zone 3 into zone 2. Therefore, the additional power flowing into zone 3 from zone 1 must equal the additional demand for power generated by new developments in zone 3 *plus* the additional flow from zone 3 into zone 2. Again, writing this constraint in words, we have

$$\left(\begin{array}{c}\text{additional demand}\\ \text{for power in zone 3}\end{array}\right) + \left(\begin{array}{c}\text{total additional flow}\\ \text{from zone 3 into zone 2}\end{array}\right) = \left(\begin{array}{c}\text{total additional flow}\\ \text{from zone 1 into zone 3}\end{array}\right)$$

The additional demand for power in zone 3 is given by $2R3 + 3I3$, and the electrical power transmitted from zone 3 into zone 2 is $UC32 + XC32$. The total additional flow of power from zone 1 into zone 3 is given by $UC13 + XC13$. The constraint is

$$2R3 + 3I3 + UC32 + XC32 = UC13 + XC13$$

Since the unused capacity of the electrical line from zone 1 to zone 3 is 1500 units, we require

$$UC13 \leq 1500$$

The complete problem formulation is shown in Table 4-14, and the analysis of the computer solution is the subject of Exercise 8 in "Check Your Understanding." This

TABLE 4-14	Land-Use Allocation Model for Capital City

Minimize $Z = 7XC12 + 2XC13 + 3XC32$

Subject to

$$R2 + R3 = 600$$
$$I2 + I3 = 400$$
$$7R2 + 9I2 \leq 3000$$
$$7R3 + 9I3 \leq 10{,}000$$
$$2R2 + 3I2 - UC12 - XC12 - UC32 - XC32 = 0$$
$$2R3 + 3I3 + UC32 + XC32 - UC13 - XC13 = 0$$
$$UC12 \leq 400$$
$$UC32 \leq 500$$
$$UC13 \leq 1500$$
$$R2, R3, I2, I3, UC12, XC12, UC13, XC13, UC32, XC32 \geq 0$$

model can be extended to consider simultaneously the expansion of several types of utility lines, including water, sewer, and natural gas. Bagby and Thesen [1976] describe an actual application of an extended version of this model for allocating land-use developments in the military installation of Fort Campbell, Kentucky. The result indicated a distribution of the anticipated land uses so that no additional utility investments were required.

School desegregation model

A school district includes two schools, A and B, located as shown on the map in Figure 4-4. The school district is divided into five census tracts. School A is roughly in the center of tract 2, and school B is in the center of tract 5. The students in the district are primarily from two major ethnic groups, X and Y. The numbers of students from each ethnic group in each census tract are also shown in Figure 4-4. For example, in census tract 1 there are 50 students from ethnic group X and 10 students from ethnic group Y. When students were assigned to schools simply on the basis of geographic distance, the proportion of students in ethnic group X enrolled in school A was substantially higher than the proportion enrolled in school B.

The district has decided to reassign the students to the schools so that the total

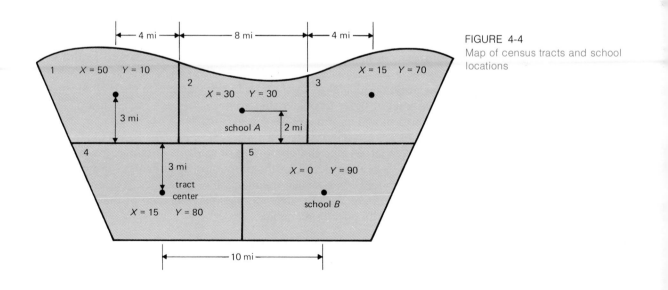

FIGURE 4-4
Map of census tracts and school locations

TABLE 4-15 Calculation of Student Miles for Each Tract and Ethnic Group

	From Tract				
	1	2	3	4	5
School A					
Distance to school	8 + 1 = 9	0 + 0 = 0	8 + 1 = 9	5 + 5 = 10	5 + 5 = 10
Student-miles for:					
X	(9)(50) = 450	(0)(30) = 0	(9)(15) = 135	(10)(15) = 150	(10)(0) = 0
Y	(9)(10) = 90	(0)(30) = 0	(9)(70) = 630	(10)(80) = 800	(10)(90) = 900
School B					
Distance to school	13 + 6 = 19	5 + 5 = 10	3 + 6 = 9	10 + 0 = 10	0 + 0 = 0
Student-miles for:					
X	(19)(50) = 950	(10)(30) = 300	(9)(15) = 135	(10)(15) = 150	(0)(0) = 0
Y	(19)(10) = 190	(10)(30) = 300	(9)(70) = 630	(10)(80) = 800	(0)(90) = 0

enrollments in the two schools are equal and so that the proportion of students in each ethnic group is identical in each school. In carrying out this reassignment, the district wishes to minimize the total number of student-miles traveled by the students. For example, if 30 students must travel 9 miles from tract 1 to school A, this corresponds to $(30)(9) = 270$ student-miles. We assume that travel distances are rectangular in the east-west and north-south directions. As a rough approximation, these distances are measured from the dot in the center of each census tract as shown in Figure 4-4. Table 4-15 contains the estimates of the distances from each tract to each school. These distances are then multiplied by the number of students in each ethnic group in the respective tract in order to obtain student-miles for each ethnic group. These calculations are also shown in Table 4-15.

Decision variables We let $XA1$ be the *proportion* of students of ethnic group X from tract 1 assigned to school A, and $XB1$ be the proportion of students of group X from tract 1 assigned to school B. In a similar manner, we would define $YA1$ and $YB1$ for ethnic group Y. Thus, there are four decision variables for each of the five census tracts, for a total of twenty decision variables.

Objective function We can minimize the student-miles traveled by minimizing the proportion of students in an ethnic group that must travel a long distance to a school. For example, if $XA1 = 1.0$, then we add 450 student-miles to the total traveled, using the student-miles figure in Table 4-15. However, if $XA1 = 0.1$, we add only $(0.1)(450)$ $= 45$ student-miles to the total. Therefore, we would like to

minimize $Z =$ the total student-miles
traveled to school A $= 450XA1 + 90YA1 + 135XA3 + 630YA3$
$\qquad\qquad\qquad\qquad\qquad\qquad + 150XA4 + 800YA4 + 900YA5$

plus the total student-
miles traveled to school $B = 950XB1 + 190YB1 + 300XB2$
$\qquad\qquad\qquad\qquad\qquad + 300YB2 + 135XB3 + 630YB3$
$\qquad\qquad\qquad\qquad\qquad + 150XB4 + 800YB4$

Constraints Since $XA1$ and $XB1$ are the proportions of students of ethnic group X from tract 1 assigned to schools A and B respectively, we must have $XA1 + XB1 = 1$ to ensure that all of the students are assigned. Similarly, we have $YA1 + YB1 = 1$ for the ethnic group Y. Two similar constraints are needed for each of the other four census tracts.

Next, we wish to ensure that the number of students assigned to each school is equal. There are a total of 390 students in the district. Thus, the enrollment in school A is $390/2 = 195$, so we have

$50XA1 + 10YA1 + 30XA2 + 30YA2 + 15XA3$
$\quad + 70YA3 + 15XA4 + 80YA4 + 90YA5 = 195$

for school A. If exactly 195 students are assigned to school A, $390 - 195 = 195$ will automatically be assigned to school B. Therefore, there is no need to include a similar constraint for school B, even though it would do no harm.

Finally, there is a total of 110 students of ethnic group X in the district. If we assign 55 to school A and 55 to school B, the proportions of the ethnic groups in each school will be identical. Thus we require that

$50XA1 + 30XA2 + 15XA3 + 15XA4 = 55$

If this constraint is satisfied, then again the identical constraint for school B would be automatically satisfied, so it is not explicitly included in the model.

The complete formulation is shown in Table 4-16, and the computer results are analyzed in Exercise 9 in "Check Your Understanding." There have been numerous examples of actual applications of linear optimization models to school desegregation problems. Two examples are described by Belford and Ratliff [1972] and Clarke and

TABLE 4-16	School Desegregation Model

Minimize $Z = 450XA1 + 90YA1 + 135XA3 + 630YA3 + 150XA4 + 800YA4 + 900YA5 + 950XB1$
$+ 190YB1 + 300XB2 + 300YB2 + 135XB3 + 630YB3 + 150XB4 + 800YB4$

Subject to

$$XA1 + XB1 = 1$$
$$YA1 + YB1 = 1$$
$$XA2 + XB2 = 1$$
$$YA2 + YB2 = 1$$
$$XA3 + XB3 = 1$$
$$YA3 + YB3 = 1$$
$$XA4 + XB4 = 1$$
$$YA4 + YB4 = 1$$
$$XA5 + XB5 = 1$$
$$YA5 + YB5 = 1$$
$$50XA1 + 10YA1 + 30XA2 + 30YA2 + 15XA3 + 70YA3 + 15XA4 + 80YA4 + 90YA5 = 195$$
$$50XA1 + 30XA2 + 15XA3 + 15XA4 = 55$$
$$XA1, XB1, YA1, YB1, XA2, XB2, YA2, YB2, XA3, XB3, YA3, YB3,$$
$$XA4, XB4, YA4, YB4, XA5, XB5, YA5, YB5 \geq 0$$

Surkis [1967]. A similar model to minimize transportation costs in a school district has been implemented by McKeown and Workman [1976].

Budget analysis of a state welfare system

A State Department of Public Welfare is attempting to develop an annual budget for three program areas: day care for children, employment services, and community services. Federal funds are provided for these services under titles to the Social Security Act, but these funds must be matched at a 1 to 3 ratio by state and local funds. The state has recently adopted a zero-base budgeting procedure that requires each program to submit two budget requests, one for operations at a lower level of funding and another for operations at a higher level of funding. The Department of Public Welfare is concerned with the development of an analytical tool that will answer such questions as how remaining funds should be allocated if funding for one program area or from one source is increased or decreased, or what the impact on all budget items will be if the constraints controlling funding are altered.

Suppose we consider formulating a linear optimization model to assist in the analysis of this budgeting problem. We could define decision variables to represent the federal funds allocated to each program area, as well as other decision variables to represent the state and local funds allocated to these programs. Constraints could be written to ensure that the total available funds were not exceeded and that lower levels of funding were provided for each program, but what would we use for an objective function?

Ideally, we would like to maximize the total welfare of the citizens of the state, but this is a very difficult concept to quantify. As an alternate strategy, we could seek an allocation of the available funds that comes the "closest" to funding each program area at its lower level of funding, and, when each program is funded at its lower level, distributes any excess funds to come "close" to the specified higher level of funding for each program. Naturally, we would like to avoid violating any budget or matching fund restrictions as a result of this allocation.

Loosely speaking, it seems that we have several "goals" in mind for this problem, but no single objective such as the minimization of costs. When such problems are encountered, it is still possible to formulate a linear optimization model that can be used to analyze an organization's ability to meet several conflicting goals. This special formulation has been given the name *goal programming,* but it is really nothing more than a special case of the linear optimization model.

Goal programming A brief digression will be useful to explain the nature of goal programming. In some cases, the objective of an organization may be expressed in terms of "goals" instead of in terms of maximizing or minimizing a single criterion. This situation is especially true in the public sector where obtaining "goals" is often considered more appropriate than maximizing profits or minimizing costs, but examples of goal programming models may be found in the private sector as well.

In the chemical production problem, suppose there are only 80 hours of time available on machine A. However, the amount of time available on machine B is flexible. The "goals" of the production planning problem are given as:

1. Use as close to 60 hours of time on machine B as possible.
2. Produce as close to a total of 30 units of chemical x and chemical y as possible.

Thus, our objective is to find values of x and y that satisfy

$$2x + 4y \leq 80 \quad \text{(machine } A \text{ constraint)}$$

$$3x + 2y \cong 60 \quad \text{(machine } B \text{ "goal")}$$

$$x + y \cong 30 \quad \text{(total production "goal")}$$

as well as the usual nonnegativity restrictions. (The symbol $\cong$ means "is approximately equal to.")

How can we write the goal constraints for machine B and for total production in terms of a linear inequality or a linear equation? Recall that if a constraint has a less than or equal to sign, a slack variable was added that represented the difference between the left-hand side of the inequality and the constant on the right-hand side. What would happen if we actually wrote the slack variable as a term in the objective function and minimized it? In an optimal solution, the slack variable would be made as small as possible, so the left-hand side of the inequality would be made very "close" to the right-hand side. Minimizing a slack variable would thus keep the left-hand side of the inequality from being smaller than the right-hand side constant, but what if it were larger? Using the same reasoning, we could introduce a surplus variable and minimize it to keep the left-hand side from being larger than the right-hand side constant.

For example, we could write the machine B goal statement as

$$3x + 2y - z_B^+ + z_B^- = 60$$

where z_B^+ corresponds to a surplus variable and z_B^- corresponds to a slack variable. Similarly, we can rewrite the total production goal statement as

$$x + y - z_T^+ + z_T^- = 30$$

by introducing z_T^+ and z_T^-. We can then find values of x and y that minimize the sum of the deviations from our two goals by solving the linear optimization model:

Minimize $\qquad\qquad Z = z_B^+ + z_B^- + z_T^+ + z_T^-$

subject to

$$
\begin{aligned}
2x + 4y &\leq 80 \\
3x + 2y - z_B^+ + z_B^- &= 60 \\
x + y - z_T^+ + z_T^- &= 30 \\
x,\, y,\, z_B^+,\, z_B^-,\, z_T^+,\, z_T^- &\geq 0
\end{aligned}
$$

That is, the objective function will ensure that the total time used on machine B is "close" to 60 and that the total number of units produced is "close" to 30.

Decision Variables for the Budget Analysis Model		TABLE 4-17
	Funding Source	
Program Area	State and Local (S)	Federal (F)
Day care for children (D)	DS	DF
Employment services (E)	ES	EF
Community services (C)	CS	CF

Decision variables We can now return to the budget analysis problem of the State Department of Public Welfare. The decision variables represent the funds allocated to the three programs from two funding sources: federal and combined state and local. These six decision variables are defined in Table 4-17.

We also need variables corresponding to slack and surplus variables that represent deviations from our budget goals. These variables are easier to understand when introduced in the context of the constraints of the model, so we will focus on the constraints next rather than on the objective function.

Constraints Suppose that Title XX federal funds totaling $78,000,000 have been made available to support activities in these three program areas, and $34,200,000 are available from a combination of state general revenue and local funds. Ordinarily, we would write a constraint for the federal funds

$$DF + EF + CF \leq 78,000,000$$

to ensure that the available funds are not exceeded, and a similar constraint for the state and local funds. Suppose we are trying to *analyze* the budget and gain insights into the alternate funding patterns that might be possible. We might wish to consider budgets that do violate these funding levels a bit, although we would like to keep these violations as small as possible.

Therefore, we can treat these funding levels as initial estimates that become *goals* for the budgeting process. Using the goal programming format, we write

$$DF + EF + CF + GFM - GFP = 78,000,000$$

as the constraint on federal funds, using *GFM* as a "slack" variable to represent the underfunding deviation from the budget goal, and GFP as a "surplus" variable to represent overfunding. If $GFM > 0$ in the optimal solution, then the actual allocation to these three projects will be less than \$78,000,000 by an amount equal to the value of *GFM*. If $GFP > 0$ in the optimal solution, then we will have allocated more than the available pool of federal funds by an amount equal to *GFP*. If this optimal solution is desirable otherwise, the Department of Public Welfare may wish to investigate the possibility of obtaining additional federal funds from a new allocation or from a reallocation of funds from other programs.

For similar reasons, the constraint on combined state and local funding can be written as

$$DS + ES + CS + GSM - GSP = \$34,200,000$$

where *GSM* and *GSP* represent deviations from this budget goal. How would you interpret the optimal solution if $GSM > 0$?

Next we must consider the requirement that federal funds be matched by state and local funds at a ratio of 1 to 3. That is, for every \$3.00 of federal monies spent on a project, state and local funds *must* increase by at least \$1.00. Since this ratio is determined by law, it cannot be violated under any circumstances. Therefore, we write the constraint

$$DF \leq 3DS$$

for the day care matching funds, which simplifies to

$$DF - 3DS \leq 0$$

To test your understanding, write the constraints for matching funds for the employment and community services programs.

Finally, we must consider the desired funding levels of the three programs. The funding budget for the three programs are shown in Table 4-18. The lower level is a minimal budgets sufficient to allow the program to operate effectively. The upper level is a desired funding level that would provide sufficient resources to operate each program at its most desirable level.

Again, we can treat these funding levels as goals that we wish to reach, and introduce four new "slack" and "surplus" variables for deviations from these two funding levels.

Lower and Upper Budget Levels for Welfare Programs		TABLE 4-18

Program	Lower Budget Level	Upper Budget Level
Day care for children	$28,785,000	$35,182,908
Employment services	18,207,877	19,698,754
Community services	47,802,290	78,320,122

For the day care program, we would have the two constraints,

$$DS + DF + GDLM - GDLP = 28{,}785{,}000$$

for the lower budget level and

$$DS + DF + GDUM - GDUP = 35{,}182{,}908$$

for the upper budget level. Similar constraints would be written for the employment and community services programs.

The complete set of constraints for this problem is shown in Table 4-19. The notation $GELM$ and $GELP$ is used for the slack and surplus variables for the employment program with respect to the lower budget level, and $GEUM$ and $GEUP$ are used for the upper budget level. How would you interpret the four variables introduced for the community services program?

Objective function In a goal programming formulation, the objective function is used to minimize either positive or negative deviations from goals. In the welfare budget analysis, we may wish to minimize any violations of the initial federal and combined state and local funding levels, and to minimize any overspending on programs above their upper budget levels. These objectives could be met by minimizing the sum of the goal deviation variables

$$GFP + GSP + GDUP + GEUP + GCUP$$

For example, GSP represents the state and local funds allocated in excess of the initial budget requirement, and $GCUP$ represents the excess of funds allocated to the community services program *above* its upper budget limit. Interpret the other variables in this summation.

TABLE 4-19   Constraints for Analyzing
                    the Annual Budget

$$DF + EF + CF + GFM - GFP = 78{,}000{,}000$$
$$DS + ES + CS + GSM - GSP = 34{,}200{,}000$$
$$DF - 3DS \leq 0$$
$$EF - 3ES \leq 0$$
$$CF - 3CS \leq 0$$
$$DF + DS + GDLM - GDLP = 28{,}785{,}000$$
$$EF + ES + GELM - GELP = 18{,}207{,}877$$
$$CF + CS + GCLM - GCLP = 47{,}802{,}290$$
$$DF + DS + GDUM - GDUP = 35{,}182{,}908$$
$$EF + ES + GEUM - GEUP = 19{,}698{,}754$$
$$CF + CS + GCUM - GCUP = 78{,}320{,}122$$

Notice that we have *not* included the goal deviation variables representing the underutilization of funds. This means that we do not care if all of the funds are *not* utilized.

In addition to avoiding overspending, we want to ensure that each program is funded at least to its lower budget level. This is accomplished by minimizing the sum

$$GDLM + GELM + GCLM$$

For example, $GDLM$ is the number of dollars that the total funding for the day care program falls short of its lower budget limit.

Once these lower limits are met, if additional funds exist, we would like to increase the funding level of each program until its upper funding level is reached. Minimizing the sum

$$GDUM + GEUM + GCUM$$

will have this effect. What does the variable $GDUM$ represent?

In summary, we would like to minimize overspending, minimize underfunding of programs below their lower budget level, and, once the lower budget levels are reached, minimize the discrepancy between the funding level of each program and its upper budget level. Are all these goals equally important? Probably not.

Suppose we consider minimizing overspending as the most important set of goals, and in fact decide that it is two times as important as meeting the lower funding limits of the programs. Meeting these lower levels for each program is five times as important as bringing the funding levels up to their upper budget levels. We can *weight* the goal deviation variables with the weights 10, 5, and 1 to reflect these ratios. With this in mind, the complete objective function becomes

$$\text{minimize } Z = 10GFP + 10GSP + 10GDUP + 10GEUP + 10GCUP$$
$$+ 5GDLM + 5GELM + 5GCLM$$
$$+ GDUM + GEUM + GCUM$$

When this objective function is added to the constraints shown in Table 4-19 the linear optimization model is complete.

The interpretation of the computer solution for this problem is the topic of Exercise 10 in "Check Your Understanding." This model is a simplification of a study by Fitzsimmons, Schwab, and Sullivan [1979] based on actual data from the State Department of Public Welfare in the State of Texas. For other examples of goal programming formulations, *see* Lee [1972]

WHAT SHOULD THE MANAGER KNOW?

There have been literally thousands of successful applications of linear optimization models in the analysis of significant managerial problems. These problems have been in virtually every functional area of the firm, and in the public and not-for-profit sectors of the economy as well as in the private sector. Thus, no matter what specialization or functional field appeals to a manager, and no matter what sector of the economy he or she is working in, the manager should be familiar with this powerful tool of analysis.

We have presented many examples of applications to emphasize this important point. In addition, a careful study of these different applications should enhance your ability to recognize potential applications in practice and to participate in the development and use of the appropriate linear optimization model.

CHECK YOUR UNDERSTANDING

1. The computer input and solution for the problem of financing the production decision were shown in Figure 4-1. The corresponding sensitivity analysis is shown

FIGURE 4-5
Sensitivity analysis
for the production
problem with
financial constraints
(Exercise 1)

DO YOU WISH SENSITIVITY ANALYSIS? YES

CONSTRAINT		SHADOW	LB	CURRENT	UB
	1	0.0000E0	6.9677E1	8.0000E1	7.2370E75
	2	1.5323E1	4.5310E1	6.0000E1	6.5300E1
	3	0.0000E0	1.2581E1	1.6000E1	7.2370E75
	4	0.0000E0	1.1129E1	1.8000E1	7.2370E75
	5	4.8387E-2	7.0400E3	8.1000E3	8.9000E3
	6	0.0000E0	-7.2370E75	4.0000E2	1.3113E3
PRICE	CHEMX		3.6250E1	6.0000E1	7.5000E1
	CHEMY		4.0000E1	5.0000E1	8.2759E1

-> END <-

in Figure 4-5. Using Figures 4-1 and 4-5, answer the following questions:
a. When the chemical production problem was analyzed in Chapter 3 (see Figures 3-7 and 3-8), an additional unit of capacity on machine A was worth $3.75. According to Figure 4-5, it is worth nothing ($0.00) when the financial constraints are added. Why?
b. What is an additional unit of machine B capacity worth to the firm when the financial constraints are considered?
c. Suppose the company changes its policy and requires a cash asset position of only $4500. Would the contribution to profit be increased? If so, by how much?

2. Figure 4-6 gives the computer input, solution, and sensitivity analysis for the portfolio selection linear optimization model discussed in the text and given in Table 4-4.
a. What is the appropriate interpretation of the objective function value of 0.097?
b. Suppose we have $100,000 to invest. How much should be purchased of each security?
c. What is the meaning of $SUR2 = 0.2$? $SLK6 = 0.1$?
d. Suppose that the upper bound on the electronics securities increased from 30 to 35 percent. How would the solution change?
e. Suppose that the yield in electronics increased from 12 to 15 percent. Would the solution change? How do you know?
f. If the yields were known for certain, we would clearly invest our entire portfolio in electronics securities. What is the purpose of the upper and lower limits on the investments? Are these limits firm or subjective? Criticize this model in terms of its practical usefulness.

```
      LPENTER
ENTER THE NAME OF THIS PROJECT PORTFOLIO SELECTION
MAXIMIZE OR MINIMIZE: MAXIMIZE
OBJECTIVE FUNCTION:Z=.12E+.08U+.1F+.09C
ENTER CONSTRAINT EQUATIONS, (STRIKE JUST A CARRIAGE RETURN TO STOP INPUT)
  (1) E+U+F+C=1
  (2) E≥.1
  (3) E≤.3
  (4) U≥.15
  (5) F≥.05
  (6) F≤.2
  (7) C≥.2
  (8) C≤.35
  (9) E+F≤.4
 (10) .5E-U+.5F≤0
 (11)
      LPRUN
```

PORTFOLIO SELECTION

THE OPTIMAL VALUE OF THE OBJECTIVE FUNCTION IS: 0.097

THE VARIABLES IN THE SOLUTION ARE

VARIABLE	E	AT LEVEL	3.0000E-1
	U		2.5000E-1
	F		1.0000E-1
	C		3.5000E-1
	SUR2		2.0000E-1
	SUR4		1.0000E-1
	SUR5		5.0000E-2
	SLK6		1.0000E-1
	SUR7		1.5000E-1
	SLK10		5.0000E-2

DO YOU WISH SENSITIVITY ANALYSIS? YES

CONSTRAINT		SHADOW	LB	CURRENT	UB
	1	8.0000E-2	9.5000E-1	1.0000E0	7.2370E75
	2	0.0000E0	-7.2370E75	1.0000E-1	3.0000E-1
	3	2.0000E-2	2.0000E-1	3.0000E-1	3.5000E-1
	4	0.0000E0	-7.2370E75	1.5000E-1	2.5000E-1
	5	0.0000E0	-7.2370E75	5.0000E-2	1.0000E-1
	6	0.0000E0	1.0000E-1	2.0000E-1	7.2370E75
	7	0.0000E0	-7.2370E75	2.0000E-1	3.5000E-1
	8	1.0000E-2	2.0000E-1	3.5000E-1	4.0000E-1
	9	2.0000E-2	3.5000E-1	4.0000E-1	4.3333E-1
	10	0.0000E0	-5.0000E-2	0.0000E0	7.2370E75
PRICE	E		1.0000E-1	1.2000E-1	7.2370E75
	U		-7.2370E75	8.0000E-2	9.0000E-2
	F		8.0000E-2	1.0000E-1	1.2000E-1
	C		8.0000E-2	9.0000E-2	7.2370E75

FIGURE 4-6
Portfolio selection
problem (Exercise 2)

3. The computer input and solution for the cash management problem are shown in Figure 4-7.

a. The optimal value of the objective function is -0.671. What does this mean?

b. Interpret the solution. Will any bank credit be needed, and, if so, how much and in what month? Should either security be sold early? When should the accounts payable be paid? Should any short-term securities be purchased?

c. The shadow price for constraint [4] is 0.025773. How do you interpret this number?

d. The shadow price for constraint [7] is -0.030928. How do you interpret this number.

e. Suppose that the short-term security yield for a 30 day maturity increases from 0.75 to 1.0 percent. Would the optimal solution change?

f. Suppose that there was no penalty on the sale of security B one month before its maturity date. Would the solution change?

g. What difficulties would you foresee in implementing this model in the real world? How might they be overcome?

```
        LPENTER
ENTER THE NAME OF THIS PROJECT CASH MANAGEMENT
MAXIMIZE OR MINIMIZE: MAXIMIZE
OBJECTIVE FUNCTION:Z=.0075SJF+.0075SFM+.016SJM-.04CRJ-.015SAJ
                -.005SBJ-.03CRF-.005SAF-.02PFJ-.02CRM-.02PMF
ENTER CONSTRAINT EQUATIONS, (STRIKE JUST A CARRIAGE RETURN  TO STOP INPUT)
 (1) PJJ+SJF+SJM-.96CRJ-.985SAJ-.995SBJ=10
 (2) 1.02PFJ+PFF+SFM-.97CRF-.995SAF-SBF-1.0075SJF=20
 (3) .98CRM+SAM+1.016SJM+1.0075SFM-1.02PMF=10
 (4) SAJ+SAF+SAM=50
 (5) SBJ+SBF=20
 (6) PJJ+PFJ=40
 (7) PFF+PMF=60
 (8)
        LPRUN

                 CASH MANAGEMENT
THE OPTIMAL VALUE OF THE OBJECTIVE FUNCTION IS:  -0.671
               THE VARIABLES IN THE SOLUTION ARE
VARIABLE   SAJ     AT LEVEL      1.0254E1
           SBJ                   2.0000E1
           CRF                   4.6653E-1
           SAF                   3.9746E1
           CRM                   1.0204E1
           PJJ                   4.0000E1
           PFF                   6.0000E1
```

DO YOU WISH SENSITIVITY ANALYSIS? YES

		SHADOW	LB	CURRENT	UB
CONSTRAINT	1	4.1394E-2	-2.9150E1	1.0000E1	1.0448E1
	2	3.0928E-2	-7.2370E75	2.0000E1	2.0453E1
	3	-2.0408E-2	0.0000E0	1.0000E1	7.2370E75
	4	2.5773E-2	1.0254E1	5.0000E1	5.0455E1
	5	3.6187E-2	0.0000E0	2.0000E1	2.0450E1
	6	-4.1394E-2	3.9552E1	4.0000E1	7.9150E1
	7	-3.0928E-2	5.9547E1	6.0000E1	7.2370E75
PRICE	SJF		-7.2370E75	7.5000E-3	1.0234E-2
	SFM		-7.2370E75	7.5000E-3	1.0367E-2
	SJM		-7.2370E75	1.6000E-2	2.0659E-2
	CRJ		-7.2370E75	-4.0000E-2	-3.9738E-2
	SAJ		-1.5268E-2	-1.5000E-2	-1.2307E-2
	SBJ		-1.0259E-2	-5.0000E-3	7.2370E75
	CRF		-3.0262E-2	-3.0000E-2	-2.7219E-2
	SAF		-7.6933E-3	-5.0000E-3	-4.7315E-3
	PFJ		-7.2370E75	-2.0000E-2	-9.8477E-3
	CRM		-2.2788E-2	-2.0000E-2	-1.0499E-2
	PMF		-7.2370E75	-2.0000E-2	-1.0112E-2
	SAM		-7.2370E75	0.0000E0	5.3650E-3
	SBF		-7.2370E75	0.0000E0	5.2593E-3
	PJJ		-1.0152E-2	0.0000E0	7.2370E75
	PFF		-9.8885E-3	0.0000E0	7.2370E75

-> END <-

FIGURE 4-7
Cash management problem (Exercise 3)

4. Figure 4-8 gives the computer input, solution, and sensitivity analysis for the advertising media selection problem discussed in the text.
   a. How many advertising units should be purchased in each media?
   b. What if the exposure rating per unit of newspapers (N) were higher? Would the solution change?
   c. The budget limitations of $250,000 on each of the media were subjectively set. If you were to consider increasing this budget allocation to one of these media, which one would you choose? Why?
   d. This model assumes that the first advertisement in each of the media has just as much impact as the second, which has the same impact as the last advertisement. Is this a reasonable assumption? Criticize this formulation in terms of its use in the real world. Can you think of ways to improve its realism?

```
        LPENTER
ENTER THE NAME OF THIS PROJECT ADVERTISING MEDIA SELECTION
MAXIMIZE OR MINIMIZE: MAXIMIZE
OBJECTIVE FUNCTION: Z= 100M+400N+200R+600TVP+150TVO
ENTER CONSTRAINT EQUATIONS, (STRIKE JUST A CARRIAGE RETURN TO STOP INPUT)
 (1)  20M+15N+5R+40TVP+10TVO≤600
 (2)  20M≤250
 (3)  15N≤250
 (4)  5R≤250
 (5)  40TVP+10TVO≤250
 (6)  20M+15N≤350
 (7)  5R—10TVP—2.5TVO≥0
 (8)  10TVO—20TVO≥0
 (9)  10M+30N+20R+15TVO+35TVP≥250
(10)
        LPRUN
                ADVERTISING MEDIA SELECTION
THE OPTIMAL VALUE OF THE OBJECTIVE FUNCTION IS:   18166.667
                THE VARIABLES IN THE SOLUTION ARE
VARIABLE   N      AT LEVEL      1.6667E1
           R                    5.0000E1
           TVP                  1.6667E0
           TVO                  3.3333E0
           SLK2                 2.5000E2
           SLK5                 1.5000E2
           SLK6                 1.0000E2
           SUR7                 2.2500E2
           SUR9                 1.3583E3


DO YOU WISH SENSITIVITY ANALYSIS? YES
```

		SHADOW	LB	CURRENT	UB
CONSTRAINT	1	1.5000E1	5.0000E2	6.0000E2	7.5000E2
	2	0.0000E0	0.0000E0	2.5000E2	7.2370E75
	3	1.1667E1	1.0000E2	2.5000E2	3.5000E2
	4	2.5000E1	1.0000E2	2.5000E2	3.5000E2
	5	0.0000E0	1.0000E2	2.5000E2	7.2370E75
	6	0.0000E0	2.5000E2	3.5000E2	7.2370E75
	7	0.0000E0	-7.2370E75	0.0000E0	2.2500E2
	8	0.0000E0	-5.0000E1	0.0000E0	1.0000E2
	9	0.0000E0	-7.2370E75	2.5000E2	1.6083E3
PRICE	M		-7.2370E75	1.0000E2	3.0000E2
	N		2.2500E2	4.0000E2	7.2370E75
	R		7.5000E1	2.0000E2	7.2370E75
	TVP		6.0000E2	6.0000E2	1.3000E3
	TVO		-1.5000E2	1.5000E2	1.5000E2

```
-> END <-
```

FIGURE 4-8
Advertising media
selection problem
(Exercise 4)

5. The computer input and solution for the sales territory determination problem are shown in Figure 4-9. (The sensitivity analysis is omitted.)
   a. Which sales zones should be assigned to Able and which to Baker?
   b. Redraw the map in Figure 4-2 and shade in the area assigned to Able. How would you suggest dividing up zone 6?
   c. Suppose the company is willing to consider an assignment of zones that gives at least 210 customers to Able and at least 210 customers to Baker. Reformulate the problem to allow for this change.
   d. Instead of simply using the number of customers in each area, are there other measures that might be more appropriate for an equitable distribution of sales zones? In other words, evaluate this model. What changes would you suggest before using it in practice?

```
      LPENTER
ENTER THE NAME OF THIS PROJECT DETERMINATION OF SALES TERRITORIES
MAXIMIZE OR MINIMIZE: MINIMIZE
OBJECTIVE FUNCTION:Z=208XA1+100XA2+244XA3+144XA4+0XA5+144XA6
          +580XB1+144XB2+0XB3+676XB4+244XB5+100XB6
ENTER CONSTRAINT EQUATIONS, (STRIKE JUST A CARRIAGE RETURN TO STOP INPUT)
  (1) XA1+XB1=1
  (2) XA2+XB2=1
  (3) XA3+XB3=1
  (4) XA4+XB4=1
  (5) XA5+XB5=1
  (6) XA6+XB6=1
  (7) 20XA1+85XA2+150XA3+40XA4+60XA5+75XA6=215
  (8)
      LPRUN
             DETERMINATION OF SALES TERRITORIES


THE OPTIMAL VALUE OF THE OBJECTIVE FUNCTION IS:   557.867


              THE VARIABLES IN THE SOLUTION ARE


VARIABLE   XA1      AT LEVEL     1.0000E0
           XA2                   1.0000E0
           XA4                   1.0000E0
           XA5                   1.0000E0
           XA6                   1.3333E-1
           XB3                   1.0000E0
           XB6                   8.6667E-1
```

FIGURE 4-9
Sales territories problems
(Exercise 5)

6. The computer input, solution, and sensitivity analysis for the nurse scheduling problem are shown in Figure 4-10.
   a. How many nurses should come on duty each period? Verify that this schedule satisfies the minimum requirements.
   b. The shadow price for constraint [2] is 0.0. How do you interpret this?
   c. Suppose nurses come on duty only at 6:00 A.M., 2:00 P.M., and 10:00 P.M. and work 8 consecutive hours. Those arriving at 6:00 A.M. and 2:00 P.M. are paid $40 per day, and those arriving at 10:00 P.M. are paid $50. Determine by hand the number of nurses needed on each shift, based on the data in the example, and compute the total daily payroll costs. Which system would you recommend?

```
      LPENTER
ENTER THE NAME OF THIS PROJECT NURSE SCHEDULING
MAXIMIZE OR MINIMIZE: MINIMIZE
OBJECTIVE FUNCTION:Z=50N1+40N2+40N3+40N4+50N5+50N6
ENTER CONSTRAINT EQUATIONS, (STRIKE JUST A CARRIAGE RETURN TO STOP INPUT)
  (1) N1+N2≥60
  (2) N2+N3≥50
  (3) N3+N4≥35
  (4) N4+N5≥55
  (5) N5+N6≥40
  (6) N1+N6≥25
  (7)
      LPRUN
```

```
                    NURSE SCHEDULING


THE OPTIMAL VALUE OF THE OBJECTIVE FUNCTION IS:    5850.000


              THE VARIABLES IN THE SOLUTION ARE


VARIABLE   N1      AT LEVEL       5.0000E0
           N2                     5.5000E1
           N4                     3.5000E1
           N5                     2.0000E1
           N6                     2.0000E1
           SUR2                   5.0000E0
```

DO YOU WISH SENSITIVITY ANALYSIS? YES

		SHADOW	LB	CURRENT	UB
CONSTRAINT	1	4.0000E1	5.5000E1	6.0000E1	7.2370E75
	2	0.0000E0	-7.2370E75	5.0000E1	5.5000E1
	3	3.0000E1	3.0000E1	3.5000E1	4.0000E1
	4	1.0000E1	5.0000E1	5.5000E1	6.0000E1
	5	4.0000E1	3.5000E1	4.0000E1	4.5000E1
	6	1.0000E1	2.0000E1	2.5000E1	3.0000E1
PRICE	N1		4.0000E1	5.0000E1	8.0000E1
	N2		1.0000E1	4.0000E1	5.0000E1
	N3		3.0000E1	4.0000E1	7.2370E75
	N4		1.0000E1	4.0000E1	5.0000E1
	N5		4.0000E1	5.0000E1	8.0000E1
	N6		2.0000E1	5.0000E1	6.0000E1

-> END <-

FIGURE 4-10
Nurse scheduling
problem (Exercise 6)

7. The computer input, solution, and sensitivity analysis for the personnel planning
problem are shown in Figure 4-11.
   a. How many trainees should be hired in January? In February?
   b. Suppose the machinists are paid $2000 per month. Would this change be
      likely to alter the solution? Why or why not?
   c. The results are not integer valued. How would you implement this solution in
      practice? In other words, if you were in charge of recruiting and training, what
      would you do?

```
      LPENTER
ENTER THE NAME OF THIS PROJECT PERSONNEL PLANNING
MAXIMIZE OR MINIMIZE: MINIMIZE
OBJECTIVE FUNCTION:Z=1000TRAINJ+1200MACHF+1000TRAINF+1200MACHM
ENTER CONSTRAINT EQUATIONS, (STRIKE JUST A CARRIAGE RETURN TO STOP INPUT
  (1) 75TRAINJ≤500
  (2) MACHF-TRAINJ=27
  (3) 150MACHF—75TRAINF≥4500
  (4) MACHM-TRAINF-.9MACHF=0
  (5) 150MACHM≥4200
  (6)
      LPRUN
                      PERSONNEL PLANNING
```

FIGURE 4-11
Personnel planning
problem (continued on
next page)

```
THE OPTIMAL VALUE OF THE OBJECTIVE FUNCTION IS:    74048.276

            THE VARIABLES IN THE SOLUTION ARE


VARIABLE   TRAINJ AT LEVEL      3.3448E0
           MACHF                3.0345E1
           TRAINF               6.8966E-1
           MACHM                2.8000E1
           SLK1                 2.4914E2


DO YOU WISH SENSITIVITY ANALYSIS? YES

                      SHADOW       LB        CURRENT      UB
CONSTRAINT    1      0.0000E0    2.5086E2    5.0000E2    7.2370E75
              2     -1.0000E3    2.3678E1    2.7000E1    3.0345E1
              3      5.9770E0    3.7725E3    4.5000E3    4.6667E3
              4     -1.4483E3   -9.6333E0    0.0000E0    1.0000E0
              5      1.7655E1    4.0500E3    4.2000E3    5.6450E3


PRICE      TRAINJ              -3.0000E2    1.0000E3    7.2370E75
           MACHF               -1.0000E2    1.2000E3    7.2370E75
           TRAINF              -2.8400E3    1.0000E3    2.4444E3
           MACHM               -1.4483E3    1.2000E3    7.2370E75
-> END <-
```

FIGURE 4-11
Continued
(Exercise 7)

8. The computer input, solution, and sensitivity analysis for the land-use allocation problem are shown in Figure 4-12.
   a. Which utility lines will require expansion? By how much?
   b. How many residential developments should be given building permits in each zone? How many industrial developments?
   c. Suppose an additional 100 residential developments (700 rather than 600) are actually needed. How much extra will it cost the city for the expansion of the utility lines?
   d. The city wishes to charge each industrial development a building permit fee equal to the marginal cost of the necessary utility line expansion. What should the fee be?
   e. How many additional units of electricity will be transmitted on each of the three electrical lines after the expansion?
   f. What other considerations might be included in a real-world application of an urban planning model?

```
      LPENTER
ENTER THE NAME OF THIS PROJECT LAND USE ALLOCATION
MAXIMIZE OR MINIMIZE: MINIMIZE
OBJECTIVE FUNCTION:Z=7XC12+2XC13+3XC32
ENTER CONSTRAINT EQUATIONS, (STRIKE JUST A CARRIAGE RETURN TO STOP INPUT)
 (1) R2+R3=600
 (2) I2+I3=400
 (3) 7R2+9I2≤3000
 (4) 7R3+9I3≤10000
 (5) 2R2+3I2-UC12-XC12-UC32-XC32=0
 (6) 2R3+3I3+UC32+XC32-UC13-XC13=0
 (7) UC12≤400
 (8) UC32≤500
 (9) UC13≤1500
(10)
      LPRUN
                   LAND USE ALLOCATION



THE OPTIMAL VALUE OF THE OBJECTIVE FUNCTION IS:   1000.000


              THE VARIABLES IN THE SOLUTION ARE


VARIABLE   XC13    AT LEVEL      5.0000E2
           UC12                  4.0000E2
           UC13                  1.5000E3
           UC32                  4.5714E2
           R2                    4.2857E2
           R3                    1.7143E2
           I3                    4.0000E2
           SLK4                  5.2000E3
           SLK8                  4.2857E1


DO YOU WISH SENSITIVITY ANALYSIS? YES

                    SHADOW        LB       CURRENT        UB
CONSTRAINT    1    4.0000E0    4.2857E2    6.0000E2    1.3429E3
              2    6.0000E0    2.3333E2    4.0000E2    9.7778E2
              3    0.0000E0    1.4000E3    3.0000E3    3.1500E3
              4    0.0000E0    4.8000E3    1.0000E4    7.2370E75
              5   -2.0000E0   -4.2857E1    0.0000E0    4.5714E2
              6   -2.0000E0   -7.2370E75   0.0000E0    5.0000E2
              7   -2.0000E0    3.5714E2    4.0000E2    8.5714E2
              8    0.0000E0    4.5714E2    5.0000E2    7.2370E75
              9   -2.0000E0    0.0000E0    1.5000E3    2.0000E3
```

FIGURE 4-12
Land-use allocation problem (continued on next page)

```
PRICE        XC12            2.0000E0    7.0000E0    7.2370E75
             XC13            0.0000E0    2.0000E0    7.0000E0
             XC32            0.0000E0    3.0000E0    7.2370E75
             UC12           -7.2370E75   0.0000E0    2.0000E0
             UC13           -7.2370E75   0.0000E0    2.0000E0
             UC32            0.0000E0    0.0000E0    0.0000E0
             R2             -7.2370E75   0.0000E0    0.0000E0
             R3              0.0000E0    0.0000E0    7.2370E75
             I2              0.0000E0    0.0000E0    7.2370E75
             I3             -7.2370E75   0.0000E0    0.0000E0
-> END <-
```

FIGURE 4-12
Continued
(Exercise 8)

9. The computer input and solution for the school desegregation problem are shown in Figure 4-13. (The sensitivity analysis is omitted.)

a. Verify that 195 students are assigned to school A and that 195 are assigned to school B. Also, verify that 55 students from ethnic group X are assigned to each school.

b. Notice that $XB1 = 0.5$, so that $(0.5)(50) = 25$ students from ethnic group X in zone 1 are assigned to school B, even though they must travel 19 miles. The 30 students from ethnic group X in zone 2 are assigned to school A, even though they would have to travel only 10 miles to school B. If 25 students from ethnic group X in zone B were assigned to school B, then the 25 in zone 1 assigned to B could be reassigned to school A. Would this be a better solution? If so, what is wrong with the model?

c. Suggest an alternate objective function and reformulate the problem (Hint: See the sales territory model.)

d. Suppose that the district wishes to ensure that there are at least 180 students enrolled in each school and that at least 45 students from ethnic group X are enrolled in each school. Reformulate the problem to impose these constraints.

10. The computer input and output for the budget analysis problem are shown in Figure 4-14.

a. What is the allocation of state and local funds to the three programs? That is, how much of the total amount of state and local dollars is allocated to the day care program? Employment services? Community services? What is the allocation of federal funds to the three programs?

b. Which budget goals are met? Which are not met by this allocation?

c. Suppose that a total of $1,000,000 was reallocated from the employment services program to the day care program. How would the "optimal solution" to this problem be changed?

```
      LPENTER
ENTER THE NAME OF THIS PROJECT SCHOOL DESEGREGATION
MAXIMIZE OR MINIMIZE: MINIMIZE
OBJECTIVE FUNCTION:Z=450XA1+90YA1+0XA2+0YA2+135XA3+630YA3
                    +150XA4+800YA4+0XA5+900YA5+950XB1+190YB1
                    +300XB2+300YB2+135XB3+630YB3+150XB4+800YB4+0XB5+0YB5
ENTER CONSTRAINT EQUATIONS, (STRIKE JUST A CARRIAGE RETURN TO STOP INPUT)
  (1) XA1+XB1=1
  (2) YA1+YB1=1
  (3) XA2+XB2=1
  (4) YA2+YB2=1
  (5) XA3+XB3=1
  (6) YA3+YB3=1
  (7) XA4+XB4=1
  (8) YA4+YB4=1
  (9) XA5+XB5=1
 (10) YA5+YB5=1
 (11) 50XA1+10YA1+30XA2+30YA2+15XA3+70YA3+15XA4+80YA4+90YA5=195
 (12) 50XA1+30XA2+15XA3+15XA4=55
 (13)
      LPRUN
                    SCHOOL DESEGREGATION

THE OPTIMAL VALUE OF THE OBJECTIVE FUNCTION IS:    2505.000

THE VARIABLES IN THE SOLUTION ARE

VARIABLE  XA1     AT LEVEL      5.0000E-1
          YA1                   1.0000E0
          XA2                   1.0000E0
          YA2                   1.0000E0
          YA3                   1.0000E0
          YA4                   3.7500E-1
          XA5                   1.0000E0
          XB1                   5.0000E-1
          XB3                   1.0000E0
          XB4                   1.0000E0
          YB4                   6.2500E-1
          YB5                   1.0000E0
```

FIGURE 4-13
School desegregation problem
(Exercise 9)

d. By how much would the "weight" on the variable *GDUM* have to increase before its value would change? Can you relate this result to your answer in c?

e. The shadow price for constraint [11] is 1.0. How do you interpret this result?

f. The federal funds must be matched by state and local funds at a ratio of 1 to 3. If this ratio were changed to 1 to 2, would the solution change. How do you know?

g. Suppose that the *weight* on *GSP* is changed from 10 to 2. Would the solution change?

```
       LPENTER
ENTER THE NAME OF THIS PROJECT BUDGET ANALYSIS
MAXIMIZE OR MINIMIZE: MIN
OBJECTIVE FUNCTION:Z=10GSP+10GFP+10GDUP+10GEUP
                   +10GCUP+5GDLM+5GELM+5GCLM+GDUM+GEUM+GCUM
ENTER CONSTRAINT EQUATIONS, (STRIKE JUST A CARRIAGE RETURN TO STOP INPUT)
 (1)  DF+EF+CF+GFM-GFP=78000000
 (2)  DS+ES+CS+GSM-GSP=34200000
 (3)  DF-3DS≤0
 (4)  EF-3ES≤0
 (5)  CF-3CS≤0
 (6)  DF+DS+GDLM-GDLP=28785000
 (7)  EF+ES+GELM-GELP=18207877
 (8)  CF+CS+GCLM-GCLP=47802290
 (9)  DF+DS+GDUM-GDUP=35182908
(10)  EF+ES+GEUM-GEUP=19698754
(11)  CF+CS+GCUM-GCUP=78320122
       LPRUN
```

```
                        BUDGET ANALYSIS
    THE OPTIMAL VALUE OF THE OBJECTIVE FUNCTION IS: 21001783.999
                 THE VARIABLES IN THE SOLUTION ARE
```

```
VARIABLE   GDUM     AT LEVEL        6.3979E6
           GCUM                     1.4604E7
           EF                       8.62+1E6
           ES                       1.1075E7
           DF                       2.1589E7
           DS                       7.1962E6
           CF                       4.7787E7
           CS                       1.5929E7
           GELP                     1.4909E6
           GCLP                     1.5914E7
           SLK4                     2.4600E7
```

DO YOU WISH SENSITIVITY ANALYSIS? YES

		SHADOW	LB	CURRENT	UB
CONSTRAINT	1	-1.0000E0	6.2086E7	7.8000E7	9.2604E7
	2	-1.0000E0	-2.6000E7	3.4200E7	4.5699E7
	3	0.0000E0	-2.4600E7	0.0000E0	2.8787E7
	4	0.0000E0	-7.2370E75	0.0000E0	2.4600E7
	5	0.0000E0	-2.4600E7	0.0000E0	3.4496E7
	6	0.0000E0	-1.4181E7	2.8785E7	3.5183E7
	7	0.0000E0	-7.2370E75	1.8208E7	1.9699E7
	8	0.0000E0	-7.2370E75	4.7802E7	6.3716E7
	9	1.0000E0	2.8785E7	3.5183E7	7.2370E75
	10	1.0000E0	1.8208E7	1.9699E7	3.5613E7
	11	1.0000E0	6.3716E7	7.8320E7	7.2370E75

PRICE	DS	0.0000E0	0.0000E0	2.0000E0
	DF	0.0000E0	0.0000E0	0.0000E0
	ES	-4.0000E0	0.0000E0	0.0000E0
	EF	0.0000E0	0.0000E0	0.0000E0
	CS	0.0000E0	0.0000E0	0.0000E0
	CF	0.0000E0	0.0000E0	0.0000E0
	GFM	-1.0000E0	0.0000E0	7.2370E75
	GFP	1.0000E0	1.0000E1	7.2370E75
	GSM	-1.0000E0	0.0000E0	7.2370E75
	GSP	1.0000E0	1.0000E1	7.2370E75
	GDLM	0.0000E0	5.0000E0	7.2370E75
	GDLP	0.0000E0	0.0000E0	7.2370E75
	GELM	0.0000E0	5.0000E0	7.2370E75
	GELP	-5.0000E0	0.0000E0	0.0000E0
	GCLM	0.0000E0	5.0000E0	7.2370E75
	GCLP	0.0000E0	0.0000E0	0.0000E0
	GDUM	-4.0000E0	1.0000E0	1.0000E0
	GDUP	-1.0000E0	1.0000E1	7.2370E75
	GEUM	1.0000E0	1.0000E0	7.2370E75
	GEUP	-1.0000E0	1.0000E1	7.2370E75
	GCUM	1.0000E0	1.0000E0	1.0000E0
	GCUP	-1.0000E0	1.0000E1	7.2370E75

FIGURE 4-14
Budget analysis
problem (Exercise 10)

SHORT CASES

A Federal Home Loan Bank makes essentially four kinds of loans, which yield the following   CASE 4-1
annual interest rates:

First mortgages	10%
Second mortgages	16%
Home improvement loans	18%
Loans against accounts	5%

The bank has a maximum lending capability of $2 million and must stay within the following
limits and policies:

a. First mortgages must be at least 45 percent of all mortgages and at least 25 percent of loans
   outstanding.
b. Second mortgages cannot exceed 30 percent of loans.

Formulate the bank's loan problem as a linear optimization model designed to maximize
interest income within the stated policy limits.

CASE 4-2   Clyde's, a men's store in a small college town, wishes to place an order for its three major lines of apparel: casual sportswear, suits and sports coats, and sweaters. Clyde's receives a greater profit per unit from suits and sports coats, but the required floor space for displays and sales time is also greater. The per unit profit for sweaters is the lowest, but the required floor space and sales time are also low.

Clyde's feels obligated to carry a full line of clothing, so the buyer feels that she must order at least 100 units of casual sportswear, 100 units of suits and sports coats, and 200 units of sweaters for the season. Otherwise, she would like to order a mix of apparel that, if sold, would maximize her profits.

The store has only 3000 square feet of floor space and only 1600 salesperson hours available for customer service. The buyer has made rough estimates of the floor space and salesperson-hour requirements per 100 units of each line of clothing. The results are shown in Table 4-20. Finally, the buyer feels that she could sell a maximum of 1000 units of the casual sportswear, 2000 units of suits and sports coats, and a virtually unlimited number of units of sweaters. How many units of each line should the buyer order for the season, assuming that she wished to maximize profits? Formulate the buyer's problem as a linear optimization model.

TABLE 4-20   Sales Data for Clyde's

Line of Clothing	Average Profit per Unit	Salesperson-Hours per 100 Sold	Floor Space (sq ft per 100 units)
Casual sportswear	$ 7.00	30	50
Suits and sports coats	20.00	100	75
Sweaters	5.00	10	40

CASE 4-3   A local power plant has had a visit from the air pollution control authorities. After considerable technical analysis, the plant has been ordered to reduce solid pollutants by 50,000 lb per year, oxides of sulfur by 40,000 lb per year, and hydrocarbons by 50,000 lb per year.

The plant currently uses coal as a fuel. Extensive engineering analysis indicates that substantial reductions in pollutants could be achieved by installing and operating precipitators, using fuel oil, or using natural gas. The annual cost of each of these control methods is as follows:

Control Method	Annual Cost
Precipitator (P)	15
Coal to oil (CO)	10
Coal to gas (CG)	18

Potential Improvement in Air Pollutants by Three Control Methods (in 1000s of lb)				TABLE 4-21
Pollutant	Precipitator	Coal to Oil	Coal to Gas	
Solids	30	32	40	
Oxides of sulfur	35	20	30	
Hydrocarbons	28	10	40	

Fractional or multiple installations of each of these methods may be used.

The engineering analysis also indicated estimates of the possible improvement in each of the three types of pollutants for each of the three control methods. These data are shown in Table 4-21. Formulate the pollution control problem as a linear optimization model.

Mr. George Overstreet has decided to run for the city council of his home town. He faces stiff opposition in the primary election as well as in the fall. The resources for his campaign are limited in terms of both time from volunteer workers and money.

CASE 4-4

Mr. Overstreet has divided the town into city blocks as a basic campaign unit. He can take three different actions on each block: door-to-door canvassing, placement of lawn signs, and a district-wide mailing. The estimated average time and cost per city block of each of these actions is shown in Table 4-22. Mr. Overstreet estimates that he can allocate a total of 8 hours of volunteer worker time and a total of $7 to each block over both the primary and the fall campaign.

After a preliminary analysis, Overstreet has made estimates of the impacts of each of the three campaign strategies. The results are shown in Table 4-23. For example, if a block is canvassed door-to-door in the primary campaign, Overstreet expects to receive a net additional 1.5 votes. We say "net additional" votes, because the door-to-door canvassing stimulates voter participation in general, with some of the additional votes going to his opponent.

Alternate Campaign Actions			TABLE 4-22
Effort	Time per Block (hr)	Dollars per Block	
Door-to-door canvassing	2	$ 0.00	
Lawn signs	1	3.50	
District-wide mailing	0	10.50	

TABLE 4-23   Net Effects of Campaign Action on Votes

	Net Additional Votes	
Effort	Primary	Fall Election
Door-to-door canvassing	1.5	4.0
Lawn signs	1.8	0.25
District-wide mailing	10.0	20.0

```
      LPENTER
ENTER THE NAME OF THIS PROJECT CAMPAIGN RESOURCE ALLOCATION
MAXIMIZE OR MINIMIZE: MAXIMIZE
OBJECTIVE FUNCTION:Z=4CF+.25SF+20MF+0CP+0SP+0MP
ENTER CONSTRAINT EQUATIONS, (STRIKE JUST A CARRIAGE RETURN TO STOP INPUT)
  (1) 2CP+SP+2CF+SF≤8
  (2) 3.5SP+10.5MP+3.5SF+10.5MF≤7
  (3) 1.5CP+1.8SP+10MP≥2
  (4)
      LPRUN
              CAMPAIGN RESOURCE ALLOCATION


THE OPTIMAL VALUE OF THE OBJECTIVE FUNCTION IS:    25.333


              THE VARIABLES IN THE SOLUTION ARE


VARIABLE   CF     AT LEVEL      4.0000E0
           MF                   4.6667E-1
           MP                   2.0000E-1


DO YOU WISH SENSITIVITY ANALYSIS? YES

                    SHADOW        LB        CURRENT        UB
CONSTRAINT     1    2.0000E0    0.0000E0    8.0000E0    7.2370E75
               2    1.9048E0    2.1000E0    7.0000E0    7.2370E75
               3   -2.0000E0    0.0000E0    2.0000E0    6.6667E0

PRICE        CF                 3.0000E0    4.0000E0    7.2370E75
             SF                -7.2370E75   2.5000E-1   8.6667E0
             MF                 1.0000E-6   2.0000E1    2.6667E1
             CP                -7.2370E75   0.0000E0    1.0000E0
             SP                -7.2370E75   0.0000E0    5.0667E0
             MP                -6.6667E0    0.0000E0    2.0000E1
-> END <-
```

FIGURE 4-15
Campaign resource
allocation (Case 4-4)

Suppose Overstreet wishes to obtain a net additional vote of at least 2.0 per block from his campaign efforts in the primary, and then maximize the net additional vote in the fall election. How should he allocate his resources?

Overstreet has formulated his problem using a linear optimization model. He defined CP as the proportion of city blocks that can be canvassed (C) during the primary (P) and CF as the proportion canvassed in the fall (F). For example, if $CP = 0.5$, then half of the blocks should be canvassed in the primary. He also assumed that he may have $CP > 1.0$. For example, he would interpret $CP = 2.5$ to mean that each block should be canvassed 2.5 times prior to the primary.

Likewise, SP and SF are the proportions receiving signs (S) in the primary and fall respectively, and MP and MF are the proportions receiving a direct mailing (M). The complete problem formulation is shown as the computer input in Figure 4-15 along with the solution.

a. How many additional votes in each block does Overstreet expect to receive from his fall campaign efforts?
b. Suppose Overstreet could *hire* additional campaign workers for $1 per hour. Should he spend $1 for an hour of campaign worker time?
c. Suppose that Overstreet would like to generate a net additional vote in each block of 5.0 from the efforts during the primary. How many net additional votes in the fall election would he be giving up?
d. Criticize the assumptions of this model. (Hint: Compare this model to the media selection model.)*

Select three or four references from the applications reference list, and read them in order to gain an understanding of the nature of the applications (do not concern yourself with mathematical details). Select one of these articles and summarize it. Include the following in the summary:

CASE 4-5

a. What was the nature of the problem analyzed?
b. What were the major decision variables in the model?
c. What was the objective function; that is, tell what was being optimized?
d. What was the nature of the important constraints?
e. How was the solution actually used?
f. If you were a manager faced with this problem, would you consider these results useful? What were the limitations of the model? Were there other considerations that should also influence the ultimate decision?

---

* This case is based on an analysis by Southwick and Zionts [1975] of Southwick's campaign for the Town Council of Amhurst, New York. (He won!) For a discussion of the actual use of a linear optimization model in planning a political campaign, see Barken and Bruno [1972].

APPLICATIONS REFERENCES

Aaker, D. A., "Management Science in Marketing: The State of the Art," *Interfaces,* Vol. 3, No. 4, August 1973.

Adelman, I, "A Linear Programming Model of Educational Planning: A Case Study of Argentina," in *The Theory of Design of Economic Development,* I. Adelman and E. Thorbecke, editors, The Johns-Hopkins Press, Baltimore, 1966.

Allman, W. P., "An Optimization Approach to Freight Car Allocation Under Fiscal-Mileage per Diem Rental Rates," *Management Science,* Vol. 18, No. 10, June 1972.

Anderson, D., "Models for Determining Least-Cost Investments in Electricity Supply," *The Bell Journal of Economics and Management Science,* Spring 1972.

Bagby, G., and A. Thesen, "A Network Flow Model for Allocation of Land Uses to Sectors," *Management Science,* Vol. 22, No. 11, July 1976.

Bammi, D., and D. Bammi, "Development of a Comprehensive Land Use Plan by Means of a Multiple Objective Mathematical Programming Model," *Interfaces,* Vol. 9, No. 2, Part 2, February 1979.

Barken, J. D., and J. E. Bruno, "Operations Research in Planning Political Campaign Strategies," *Operations Research,* September-October 1972.

Bass, F. M., and R. T. Lonsdale, "An Exploration of Linear Programming in Media Selection," *Journal of Marketing Research,* Vol. 3, 1966.

Belford, P. C., and D. Ratliff, "A Network-Flow Model for Racially Balancing Schools," *Operations Research,* Vol. 20, No. 3, 1972.

Bertoletti, M. E., J. Chapiro, and H. R. Rieznik, "Optimization of Investment—A Solution by Linear Programming," *Management Technology,* No. 1, January 1960, pp. 64–75.

Bruno, J., "An Alternative to Uniform Expenditure Reductions in Multiple Resource State Finance Programs," *Management Science,* Vol. 17, No. 6, February 1971, pp. 386–98.

Bruno, M., "A Programming Model for Israel," in *The Theory and Design of Economic Development,* I. Adelman, and E. Thorbecke, editors, The Johns-Hopkins Press, Baltimore, 1966.

Byrd, J., and L. T. Moore, "The Application of a Product Mix Linear Programming Model in Corporate Policy Making," *Management Science,* September 1978.

Carleton, W., "An Analytical Model for Long-Range Financial Planning," *Journal of Finance,* May 1970.

Charnes, A., W. W. Cooper, and R. Ferguson, "Blending Aviation Gasolines, A Study in Programming Interdependent Activities," *Econometrica,* Vol. 20, No. 2, April 1952, pp. 135–59.

———, "Optimal Estimation of Executive Compensation by Linear Programming," *Management Science,* Vol. 1, No. 2, January 1955, pp. 138–51.

Charnes, A., W. W. Cooper, K. A. Lewis, and R. J. Niehaus, "A Multi-Objective Model for Planning Equal Employment Opportunities," OCMM Research Report No. 23, Office of Civilian Manpower Management, Washington, D.C., October 1975.

Charnes, A., W. W. Cooper, and R. J. Niehaus, *Studies in Manpower Planning,* U. S. Navy Office of Civilian Manpower Management, Washington, D.C., July 1972.

Chenery, H. B., and A. MacEwan, "Optimal Patterns of Growth and Aid: The Case of Pakistan," in *The Theory and Design of Economic Development,* I. Adelman, and E. Thorbecke, editors, The Johns-Hopkins Press, Baltimore, 1966.

Clarke, S., and J. Surkis, "An Operations Research Approach to Racial Desegregation of School Systems," *Socio-Economic Planning Sciences,* Vol. 1, 1967.

Cohen, K. J., and F. S. Hammer, "Linear Programming and Optimal Bank-Asset Management Decisions," *Journal of Finance,* Vol. 21, 1967.

Cohen, R., C. McBride, R. Thornton, and T. White, *Letter Mail System Reference Design: An Analytical Method for Evaluating Candidate Mechanization,* Institute for Defense Analyses, Report R-168, 1970.

Crane, D. B., F. Knoop, and W. Pettigrew, "An Application of Management Science to Bank Borrowing Strategies," *Interfaces,* Vol. 8, No. 1, Part 2, November 1977.

Darnell, D., and C. Loflin, "National Airlines Fuel Management and Allocation Model," *Interfaces,* Vol. 7, No. 2, February 1977, pp. 1–16.

Debanne, J. G., and J. N. Lavier, "Management Science in the Public Sector — The Estevan Case," *Interfaces,* Vol. 9, No. 2, Part 2, February 1979.

Dickens, J. H., "Linear Programming in Corporate Simulation," in *Corporate Simulation Models,* A. H. Schrieber, editor, University of Washington, Seattle, 1970.

Drayer, W., and S. Seabury, "Facilities Expansion Model," *Interfaces: Practice of Management Science,* Vol. 5, No. 2, February 1975.

Eisemann, K., and W. N. Young, "Study of a Textile Mill with the Aid of Linear Programming," *Management Technology,* No. 1, January 1960, pp. 52–63.

Engle, J. F., and M. W. Warshaw, "Allocating Advertising Research," *Journal of Advertising Research,* Vol. 4, No. 3, 1964, pp. 42–48.

Fabian, T., "Blast Furnace Production Planning — A Linear Programming Example," *Management Science,* Vol. 14, No. 2, October 1967, pp. 1–27.

Fetter, R. B., "A Linear Programming Model for Long Range Capacity Planning," *Management Science,* Vol. 7, No. 4, 1961, pp. 372–78.

Fitzsimmons, J. A., A. J. Shawab, and R. S. Sullivan, "Goal Programming for Holistic Budget Analysis," *Administration in Social Work,* Vol. 3, No. 1, Spring 1979, pp. 33–43.

Franklin, A. D., and E. Koenigsberg, "Computed School Assignments in a Large District," *Operations Research,* Vol. 21, No. 2, March-April 1973, pp. 413–26.

Garvin, W. W., H. W. Crandall, J. B. John, and R. A. Spellman, "Applications of Linear Programming in the Oil Industry," *Management Science,* Vol. 3, No. 4, July 1957, pp. 407–30.

Gilmore, P. C., and R. E. Gomory, "A Linear Programming Approach to the Cutting Stock Problem," *Operations Research,* Vol. 9, 1961, pp. 849–59.

———, "A Linear Programming Approach to the Cutting Stock Problem — Part II," *Operations Research,* Vol. 11, No. 6, November-December 1963, pp. 863–88.

———, "Multistage Cutting Stock Problems of Two and More Dimensions," *Operations Research,* Vol. 13, No. 1, January-February 1965, pp. 94–120.

Glassey, C. R., and V. K. Gupta, "A Linear Programming Analysis of Paper Recycling," *Management Science,* Vol. 21, No. 4, December 1974, pp. 392–408.

Gray, P., and C. Cullinan-James, "Applied Optimization — A Survey," *Interfaces,* Vol. 6, No. 3, May 1976.

Greene, J. H., K. Chatto, C. R. Hicks, and C. B. Cox, "Linear Programming in the Packing Industry," *Journal of Industrial Engineering,* Vol. 10, No. 5, 1959, pp. 364–72.

Hamilton, W. F., and M. A. Moses, "An Optimization Model for Corporate Financial Planning," *Operations Research,* Vol. 21, No. 3, May-June 1973, pp. 677–92.

Hanssmann, F., and S. W. Hess, "A Linear Programming Approach to Production and Employment Scheduling," *Management Technology,* No. 1, January 1960, pp. 46–52.

Heady, E. O., et al., "Programming Models for the Planning of the Agricultural Sector," in *The Theory and Design of Economic Development,* I. Adelman, and E. Thorbecke, editors, The Johns-Hopkins Press, Baltimore, 1966.

Heller, N. B., R. E. Markland, and J. A. Brockelmeyer, "Partitioning Police Districts into Optimal Patrol Beats Using a Political Districting Algorithm: Model Design and Validation," School of Business Administration, University of Missouri, St. Louis, 1971.

Heroux, R. L., and W. A. Wallace, "Linear Programming and Financial Analysis of the New Community Development Process," *Management Science,* Vol. 19, No. 8, April 1973, pp. 857–72.

Hess, W. H., and S. A. Samuels, "Experience with a Sales Districting Model: Criteria and Implementation," *Management Science,* Vol. 18, No. 4, Part II, December 1971.

Hess, W. H., J. Weaverm, H. Siegfeldt, J. Whelan, and P. Zitau, "Nonpartisan Political Redistricting by Computer," *Operations Research,* Vol. 13, No. 6, November-December 1965.

Hughes, J. S., and W. G. Lewellen, "Programming and Solutions to Capital Rationing Problems," *Journal of Business, Finance and Accounting,* Vol. 1, No. 1, Spring 1974.

Ignall, E., P. Kolesar, and W. Walker, "Linear Programming Models of Crew Assignments for Refuse Collection," P-4717, The Rand Corporation, Santa Monica, Calif., November 1972.

Ijiri, Y., F. K. Levy, and R. C. Lyon, "A Linear Programming Model for Budgeting and Financial Planning," *Journal of Accounting Research,* Autumn 1963.

Jain, S. K., K. L. Scott, and E. G. Vasold, "Orderbook Balancing Using a Combination of Linear Programming and Heuristic Techniques," *Interfaces,* Vol. 9, No. 1, November 1978.

Jewell, W. S., "Warehouse and Distribution of a Seasonal Product," *Naval Research Logistics Quarterly,* Vol. 4, 1957.

Kohn, R. E., "Application of Linear Programming to a Controversy on Air Pollution Control," *Management Science,* Vol. 17, No. 10, June 1971, pp. 609–21.

Kotak, D. B., "Application of Linear Programming to Plywood Manufacturing," *Interfaces,* Vol. 7, No. 1, Part 2, November 1976.

Kotler, P., *Marketing Decision Making: A Model Building Approach,* Holt, Rinehart & Winston, New York, 1971.

Lee, S. M., *Goal Programming for Decision Analysis,* Auerback, Philadelphia, 1972.

Lee, S. M., and L. J. Moore, "Optimizing Transportation Problems with Multiple Objectives," *AIIE Transactions,* Vol. 5, No. 4, December 1973, pp. 333–38.

Loucks, D. P., C. S. ReVelle, and W. R. Lynn, "Linear Programming Models for Water Pollution Control," *Management Science,* Vol. 14, No. 4, December 1957, pp. 166–81.

Manne, A. S., "A Linear Programming Model for the U.S. Petroleum Refining Industry," *Econometrica,* January 1958.

———, "Key Sectors of the Mexican Economy, 1962–72," in *The Theory and Design of Economic Development,* I. Adelman, and E. Thorbeck, editors, The Johns-Hopkins Press, Baltimore, 1966.

Manne, A. S., and T. A. Weisskopf, "A Dynamic Multisectoral Model for India, 1967–75," in *Input-Output Techniques,* Vol. 2, A. P. Carter and A. Brody, editors, North-Holland, Amsterdam, 1970.

Mao, J. C. T., *Quantitative Analysis of Financial Decisions,* Collier-MacMillan, London, 1969.

Masse, P., and R. Gibrat, "Application of Linear Programming to Investments in the Electric Power Industry," *Management Science,* Vol. 3, No. 2, January 1957, pp. 149–66.

McBride, C. C., "Post Office Mail Operations," in *Analysis of Public Systems,* edited by A . W. Drake, R. L. Keeney, and P. M. Morse, MIT Press, Cambridge, Mass., 1972.

McKeown, P., and B. Workman, "A Study in Using Linear Programming to Assign Students to Schools," *Interfaces,* Vol. 6, No. 4, August 1976.

Metzger, R. W., and R. Schwarzbek, "A Linear Programming Application to Cupola Charging," *Journal of Industrial Engineering,* Vol. 12, No. 2, March-April 1961, pp. 87–93.

Meyer, M., "Applying Linear Programming to the Design of Ultimate Pit Limits," *Management Science,* Vol. 16, No. 2, October 1969, pp. 121–35.

Orgler, Y. E., "An Unequal-Period Model for Cash Management Decisions," *Management Science,* Vol. 16, No. 2, October 1969, pp. 77–92.

Revelle, C., F. Feldmann, and W. Lynn, "An Optimization Model for Tuberculosis Epidemiology," *Management Science,* Vol. 16, No. 4, December 1969, pp. 190–211.

Revelle, C., et al., "Linear Programming Applied to Water Quality Management," *Water Resources Research,* February 1968.

Robichek, A. A., D. Teichroew, and J. M. Jones, "Optimal Short Term Financing Decisions," *Management Science,* Vol. 12, No. 1, September 1965, pp. 1–36.

Ray, E., and E. Duckworth, "Linear Programming in Practice," *Applied Statistics,* March 1957.

Reddy, J., "A Model to Schedule Sales Optimally Blended From Scarce Resources," *Interfaces,* Vol 6, No. 2, Part 2, November 1975.

Rutenburg, D. R., "Maneuvering Liquid Assets in a Multi-National Company: Formulation and Deterministic Solution Procedure," *Management Science,* Vol. 16, No. 10, June 1970, pp. 671–84.

Sharpe, W. F., "A Linear Programming Algorithm for Mutual Fund Portfolio Selection," *Management Science,* Vol. 13, No. 7, 1967, pp. 499–510.

Smith, K. V., editor, *Management of Working Capital,* West Publishing Company, St. Paul, 1974.

Smith, S. B., "Planning Transistor Production by Linear Programming," *Operations Research,* Vol. 13, No. 1, January-February 1965, pp. 132–39.

Southwick, L., and S. Zionts, "Optimal Resource Allocation in a Local Election Campaign," *Interfaces,* Vol. 6, No. 1, November 1975.

Thomas, J., "Linear Programming Models for Production-Advertising Decisions," *Management Science,* Vol. 17, No. 8, April 1971, pp. 474–84.

Tsao, C. S., and R. H. Day, "A Process Analysis Model for the U.S. Steel Industry," *Management Science,* Vol. 19, No. 10, June 1971, pp. 588–608.

CHAPTER 5

Introduction to
the Simplex Method

In the previous two chapters we discussed the formulation and interpretation of linear optimization models, assuming that the solution was provided by a computer program. Now let us look inside the linear programming solution technique, the *simplex method*. An understanding of how the simplex algorithm functions will contribute to a more effective interpretation of results.

We first present an algebraic development of the solution strategy as an aid to understanding the solution process. Next, the simplex algorithm is explained as a series of steps that can be formulated for computer solution. In effect, the algorithm is reduced to a series of mechanical steps, based on organizing the data into a special table that is traditionally called a tableau.

We will use the chemical production problem as a vehicle for discussion. Since we can represent that problem in graphic form, and since we already know the optimal solution, we can see readily what is happening at each stage of the algorithm. We will simplify the problem slightly by eliminating the demand constraints. Recall that, for the stated problem, these constraints were not effective in dictating the optimal solution anyway. Eliminating them provides a simpler, more direct explanation of the procedure.

Formulation

The statement of the problem was one of allocating time on machines A and B to the two products, x and y, in such a way that contribution to profit and overhead would be maximized. The time requirements on the two machines for each product were given and the total available time on the two machines was limited. (Rereading the Chapter 3 formulation may help, but all conditions for the problem are the same except that we will assume we can sell all products produced within the limits of machine capacity.) Therefore, the resulting linear optimization model is

maximize $Z = 60x + 50y$

subject to

$$2x + 4y \leq 80 \qquad \text{(machine } A\text{)}$$

$$3x + 2y \leq 60 \qquad \text{(machine } B\text{)}$$

$$x \geq 0 \qquad\qquad \text{(minimum production for chemical } x\text{)}$$

$$y \geq 0 \qquad\qquad \text{(minimum production for chemical } y\text{)}$$

Graphic solution

Figure 5-1 shows the constraints plotted on a graph and identifies the feasible solution space, *abcd,* and the previously determined optimal allocation of machine time at point *c;* that is, produce $x = 10$ units and $y = 15$ units. Recall also that the contribution for the optimal solution was $1350.

We have plotted in Figure 5-1 the linear objective function for two values of total contribution, $Z = \$900$ and $Z = \$1200$. It is now rather obvious for the simple problem that if we substituted larger and larger values of Z in the objective function, lines parallel to the $900 and $1200 lines would result, and a line through point *c* would define a combination of *x* and *y* with the maximum possible contribution within the

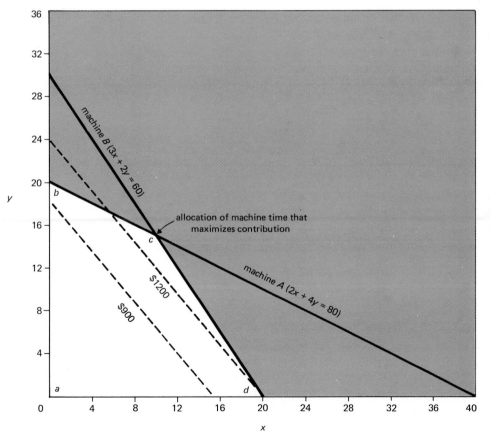

FIGURE 5-1
Graphic solution of example used for algebraic interpretation of the simplex method.

feasible solution space. Figure 5-1 provides us with a clear picture of the problem and the relationships for various solutions evaluated by the objective function.

ALGEBRAIC SOLUTION

Let us now proceed through the algebraic steps of the simplex solution to the chemical production problem.

Slack variables

First, let us note the physical meaning of the constraints on available time for machines A and B. For machine A, since x requires 2 hours per unit and y requires 4 hours per unit, and we are limited to a total of 80 hours, we wrote the inequality constraint

$$2x + 4y \le 80 \tag{1}$$

and for machine B,

$$3x + 2y \le 60 \tag{2}$$

The inequalities state that the use of machines A and B is less than or equal to 80 and 60 hours respectively; that is, there *could* be idle machine time. If we take up the slack available, we could convert inequalities (1) and (2) into equations by defining *slack variables* to represent the possible idle time. Therefore,

$$2x + 4y + W_A = 80 \tag{3}$$
$$3x + 2y + W_B = 60 \tag{4}$$

where W_A is the idle time for machine A, and W_B the idle time for machine B. We also require W_A and W_B to be nonnegative (W_A, $W_B \ge 0$). The constraints plotted in Figure 5-1 are lines that indicate the full use of machine A when $W_A = 0$ and of machine B when $W_B = 0$. Solutions that involve some idle time are permissible and would fall below one or both of the constraint lines, and would be within the solution space *abcd*.

The effect of solutions involving slack (idle machine time) is easy to see through examples. Assume that the production schedule is 9 units of chemical x, and 14 units of chemical y. Since 2 hours per unit of x and 4 hours per unit of y are required of machine A time, and machine A has a total of 80 hours available, we have from equation (3)

$$W_A = 80 - (2)(9) - (4)(14) = 80 - 74 = 6 \text{ hours}$$

There are 74 productive hours, and the slack in machine A time is taken up as idle time of 6 hours.

Similarly, the idle time on machine B from equation (4) would be

$$W_B = 60 - (3)(9) - (2)(14) = 60 - 55 = 5 \text{ hours}$$

Now examine Figure 5-1 and note that the point ($x = 9$, $y = 14$) falls inside the feasible solution space, but not on any of the constraint lines. This type of solution is called *nonbasic*.

With the slack variables now in the formulation, the objective function is actually

$$\text{maximize } Z = 60x + 50y + (0)W_A + (0)W_B$$

The zero coefficients for the slack variables are appropriate, since they make no contribution to profit. The total contribution of the nonbasic solution is

$$Z = (60)(9) + (50)(14) + (0)(6) + (0)(5) = 540 + 700 + 0 + 0 = 1240$$

Let us return to our two equations, (3) and (4), with four unknown variables, plus the objective function. Now, recall from simple algebra that we can solve equations simultaneously if there are the same number of unknowns as equations. If we set any two of the four variables to zero, we can solve the two equations simultaneously to find the values of the other two. This is exactly what we will be doing in the following step-by-step procedure.

Solution procedure

Step 1. Establish an initial solution To start, let us develop a trivial solution whose implications we know and understand — the worst possible solution. We assume no production; that is, $x = y = 0$. We know then that all the available time on the two machines will be idle, and, using the objective function to evaluate the solution, we know that $Z = 0$, since we have produced nothing. Let us solve equations (3) and (4) for W_A and W_B as follows:

$$W_A = 80 - 2x - 4y \tag{5}$$

$$W_B = 60 - 3x - 2y \tag{6}$$

and our statement of the objective function is

$$Z = 60x + 50y + (0)W_A + (0)W_B$$

When rearranged with all the variables on the left of the equal sign, the objective function is

$$Z - 60x - 50y - (0)W_A - (0)W_B = 0 \tag{7}$$

If x and y are zero, the values of W_A and W_B are

$$W_A = 80 - 2(0) - 4(0) = 80$$

$$W_B = 60 - 3(0) - 2(0) = 60$$

The evaluation of this solution by the objective function is

$$Z - 60(0) - 50(0) - 80(0) - 60(0) = 0$$

which is the contribution expected when nothing is produced. Note that this is point a in Figure 5-1.

Step 2. Can the initial solution be improved? We now need a test for optimality in order to know whether to stop or to continue in search of a better solution. Recall that x and y provide positive contributions to profit of \$60 and \$50 respectively. In the last statement of the objective function, equation (7), these contributions appear with *negative signs*. These negative signs occur because we have rewritten equation (7) so that all the terms involving variables appear on the left-hand side of the equal sign. This is a standard format for writing linear equations. Using this format, a variable in the objective function equation with a negative coefficient will actually improve a trial solution if it can be increased from its current value. Therefore, we can improve the initial solution by introducing either x or y into the solution with nonzero values.

This is the test: if we examine the last statement of the objective function and find variables in it with *negative coefficients,* then the solution can be improved by increasing one of these variables from its current value of zero. If at some point in the procedure we find only variables with nonnegative coefficients in the objective function, then no improvement is possible and we have an optimal solution.

Step 3. Selecting the incoming variable We can improve the solution by making either x or y nonzero. Let us choose the variable that provides the greatest improvement per unit. Since in equation (7), a unit of x earns \$60 and a unit of y only \$50, we select x as the variable to enter the solution with a nonzero value. We refer to x as the *incoming variable.* In doing so, we have determined the direction of change in our solution, since x will *increase* from its initial value of zero.

Step 4. Determine the amount of change in x We know that allocating productive time to x will improve the objective function value. For each unit of x produced, we obtain a contribution of \$60. How many units of x should we produce? Since we have found an advantageous direction of change, we wish to press this advantage by producing the maximum possible amount of x, within the constraints of the problem. Suppose we solve equations (3) and (4) for x. From (3) we obtain

$$x = 40 - 2y - \frac{W_A}{2} \tag{8}$$

and from (4),

$$x = 20 - \frac{2y}{3} - \frac{W_B}{3} \tag{9}$$

In the initial solution, $y = 0$. What if W_A were set equal to 0 along with y? From (8), x would equal 40. If W_B were set equal to zero along with y, x would equal 20 in (9).

The smaller of these two numbers, 20, determines how large x can become. From (9), there is no way that x can become larger than 20 without either y or W_B being a negative number, and this is not permitted. This can also be seen in Figure 5-1, since equation (8) refers to the constraint for machine A and equation (9) to the constraint for machine B. Note that $x = 40$ is not in the feasible solution region, but that 20 is the maximum value of x in the feasible region. Therefore, equation (4) determines how large we can make x.

Now let us pause to examine the logic of what we have done in terms of the actual chemical production problem. Machine A has 80 hours available and the time to process chemical x is 2 hours per unit, so if all the machine A time were allocated to chemical x, as proposed by the solution at this stage, we can produce

$$\frac{80 \text{ hours available}}{2 \text{ hours per unit}} = 40 \text{ units of chemical } x$$

This is the result obtained from equation (8), if $y = 0$ and $W_A = 0$.

Now let us examine machine B in a similar way. Machine B has 60 hours available, and the time to process chemical x is 3 hours per unit. If all the machine B time were allocated to the production of chemical x, then the maximum output would be

$$\frac{60 \text{ hours available}}{3 \text{ hours per unit}} = 20 \text{ units of chemical } x$$

This is the result obtained from equation (9), if $y = 0$ and $W_B = 0$.

Therefore, when machines A and B are considered as a system, the output is limited by machine B to 20 units of chemical x. Also, since the solution at this stage limits x to 20 units, there will be some idle time in machine A because it will produce somewhat less than it could. The values of the slack variables from equations (5) and (6) are

$$W_A = 80 - (2)(20) - (4)(0) = 40 \text{ hours}$$
$$W_B = 60 - (3)(20) - (2)(0) = 0 \text{ hours}$$

In order to increase x to 20, we must reduce W_B to 0, as seen in equation (9). Thus, we will again have a solution with two nonzero values, x and W_A, and with two variables, y and W_B, set equal to zero. To determine the effect on W_A of setting x equal to $20 - 2y/3 - W_B/3$ as required by (9), we substitute $20 - 2y/3 - W_B/3$ from (9) into (5), and obtain

$$W_A = 80 - 2\left(20 - \frac{2y}{3} - \frac{W_B}{3}\right) - 4y$$

which simplifies to

$$W_A = 40 - \frac{8y}{3} + \frac{2W_B}{3} \tag{10}$$

Thus, with $y = W_B = 0$, we have $W_A = 40$.

Expressions (9) and (10) would be obtained if we simply solved equations (3) and (4) simultaneously for the common values of x and W_A, when y and W_B are assumed to be constants. To accomplish this, we would rewrite (5) and (6) as

$$2x + W_A = 80 - 4y \tag{11}$$

$$3x \qquad = 60 - 2y - W_B \tag{12}$$

To solve these equations, we divide (12) by 3, the coefficient of x, so it becomes

$$x = 20 - \frac{2y}{3} - \frac{W_B}{3}$$

Notice that this is equation (9). Now, we multiply (9) by -2, the negative of the coefficient of x in (11), and add the result to (11) as shown below:

$$2x + W_A = \quad 80 - 4y \tag{11}$$

$$-2x \qquad = -40 + \frac{4y}{3} + \frac{2W_B}{3} \qquad \text{[(9) multiplied by } -2]$$

$$\overline{\qquad W_A = \quad 40 - \frac{8y}{3} + \frac{2W_B}{3}} \tag{10}$$

The result is equation (10).

We also substitute (9) as the value of x in the last statement of the objective function, equation (7). The objective function then becomes

$$Z - 60\left(20 - \frac{2y}{3} - \frac{W_B}{3}\right) - 50y - (0)W_A - (0)W_B$$

$$= Z - 1200 - 10y + 20W_B = 0$$

which can be written

$$Z - 10y + 20W_B = 1200 \tag{13}$$

With y and W_B set to zero, (13) gives the total contribution of the solution $x = 20$ and $W_A = 40$, which is $Z = 1200$.

To summarize, by letting y and W_B be zero, we obtain the solution

$x \quad = 20$, from (9)

$W_A = 40$, from (10)

$y \quad = 0$

$W_B = 0$

$Z \quad = 1200$, from (13)

This solution is an obvious improvement over the first solution, since the value of the objective function has now increased from zero to $1200. We can see from Figure 5-1 that the second stage of our solution is represented by point d.

Now you may be asking yourself the question: "If we are going to set y and W_B equal to zero anyway, why do we carry them along as excess baggage in equations (9), (10), and (13)?" The answer is that we obtain additional information from having them in (9), (10), and (13). For example, in (13) we now see that an additional unit of y will increase the value of the objective function Z by $10 per unit, because it has a negative coefficient of $-$10. Why is the increase only $10 per unit, since the contribution per unit from y as shown in the original formulation is $50 per unit? To increase y from its current value of zero, we will have to decrease x, which has a per unit contribution of $60. However, (13) tells us that the *net effect* of increasing y from the *current solution* will be worth $10 per unit. We can use the "excess baggage" in (9) and (10) to quickly determine how large to make y.

Let us reflect on these marginal values in the objective function in the context of the actual chemical production problem. From equation (13) the contributions are $10 per unit for chemical y, and $-$20 per hour for W_B. Since all the available time for machine B is allocated to chemical x in the current solution, we cannot process units of chemical y unless we process fewer units of chemical x. Chemical y requires 2 hours per unit on machine B, and chemical x requires 3 hours per unit. If we process one unit of y, we must reduce x by 2/3 units, since y requires 2/3 the time of x on machine B. The result is that while we gain $50 by producing a unit of y, we lose $(2/3)$60 = $40 by processing 2/3 units less of x. The net gain is, therefore, only $50 - $40 = $10, as indicated in equation (13).

Now, how about the $-$20 contribution for W_B shown in equation (13)? It says, if we reduce the idle time of $W_B = 60$ hours to only 59 hours, the net cost will be $20.

The physical significance of this action is as follows: if we increase the idle time in machine B from $W_B = 0$ to $W_B = 1$, we forego the contribution of 1/3 unit of chemical x (it requires 3 hours per unit of x on machine B), or $(1/3)\$60 = \$20$.

Thus, the revised objective function of equation (13) states the marginal values of changing the production plan from the present solution. We could gain \$10 per unit by producing chemical y and sacrificing some production of chemical x. We would lose \$20 per hour if idle time were introduced into machine B's operations. Obviously, the best next step is to change the production plan by introducing the processing of some of chemical y, even though we sacrifice some output of chemical x. Of course, the question is: how many units of chemical y?

Step 5. Repeat steps 2, 3, and 4 Since y has a negative coefficient in (13), we would like to increase it from its current solution value of zero. Notice that W_B has a positive coefficient in (13). The value of the objective function would increase if we could *decrease* W_B. However, W_B is zero in the current solution, and so it cannot be reduced any further. Therefore, we select y as our entering variable.

Using the "excess baggage" in (9) and (10), we solve for y and obtain

$$y = 30 - \frac{3x}{2} - \frac{W_B}{2} \tag{14}$$

from (9) and

$$y = 15 - \frac{3W_A}{8} + \frac{W_B}{4} \tag{15}$$

from (10). W_B is equal to zero in the current solution; setting $x = 0$ gives $y = 30$ from (14), while setting $W_A = 0$ gives $y = 15$ from (15), which is more restrictive. Therefore, we can make $y = 15$ in the revised solution.

Substituting the right-hand side of (15) for y in (9) gives

$$x = 20 - \frac{2}{3}\left(15 - \frac{3W_A}{8} + \frac{W_B}{4}\right) - \frac{W_B}{3}$$

which simplifies to

$$x = 10 + \frac{W_A}{4} - \frac{W_B}{2} \tag{16}$$

Again, we would obtain (15) and (16) by solving (3) and (4) simultaneously for x and y while treating W_A and W_B as constants (check this yourself).

We also substitute the value of y given by equation (14) in the last statement of the objective function (13), and we obtain

$$Z + \frac{15W_A}{4} + \frac{35W_B}{2} = 1350 \qquad (17)$$

or, alternately, we can substitute the values of x and y given by equations (15) and (16) in the original statement of the objective function that includes slack variables, $Z = 60x + 50y + (0)W_A + (0)W_B$, and obtain

$$Z = 60\left(10 + \frac{W_A}{4} - \frac{W_B}{2}\right) + 50\left(15 - \frac{3W_A}{8} + \frac{W_B}{4}\right) + 0 + 0$$

$$= 600 + \frac{60W_A}{4} - 30W_B + 750 - \frac{150W_A}{8} + \frac{50W_B}{4}$$

$$= 1350 - \frac{15W_A}{4} - \frac{35W_B}{2}$$

Of course, this is identical with equation (17).

When W_A and W_B are zero, the values of the variables and of the objective function are then as follows:

$y \quad = 15$, from (15)

$x \quad = 10$, from (16)

$W_A = 0$

$W_B = 0$

$Z \quad = 1350$, from (17)

We see that this is point c in Figure 5-1, and we know that this is the optimal solution by inspecting Figure 5-1. According to our procedure, however, we know this is true by examining the last statement of the objective function, equation (17). We note that the only possible way the contribution could be increased is by decreasing either W_A, W_B, or both, since their respective coefficients in (17) are positive. Since the solution at this stage already specifies that W_A and W_B are at their minimum values of zero, and since none of the variables can take on negative values, there is no way to increase contribution, and we have met the requirements for the test of optimality.

Shadow prices

Recall that the sensitivity analysis provided by the computer program in Figure 3-8 indicated that the value for a marginal unit of capacity for machine A was $3.75 and for machine B, $17.50. Where do we find these values in the algebraic solution? They are contained in the last statement of the objective function, equation (17). The significance of the coefficients 15/4 and 35/2 for W_A and W_B is that they are the shadow prices for marginal units of capacity. In other words, for every unit of W_A added in the solution at this point (idle time on machine A), contribution declines by $15/4 = \$3.75$. But conversely, if the original capacity of machine A had been 81 hours instead of 80, net contribution could have been increased by $3.75.

Thus, the coefficients of the slack variables in the objective function are the shadow prices and, indeed, had this equivalent meaning at every stage of the solution. In the initial statement of the objective function, equation (7), x and y had marginal contribution rates per unit of 60 and 50 and W_A and W_B had zero rates. In the second stage of solution the objective function was represented by equation (13), and y had a contribution rate of 10 and W_B a rate of -20.

Characteristics of the simplex solution

The optimizing model we have developed involved a trial solution of the constraint equations, an evaluation of that solution by the objective function, and a test for optimality. If the optimality test indicated that improvement was possible, we determined the direction of change of the solution (selection of the entering variable) and the amount of change (testing constraints to see how much the entering variable could be increased and selecting the most restrictive equation). This generated a new solution, which was subjected to the same procedure until the test for optimality indicated that no further improvement was possible.

Note that, in fact, we did not consider all possible feasible solutions. Instead, we proceeded to the optimum solution by considering only three alternate solutions: points a, d, and finally c in Figure 5-1. There are an infinite number of combinations of the four variables that we did not bother with as we converged on the optimum solution. For example, proceeding from a to d, we considered none of the feasible solutions along the line *ad,* which would have yielded progressively larger values of contribution as *x* increased. Instead, we jumped from *a* to *d.* Similarly, we did not consider any of the feasible solutions along the line *dc,* although each one would have progressively yielded a larger contribution as we converged on the optimum. For example, the point ($x = 16$, $y = 6$) results in $W_A = 24$, $W_B = 0$, and a contribution of $1260.

Also, we did not consider any of the feasible solutions that fell inside the solution space *abcd.* We should note that all these other solutions we did not consider — those that lie inside the solution space but not on constraint lines — are feasible solutions that involve more than two of the four variables with positive values. By requiring that we deal only with solutions where two, and only two, variables could be positive, we jumped from corner to corner, rather than moving more slowly in a larger number of steps along the sides of the solution space or even within its interior. The solutions that involve only two of the four variables are called *basic solutions.* There are only four basic solutions in our example, at points *a, b, c,* and *d.* Feasible solutions that involve more than two of the four variables are nonbasic solutions.

In the larger scale problems, we are doing a similar thing; that is, moving from one basic solution to a better one, jumping over an entire set of other feasible solutions that are in-between. These basic solutions are always at the corners of two- and three-dimensional problems, and conceptually at the equivalent of corners of multidimensional problems. This solution strategy is advantageous, since it can be shown that if a linear optimization model actually has an optimal solution, it will lie at a corner point. The proof of this important result is beyond our scope in this discussion, but it provides the rationale for the simplex algorithm.

THE SIMPLEX ALGORITHM

We used simple problems to explain linear optimization models and the simplex solution technique. The power of linear programming, however, is in the solution of large-scale problems, and the key to their solution has been the simplex algorithm. The simplex algorithm uses the algebraic logic we have just discussed, but reduces this logic to a very efficient set of arithmetic and logical operations so that computing effort is minimized. When the algorithm has been developed in a rigorous way, the computing effort can be further reduced by programming the algorithm for computers. Large-scale problems of resource allocation can then be formulated and solved at reasonable cost. Without the simplex algorithm and without computers, the solution of large-scale problems would be entirely out of reason.

We will now present a more rigorous description of the simplex method, so that the logic can be programmed on a computer. This description is based on an approach for solving several simultaneous linear equations.

In reducing the simplex algorithm to a set of rigorous rules, there is a risk that we may begin to think of it as a mechanical procedure, losing contact with what is being accomplished at each stage of solution. We will try to maintain contact with the meaning of each step by using the chemical production problem as an example again, and relating our manipulations to the process of the preceding algebraic development and to the graphic solution shown in Figure 5-1.

Recall that after the addition of the slack variables to account for idle time, our two restricting equations for machines A and B were

$$2x + 4y + W_A = 80 \tag{18}$$

$$3x + 2y + W_B = 60 \tag{19}$$

An initial solution to this set of equations is found by setting $x = y = 0$, which gives $W_A = 80$ and $W_B = 60$. This solution is easy to see, since W_A has a coefficient of $+1$ in (18) but does not appear in (19), and W_B has a coefficient of $+1$ in (19) but does not appear in (18).

The objective function for this problem can be written as

$$Z = 60x + 50y + (0)W_A + (0)W_B \tag{20}$$

since idle time contributes nothing to profits or overhead. Substituting the initial solution of $W_A = 80$ and $W_B = 60$ into 20 gives

$$Z - 60x - 50y = (0)80 + (0)60 = 0 \tag{21}$$

as the corresponding value of the objective function.

Since (21) is also an equation, we can combine it with (18) and (19) and write

$$Z - 60x - 50y = \quad 0 \qquad \text{(row 0)}$$

$$2x + 4y + W_A = 80 \qquad \text{(row 1)}$$

$$3x + 2y + W_B = 60 \qquad \text{(row 2)}$$

where all the variables must also be nonnegative. This is our set of *initial equations* that are associated with the initial solution $x = y = 0$, $W_A = 80$, and $W_B = 60$.

Improving the initial solution

To improve the initial solution, we use the test for optimality: "Are there coefficients in the objective function that indicate that Z can be increased?" If there are, we know we can substitute a variable in the solution that has a higher contribution rate to the objective function than one of the variables now in the solution.

Row 0 is the same as equation (7) developed during the algebraic solution. Thus, variables with *negative* coefficients in row 0 will improve the objective function if they are brought into the solution.

Identifying the entering variable and key column Any variable with a negative coefficient in row 0 will improve (increase) the objective function if its value is increased from 0. The following rule is useful in selecting the entering variable:

> RULE I. If there are variables with negative coefficients in row 0, choose the one with the most negative coefficient as the *entering variable*. If there are no variables with negative coefficients in row 0, the solution is optimal.

In this example, we chose x as the entering variable according to Rule I. This choice determines the "direction of change" in the solution.

The coefficients of the entering variable x, -60 in row 0, 2 in row 1, and 3 in row 2, will play a key role in the computations of the simplex algorithm. Since these coefficients are arranged vertically as a column of numbers in rows 0, 1, and 2, we designate them as the *key column*.

Identifying the key row If x increases by 1 unit, W_A must decrease by 2 units (the coefficient of x in row 1) in order to maintain the equality in row 1, and W_B must decrease by 3 units (the coefficient of x in row 2) to maintain the equality in row 2. If W_A decreases from its initial value of 80 units to 0, x could increase to $80/2 = 40$; if W_B decreases from its initial value of 60, x could increase to $60/3 = 20$. The latter, 20, would be reached first as x increases. Therefore, the relationship between W_B and x in row 2 *limits* the size of x, so we designate row 2 as the *key row* in our calculations.

Notice that this result was determined by dividing the right-hand side of each row (ignoring row 0) by the corresponding number in the key column. If the coefficient in the key column in a row were negative or zero, the row would be ignored, since increasing the entering variable would not force another variable to zero. This idea can be implemented in the simplex algorithm with a second rule.

RULE II. Taking the ratios of the right-hand sides of the rows to the corresponding coefficients of the key column (ignoring zero or negative coefficients), choose the row with the smallest ratio as the *key row.*

In the algebraic solution, we solved each constraint equation for the entering variable, then set the remaining variables equal to zero. The constraint that gave the minimum value for the entering variable was identified as the limiting constraint. Rule II achieves exactly the same result and determines the "amount of change" in the solution.

Pivoting We now know the entering variable x, the key column of the coefficients of x, and the key row, row 2. The coefficient of the entering variable x that is in the key column and in the key row, 3, also plays a special role in the simplex algorithm, so we call it the *key number.* We are prepared to carry out the *pivoting operation* that determines a revised solution to our linear optimization problem.

The key row was determined by identifying the first nonzero variable to be *decreased to zero* as the entering variable is *increased from zero.* From our Rule II calculations, we know that the variable x will be increased to 20 and the variable W_B will be decreased to 0 in the new solution.

Pivoting requires the following steps:

1. Divide each coefficient in the key row and its right-hand side by the key number.
2. For each row *except* the key row:
   a. Multiply each coefficient of the newly transformed key row (found in step 1 above) by the negative of the coefficient in the key column in the nonlimiting row.
   b. Add the result to the nonlimiting row.

In our example problem, we carry out these steps by dividing row 2 (the key row) by the key number, 3. The result is

$$x + \frac{2y}{3} + \frac{W_B}{3} = 20 \tag{22}$$

Next, we modify rows 0 and 1 as indicated.

Row 0: multiply (22) by 60 and add to row 0

Row 1: multiply (22) by -2 and add to row 1

For row 0, the calculations would be

$$
\begin{array}{llll}
Z - 60x - 50y & = 0 & \text{(row 0)} \\
\underline{ \; 60x + 40y \quad + 20W_B = 1200} & & \text{[Eq. (22) multiplied by 60]} \\
Z \qquad\quad - 10y \quad + 20W_B = 1200 & &
\end{array}
$$

After carrying out similar calculations for row 1 (check them for yourself), the revised set of equations is

$$
\begin{array}{lll}
Z \qquad\quad - 10y \qquad + 20W_B = 1200 & \qquad \text{(row 0)} \\[2mm]
\dfrac{8y}{3} + W_A - \dfrac{2W_B}{3} = 40 & \qquad \text{(row 1)} \\[2mm]
x + \dfrac{2y}{3} \qquad + \dfrac{W_B}{3} = 20 & \qquad \text{(row 2)}
\end{array}
$$

Notice that in each row there is one variable with a coefficient of 1 and with coefficients of 0 in the other rows (including row 0). This variable is "in the solution" with a value equal to the number on the right-hand side of the equal sign. In row 0, this variable is Z, which equals 1200; in row 1, $W_A = 40$; and in row 2, $x = 20$. The variables that are "in the solution" are called *basic variables.* The other variables, y and W_A in this case, are required to equal 0, and are called *nonbasic variables.*

This is the solution we obtained after solving for x using the limiting equation, and substituting back into the other equations in the algebraic development. We also demonstrated the same result using another solution technique for simultaneous equations [equations (11) through (13)]. When examined closely, pivoting is simply an approach for solving a system of simultaneous equations. Although the arithmetic is a bit tedious, there is nothing at all that is particularly sophisticated or mathematically "advanced" about this basic solution strategy.

In fact, Step 2 of the pivoting procedure can be made even more mechanical by using a simple formula. For each row *except* the key row, all the numbers in the revised row can be obtained from the following relationship:

$$
\text{New number} = \text{Old number} - \frac{\begin{pmatrix} \text{Corresponding} \\ \text{number of} \\ \text{key row} \end{pmatrix} \times \begin{pmatrix} \text{Corresponding} \\ \text{number of} \\ \text{key column} \end{pmatrix}}{\text{Key number}} \tag{23}
$$

For example,

1. row 1, constant column
   new number $= 80 - (60 \times 2)/3 = 40$

2. row 1, x column
   new number $= 2 - (3 \times 2)/3 = 0$

3. row 0, x column
   new number $= -60 - (3 \times -60)/3 = 0$

The remaining coefficients in row 0 and row 1 can be calculated in the same way (check this yourself).

Accomplishing the pivoting operation completes one *iteration* of the simplex algorithm. Thus, an iteration corresponds to a movement from one corner point of the solution space to another corner point, or from one basic solution to another.

Improving the solution

The variable y has the only negative coefficient in row 0, and so we know that it should enter the solution by Rule I. The coefficients of y, -10 in row 0, 8/3 in row 1, and 2/3 in row 2, become the key column. We can determine the key row from the ratios shown in Table 5-1. The minimum ratio of 15 corresponds to row 1, which is designated as the key row according to Rule II. The key number is the coefficient in both the key row and the key column, 8/3.

Performing the pivoting operation, we first divide each coefficient in the key row, row 1, by the key number, 8/3, and obtain

$$y + \frac{3W_A}{8} - \frac{W_B}{4} = 15 \tag{24}$$

We modify rows 0 and 2 as indicated.

Applying Rule II			TABLE 5-1
Row	Current Right-Hand Side	Coefficient of y	Ratio
1	40	8/3	15
2	20	2/3	30

Row 0: multiply (24) by 10 and add to row 0.

Row 2: multiply (24) by $-2/3$ and add to row 2.

Alternately, rows 1 and 2 could be determined by applying formula (23). The resulting system of equations is

$$Z \qquad\qquad + \frac{15W_A}{4} + \frac{35W_B}{2} = 1350 \qquad \text{(row 0)}$$

$$y \quad + \frac{3W_A}{8} - \frac{W_B}{4} = 15 \qquad \text{(row 1)}$$

$$x \qquad - \frac{W_A}{4} + \frac{W_B}{2} = 10 \qquad \text{(row 2)}$$

By identifying the variable in each row with a coefficient of 1 and with coefficients of 0 in the other rows, we see that the solution is $Z = 1350$, $x = 10$, and $y = 15$, with $W_A = W_B = 0$. Now both x and y are basic variables, while W_A and W_B are nonbasic.

Since there are no variables in row 0 with negative coefficients, this solution is optimal. As we expected, these values coincide with our previous algebraic solution and with the graphic solution. Note also that the coefficients in row 0 yield the shadow prices obtained previously for W_A and W_B.

Summary of the procedure

The steps of the simplex algorithm may be summarized as follows:

1. Formulate the constraints and the objective function.
2. Develop the set of *initial equations,* using the slack variables in the initial solution.
3. Identify the *entering variable,* the variable with the most negative coefficient in row 0, and the *key column* of coefficients of the entering variable.
4. Identify the *key row,* the row with the minimum ratio, determined by dividing the right-hand side of each row by the positive coefficient in the key column in that row (if the coefficient is zero or negative, the row is ignored).
5. Perform the *pivoting operation.*
   a. Divide the key row by the *key number,* the coefficient at the intersection of the key row and the key column.

b. For each nonlimiting row:

(1) Multiply the newly transformed key row (found in a. above) by the negative of the coefficient in the key column of the nonlimiting row.

(2) Add the result to the nonlimiting row.

Alternately, the coefficients for the nonlimiting rows can be calculated from the formula:

$$\text{New number} = \text{Old number} - \frac{\left(\begin{array}{c}\text{Corresponding}\\ \text{number of}\\ \text{key row}\end{array}\right) \times \left(\begin{array}{c}\text{Corresponding}\\ \text{number of}\\ \text{key column}\end{array}\right)}{\text{Key number}}$$

6. Repeat steps 3 through 5 until all the coefficients in row 0 are nonnegative. An optimal solution then results.

7. The resulting optimal solution is interpreted in the following manner: in each row there is exactly one basic variable with a coefficient of 1 and with coefficients of 0 in the other rows. This variable is equal to the right-hand side of the row. The value of the objective function is given by the value of Z. All other nonbasic variables are zero. The shadow prices, which indicate the value of a marginal unit of each variable not in the solution, are the coefficients of the slack variables in row 0.

The output for the computer solution, including sensitivity analysis for the simplified chemical production problem, is shown in Figure 5-2. Note that the format is the same as the computer output illustrated in Chapter 3, showing the optimal value of the objective function, the optimal value of the decision variables, the shadow prices, and the upper and lower bounds on the right-hand values of the constraints and of the prices in the objective function.

THE SIMPLEX TABLEAU

The logic and calculations of the simplex algorithm can be simplified even further by the use of the simplex tableau format for organizing the data. To minimize recopying of x, y, W_A, W_B, and Z, let us rearrange the two restricting equations (18) and (19) and the objective function equation (21) with the variables at the heads of columns and

```
LPRUN
                    CHEMICAL PRODUCTION


THE OPTIMAL VALUE OF THE OBJECTIVE FUNCTION IS:    1350.000


         THE VARIABLES IN THE SOLUTION ARE


VARIABLE   X        AT LEVEL       1.0000E1
           Y                       1.5000E1


DO YOU WISH SENSITIVITY ANALYSIS? Y
                      SHADOW      LB       CURRENT      UB
CONSTRAINT     1     3.7500E0   4.0000E1   8.0000E1   1.2000E2
               2     1.7500E1   4.0000E1   6.0000E1   1.2000E2

PRICE      X                    2.5000E1   6.0000E1   7.5000E1
           Y                    4.0000E1   5.0000E1   1.2000E2
```

FIGURE 5-2
Computer solution and sensitivity analysis for the simplified chemical production problem.

the coefficients of these variables in rows to represent the equations. The equal signs have also been dropped.

Z	x	y	W_A	W_B		
1	−60	−50	0	0	0	(row 0)
0	2	4	1	0	80	(row 1)
0	3	2	0	1	60	(row 2)

Next, to the right beside the constants 80 and 60, we place two columns that identify the variables in the solution and their contribution rates in the objective function, as shown in Table 5-2. This format for a linear optimization model is called the *simplex tableau*. The column of constants plus these two new columns are called the *stub* of the tableau.

Before proceeding, let us name the various parts of the tableau shown in Table 5-2. The variable row simply identifies the variable associated with each of the coefficients in the various columns. Row 0 is the objective function row and contains the

Initial Simplex Tableau   TABLE 5-2

					Solution Stub			
Z	x	y	W_A	W_B				(variable row)
1	−60	−50	0	0	0	Z	1	(row 0)
0	2	4	1	0	80	W_A	0	(row 1)
0	3	2	0	1	60	W_B	0	(row 2)

Constant column (value of variables in solution)⎓

Variable column (variables in solution; variables not shown in this solution are zero)⎓

Objective column (contribution rates of solution variables in the objective function)⎓

negative of the coefficients that show the contribution rates for each of the variables in the objective function. For example, the contribution of each unit of x is $60 per unit, y is $50 per unit, W_A is zero, and so on.

The solution stub always contains three columns. The variable column shows the variables that have positive values (basic variables) at a given stage of solution, *and the variables not shown in the variable column have a value of zero.* The constant column shows the value of each of the variables in the solution. The objective column shows the contribution rates of the variables in the solution, and these coefficients come from the objective row. For example, in the initial solution, the coefficients below W_A and W_B are zeros.

We must not lose sight of the fact that the numbers in the tableau are the coefficients of the variables in the variable row, and that the numbers in the constant column are the numerical values of the right-hand side of the objective function row 0 and of the constraint equations, rows 1 and 2.

Improving the initial solution

The simplex algorithm can be applied just as before, except that the tableau format allows some additional streamlining of the calculations.

Selecting the key column, key row, and key number We can apply Rule I of the simplex algorithm to the tableau, which says that we should select the variable with the most negative contribution in row 0 as the *entering variable*. From Table 5-2, we can see that the most negative coefficient is $-\$60$, which is associated with the variable x. Therefore, we designate the column of coefficients of x as the *key column*.

We select the *key row* by applying Rule II of the simplex algorithm. That is, *we divide each number in the constant column by the corresponding number in the key column* (ignoring zero or negative entries in the key column). The key row is the row yielding the smallest quotient. For our problem, the quotients are:

first row, $80/2 = 40$

second row, $60/3 = 20$ (key row)

The number at the intersection of the key row and the key column is designated the *key number*. Table 5-3 shows the initial tableau with the key column, key row, and key number identified.

The pivoting operation can now be accomplished in a mechanistic fashion by creating a new tableau. The first step in developing the new tableau is to calculate the coefficients for the *main row*. The main row appears in the same relative position in the new tableau as the key row in the preceding tableau. It is computed by dividing the coefficients of the key row by the key number; Table 5-4 shows this development. The variable and its objective number from the head of the key column — that is, x and 60 — are placed in the stub of the main row, replacing W_B and 0 from the previous

---

TABLE 5-3   Initial Simplex Tableau with Key Column, Key Row, and Key Number Identified

Tableau I

	Z	x	y	W_A	W_B				
	1	-60	-50	0	0	0	Z	1	(row 0)
	0	2	4	1	0	80	W_A	0	(row 1)
Key row⟶	0	3	2	0	1	60	W_B	0	(row 2)

Key column⎯⎯⎯⎯   Key number

Simplex Tableau with Main Row of New Tableau   TABLE 5-4

Tableau I

	Z	x	y	W_A	W_B					
	1	-60	-50	0	0	0	Z	1	(row 0)
	0	2	4	1	0	80	W_A	0	(row 1)
	0	3	2	0	1	60	W_B	0	(row 2)

Tableau II

	0	1	2/3	0	1/3	20			Main row

Simplex Tableau with Variable and Objective Columns Completed   TABLE 5-5

Tableau I

	Z	x	y	W_A	W_B					
	1	-60	-50	0	0	1200	Z	1	(row 0)
	0	2	4	1	0	80	W_A	0	(row 1)
	0	3	2	0	1	60	W_B	0	(row 2)

Tableau II

							Z	1
							W_A	0
	0	1	2/3	0	1/3	20	x	60

tableau. The balance of the objective and variable columns in the stub is copied from the previous tableau and the new tableau developed to this point now appears in Table 5-5.

Now all the remaining coefficients in the new tableau can be calculated by applying formula (23). The completed improved solution is shown in Tableau II in Table 5-6. Note that the solution at this stage is $x = 20$, $W_A = 40$, $y = 0$, and $W_B = 0$, and that the value of the objective function is 1200, as shown in the solution stub.

TABLE 5-6

Simplex Tableau with First Iteration Completed

Tableau I

Z	x	y	W_A	W_B					
1	−60	−50	0	0	0	Z	1	(row 0)
0	2	4	1	0	80	W_A	0	(row 1)
0	3	2	0	1	60	W_B	0	(row 2)

Tableau II

1	0	−10	0	20	1200	Z	1	(row 0)
0	0	8/3	1	−2/3	40	W_A	0	(row 1)
0	1	2/3	0	1/3	20	x	60	(row 2)

Third and optimal solution

Next, we examine row 0 of Tableau II in Table 5-6, and we see that potential improvement still exists, since the coefficient −10 appears under the variable y. Thus, y is selected as the key column of the tableau. Proceeding as before, we obtain the new solution in Tableau III of Table 5-7, which is optimal.

To summarize, the use of the tableau helps to organize the data and calculations of the simplex algorithm, but the results obtained are identical.

The optimum solution is interpreted in the following manner: the solution appears in the stub. The variables shown in the variable column have the values shown in the corresponding rows of the constant column. The value of the objective function is shown in the constant column, row 0. All variables not shown in the stub are zero. The shadow prices that indicate the value of a marginal unit of each variable not in the solution are shown in row 0 of the final solution.

EXTENSIONS OF THE SIMPLEX METHOD

In our initial presentation of the simplex algorithm, we solved a maximization problem subject to constraints with less than or equal to signs. The simplex algorithm may be extended to deal with other forms of the objective function and constraints. These extensions are of definite interest to the manager in solving practical managerial problems.

Simplex Tableau, Second and Third Iterations Completed

TABLE 5-7

Tableau I

Z	x	y	W_A	W_B				
1	−60	−50	0	0	0	Z	1	(row 0)
0	2	4	1	0	80	W_A	0	(row 1)
0	3	2	0	1	60	W_B	0	(row 2)

Tableau II

1	0	−10	0	20	1200	Z	1	(row 0)
0	0	8/3	1	−2/3	40	W_A	0	(row 1)
0	1	2/3	0	1/3	20	x	60	(row 2)

Tableau III

1	0	0	15/4	35/2	1350	Z	1	(row 0)
0	0	1	3/8	−1/4	15	y	50	(row 1)
0	1	0	−1/4	1/2	10	x	60	(row 2)

Minimizing an objective function

The simplex algorithm can be applied to minimize an objective function as easily as to maximize one. To illustrate this point, we use a different version of the chemical production problem. As before, we produce two chemicals, x and y, on machines A and B. Each unit of chemical x requires 2 worker-hours on machine A and 3 worker-hours on machine B, where a total of 80 worker-hours is available. Each unit of chemical y requires 4 worker-hours on machine A and 2 worker-hours on machine B, where 60 worker-hours are available. The variable cost of producing a unit of chemical x is $290, while the variable cost of producing a unit of chemical y is $400.

Now suppose that we have signed a fixed fee contract with a major firm to supply them with a *total* of 22 units of chemicals x and y. Our objective, therefore, is to *minimize* the total variable production costs subject to the constraints on worker-hours and on the total number of units produced. The appropriate formulation of the problem would be

minimize $Z = 290x + 400y$

subject to

$$2x + 4y \leq 80$$

$$3x + 2y \leq 60$$

$$x + y = 22$$

$$x, y \geq 0$$

In order to apply the simplex algorithm to this minimization problem, we can adopt one of two strategies. First, we can simply multiply the objective function by -1 and obtain

maximize $Z = -290x - 400y$

It should be clear that maximizing a function (making it as large as possible) is equivalent to minimizing its value when the signs are changed (making the negative of the function as small as possible). This change allows us to apply the same algorithm as before to the problem with the modified objective function.

We may also alter the procedure to minimize an objective function by changing one simple rule in the algorithm, Rule I. When selecting the entering variable (or key column), the variable with the most positive coefficient in the objective function row (row 0) is chosen, rather than the one with the most negative number. An optimal solution is determined when all the coefficients in the objective function row are negative or zero. All other steps remain exactly the same.

To understand the logic behind this modification of Rule I, recall our previous interpretation of the coefficients in row 0. A negative coefficient in row 0 indicates how much the objective function will *increase* if the corresponding variable is increased by one unit; a positive coefficient in row 0 indicates how much the objective function will *decrease* if the corresponding variable is increased by one unit. If we are attempting to minimize the objective function, then we wish to identify those variables with positive coefficients in row 0, since bringing them into the solution will decrease the objective function.

We would illustrate this approach with our minimization problem except for one additional complication: it contains an equality constraint. Adapting the simplex algorithm to solve a problem with an equality constraint is our next topic.

Equality and requirement constraints

The initial solution for the simplex algorithm was found by introducing slack variables into each constraint involving a less than or equal to ($\leq$) sign, and setting each slack variable equal to the right-hand side of the resulting equation. If a constraint is written with an equality ($=$) sign or a greater than or equal to ($\geq$) sign, this strategy must be modified.

Equality constraints To fit into the requirements of the simplex format we must have a variable in each row with a coefficient of $+1$ in that row and coefficients of 0 in the other rows. Recall that these variables are the *basic variables* with nonzero values at each iteration of the simplex algorithm. Suppose the problem formulation includes the equation

$$x + y = 22$$

in addition to constraints with less than or equal to inequalities. To provide an initial solution for the simplex algorithm, we would like to let $x = y = 0$, and set the slack variables equal to the right-hand side constants. However, it does not seem to make sense to add a slack variable to this equality constraint, since the sum of $x + y$ *must* equal 22 or the constraint will be violated.

Nevertheless, we need an initial solution, so we will add a variable to this equation that plays the role of a slack variable in the initial solution, but that we force to be equal to 0 in the optimal solution. The equation

$$x + y = 22$$

can be modified to fit into the simplex format by adding an *artificial variable U*. The equation then becomes

$$x + y + U = 22$$

Notice that the artificial variable U plays precisely the same role as the slack variable in a constraint with a less than or equal to ($\leq$) sign; that is, in the initial solution we can let $U = 22$ when x and y are set equal to 0.

The artificial variable is included simply as a computational device that permits us to stay within the rules of the simplex algorithm. However, if U does not equal 0 in the final (optimal) solution to the linear optimization model, then $x + y$ would not equal 22 so the constraint $x + y = 22$ would be violated. To ensure that this variable will always be equal to 0 in the optimal solution, we assign it an arbitrarily large coefficient in the objective function, which we call M (for "mighty big" perhaps). If we are maximizing the objective function, we assign the artificial variable a coefficient of $-M$ in the objective function. Since $-M$ is an overwhelming large cost in relation to the positive contribution in the objective function, when the objective function is maximized through the use of the simplex algorithm, the artificial variable will be driven to 0. If this does not occur, we know that there is no feasible solution to the problem. If we are minimizing an objective function, we assign an artificial variable a coefficient of $+M$. Again, the value of the artificial variable will be driven to 0 by the simplex algorithm if a feasible solution exists.

Example We can illustrate both the minimization of an objective function and the use of an artificial variable in an equality constraint by solving the example problem involving a fixed fee contract. When we add slack variables to the inequality constraints and the artificial variable to the equality constraint, the problem formulation becomes

$$\text{minimize } Z = 290x + 400y \qquad + MU$$

subject to

$$2x + 4y + W_A \qquad\qquad = 80$$
$$3x + 2y \qquad + W_B \qquad = 60$$
$$x + y \qquad\qquad + U \; = 22$$
$$x, y, W_A, W_B, U \geq 0$$

Notice that the artificial variable U has a coefficient of $+M$ in the objective function since we are minimizing it. Clearly, any variable with a relatively large positive coefficient will be made as small as possible in the optimal solution.

Before proceeding, let us gain some additional insight into this problem by looking at its graphical portrayal in Figure 5-3. The feasible region for the problem is restricted to the points on the equality constraint, $x + y = 22$, between the extreme points c and d shown on the graph. Notice that an equality constraint restricts the feasible region to points on the line corresponding to the constraint, rather than simply to points on one side of the line as with an inequality constraint. The only corner points in the feasible region illustrated in Figure 5-3 are at c and d. Therefore, the simplex algorithm should find the optimal solution at one of these two points.

The initial tableau for applying the algorithm is shown in Table 5-8. Recall that in the application of the simplex algorithm with slack variables, each slack variable had a coefficient of 0 in the objective function row, row 0. This is also true in Table 5-8 for the slack variables W_A and W_B, but not for the artificial variable U, which has a coefficient of $-M$! Therefore, our first iteration is a step that *eliminates the coefficient(s) of*

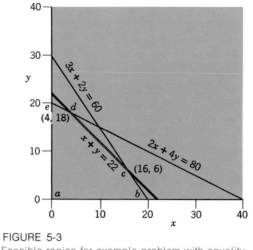

FIGURE 5-3
Feasible region for example problem with equality
constraints falls only on the line $x + y = 22$
between points c and d.

the artificial variable(s) in the objective function row, row 0. This is accomplished by
multiplying row 3 by M and adding the result to row 0, as shown in Table 5-8. Notice
that M is treated just like any other number in the calculations.

The result of the first iteration shown in Table 5-8 is an initial solution with $x = 0$,
$y = 0$, $W_A = 80$, $W_B = 60$, $U = 22$, and an objective function value of $22M$. Since M

Initial Tableau and First Iteration for the Example of Equality Constraints									TABLE 5-8
Z	x	y	W_A	W_B	U				
Initial Tableau									
1	-290	-400	0	0	$-M$	0	Z	1	(row 0)
0	2	4	1	0	0	80	W_A	0	(row 1)
0	3	2	0	1	0	60	W_B	0	(row 2)
0	1	1	0	0	1	22	U	M	(row 3)
First Iteration									
1	$-290 + M$	$-400 + M$	0	0	0	$22M$	Z	1	(row 0)
0	2	4	1	0	0	80	W_A	0	(row 1)
0	3	2	0	1	0	60	W_B	0	(row 2)
0	1	1	0	0	1	22	U	M	(row 3)

is very large and we are trying to minimize the objective function, this solution is clearly unsatisfactory so we must improve it. In Figure 5-3, this solution corresponds to point a on the graph, which is not even a feasible point, since $U = 22$. To find a feasible point, we must force $U = 0$.

Now we will simply apply the simplex algorithm to the tableau created by the first iteration. Since we are minimizing, we will select the key column by identifying the *most positive* coefficient in row 0, rather than the most negative number. Since M is an arbitrarily large number, both $-290 + M$ and $-400 + M$ are greater than 0, and $-400 < -290$, so $-290 + M$ is the most positive coefficient in row 0. Therefore, the column corresponding to x is the key column.

The remainder of the calculations are carried out according to the standard rules of the simplex algorithm, as shown in Table 5-9. The solution determined by the second iteration is $x = 20$, $y = 0$, $W_A = 40$, $W_B = 0$, and $U = 2$. This solution corresponds to point b in Figure 5-3, another infeasible point. However, the third iteration yields the result $x = 16$, $y = 6$, $W_A = 24$, $W_B = 0$, and $U = 0$. This third solution is feasible since it corresponds to point c in Figure 5-3. Since all the nonzero coefficients in row 0 are negative (because $-M$ is a negative number), this solution is also optimal.

Carefully review the calculations in Table 5-9. The important point to be made is that the algorithm forced U to be equal to 0 in the optimal solution. The introduction of the coefficient M made the calculations a bit more tedious, but the simplex rules were followed in a straightforward way.

The shadow prices of the slack variables are interpreted exactly as before. The coefficient of W_B in row 0 in the optimal solution is -110. This indicates that introducing one unit of W_B into the optimal solution would *increase* the value of the objective function by $110. Alternately, it may be interpreted to mean that an extra unit of capacity for machine B would have *reduced* the objective function by $110.

To obtain a shadow price for the right-hand side of the third constraint representing our contractual agreement, we use the coefficient of its artificial variable in row 0 except we ignore the M. Since the row 0 coefficient of U in the optimal solution is $620 - M$ as shown in Table 5-9, we know that increasing the contractual production agreement from 22 to 23 units would increase cost by $620, which is more than the unit costs of either chemical x or chemical y. This is because this increase in production of one unit could only be accomplished by increasing the number of units of y by 3 and reducing the number of units of x by 2, for a net change of one unit. This change is indicated by the coefficients of U of -2 in row 2, and of $+3$ in row 3 in the optimal solution. Verify that this change in the production schedule would increase the total costs by $620.

Calculation of Optimal Solution for the Example of Equality Constraints   TABLE 5-9

Z	x	y	W_A	W_B	U				
Initial Tableau									
1	-290	-400	0	0	$-M$	0	Z	1	(row 0)
0	2	4	1	0	0	80	W_A	0	(row 1)
0	3	2	0	1	0	60	W_B	0	(row 2)
0	1	1	0	0	1	22	U	M	(row 3)
First Iteration									
1	$-290+M$	$-400+M$	0	0	0	22M	Z	1	(row 0)
0	2	4	1	0	0	80	W_A	0	(row 1)
0	3	2	0	1	0	60	W_B	0	(row 2)
0	1	1	0	0	1	22	U	M	(row 3)
Second Iteration									
1	0	$-620/3+M/3$	0	$290/3-M/3$	0	$5800+2M$	Z	1	(row 0)
0	0	8/3	1	$-2/3$	0	40	W_A	1	(row 1)
0	1	2/3	0	1/3	0	20	x	290	(row 2)
0	0	1/3	0	$-1/3$	1	2	U	M	(row 3)
Third Iteration									
1	0	0	0	-110	$620-M$	7040	Z	1	(row 0)
0	0	0	1	2	-8	24	W_A	0	(row 1)
0	1	0	0	1	-2	16	x	290	(row 2)
0	0	1	0	-1	3	6	y	400	(row 3)

The value of M in row 0 is ignored when interpreting the shadow price because M is the coefficient of an artificial variable, and did not appear in the original objective function. However, the constant added or subtracted to M in row 0 indicates the effect of an increase or decrease in the artificial variable on the value of the original objective function (prior to the addition of artificial variables). As in the case of the slack variable, an increase of one unit in the value of the artificial variable corresponds to the decrease of one unit in the right-hand side of its corresponding constant, so its shadow price implicitly places a value on an additional unit of this right-hand side constant.

In our simple example, a manager negotiating this fixed fee contract might be very interested in the fact that agreeing to produce 23 total units rather than 22 would cost an additional $620!

Requirement constraints In many linear programming problems, a constraint may be required to ensure that some combination of terms must be greater than or equal to a given number. For example, the inequality

$$x - y \geq 15$$

has a requirement of at least 15 for the difference between x and y.

Recall that when the inequality sign is less than or equal to ($\leq$), we add a slack variable to the left-hand side that represents the *difference* between the sum of the variables on the left of the inequality and the constant on the right. Since the sum of the variables must be less than or equal to this constant, the slack variable must be nonnegative.

Suppose we use a similar strategy with a constraint involving a greater than or equal to sign, except that this time we must *subtract* a variable from the left-hand side to represent the difference. This variable is called a *surplus variable* since it is the surplus on the left-hand side of the inequality. The example inequality would become

$$x - y - S = 15$$

where S is a surplus variable.

Now to obtain an initial feasible solution for the simplex algorithm, we previously let x and y equal zero, and let the slack variable equal to the right-hand side. Since the surplus variable has a negative sign, this strategy would require it to be a negative number when the right-hand side constant is positive. This violates the rules of the simplex algorithm.

Therefore, we treat each requirement constraint with its surplus variable exactly like an equality constraint, and add to it an artificial variable as well. The example constraint would become

$$x - y - S + U = 15$$

In the initial solution we can let $U = 15$ when x, y, and S are set equal to 0. By again assigning the artificial variable U a coefficient in the objective function of $+M$ if we are minimizing, or $-M$ if we are maximizing, we can ensure that U will be equal to 0 in the final optimal solution, assuming that a feasible solution to the problem exists.

Example Suppose we wish to solve the linear optimization model

$$\text{maximize } Z = 60x + 50y$$

subject to

$$2x + 4y \leq 80$$
$$3x + 2y \leq 60$$
$$x - y \geq 15$$
$$x, y \geq 0$$

When slack variables are added to the constraints with less than or equal to signs, and a surplus variable and an artificial variable are added to the constraint with a greater than or equal to sign, the problem formulation is

maximize $Z = 60x + 50y \qquad\quad - MU$

subject to

$$2x + 4y + W_A \qquad\qquad\qquad = 80$$
$$3x + 2y \qquad + W_B \qquad\qquad = 60$$
$$x - \ y \qquad\qquad\quad - S + U \ = 15$$
$$x, y, W_A, W_B, S, U \geq 0$$

Notice that the surplus variable has a coefficient of 0 in the objective function, and the artificial variable has a coefficient of $-M$, since we are maximizing.

The graphical portrayal again provides some insight into the solution strategy. The feasible region shown in Figure 5-4 is determined by the three corner points b, c, and d, so one of these points should be the optimal solution.

The calculations of the simplex algorithm are shown in Table 5-10. As in the case of the equality constraint, the first iteration is made to eliminate the $-M$ as a coefficient of the artificial variable. This gives the solution $x = 0$, $y = 0$, $W_A = 80$, $W_B = 60$, $S = 0$, and $U = 15$, and an objective function value of $-15M$, corresponding to point a in Figure 5-4. Notice that this solution is not in the feasible region shown in Figure 5-4, as we would expect since the artificial variable is not equal to 0. Applying the simplex algorithm as before, we obtain the optimal solution $x = 18$, $y = 3$, $W_A = 32$, $W_B = 0$, $S = 0$, and $U = 0$, at corner point c.

Again it is important to note that the artificial variable U was forced to be equal to 0 in the optimal solution by the use of an arbitrarily large coefficient, M, in the objective function.

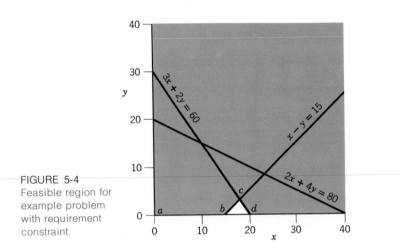

FIGURE 5-4
Feasible region for
example problem
with requirement
constraint.

TABLE 5-10 | Calculation of Optimal Solution for Requirement Constraint Example

Z	x	y	W_A	W_B	S	U				
Initial Tableau										
1	−60	−50	0	0	0	M	0	Z	1	(row 0)
0	2	4	1	0	0	0	80	W_A	0	(row 1)
0	3	2	0	1	0	0	60	W_B	0	(row 2)
0	1	−1	0	0	−1	1	15	U	M	(row 3)
First Iteration										
1	−60 − M	−50 + M	0	0	M	0	−15M	Z	1	(row 0)
0	2	4	1	0	0	0	80	W_A	0	(row 1)
0	3	2	0	1	0	0	60	W_B	0	(row 2)
0	1	−1	0	0	−1	1	15	U	M	(row 3)
Second Iteration										
1	0	−110	0	0	−60	60 + M	900	Z	1	(row 0)
0	0	6	1	0	2	−2	50	W_A	0	(row 1)
0	0	5	0	1	3	−3	15	W_B	0	(row 2)
0	1	−1	0	0	−1	1	15	x	60	(row 3)
Third Iteration										
1	0	0	0	22	6	−6 + M	1230	Z	1	(row 0)
0	0	0	1	−6/5	−8/5	8/5	32	W_A	0	(row 1)
0	0	1	0	1/5	3/5	−3/5	3	y	50	(row 2)
0	1	0	0	1/5	−2/5	2/5	18	x	60	(row 3)

The surplus variable S is also equal to 0 in the optimal solution to this problem, although the surplus variable may be positive in the optimal solutions of other problems.

The shadow price for the requirement constraint is obtained from the row 0 coefficient of its artificial variable, as in the case of the equality constraint. In this example, this coefficient is $M - 6$. Again we ignore the M, and recognize that an increase in the right-hand side of the requirement constraint from 15 to 16 units would *reduce* the objective function by $6.00!

WHAT SHOULD THE MANAGER KNOW?

In Chapter 3 we argued that the manager need not be concerned with the mathematical complexities of the linear programming solution technique. Yet, in this chapter, we have presented that technique in some detail. The relevant question at this point is, "What should the manager know about the simplex algorithm?"

It is most unlikely that a manager would ever consider solving a practical linear programming problem by hand. The computational effort would not be justified, since standard computer codes are available that can efficiently handle problems involving more than 1000 constraints. Therefore, the rationale for studying the algorithm must be based on other considerations.

A manager should not be intimidated by the techniques of management science. Understanding the basic strategy of the simplex algorithm may be helpful in appreciating what linear programming can and cannot do. After all, when reduced to simplest terms, the nature of the simplex technique is to solve simultaneous equations successively in a sequence controlled by a test for optimality. The logic of the method is straightforward and relatively simple to comprehend. This knowledge may make the manager more comfortable in dealing with technical analysts and more confident in using the results of computerized solutions to linear optimization models.

CHECK YOUR UNDERSTANDING

1. The Elmore Electronics Corporation was presented as Case 3-1 in Chapter 3. Continue your study of that problem by creating a graphic means of solution.
   a. Plot the constraints on a graph, using the number of oscilloscopes (O) for the horizontal axis, and the number of voltmeters (V) for the vertical axis.

b. Plot the objective function on the same graph for the value of $Z = \$36,000$. Which two constraints appear to limit the size of the contribution?

c. Solve simultaneously for values of O and V the two equations that limit the size of total contribution.

d. Look at your graph of constraints. Are there any constraints that can be ignored completely since they have no possible effect, that is, they are redundant?

2. What is the function of slack variables in the simplex method of solution?

3. What is the physical meaning of slack variables in the following types of constraints?

a. Constraint on the capacity of a machine

b. Constraint on the size of the market

c. Constraint on the total expenditure on advertising in various media

4. Explain the rationale of step 1, "establish an initial solution," in the algebraic solution. Why start with the worst possible solution?

5. In the algebraic solution procedure, what is the test for determining whether or not an initial or other solution can be improved?

6. Suppose, in attempting to improve a solution, we have several variables with positive contributions in the objective function. How do we select the incoming variable?

7. Given that we have selected the incoming variable, which indicates the variable that will increase from its initial value of zero, how do we determine how much to increase the value of that variable? What limits the size of the incoming variable?

8. When we have decided on the limiting size of the incoming variable by testing to determine the maximum value it can have in either of the constraints, how do we modify the objective function in order to determine whether or not we now have an optimum solution?

In the text example, the original contribution y in the objective function was $\$50$ per unit. Why is the contribution of y only $\$10$ at the end of the first iteration?

9. What is the test for optimality in the algebraic procedure?

10. Following is a linear optimization model for a simplified version of the Elmore Electronics Corporation problem that you solved graphically in exercise 1. Now solve it using the algebraic procedure we have outlined:

maximize $Z = 100O + 40V$

subject to

$$6.3O + 1.5V \leq 2500$$
$$7O + 3V \leq 3000$$
$$O, V \geq 0$$

11. What is a feasible solution? A basic solution? Identify both kinds of solutions in Figure 5-1. Can a feasible solution be basic? Must a feasible solution be basic?

12. The Two-Product Company was formulated as a linear optimization model in Chapter 3, with computer input and solution given in Figure 3-13. With that formulation, solve the problem by the simplex methods of this chapter.

13. A manufacturer has two products, both of which are made in two steps by machines A and B. The process times for the two products on the two machines are as follows:

Product	Machine A (hr)	Machine B (hr)
1	4	5
2	5	2

For the coming period, machine A has 100 hours available and B has 80 hours available. The contribution for product 1 is $10 per unit and for product 2, $5 per unit. Using the methods of the simplex algorithm, formulate and solve the problem for maximum contribution.

14. Consider the following linear optimization model:
maximize $Z = 3x_1 + x_2 + 4x_3$
subject to $6x_1 + 3x_2 + 5x_3 \leq 25$
$3x_1 + 4x_2 + 5x_3 \leq 20$
$x_1, x_2, x_3 \geq 0$
After adding slack variables and performing one simplex iteration, we have the following tableau:

1	$-3/5$	11/5	0	0	4/5	16	Z	1
0	3	-1	0	1	-1	5	S_1	0
0	3/5	4/5	1	0	1/5	4	x_3	4

If the above result is not optimal, perform the next iteration. Indicate the resulting values of the variables and the objective function.

15. Consider the following linear optimization model:
maximize $Z = 3x_1 + 6x_2 + 2x_3$
subject to

$$3x_1 + 4x_2 + x_3 \leq 2 \quad \text{(resource } A)$$
$$x_1 + 3x_2 + 2x_3 \leq 1 \quad \text{(resource } B)$$
$$x_1, x_2, x_3 \geq 0$$

Solve this problem for the optimal solution using the simplex method.

16. Consider the following linear optimization model:
minimize $Z = 3x + 6y$
subject to

$$8x + 6y \geq 15$$
$$3x - y \leq 12$$
$$x + y = 4$$
$$x, y \geq 0$$

a. Analyze the problem graphically. What is the optimal solution?
b. Solve the problem for the optimal solution using the simplex method.

17. Consider the following linear optimization model:
maximize $Z = 15x_1 - 12x_2 - 4x_3 + 3x_4$
subject to

$$8x_1 - 3x_2 - x_3 + x_4 \leq 3$$
$$-6x_1 - x_2 + x_3 - x_4 \geq 6$$
$$x_1, x_2, x_3, x_4 \geq 0$$

Solve the problem for the optimal solution using the simplex method.

18. The computer input and output for the example problem with an equality constraint is shown in Figure 5-5. Compare the results with those in Table 5-9. Notice that the shadow price for constraint [3] is $620, while the shadow price for constraint [2] is $-$110.
a. Suppose that we could purchase an extra 5 hours on machine B (constraint [2]) for $100 per hour. Would this reduce costs?
b. Suppose that we could increase our contract to a total of 24 units to be produced, and we would be paid $450 per unit for these marginal units. Would this be a wise decision?

```
      LPENTER
ENTER THE NAME OF THIS PROJECT EQUALITY
MAXIMIZE OR MINIMIZE:MIN
OBJECTIVE FUNCTION:Z=290X+400Y
ENTER CONSTRAINT EQUATIONS, (STRIKE JUST A CARRIAGE RETURN TO STOP INPUT)
  (1) 2X+4Y≤80
  (2) 3X+2Y≤60
  (3) X+Y=22
  (4)
      LPRUN

THE OPTIMAL VALUE OF THE OBJECTIVE FUNCTION IS:   7040.000

              THE VARIABLES IN THE SOLUTION ARE

VARIABLE   X        AT LEVEL      1.6000E1
           Y                      6.0000E0
           SLK1                   2.4000E1

DO YOU WISH SENSITIVITY ANALYSIS? YES

                      SHADOW        LB        CURRENT       UB
CONSTRAINT      1    0.0000E0     5.6000E1    8.0000E1    7.2370E75
                2   -1.1000E2     4.8000E1    6.0000E1    6.6000E1
                3    6.2000E2     2.0000E1    2.2000E1    2.5000E1

PRICE      X                     -7.2370E75   2.9000E2    4.0000E2
           Y                      2.9000E2    4.0000E2    7.2370E75

-> END <-
```

FIGURE 5-5
Example problem with equality constraint (Exercise 18).

19. Consider the following linear optimization model:
maximize $Z = 0.10F + 1.60S + 1.80H + 0.50A$
subject to

$$F + S + H + A = 2$$
$$0.75F - 0.25S - 0.25H - 0.25A \geq 0$$
$$0.55F - 0.45S \qquad\qquad \geq 0$$
$$0.30F + 0.70S - 0.30H - 0.30A \leq 0$$
$$F, S, H, A \geq 0$$

a. Set up the initial tableau. *Do not work the problem.*
b. Generate a tableau with zero as the coefficient in the objective function row of each of the basic variables.

GENERAL REFERENCES

Charnes, A., and W. W. Cooper, *Management Models and Industrial Applications of Linear Programming,* Vols. 1 and 2, John Wiley & Sons, New York, 1961.

Dallenbach, H. G., and E. J. Bell, *User's Guide to Linear Programming,* Prentice-Hall, Englewood Cliffs, N.J., 1970.

Dantzig, G. B., *Linear Programming and Extensions,* Princeton University Press, Princeton, N.J., 1963.

Hillier, F. S., and G. J. Lieberman, *Introduction to Operations Research,* third edition, Holden-Day, San Francisco, 1980.

Wagner, H. M., *Principles of Operations Research,* second edition, Prentice-Hall, Englewood Cliffs, N.J., 1975.

CHAPTER 6

Linear Programming: Special Situations, Sensitivity Analysis, and Duality

As we have seen in Chapter 5, the simplex algorithm may be used to calculate the optimal solution to a linear optimization problem. The example problems that we used to illustrate the simplex algorithm were all simple, and could be solved in a straightforward manner. Occasionally, situations that require special attention are encountered when the simplex algorithm is applied. For example, what happens when a linear optimization model is formulated so that no values of the decision variables will simultaneously satisfy all the constraints? Or what happens if the constraints do not actually bound the value of the objective function so that it can be increased without an upper limit? We begin this chapter by reviewing these two special situations, as well as others.

From a manager's point of view, the actual solution to a linear optimization model may be much less significant than the *insight* gained from analyzing the sensitivity of the solution to changes in the objective function coefficients and in the right-hand side constants. The objective function coefficients often represent prices, contributions to profit and overhead, or costs. The manager may wish to know whether an increase in costs, or a change in pricing strategy, will affect the choice of the optimal solution. The right hand-side constants often represent the manager's available resources. The manager may wish to know if additional units of any resource should be acquired. If so, how much? At what price? These questions may all be answered by a sensitivity analysis of the optimal solution.

An alternate perspective on the value of the resources may be obtained by seeking the optimal price to charge for each resource. As we will see, this problem may be formulated as a special linear optimization model called the dual problem. A thorough understanding of the economic concepts underlying the dual problem may assist a manager in understanding the value of each scarce resource.

SPECIAL SITUATIONS

We begin by reviewing four special situations that can occur when a linear optimization model is solved by the simplex algorithm. The manager should be able to recognize these situations when they occur, and take action to exploit or remedy the situations.

Alternate optimal solutions

The identification of alternate optimal solutions is important, since they provide flexibility for managerial decisions. What if we are maximizing an objective function and one of the coefficients of a nonbasic variable is 0 in row 0 of an iteration of the simplex algorithm, and the other coefficients are all positive? Recall that the coefficients of the nonbasic variables in row 0 indicate how much the objective function will change with a unit increase in the associated variable. If the coefficient in row 0 is 0, then the corresponding variable can enter the solution without changing the value of the objective function. If this occurs when there are no negative coefficients in row 0, the existing solution is optimal, but the solution that would be found by "bringing in" the variable with the 0 coefficient would also be optimal. It would have the same objective function value since the change per unit is 0.

Alternate optimal solutions, if they exist, will interest a manager since they offer a choice among operating decisions without affecting the primary objective. The manager may actually prefer one of the alternate optimal solutions because of considerations not explicitly represented in the objective function.

For example, suppose that each unit of chemical x had a sales price of $365 rather than $350. Subtracting the variable costs of $290 provides a profit margin of $75 per unit. The modified formulation of the linear optimization problem becomes

maximize $Z = 75x + 50y$

subject to

$$2x + 4y \leq 80$$

$$3x + 2y \leq 60$$

$$x, y \geq 0$$

The first iteration of the simplex algorithm is shown in Table 6-1. Notice that we have precisely the same result as the one found earlier in Table 5-6, with one important exception. The coefficient of y in row 0 is equal to 0. Therefore, there are no negative coefficients in row 0, so the solution $x = 20$, $y = 0$, $W_A = 40$, $W_B = 0$, and $Z = 1500$ is optimal!

Since the coefficient of y in row 0 is 0, this means that a unit increase in the value of y will not affect the objective function value. Suppose we choose y as our incoming variable and complete another iteration of the simplex algorithm. The result is shown in Table 6-2, where the alternate optimal solution is $x = 10$, $y = 15$, $W_A = 0$, $W_B = 0$, and $Z = 1500$.

To verify that these are alternate optimal solutions, we can substitute the results in the objective function and obtain

$$75(20) + 50(0) = 1500$$

TABLE 6-1

First Iteration of Example with an Alternate Optimal Solution

Initial Tableau

Z	x	y	W_A	W_B				
1	−75	−50	0	0	0	Z	1	(row 0)
0	2	4	1	0	80	W_A	0	(row 1)
0	3	2	0	1	60	W_B	0	(row 2)

First Iteration

1	0	0	0	25	1500	Z	1	(row 0)
0	0	8/3	1	−2/3	40	W_A	0	(row 1)
0	1	2/3	0	1/3	20	x	75	(row 1)

for the first optimal solution, and

$$75(10) + 50(15) = 1500$$

for the alternate optimal solution.

Figure 6-1 illustrates why the alternate optimal solutions occur with this modified objective function. The dotted lines represent plots of the objective function for $Z =$ $750, $1000, $1250, and $1500. Notice that the dotted lines are *parallel* to the constraint line determined by the equation $3x + 2y = 60$. When $Z = \$1500$, the "$1500 line" lies directly on the line $3x + 2y = 60$, and intersects *two* corner points, $x = 20$, $y = 0$ and $x = 10$, $y = 15$. These points correspond to our two alternate optimal solutions. When only two decision variables are involved in the problem, alternate optimal solutions may occur when the objective function line is parallel to one of the constraints. When there are more than two decision variables, the constraints and the objective function may be represented geometrically by planes or hyperplanes, but the reasoning is the same. That is, the objective function is parallel to one of the constraints.

The two preceding alternate optimal solutions are basic solutions, occurring at corners of the polygon of feasible solutions. But, note that the constraint line and the $1500 contribution line coincide over the entire range of solutions between these corner points. All combinations of x and y that fall on the constraint line between the corner points will also be optimal, yielding a contribution of $1500. These solutions are nonbasic, and provide the manager with even more flexibility in making decisions concerning the programming of the production of the two chemicals.

Second Iteration Showing Alternate Optimal Solution									TABLE 6-2

Initial Tableau

Z	x	y	W_A	W_B					
1	−75	−50	0	0	0	Z	1	(row 0)	
0	2	4	1	0	80	W_A	0	(row 1)	
0	3	2	0	1	60	W_B	0	(row 2)	

First Iteration

1	0	0	0	25	1500	Z	1	(row 0)
0	0	8/3	1	−2/3	40	W_A	0	(row 1)
0	1	2/3	0	1/3	20	x	75	(row 2)

Second Iteration

1	0	0	0	25	1500	Z	1	(row 0)
0	0	1	3/8	−1/4	15	y	50	(row 1)
0	1	0	−1/4	1/2	10	x	75	(row 2)

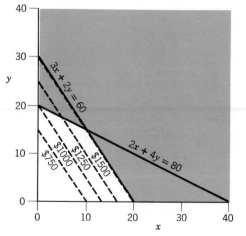

FIGURE 6-1
Plot of objective function lines for the problem with alternate optimal solutions.

Degenerate solutions

In our previous discussion of the simplex algorithm, we distinguished the basic variables from the nonbasic variables by saying that the basic variables have positive values in a solution. On the other hand, nonbasic variables are always equal to zero at any iteration. An exception to this statement occurs occasionally, and a basic variable will actually be equal to zero rather than to a positive value. This situation is of sufficient interest to have a special name. When one of more of the basic variables are actually "in the solution" with a value of 0, the solution is said to be degenerate. This condition was the cause for alarm in the early days of the development of the simplex algorithm, since it is theoretically possible for the algorithm to fail when a degenerate solution is encountered. As a practical matter, experience has shown that the algorithm seldom fails. However, several iterations may occur with no change in the objective function value. Finding an efficient means of moving away from a degenerate solution to one that improves the objective function value is a topic of considerable interest to analysts.

Suppose we modify the chemical production problem by assuming that each unit of chemical x requires 4 worker-hours of processing time on machine A rather than 2 worker-hours. The formulation becomes

maximize $Z = 60x + 50y$

subject to

$$4x + 4y \leq 80$$

$$3x + 2y \leq 60$$

$$x, y \geq 0$$

The first iteration of the simplex method is shown in Table 6-3. As before, x is identified as the entering variable, so its column of coefficients is the key column.

To identify the key row, we compute the ratios of the right-hand side constants to the corresponding coefficients in the key column. In row 1, we have $80/4 = 20$, and in row 2 we have $60/3 = 20$, a *tie!* Therefore, we arbitrarily select one of these rows as the key row. In Table 6-3 we have chosen row 2 as the key row and the first iteration gives the solution $x = 20$, $y = 0$, $W_A = 0$, $W_B = 0$, and the objective function value of $Z = 1200$.

Look closely at the result after the first iteration. The basic variables are x and W_A. Ordinarily, basic variables have values greater than 0, but $W_A = 0$ in this solution.

We still have a negative coefficient in the objective function row, so another iteration must be performed. This time y is the entering variable. Taking the ratios of the right-hand side constants to the coefficients of y we find $0/(4/3) = 0$ in row 1, and $20/(2/3) = 30$ in row 2. The smaller of these two ratios is 0 in row 1. Recall that this

First Iteration with a Degenerate Solution

TABLE 6-3

Initial Tableau

Z	x	y	W_A	W_B				
1	−60	−50	0	0	0	Z	1	(row 0)
0	4	4	1	0	80	W_A	0	(row 1)
0	3	2	0	1	60	W_B	0	(row 2)

First Iteration

1	0	−10	0	20	1200	Z	1	(row 0)
0	0	4/3	1	−4/3	0	W_A	0	(row 1)
0	1	2/3	0	1/3	20	x	60	(row 2)

Second Iteration with a Degenerate Solution

TABLE 6-4

Initial Tableau

Z	x	y	W_A	W_B				
1	−60	−50	0	0	0	Z	1	(row 0)
0	4	4	1	0	80	W_A	0	(row 1)
0	3	2	0	1	60	W_B	0	(row 2)

First Iteration

1	0	−10	0	20	1200	Z	1	(row 0)
0	0	4/3	1	−4/3	0	W_A	0	(row 1)
0	1	2/3	0	1/3	20	x	60	(row 2)

Second Iteration

1	0	0	15/2	10	1200	Z	1	(row 0)
0	0	1	3/4	−1	0	y	50	(row 1)
0	1	0	−1/2	11/9	20	x	60	(row 2)

ratio determines the value of the entering variable in the next tableau, so we expect to find $y = 0$ as a basic variable.

The second iteration is shown in Table 6-4. The solution is $x = 20$, $y = 0$, $W_A = 0$, $W_B = 0$, and $Z = 1200$.

Notice that the solution after the second iteration is identical to the solution after the first iteration. The only difference is that y replaced W_A as a basic variable with a value of 0. However, the solution in Table 6-4 has no negative coefficients in row 0, so it is identified as the optimal solution.

This example illustrates the problem caused by a degenerate solution. An extra iteration was required that did not change the values of the variables or the value of the objective function. In this simple example, the degenerate solution occurred at the optimal value of the objective function. In large practical problems, degenerate solutions are often encountered before the optimal value of the objective function is found, and several iterations may occur with the value of the objective function unchanged. Eventually the objective function will begin to improve again, but a considerable amount of computer time may have been used to overcome the degenerate solution.

Infeasible solutions

In some cases there are no values for the decision variables that simultaneously satisfy all the constraints of a linear optimization model. When this occurs, we say that there is no feasible solution to the problem, or that the solution is *infeasible*.

Suppose we reconsider the chemical production problem with the fixed fee contract, except that this time the contract requires a total of at least 30 units of chemicals x and y. The formulation of the linear optimization model is

minimize $Z = 290x + 400y$

subject to

$$2x + 4y \leq 80$$
$$3x + 2y \leq 60$$
$$x + y \geq 30$$
$$x, y \geq 0$$

The solution to this problem is shown in Table 6-5.

First notice that the solution in the final iteration of Table 6-5 is optimal according to the rules of the simplex algorithm, since all the coefficients in row 0 are 0 or they are negative. However, this solution has an artificial variable in the final basic solution with a positive value; that is, $U = 5$! Recall that the purpose of the large coefficient M assigned to the artificial variable was to ensure that $U = 0$ in the optimal solution, but this has not occurred.

Calculations Leading to an Infeasible Solution

TABLE 6-5

Z	x	y	W_A	W_B	S_i	U				
Initial Tableau										
1	−290	−400	0	0	0	−M	0	Z	1	(row 0)
0	2	4	1	0	0	0	80	W_A	0	(row 1)
0	3	2	0	1	0	0	60	W_B	0	(row 2)
0	1	1	0	0	−1	1	30	U	M	(row 3)
First Iteration										
1	M − 290	M − 400	0	0	−M	0	30M	Z	1	(row 0)
0	2	4	1	0	0	0	80	W_A	0	(row 1)
0	3	2	0	1	0	0	60	W_B	0	(row 2)
0	1	1	0	0	−1	1	30	U	M	(row 3)
Second Iteration										
1	0	M/3 − 620/3	0	290/3 − M/3	−M	0	5800 + 10M	Z	1	(row 0)
0	0	8/3	1	−2/3	0	0	40	W_A	0	(row 1)
0	1	2/3	0	1/3	0	0	20	x	290	(row 2)
0	0	1/3	0	−1/3	−1	1	10	U	M	(row 3)
Third Iteration										
1	0	0	155/2 − M/8	45 − M/4	−M	0	8900 + 5M	Z	1	(row 0)
0	0	1	3/8	−1/4	0	0	15	y	400	(row 1)
0	1	0	−1/4	1/2	0	0	10	x	290	(row 2)
0	0	0	−1/8	−1/4	−1	1	5	U	M	(row 3)

The fact that this final iteration is "optimal" with respect to the row 0 coefficients simply means that the objective function cannot be reduced further. Since an artificial variable is still in the solution, we know that the constraint corresponding to this artificial variable, $x + y \geq 30$, is violated, so there is no feasible solution to the problem.

The graph of the problem is shown in Figure 6-2. Notice that the set of feasible points that satisfy the worker-hour constraints on machines A and B do not intersect the set of feasible points that satisfy the contract constraint of a total of 30 units. The optimal infeasible solution found by the simplex algorithm is at corner point c, which satisfies the machine constraints but not the contract constraint.

The practical implication of an infeasible solution is that the manager must take

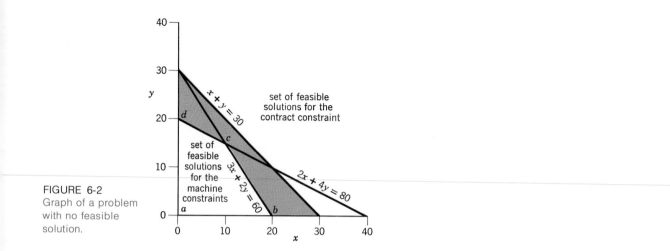

adequate action to increase the availability of resources or to otherwise modify the constraints so that a feasible solution can be obtained. In our simple example, the manager could either allocate more worker-hours to machines A and B until at least 30 units could be produced, or attempt to renegotiate the contract so that a smaller total number of units would be acceptable.

Unbounded solution

An unbounded solution occurs when an objective function being maximized can equal infinity, or when an objective function being minimized can equal minus infinity. A simple numerical example will illustrate this possibility.

Suppose we wish to solve the linear optimization problem

maximize $Z = x + 2y$

subject to

$$x - y \leq 5$$
$$x \leq 10$$
$$x, y \geq 0$$

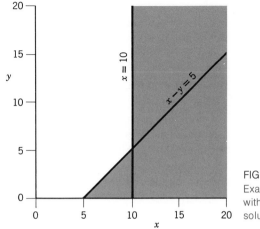

FIGURE 6-3
Example problem
with an unbounded
solution.

Initial Tableau for a Problem with an Unbounded Solution   TABLE 6-6

Z	x	y	W_1	W_2					
1	−1	−2	0	0	0	Z	1	(row 0)
0	1	−1	1	0	5	W_1	0	(row 1)
0	1	0	0	1	10	W_2	0	(row 2)

A graphical analysis of this problem is shown in Figure 6-3. Notice that the feasible region extends along the y axis to infinity. Since the objective function included y with a positive coefficient, the objective function would increase without a bound as y increases.

The initial tableau for this problem is shown in Table 6-6. The variable with the most negative coefficient in row 0 is y, so we identify it as the entering variable.

Now suppose we try to identify the key row. The coefficients of y in the key column are −1 and 0. Recall that the rules of the simplex algorithm said to ignore any coefficients that are zero or negative. Since *both* these coefficients must be ignored, we cannot determine a key row. This is an indication that the solution is unbounded. That is, when all the coefficients in the key column are negative or zero, the optimal solution is unbounded.

In practical problems, an unbounded solution will be an indication that the problem is not formulated correctly. The formulation should be carefully examined to determine if a constraint has been written incorrectly or simply omitted.

SENSITIVITY ANALYSIS

To an alert manager, the optimum solution not only provides answers—given assumptions about resources, prices, and capacities—but should raise questions about what would happen *if* conditions should change. Some of these changes might be imposed by the environment, such as changes in resource costs and market constraints, or they might occur if resources were curtailed. Some, however, represent questions raised by the manager because they are changes that he or she can initiate, such as enlarging capacities or adding new activities. Obviously, it is possible to answer some of these questions by new computer runs, but why make the added runs if the information is already available in the present optimal solution? Sensitivity analysis is focused on the objective function and on the values for the right-hand sides of the constraints. Let us now consider how these analyses are developed.

To illustrate these ideas, we will again use the formulation of the simplified chemical production problem introduced in Chapter 5. For ease of reference, the formulation is

maximize $Z = 60x + 50y$

subject to

$$2x + 4y \le 80$$
$$3x + 2y \le 60$$
$$x, y \ge 0$$

The output for the computer solution, including sensitivity analysis for this problem is shown in Figure 6-4. Note that the format is the same as the computer output illustrated in Chapter 3, showing the optimal value of the objective function, the optimal value of the decision variables, the shadow prices, and the upper and lower bounds on the right-hand values of the constraints and of the prices in the objective function.

The initial and final tableaus for this same problem are shown in Table 6-7. Those tableaus are identical to Tableaus I and III from Table 5-7.

```
LPRUN
                    CHEMICAL PRODUCTION


THE OPTIMAL VALUE OF THE OBJECTIVE FUNCTION IS:   1350.000


          THE VARIABLES IN THE SOLUTION ARE


VARIABLE   X       AT LEVEL        1.0000E1
           Y                       1.5000E1


DO YOU WISH SENSITIVITY ANALYSIS? YES

                     SHADOW        LB        CURRENT       UB
CONSTRAINT     1     3.7500E0    4.0000E1    8.0000E1    1.2000E2
               2     1.7500E1    4.0000E1    6.0000E1    1.2000E2

PRICE      X                     2.5000E1    6.0000E1    7.5000E1
           Y                     4.0000E1    5.0000E1    1.2000E2
```

FIGURE 6-4
Computer solution
and sensitivity
analysis for
the simplified
chemical produc-
tion problem.

Analysis of the objective function

We have already referred to the shadow prices and their significance. What happens
if the unit prices (contributions or costs) in the objective function change? Would the

Initial and Final Tableaus for the Simplified Chemical Production Problem									TABLE 6-7
Z	x	y	W_A	W_B					
Tableau I									
1	−60	−50	0	0	0	Z	1	(row 0)	
0	2	4	1	0	80	W_A	0	(row 1)	
0	3	2	0	1	60	W_B	0	(row 2)	
Tableau III									
1	0	0	15/4	35/2	1350	Z	1	(row 0)	
0	0	1	3/8	−1/4	15	y	50	(row 1)	
0	1	0	−1/4	1/2	10	x	60	(row 2)	

optimal solution remain comprised of the same combination of decision variables? (Of course, the *value* of the objective function would change if the prices of the basic variables changed.)

Changes in nonbasic variables For our example, let us first consider the prices for the nonbasic variables W_A and W_B, which are not in the optimal solution. If we could sufficiently increase the profitability of idle time, the solution could change. (This is seemingly ridiculous for the chemical production example, but consider other cases where a value is placed on idle resources, for example, government agricultural subsidies. Of course, another company might be willing to pay rent on available capacity.)

Recall that the rows in the simplex tableau actually represent equations at every stage of the solution. If the W_A contribution were increased by Δ, an arbitrary amount, then row 0 in the initial tableau becomes

$$1 \quad -60 \quad -50 \quad -(0 + \Delta) \quad 0 \quad 0$$

For convenience in this section, we rewrite this row inserting the variables, and the corresponding equation is

$$Z \quad -60x - 50y - (0 + \Delta)W_A - (0)W_B = 0$$

If we perform the simplex transformations at each iteration as before, the row 0 in the final tableau would become

$$Z + (0)x + (0)y + \left(\frac{15}{4} - \Delta\right)W_A + \frac{35W_B}{2} = 1350$$

Notice that these are the coefficients of row 0 of Tableau III in Table 6-7, except that $-\Delta$ is subtracted from the coefficient of W_A. For the solution in Table 6-7 to remain optimal, the coefficient of W_A must be positive or zero. This means that

$$\frac{15}{4} - \Delta \geq 0$$

or $\Delta \leq \frac{15}{4}$. Otherwise, if $\Delta > \frac{15}{4}$ the coefficient of W_A becomes negative, and by the rules of the simplex algorithm, W_A would enter the solution in exchange for x or y.

The final row 0 coefficients of the nonbasic variables represent the largest positive increments to the original objective function coefficients for those variables that would not alter the current solution.

Basic variables Now what is the effect of changing the contribution of basic variables in the final solution, such as x and y? For example, within what range is the coefficient for x valid for the current solution? If we add an increment Δ_x to the contribution for x in the initial row 0, we have

$$Z - (60 + \Delta_x)x - 50y - (0)W_A - (0)W_B = 0$$

Again, if we perform the simplex arithmetic transformations at each iteration, the final row 0 is

$$Z - \Delta_x x + \frac{15W_A}{4} + \frac{35W_B}{2} = 1350 \tag{1}$$

However, since x is a basic variable, its coefficient must equal 0 in every row, including row 0, except for the row in which its coefficient is 1 (row 2 in this example). If we alter row 0 of Tableau III in Table 6-7, according to equation (1), we have the revised Tableau III shown in Table 6-8.

Note now that there is a negative contribution of $-\Delta_x$, so we must perform an-

Z	x	y	W_A	W_B					
Tableau III									
1	$-\Delta_x$	0	15/4	35/2	1350	Z	1	(row 0)
0	0	1	3/8	−1/4	15	y	50	(row 1)
0	1	0	−1/4	1/2	10	x	60	(row 2)
Tableau IV									
1	0	0	$15/4 - \Delta_x/4$	$35/2 + \Delta_x/2$	$1350 + 10\Delta_x$	Z	1	(row 0)
0	0	1	3/8	−1/4	15	y	50	(row 1)
0	1	0	−1/4	1/2	10	x	60	(row 2)

Final Iteration with the Contribution of Basic Variable x Increased by Δ_x TABLE 6-8

other iteration in the usual way. The key column and row are determined and shown in Table 6-8, and the coefficients of Tableau IV are generated according to the simplex rules.

Examine row 0 of Tableau IV in Table 6-8. For this current solution to remain optimal, the coefficients of W_A and W_B must remain positive or zero. Therefore, we require

$$\frac{15}{4} - \frac{\Delta_x}{4} \geq 0$$

for W_A. Simplifying, we obtain $\Delta_x \leq 15$. Similarly, we have

$$\frac{35}{2} + \frac{\Delta_x}{2} \geq 0$$

for W_B, so $\Delta_x \geq -35$. Thus, the *change* to the original contribution of *x*, 60, must be between -35 and 15 units. This means that the same solution will be optimal if the contribution of *x* is any number as small as $60 - 35 = 25$ or as large as $60 + 15 = 75$, as long as the other data in the problem remain unchanged. A similar analysis for chemical *y* indicates its range to be 40 to 120. Check these bounds on *x* and *y* with the computer sensitivity analysis in Figure 6-4.

Sensitivity of the right-hand side of the constraints

If the resources were to change, under what conditions would the solution change? These resources for our problem were the available hours on machines *A* and *B* of 80 and 60 hours. First, let us consider the machine *A* constraint. If we added an increment of hours, Δ_A, to the 80-hour limit, the initial tableau becomes

1	−60	−50	0	0	$(0 + 0\Delta_A)$	Z	1	(row 0)
0	2	4	1	0	$(80 + 1\Delta_A)$	W_A	0	(row 1)
0	3	2	0	1	$(60 + 0\Delta_A)$	W_B	0	(row 2)

Notice that we have added a new variable to this problem on the right-hand side of the equations. The coefficients of this new variable are 1 in row 1, and 0 in row 0 and in row 2. These are the same coefficients as for the variable W_A, the slack variable for row 1. In applying the simplex method, we divide every coefficient in a row by the same constant, or we multiply every coefficient in a row by the same constant. The result is that if the coefficients of two different variables are identical in *every* row in the initial tableau, they will be identical after every iteration, including the final one. Therefore, it is not necessary to re-solve the initial tableau with Δ_A added to the right-hand side. We know that the solution would be

1	0	0	$\dfrac{15}{4}$	$\dfrac{35}{2}$	$1350 + \dfrac{15\Delta_A}{4}$	Z	1	(row 0)
0	0	1	$\dfrac{3}{8}$	$-\dfrac{1}{4}$	$15 + \dfrac{3\Delta_A}{8}$	y	50	(row 1)
0	1	0	$-\dfrac{1}{4}$	$\dfrac{1}{2}$	$10 - \dfrac{\Delta_A}{4}$	x	60	(row 2)

where the coefficients of Δ_A are identical to those of W_A.

For the optimal solution to be feasible, the optimal values of the basic variables must be nonnegative. Therefore, we have the relation

$$15 + \frac{3}{8}\,\Delta_A \geq 0$$

from row 1, which simplifies to $\Delta_A \geq -40$. From row 2,

$$10 - \frac{1}{4}\,\Delta_A \geq 0$$

or $\Delta_A \leq 40$. The same basic variables will be "in the solution" as long as $-40 \leq \Delta_A \leq 40$, or as long as the available hours on machine A are between $80 - 40 = 40$ and $80 + 40 = 120$. However, in this case the *values* of these basic variables would change.

Note in row 0 the value of the objective function, Z, is $1350 + (15/4)\Delta_A$. This value emphasizes that $15/4$ is the shadow price, or marginal value, of an additional hour on machine A. This shadow price is valid for any number of machine hours within the range of 40 and 120.

For example, suppose we can obtain 10 additional hours of time on machine A by changing our maintenance techniques. Thus, $\Delta_A = 10$, which is within the range -40 to $+40$. The new values of the basic variables are given by

$$y = 15 + \frac{3\Delta_A}{8}$$

$$x = 10 - \frac{\Delta_A}{4}$$

Substituting $\Delta_A = 10$, we obtain

$$y = 15 + \frac{3(10)}{8} = 18.75$$

$$x = 10 - \frac{10}{4} = 7.50$$

and the new value of the objective function is

$$Z = 1350 + \frac{15(10)}{4} = 1387.5$$

We can apply the same type of analysis for the machine B constraint. Suppose we add an increment of Δ_B to the 60-hour limit on machine B in the initial set of equations. Then the coefficients for Δ_B in the final set of equations will be the same as the coefficients for W_B in the final set of equations. Therefore, the right-hand sides of the final set of equations and the associated values of Δ_B will be

$$15 - \frac{\Delta_B}{4} \geq 0$$

which gives $\Delta_B \leq 60$ from row 1, and

$$10 + \frac{\Delta_B}{2} \geq 0$$

which gives $\Delta_B \geq -20$ from row 2. The range for the right-hand side constant for machine B is then $60 - 20 = 40$, and $60 + 60 = 120$, or 40 to 120. Check these ranges with the computer sensitivity analysis in Figure 6-4. (Note that these ranges are not the same as those given in Figure 3-8 because the constraint set included market limitations in that problem.)

These bounds apply when each right-hand side constant is varied independently. A similar, but more complex analysis is called for when several changes are made simultaneously [see Wagner, 1975].

Sensitivity analysis with requirement and equality constraints

Sensitivity analysis of linear optimization models with requirement and equality constraints can be performed in precisely the same manner as we have illustrated with the less than or equal to constraints with one important exception. The artificial variable associated with the requirement or equality constraint plays the role of the slack variable when the sensitivity of the optimal solution to its right-hand constant is calculated. That is, if we add an increment Δ to the right-hand side constant of a requirement or equality constraint in the initial tableau, then the coefficients of Δ in the final tableau will be identical to those of the corresponding artificial variable, except for row 0. The coefficient of an artificial variable in row 0 usually involves two terms: one is a constant and the other is a constant multiplied by M. When performing the sensitivity analysis, we simply ignore the term involving M, and use the constant term as our shadow price for additional units of the resource.

DUALITY

In the chemical production problem, we were given information concerning two productive processes, A and B, and limitations on the resources available to be utilized by these processes. Given prices for the products that these processes produce, the objective of our linear optimization model was to determine the number of units of each product to produce so that the total contribution to profit was maximized.

There is an alternate way to think about this problem. The resources to be utilized by the two productive processes in the chemical production problem were hours on machines A and B. Suppose we wished to determine *prices* for these resources that are optimal in the following sense: if we are offered *more* than these prices for the resources, we should sell them; if we are offered *less* than these prices, we should not sell the resources. Instead we should utilize them to produce our two products, chemicals x and y.

An example

To make this discussion more concrete, suppose you are the manager of the chemical production process. Again ignoring the demand constraints, the relevant data are shown in Table 6-9. You have just received an urgent telephone call from Gilbert Testor of the Gilbert Chemical Company. They have received a number of large orders recently, and are operating at their plant capacity. He offers to lease your production capacity for the next month for a "fair price." He asks you to analyze your operations, and determine your prices for leasing time on machines A and B.

Thinking about this problem, you decide that a fair price for these hours would provide at least as much contribution as you could obtain if you used the resources to

TABLE 6-9

Productivity Data for the Chemical Production Problem

	Contribution	Machine A (80 hours available)	Machine B (60 hours available)
Chemical x	$60	2	3
Chemical y	50	4	2

manufacture chemicals x and y. Suppose we let P_A be the lease price for an hour on machine A, and P_B be the lease price for an hour on machine B. If you produce one unit of chemical x, you will receive a contribution to profit of $60. The production of one unit of chemical x requires 2 hours from machine A and 3 hours from machine B. Given the lease prices P_A and P_B, the total return from leasing 2 hours on machine A and 3 hours on machine B is $2P_A + 3P_B$. In order to ensure that these hours could not be better used to produce one unit of chemical x, you require that

$$2P_A + 3P_B \geq 60 \tag{1}$$

so that the total return from leasing these hours will be at least as great as the contribution that you could generate by using them to produce one unit of chemical x.

According to Table 6-9, one unit of chemical y can be produced by the input of 4 hours on machine A and 2 hours on machine B. Using the same reasoning as you did with chemical x, you would require lease prices P_A and P_B to satisfy the inequality

$$4P_A + 2P_B \geq 50 \tag{2}$$

since $50 is the contribution to profit from one unit of chemical y.

Finally, the total contribution from leasing the 80 available hours on machine A and the 60 available hours on machine B would be given by the expression

$$Z = 80P_A + 60P_B \tag{3}$$

It seems clear that any combination of prices P_A and P_B that satisfy both inequalities (1) and (2) would be advantageous to you. That is, you would receive more total contribution to profit computed by plugging these prices into (3) and leasing the hours than by utilizing the hours to produce chemicals x and y.

You hesitate to be too greedy, however. After all, Mr. Testor might be able to lease hours at some other plant, or simply reject your offer if your prices are too high.

Therefore, you would like to determine the *minimum* prices that you could afford to charge for the available hours, and not lose money relative to your alternative of producing chemicals x and y. After some additional thought, you recognize that these minimum prices would solve the linear optimization model.

minimize $Z = 80P_A + 60P_B$

subject to   (D)

$$2P_A + 3P_B \geq 60$$
$$4P_A + 2P_B \geq 50$$
$$P_A, P_B \geq 0$$

The constraints of this problem ensure that you will receive at least as much for the leased hours as they could generate in their alternate use in producing chemicals x and y. The solution to the problem will be the minimum total return you could receive while satisfying these constraints. In this sense, the optimal prices P_A and P_B that solve this linear optimization problem will be the minimum prices for your resources that you should accept in your negotiations with Mr. Testor. If he will not pay *at least* these prices you should refuse his offer and produce chemicals x and y instead.

Before looking at the solution to the linear optimization model D, let us compare it to our original formulation of the simplified chemical production problem, reproduced below for ease of comparison and labeled problem P.

maximize $Z = 60x + 50y$

subject to

$$2x + 4y \leq 80$$ (P)
$$3x + 2y \leq 60$$
$$x, y \geq 0$$

The optimal solution to the linear optimization model P is the maximum contribution that we could obtain using the available hours on machines A and B to produce chemicals x and y. The optimal solution to the linear optimization model D is the minimum contribution that we could obtain leasing the available hours on machines A and B while receiving at least as much contribution as generated by the alternative of using the hours to produce chemicals x and y.

Now, if you think about this for a moment, the following relationships between problems P and D should be intuitively obvious:

1. The optimal solution to P equals the optimal solution to D.
2. Any feasible solution to P is less than or equal to any feasible solution to D.

The second statement follows immediately from the first, since any feasible solution to P is always less that or equal to its optimal value, and a feasible solution to D is greater than or equal to its optimal value.

The computer solution to D is shown in Figure 6-5. Comparing the result to the solution of the simplified chemical production problem P in Figure 6-4, we find that the optimal solution to both linear optimization problems is equal to $1350, as we expected. There is another important observation to be made by comparing the solu-

```
        LPENTER
ENTER THE NAME OF THIS PROJECT DUAL PROBLEM
MAXIMIZE OR MINIMIZE: MIN
OBJECTIVE FUNCTION:Z=80PA+60PB
ENTER CONSTRAINT EQUATIONS, (STRIKE JUST A CARRIAGE RETURN TO STOP INPUT)
  (1)  2PA+3PB≥60
  (2)  4PA+2PB≥50
  (3)
        LPRUN
                          DUAL PROBLEM


THE OPTIMAL VALUE OF THE OBJECTIVE FUNCTION IS:    1350.000


              THE VARIABLES IN THE SOLUTION ARE


VARIABLE   PA      AT LEVEL     3.7500E0
           PB                   1.7500E1


DO YOU WISH SENSITIVITY ANALYSIS? YES

                        SHADOW       LB        CURRENT       UB
CONSTRAINT      1     1.0000E1    2.5000E1    6.0000E1    7.5000E1
                2     1.5000E1    4.0000E1    5.0000E1    1.2000E2

PRICE         PA                  4.0000E1    8.0000E1    1.2000E2
              PB                  4.0000E1    6.0000E1    1.2000E2
-> END <-
```

FIGURE 6-5
Computer solution
for Problem D.

tions to P and D, however. Notice that the optimal solution to D is a price of P_A = $3.75 for the hours available on machine A, and P_B = $17.5 for the hours available on machine B. *These values are the same as the values for the shadow prices for the constraints of P as shown in the sensitivity analysis of P in Figure 6-4.*

In retrospect this result should not be surprising. Recall that the shadow prices of the chemical production problem were interpreted as the *marginal price* or *value* of an additional unit of each resource. Since the optimal prices found as the solution to D are interpreted in precisely the same way as the optimal price or value of each resource, we should expect them to be identical to the shadow prices of the original problem P. Finally, notice also that the shadow prices of D shown in the optimal solution of Figure 6-5 are identical to the optimal values of the decision variables *CHEMX* and *CHEMY* in Figure 6-4.

A generalization This intimate relationship between the linear optimization models P and D is no accident. Since we began the analysis of the chemical production problem with formulation P, we call it our *primal* problem. Formulation D is called the *dual* problem corresponding to this primal problem.

Every linear optimization problem may be viewed as a primal problem, and each one has an associated dual problem. If the primal problem is a maximization problem like P, then the dual problem is a minimization problem like D, and vice versa. If we choose formulation D as our primal problem, *then its dual problem is P!*

We presented an intuitive explanation of the formulation of D given P. In general, a set of straightforward rules may be followed to formulate the dual of any primal problem. These rules are simplified by the concept of a *standard form* for a linear optimization problem.

Standard form If a linear optimization problem is a maximization problem, then it is in *standard form* if all its constraints are written with less than or equal to signs ($\leq$), except for the nonnegativity constraints on the decision variables. If a linear optimization problem is a minimization problem, then it is in *standard form* if all its constraints are written with greater than or equal to signs ($\geq$).

Notice that any inequality sign in a constraint may be reversed by multiplying the constraint through by minus one. For example, the constraint

$$2x - 3y \leq 4$$

may be replaced by its equivalent form

$$-2x + 3y \geq -4$$

derived by multiplying both sides of the inequality by minus one.

Also, any equality constraint may be replaced by two inequality constraints. That is, the constraint

$$3x + 6y = 14$$

can be replaced by the inequalities

$$3x + 6y \leq 14$$

and

$$3x + 6y \geq 14$$

These two observations allow us to write any arbitrary linear optimization problem in standard form. For example, suppose we are given the primal problem:

minimize $Z = 3x - 6y$

subject to

$$8x + 6y \geq 15$$
$$3x - y \leq 12$$
$$x + y = 4$$
$$x, y \geq 0$$

Since this is a minimization problem, we would like to write all the constraints with greater than or equal to signs. The second constraint may be replaced with its equivalent

$$-3x + y \geq -12$$

and the third constraint may be replaced by the two inequalities:

$$x + y \leq 4$$

and

$$x + y \geq 4$$

Finally, the first of the two preceding inequalities, $x + y \leq 4$, may be multiplied by minus one to reverse the inequality. The result, in standard form, is

minimize $Z = 3x - 6y$

subject to

$$
\begin{aligned}
8x + 6y &\geq 15 \\
-3x + y &\geq -12 \qquad\qquad \text{(S)} \\
-x - y &\geq -4 \\
x + y &\geq 4 \\
x, y &\geq 0
\end{aligned}
$$

Writing the dual If the primal problem is in standard form, then the dual problem can also be written in standard form by following some simple rules. If the primal problem is a maximization problem, the dual problem is a minimization problem, and vice versa. The rules for writing the dual problem are the following:

1. The dual problem will have as many decision variables as the primal problem has constraints. The decision variables of the dual problem are called *dual variables.*

2. Associate each dual variable uniquely with one constraint in the primal problem.

3. The objective function of the dual problem is obtained by multiplying the right-hand side of each constraint in the primal problem by the dual variable associated with its constraint, and summing the results.

4. The dual problem will have as many constraints as the primal problem has variables. The constraints are determined as follows: Select each variable from the primal problem in turn. The coefficient of the selected primal decision variable in each constraint is multiplied by the dual variable associated with its constraint, and the results are summed to obtain the left-hand side of a dual constraint. The right side of this dual constraint is the coefficient of this same primal problem variable in the objective function.

These rules may seem more complicated than they actually are. Suppose we think of a linear optimization problem as a table of numbers with its rows and columns corresponding to the coefficients of the constraints. Loosely speaking, the dual problem is formed by writing the rows of the primal problem as the columns of the dual. The coefficients of the objective function of the dual are the right-hand side of the constraints of the primal, and the right-hand side of the dual constraints are the objective function coefficients of the primal problem.

To illustrate these rules, suppose we take formulation S as our primal problem. Since S is a minimization problem with greater than or equal to inequalities, its dual formulation will be a maximization problem with less than or equal to inequalities. Since S has four constraints, its dual formulation will have four dual variables, P_1, P_2, P_3, and P_4, as noted in step 1.

Following step 2, we will associate dual variable P_1 with the first constraint of the primal, $8x + 6y \geq 15$; P_2 with the second constraint, and so forth. From step 3, the objective function of the dual problem is

$$\text{maximize } Z = 15P_1 - 12P_2 - 4P_3 + 4P_4$$

using the right-hand sides of the constraints as the coefficients.

Finally, from step 4, we select the variable x from the primal S to determine the first dual constraint. The constraint corresponding to x in the dual is

$$8P_1 - 3P_2 - P_3 + P_4 \leq 3$$

where the coefficients of the dual variables are the coefficients of x in the four constraints of the primal problem and the right-hand side is the coefficient of x in the objective function of the primal problem.

In the same manner, we obtain the dual constraint corresponding to the decision variable y in the primal problem. The resulting formulation of the dual problem for S is

$$\text{maximize } Z = 15P_1 - 12P_2 - 4P_3 + 4P_4$$

subject to

$$8P_1 - 3P_2 - P_3 + P_4 \leq 3$$
$$6P_1 + P_2 - P_3 + P_4 \leq -6$$
$$P_1, P_2, P_3, P_4 \geq 0$$

Notice also that formulation D may be obtained from P by following the same rules.

Properties of the dual formulation

The relationship between the solutions of the problems P and D can also be generalized. For simplicity, let us suppose that the primal problem has a feasible finite optimal solution. Recall that it is possible to write constraints that have no feasible solution. For example, there is no value of the variable x that would simultaneously satisfy the two simple constraints $x \geq 5$ and $x \leq 3$. Therefore, a linear optimization problem with these two constraints would not have a feasible solution. It is also possible to have an unbounded, or infinite, solution to a linear optimization model.

In practical applications, problems with infeasible or unbounded solutions are probably formulated incorrectly. Therefore we are primarily interested in the following result: *If either the primal problem or its dual formulation has a feasible finite optimal solution, the other will have the identical optimal solution.*

The relationship between the shadow prices of P and D can be generalized as follows: *The shadow prices for the optimal solution to a linear optimization problem in standard form are the optimal values of its dual variables.* What if the problem is not written in standard form? Then there may be a sign reversal in the relationship between a shadow price and its corresponding dual variable, but the *absolute value* of the shadow price will equal the *absolute value* of the dual variable. For example, suppose we solve a maximization problem with our computer code and one of the constraints contains a greater than or equal to sign. The corresponding shadow price will be either zero or negative, since increasing the right-hand side of the constraint by one unit actually "tightens" a constraint with a greater than or equal to sign, making it relatively more restrictive and reducing the objective function. Therefore, it will have a negative shadow price if it constrains the optimal solution. The dual variable corresponding to this constraint *if* it were transformed into standard form is the negative of this negative shadow price, which is a positive number. A similar interpretation is required for a minimization problem with a less than or equal to constraint.

Recall that a zero shadow price indicates that a constraint is not a controlling constraint at the optimal solution; that is, the slack or surplus variable associated with the constraint is positive in the optimal solution. This relationship is formalized by the *principle of complimentary slackness: If an inequality constraint is not a controlling constraint at the optimal solution, then its corresponding dual variable will be zero in any optimal solution to the dual problem.*

Use of the dual formulation

The dual formulation can be used to great advantage by the technical specialist. According to our rules for writing the dual formulation, a primal problem with m constraints and n variables has a corresponding dual formulation with n constraints and m variables. For technical reasons beyond our scope, the efficiency of computer codes for solving large linear optimization problems depends more on the number of constraints than on the number of variables. Therefore, if a large linear optimization problem has many more constraints than variables, it may be more efficient to formulate and solve its dual problem and then determine the optimal solution to the primal problem from the shadow prices of the optimal dual solution.

These are issues that managers should recognize as important, but they are unlikely to be intimately involved in such details in practice. Perhaps the most important aspect of the concept of the dual formulation for a manager is the following: The allocation of scarce resources to productive processes *implicitly* imputes a price on these resources. This price is an important guide to decisions concerning the acquisition and utilization of these resources.

WHAT SHOULD THE MANAGER KNOW?

The manager should know how to obtain the maximum insight and knowledge from a linear optimization model. This requires an understanding of both the optimal solution to the model and all its implications. A richer understanding of a problem is a much more useful result from a model than a computer printout of numbers.

In order to milk the most insight from a linear optimization model, the manager should be able to recognize, exploit, and remedy special situations that may occur during the solution of the model. The manager needs to understand how to interpret a sensitivity analysis of the optimal solution, and how resource allocation decisions implicitly place a price (or value) on scarce resources.

Special situations

The manager should be sufficiently familiar with linear programming to be able to exploit certain simple extensions in problem formulation. For example, if the solution indicates that an alternate optimal solution exists, it should be welcomed as providing additional flexibility and a further opportunity to exercise judgment. If there is no feasible solution then the manager must take action to acquire more resources or to modify the problem in some other way.

Sensitivity analysis

An understanding of the simplex algorithm is necessary to truly understand how the results of a sensitivity analysis are generated. Since these results are extremely important for managers, they should have confidence in their ability to interpret them properly.

Shadow prices indicate the value of a marginal unit of a resource, and the sensitivity analysis of the right-hand side of the constraints can determine the ranges over which these shadow prices are valid. The analysis of the objective function can be important in identifying coefficients to which the solution is especially sensitive. This identification may help focus effort on refining estimates of those coefficients to which the solution is extremely sensitive.

Duality

Duality theory offers an alternate interpretation of how the price or value of a scarce resource should be determined. The economic concepts behind this theory may aid a manager in intuitively assessing the value of resources even when no formal analysis is performed.

CHECK YOUR UNDERSTANDING

1. Solve the following problem graphically and by the simplex method:

maximize $Z = 25x + 50y$
subject to

$$2x + 4y \leq 80$$
$$3x + 2y \leq 60$$
$$x, y \geq 0$$

If an alternate optimal solution is indicated by the simplex tableau, find it by performing another iteration.

2. The computer input and solution for the linear optimization model

maximize $Z = 75x + 50y$
subject to

$$2x + 4y \leq 80$$
$$3x + 2y \leq 60$$
$$x, y \geq 0$$

are shown in Figure 6-6. Notice that the upper bound on the current objective function coefficient of y is 50. Can you relate this to the existence of an alternate optimal solution?

```
      LPENTER
ENTER THE NAME OF THIS PROJECT ALTERNATE SOLUTION
MAXIMIZE OR MINIMIZE: MAX
OBJECTIVE FUNCTION:Z=75X+50Y
ENTER CONSTRAINT EQUATIONS, (STRIKE JUST A CARRIAGE RETURN TO STOP INPUT)
 (1) 2X+4Y≤80
 (2) 3X+2Y≤60
 (3)
      LPRUN
                         ALTERNATE SOLUTION

THE OPTIMAL VALUE OF THE OBJECTIVE FUNCTION IS:    1500.000

                   THE VARIABLES IN THE SOLUTION ARE


VARIABLE   X      AT LEVEL       2.0000E1
           SLK1                  4.0000E1


DO YOU WISH SENSITIVITY ANALYSIS? YES

                        SHADOW       LB        CURRENT       UB
CONSTRAINT    1       0.0000E0    4.0000E1    8.0000E1    7.2370E75
              2       2.5000E1    0.0000E0    6.0000E1    1.2000E2

PRICE      X                      7.5000E1    7.5000E1    7.2370E75
           Y                     -7.2370E75   5.0000E1    5.0000E1
-> END <-
```

FIGURE 6-6
Alternate optimal solution (Exercise 2).

3. Explain why a manager might prefer one of two alternate optimal solutions.

4. Solve the following problem by the simplex method:

maximize $Z = 60x + 50y$
subject to

$$2x + 4y \le 80$$
$$3x + 2y \le 60$$
$$x \le 10$$
$$x, y \ge 0$$

Is the optimal solution degenerate? How do you know?

5. From a manager's point of view, what difference does it make if an optimal solution is degenerate?

```
     LPENTER
ENTER THE NAME OF THIS PROJECT DEGENERATE PROBLEM
MAXIMIZE OR MINIMIZE: MAX
OBJECTIVE FUNCTION:Z=60X+50Y
ENTER CONSTRAINT EQUATIONS, (STRIKE JUST A CARRIAGE RETURN TO STOP INPUT)
 (1) 4X+4Y≤80
 (2) 3X+2Y≤60
 (3)
    LPRUN
                    DEGENERATE PROBLEM

THE OPTIMAL VALUE OF THE OBJECTIVE FUNCTION IS:    1200.000

             THE VARIABLES IN THE SOLUTION ARE


VARIABLE  X        AT LEVEL      2.0000E1
          SLK2                   0.0000E0


DO YOU WISH SENSITIVITY ANALYSIS? YES

                   SHADOW        LB         CURRENT       UB
CONSTRAINT    1    1.5000E1   0.0000E0    8.0000E1    8.0000E1
              2    0.0000E0   6.0000E1    6.0000E1    7.2370E75

PRICE       X                 5.0000E1    6.0000E1    7.2370E75
            Y              -7.2370E75     5.0000E1    6.0000E1
-> END <-
```

FIGURE 6-7
Degenerate solution (Exercise 6).

6. The computer input and output for the linear optimization model

maximize $Z = 60x + 50y$
subject to

$$4x + 4y \leq 80$$
$$3x + 2y \leq 60$$
$$x, y \geq 0$$

are shown in Figure 6-7.

a. How do you recognize that the solution shown in Figure 6-7 is degenerate?

b. Analyze the problem graphically. Can you understand why a degenerate solution occurs?

c. Notice that the sensitivity analysis shown in Figure 6-7 indicates a "tight" upper bound on the first constraint and a "tight" lower bound on the second constraint. Relate this to your graphical analysis and explain whether you would expect tight bounds any time a degenerate solution occurs.

7. Suppose that a manager has formulated the linear optimization model shown in Table 6-5 that leads to an infeasible solution. What are the options available to the manager? What actions should be considered?

8. Solve the following problem graphically and by the simplex algorithm:

maximize $Z = 2x + 3y$
subject to

$$
\begin{aligned}
x + 2y &\le 10 \\
x &\ge 5 \\
y &\ge 6 \\
x, y &\ge 0
\end{aligned}
$$

Verify that the solution is infeasible.

9. Solve the following problem graphically and by the simplex algorithm:

maximize $Z = x + 2y$
subject to

$$
\begin{aligned}
x - y &\le 5 \\
-2x + y &\le 10 \\
x, y &\ge 0
\end{aligned}
$$

10. Suppose that a manager has formulated the linear optimization model given in Exercise 9. Why do we say that this problem was not formulated correctly? Can you think of any real-world problems that would be unbounded?

11. In analyzing the sensitivity of the cost coefficients of *nonbasic* variables in the objective function, suppose that the initial objective function that we are maximizing is $Z = 10x + 5y + (0)W_A + (0)W_B$. After all the simplex transformations, the equation representing row 0 in the final simplex tableau is $Z = (0)x + (0)y + 5W_A/17 + 30W_B/17 = 2900/17$.

If the contribution for W_A were increased from zero to $(0 + \Delta)$, what would the coefficient for W_A be in the objective function row (row 0) of the final tableau? If $\Delta = 1/2$, would the solution change?

12. Now, let us consider sensitivity analysis for the *basic* variables in the objective function indicated in Exercise 11. Suppose that an increment, Δ, is added to the contribution for y. The initial objective function becomes $Z = 10x + (5 + \Delta_y)y + (0)W_A + (0)W_B$. After we perform the simplex arithmetic transformations, the final row 0 is $Z = (0)x - \Delta_y y + (5W_A/17) + (30W_B/17) = 2900/17$. The simplex tableau at this stage of solution would then be

Z	x	y	W_A	W_B				
1	0	$-\Delta_y$	5/17	30/17	2900/17	Z	1	(row 0)
0	0	1	5/17	−4/17	180/17	y	5	(row 1)
0	1	0	−2/17	5/17	200/17	x	10	(row 2)

a. Is the solution still optimal? Why?
b. If the solution is not optimal, perform the necessary simplex iterations to make it optimal.
c. From b., what is the sensitivity of the basic variable y in the objective function; that is, what is the range in the value of the cost coefficients of y that will maintain the same final simplex solution?

13. In sensitivity analysis of the right-hand side constants of the constraints, why is it not always necessary to re-solve the initial tableau if an increment Δ is added to one of the right-hand side constants?

14. Suppose that the initial and final simplex tableaus for a problem were as follows:

Z	x	y	W_A	W_B			
Initial Tableau							
1	−10	−5	0	0	0	Z	1
0	4	5	1	0	100	W_A	0
0	5	2	0	1	80	W_B	0
Final Tableau							
1	0	0	5/17	30/17	2900/17	Z	1
0	0	1	5/17	−4/17	180/17	y	5
0	1	0	−2/17	5/17	200/17	x	10

a. Notice that the right-hand side constant limits resource A to 100 units. If resource A were increased to $100 + \Delta_A$, what is the range in the size of Δ_A that would keep the same basic variables in the solution shown in the final tableau?

b. What is the range in the value of the right-hand side of the resource A constraint?

c. What is the shadow price on resource A that is associated with the right-hand side range?

15. Compare the computer solutions in Figures 6-4 and 6-5. Notice that the lower and upper bounds on the constraints in Figure 6-4 are the lower and upper bounds on the prices in Figure 6-5, and vice versa. Can you rationalize why?

```
        LPENTER
ENTER THE NAME OF THIS PROJECT PRIMAL PROBLEM
MAXIMIZE OR MINIMIZE: MIN
OBJECTIVE FUNCTION:Z=3X-6Y
ENTER CONSTRAINT EQUATIONS, (STRIKE JUST A CARRIAGE RETURN TO STOP INPUT)
 (1) 8X+6Y≥15
 (2) 3X-Y≤12
 (3) X+Y=4
 (4)
        LPRUN
                        PRIMAL PROBLEM


THE OPTIMAL VALUE OF THE OBJECTIVE FUNCTION IS:    -24.000


                THE VARIABLES IN THE SOLUTION ARE


VARIABLE   Y        AT LEVEL      4.0000E0
           SUR1                   9.0000E0
           SLK2                   1.6000E1


DO YOU WISH SENSITIVITY ANALYSIS? YES

                        SHADOW        LB          CURRENT        UB
CONSTRAINT      1      0.0000E0    -7.2370E75    1.5000E1     2.4000E1
                2      0.0000E0    -4.0000E0     1.2000E1     7.2370E75
                3     -6.0000E0     2.5000E0     4.0000E0     7.2370E75

PRICE          X                  -6.0000E0     3.0000E0     7.2370E75
               Y                  -7.2370E75   -6.0000E0     3.0000E0
 -> END <-
```

FIGURE 6-8
Primal linear optimization model (Exercise 17).

16. Solve both the simplified chemical production problem and its dual problem by the simplex method. Verify the results shown in Figures 6-4 and 6-5, including the sensitivity analysis.

17. The computer solutions of a linear optimization problem and its dual problem are shown in Figures 6-8 and 6-9.
    a. Notice that the primal problem has only three constraints, but its dual problem has four variables. Why?
    b. The optimal values of the decision variables in Figure 6-8 are $x = 0$ and $y = 4$, but the shadow prices for the dual problem are 0 and -4. Why is the sign of the shadow price minus?
    c. What is the economic interpretation of the optimal solution for the dual problem shown in Figure 6-9?

```
        LPENTER
ENTER THE NAME OF THIS PROJECT DUAL PROBLEM
MAXIMIZE OR MINIMIZE: MAX
OBJECTIVE FUNCTION:Z=15P1-12P2-4P3+4P4
ENTER CONSTRAINT EQUATIONS, (STRIKE JUST A CARRIAGE RETURN TO STOP INPUT)
  (1) 8P1-3P2-P3+P4≤3
  (2) -6P1-P2+P3-P4≥6
  (3)
        LPRUN
                        DUAL PROBLEM


THE OPTIMAL VALUE OF THE OBJECTIVE FUNCTION IS:   -24.000


                    THE VARIABLES IN THE SOLUTION ARE


VARIABLE   P3      AT LEVEL      6.0000E0
           SLK1                  9.0000E0


DO YOU WISH SENSITIVITY ANALYSIS? YES

                        SHADOW       LB          CURRENT       UB
CONSTRAINT       1     0.0000E0   -6.0000E0     3.0000E0    7.2370E75
                 2    -4.0000E0    0.0000E0     6.0000E0    7.2370E75

PRICE         P1                 -7.2370E75    1.5000E1     2.4000E1
              P2                 -7.2370E75   -1.2000E1     4.0000E0
              P3                 -7.2370E75   -4.0000E0    -4.0000E0
              P4                 -7.2370E75    4.0000E0     4.0000E0
-> END <-
```

FIGURE 6-9
Dual linear optimization model
(Exercise 17).

PROBLEMS

18. Consider the following linear optimization model:

maximize $Z = 3x_1 + x_2 + 4x_3$
subject to

$$5x_1 + 3x_2 + 5x_3 \leq 25$$
$$4x_1 + 4x_2 + 4x_3 \leq 20$$
$$x_1, x_2, x_3 \geq 0$$

   a. Solve the linear optimization model by the simplex method. Did you encounter a degenerate problem?
   b. Write the dual linear optimization problem.
   c. Verify that the shadow prices for the constraints obtained in a. are the optimal solution to the dual problem formulated in b.

19. Consider the following linear optimization model:
maximize $Z = 3x_1 + 6x_2 + 2x_3$
subject to

$$3x_1 + 4x_2 + x_3 \leq 2 \qquad \text{(resource } A)$$
$$x_1 + 3x_2 + 2x_3 \leq 1 \qquad \text{(resource } B)$$
$$x_1, x_2, x_3 \geq 0$$

If you add W_A and W_B as slack variables, you have at the final iteration of the simplex method the following tableau:

Z	x_1	x_2	x_3	W_A	W_B			
1	0	0	1	3/5	6/5	12/5	Z	1
0	1	0	−1	3/5	−4/5	2/5	x_1	3
0	0	1	1	−1/5	3/5	1/5	x_2	6

   a. State the optimal values of the decision variables and the value of the objective function.
   b. Suppose that the number of units of resource A is increased to 3. What are the optimal values for each decision variable and the value of the objective function? (*Note:* Do not rework the problem. Use the techniques of sensitivity analysis.)

c. Suppose that the company can only guarantee that the price of x_3 is between 1.5 and 2.5. Should additional study be undertaken to determine the exact figure, or will the solution remain unchanged if the price of x_3 falls within this range? Show why.

d. Suppose that the company can purchase additional units of resource A at a cost of $0.75 per unit. Would this be a wise investment? Why or why not?

20. Consider the following linear optimization model:

maximize $Z = 4x + 6y$
subject to

$$
\begin{aligned}
x - y &\geq 5 \qquad \text{(constraint 1)} \\
2x + 3y &\leq 24 \qquad \text{(constraint 2)} \\
x, y &\geq 0
\end{aligned}
$$

After adding slack, excess, and artificial variables and performing *three* iterations of the simplex algorithm, we obtain

Z	x	y	S_1	U_1	W_2				
1	0	0	0	M	2	48	Z	1
0	1	0	−3/5	3/5	1/5	39/5	x	4
0	0	1	2/5	−2/5	1/5	14/5	y	6

a. State the optimal values of the variables and of the objective function.

b. Suppose that the right-hand side constant in constraint 1 is increased by 2 from 5 to 7 units. What are the optimal values of all the variables and of the objective function? (*Note:* Do not rework the problem; use the techniques of sensitivity analysis.)

c. The objective function row of the preceding result indicates that there is an *alternate optimal solution*. Perform *one more* iteration to discover an alternate optimal solution and indicate the resulting values of the variables and of the objective function.

d. Suppose that your accountant announces that the contribution of x has increased by 1 from 4 to 5. Will the optimal solution be affected? If so, calculate the new optimal values of all the variables and of the objective function. Use the tableau in the original statement of the problem rather than the one obtained in (c).

e. Write the dual linear optimization problem. What are the optimal values of the dual variables.

21. Refer to Tableaus I and III in Table 6-7, and answer the following question: What are the optimal values of the variables and of the objective function if the contribution of chemical x falls to only $20 per unit? Revise Tableau III and perform another iteration if necessary.

22. Mesa Plastics Company was formulated as Case 3-8 in Chapter 3 with computer input and output given. Using the simplex algorithm, we obtained the simplex tableau shown in Table 6-10. Use the methods of the simplex algorithm and of sensitivity analysis discussed in this chapter to answer the following questions:
   a. Identify the optimal solution.
   b. The last three constraints are demand constraints. If you could increase demand for one of the products by a concentrated advertising effort, which product would you choose? Why?
   c. If we expand capacity in one of the two plants, which one would we select? Why? How much should that plant be expanded at this price?
   d. In the optimal solution, all of size 2 is produced in plant B. The variable cost of producing 100 pounds of size 2 in plant B is $0.25 \times \$300 = \$75$. If we improve the efficiency of plant A for size 2, how low do the variable costs have to fall before we would want to produce size 2 in plant A? (Assume the sales revenue per 100 pounds for size 2 stays constant at $120.)

23. Use the initial and optimal tableaus shown in Table 5-9 of Chapter 5 to obtain the upper and lower bounds on the prices and the resources. Apply the methods of

TABLE 6-10   Simplex Tableau for Mesa Plastics

Z	x_{1A}	x_{1B}	x_{2A}	x_{2B}	x_{3A}	x_{3B}	W_A	W_B	W_1	W_2	W_3			
1	0	0	21.875	0	0	37.5	0	12.5	37.5	41.875	62.5	33,250	Z	1
0	0	0	0.0875	0	0	0.15	1	1.25	−0.25	−0.3125	−0.35	10	W_A	0
0	0	1	−1.25	0	0	2	0	5	0	−1.25	0	125	x_{1B}	40
0	1	0	1.25	0	0	−2	0	−5	1	1.25	0	185	x_{1A}	37.5
0	0	0	1	1	0	0	0	0	0	1	0	300	x_{2B}	45
0	0	0	0	0	1	1	0	0	0	0	1	125	x_{3A}	62.5

```
       LPENTER
ENTER THE NAME OF THIS PROJECT REQUIREMENTS
MAXIMIZE OR MINIMIZE: MAX
OBJECTIVE FUNCTION:Z=60X+50Y
ENTER CONSTRAINT EQUATIONS, (STRIKE JUST A CARRIAGE RETURN TO STOP INPUT)
 (1) 2X+4Y≤80
 (2) 3X+2Y≤60
 (3) X-Y≥15
 (4)
       LPRUN
                        REQUIREMENTS


THE OPTIMAL VALUE OF THE OBJECTIVE FUNCTION IS:    1230.000


             THE VARIABLES IN THE SOLUTION ARE


VARIABLE   X      AT LEVEL      1.8000E1
           Y                    3.0000E0
           SLK1                 3.2000E1


DO YOU WISH SENSITIVITY ANALYSIS? YES

                        SHADOW        LB        CURRENT       UB
CONSTRAINT      1     0.0000E0     4.8000E1    8.0000E1    7.2370E75
                2     2.2000E1     4.5000E1    6.0000E1    8.6667E1
                3    -6.0000E0    -5.0000E0    1.5000E1    2.0000E1

PRICE       X                    -5.0000E1    6.0000E1    7.5000E1
            Y                     4.0000E1    5.0000E1    7.2370E75
-> END <-
```

FIGURE 6-10
Computer solution with requirement constraints (Exercise 24).

sensitivity analysis discussed in this chapter. Check your answers with the sensitivity analysis given in the computer output shown in Figure 5-5 of Chapter 5.

24. Apply the methods of sensitivity analysis to the initial and optimal tableaus of the results shown in Table 5-10 of Chapter 5. Obtain the upper and lower bounds on prices and resources. Compare your answers with the computer output shown in Figure 6-10.

25. Consider the following linear optimization model:

minimize $Z = 4x + 2y$
subject to

$$4x + y \geq 12$$
$$2x - y = 0$$
$$x, y \geq 0$$

a. Analyze the problem graphically. What is the optimal solution?
b. Solve the problem by the simplex method. Notice that the initial solution is degenerate.
c. Write the dual linear optimization model. Verify that the shadow prices obtained in b. are the optimal solution to the dual problem.

CHAPTER 7

Network Models — Transportation and Transshipment

Network models are an important special case of linear optimization models for three reasons. First, many real-world problems can be modeled by using networks. Problems related to the determination of transportation and distribution systems are routinely solved in many organizations by this method. A special form of a network, known as the *transportation model,* takes its name from this use. A generalization of the transportation model is the *transshipment model,* that allows greater flexibility in the nature of the distribution system being analyzed. These models can also be used as aids in assigning workers to jobs. Other network models can be used to determine the longest or *shortest path* through a network. These models can be applied to determining equipment replacement policies and in scheduling activities in large-scale projects. The latter models include the network scheduling techniques PERT and CPM. This chapter presents the transportation and transshipment network models. The shortest path models are discussed in Chapter 8.

A second important feature of the network is that the model has a visual interpretation in addition to the mathematical formulation. The ability to visualize a network significantly reduces problems of communication between managers and technical analysts and among managers. Since one of the most important factors limiting the use of management science models by managers is their confidence in the model, this feature cannot be overemphasized.

Finally, the third advantage of the network is that the corresponding mathematical formulation has a special structure that allows extremely large problems to be solved very quickly by using specialized versions of the simplex algorithm for solving linear programming problems. The resulting low cost encourages the user to run the model many times to gain full advantage of it. An additional bonus is that integer-valued optimal solutions are obtained automatically. When a problem cannot be formulated as a network problem and an integer-valued solution is required, the additional computational effort can become quite burdensome, as we explain in Chapter 9.

These three advantages of network models — the large number of potential real-world applications, the visual interpretation, and an efficient solution strategy — are so important that the modern manager should be familiar with problems that can be analyzed with networks. Therefore, we present several examples of these models and concentrate on how they are formulated.

THE TRANSPORTATION MODEL

The transportation model is a special form of network optimization model that is routinely applied to problems of allocating the production from several factories to different warehouses or other distribution centers. The purpose of the model is to aid in selecting the most economical transportation routes for the required shipments. Such decisions must be made regularly in many large organizations. *This same model can also be used to analyze other problems with a similar mathematical structure that do not involve the selection of transportation routes.*

An introductory example

Suppose we have three different factories that can ship our product to three different retail outlets, as shown in Figure 7-1. The weekly capacity in terms of units produced varies among the factories as follows:

Factory	Supply (units/week)
(Chicago) 1	50
(New York) 2	70
(Dallas) 3	20

The average weekly shipment required by each retail outlet is

Outlet	Demand (units/week)
(Kansas City) 1	50
(Atlanta) 2	60
(Detroit) 3	30

However, the costs of shipping depend on which factories ship to which outlets, as the shipping distances vary. These costs are as follows:

From Factory	Per-Unit Costs to Outlet: 1	2	3
1	$ 3	$2	$ 3
2	10	5	8
3	1	3	10

As the table shows, factory 1 can ship one unit to outlet 2 for $2. Our problem is to determine how much should be shipped to where by whom.

Let us first consider whether this problem might be formulated as a linear optimization model. It is a *resource allocation problem,* since we are trying to allocate shipments of the product among nine different routes. Further, there are constraints on our decisions. We assume that we must meet the demand at each

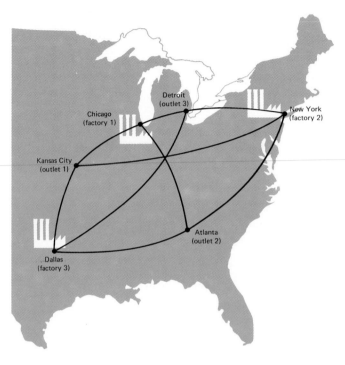

FIGURE 7-1
Geographical locations of factories
and retail outlets

retail outlet, and we cannot ship more than the available supply from each factory.

What are the decision variables? We are trying to determine how much to ship from each factory i ($i = 1, 2, 3$) to each retail outlet j ($j = 1, 2, 3$). Thus, it is convenient to use double subscripts and to denote our decision variables as x_{ij}, equaling the amount shipped from factory i to outlet j. If we discover that the optimum solution indicates $x_{31} = 20$, then 20 units should be shipped from factory 3 to outlet 1.

We can now write down our objective function. Using the data in the cost table, we wish to minimize

the total cost of
shipping from factory $1 = \quad 3x_{11} + 2x_{12} + \quad 3x_{13}$

plus the total cost of
shipping from factory $2 = 10x_{21} + 5x_{22} + \quad 8x_{23}$

plus the total cost of
shipping from factory $3 = \quad x_{31} + 3x_{32} + 10x_{33}$

Given specific values for the decision variables, this expression predicts the costs.

Next, we need the constraints on the decision variables. For factory 1, we must have $x_{11} + x_{12} + x_{13} \leq 50$, which says that the total amount shipped from factory 1 per week cannot exceed the weekly capacity of that factory. We have similar expressions corresponding to factories 2 and 3. Finally, for each retail outlet, we need a logical relationship that states that the total number of units shipped to the outlet each week is equal to the weekly demand. For outlet 2, we have $x_{12} + x_{22} + x_{32} = 60$. Two similar constraints can be determined for outlets 1 and 3. The six constraints, three for the factories and three for the retail outlets, along with the requirements that the decision variables cannot take on negative values, determine the set of feasible alternatives for our problem.

Thus, the linear optimization model appropriate for solving this problem is

minimize

$$3x_{11} + 2x_{12} + 3x_{13} + 10x_{21} + 5x_{22} + 8x_{23} + x_{31} + 3x_{32} + 10x_{33}$$

subject to

$$
\begin{aligned}
x_{11} + x_{12} + x_{13} & \qquad\qquad\qquad\qquad \leq 50 \\
x_{21} + x_{22} + x_{23} & \qquad\qquad \leq 70 \\
x_{31} + x_{32} + x_{33} & \leq 20 \\
x_{11} \qquad\qquad + x_{21} \qquad\qquad + x_{31} \qquad\qquad & = 50 \\
x_{12} \qquad\qquad + x_{22} \qquad\qquad + x_{32} \qquad & = 60 \\
x_{13} \qquad\qquad + x_{23} \qquad\qquad + x_{33} & = 30 \\
x_{ij} \geq 0, \; i = 1, 2, 3; \; j = 1, 2, 3
\end{aligned}
$$

Notice, however, that this model has a special form. The coefficients in the constraints of all the decision variables are equal to 1. Also, each decision variable appears in only two constraints. These characteristics suggest that a special version of the simplex method for solving linear optimization models may be applied to this problem — a version that is extremely efficient for solving models such as this one. Further, these same characteristics also indicate that the linear optimization model may be given a visual interpretation as a network.

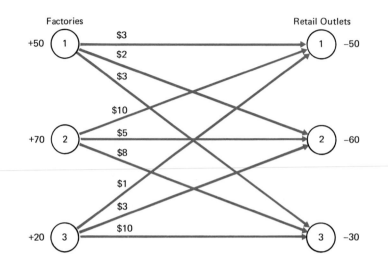

FIGURE 7-2
Network formu-
lation of the
transportation
problem

The network Now let us see how this same problem may be modeled as a network. Suppose we take the map in Figure 7-1 and rearrange it by placing all the factories on the left and all the outlets on the right. Rather than using pictures of the factories and outlets, we will use circles to represent each one. The routes between the factories and the outlets will be represented by arrows. This is illustrated in Figure 7-2.

Now we can write the number of units available at each factory with a plus sign in front of it, and the number of units required at each warehouse with a minus sign in front of it. The plus sign indicates that units are placed into the system at the corresponding circle, while the minus sign indicates that units are removed. Finally, we can write the cost per unit of shipping on each of the corresponding arrows. For example, the cost of shipping from factory 1 to outlet 3 is $3 per unit, which is written on the arrow from the factory circle 1 to the outlet circle 3 (see Figure 7-2).

Now look carefully at both the linear optimization formulation of this problem, and the diagram in Figure 7-2. Which do you understand more easily? Unless you are an extremely sophisticated mathematician, Figure 7-2 probably conveys more easily understood information than the mathematical relationships. This ability to portray the logic of the model graphically is one of the important advantages of network models. Thus, the problem of communication between a manager and an analyst is greatly simplified when network models are used.

More formally, the circles in Figure 7-2 are called *nodes,* and the arrows are called *arcs.* We will use these terms in the following discussion.

The Transportation Table
TABLE 7-1

To Outlet / From Factory	1 (Kansas City)	2 (Atlanta)	3 (Detroit)	Available at Factories
1 (Chicago)	3*	2	3	50
2 (New York)	10	5	8	70
3 (Dallas)	1	3	10	20
Required at Outlets	50	60	30	140

* Per unit cost ($) of shipping from factory to outlet.

The transportation table The information in Figure 7-2 can also be entered in a table especially suited for analyzing transportation problems, as shown in Table 7-1. There is one row for each factory, and one column for each outlet. The number of units available from the factory is written at the right of each row, and the number of units required at each outlet is written at the bottom of each column. Further, the costs are written in the small boxes; for example, the cost of shipping one unit from factory 2 to outlet 1 is $10.

We can now begin our analysis of this problem by writing down an initial solution as shown in Table 7-2. This alternative must satisfy the restrictions on capacity at each factory and the demand at each retail outlet. Further, since we are trying to minimize costs, we might start with factory 1. The cheapest means of shipping from factory 1 is to send units to outlet 2. Since we have 50 units available at factory 1, and outlet 2 requires 60, we can ship all 50 units from factory 1 to outlet 2. To fill the demand at outlet 2, we can ship an additional 10 units from factory 2. As luck would have it, this is also the cheapest route for shipping from factory 2 to any of the outlets.

TABLE 7-2   An Initial Solution

From Factory \ To Outlet	1 (Kansas City)		2 (Atlanta)		3 (Detroit)		Available at Factories
1 (Chicago)	(+1)	3	(−1)	2		3	50
			50				
2 (New York)	(−1)	10	(+1)	5		8	70
	30		10		30		
3 (Dallas)		1		3		10	20
	20						
Required at Outlets	50		60		30		140

So far so good. Now let us consider the remaining supply of units at factory 2 $(70 - 10 = 60)$. Since the demand at outlet 2 is satisfied, the next cheapest route for factory 2 is to ship to outlet 3, which requires 30 units. We can ship 30 units to outlet 3 and still have an additional 30 units of supply to ship to outlet 1.

Finally, consider factory 3. We are shipping 30 units from factory 2 to outlet 1, which has a demand of 50. The remaining demand $(50 - 30 = 20)$ is the supply at factory 3. Notice that shipping from factory 3 to outlet 1 is also the cheapest route, so this seems attractive.

As our initial solution in Table 7-2 shows, we began by shipping from factory 1 on the cheapest route and ended by shipping from factory 3 on the cheapest route. *The second was a matter of luck,* but it suggests that we may have found a good solution by using our intuition. Notice also that this solution satisfies the original set of constraints. We can easily check the solution by summing the entries in each row and in each column.

Using our objective function, we find the total cost of this alternative to be:

Units		Cost per Unit		
50	×	$ 2	=	$100
30	×	10	=	300
10	×	5	=	50
30	×	8	=	240
20	×	1	=	20
				$710

Now we consider whether the initial solution can be improved.

Improving the solution   To investigate the possibility of improving the solution, let us suppose we ship along the route from factory 1 to outlet 1. Just for the moment, suppose we ship only 1 unit along this route. We can indicate this shipment by placing a small +1 in the upper right-hand corner of the cell in the transportation table corresponding to factory 1 and outlet 1, as shown in Table 7-2. What does this additional unit do to our supply and demand constraints?

The supply at factory 1 is only 50 units, but this additional unit plus the 50 shipped from factory 1 to outlet 2 sum to 51. In order to observe this supply restriction of 50 units, let us reduce the number of units shipped from factory 1 to outlet 2 by 1 unit, and denote this by placing a −1 in the corresponding cell of the transportation table (Table 7-2).

However, when we remove 1 unit from the demand at outlet 2, we need to compensate. Notice that if we add 1 unit in row 2, column 2 of the transportation table and subtract 1 unit from row 2, column 1, all our original constraints on supplies and demands will be met. Thus, we again have a feasible solution, as shown in Table 7-2.

Now, in the cells with the +1s, we will incur additional costs of $3 + $5 = $8. However, the cells with −1s indicate savings since 1 less unit will be shipped in each. The savings from this trial solution are $2 + $10 = $12. Thus, we would incur an additional cost of $8 but a savings of $12, resulting in a *net* savings of $4 for each additional unit we ship from factory 1 to outlet 1. This fact suggests that a desirable *change* in the initial solution would be to increase the number of units shipped from factory 1 to outlet 1 from its initial value of 0 units.

We clearly want to ship as many units as possible on this route by shifting them away from the routes between factory 1 and outlet 2, and between factory 2 and outlet 1. How many units can we shift around? In the cells in Table 7-2 with the minus signs, we are removing units. We cannot remove more than 50 units from the route of factory 1 to outlet 2, or more than 30 units from the route of factory 2 to outlet 1. The smaller of these numbers is 30, so the most we can shift around is 30 units. This 30 units is the appropriate *amount of change* in the desirable direction. The results of a shift of 30 units are shown in Table 7-3. Notice that there are 30 additional units in each of the cells that have +1s in Table 7-2, and 30 fewer units in each cell with a −1. The net savings for this change is $4 (net savings/unit shifted) × 30 (units shifted) = $120.

What about other changes in the solution? Suppose one unit is shipped from factory 1 to outlet 3. You should verify, using the approach described above, that the net savings will be $2 per unit shifted. This time, the maximum number of units that can be shifted among transportation routes is 20. The new solution is shown in Table 7-4.

The result shown in Table 7-4 is actually the optimal solution to the problem, since no further improvements can be made by shifting units (check this yourself). The

TABLE 7-3   A Revised Solution

To Outlet / From Factory	1 (Kansas City)	2 (Atlanta)	3 (Detroit)	Available at Factories
1 (Chicago)	3 ⃝30	2 ⃝20	3	50
2 (New York)	10	5 ⃝40	8 ⃝30	70
3 (Dallas)	1 ⃝20	3	10	20
Required at Outlets	50	60	30	140

The Final Solution   TABLE 7-4

From Factory \ To Outlet	1 (Kansas City)	2 (Atlanta)	3 (Detroit)	Available at Factories
1 (Chicago)	3 (30)	2	3 (20)	50
2 (New York)	10	5 (60)	8 (10)	70
3 (Dallas)	1 (20)	3	10	20
Required at Outlets	50	60	30	140

search for further improvements corresponds to the "test for optimality" in the simplex method of solving linear optimization models. Notice also that all the shipments are integer-valued, although we did not specify this as a restriction.

The total cost of shipping according to this solution is as follows:

Units		Cost per Unit		
30	×	$3	=	$ 90
20	×	3	=	60
60	×	5	=	300
10	×	8	=	80
20	×	1	=	20
				$550

Thus, through a simple analysis, we have reduced the cost by $710 − $550 = $160. This represents a 22.5 percent cost reduction. Furthermore, our original solution was determined by using an apparently reasonable strategy, and the problem was relatively simple with only three factories and three outlets. The strategy we employed to improve the initial solution can be formalized as an algorithm. This algorithm and another example problem are presented in the appendix to this chapter.

In a much more realistic problem in terms of size, determining a good solution by hand would be much more difficult; however, the potential cost savings are even greater than in this example. These much larger problems can be solved efficiently using a modified version of the simplex method for linear programming.

Unequal supply and demand Suppose that the capacities at the three factories in this example had been 60, 80, and 30. Then the total potential supply of $60 + 80 + 30 = 170$ units is 30 more than the total demand of $50 + 60 + 30 = 140$ units. How do we adjust for the unequal supply and demand totals? We can define a "dummy" outlet with a demand equal to the difference between the total supply and the total demand; that is, with a demand of $170 - 140 = 30$ units. The cost of shipping from each factory to this "dummy" outlet will be zero. Naturally, any units assigned by our solution strategy to this nonexistent outlet would not actually be produced and shipped, which justifies the use of the zero costs. This process will help us in determining the appropriate production schedule in each factory. The resulting initial table, corresponding to Table 7-1, is shown in Table 7-5.

If the demand in a problem exceeds the supply, a similar strategy could be adopted by adding a "dummy" row with zero costs of shipping. These "dummy" shipping routes correspond to slack variables in the equivalent linear programming formulation of the problem.

The practical use of the transportation model

The transportation model is routinely used in determining transportation and distribution policies for many large organizations. When production capacity exceeds the demand for a product, this same model can also be used to determine the production schedule at each of the factories. Excellent discussions of the analysis of large distribution systems are provided by Geoffrion [1976] and by Zierer, Mitchell, and White [1976]. In actual practice, organizations may use these models on an annual or semiannual basis to revise their transportation and distribution policies.

One obvious limitation of the transportation model is that it assumes that the units to be shipped from each source to each destination are identical and interchangeable. However, many organizations have multiple products with different demands in the different market areas. It may not be appropriate to solve the distribution problem for

A Transportation Table With a Dummy Outlet
to Adjust for Unequal Total Supplies and Demands

TABLE 7-5

To Outlet / From Factory	1 (Kansas City)	2 (Atlanta)	3 (Detroit)	4 (Dummy)	Available at Factories
1 (Chicago)	3	2	3	0	60
2 (New York)	10	5	8	0	80
3 (Dallas)	1	3	10	0	30
Required at Outlets	50	60	30	30	170

each product independently of the others because it is cheaper per unit when large quantities are shipped on the same routes. The transportation problem with multiple products (the multicommodity problem) can be formulated mathematically, and algorithms for its solution have been proposed. However, the multicommodity problems cannot be represented by a network. Consequently, they are much harder to solve computationally and require much more computer time. For these reasons their practical usefulness is limited.

An alternative is to define a *standard commodity bundle* for the organization that represents a combination of the multiple products proportional to their respective market demands. This strategy works well when the relative market demands for the products do not differ significantly in each market area. For example, suppose a firm manufactures two products. The total demand for product 1 is 1500 units, while the total demand for product 2 is 500 units. Thus, product 1 outsells product 2 at a ratio of 3 to 1. Further, this sales proportion is relatively constant in each of the different market areas. Then the organization can solve its transportation and distribution problems by assuming a standard commodity bundle with a total demand of 1500 + 500 = 2000 units. Suppose the cost of shipping product 1 from a particular factory to a specific outlet is $2 per unit, while the cost of shipping product 2 from the same factory to the same outlet is $1 per unit. Then, the cost of shipping each unit of the standard commodity bundle from this factory to this outlet would be ($2) (0.75) + ($1) (0.25) = $1.75. The transportation model could then be applied to analyze this problem.

It is also possible to add lower and upper bounds on the number of units to be shipped along each route (or arc). For example, we might require that the number of units shipped from factory 1 to distribution center 2 be at least 30 but no more than 40. We could write these lower and upper bounds as the pair (30, 40), and place them next to the appropriate arc in the network. Mathematically, this corresponds to adding very simple constraints to the linear programming formulation of the problem. The simple form of these constraints means that they can be satisfied with little additional computational burden. When lower and upper bounds are placed on the routes, the resulting model is often called a *capacitated* transportation problem.

It is also important to recognize that an optimizing model, such as the transportation model, may be used to answer *what if* questions and to provide data for a more extensive analysis of a broader problem. For example, suppose a firm is currently producing a product at three different factories, each of which is operating at near capacity. Further, a market analysis shows that the demand for the product is expected to grow even higher over the next ten years before leveling off. The company may be trying to decide (1) whether or not to build a new factory, and (2) if so, in which of several alternate locations.

In order to analyze this problem, the company could estimate the total production and distribution costs associated with manufacturing the product in the three existing factories over the expected market life of the product. This estimate could be made by solving the transportation problem with the new market forecasts for each year in the estimated market life of the product and discounting the results to determine the equivalent present values of the costs. Next, the assumption could be made that a factory was built at one of the locations under consideration and the transportation problem could be re-solved for each of the years in the market life of the product, given this new factory. The estimated costs of producing and distributing with this new factory, plus the cost of constructing it, could then be compared with the cost of operating the existing factories, perhaps using overtime.

By repeating the analysis for the alternate sites under consideration, the cost implications of the various choices could be estimated. These results would play an important role in the determination of the new plant site, if a plant is to be built. Naturally, we recognize that the president of the company may still choose to construct a new plant in Columbus, Ohio, because he or she has relatives there, but at least the opportunity costs of such a decision would be clear.

THE TRANSSHIPMENT MODEL

Another limitation of the transportation model is the assumption that direct routes exist from each factory (or supply point) to each distribution center (or demand point). Again, in the real world, things are not always so simple. Major transportation routes actually pass through major distribution centers before going to smaller market areas.

Suppose we wish to redistribute goods among eight cities (the circled letters) as shown in Figure 7-3. The arrows, or arcs, indicate possible shipping routes. The arcs point in a specific direction indicating that goods can only be shipped along the route in that direction. In some cases, as for example between cities d and e, there are arcs pointing in two different directions indicating that goods can be shipped from e to d, or from d to e. The number associated with each city is the supply (plus) or demand (minus) at that location. For example, city a has a supply of 10, city c has a demand

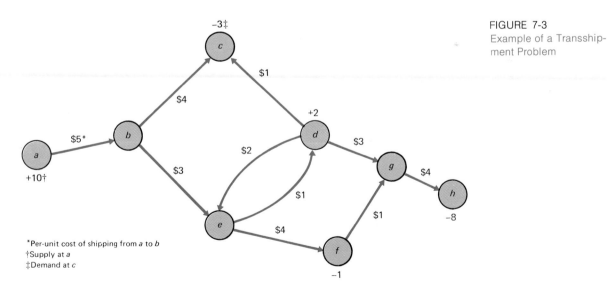

FIGURE 7-3
Example of a Transshipment Problem

*Per-unit cost of shipping from a to b
†Supply at a
‡Demand at c

of -3, and city *e* has neither a supply nor a demand. Notice that some cities may have goods shipped *through* them. These cities, *b, d, e, f,* and *g,* have arrows pointing into and out of them, and are called transshipment points.

A network such as this one that includes transshipment points is called a *transshipment problem.* As in the case of the transportation problem, the fact that the model can be represented as a network means that extremely efficient computer codes exist for its solution. Furthermore, there is a strong relationship between the mathematical structures of the transshipment and the transportation models. This relationship makes it possible to treat the transshipment problem as a transportation problem, and to develop a transportation table for it. The simple rules that allow this transformation of a transshipment problem into a transportation problem are omitted here, but they may be found in Wagner [1975].

AN EXAMPLE OF THE USE OF A NETWORK MODEL

We will now present an example of the actual use of a network model to aid in solving a real-world problem. This example illustrates the following points:

1. A network model may be used for problems other than those related to transportation and distribution issues.
2. Optimizing management science models can be successfully applied to problems in the public and not-for-profit sectors.
3. The visual interpretation of a network model is an important advantage in communicating its logic to individuals who have not been formally exposed to management science techniques.
4. The computational advantage of a particular model formulation can significantly enhance its practical usefulness.
5. An optimizing model does not always "solve" the problem, but it can be a helpful aid to the decision maker.

The problem is the assignment of faculty members to courses during the three quarters of an academic year. The particular implementation we describe took place in the Graduate School of Management (GSM) at UCLA (for further details, see Dyer and Mulvey [1976]).

The faculty/course scheduling problem is complicated by the lack of a clearly defined objective to serve as a guide for the solution process. The preferences of the faculty members must be balanced against the needs and desires of the students, while administrative policies and resource constraints must also be considered. Even these constraints are "loose," and some may be recognized only as the solution evolves.

How can one go about formulating an optimizing model for aiding a decision maker in analyzing a problem such as this one? First, the model builder may look for analogies with more familiar models. For example, one might note that each faculty member teaches a specific number of courses per academic year (usually five quarter courses per year at GSM). Thus, a typical faculty member might be viewed as "supplying" five course section equivalents, one unit of which is defined as the time and effort equal to the actual teaching of one course section. Further, each course "demands" one course section equivalent for each section that is to be offered. Thus, if three sections of course MGT 240 are to be offered during the year, the annual demand is three course section equivalents. This analogy suggests that the problem might be modeled as a transportation problem, with each faculty member being represented as a supply point that supplies course section equivalents into the system, and with each course viewed as a demand point that takes course section equivalents out of the system. An arc from a particular faculty member to a particular course would indicate that the faculty member could teach that course. Otherwise, the arc would be omitted.

In addition, the courses are taught over three quarters, and the schedule must be determined by quarters. Thus, the analogy went further. The quarters could be viewed as transshipment points, with the course section equivalents of the faculty "shipped" through particular quarters to corresponding quarter transshipment points for the courses. The network model that resulted from this analogy is shown in Figure 7-4 for a department with two faculty and three courses.

The flow on the arcs of the network is in course section equivalents. The nodes in the network are either faculty or course related. For each faculty member, there are up to four nodes corresponding to the annual, fall, winter, and spring schedules. However, if a faculty member is not teaching during a particular quarter, the corresponding node is deleted. There are similar sets of nodes for the courses. Figure 7-5 portrays several examples of how lower and upper bounds of the flows on the arcs can be useful in achieving various objectives. As illustrated in Figure 7-5(a), the total number of course sections to be offered by teaching assistants during the year is restricted to between 20 and 30. However, any one quarter cannot have more than 15 course sections offered by teaching assistants because of the capacity restrictions of the other arcs.

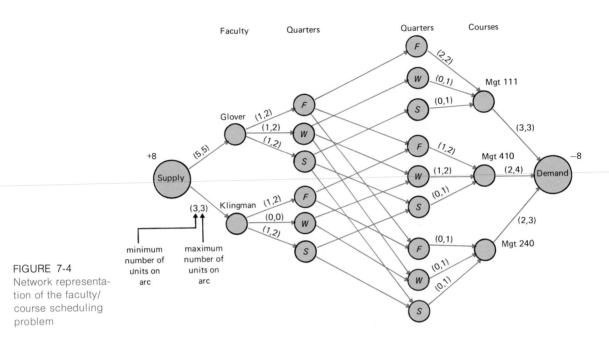

FIGURE 7-4
Network representation of the faculty/course scheduling problem

Similar restrictions determine the number of offerings of the courses. For example, MGT 200A will be offered either two or three times during the academic year as shown in Figure 7-5(b). One section will be offered during the fall as indicated by the corresponding minimum and maximum flow restrictions of one. At least one section will be offered during the spring quarter, and a third section *may* be offered during either the winter or the spring. The determination of whether this third section will actually be offered, and during which of the two quarters, will be made by the model, based on the availability of faculty resources. Thus, the user is able to incorporate many options within the context of a simple network model. Further, this visual interpretation makes it easy to convey the logic of the model to actual users.

The desires of the faculty members receive consideration in the model in two ways. Subject to administrative policies, a faculty member may determine the number of courses he or she will teach each quarter by manipulating the lower and upper bounds of the flow restrictions as illustrated in Figure 7-5(c). Jones will be assigned all five of her courses in the fall and winter and be free from formal teaching duties in the spring. In addition, the optimization in the model is carried out with respect to the "preference weights" of the faculty members for teaching the various courses. These preference weights range from -2 to $+2$, and are assigned by the faculty members.

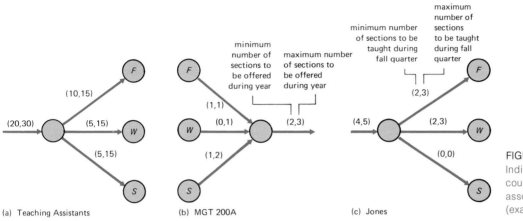

FIGURE 7-5
Individual faculty/
course nodes and
associated arcs
(examples)

Thus, it would appear that the evaluation model for this formulation is "maximize faculty happiness." However, it was assumed that the objective of maximizing faculty "happiness" and student "satisfaction" are complementary. Faculty members generally prefer teaching courses that are consistent with their professional abilities and teaching styles. Similarly, students generally prefer instructors who are enthusiastic about a course and its contents. While there may be some exceptional cases, it was not felt that these occurrences justify the burden of collecting additional information beyond simple expressions of faculty preference. In addition, information concerning the needs and desires of the students can be used to determine the lower and upper bounds on the number of sections of each course offered per academic year, and by quarter.

This network formulation is extremely attractive from a computational standpoint. The current costs of solving this model for GSM (with approximately 1000 nodes and 4500 arcs*) is in the range of $0.50 to $1 for the optimization, and $4 to $7 for a complete run, including input and output charges. Prior to recent developments in the field of network optimization, the cost of solving the same model would have been approximately $50 per run, which would have greatly inhibited its usefulness. The advantage of this low cost encourages the scheduler to make use of the model much more freely.

* Note that each arc in a network corresponds to a variable in the equivalent linear programming formulation.

Although a number of considerations relevant to the faculty/course scheduling problem can be incorporated into this network model, and it has an obvious computational advantage, this formulation is only a crude approximation to the "ideal" model that would actually solve the scheduling problem in a single run. Therefore, the actual solution strategy for the problem is iterative, with the model producing a "first cut," an approximate solution that must be modified by the decision maker to include more subtle issues not considered in the model.

We emphasize again that a model need not be sufficiently detailed to "solve" a problem in a single computer run in order to be useful. Instead, managers should view it as a decision-making aid that efficiently does much of the required computational work for them, but must be used intelligently to actually provide some benefit.

WHAT SHOULD THE MANAGER KNOW?

Network models are among the most practical and useful management science models because they have many advantageous characteristics.

1. Many real-world problems can be formulated with network models.
2. The visual interpretation of the network reduces the problem of communication between the manager and the analyst.
3. Efficient computer codes are available to analyze the networks, and integer valued solutions are obtained automatically.

These advantages enhance the practical usefulness of the transportation and transshipment models.

Problem characteristics

The transportation and transshipment models may be applied to problems that require the allocation of units from sources of supply to sources of demand. The most obvious examples of such problems are the product distribution problems of large organizations. Certainly these models have been used to advantage for analyzing such problems in many instances. In addition, by solving transportation or transshipment problems several times for new facilities located on alternate sites, the problem of locating new facilities can also be analyzed.

It is also possible to use this model to assign workers to tasks, as illustrated in the description of the actual application of this methodology to the problem of faculty/

course scheduling. This methodology is the basis for assigning military manpower to different jobs, as described by Charnes, Cooper, Niehaus and Sholtz [1970], and assigning workers to shifts as described by Segal [1974].

Thus, if the manager is studying any problem and recognizes that the task is to allocate units of a resource from sources of supply to sources of demand, he or she should consider formulating the problem with a transportation or transshipment model.

Formulation and information requirements

The formulation of large-scale transportation and transshipment problems will probably be the responsibility of an analyst with specialized skills in management science. However, the visual interpretation of these models makes it easy for the manager to get involved in this task and to be satisfied that the logic of the model is correct. This involvement on the part of the manager significantly reduces the problem of validating the model.

The information requirements are the shipping costs per unit on each route, the supply capacities at the supply points, and the demands. These demands may be market demands, which are based on market surveys or other marketing estimates. Sensitivity analysis can be used to determine if the solution is particularly sensitive to changes in any one of these estimates. Then, when changes occur in the estimates, the sensitivity analysis can be used to determine whether a new solution needs to be calculated, or what the potential costs of *not* changing an existing distribution policy actually are.

Computational considerations

The computational advantage of the network formulation is significant. Table 7-6 shows the time required to solve several transshipment problems on a CDC 6600 computer and gives an estimate of the costs of solving these problems based on computer charges of $0.04 per second [Mulvey, 1975]. A transportation problem with 8000 nodes would require a transportation table with a total of 8000 rows and columns. Yet it is possible to solve such a problem in approximately 80.5 seconds on a large computer at an estimated cost of $3.22. This result is not only of interest to technical analysts. The important practical implication is that the manager can use such a model freely once it has been formulated. Making 50 different runs to explore *what if* questions under various scenarios would cost only $161. The potential savings

TABLE 7-6

Solution Times and Costs for
Large Transshipment Problems

Problem	No. of Nodes	No. of Arcs	Solution Time[a] (seconds)	Solution Cost[b]
1	8000	15,000	80.5	$3.22
2	5000	23,000	80	3.20
3	3000	35,000	63	2.52
4	5000	15,000	51	2.04
5	3000	23,000	37.5	1.50

[a] On a CDC 6600.

[b] Assuming $0.04 per second.

from such analyses can run into millions of dollars (for examples see Geoffrion [1976] and Glover, Hultz, and Klingman [1978, 1979]).

One of the problems in Table 7-6 includes 35,000 arcs. Recall that an arc corresponds to a variable in a linear programming formulation. Can you imagine keypunching in the data for this problem! Naturally, special computer programs called *matrix generators* have been written to develop the input data for problems of this size.

In order to emphasize again the power of these solution methods, we suggest that when you are solving a transportation problem by hand with a total of 8 or 10 rows *and* columns and perhaps 16 variables, you should take a second look at the solution times and costs in Table 7-6.

Advantages and disadvantages of the model

The advantages of the transportation and transshipment models have been discussed. The only disadvantage is that they are somewhat restricted in the amount of problem detail that can be incorporated. Some important logic in a problem may not lend itself to formulation in the network format. This situation occurred in the faculty/ course scheduling problem, but the computational advantage of the network formulation suggested that a man-machine solution strategy would be successful. The network model could be used to provide an "approximate" solution, that could then be adjusted by hand to determine the final solution. This same strategy might be of value in other practical situations.

APPENDIX TO CHAPTER 5
THE TRANSPORTATION ALGORITHM

In this appendix, we will provide one algorithm for solving transportation problems by hand. This algorithm is presented to emphasize that the special structure of the transportation problem makes its solution much easier than ordinary linear programming problems. While other more efficient algorithms for solving transportation problems by hand are available, they are more complex conceptually. Since the chances that you will ever have to solve a real-world transportation problem by hand are remote, we have selected this particular algorithm because of its intuitive appeal. For reasons that will become apparent as you study the algorithm, it is called the "stepping-stone method" for solving transportation problems. Details regarding alternate solution strategies are provided in Dantzig [1963] and Wagner [1975].

The problem A company with factories at cities A and B supplies warehouses at cities C, D, E, and F. Monthly factory capacities are 150 at A and 200 at B. If overtime production is utilized, the capacities can be increased to 250 at A and 300 at B. Incremental unit overtime costs are \$5 at A and \$3 at B. Contributions to profit and overhead per unit excluding shipping costs are \$14 at A and \$16 at B for regular production. The current monthly warehouse requirements are 110 at C, 70 at D, 160 at E, and 130 at F. Unit shipping costs are as follows:

	To:			
From	C	D	E	F
A	\$3	\$4	\$5	\$7
B	5	8	3	4

Notice that the total monthly capacity with overtime is $250 + 300 = 550$, while the total demand is only $110 + 70 + 160 + 130 = 470$. Thus, the questions are: How much should be produced during regular production? How much should be produced during overtime at each factory? To which warehouses should the units be shipped?

Unequal supply and demand Each factory is a source of supply with a regular capacity at one contribution to profit per unit and an overtime capacity at another contribution to profit per unit. Thus, we can define two rows in a transportation table for each factory, corresponding to regular and overtime capacity respectively. For example, the "supply" for factory A operating at regular production capacity is 150 units, while the overtime "supply" of factory A is $250 - 150 = 100$ units. We label the row in the transportation table corresponding to regular production as AR, and the row corresponding to overtime production as *AO*. Similarly we define two rows for factory *B*.

We have a column in the transportation table corresponding to each warehouse. However, how do we adjust for the fact that the total supply capacity of 550 units does not equal the total demand of 470 units? To account for this fact, we define a "dummy" warehouse with a demand equal to the difference between the total supply and the total demand; that is, with a demand of $550 - 470 = 80$ units. The cost of shipping from each factory to this "dummy" warehouse will be zero.

To complete the information for the transportation table, we need the costs of shipping. However, in this example, we actually have the contribution to profit and overhead per unit at each factory, and these values should be taken into account. For example, units produced at factory *A* and shipped to warehouse *C* will bring a net contribution of $14 - $3 = 11 if produced during regular hours, and $11 - $5 = 6 if produced during overtime. The transportation table for this problem is shown in Table 7-7.

To facilitate the discussion of the algorithm, we have labeled the cells in the transportation table in the upper left-hand corner, as shown in Table 7-7. For example, the cell *AO, D* corresponds to a shipment of units made during overtime in plant *A* to warehouse *D*.

The algorithm

We now present an algorithm for solving this problem. This algorithm is simply a formal presentation of the logic used in solving the example problem presented earlier in the chapter. In order to be effective, the algorithm must determine the following:

1. An initial solution
2. A test for improvement
3. A means of improving the solution

We will now consider each of these requirements.

An initial solution The simplest approach to obtaining an initial solution is to ignore the distribution costs (or contributions to profit and overhead as in this example). This initial solution is obtained by the following step-by-step procedure, sometimes called the northwest corner rule.

> STEP 1. Start allocating supply to demand in the upper left-hand corner (the northwest corner) of the transportation table.

The Transportation Table With a Dummy Warehouse   TABLE 7-7

To Warehouse / From Factory	C		D		E		F		Dummy (Dum)		Available at Factories
AR (regular)	AR,C	11*	AR,D	10	AR,E	9	AR,F	7	AR, Dum	0	150
AO (overtime)	AO,C	6	AO,D	5	AO,E	4	AO,F	2	AO, Dum	0	100
BR (regular)	BR,C	11	BR,D	8	BR,E	13	BR,F	12	BR, Dum	0	200
BO (overtime)	BO,C	8	BO,D	5	BO E	10	BO,F	9	BO, Dum	0	100
Required at Outlets	110		70		160		130		80		550

* Net contribution to profit and overhead.

STEP 2. Allocate as many units as possible while observing the restrictions on total supply for the row and on total demand for the column.

STEP 3. If the demand in the column is met, move to the right to the cell in the next column. Go to step 2.

STEP 4. If the supply for the row is exhausted, move down to the cell in the next row. Go to step 2.

Applying these rules to Table 7-8, we begin with cell AR, C (step 1), and we see that factory A operating at regular capacity has 150 units available, while warehouse C

TABLE 7-8   Initial Solution by the Northwest Corner Rule

To Warehouse / From Factory	C		D		E		F		Dummy (Dum)		Available at Factories
AR (regular)	AR,C	11	AR,D	10	AR,E	9	AR,F	7	AR, Dum	0	150
	(110)		(40)								
AO (overtime)	AO,C	6	AO,D	5	AO,E	4	AO,F	2	AO, Dum	0	100
			(30)		(70)						
BR (regular)	BR,C	11	BR,D	8	BR,E	13	BR,F	12	BR, Dum	0	200
					(90)		(110)				
BO (overtime)	BO,C	8	BO,D	5	BO,E	10	BO,F	9	BO, Dum	0	100
							(20)		(80)		
Required at Outlets	110		70		160		130		80		550

AR,C: 11 × 110 = 1210	BR,E : 13 × 90 = 1170
AR,D: 10 × 40 = 400	BR,F : 12 × 110 = 1320
AO,D: 5 × 30 = 150	BO,F : 9 × 20 = 180
AO,E: 4 × 70 = 280	BO,Dum: 0 × 80 = ___0
	4710

requires 110. We assign 110 units from *AR* to *C*, and circle this number, completing step 2. We have met the demand at *C*, so we move to the right under column *D* (step 3), and assign the balance of the supply from *AR*, 40 units, to *D* (step 2). Now that the supply has been exhausted, we drop down to row *AO* (step 4), and assign the balance of *D*'s requirement, 30 units, from the overtime capacity at factory *A* (step 2). We continue in this fashion, stair-stepping down the table until all of the assignments have been made, as shown in Table 7-8. The total contribution associated with this solution, $4710, is also calculated in Table 7-8 by multiplying the

number of units shipped to each warehouse from each factory using regular or over-time production, by the appropriate net contribution per unit.

Notice that the application of the northwest corner rule determines a solution that satisfies the restrictions on supply and demand at each factory and at each warehouse. Thus, the solution is feasible. Also, there are four rows and five columns in Table 7-8. The number of cells in the table with assignments is $4 + 5 - 1 = 8$. In general, if n is the number of rows in a transportation table, and m is the number of columns, we want $n + m - 1$ assignments in the table. Otherwise, we call the solution *degenerate*, and we discuss special procedures for dealing with degenerate solutions later in this appendix.

According to this initial solution, the regular and overtime capacities of factory A will be utilized completely. However, the 80 units in cell *BO, Dum* indicates that the overtime capacity of factory B is not completely utilized. The 20 units actually produced during overtime at factory B are shipped to warehouse F (cell *BO, F*).

A test for improvement Is the initial northwest corner solution in Table 7-8 the best possible solution? We can answer this question by examining each of the open cells in the transportation table to determine whether it would be better to move some of the units into it. In doing so, we want to be sure that any new solution satisfies the supply and demand restrictions shown in the right column and in the bottom row in the transportation table.

In evaluating each open cell, the following steps are used:

STEP 1. Determine a closed path, starting at the open cell being evaluated, and "stepping" from cells with assignments back to the original cell. Right angle turns in this path are permitted only at cells with assignments and at the original open cell. Since only the cells at the turning points are considered to be on the closed path, both open and assigned cells may be skipped over.

STEP 2. Beginning at the cell being evaluated, assign a plus, then alternate minus and plus signs at the assigned cells on the corner points of the path.

STEP 3. Add the unit costs in the squares with plus signs, and subtract the unit costs in the squares with minus signs. If we are minimizing costs (maximizing profits), the result is the net change in the cost (profit) per unit from the changes made in the assignments.

STEP 4. Repeat this procedure for each open cell in the transportation table.

TABLE 7-9   Closed Path for *AR,E* and Cell Evaluations

To Warehouse / From Factory	C		D		E		F		Dummy (Dum)		Available at Factories
AR (regular)	AR,C	11	AR,D	10	AR,E	9	AR,F	7	AR, Dum	0	150
	(110)		(40) (−)		(+) 0		−1		+1		
AO (overtime)	AO,C	6	AO,D	5	AO,E	4	AO,F	2	AO, Dum	0	100
	0		(30) (+)		(70) (−)		−1		+6		
BR (regular)	BR,C	11	BR,D	8	BR,E	13	BR,F	12	BR, Dum	0	200
	−4		−6		(90)		(110)		−3		
BO (overtime)	BO,C	8	BO,D	5	BO,E	10	BO,F	9	BO, Dum	0	100
	−4		−6		0		(20)		(80)		
Required at Outlets	110		70		160		130		80		550

Steps 1 and 2 correspond to the intuitively appealing strategy of assigning a single unit to the open square, then adjusting the shipments in the squares with assignments until all the row supply and column demand constraints are satisfied. Step 3 simply calculates the cost (or contribution to profit) that would result from such a modification in the assignments.

If the net changes are all greater than or equal to 0, and if we are minimizing costs, or if they are all less than or equal to 0, and we are maximizing profits, we have found an optimal solution.

The application of these steps to the open square *AR, E* is shown in Table 7-9. Notice that the closed path forms a simple rectangle. The net change associated with a single unit being shipped from factory *A* using regular capacity to warehouse *E* is

Closed Path for Cell *BO,C*   TABLE 7-10

To Warehouse / From Factory	C		D		E		F		Dummy (Dum)		Available at Factories
AR (regular)	AR,C (−) (110)	11	AR,D (+) (40)	10	AR,E	9	AR,F	7	AR, Dum	0	150
AO (overtime)	AO,C	6	AO,D (−) (30)	5	AO,E (+) (70)	4	AO,F	2	AO Dum	0	100
BR (regular)	BR,C	11	BR,D	8	BR,E (−) (90)	13	BR,F (+) (110)	12	BR, Dum	0	200
BO (overtime)	BO,C (+) −4	8	BO,D	5	BO,E	10	BO,F (−) (20)	9	BO, Dum (80)	0	100
Required at Outlets	110		70		160		130		80		550

$$9 - 4 + 5 - 10 = 0.$$

This value is written in the bottom left-hand corner of cell *AR, E* in Table 7-9. The net changes in profit for all of the open cells are also shown in Table 7-9.

The evaluation of all open squares is not so easy. For example, the closed path for evaluating cell *BO, C* is shown in Table 7-10, and the net change is

$$8 - 9 + 12 - 13 + 4 - 5 + 10 - 11 = -4$$

Since we are trying to maximize profits in this example, this would not be a desirable cell in which to switch some units.

Improving the solution Each negative net change indicates the amount by which the total solution will be reduced if one unit were shipped in the corresponding cell, while each positive net change indicates the amount by which it will be increased.

Notice that in Table 7-9, two open cells, *AR* to the dummy warehouse and *AO* to the dummy warehouse, have positive net changes. Which one should we choose in determining the new solution? One reasonable rule for small problems and hand solutions is always to select the one with the most negative (if minimizing costs) or the most positive net change (if maximizing profits). Therefore, we choose the cell *AO, Dum.*

To improve the solution, carry out the following steps:

STEP 1. Identify again the closed path for the chosen open cell, and assign the plus and minus signs as before. Determine the minimum number of units assigned to a cell on this path that is marked with a minus sign.

STEP 2. Add this number to the open cell and to all other cells on the path marked with a plus sign. Subtract this number from cells on the path marked with a minus sign.

The closed path for *AO, Dum* is + *AO, Dum* − *BO, Dum* + *BO, F* − *BR, F* + *BR, E* − *AO, E.* The minimum number of units in a cell with a minus sign is the 70 in *AO, E.* Thus, we add 70 units to cells *AO, Dum; BO, F;* and *BR, E,* and subtract 70 units from cells *BO, Dum; BR, F;* and *AO, E.* This reassignment of units determines a new alternative, as shown in Table 7-11. This new solution corresponds to switching 70 units from overtime production in factory *A* to overtime production in factory *B.*

Now we repeat the process for the evaluation of each unused cell. The results are also shown in Table 7-11. The cells with the largest net change are *BR, C* and *BO, C.* Since these net changes are equal, suppose we arbitrarily choose cell *BR, C,* and improve the solution again. The result, shown in Table 7-12, again corresponds to switching some additional units from overtime production at factory *A* to overtime production in factory *B.*

The evaluation of the open cells in Table 7-12 reveals that there are no positive net changes, so there are no switches in shipments that will lead to a further improvement in the solution. Therefore, this is an *optimal solution* to the problem. The total incremental contribution to profit and overhead associated with this solution is $5150, as calculated in Table 7-12. This compares with the total incremental contribution of $4710 associated with the initial solution, for an increase of $440, or approximately 9 percent.

New Solution (First Iteration)

TABLE 7-11

To Warehouse / From Factory	C		D		E		F		Dummy (Dum)		Available at Factories
AR (regular)	AR,C (110)	11	AR,D (40)	10	AR,E −6	9	AR,F −7	7	AR, Dum −5	0	150
AO (overtime)	AO,C 0	6	AO,D (30)	5	AO,E −6	4	AO,F −7	2	AO, Dum (70)	0	100
BR (regular)	BR,C +2	11	BR,D 0	8	BR,E (160)	13	BR,F (40)	12	BR, Dum −3	0	200
BO (overtime)	BO,C +2	8	BO,D 0	5	BO,E 0	10	BO,F (90)	9	BO, Dum (10)	0	100
Required at Outlets	110		70		160		130		80		550

Alternate optimal solutions

The fact that open cells AO, C; BO, C; and BO, E have zero evaluations in Table 7-12 is important, and gives us flexibility in determining the final plan of action. These zero evaluations allow us to generate other solutions that have the same total net contribution as the optimal solution shown in Table 7-12. For example, since open cell AO, C has a zero evaluation, we may make the shifts in assignments as indicated by its closed path and generate the alternate optimal solution shown in Table 7-13. The managerial implication of this result is that in the optimal solution, a total of 150 units should be produced using regular capacity at factory A, while an additional 20 units should be produced on overtime at factory A. Of this total of 170 units, 100 should be shipped to warehouse C, and 70 units should be shipped to warehouse D.

TABLE 7-12   An Optimal Solution

To Warehouse / From Factory	C		D		E		F		Dummy (Dum)		Available at Factories
AR (regular)	AR,C (100)	11 (−)	AR,D (+) (50)	10	AR,E −4	9	AR,F −5	7	AR, Dum −5	0	150
AO (overtime)	AO,C (+) 0	6	AO,D (−) (20)	5	AO,E −4	4	AO,F −5	2	AO, Dum 80	0	100
BR (regular)	BR,C (10)	11	BR,D −2	8	BR,E (160)	13	BR,F (30)	12	BR, Dum −5	0	200
BO (overtime)	BO,C 0	8	BO,D −2	5	BO,E 0	10	BO,F (100)	9	BO, Dum −2	0	100
Required at Outlets	110		70		160		130		80		550

```
AR,C   : 11 × 100 = 1100      BR,C: 10 ×  11 =  110
AR,D   : 10 ×  50 =  500      BR,E: 13 × 160 = 2080
AO,D   :  5 ×  20 =  100      BR,F: 12 ×  30 =  360
AO,Dum:  0 ×  80 =    0       BO,F:  9 × 100 =  900
                                              5150
```

As the alternate optimal solution indicates, it makes no difference in the total contribution of the solution whether the 20 units produced on overtime are shipped to C or D. Give your own interpretation of the managerial implications of the alternate optimal solutions afforded by the zero evaluations in open cells BO, C and BO, E.

Degeneracy

If n is the number of rows, and m is the number of columns in a transportation table, we want $n + m - 1$ assignments in the table. A solution with fewer than $n + m - 1$

An Alternate Optimal Solution

TABLE 7-13

To Warehouse / From Factory	C		D		E		F		Dummy (Dum)		Available at Factories
AR (regular)	AR,C	11	AR,D	10	AR,E	9	AR,F	7	AR, Dum	0	150
	(80)		(70)								
AO (overtime)	AO,C	6	AO,D	5	AO,E	4	AO,F	2	AO, Dum	0	100
	(20)								(80)		
BR (regular)	BR,C	11	BR,D	8	BR,E	13	BR,F	12	BR, Dum	0	200
	(10)				(160)		(30)				
BO (overtime)	BO,C	8	BO,D	5	BO,E	10	BO,F	9	BO, Dum	0	100
							(100)				
Required at Outlets	110		70		160		130		80		550

assignments is called a *degenerate solution*. Such a solution may arise when the rules for improving the solution are applied, or even in determining an initial solution by the northwest corner rule.

An example in Table 7-14 shows that a degenerate solution will arise if the rule for improving the solution is followed by shifting the minimum number of units in a cell marked with a minus sign. This minimum number, 80, occurs in two cells, *AO, E* and *BO, Dum*.

Note that the problem in Table 7-14 is only a slight modification of the problem we have been using. The overtime capacity of factory *A* and the demand at warehouse *E* have each been increased by 10 units. Otherwise, the northwest corner rule was applied to determine the initial solution as before.

TABLE 7-14 Transportation Table Where Degeneracy Will Occur

To Warehouse / From Factory	C		D		E		F		Dummy (Dum)		Available at Factories
AR (regular)	AR,C	11	AR,D	10	AR,E	9	AR,F	7	AR, Dum	0	150
	(110)		(40)								
AO (overtime)	AO,C	6	AO,D	5	AO,E	4	AO,F	2	AO, Dum	0	110
			(30)		(80) (−)				(+) +6		
BR (regular)	BR,C	11	BR,D	8	BR,E	13	BR,F	12	BR, Dum	0	200
					(90) (+)		(110) (−)				
BO (overtime)	BO,C	8	BO,D	5	BO,E	10	BO,F	9	BO, Dum	0	100
							(20) (+)		(80) (−)		
Required at Outlets	110		70		170		130		80		560

When the shift of 80 units occurs, the assignments in cells *AO, E* and *BO, Dum* both go to 0, as shown in Table 7-15. We have only 7 assignments in Table 7-15 rather than the $4 + 5 - 1 = 8$ assignments we obtain in a nondegenerate solution. The practical effect is that several of the open cells in Table 7-15 cannot be evaluated in the usual way since a closed path cannot be established for them. For example, try to devise a closed path for evaluating cell *AR, E.*

The degeneracy can be resolved, however, by regarding one of the two cells where assignments have disappeared as an assigned cell with an extremely small allocation, that we call an ϵ (epsilon) allocation. This is illustrated in Table 7-16, where the ϵ is placed in cell *BO, Dum.* Table 7-16 also shows the closed path for cell *AR, E.* Conceptually, we regard the ϵ allocation as being infinitesimally small, so that it does

A Degenerate Solution

TABLE 7-15

To Warehouse / From Factory	C		D		E		F		Dummy (Dum)		Available at Factories
AR (regular)	AR,C	11	AR,D	10	AR,E	9	AR,F	7	AR, Dum	0	150
	(110)		(40)								
AO (overtime)	AO,C	6	AO,D	5	AO,E	4	AO,F	2	AO, Dum	0	110
			(30)						(80)		
BR (regular)	BR,C	11	BR,D	8	BR,E	13	BR,F	12	BR, Dum	0	200
					(170)		(30)				
BO (overtime)	BO,C	8	BO,D	5	BO,E	10	BO,F	9	BO, Dum	0	100
							(100)				
Required at Outlets	110		70		170		130		80		560

not affect the supply and demand totals. The ϵ allocation, however, does make it possible to meet the $n + m - 1$ restriction on the number of assignments so that evaluation paths may be established for all open cells. The ϵ allocation is then manipulated as though it were no different from any other allocation. If in subsequent manipulations, the ϵ cell is the one that limits shifts of units, the ϵ is simply shifted to the cell being evaluated, and the usual procedure is then continued (see p. 298: Table 7-16).

Summary

The application of the stepping-stone method to the transportation model is equivalent to the use of the simplex method. However, the special structure of the transpor-

TABLE 7-16   The ε Allocation and the Closed Path for Cell AR,E

To Warehouse From Factory	C		D		E		F		Dummy (Dum)		Available at Factories
AR (regular)	AR,C	11	AR,D	10 (−)	AR,E	9	AR,F	7	AR, Dum	0	150
	(110)		(40) ←		(+)						
AO (overtime)	AO,C	6	AO,D	5 (+)	AO,E	4	AO,F	2	AO, Dum	0 (−)	110
			(30)						(80)		
BR (regular)	BR,C	11	BR,D	8	BR,E	13 (−)	BR,F	12 (+)	BR, Dum	0	200
					(170) ←		(30)				
BO (overtime)	BO,C	8	BO,D	5	BO,E	10	BO,F	9 (−)	BO, Dum	0 (+)	100
							(100) ←		(ε)		
Required at Outlets	110		70		170		130		80		560

tation model provides certain computational advantages that are exploited in the stepping-stone algorithm. For example, in a transportation problem, it is very easy to find an initial starting solution involving only decision variables, rather than the starting solution with all slack variables or with some artificial variables as in the general simplex algorithm.

The evaluation of the open cells in the transportation table is equivalent to the calculation of row 0 coefficients for the corresponding variables in the linear programming formulation. Again, the special structure of the transportation model simplifies the calculations so much that they can easily be accomplished by hand. Likewise, the shift of units to improve a solution is equivalent to a pivot in the simplex algorithm.

As we have argued, it is most unlikely that you will ever be involved in solving a practical transportation problem by hand. Therefore, the motivation for your learning how to apply the stepping-stone algorithm must lie elsewhere. Learning to solve these simple problems emphasizes how the special structure of the network simplifies the computations of linear programming, and may provide some additional insights regarding the economic interpretation and logic of linear programming. This awareness should make you even more sensitive to possible applications of network models.

CHECK YOUR UNDERSTANDING*

1. Explain the significance of the visual interpretation of a network.
2. Comment on the following statement: "A manager does not need to worry about how efficient a computer program is for solving a problem. The machine can run all night so long as it finally gets *the* answer."
3. Compute the net savings (costs) associated with shipping one additional unit in each open cell in Table 7-4. That is, compute the net savings (costs) associated with shipping from factory 1 to outlet 2, from factory 2 to outlet 1, and from factory 3 to outlets 2 and 3. Why do we say that the solution in Table 7-4 is optimal?
4. Suppose we begin the introductory example problem with the initial solution shown in Table 7-17.
   a. Compute the total shipping costs associated with this initial solution.
   b. Suppose we ship one unit from factory 1 to outlet 1. Compute the *net savings* that result. Have you found a desirable *direction of change?*
   c. How many units can be shifted around to the route from factory 1 to outlet 1. In other words, what is the appropriate *amount of change* in the desirable direction?
   d. Revise the solution by shifting the necessary units. Check to see that the supply and demand restrictions are satisfied.
   e. Now compute the *net savings* from shipping one unit from factory 2 to outlet 3 while observing the supply and demand restrictions. If this is a desirable direction of change, compute the appropriate amount of change and shift the

---

* Questions that require an understanding of the materials in the preceding appendix are introduced with the notation (Appendix).

TABLE 7-17   An Alternate Initial Solution

To Outlet / From Factory	1 (Kansas City)	2 (Atlanta)	3 (Detroit)	Available at Factories
1 (Chicago)	3	2 ⟨20⟩	3 ⟨30⟩	50
2 (New York)	10 ⟨30⟩	5 ⟨40⟩	8	70
3 (Dallas)	1 ⟨20⟩	3	10	20
Required at Outlets	50	60	30	140

necessary units. Compare your result with the optimal solution in Table 7-4.

5. What is the significance of the notion of a "standard commodity bundle"? When can it be used?

6. In the solution strategy for the faculty/course scheduling problem shown in Figure 7-4, why is the solution of an optimizing model only an "approximation"?

7. (Appendix) Modify steps 1 through 4 of the northwest corner rule for finding an initial solution so that it becomes the "northeast" corner rule. That is, modify the steps so that you begin in the upper right-hand corner (the northeast corner) of the transportation table. Apply this new northeast corner rule to the introductory example shown in Table 7-1. Verify that you obtain the initial solution shown in Table 7-17.

8. (Appendix) Apply the *northwest* corner rule to the introductory example shown in Table 7-1. What happens? The supply in row 1 and the demand in column 1 are met simultaneously by an allocation of 50 units. If no entry appears in row 1, column 2 or in row 2, column 1, the solution will be *degenerate*. Place an ϵ in row 1, column 2 (the shipment from factory 1 to outlet 2), and continue to allocate the remainder of the units to the cells using the northwest corner rule.
   a. Evaluate the open cell in row 1, column 3.
   b. How many units can be shifted into the cell in row 1, column 3 (hint: not zero, but a "very small" number)?
   c. Make this shift, and continue to apply the stepping-stone algorithm until the optimal solution is obtained.

9. Factories 1 and 2 distribute an identical product through two regional warehouses. Normal production costs are $2 per unit at factory 1, and $4 per unit at factory 2. Normal capacity is 100 units at each plant. Shipping costs are given below:

Factory	Warehouse 1	2
1	$2	$4
2	3	1

The demand at warehouse 1 is 75 units, and demand at warehouse 2 is 125 units.
   a. Set up the transportation table that you would use to determine the optimal production-shipping schedule. Do *not* work the problem.
   b. Now assume that the demand at warehouse 2 has increased to 150 units. Suppose that additional overtime capacity of 20 units is available at each plant. Overtime production costs are $3 per unit at plant 1, and $5 per unit at plant 2. Set up the new transportation table that you would use to determine the optimal production-shipping schedule, utilizing both regular and overtime capacity. Do *not* work the problem.
   c. (Appendix) Use the northwest corner rule to obtain an initial solution and solve for the optimal production-shipping schedules for (a) and (b) above.

10. Temple-Stark, Inc., produces a cleaning fluid at its plants in Albuquerque and Boston. Cleaning fluid sells for $0.50 a can in the Midwest and Southwest (serviced by warehouses located in Omaha and Houston) and for $0.55 a can in the Rocky Mountains, which are served by a warehouse in Salt Lake City.

Transportation costs per can are as follows:

	Transportation Cost to:		
From	Salt Lake City	Omaha	Houston
Albuquerque	$0.07	$0.08	$0.05
Boston	0.10	0.05	0.09

Production information is as follows:

Plant	Monthly Capacity	Unit Production Cost
Albuquerque	1700	$0.35
Boston	1800	0.29

a. Suppose the monthly demand is for 1300 cans in Salt Lake City, 1200 cans in Omaha, and 1000 cans in Houston. Set up a transportation table that could be used to determine the optimum production-shipping schedule. Do *not* work the problem.

b. Suppose the monthly demand is for 1200 cans in Salt Lake City, 1000 cans in Omaha, and 1000 cans in Houston. Set up a transportation table that could be used to determine the optimum production-shipping schedule. Do *not* work the problem.

c. (Appendix) Use the northwest corner rule to obtain an initial solution and solve for the optimal production-shipping schedules for cleaning fluid for (a) and (b) above.

11. Factories A, B, and C distribute an identical product through three regional warehouses, X, Y, and Z. Monthly factory capacities are 160, 190, and 150 units, respectively. Monthly warehouse requirements average 150, 160, and 90 units, respectively. The unit distribution costs differ and are shown below:

From	To:		
	X	Y	Z
A	$ 3	$5	$ 8
B	5	6	15
C	12	7	4

The current shipping schedule is as follows:

From	To	No. of Units
A	X	150
A	Y	10
B	Y	150
B	Z	40
C	Z	50

a. Set up a transportation table that could be used to determine the optimum shipping plan.

b. Use the current shipping schedule as the initial solution. Evaluate the net savings (cost) associated with shipping one additional unit on each of the following routes while observing the supply and demand restrictions:

From	To
A	Z
A	dummy warehouse
B	X
B	dummy warehouse
C	X
C	Y

c. If one or more of the evaluations in (b) reveals a net savings, shift the units in the transportation table. Interpret the results.

d. Evaluate the net savings (cost) associated with shipping one additional unit on each of the unused routes in the revised table. Is the solution optimal? How do you know?

12. Four workers are available, each of whom may be assigned to only one of four jobs. The number of minutes required to perform each job by each worker is shown in the table below:

Worker	Job 1	2	3	4
1	2	4	5	—
2	7	3	2	3
3	9	—	8	6
4	—	6	2	3

The empty cells indicate that the worker does not have the necessary skills to do the particular job.

a. Set up a transportation problem that can be used to assign one worker to each job so that the *sum* of the minutes required for the jobs is minimized. What is the appropriate interpretation of the supply and the demand in this case?

b. Draw the network corresponding to this problem.

c. (Appendix) Use an initial solution of 1s in row 1, column 1; row 2, column 2; row 3, column 3; and row 4, column 4. This solution is degenerate. Place ϵ's in row 1, column 2; row 2, column 3; and row 3, column 4. Solve by the stepping-stone method.

d. (Appendix) If, after a little practice, worker number four can perform job two in two minutes instead of six, should the solution be changed? If so, what should it become?

SHORT CASES

CASE 7-1   Texas Electronics, Inc., has just received a large government contract to deliver radar units to three different locations over a three-year period. The radar units are currently manufactured in plants in Atlanta (*A*) and Boston (*B*). Each plant has a normal capacity of 100 units per year. However, an extra shift could be added in either or in both plants that could boost the annual capacity by an additional 75 units in each plant. Any units produced on an extra shift would cost an additional $2 per unit (these costs are "scaled" so they are simple numbers).

The units must be shipped to Rhode Island (*R*), South Dakota (*S*), and Tennessee (*T*). The annual demands vary over the three year period of the contract as shown in the following table:

Demand in Year:	Location		
	R	*S*	*T*
1	50	60	100
2	75	70	120
3	100	80	150

The per-unit costs of shipping also vary as follows:

From	To:		
	R	*S*	*T*
A	$3	$1	$5
B	8	2	4

Production-Shipping Schedule for Texas Electronics			TABLE 7-18

	To:		
From	R	S	T
Year 1			
A (normal)	50	50	0
A (extra shift)	0	10	0
B (normal)	0	0	100
B (extra shift)	0	0	0
Year 2			
A (normal)	75	25	0
A (extra shift)	0	45	0
B (normal)	0	0	100
B (extra shift)	0	0	20
Year 3			
A (normal)	100	0	0
A (extra shift)	0	75	0
B (normal)	0	0	100
B (extra shift)	0	5	50

On the basis of these data, a management science analyst has determined the optimum pro-duction-shipping schedule for each of the three years by using the transportation model and a special-purpose computer program. The results are shown in Table 7-18.

As an alternative, Texas Electronics, Inc., can purchase a new plant in Chicago (C), operate it for three years, and sell it at an estimated total net loss of $1000. This new plant has a normal capacity of 130 units per year, and an extra shift could produce an additional 100 units per year, although there would be an estimated incremental cost of $2 per unit manufactured on the second shift. It costs $2 per unit to ship from Chicago to Rhode Island, $6 to ship to South Dakota, and $3 to ship to Tennessee.

The management science analyst has also performed a *what if* analysis of the optimum production-shipping schedule, based on the assumption that the plant in Chicago has been purchased. The results are shown in Table 7-19. Should Texas Electronics, Inc., purchase this new plant? Based on the monetary criterion alone, what is the appropriate decision? What other factors might alter this decision? (See p. 306: Table 7-19.)

(Appendix) The Stellar Steel Company makes automotive parts that are used in the assembly   CASE 7-2
of automobiles. At present, the company has three plants, one in Cleveland, one in Denver,

TABLE 7-19   Production-Shipping Schedule for
Texas Electronics with Chicago Plant

From	To:		
	R	S	T
Year 1			
A (normal)	0	60	0
A (extra shift)	0	0	0
B (normal)	0	0	20
B (extra shift)	0	0	0
C (normal)	50	0	80
C (extra shift)	0	0	0
Year 2			
A (normal)	0	70	0
A (extra shift)	0	0	0
B (normal)	0	0	65
B (extra shift)	0	0	0
C (normal)	75	0	55
C (extra shift)	0	0	0
Year 3			
A (normal)	20	80	0
A (extra shift)	0	0	0
B (normal)	0	0	100
B (extra shift)	0	0	0
C (normal)	80	0	50
C (extra shift)	0	0	0

and one in Philadelphia. These plants supply four automobile assembly plants in Oakland, Gary, Houston, and Newark. Of late, the output from the company's plants has not been able to keep pace with its orders. As a result, the company has decided to build a new plant to expand its productive capacity. It is considering San Francisco and Atlanta as possible sites; both appear to be excellent choices in terms of subjective, noncost factors.

The production and output requirements for each of the existing plants, together with the estimated production costs of the two locations are shown in Table 7-20. Transportation costs from all these plants to the assembly plants are also given. Which of the two new locations should be selected on the basis of the cost criterion?

Production-Distribution Data for the Stellar Steel Company   TABLE 7-20

Demand			Production		
	Assembly Plant Requirements (units per month)			Normal Production Load (units per month)	Production Costs (per unit)
Oakland	9,000	Denver		6,000	$0.48
Gary	10,000	Philadelphia		14,000	0.50
Houston	12,000	Cleveland		15,000	0.52
Newark	15,000	Atlanta (estimate)		—	0.49
	46,000	San Francisco (estimate)		—	0.53
				35,000	

Transportation Costs ($ per unit)

	To:			
From	Gary	Houston	Newark	Oakland
Cleveland	$0.25	$0.55	$0.40	$0.60
Denver	0.35	0.30	0.50	0.40
Philadelphia	0.36	0.45	0.26	0.66
Atlanta	0.35	0.30	0.41	0.50
San Francisco	0.60	0.38	0.65	0.27

A firm is attempting to manage its cash balance so that it obtains the maximum return on its   CASE 7-3
assets.* It has forecasted the cash payments it can expect from its accounts receivables, and the
accounts payable from its own commitments in each of the next three months as shown:

Month	Forecasted Cash Inflow (in $ thousands)	Forecasted Accounts Payable (in $ thousands)
1 (Jan.)	10	40
2 (Feb.)	20	60
3 (Mar.)	40	50
	70	150

* Based on V. Srinivasan, "A Transshipment Model for Cash Decisions," *Management Science,*
Vol. 20, No. 10, June 1974.

The firm can delay payment of an account by one month and pay a penalty of 2 percent. However, it cannot delay payment by more than one month.

The firm also has two marketable securities. Security A matures on March 1 with a face value of $50,000, while security B matures on February 1 with a face value of $20,000. These securities could be sold early, if necessary, to provide cash for the accounts receivable. The penalties are as follows:

Number of Months Before Maturity	Penalty (percent)
1	0.5
2	1.5

In addition, the firm has a line of credit with a bank. The interest charges for borrowing are as follows:

Borrow in Month	Interest Charge (percent)
1 (Jan.)	4.0
2 (Feb.)	3.0

This credit can be used to cover the excess cash demands over the total cash availabilities during this three-month period.

Finally, any excess cash available during one month may be invested in short-term securities which mature in 30 days or 60 days. The returns from these securities are as follows:

Maturity (days)	Return (percent)
30	0.75
60	1.60

a. Formulate the cash management problem as a transshipment problem. Assume that all the accounts payable, including those for March, must be paid before April 1. (Hint: Define nodes representing "cash" in each month that are the transshipment nodes. The other nodes will be either "sources" or "sinks.")

b. Compare this network formulation with the linear optimization model for the cash management problem that was presented in Chapter 4. What are the pros and cons of each formulation?

GENERAL REFERENCES

Bradley, G. H., G. G. Brown, and G. W. Graves, "Design and Implementation of Large Scale Primal Transshipment Algorithms," *Management Science,* Vol. 24, No. 1, September 1977.

Dantzig, G., *Linear Programming and Extensions,* Princeton University Press, Princeton, N.J., 1963.

Klingman, A., A. Napier, and J. Stutz, "Netgen: A Program for Generating Large Scale Capacitated Assignment, Transportation, and Minimum Cost Flow Network Problems," *Management Science,* Vol. 20, No. 5, January 1974.

Wagner, H., *Principals of Management Science,* Prentice-Hall, Englewood Cliffs, N.J., 1975.

APPLICATIONS REFERENCES

Charnes, A., W. Cooper, R. Niehaus, and D. Sholtz, "A Model for Civilian Manpower Management in the U.S. Navy," in *Models of Manpower Systems,* edited by A. Smith, English Universities Press, 1970.

Dyer, J., and J. Mulvey, "An Integrated Optimization/Information System for Academic Planning," *Management Science,* Vol. 22, No. 12, August 1976.

Geoffrion, A., "Better Distribution Planning with Computer Models," *Harvard Business Review,* Vol. 54, No. 4, July–August 1976.

Glover, F., J. Hultz, and D. Klingman, "Improved Computer-Based Planning Techniques, Part I," *Interfaces,* Vol. 8, No. 4, August 1978.

———, "Improved Computer-Based Planning Techniques, Part II," *Interfaces,* Vol. 9, No. 4, August 1979.

———, and D. Klingman, "Network Application in Industry and Government," *AIIE Transactions,* Vol. 9, No. 4, 1977.

Mulvey, J., "Special Structures in Network Models and Associated Applications," Ph.D. dissertation, The Graduate School of Management, The University of California, Los Angeles, 1975.

Segal, M., "The Operator Scheduling Problem: A Network Flow Approach," *Operations Research,* Vol. 22, No. 4, July–August 1974, pp. 808–823.

Srinivasan, V., "A Transshipment Model for Cash Decisions," *Management Science,* Vol. 20, No. 10, June 1974.

Zierer, T. K., W. A. Mitchell, and T. R. White, "Practical Applications of Linear Programming to Shell's Distribution Problems," *Interfaces,* Vol. 6, No. 4, August 1976.

CHAPTER 8

Network Models — Shortest Path and Network Scheduling

Another important class of network models involves the determination of the longest or the shortest path through a network. In most real-world applications, the length of the path is not actually a measure of distance, but rather a measure of money or of time. If the measure is money, the shortest path algorithm can be applied to determine the least cost route through a network. This strategy is often employed in developing a policy for replacing equipment. If the measure is time, the "longest path" through the network may be of interest as an estimate of the duration of a large-scale project. This concept is the basis for the well-known network scheduling techniques PERT and CPM. Examples of these applications will be provided.

These network models also share the following important characteristics mentioned in Chapter 7.

1. Many real-world problems can be formulated with shortest path or network scheduling models.

2. The visual interpretation of the network reduces the problems of communication.

3. Efficient computer codes are available to analyze the networks, and integer valued solutions are obtained automatically.

Therefore, a manager should be able to recognize opportunities for using these models.

THE SHORTEST PATH MODEL

The problem of finding the shortest path from the beginning to the end of a large network may be viewed as a special case of the transshipment problem. All the nodes in the network are viewed as transshipment points except for the starting and ending nodes. A supply of one unit is assumed at the start, and a demand of one is assumed at the end, or terminal node. The problem can be solved as a normal transshipment problem, which means it can also be restructured into an equivalent transportation problem. The path over which the single unit is shipped is actually the "shortest path" when the costs are interpreted as distances. This model can be used to analyze several commonly occurring real-world problems.

The shortest path algorithm

As we have said, the shortest path problem can be formulated as a transshipment problem. The problem can then be solved efficiently by using a specially modified

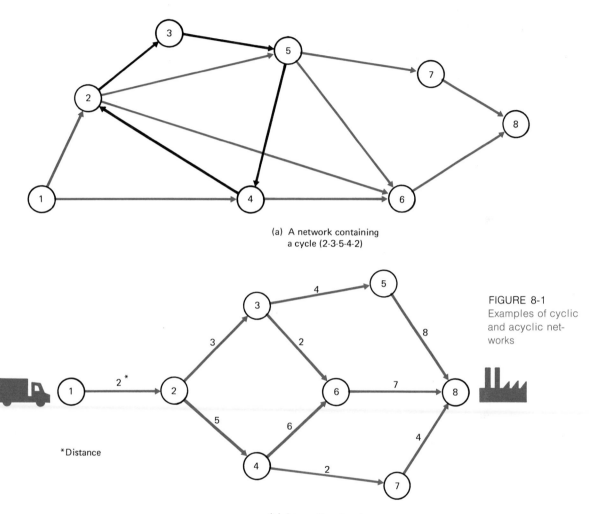

(a) A network containing
a cycle (2-3-5-4-2)

FIGURE 8-1
Examples of cyclic
and acyclic net-
works

*Distance

(b) An acyclic network

computer program for linear programming problems. However, the special nature of the shortest path problem makes it possible to develop an *especially simple algorithm* for its solution. This is particularly true when the network is *acyclic*.

A network is *acyclic* if it contains no cycles. A cycle is a path from a node that eventually returns to the same node. For example, the network in Figure 8-1(a) contains a cycle, since it is possible to travel from node 2 to node 3, from node 3 to node 5, from node 5 to node 4, and from node 4 back to node 2. However, the network shown in Figure 8-1(b) contains no cycles, and is therefore acyclic.

To find the shortest path in an acyclic network, we can take the following steps:

STEP 1. Begin at the terminal node in the network (node 8 in Figure 8-1(b)). Label it with a zero.

STEP 2. Consider a node whose outward pointing arcs all go into labeled nodes. Add the distance on each outward arc to the label value on the node it goes into. Label this new node with the minimum of these sums.

STEP 3. Repeat step 2 until the beginning node is labeled. This label is the length of the shortest path.

STEP 4. To identify the shortest path, trace forward through the network from the beginning node, selecting at each node the outgoing arc with the minimum sum in step 2. If a tie occurs, there are alternate paths.

Let us apply this algorithm to the acyclic network shown in Figure 8-1(b). At step 1, we first label node 8 with a 0, placing the label in a box below the node. Next, for step 2, we choose a node whose outgoing arcs all go into labeled nodes. Since node 8 is labeled, nodes 5, 6, and 7 are eligible. Suppose we choose node 6. The distance on the arc from node 6 to node 8 is 7, plus the label value of 0, equals 7. This is the label we place on node 6 in Figure 8-2.

Now we repeat step 2. Nodes 5 and 7 are still eligible to be labeled. What about node 3, since an outgoing arc goes from node 3 to the now labeled node 6? No, it is *not* eligible, because another outgoing arc goes from node 3 to node 5, and node 5 has not been labeled yet. So, let us label node 5 with the value $8 + 0 = 8$, and we now obtain the labeling shown in Figure 8-2.

Since both nodes 5 and 6 have been labeled, node 3 is eligible, as is node 7. Choosing node 3, we add the distance on the arc from node 3 to node 5, 4, plus the label on node 5, 8, and obtain $4 + 8 = 12$. Similarly, for the arc from node 3 to node 6, we obtain $2 + 7 = 9$. Now, we take the minimum of these two numbers, 9, as the label for node 3, since the minimum of the lengths on the alternate paths identifies the shortest path.

Continuing this process, we eventually label the beginning node 1, as shown in

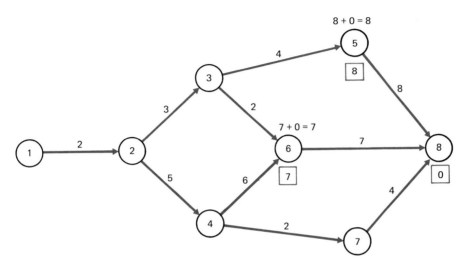

FIGURE 8-2
Partially labeled
network

Figure 8-3. Thus, the length of the shortest path is given by the label on node 1, 13. To find the path, we trace forward through the network. Obviously, it includes the arc from node 1 to node 2. At node 2, we note that the minimum sum in step 2 was for the arc from node 2 to node 4 (the distance of 5 plus the label value on node 4 gives the label value on node 2). Thus, the arc from node 2 to node 4 is on the path. Tracing forward to the terminal node, we determine that the shortest path is from node 1 to node 2, node 2 to node 4, node 4 to node 7, and node 7 to node 8. In this simple network, you could have discovered this solution without the aid of the algorithm. However, the algorithm can be computerized and applied to much more complicated networks.

The equipment replacement problem

In the most common applications of the shortest path algorithm, the "distances" are actually either costs or measures of time. The problem of determining when to replace a piece of equipment can often be analyzed through use of this model by allowing the distances to be costs.

Suppose a company has just received a contract for producing a new product for five years. The production of this new product requires the purchase of a new piece of machinery that can be used only for this product. The cost of this machinery is

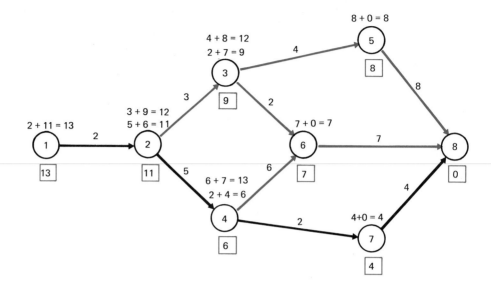

FIGURE 8-3
The shortest path
(1-2-4-7-8)

$200 now. However, the company estimates that after two more years, the price will increase to $250 for the same piece of equipment. The salvage value of the equipment depends on the number of years it has been used, as shown in Table 8-1. Similarly, the operating costs depend on its age, since maintenance increases as the machine becomes older. These costs are also shown in Table 8-1.

How can we best analyze this problem? One way might be to assume that we purchase the machine at the start of the first year (which we must do) and compute

TABLE 8-1	Salvage Value and Annual Operating Costs		
	Number of Years Used	Salvage Value at End of Year	Annual Operating Costs
	1	$100	$ 10
	2	75	50
	3	50	100
	4	25	120
	5	0	130

Costs of Purchasing a Machine at the Beginning of Year 1					TABLE 8-2
	Keep Machine Until End of Year:				
	1	2	3	4	5
Purchase price	$200	$200	$200	$200	$200
Operating cost					
Year 1	10	10	10	10	10
Year 2	—	50	50	50	50
Year 3	—	—	100	100	100
Year 4	—	—	—	120	120
Year 5	—	—	—	—	130
Total cost	210	260	360	480	610
Less salvage value	100	75	50	25	0
Net cost	110	185	310	455	610

the cost of keeping it for each of one, two, three, four, or five years. These calculations are shown in Table 8-2. Next, we might suppose we purchase a new machine at the beginning of the second year and keep it for one, two, three, or four years. We can calculate these costs in a similar manner, as shown in Table 8-3. We can do the same for the assumption that we purchase a new machine at the beginning of the third year, using the new purchase price of $250, and for years four and five also, as shown in Table 8-4. Notice that if we purchase a machine at the beginning of the fifth year, the total cost will be $250 for the purchase plus $10 for operating expenses and minus the $100 salvage value, since we must sell it at the end of the fifth year. This gives $250 + $10 − $100 = $160.

Now, the problem is to determine a strategy that takes us from the beginning of year 1 to the end of year 5 as cheaply as possible. We know the cost of purchasing a new machine at the beginning of any year and holding it until the beginning of any other year. If we look at the problem closely, we can see an analogy with the shortest path problem.

Suppose we construct a network by defining nodes as the beginnings of each of the five years in the time horizon of this study, plus one additional node to mark the beginning of the sixth year (or the end of the fifth year). We can draw arcs from the beginning of each year to the beginning of each of the subsequent years, as shown in

TABLE 8-3

Costs of Purchasing a Machine at the Beginning of Year 2

	Keep Machine Until End of Year:			
	2	3	4	5
Purchase price	$200	$200	$200	$200
Operating cost				
Year 2	10	10	10	10
Year 3	—	50	50	50
Year 4	—	—	100	100
Year 5	—	—	—	120
Total cost	210	260	360	480
Less salvage value	100	75	50	25
Net cost	110	185	310	455

Figure 8-4. For example, the arc from node 1 to node 4 represents the decision to purchase a machine at the beginning of year 1 and keep it three years, until the beginning of year 4. The cost of this strategy from Table 8-2 is $310, which appears on the arc from node 1 to node 4. Notice how the other costs on the arcs in Figure 8-4 correspond to the costs in Tables 8-2, 8-3, and 8-4.

The network in Figure 8-4 is acyclic, so it can be solved using the shortest path algorithm for minimizing total costs. Using the four-step manual procedure, verify that the minimum total cost of the optimal equipment replacement strategy is $530, and the strategy is to purchase a machine at the beginning of year 1 and sell it at the end of year 1; then purchase a second machine to be held for two years, and finally, purchase a third machine also to be held for two years. Notice that it is not obvious that such a strategy would be optimal.

Since these costs are incurred over several years, it might be appropriate to discount them by the proper rate for the firm. The length of the shortest path would then correspond to the present value of the optimal equipment replacement policy. An example of this approach is given as an exercise at the end of the chapter.

NETWORK SCHEDULING MODELS

One of the most practical and important uses of the concepts of the length of the path through a network is found in network scheduling models. Network scheduling

Costs of Purchasing a Machine at the Beginning of Years 3, 4, and 5   TABLE 8-4

	Purchased Year 3			Purchased Year 4		Purchased Year 5
	Keep Machine Until End of Year:					
	3	4	5	4	5	5
Purchase price	$250	$250	$250	$250	$250	$250
Operating cost						
Year 3	10	10	10	—	—	—
Year 4	—	50	50	10	10	—
Year 5	—	—	100	—	50	10
Total cost	260	310	410	260	310	260
Less salvage value	100	75	50	100	75	100
Net cost	160	235	360	160	235	160

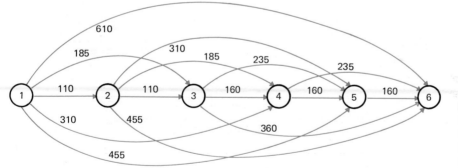

FIGURE 8-4
Shortest path network for analyzing the equipment replacement problem

models are used to plan, schedule, control, and evaluate complex projects and tasks. The basic idea is to analyze a complex project—for example, the development of a new weapons system, the construction of a large building, or the production of a motion picture—by identifying the specific tasks that must be accomplished to complete the project and interrelating them in a network.

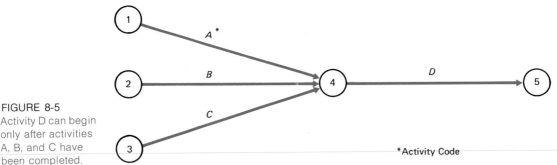

FIGURE 8-5
Activity D can begin
only after activities
A, B, and C have
been completed.

The network planning techniques known as the critical path method (CPM) and the Program Evaluation and Review Technique (PERT) were originally developed in the 1950s. PERT was first used to help manage the successful Polaris project, and since that time, some form of network scheduling model has been required for every government defense contract.

The nodes in the network scheduling models represent "events" in the project.* An event generally corresponds to the beginning or end of a specific task, or "activity," that must be performed as part of the project. The activities are represented by the arcs in the network.

The rules of logic in the network are relatively simple. Suppose an activity D can be started only after activities A, B, and C have been completed. This situation would be diagrammed as shown in Figure 8-5. Thus, all activities represented by arcs into an event node must be completed before an activity represented by an arc out of an event node can begin.

In addition, because of restrictions imposed by most computer routines that analyze network schedules, two activities cannot have the same beginning and ending event nodes. Thus, if activities B and C can begin after activity A, and activity D can begin after activities B and C have been completed, we might be tempted to diagram this relationship as shown in Figure 8-6(a). However, since computer codes identify activities by their beginning and ending nodes, they could not distinguish between activity B and activity C, which both begin with event 2 and end with event 3. Therefore, a "dummy" activity is used as shown in Figure 8-6(b). The dummy activity has a time duration of zero and is used for logical purposes in the network.

---

* We are presenting the "activity on the arcs" approach to network scheduling, although it is also possible to develop "activities on the nodes" models.

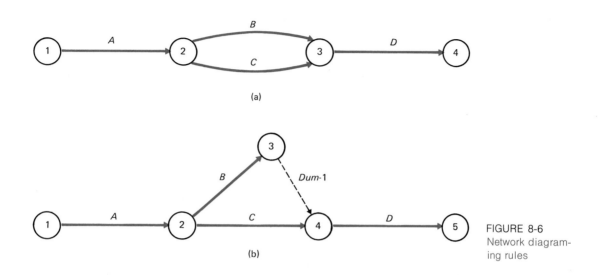

(a)

(b)

FIGURE 8-6
Network diagram-
ing rules

Now, consider a simple example of a project that might be analyzed by using network scheduling. Suppose we wish to conduct a market survey. Our first activity, A, will be to study the purpose of the survey. After completing this task, we can hire data collection personnel (B) and design the questionnaire (C). After both B and C are completed, we can train the personnel (D). However, after completing only the design of the questionnaire (C), we can begin selecting households for our survey

Activities Required and Immediate Predecessors   TABLE 8-5
for the Market Survey

Activity Code	Description	Immediate Predecessors
A	Study purpose	—
B	Hire personnel	A
C	Design questionnaire	A
D	Train personnel	B, C
E	Select households	C
F	Survey	D, E

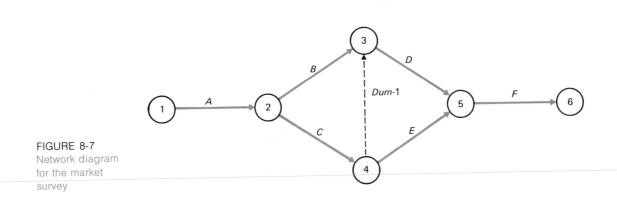

FIGURE 8-7
Network diagram
for the market
survey

(E), even before the personnel have been hired (B). Finally, after completing tasks (D) and (E) we can take the survey (F). These tasks and the precedence relationships are shown in Table 8-5. Try to construct your own network for analyzing this problem before looking at the solution in Figure 8-7. Notice that one dummy activity was required to indicate that activity D cannot start until *both* activities B and C have been completed, but activity E depends only on activity C.

Just the construction of such a network could be a significant managerial aid in dealing with a complex problem. In preparing Table 8-5, it was necessary to do an *activity analysis*; that is, the activities required to complete the project had to be identified and the technical precedence relationships among the activities had to be determined. These precedence relationships are the statements of which activities must immediately precede an activity. The value from the network can be enhanced if the activity analysis also uses estimates of the time required to complete each activity, and these are included in the network. To determine these time estimates, decisions must be made regarding the methods and tools to be used in completing each activity. Again, this forces the manager to break down the project into its individual tasks, and to plan each of these in detail before beginning the project. Suppose that the time estimates for the activities in the market survey are 2 weeks for A, 4 weeks for B, 2 weeks for C, 1 week for D, 2 weeks for E, and 3 weeks for F. These time estimates are shown in parentheses on the network in Figure 8-8.

Network analysis

Given these time estimates, the network may be analyzed to provide additional information of importance to managers. The most obvious information of interest is the total length of time required for the project. This time is computed by applying a

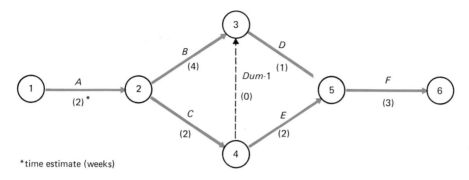

FIGURE 8-8
Time estimates for
the activities in the
network diagram

*time estimate (weeks)

modified version of the shortest path algorithm. However since we are interested in completing each of the activities, the total time for the project will be equal to the *longest path* through the network. Thus, we apply a suitably modified algorithm to obtain this estimate.

This algorithm computes the "earliest" and "latest" start and finish times for each of the activities. The early start and finish times are simply the earliest that each activity can be started and finished, given the technical precedence relationships in the network. The latest start and finish times are the latest that an activity can be started and finished, *without delaying the total time to complete the project.* The difference between the early and late start (finish) time is the "slack" associated with an activity.

This slack is the amount of time that a particular activity could be delayed without delaying the completion of the project. This information can be very useful to managers in scheduling work and the use of equipment. The activities with zero slack cannot be delayed without delaying the entire project. These activities are on the longest path through the network, which is called the *critical path*.

Earliest start and finish times We can begin with zero as the starting time for the project, which becomes the earliest start time (*ES*) for the first activity. Given *ES* for an activity, the earliest finish time (*EF*) is simply *ES* + activity time. The procedure for computing *ES* and *EF*, which is similar to the shortest path algorithm, is as follows:

STEP 1. Place the value of the project start time to the left of the beginning activity in the position shown for the early start time in Figure 8-9. In Figure 8-9 we see a zero for the *ES* of activity *A*. The early finish time is then *ES* + activity time, or 2 weeks for activity *A*. This *labels* activity *A*.

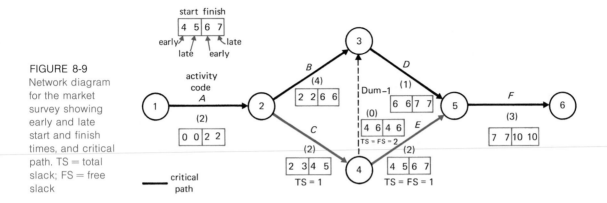

FIGURE 8-9
Network diagram
for the market
survey showing
early and late
start and finish
times, and critical
path. TS = total
slack; FS = free
slack

STEP 2. Consider any activity not yet labeled, all of whose predecessors have been labeled with their *ES*'s and *EF*'s. The *ES* for this activity is the *largest number* in the *EF* position of its immediate predecessors. That is to say, the earliest an activity can begin is the earliest that *all* of its predecessor activities are finished. The *ES* for activity *B* in Figure 8-9 is 2 weeks.

STEP 3. The *EF* for this activity is *ES* + activity time. For activity *B*, $EF = 2 + 4 = 6$ weeks.

STEP 4. Repeat steps 2 and 3 until the last activity is labeled. This label is the *length* of the critical (longest) path in the network, and the total duration for the project.

In our simple example, the length of the critical path is 10 weeks, which is the minimum amount of time required to complete the market survey.

Latest start and finish times If we assume that the target for completing the market survey is the *EF* time of 10 weeks, then we have defined the latest finish time (*LF*) of 10 weeks, allowing no slack in the project as a whole. Therefore, the latest start time (*LS*) for the final activity is *LF* − activity time. The procedure for computing *LS* and *LF* for the remaining activities is as follows:

STEP 1. Label the *LF* and *LS* values for the terminal activities as shown in Figure 8-9. For the market survey, *LF* = 10, and *LS* = 7 for activity *F*.

STEP 2. Consider any activity not yet labeled, all of whose successors have been labeled with these *LS*'s and *LF*'s. The *LF* for this activity is the *smallest number* in the *LS* position of its immediate successors. That is to say, the latest that an activity can be finished is the latest that *any* of its successors can start. The *LF* for activity *E* in Figure 8-9 is 7 weeks.

STEP 3. The *LS* for this activity is *LF* − activity time. For activity *E*, *LS* = 7 − 2 = 5 weeks.

STEP 4. Repeat steps 2 and 3 until the initial activity is labeled.

Slack and critical path Total slack (*TS*) for an activity is the maximum time that the activity can be delayed beyond its *ES* without delaying the project completion time. The critical activities are those that are in the sequence of the longest time path through the network, and therefore the activities on this path all have minimum possible *TS*. Since for our example the target date and the *EF* for activity *F* (the finish activity) are the same, all critical activities will have zero *TS*. The project target date may of course be later than the *EF* of the finish activity, in which case all activities on the critical path would have the same *TS* equal to the difference. Then all noncritical activities will have greater *TS* than critical activities.

Free slack (*FS*) is the amount of time that an activity can be delayed without delaying the *ES* of any other activity. Free slack for an activity never exceeds its *TS*. Free slack is computed as the difference between the *EF* for that activity and the earliest of the *ES* times of all of its immediate successors. For example, activity *E* has *FS* = 1, since the *ES* of its successor is 7 and its own *EF* is 6. To compute FS manually, one should examine the network diagram in order to take account of the precedence relationships.

An example Network scheduling techniques are often applied to large-scale projects, such as the development of the Polaris missile or the construction of the Mexico City subway. However, they can also be used to analyze relatively simple operations, such as rebuilding a device known as a tool cutter-grinder. This latter example is realistic, yet simple enough to present in its entirety.

The first step is the activity analysis, which generates the activities required, the activity time requirements in days, and the technical precedence requirements to build a tool cutter-grinder, as shown in Table 8-6. The network corresponding to this activity analysis is then generated, and the critical path analysis is performed, as illus-

TABLE 8-6

Rebuilding a Tool Cutter-Grinder

Activity Code	Description	Days Required	Immediate Predecessors
A	Disconnect and move	0.2	—
B	Connect power and pretest	0.2	A
C	Remove electrical units	0.2	B
D	Clean machine	0.3	C
E	Remove and disassemble mechanical units	0.2	C
F	Clean machine parts	0.4	D
G	List mechanical parts	0.5	F
H	Order machine parts	0.5	G
I	Receive machine parts	1.0	H
J	Paint cross slides	25.0	I
K	Machine parts	1.5	G
L	Inspect and list electrical parts	1.0	K
M	Paint motor	1.0	L
N	Assemble motor	0.8	P, Q, R
O	Machine saddle	2.5	H
P	Machine slides	2.0	V
Q	Machine table	.2.0	L
R	Paint machine	2.0	M
S	Scrape slides	1.0	N
T	Scrape table	1.0	G
U	Scrape saddles	0.5	E
V	Machine gibs	2.0	K
W	Install spindle	1.0	J, O, T
X	Assemble parts	1.0	J, O, S, T
Y	Scrape gibs	0.5	U
Z	Assemble head	1.0	J, O, T
AA	Install motor and electrical parts	0.3	Y
BB	Assemble cross slides	0.4	J, O, T
CC	Connect power and test	0.5	AA, BB, Z, W, X
DD	Touch up, move, reinstall	0.3	CC

Source: data from R. D. Archibald and R. L. Villoria, *Network-Based Management Systems*, John Wiley & Sons, New York, 1967. Used by permission.

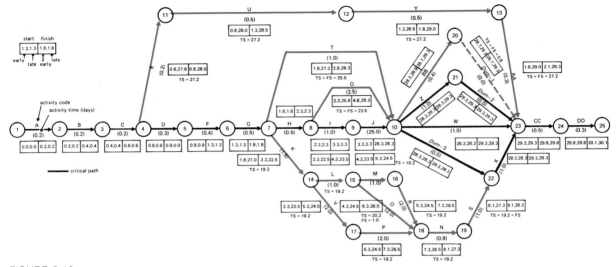

FIGURE 8-10
Arrow diagram for rebuilding Cincinnati No. 2 cutter-grinder showing early and late start and
finish times, and critical path. TS = total slack; FS = free slack

trated in Figure 8-10. For practical problems, these computations are actually performed by computer codes. The output from a computer code that has analyzed the
tool cutter-grinder network is shown in Figure 8-11.

Extensions and managerial uses of network scheduling techniques

There are numerous extensions of the network scheduling techniques that enhance
their practical usefulness to managers. One important extension is the use of probabilistic time estimates. The time estimate for completing a particular activity may be
uncertain, especially in research and development activities where there is no previous experience to use as a guide. Therefore, instead of a single time estimate for an
activity, *three* time estimates are obtained. The three different time estimates are:

1. The *optimistic time, a,* is the shortest possible time in which the activity may be
   accomplished if all goes well. The estimate is based on the assumption that the
   activity would have no more than one chance in 100 of being completed in less
   than this time.

FIGURE 8-11   Critical Path Schedule Job No. 50787, Date issued 7-17-81, Page 1

Operation Code	i	j	Days Req'd.	Earliest		Latest		Days Slack	Free Slack
				Start	Finish	Start	Finish		
A	1	2	.2	.0	.2	.0	.2	.0**	—
B	2	3	.2	.2	.4	.2	.4	.0**	—
C	3	4	.2	.4	.6	.4	.6	.0**	—
D	4	5	.3	.6	.9	.6	.9	.0**	—
E	4	11	.2	.6	.8	27.8	28.0	27.2	.0
F	5	6	.4	.9	1.3	.9	1.3	.0**	—
G	6	7	.5	1.3	1.8	1.3	1.8	.0**	—
H	7	8	.5	1.8	2.3	1.8	2.3	.0**	—
I	8	9	1.0	2.3	3.3	2.3	3.3	.0**	—
J	9	10	25.0	3.3	28.3	3.3	28.3	.0**	—
K	7	14	1.5	1.8	3.3	21.0	22.5	19.2	.0
L	4	15	1.0	3.3	4.3	22.5	23.5	19.2	.0
M	15	16	1.0	4.3	5.3	23.5	24.5	19.2	.0
N	18	19	.8	7.3	8.1	26.5	27.3	19.2	.0
O	8	10	2.5	2.3	4.8	25.8	28.3	23.5	23.5
P	17	18	2.0	5.3	7.3	24.5	26.5	19.2	.0
Q	15	18	2.0	4.3	6.3	24.5	26.5	20.2	1.0
R	16	18	2.0	5.3	7.3	24.5	26.5	19.2	.0
S	19	22	1.0	8.1	9.1	27.3	28.3	19.2	19.2
T	7	10	1.0	1.8	2.8	27.3	28.3	25.5	25.5
U	11	12	.5	.8	1.3	28.0	28.5	27.2	.0
V	14	17	2.0	3.3	5.3	22.5	24.5	19.2	.0
W	10	23	1.0	28.3	29.3	28.3	29.3	.0**	—
X	22	23	1.0	28.3	29.3	28.3	29.3	.0**	—
Y	12	13	.5	1.3	1.8	28.5	29.0	27.2	.0
Z	10	21	1.0	28.3	29.3	28.3	29.3	.0**	—
AA	13	23	.3	1.8	2.1	29.0	29.3	27.2	27.2
BB	10	20	.4	28.3	28.7	28.9	29.3	.6	.0
CC	23	24	.5	29.3	29.8	29.3	29.8	.0**	—
DD	24	25	.3	29.8	30.1	29.8	30.1	.0**	—
Dum-1	20	23	.0	28.7	28.7	29.3	29.3	.6	.6
Dum-2	21	23	.0	29.3	29.3	29.3	29.3	.0**	—
Dum-3	10	22	.0	28.3	28.3	28.3	28.3	.0**	—

** Critical Operations.

2. The *pessimistic time, b,* is the longest time that an activity could take under adverse conditions, barring acts of nature. This time estimate is based on the assumption that the activity would have no more than one chance in 100 of taking longer than time *b.*

3. The *most likely time, m.*

These three time estimates are reduced to a single time estimate t_e, the *mean* of the implied probability distribution for the activity time. In addition, the *variance* of this distribution, σ^2, can also be estimated. The formulas are:

$$t_e = \frac{1}{6}(a + 4m + b) \tag{1}$$

$$\sigma^2 = \left[\frac{1}{6}(b - a)\right]^2 \tag{2}$$

The t_e estimates are then used in the computation of the critical path for a project exactly as before. However, the total time for the critical path is now interpreted as the *mean* estimate.

When we add several random variables, the sum is also a random variable with a normal probability distribution, even if the random variables that are added are not normally distributed. The mean of this normal distribution is equal to the sum of the means of the individual random variables, and the variance is equal to the sum of the variances of the random variables if the random variables are independent. Therefore, the length of the critical path is the mean of a normal probability distribution whose variance is equal to the sum of the variances of the individual activities on the critical path.

Management can then compute the *probability* of completing the project in any specified length of time. For example, since the length of the critical path is only the mean of a normal probability distribution for the total project time, there is only a 50 percent chance that the project will actually be completed by this time. Management can plan, reschedule, or even renegotiate contracts on the basis of the expected outcomes and risk levels. Obviously, however, the output is no better than the input data, and there is a danger that the very existence of such precise probability statements will give an aura of accuracy that may not be justified.

The network schedule can also be used to study questions of time/cost trade-offs. In order to estimate the time required to complete an activity, assumptions regarding the level of labor and the resources to be used must be made. In some cases, it may be advantageous to develop multiple time estimates for multiple levels of resource input. The critical path analysis could be performed with each activity by using a maximum of its resources. Then, for activities with slack, resources could be reduced, extending the time for the activity but not increasing the time for the network, as long as the time extension does not exceed the slack on the activity's path.

In some cases, even activities on the critical path may be extended when the cost savings exceed the costs of delaying the project completion. Computer algorithms are also available to perform such analyses. Managers may also wish to use the early start/late start information for activities not on the critical path to schedule their start in such a way as to smooth the labor requirements over the total life of the project, or to make the most efficient use of other limited resources, such as special-purpose machinery.

Finally, the network schedule can be used for project control. Cost estimates can be developed for the activities and these data can be entered into computer programs along with the time estimates. As work on a project progresses, the actual cost and time figures can be compared with the estimates. Areas in which significant cost or time overruns are occurring can be identified easily, and managerial actions can be considered to overcome them. For example, if a time overrun is occurring on a network path that has a relatively large slack value, the manager may choose to do nothing. However, if the time overrun is on the critical path or on one with little slack, a manager may wish to take immediate action. These topics are treated in further detail at a managerial level in Weist and Levy [1977], while more technical issues are examined in Moder and Phillips [1970] and in Archibald and Villoria [1967].

WHAT SHOULD THE MANAGER KNOW?

The shortest path model may be viewed as a special case of the transshipment problem. In pure form, the most obvious application of the shortest path problem is to capital budgeting and equipment replacement problems. However, a modification of the shortest path algorithm may be applied to network representations of large-scale projects to determine the critical path in the network and other information of managerial significance. Therefore, we will confine this discussion to the network scheduling techniques.

Problem characteristics

Network scheduling methods are advantageously applied to complex, large-scale projects. Generally, these are one-of-a-kind projects, so that previous plans and experience for completing this type of effort are not available. Among the successful applications that have been reported are the following cases:

1. Construction of new homes, shopping centers, subways, etc. [Glasser and Young, 1961; O'Brian, 1965]
2. Introduction of new products [Wong, 1964]
3. Major maintenance efforts [Reeves, 1960]
4. Pilot production runs [Odom and Blystone, 1964]
5. Development of new weapon systems [Fazar, 1961]
6. Moving an entire hospital, including its patients, to a new location [Hanson, 1972]

Thus, any time the manager confronts a problem that is complex in that it requires the completion of several interrelated activities, is relatively large in terms of the resource requirements, and is nonroutine (no one in the organization has had significant experience in dealing with this type of problem previously), a network scheduling technique should be considered as a managerial aid.

Formulation

The manager and all persons who will be responsible for some of the activities to be performed should be involved in formulating the initial network. *Some experts claim that 90 percent of the benefits of the technique are obtained from this exercise.* The activities must be identified and the interrelationships must be clarified. Responsibility for accomplishing each activity must be assigned to individuals, and the person responsible should be involved in determining how to conduct the activity and in estimating the time required for its completion. This involvement provides the participants with an overview of the entire project and an understanding of how their activities relate to others.

Computational considerations

Once the initial network has been formulated, it can be entered into the computer for analysis. Instead of providing the answer, the result of this analysis should be the basis for another round of planning with the managers involved in the project. Issues of trading off costs versus time and of labor smoothing can be raised. Alternate solutions can be generated by moving activities from their early start to their late start times. Several computer runs would doubtless be required before the final plan is determined.

When the project is under way, the actual time and cost performances can be entered into the computer to compare against the initial estimates. Potentially, areas of cost or time overruns can be identified early, and managerial action can be taken.

Interpretation

The manager must be careful not to put too much reliance on the network. Just because the network terminates before the project due date does not mean that the actual project will. Thus, the manager must ensure that the data used in the analysis are an accurate portrayal of what is actually occurring in the project.

Disadvantages of the network scheduling models

Network scheduling, especially for the control of a project, can be relatively costly. The costs of obtaining information and updating the network may not justify the benefits of the method in relatively small projects. As a rough rule of thumb, O'Brian [1965] suggests that computer network scheduling techniques are probably not justified on projects involving costs of $100,000 or less and should be questioned on projects even up to $500,000 in costs. However, the hand calculations for these networks are so straightforward that smaller projects can be organized with a simple analysis and "back of the envelope" calculations.

Even if computer network scheduling and control techniques are not used, the manager should always consider an initial planning session devoted to the construction of a network. Again, much of the value of a management science model is not in the solution it provides, but in the knowledge gained in the process of its formulation.

CHECK YOUR UNDERSTANDING

1. Distinguish between an acyclic and a cyclic network. Give a real-world example of a problem in which each might be encountered.
2. In applying the steps to find the shortest path in an acyclic network, why do we begin at the *terminal* node rather than the *beginning* node?
3. At node 3 in Figure 8-3, what is the length of the shortest path from node 3 to node 8? How does this length relate to the label value on node 3? Answer the same question for node 2. See if you can use this insight to summarize the logic of the solution strategy in one or two sentences.

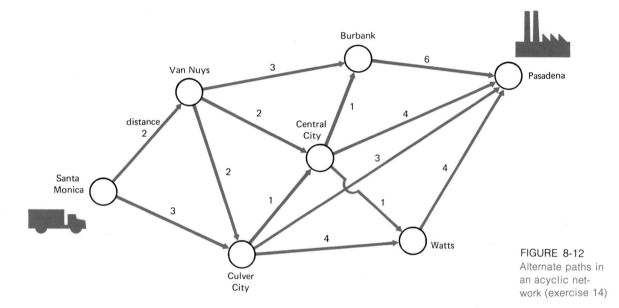

FIGURE 8-12
Alternate paths in
an acyclic net-
work (exercise 14)

4. Apply the four-step procedure for solving shortest path problems to the network shown in Figure 8-4, labeling the nodes. Interpret the results.

5. What is an "event" in a project? How does it relate to an "activity"?

6. What is the function of a "dummy" activity?

7. What is the managerial significance of information regarding the "slack" associated with an activity? How might this information be used?

8. What is the "critical path"? What is its managerial significance?

9. What is the difference between "free slack" and "total slack" for an activity? What is its managerial significance?

10. Suppose that the target for completing the market survey shown in Figure 8-9 is twelve weeks, so that the late finish time (LF) for the terminal activity F is 12. Compute the revised late start and late finish times for the activities. Also compute the revised total slack and free slack for each activity.

11. The following comment was heard in industry: "Every time the PERT chart is revised, the management sends a bunch of supervisors to check on the activities on the critical path. When they ask us for time estimates for our activity, we

always revise our actual estimates to ensure that our activity won't be on the critical path. We don't want a bunch of supervisors hanging around!'' What are the implications of this comment for the proper use of network scheduling techniques in real-world situations?

12. Suppose the critical path of a project was determined by using probabilistic time estimates. The mean length of the critical path is 12 days, and the variance (determined by summing the variance of each activity on the critical path) is 4 days. Thus, the standard deviation associated with the critical path is $\sqrt{4} = 2$ days. Using the area under the standardized normal curve in Table C-1 of Appendix C, compute the probability that the project will actually be completed in 10 days, 12 days, 14 days, 16 days.

13. Describe how the network schedule may be used to accomplish each of the following:
   a. a time/cost trade-off analysis
   b. a resource scheduling and allocation analysis
   c. cost control

14. Find the shortest path in the acyclic network shown in Figure 8-12 by labeling all of the nodes in the manner illustrated in Figures 8-2 and 8-3.

SHORT CASES

CASE 8-1   Suppose the company considering the purchase of a new piece of equipment applies a 15 percent discount factor to the costs shown in Tables 8-2, 8-3, and 8-4.

The results for purchasing at the beginning of the year 1 are as follows:

	Keep Until End of Year:				
	1	2	3	4	5
Net discounted cost	$121.79	$189.78	$279.37	$366.56	$445.48

For purchasing at the beginning of year 2:

	Keep Until End of Year:			
	2	3	4	5
Net discounted cost	$105.86	$165.03	$242.92	$318.74

For purchasing at the beginning of years 3, 4, and 5:

	Purchase at Beginning of Year:					
	Year 3			Year 4		Year 5
	Keep Until End of Year:					
	3	4	5	4	5	5
Net discounted cost	$129.85	$181.31	$249.05	$112.92	$157.66	$98.19

Using the four-step strategy for finding the shortest path in an acyclic network, find the optimum equipment replacement policy for this company, using these discounted costs. Does the solution change when the costs are discounted? Is this surprising? Why or why not?

The South Bay Company must purchase a new truck to haul heavy rocks from a large construction site. The truck will only be used for four years. The cost of the truck is $20,000 now, but it is estimated that the cost will jump to $22,000 after two more years. The operating costs and salvage values are shown below: CASE 8-2

Number of Years Used	Salvage Value at End of Year	Annual Operating Costs
1	$15,000	$1,000
2	10,000	2,000
3	8,000	4,000
4	7,000	8,000

a. Set up tables similar to Tables 8-2, 8-3, and 8-4 to estimate the net cost of purchasing a truck at the beginning of each year.
b. Using the shortest path approach, determine the optimum purchasing plan for this truck.

A small maintenance project consists of ten jobs, whose precedence relationships are identified by their node numbers as shown in Table 8-7.   CASE 8-3
a. Draw a network diagram representing the project.
b. Calculate early and late start and finish times for each job.
c. How much total slack does job d have? Job f? Job j?
d. Which jobs are critical?
e. If job b were to take six days instead of three, how would the project finish date be affected?

TABLE 8-7	Jobs for a Small Maintenance Project	
Job	Network Description (initial node, final node)	Estimated Duration (days)
a	(1, 2)	2
b	(2, 3)	3
c	(2, 4)	5
d	(3, 5)	4
e	(3, 6)	1
f	(4, 6)	6
g	(4, 7)	2
h	(5, 8)	8
i	(6, 8)	7
j	(7, 8)	4

CASE 8-4   An architect has been awarded a contract to prepare plans and specifications for an urban renewal project. The job consists of the following activities and their estimated times.

Activity	Description	Immediate Predecessors	Time (days)
a	Preliminary sketches	—	2
b	Outline of specifications	—	1
c	Prepare drawings	a	3
d	Write specifications	a, b	2
e	Run off prints	c, d	1
f	Have specifications printed	c, d	3
g	Assemble bid packages	e, f	1

a. Draw a network diagram for this job, indicate the critical path and calculate the total slack and free slack for each activity.

b. During the first day of work it is learned that activity c (Prepare drawings) will take 4 days instead of 3. What effect does this delay have on the project completion date and project management?

The following tasks are required for the production of a play: CASE 8-5

Activity	Description	Immediate Predecessors	Time (weeks)
a	Play selection	—	3
b	Casting	a	4
c	Costume design	a	3
d	Set design	a	2
e	Set construction	d	4
f	Rehearsals	b	3
g	Dress rehearsals	c, e, f	2
h	Printing tickets and programs	b	6

a. Draw the network diagram for this play.
b. Calculate the early and late start and finish times for each activity, and the total slack and free slack for each activity.
c. Indicate the critical path.

Consider the project network shown in Figure 8-13.   CASE 8-6
a. Supply the information indicated in the following table:

Activity	Network Description (initial node, terminal node)	Time (weeks)	ES	EF	LS	LF	TS	FS
a	(1, 2)	2						
b	(1, 3)	3						
c	(2, 4)	4						
d	(3, 4)	1						
e	(4, 5)	3						
f	(4, 6)	2						
g	(5, 6)	0						
h	(5, 7)	3						
i	(6, 7)	1						
j	(7, 8)	2						

b. If activities e and f both require the use of a special piece of equipment (i.e., cannot be

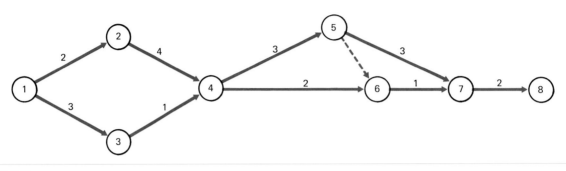

FIGURE 8-13
Project network (case 8-6)

performed at the same time), what adjustment would you make? In particular, how would the project duration be affected?

CASE 8-7 An established company has decided to add a new product to its line. It will buy the product from a manufacturing concern, package it, and sell it to a number of distributors selected on a geographical basis. Market research has indicated the volume expected and size of sales force

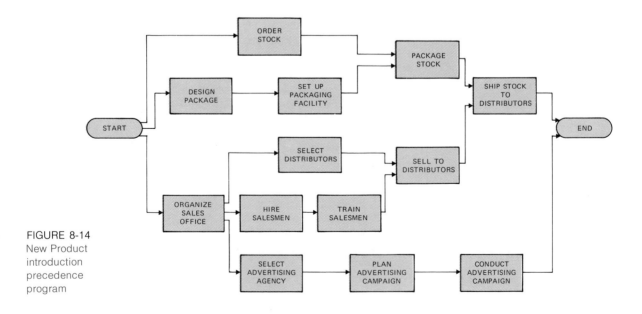

FIGURE 8-14
New Product
introduction
precedence
program

required. The steps shown in Table 8-8 are to be planned. The precedence relationships among these activities are shown in Figure 8-14. As the figure shows, the company can begin to organize the sales office, design the package, and order the stock immediately. Also, the stock must be ordered and the packaging facility must be set up before the initial stocks are packaged.

a. Draw the network diagram for this project.
b. Calculate the early and late start and finish times for each activity, and the total and free slack for each activity.
c. Indicate the critical path.

Planning Activities for New Product Introduction   TABLE 8-8

Activity	Description	Time (weeks)
a	Organize Sales Office	6
b	Hire Salesmen	4
c	Train Salesmen	7
d	Select Advertising Agency	2
e	Plan Advertising Campaign	4
f	Conduct Advertising Campaign	10
g	Design Package	2
h	Set Up Packaging Facilities	10
i	Package Initial Stocks	6
j	Order Stock from Manufacturer	13
k	Select Distributors	9
l	Sell to Distributors	3
m	Ship Stock	5

Probabilistic time estimates have been obtained for the activities in the simple project network   CASE 8-8
shown in Figure 8-15. For example, the estimate of the "optimistic time," a, for job a is 1; the estimate of the "most likely time," m, for job a is 2; and the estimate of the "pessimistic time," b, for job a is 3.

a. Using the formulas (1) and (2), calculate the mean and variance for each activity time.
b. Using the mean values, determine the critical path and its mean duration.
c. Sum the variances of the times of the activities on the critical path to obtain the variance associated with the mean duration of the project.
d. Using the area under the standardized normal curve in Table C-1 of Appendix C, compute the probability that the project will actually be completed in 10 days, 12 days, 14 days, 16 days.

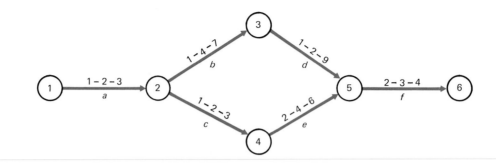

Figure 8-15
Project network
(Case 8-8)

e. A penalty cost of $50,000 must be paid if the project is not completed in 12 days. For an additional cost of $20,000, the management can guarantee that activity *d* can be completed in exactly 1 day. Should they pay the $20,000 for sure, or accept the risk regarding the penalty cost?

CASE 8-9   For the network shown in Figure 8-16, determine the critical path and the probability of finishing the project in less than 32 time periods. The optimistic, most likely, and pessimistic time estimates are shown above each activity.

FIGURE 8-16
Project network
(Case 8-9)

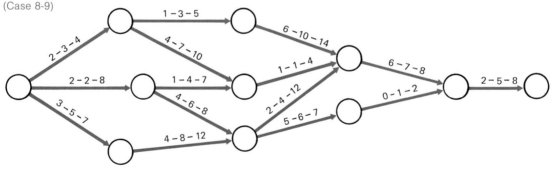

CASE 8-10   Miller Manufacturing Company is engaged in the small project shown in Figure 8-17.

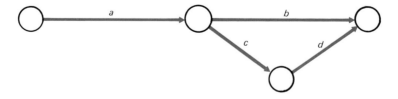

FIGURE 8-17
Project network
(Case 8-10)

The times required to accomplish each activity depend on the level of resources allocated to it. For example, activity *a* can be accomplished in 3 days with a normal allocation of resources. However, for an additional $400 worth of resources, the time can be reduced to 2 days, and for another allocation of $400 worth of resources, it can be cut to 1 day. No further reductions are possible. Similar reductions in time are possible for the other activities. The data for each activity are as follows:

Activity	Minimum Time (days)	Normal Time (days)	Cost to Reduce Time by 1 Day
a	1	3	$400
b	3	7	100
c	2	4	400
d	2	5	200

a. What are the normal project duration and the minimum project duration?
b. Overhead costs of $450 per day are incurred for *every* day the project is not completed. What is the optimum duration of the project considering both overhead costs and the costs to reduce the time on each activity?

A small maintenance project consists of the jobs in the following table. With each job is listed   CASE 8-11
its normal time and a minimum time (in days). The cost in dollars per day of reducing the time for each job is also given.

Job	Network Description (initial node, terminal node)	Minimum Time (days)	Normal Time (days)	Cost to Reduce Time by 1 Day
a	(1, 2)	6	9	$20
b	(1, 3)	5	8	25
c	(1, 4)	10	15	30
d	(2, 4)	3	5	10
e	(3, 4)	6	9	15
f	(4, 5)	1	2	40

a. What is the normal project duration and the minimum project duration?
b. Overhead costs are $50 per day. What is the optimum length schedule in terms of both time reduction and overhead costs? List the scheduled durations for each job for your solution.

GENERAL REFERENCES

Archibald, R., and R. Villoria, *Network-Based Management Systems,* John Wiley & Sons, New York, 1967.

Levy, F., G. Thompson, and J. Wiest, "The ABC's of the Critical Path Method," *Harvard Business Review,* Vol. 41, No. 5, October 1963.

Moder, J., and C. Phillips, *Project Management with CPM and PERT,* second edition, Reinhold Corporation, New York, 1970.

Paige, H. W., "How PERT-Cost Helps the General Manager," *Harvard Business Review,* Vol. 40, No. 2, March–April 1962.

Weist, J., and F. Levy, *A Management Guide to PERT/CPM,* second edition, Prentice-Hall, Englewood Cliffs, N.J., 1977.

APPLICATIONS REFERENCES

Fazar, W., "Navy's PERT System," *Federal Accountant,* Vol. 11, December 1961.

Glasser, L., and R. Young, "Critical Path Planning and Scheduling: Application to Engineering and Construction," *Chemical Engineering Progress,* Vol. 57, November 1961.

Hanson, R. S., "Moving a Hospital to a New Location," *Industrial Engineering,* Vol. 4, No. 11, November 1972.

O'Brian, J., *CPM in Construction Management,* McGraw-Hill, New York, 1965.

Odom, R., and E. Blystone, "A Case Study of CPM in a Manufacturing Situation," *Journal of Industrial Engineering,* Vol. 15, No. 6, November–December 1964.

Reeves, E., "Critical Path Speeds Refinery Revamp," *Canadian Chemical Processing,* Vol. 44, October 1960.

Wong, Y., "Critical Path Analysis for New Product Planning," *Journal of Marketing,* Vol. 28, No. 4, October 1964.

CHAPTER 9

Optimization Models
with Integer Variables

The solution to the two-product linear optimization model in Chapter 3 indicated that 10 units of chemical x and 15 units of chemical y should be produced. This is an integer solution; that is, the solution values have no fractional components. In our formulation of this two-product linear optimization model, we did not require that the solution should be in integer values; it happened by chance. In this example, obtaining an integer-valued solution may not have been particularly important. It might be possible to produce 10.5 units of chemical x during each time period, so that a total of 21 units would be produced over two time periods. However, in some real-world problems, it will be desirable, perhaps even necessary, to obtain integer-valued solutions.

Solutions obtained from linear programming are not always integer valued, and the strategy of "rounding off" the linear programming solution may not provide the optimal integer solution. Glover and Sommers [1975] describe examples of real-world problems for which the strategy of rounding the linear programming solution cannot even be used to find a *feasible* integer solution.

The network models of the previous chapters have natural integer solutions that are obtained automatically by the solution techniques. If the supplies and demands and the upper and lower bounds on the flows in the network are originally stated as integers, an integer solution will result. However, it is not possible to use network models for all analyses, so special modeling strategies and solution algorithms have been developed.

This chapter discusses optimization models with integer values. These models are generally formulated in the same format as linear optimization models, with the additional constraint that some or all of the decision variables must be integer valued in the final solution. Several examples of such models will be presented first, then a solution strategy for these models will be discussed. The section on solution strategies may be omitted by readers primarily interested in model formulation and interpretation.

EXAMPLES OF MODELS WITH INTEGER VARIABLES

There are two important types of integer variables that appear in optimization models. The first, integer decision variables, simply represents the number of units of a product, a machine, or of some other resource that should be produced or allocated, much like the ordinary decision variables in linear optimization models. The second type of integer variable is a *logical* variable that allows the optimization model to evaluate mutually exclusive alternate decisions and to analyze various combinatorial problems. An example of a combinatorial problem is the selection of three of ten alternate sites for new warehouses.

Integer decision variables

Integer decision variables may simply be the number of units of a particular product that are produced or the number of pieces of equipment that are purchased. The problem formulations would be identical to linear optimization models with one exception: instead of nonnegativity requirements for the variables in the form $x \geq 0$, integer requirements would be written in the form $x = 1, 2, 3, \ldots$.

If all the variables in the model are required to have integer values, the formulation is called an *integer programming* model. If some of the variables are required to be integer while others can have any nonnegative values as in an ordinary linear optimization model, the problem is termed a *mixed integer programming* model.

Variables that are required to have integer values often represent expensive resources. For example, a company planning a product distribution system will not consider a solution requiring them to build 3.5 warehouses to be particularly meaningful. Similarly, an oil company may wish to purchase either 4 or 5 supertankers, but not 4.3 supertankers. In some cases, a linear programming problem can be solved by ignoring the integer restrictions, and the variables that are required to have integer values can be "rounded off" to the nearest integer solution. This procedure may or may not give the best integer solution that can actually be obtained. When significant costs or other resources are involved, the additional computational burden generally associated with integer programming models may be justified in order to find the best integer solution.

Example of an integer programming formulation The objective of the two-product model of Chapter 3 was to determine the number of units of chemical x and of chemical y to be produced over a two-week period. Suppose that, at the end of the two-week period, new products must be produced. Any unfinished units of chemical x or chemical y cannot be completed and must be destroyed since there are no adequate storage facilities. Therefore, the problem is to determine the number of *integer valued* units of chemical x and chemical y to be produced.

Using the data from Chapter 3, the problem would be formulated as
maximize $Z = 60x + 50y$

subject to

$2x + 4y \leq 80,$	(machine A)
$3x + 2y \leq 60,$	(machine B)
$x \quad \leq 16,$	(demand for chemical x)
$y \leq 18,$	(demand for chemical y)
$x \quad = 0, 1, 2, \ldots$	(integer value for chemical x)
$y = 0, 1, 2, \ldots$	(integer value for chemical y)

This integer programming problem formulation is identical to the linear programming problem formulation of Chapter 3 except that the integer valued restrictions $x = 0, 1, 2, \ldots$ and $y = 0, 1, 2, \ldots$ have replaced the nonnegativity constraints $x \geq 0$ and $y \geq 0$.

Notice that the integer requirements are more *restrictive* than the nonnegativity requirements, since the nonnegativity requirements allow the decision variables to assume both integer and noninteger values. Thus, this integer programming formulation is called a *restriction* of the linear programming formulation. Likewise, the linear programming formulation is called a *relaxation* of the integer programming formulation since its constraint set includes all of the feasible solutions to the integer programming problem and other noninteger solutions as well. These concepts will be important in understanding the solution strategy for integer programming problems.

Example of a mixed integer programming formulation The machines that provide radiology services in a hospital are expensive to purchase and operate. Suppose a hospital is attempting to determine the number of machines of each type to purchase for a radiology department. The department provides two services, X-rays and radiation therapy.

There are four different machines that the hospital could use. Two of these machines can be used for normal X-rays only, one for radiation therapy only, and the other for either X-rays or radiation therapy. The average daily costs for each machine, that include both depreciation and operating costs, are shown in Table 9-1. Also shown in Table 9-1 are the estimates of the average time required to provide each

Costs and Times for the Machines

TABLE 9-1

	Machines			
	X-ray Only (1)	X-ray Only (2)	X-ray and Radiation (3)	Radiation Only (4)
Cost per day ($)	200	300	350	250
Time per X-ray (hr)	0.50	0.25	0.50	—
Time per radiation (hr)	—	—	0.75	0.50

service on each machine. The hospital estimates that each machine is available for only 5 hours of productive work each day because of maintenance requirements and other interruptions.

The average daily demand for the services is relatively constant at 30 for normal X-rays and at 20 for radiation therapy treatments. If these services are not provided in the hospital, they can be purchased externally at a cost to the hospital of $20 for each X-ray and $40 for each radiation therapy treatment.

The problem is to minimize the total cost to the hospital of operating the machines plus any charges for outside services. Suppose we define $MACH1$, $MACH2$, $MACH3$, and $MACH4$ as the number of machines of type 1, type 2, type 3, and type 4 that are purchased. Then the daily cost of operating the machines will be given by

$$200\ MACH1 + 300\ MACH2 + 350\ MACH3 + 250\ MACH4$$

Letting $XEXT$ be the number of X-rays purchased externally, and $REXT$ the number of radiation therapy treatments purchased externally, the cost of these external purchases will be

$$20\ XEXT + 40\ REXT$$

Therefore, the objective function for the optimization model for this problem would be

$$
\begin{aligned}
\text{minimize } Z = {}& 200\ MACH1 + 300\ MACH2 + 350\ MACH3 \\
& + 250\ MACH4 + 20\ XEXT + 40\ REXT
\end{aligned}
\tag{1}
$$

The constraints require that we define some additional decision variables. Let $XMACH1$, $XMACH2$, $XMACH3$ be the number of X-rays performed on machines of type 1, type 2, and type 3. Likewise, $RMACH3$ and $RMACH4$ are the number of radiation therapy treatments performed on the type 3 and type 4 machines. Now, since each X-ray on a machine of type 1 takes 0.5 hours, and each machine of type 1 is productive for only 5 hours per day, we must have

$$0.5\ XMACH1 \le 5\ MACH1 \qquad\qquad\qquad\qquad \text{(type 1)} \quad (2)$$

since $MACH1$ is the number of machines of type 1 that are available. Similarly, we have for the other three machines,

$$0.25\ XMACH2 \le 5\ MACH2 \qquad\qquad\qquad\qquad \text{(type 2)} \quad (3)$$

$$0.5\ XMACH3 + 0.75\ RMACH3 \le 5\ MACH3 \qquad\qquad \text{(type 3)} \quad (4)$$

$$0.5\ RMACH4 \le 5\ MACH4 \qquad\qquad\qquad\qquad\quad \text{(type 4)} \quad (5)$$

In order to meet the daily demand of 30 X rays, we require

$$XMACH1 + XMACH2 + XMACH3 + XEXT = 30 \qquad\qquad\qquad (6)$$

and for the radiation therapy treatment demand,

$$RMACH3 + RMACH4 + REXT = 20 \qquad\qquad\qquad\qquad\qquad (7)$$

Finally, suppose that space availabilities limit the total number of machines that can be used to a maximum of 7, and the number of machines of type 1 (which is especially cumbersome) to 2. Then we would need the constraints

$$MACH1 + MACH2 + MACH3 + MACH4 \le 7 \qquad\qquad\qquad\quad (8)$$

and

$$MACH1 \le 2 \qquad\qquad\qquad\qquad\qquad\qquad\qquad\qquad\qquad (9)$$

Using these relationships, we could now write down a formulation of a linear optimization model to solve this problem *if* noninteger values for the decision variables are acceptable solutions. In this problem, that seems unlikely. We need to know how many machines of each type to purchase, and a solution with $MACH1 = 1.5$

would be of limited usefulness. Thus, it seems clear that we should restrict the variables *MACH*1, *MACH*2, *MACH*3, and *MACH*4 to integer values.

What about the other variables? Again, we cannot perform half an X-ray or provide a fractional radiation treatment during a day. Therefore, it would seem that the variables corresponding to the number of treatments provided on each machine should be integer valued also. But, is this really necessary?

The answer to this question is a matter of judgment. This example shows why we argue that the manager should be involved in model formulation. What is the true purpose of this model? If it is to provide guidance regarding the number of machines of each type to purchase, then it may not be necessary to require the treatment variables to be integer valued. After all, each X-ray treatment *averages* 0.5 hours on machine 1, and machine 1 is available approximately 5 hours per day. Thus, if the model sets *XMACH*1 = 8.5, we could interpret this to mean that *about* 8.5 X-rays will be performed on machine 1 each day, with more on some days and less on others. The issue of integer values for these variables does not seem to be critical for the assumed purpose of the model. On the other hand, if we were developing a model to assist in actually *scheduling* treatments, then we would require the treatment variables to be integer valued.

It is important not to require integer values for variables unless it is critical for the use of the model, because such a requirement introduces additional computational difficulties in the solution algorithm. If problems have a large number of integer variables, it may be impractical to solve them even with the most sophisticated computers and algorithms.

In the standard format for the constraints to a linear or integer programming model, all the decision variables are written to the left of the equality or inequality sign, so that only a constant appears to the right. Therefore, we transpose a decision variable in each of the constraints (2)–(5), and state the *mixed integer* programming problem as follows:

minimize $Z = 200\ MACH1 + 300\ MACH2 + 350\ MACH3$
$+ 250\ MACH4 + 20\ XEXT + 40\ REXT$

subject to

$$0.5\ XMACH1 - 5\ MACH1 \leq 0$$
$$0.25\ XMACH2 - 5\ MACH2 \leq 0$$
$$0.5\ XMACH3 + 0.75\ RMACH3 - 5\ MACH3 \leq 0$$
$$0.5\ RMACH4 - 5\ MACH4 \leq 0$$

(capacity restrictions)

$$XMACH1 + XMACH2 + XMACH3 + XEXT = 30 \quad \left.\right\}\text{ (demand}$$
$$RMACH3 + RMACH4 + REXT = 20 \qquad\qquad \text{restrictions)}$$

$$MACH1 + MACH2 + MACH3 + MACH4 \le 7 \quad \left.\right\}\text{ (space}$$
$$MACH1 \le 2 \qquad\qquad\qquad\qquad\qquad \text{restrictions)}$$

$$XMACH1, XMACH2, XMACH3, XEXT \ge 0 \quad \left.\right\}\text{ (nonnegativity}$$
$$RMACH3, RMACH4, REXT \ge 0 \qquad\qquad \text{restrictions)}$$

$$MACH1, MACH2, MACH3, MACH4 = 0, 1, 2, \ldots \quad \left.\right\}\text{ (integer-value}$$
$$\qquad\qquad\qquad\qquad\qquad\qquad\qquad\qquad \text{restrictions)}$$

This model is a simple version of a more complex mixed integer model developed by Vora [1974] to plan the facilities for a diagnostic radiology department of a general hospital in upstate New York.

Logical integer variables

Perhaps the most important use of integer variables in optimization models is as logical variables. As such, the integer variables generally indicate "yes" or "no" decisions instead of the number of units used or produced.

Capital budgeting The simplest example is a capital budgeting problem in which we have several alternate investments. We can define integer variables restricted to 0 or 1 (simply called 0–1 variables) and corresponding to each alternative. If the optimal value for the variable corresponding to an alternative is 0, the investment is not accepted; if the value is 1, it is accepted.

For example, suppose we have the investment opportunities shown in Table 9-2 and a total available budget of 22 units. We can let x_1, x_2, and x_3 be defined as 0–1 variables corresponding to investment opportunities 1, 2, and 3 respectively. With the expected return values from Table 9-2, the objective function for the optimizing model for this problem would be

$$\text{maximize } Z = 20x_1 + 30x_2 + 15x_3 \tag{10}$$

If the proposed solution values of the variables are $x_1 = x_2 = 1$ and $x_3 = 0$, then investments 1 and 2 should be accepted and investment 3 should be rejected. The value of the objective function (10) would be $(20)(1) + (30)(1) + (15)(0) = 50$, the total expected return from accepting opportunities 1 and 2.

Investment Opportunities			TABLE 9-2
Investment Opportunity	Expected Return	Cost	
1	20	10	
2	30	20	
3	15	12	

The constraint on the budget is incorporated into the model by using the cost data from Table 9-2,

$$10x_1 + 20x_2 + 12x_3 \leq 22 \tag{11}$$

Also required is the integer-value restriction on the variables,

$$x_1, x_2, x_3 = 0, 1 \tag{12}$$

Notice that the solution $x_1 = x_2 = 1$ and $x_3 = 0$ does not satisfy the budget constraint (11), so it is not a feasible solution. Similarly, the integer solution $x_1 = 0$, $x_2 = x_3 = 1$ does not satisfy (11). However, the solution $x_1 = x_3 = 1$, $x_2 = 0$ is feasible, and the corresponding value of the objective function (10) is larger than for any other feasible integer solution. (Convince yourself of this.) Therefore, the optimal feasible solution is to accept investment opportunities 1 and 3 and to reject opportunity 2. Although this solution is obvious from a careful analysis of the data in Table 9-2, much more complex problems that do not have obvious solutions can be formulated in a similar manner.

Additional logical complexity can be introduced into this problem through the use of the appropriate constraints. *Either/or* decisions can be enforced very simply. For example, suppose investment opportunities 2 and 3 in Table 9-2 are mutually exclusive. That is, we could invest in *either* opportunity 2 *or* opportunity 3, but not in both. This logic could be incorporated into our formulation of the problem [(10), (11), (12)] by adding the constraint

$$x_2 + x_3 \leq 1 \tag{13}$$

Notice, if $x_2 = 1$, then x_3 must equal 0 to satisfy this inequality, and vice versa. Of course, both x_2 and x_3 could equal 0. We could *require* that one or the other of the opportunities be accepted by changing the inequality sign in (13) to an equality.

A slightly more complex example of logic that can be imposed through constraints on 0–1 variables is the *if-then* requirement. Suppose we require that investment opportunity 1 be accepted *if* opportunity 3 is accepted; that is, if we accept opportunity 3, *then* we must accept opportunity 1. We can impose this restriction through the constraint

$$x_3 - x_1 \leq 0$$

If $x_3 = 0$, then x_1 can be either 0 or 1; however, *if* $x_3 = 1$, signifying that x_3 is accepted, *then* x_1 must equal 1 in order to satisfy this constraint.

Using similar reasoning, many other logical interdependencies can be represented by constraints on 0–1 variables.

The fixed-charge problem Several real-world problems require that certain continuous variables either be set equal to 0 or that they be greater than some number N. For example, a variable x may represent the capacity of a warehouse, and we may require that either the warehouse not be built at all (in which case $x = 0$), or that the capacity be larger than some minimum value ($x \geq N$). Similarly, if x represents the number of units of a product produced during a particular time period, we may require either $x = 0$ or $x \geq N$ to ensure a minimum "lot size" for production.

This type of restriction can be imposed by introducing a 0–1 variable, y, and an arbitrarily large number M, and writing the constraints

$$x - My \leq 0 \tag{14}$$

and

$$x - Ny \geq 0 \tag{15}$$

where $N \leq M$, and M is selected so that x will be less than M for any feasible solution to the original problem. If $y = 0$ in the optimal solution, (14) constrains $x \leq 0$, but if $y = 1$, then (15) requires $x \geq N$, as we have stipulated. Notice that the only purpose of introducing the 0–1 variable y into this problem is to enforce this restriction; y has no other meaning in the problem.

To illustrate this concept, suppose x is defined as the capacity of a proposed warehouse. Because of company policy and other considerations, we require that either $x = 0$ or $x \geq 200$ units. From an analysis of other information, including the product demand, it is clear that the largest feasible value of x will be less than 1000 units. We impose this minimum capacity restriction by introducing the 0–1 variable y, and the constraints

$$x - 1000y \leq 0$$

and

$$x - 200y \geq 0$$

Facility location An important example of a real-world problem common to many organizations is the facility location problem. We can illustrate this problem by modifying the data for the transportation problem (introductory example) of Chapter 7. Suppose we currently have two facilities in operation and are trying to decide where to locate a third facility. The weekly capacities for the existing and proposed facilities are as follows:

Factory	Supply (units/week)
1	50
2	70
3 (proposed)	20
4 (proposed)	20

Factories 1 and 2 are currently in operation, while factories 3 and 4 represent new facilities at different locations, only one of which will actually be constructed. The projected weekly demand at each retail outlet is given below.

Outlet	Demand (units/week)
1	50
2	60
3	30

The costs for shipping follow, with estimates for the proposed factories 3 and 4.

Factory	Outlet 1	2	3
1	3	2	3
2	10	5	8
3 (proposed)	1	3	10
4 (proposed)	4	5	3

Further, the estimated weekly cost of operating the proposed factory 3, including depreciation, is 100, while the estimated operating cost of factory 4 is 120. Which of the two proposed plants should be constructed?

In this simple example, the most obvious and efficient solution strategy would be to solve the problem by using the specialized network code for the distribution problem, assuming factory 3 had been built (ignoring factory 4), then solve again, assuming factory 4 had been built (ignoring factory 3). The transportation costs in each case should be compared to the operating costs of the new facility, and the better alternative could be identified.

In real-world problems, the number of feasible alternatives often increases to the point that it is impractical to solve individual problems for each alternative. In such cases, integer programming is the appropriate solution strategy, so it will be worthwhile to study the integer programming formulation of this problem.

We must introduce two logical, 0–1 variables, y_3 and y_4, such that $y_3 = 1$ indicates factory 3 should be built, while $y_3 = 0$ indicates that it should not be built. A similar interpretation holds for y_4.

Thus, the objective function for this problem would be (refer to Chapter 7 for additional details):

minimize $Z =$

$$
\begin{array}{ll}
3x_{11} + 2x_{12} + 3x_{13} & \text{(total cost of shipping from factory 1)} \\
+ 10x_{21} + 5x_{22} + 8x_{23} & \text{(total cost of shipping from factory 2)} \\
+ x_{31} + 3x_{32} + 10x_{33} & \text{(total cost of shipping from factory 3)} \\
+ 4x_{41} + 5x_{42} + 3x_{43} & \text{(total cost of shipping from factory 4)} \\
+ 100y_3 + 120y_4 & \text{(operating costs of factories 3 and 4)} \qquad (16)
\end{array}
$$

The operating costs for factory 3 or factory 4 will be incurred if $y_3 = 1$ or $y_4 = 1$.

The supply constraints for factories 1 and 2 will be identical to the original formulation of this problem; that is,

$$x_{11} + x_{12} + x_{13} \le 50 \qquad (17)$$

$$x_{21} + x_{22} + x_{23} \le 70 \qquad (18)$$

The demand constraints will be modified by the addition of variables representing potential supply from factories 3 and 4, so we have

$$x_{11} + x_{21} + x_{31} + x_{41} = 50 \tag{19}$$

$$x_{12} + x_{22} + x_{32} + x_{42} = 60 \tag{20}$$

$$x_{13} + x_{23} + x_{33} + x_{43} = 30 \tag{21}$$

The only significant change is in the supply constraints for the proposed facilities, 3 and 4.

If facility 3 is built, it can supply 20 units, and $y_3 = 1$; otherwise, if $y_3 = 0$, its supply must equal 0 also. This restriction can be incorporated easily by writing

$$x_{31} + x_{32} + x_{33} \leq 20y_3 \tag{22}$$

If $y_3 = 1$, the right hand side of this inequality is 20; otherwise, it is 0 as desired. Similarly, we would write

$$x_{41} + x_{42} + x_{43} \leq 20y_4 \tag{23}$$

for factory 4.

We might wish to ensure that only factory 3 or factory 4 will be included in the final solution. This restriction could be imposed by the additional constraint

$$y_3 + y_4 \leq 1 \tag{24}$$

The solution to this *mixed integer* programming model, (16) through (24), non-negativity restrictions on the x_{ij} variables, and 0–1 integer restrictions on y_3 and y_4, would yield the optimum solution in terms of the best distribution policy *and* the appropriate new factory to open.

THE DESIGN OF A DISTRIBUTION SYSTEM
WITH A MIXED INTEGER OPTIMIZATION MODEL

Geoffrion [1976] presents a case study of an application of a mixed integer optimization model to the analysis and design of the distribution system for Hunt-Wesson Foods. We will briefly summarize this study; however, the article is written for managers and is highly recommended as supplemental reading.

At the beginning of the study, Hunt-Wesson Foods produced several hundred products at 14 locations and distributed nationally through 12 distribution centers. Annual sales were in the neighborhood of $450 million. Transportation was by rail and by truck carriers. The firm's policy was to service each customer from a single distribution center for all products. This policy was intended to simplify operations for the firm and to be convenient for the customer.

The questions to be answered by the study included the following:

- How many distribution centers should there be?
- In which cities should they be located?
- What size should each distribution center be, and which products should it carry?
- Which distribution center(s) or plant(s) should service each customer?
- How should each plant's output of each product be allocated among distribution centers or customers?
- What should the annual transportation flows be throughout the system?
- For a given level of customer service, what is the breakdown of total annual cost for the best distribution system as compared with a projection of the current system to the target period?

Obviously, there were numerous restrictions and constraints that had to be imposed on the problem. Examples include:

- No plant can produce above its stipulated production capacity for each product.
- The size of each open distribution center must be within a prescribed range.
- Each customer must be served by a single distribution center for all products.
- A distribution center can be assigned to serve a customer only if it is sufficiently close to permit the desired standard of customer service.
- There must be between 10 and 15 distribution centers.
- There are certain subsets of distribution centers among which no more than one may be open, exactly one must be open, and so on.

Notice that several of these constraints imply the need for logical integer variables, as discussed in the presentation of the simple facility location problem and in the capital budgeting example.

A mixed integer optimization model was formulated to analyze this problem. The model was run many times to check solution sensitivity to the various assumptions, to balance total costs against service levels, to answer *what if* questions regarding possible future events, and to develop a priority ranking for the implementation of the various recommendations. As a result of this analysis, five changes were recommended in the locations of the firm's distribution centers, and at least three of these changes were made. Improvements in the assignment of customers to distribution centers were also implemented. Annual cost savings directly attributable to this study were estimated to be *several million dollars.*

A SOLUTION STRATEGY

There are many different strategies for solving integer programming problems, only one of which we will present. Some of these strategies are most appropriate for all integer programming problems, while others are designed for mixed integer programming problems. Some strategies allow the integer variables to take on any nonnegative integer values, while others treat only 0–1 integer variables.

The choice of a solution strategy for a particular integer or mixed integer programming problem is best left to an expert in the field of management science. However, we present the solution strategy known as "branch and bound" to illustrate some basic concepts and some of the difficulties associated with solving integer programming problems.

Branch and bound

The branch and bound solution strategy can be used for integer or mixed integer programming problems. As an example, we consider the integer programming formulation of the chemical production problem with the total time on machine B reduced to 55 hours instead of 60 hours. The formulation is

$$\text{maximize } Z = 60x + 50y \tag{25}$$

subject to

$$2x + 4y \leq 80, \tag{26}$$

$$3x + 2y \leq 55, \tag{27}$$

$$x \quad\;\; \leq 16, \tag{28}$$

$$y \leq 18, \tag{29}$$

$$x, y = 0, 1, 2, \ldots \tag{30}$$

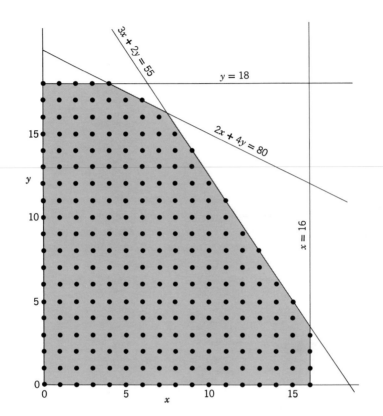

FIGURE 9-1
Solutions to the
integer program-
ming problem

which we will call $\overline{IP}$. The only differences between this formulation and the original linear programming formulation are constraint (27) with a right-hand side of 55 instead of 60 and constraint (30), which replaces the nonnegativity constraints $x, y \geq 0$.

The solution set for this problem is shown in Figure 9-1. This set consists of all pairs of integer values, denoted by the dots in Figure 9-1, that satisfy the constraints of the problem. If you count these dots, you will find 240 alternate feasible solutions. In this example it would be possible, but time consuming, to evaluate each of these alternate solutions with the objective function of the model and choose the one that maximizes this objective function. In practical problems, such a strategy would be most inefficient.

The logic of branch and bound is really quite simple, and is based on the general concepts of *relaxation* and *separation* [Geoffrion and Marsten, 1972].

Relaxation We begin with the initial integer programming problem formulation $\overline{IP}$, as shown in expressions (25) through (30). First, we note that this problem is identical to a linear programming problem except for the integer value restrictions (30). We can relax $\overline{IP}$ by replacing the integer constraints (30) by the less restrictive nonnegativity constraints

$$x, y \geq 0 \tag{31}$$

By less restrictive, we mean that all values of the variables feasible in the original problem will also be feasible in the relaxed problem, as well as additional values of these variables.

The set of feasible solutions for the relaxed $\overline{IP}$ with (31) replacing (30) is the shaded portion of Figure 9-1 that contains all of the feasible solutions to the original $\overline{IP}$ as well as noninteger solutions. Thus, the optimal solution to the relaxed problem will be at least as good as the optimal solution to the original problem. Further, it follows that if the optimal solution to the relaxed problem is feasible in the original problem, that is, integer valued, it is also the optimal solution in the original problem. (Think about this for a moment.)

Now we can solve the relaxed $\overline{IP}$ with (31) replacing (30), using the simplex algorithm. If we happen to obtain an all integer solution, we know we have also found the optimal integer solution to $\overline{IP}$ since the optimal solution in the relaxed problem is feasible in the original problem.

What if we do not obtain an integer solution when we solve the relaxed $\overline{IP}$ using the simplex method? Then we must use the concept of *separation*.

Separation When using the branch and bound solution strategy, we *separate* a problem by creating two new problems with the following characteristics:

1. Every feasible integer solution to the original problem is a feasible integer solution to *exactly one* of the subproblems.

2. Any feasible integer solution to one of the subproblems is a feasible integer solution to the original problem.

3. Some of the feasible noninteger solutions to the relaxed version of the original problem are no longer feasible noninteger solutions of the relaxed version of either subproblem.

In other words, we divide up the feasible set of solutions to the relaxed (linear programming) version of the original (integer) problem so that all the feasible integer solutions are retained in one or the other of the subproblems, but some of the noninteger solutions have been eliminated. When we eliminate enough of the noninteger solutions, we will obtain an integer solution.

The two subproblems are called *descendants* of the original problem. The descendants are placed in a *candidate* list of new problems to be solved. Eventually, the solution to the relaxed version of one of the problems from this candidate list will be the optimal solution to the original integer programming problem.

Separation is implemented by adding additional constraints to the original problem. For example, suppose we separate $\overline{IP}$ by adding the constraint $x \leq 10$ to the original constraint set, expressions (25) through (30), to create descendant 1, and $x \geq 11$ to expressions (25) through (30) to create descendant 2. The feasible regions for these two descendants of $\overline{IP}$ are shown in Figure 9-2. The feasible solutions to descendant 1 are the dots in the lightly shaded area, while the feasible solutions to descendant 2 are the dots in the heavily shaded area. Notice that characteristics 1, 2, and 3 above are satisfied by this problem separation. That is, every feasible solution to $\overline{IP}$ is a feasible solution to either descendant 1 or descendant 2 but not to both, any feasible solution to descendant 1 or descendant 2 is a feasible solution to $\overline{IP}$, and a portion of the feasible region for the linear programming solution of the relaxed version of $\overline{IP}$ is excluded from consideration by this restriction. Notice also that no integer solutions are excluded.

The steps The branch and bound algorithm searches the set of all possible integer solutions in such a way that all the possibilities do not have to be considered explicitly. It creates a list of candidate problems by separating the original integer programming problem into descendants. The candidate problems are solved by relaxing the integer constraints. The best solution for each candidate problem is compared, and the overall optimal integer solution is identified.

When we speak in general of an integer or mixed integer programming model, we will refer to it simply as *IP*, omitting the "bar" used in referring to the specific problem of expressions (25) through (30). The steps for the branch and bound as suggested by Dakin [1965] for maximizing *IP* are as follows:

STEP 1. The original candidate list consists of *IP* only, and the best feasible integer solution obtained so far (Z^*) is set at an arbitrarily small number (if we are minimizing *IP*, Z^* is set at an arbitrarily large number).

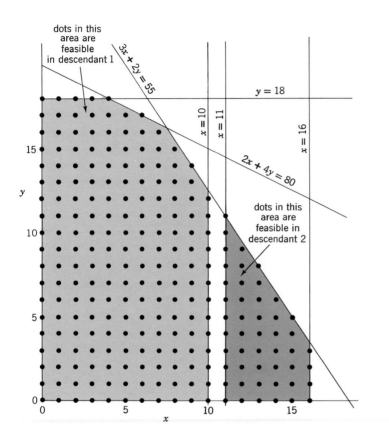

FIGURE 9-2
Feasible solutions
to the two descen-
dants of IP

STEP 2. Stop if the candidate list is empty. The best feasible integer solution previously discovered is the optimal solution.

STEP 3. The last problem placed into the candidate list is selected (last in, first out, or LIFO).

STEP 4. Relax all integer requirements.

STEP 5. Solve by the simplex method.

STEP 6. If there is no feasible solution to the relaxed problem, go to step 2.

STEP 7. If step 5 reveals that the problem selected from the candidate list has no feasible solution better than the best solution obtained so far (Z^*), go to step 2.

STEP 8. If step 5 reveals an optimal integer solution to the problem selected from the candidate list, go to step 10.

STEP 9. Separate the problem from the candidate list by selecting a fractional valued variable $\bar{x}_j$ in the solution determined in step 5. Let $[\bar{x}_j]$ denote the largest integer smaller than $\bar{x}_j$ (e.g., if $\bar{x}_j = 3.6$, $[\bar{x}_j] = 3$). Create the first descendant by adding the constraint $x_j \leq [\bar{x}_j]$, and create the second descendant by adding the constraint $x_j \geq [\bar{x}_j] + 1$. Add these descendants to the candidate list and go to step 2.

STEP 10. A new feasible solution to *IP* has been found. If the value of the objective function is greater than the best solution obtained so far, set Z^* equal to this value and go to step 2.

The result of applying step 9 is the creation of two descendants, as illustrated in Figure 9-2. In actual implementations of the branch and bound algorithm, a particular rule for choosing the fractional valued variable is included. For our purposes, we shall assume that this selection is arbitrary.

A flow chart portraying these ten steps is shown in Figure 9-3. In order to understand the logic of these steps, it may be helpful to refer to the general framework of an optimization model. According to this general framework, an optimizing model consists of an alternative generator, a predictive model, and an evaluation model, with feedback flowing from the evaluation model to the alternative generator. As indicated in Figure 9-3, steps 1 through 4 may be viewed as the alternative generator, since the candidate list contains the alternate problems to be analyzed.

In step 5, the simplex algorithm is applied to a relaxed version of a problem from the candidate list to *predict* its objective function value. If the application of this algorithm to the relaxed problem leads to an integer-valued solution, this prediction is exact. Otherwise, it is only a *bound* on the actual optimal integer solution to the problem from the candidate list.

Steps 6, 7, 8, and 10 *evaluate* the solution obtained from the prediction of step 5. Finally, step 9 provides *feedback* to the alternative generating steps by producing new descendants for the candidate list.

Now let us see how our particular example $\overline{IP}$ [expressions (25) through (30)] might be solved using this framework. We would perform the following steps:

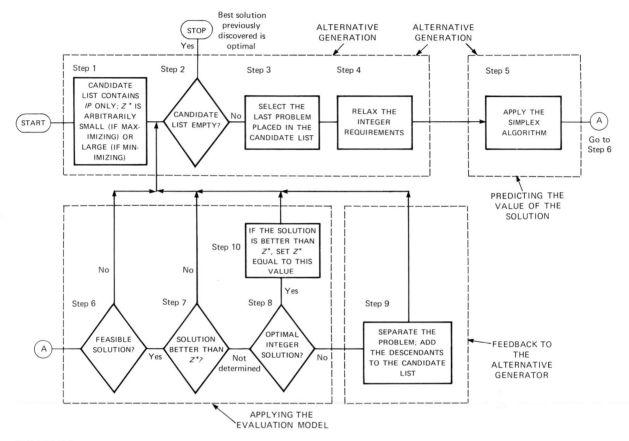

FIGURE 9-3
The general framework for solving integer programming problems

STEP 1. The candidate list consists of *IP*, and let $Z^* = 0$.

STEP 2. Continue to step 3.

STEP 3. Select $\overline{IP}$ from the candidate list.

STEP 4. Relax $\overline{IP}$ by substituting (31) for (30), thus relaxing the integer restrictions by substituting the nonnegativity constraints.

STEP 5. Apply the simplex algorithm to the resulting linear optimization model. The solution is $x = 7.5$, $y = 16.25$, $Z = 1262.5$.

STEPS 6, 7, 8. Continue.

STEP 9. Separate $\overline{IP}$. We choose $x = 7.5$ as the fractional valued variable on which to separate, and $[7.5] = 7$. Descendant $D1$ is created by adding $x \le 7$ to the constraints, and descendant $D2$ is created by adding $x \ge 8$. The feasible solutions to these descendants are shown in Figure 9-4. These problems are added to the candidate list.

STEP 2. Continue.

STEP 3. The candidate list contains $D1$ and $D2$. Select $D2$ (LIFO) from the candidate list.

STEP 4. Relax the integer requirements in $D2$.

STEP 5. Applying the simplex algorithm gives $x = 8$, $y = 15.5$, $Z = 1255$.

STEPS 6, 7, 8. Continue.

STEP 9. Separate $D2$ by adding $y \le 15$ to the constraints of $D2$ to create $D3$, and by adding $y \ge 16$ to the constraints of $D2$ to create $D4$. These two problems are added to the candidate list.

STEP 2. Continue the process.

Instead of continuing this step-by-step description of the application of branch and bound, we have summarized the process in Figure 9-5. Each square in Figure 9-5 corresponds to a problem, with the initial integer programming problem $\overline{IP}$ at the top and the various descendants labeled below it. We can see from this diagram the origin of the term "branch" in the name of this approach, since the creation of the descendants can be visualized as creating branches of alternate solutions. The problem number in the squares indicates the order in which the problems on the candidate list were solved using the simplex algorithm, since we are using the LIFO strategy in step 3. The value of Z^* is the value of the best feasible integer solution found prior to the solution of the associated problem from the candidate list.

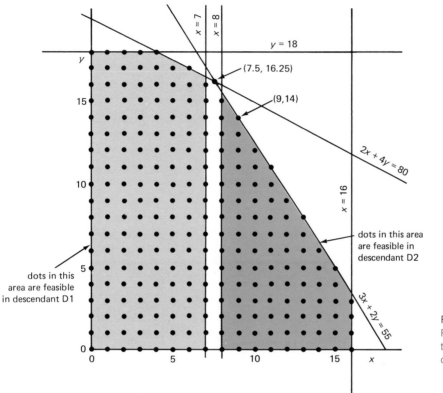

FIGURE 9-4
Feasible solutions
to the first two
descendants of $\overline{\text{IP}}$

In our verbal discussion, the descendants $D3$ and $D4$ had been created from $D2$ and added to the candidate list. The candidate list at this point contains $D1$, which was added to the list "first"; $D3$, which was added next; and $D4$, which was added "last." The next problem selected from the candidate list is $D4$, again using the "last in, first out" LIFO rule. As we can see from Figure 9-5, there is no feasible solution to the linear programming relaxation corresponding to $D4$ (study Figure 9-4 carefully to see why). We return immediately to the candidate list (step 6) and select $D3$ (LIFO). Again, the solution to the linear programming relaxation is noninteger, so we create the two descendants $D5$ and $D6$. The solution to the linear programming relaxation corresponding to $D6$ gives the first all integer solution, $x = 9$, $y = 14$, $Z = 1240$. Thus, Z^* is set equal to 1240 prior to selecting $D5$ from the candidate list. The solution to $D5$ is also integer valued, but since $Z = 1230$ is less than Z^*, it is ignored as a inferior solution.

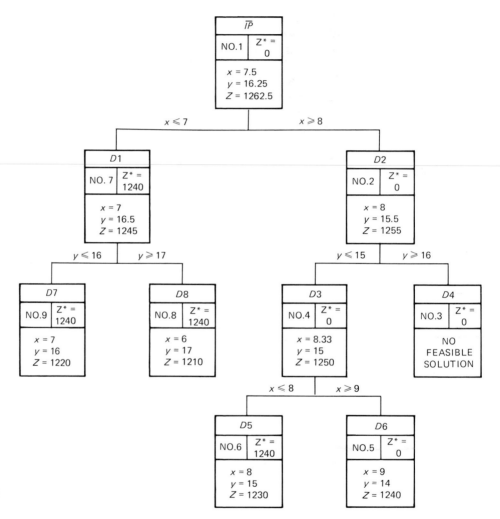

FIGURE 9-5
Summary of the
branch and bound
solution of $\overline{IP}$

What if the solution to $D5$ had *not* been integer valued? We would *not* have created descendants of $D5$ because the objective function value of 1230 is less than Z^*. Notice that the objective function values of descendants are always less than or equal to the objective function values of the problem that was separated to produce them. Thus, any descendants of $D5$ would have had objective function values of less than or equal to 1230. These values would be less than the objective function value of a previously discovered integer solution. This branch is therefore *bounded,* and would not be pursued further. Thus, the term "branch and bound" is descriptive of the solution strategy.

After $D5$ was eliminated, only $D1$ remained in the candidate list, so it was selected. The solution was noninteger, but the objective function value $Z = 1245$ is greater than $Z^* = 1240$. Therefore, we cannot bound this branch, and we must create two more descendants, $D7$ and $D8$. The objective function values for $D7$ and $D8$ are both less than Z^*, so we can eliminate them from further consideration. Notice that both $D7$ and $D8$ have all integer solutions. Since there are no more problems in the candidate list, the procedure stops (Step 2), and the solution corresponding to $Z^* = 1240$ is $x = 9$, $y = 14$, the optimal integer solution.

There are several points worth noting regarding this solution strategy. First, the solution of an integer optimization model is considerably more work than the solution of the corresponding linear optimization model created by relaxing the integer constraints. To solve this integer programming problem, we were required to solve *nine* linear programming problems, as well as do the bookkeeping regarding the candidate list and the value of Z^*. However, a careful count of the feasible solutions to this integer optimization model (the "dots" in Figure 9-4) reveals 240 alternatives. We evaluated only four of these ($x = 6$ and $y = 17$, $x = 7$ and $y = 16$, $x = 8$ and $y = 15$, and $x = 9$ and $y = 14$), or 1.7 percent, using the branch and bound strategy.

Also, consider the results of the "common sense" strategy: find the best solution to the relaxed linear optimization model, and round off to the nearest feasible integer value. The optimal solution to the relaxed linear optimization model corresponding to $\overline{IP}$ is $x = 7.5$, $y = 16.25$, and the "closest" feasible integer solution is $x = 7$, $y = 16$. Notice that this is *not* the optimal integer solution determined by branch and bound, although it was the solution for a descendant problem $D7$ (see Figure 9-5), and has an objective function value of 1220. This value compares with the optimal objective function value of 1240. In this case, the difference might not be considered significant, although in many real-world problems, the difference between this "common sense" solution and the actual optimal integer solution can be dramatic.

WHAT SHOULD THE MANAGER KNOW?

Optimization models with integer variables provide powerful tools of analysis for managers. However, the computational burden associated with these problems has inhibited their widespread use until recently. Extremely large linear optimization models can be solved on the computer by efficiently programmed versions of the simplex algorithm, but there is no single algorithm that is equally general when applied to integer or mixed integer optimization models. The branch and bound strategy described in this chapter may perform satisfactorily for some problems, but not so well for others.

The choice of a particular integer programming algorithm is an issue for the technical analyst. However, it is important that the manager work closely with the analyst so that the formulation of the model with integer variables can be as efficient as possible.

Problem formulation

As we noted in the example of the selection of machines for the radiology department of a hospital, it is important that as few variables be required to have integer values as are actually necessary to analyze the problem. Only variables that are associated with significant costs, like the number of expensive machines to be purchased or the number of warehouses to be built, should be forced to achieve an integer value in a model. Logical variables also must be integer valued, but they should be used sparingly. By working with the technical analyst, the manager can help to ensure that the formulation of the model is efficient in the sense that extraneous integer variables or logical variables are not included. This efficiency will increase the usefulness of the model, since it can be used more often.

Problem characteristics

Problems that are obviously candidates for analysis with integer models are those involving expensive items such as capital budgeting projects, machines, or facilities. Logical variables also occur in many facility design problems and can be used to advantage.

Scheduling problems can also be analyzed by using integer optimization models. Since many scheduling problems can also be formulated as network models, such as the example of scheduling faculty members to teach courses, this alternative should be explored first, because the network solution algorithms are much more efficient. However, if there is additional complexity that cannot be captured in a network, an integer model may be appropriate and useful.

Computational algorithms

The specific algorithms for solving integer optimization models are relatively complex and of little interest to the practicing manager (for further details, see Salkin [1975]). However, it should be helpful for the manager to understand the specific example of the branch and bound approach. This understanding should provide some appreciation of the logic of the solution strategy and should emphasize the need for cooperation with the technical analyst in the task of problem formulation.

CHECK YOUR UNDERSTANDING

1. Comment on the following statement: "To find the optimal integer solution, simply ignore the integer restrictions and solve the equivalent linear programming problem. Then round off this solution to the closest set of integer values."
   a. Give an example of a problem in which this might be a reasonable solution strategy.
   b. Give an example of a problem in which this might *not* be a reasonable solution strategy.
2. Distinguish between integer "decision variables" and integer "logical" variables. Give an example of each.
3. What is meant by the terms "restriction" and "relaxation" when applied to mathematical programming problems?
4. What is the basis for determining whether a particular variable should be required to have integer values in an optimization model?
5. Refer to the capital budgeting problem [expressions (10) through (12)] with three logical 0–1 variables. Write the constraints that impose the following restrictions:
   a. We cannot invest in more than two of the opportunities.
   b. Opportunity 1 can be accepted only *if* opportunity 3 is accepted; that is, if opportunity 3 is not accepted, neither is opportunity 1, but if opportunity 3 is accepted, then we have the option of accepting opportunity 1.
   c. Opportunity 1 can be accepted only if *either* opportunity 2 or opportunity 3 is accepted.
   d. Opportunity 1 can be accepted only if *both* opportunities 2 and 3 are accepted. (Hint: This restriction may require two constraints.)

6. Suppose we define x as the number of units of a product that are to be produced during the next month. The maximum capacity of the plant for this product is 2500 units. However, we require that a minimum production run of at least 500 units must be produced, if any are produced at all, to avoid scheduling production for a large number of different products during the month. Write the appropriate constraints to impose these restrictions, defining any new variable(s) that you introduce.

7. We can "relax" an integer programming problem by ignoring the integer value restrictions on the variables, but the concept of *relaxation* is a general one. Describe at least one other way that a mathematical programming problem (not necessarily an integer programming problem) could be "relaxed."

8. Justify the following statement: "If the optimal solution to the relaxed problem is feasible in the original problem, it is also the optimal solution in the original problem."

9. Suppose we attempt to *separate* $\overline{IP}$ [expressions (25) through (30)] by adding the constraint $x \leq 9$ to create one subproblem, and the constraint $x \geq 11$ to create another subproblem. Does this procedure satisfy the characteristics of a legitimate problem separation? (Graph the problem and these new constraints.)

10. Suppose we attempt to *separate* $\overline{IP}$ by adding the constraints $x + y \leq 3$ to create one subproblem and $x + y \geq 4$ to create another subproblem. Does this procedure satisfy the characteristics of a legitimate problem separation? (Graph the problem and these new constraints.)

11. The branch and bound algorithm described in steps 1 through 10 used the LIFO (last in, first out) strategy to select problems from the candidate list. Redraw Figure 9-5 assuming that a FIFO (first in, first out) strategy is used to select the problems. This change will affect the order in which the various candidate problems are solved.

12. Justify the following statement: "If the solution to D5 had *not* been integer valued, we would not have created its descendants, because the objective function value of 1230 is less than Z*." How would we know that one of the descendants of D5 does not contain an *integer solution* with an objective function value greater than Z*? Use the properties of the techniques of separation and relaxation in your argument.

13. Consider Exercise 9 in Check Your Understanding in Chapter 7. Suppose we decide that we should not use overtime at either of the existing plants. Therefore,

we consider a second alternative for meeting the increase in demand to 150 units at warehouse 2. This alternative is the construction of a third plant (plant 3) with a capacity of 200 units. Being modern, the normal production costs would be only $1 per unit, and the cost per unit of shipping to warehouse 1 would be $2, and the cost to warehouse 2, $3. *If* we construct this new plant, we incur a fixed operating cost of $100. However, because of the third plants' capacity, we have the option of closing plants 1 and 2. Closing plant 1 would *save* the fixed operating cost of $75, while closing plant 2 would *save* the fixed operating cost of $50. Assume that we must meet the demand requirements at the warehouses using normal production capacities only.

Formulate the problem. (Hint: The formulation would be similar to one for considering three potential plant locations.)

14. A manufacturer has two products, *x* and *y*, both of which are made in two steps by machines *A* and *B*. Process times per 100 are:

	x (hr)	y (hr)
Machine A	4	5
Machine B	5	2

For the coming period machine *A* has 100 hours available and machine *B* 80 hours. The sales prices and variable cost components per 100 units for the two products are:

	x	y
Price	$20	$10
Variable cost	10	5

The organization can sell all it can make in the current market and wishes to know the quantities of each product to make in order to maximize some function that approximates profit.

a. Write the constraints and objective function to describe the situation as a linear programming problem.

b. Suppose that the total "set-up" costs to produce *x* are $100 and the "setup" costs for *y* are $75. This means that these costs are incurred in *full* if any of *x* or *y* respectively are produced. Write the constraints and objective function to describe this modified situation. Be sure to define any variables you introduce.

15. (Requires the use of the simplex algorithm) In the analysis preceding the launch of astronauts for the first space shuttle mission, the following problem was discussed: The spacecraft was limited to 8 cubic feet of storage for the added supplies to be used in case of an emergency. To deal with the problem of allocating these supplies, "packages" of supplies were created and valued.

Package Description	Cubic Feet Required per Package	Value
Medical supplies	2	3
Repair devices	3	6
Safety devices	3	4

Each additional package of each type was considered to have the same value as the first one placed on board. The problem was to determine how many of each type of package to take so as to maximize the total value obtained.
a. Formulate the appropriate integer programming problem.
b. Solve this formulation for the optimal integer solution using the branch and bound algorithm.

SHORT CASES

CASE 9-1   Suppose we have a metropolitan area where we are trying to locate several Health Maintenance Organizations (HMO's) that provide prepaid health care. There are 3 potential site locations and 5 census tracts to be served by these sites. If we open an HMO at a particular site, we can estimate the number of subscribers from each tract who would go to that site *if the persons in the tract were assigned* to go to the HMO at that site. These numbers will vary from site to site depending on how close it is to a census tract and how close it is to major public transportation routes. The tracts are to be assigned to *only one* of the HMO's that is actually built. The estimated number of subscribers are shown below:

Site	Census Tract 1	2	3	4	5
1	50,000	10,000	25,000	12,000	20,000
2	20,000	15,000	20,000	20,000	40,000
3	25,000	20,000	10,000	20,000	25,000

In addition, we know that it will cost $5 million to construct an HMO at site 1, $3 million to construct one at site 2, and $2 million to construct one at site 3. The total available budget for construction is $7 million. Finally, each new HMO requires a minimum enrollment of 70,000 subscribers or it should not be built.

Formulate a model to maximize the total number of subscribers in the metropolitan area subject to the constraints described above.

Study the network formulation of the faculty/course scheduling problem described in Chapter 7 and illustrated in Figures 7-4 and 7-5. In the network formulation, we can place upper and lower bounds on the following:

CASE 9-2

(1) The total number of courses taught by a faculty member each academic year

(2) The number of courses taught by a faculty member each quarter

(3) The total number of sections of a particular course offered each academic year

(4) The number of sections of a particular course offered each quarter

However, there are some types of constraints that *cannot* be included in the network formulation.

Suppose we consider a scheduling problem with only the following courses and four faculty members:

Course Number	Name of Course	Faculty Member Number	Name
1	Introduction to Management Science	1	Janes
2	Advanced Management Science	2	Gillespie
3	Basic Mathematical Concepts	3	Mitoff
4	Elective	4	Pulliam

All four faculty members can teach courses 1 and 4, Introduction to Management Science and the elective. However, only Janes and Pulliam can teach course 3, Basic Mathematical Concepts, and Mitoff does not have the background to offer course 2, Advanced Management Science.

Let x_{ij}, y_{ij}, and z_{ij} be the number of sections of course i ($i = 1, 2, 3,$ or 4) offered by faculty member j ($j = 1, 2, 3,$ or 4) in the fall, winter, and spring respectively. For example, $y_{24} = 2$ would signify that two sections of course 2, Advanced Management Science, should be offered by faculty member 4, Pulliam, in the winter.

a. Formulate constraints to impose the following restrictions:
   (1) Course 2 should be offered in the winter *only* if course 1 is offered in the fall.
   (2) Pulliam is willing to teach as many as two sections of either course 1 or course 3 in the winter, but not one or more sections of both courses.

(3) If Jane teaches course 1 in the fall, he must offer course 4 in the spring.

(4) No sections of course 4 should be offered unless at least one section of each of courses 1, 2, and 3 is offered.

b. None of the above constraints can be introduced explicitly in the network formulation, which is why the solution to the network model was called an approximate solution in Chapter 7.

(1) In what ways does an integer programming formulation of the faculty/course scheduling problem have an advantage over the network formulation?

(2) In what ways does the network formulation have an advantage?

(3) What is the appropriate basis for preferring one formulation over the other?

CASE 9-3   Hypol Industries makes large industrial machines that are used to manufacture other products. The existing Hypol plant is cramped and outdated. It must either be modernized or a new plant must be purchased. If a new facility is purchased, management must decide whether to install a fully automated production line or to stay with the cheaper, more conventional methods.

The completed products are initially shipped on a company-owned barge to a major shipping area. Another investment alternative would be a new, more efficient barge. If a new

TABLE 9-3   Project List for Hypol Industries

Project Number	Description	Net Present Value of Future Income	Worker Hours	Expenditures Year 1	Year 2
1	Modernize existing facility	$100,000	7,000	$200,000	$100,000
2	Purchase new facility	200,000	6,000	500,000	0
3	Add fully auto-mated assembly line to new facility	40,000	1,000	50,000	0
4	Modernize sales offices	200,000	2,000	100,000	100,000
5	Purchase a new shipping barge	75,000	1,000	0	200,000
6	Add new shipping dock to existing facility	50,000	3,000	50,000	25,000

barge were purchased *and* the old facility were modernized, a new shipping dock would have to be built.

Finally, the company could also invest in modernizing the sales offices in the cities where the sales representatives are based.

The alternate projects are shown in Table 9-3 along with the net present values of their associated future income streams. All of the projects are desirable in the sense that they have positive net present values. However, they also consume worker hours and cash. Hypol must observe the following limitations, which were estimated by the accounting department:

Worker hours: 15,000

Expenditures: Year 1 $600,000
               Year 2 $300,000

a. Formulate the appropriate optimization model for analyzing this problem.

b. Other than being computationally more efficient, why might a simple linear programming formulation be useful in analyzing this problem? (Hint: What if the constraints in expenditures are not absolutely fixed, but they could vary a bit. What information would you like to have to determine the appropriate expenditure level?)

GENERAL REFERENCES

Dakin, R., "A Tree Search Algorithm for Mixed Integer Programming Problems," *Computer Journal,* Vol. 8, No. 3, 1965.

Garfinkel, R., and G. Nemhauser, *Integer Programming,* John Wiley & Sons, New York, 1972.

Geoffrion, A., and R. Marsten, "Integer Programming Algorithms: A Framework and State-of-the-Art Survey," *Management Science,* Vol. 18, No. 7, March 1972.

Salkin, H., *Integer Programming,* Addison-Wesley Publishing Co., Reading, Mass., 1975.

Zionts, S., *Linear and Integer Programming,* Prentice-Hall, Inc., Englewood Cliffs, N.J., 1974.

APPLICATIONS REFERENCES

Atkins, R., and R. Shriver, "New Approach to Facilities Location," *Harvard Business Review,* May–June 1968.

Gaballa, A., and W. Pearce, "Telephone Sales Manpower Planning at Quantas," *Interfaces,* Vol. 9, No. 3, May 1979.

Geoffrion, A., "Better Distribution Planning with Computer Models," *Harvard Business Review,* Vol. 54, No. 4, July–August 1976.

Glover, F., "Management Decisions and Integer Programming," *The Accounting Review,* January 1972.

Glover, F., and D. Sommers, "Pitfalls of Rounding in Discrete Management Decision Problems," *Decision Sciences,* Vol. 6, May–June 1975.

Markland, R. E., and R. J. Newett, "Production-Distribution Planning in a Large-Scale Commodity Processing Network," *Decision Sciences,* Vol. 7, No. 4, October 1976.

Noonan, F., and R. J. Giglio, "Planning Electric Power Generation: A Non-Linear Mixed Integer Model Employing Benders Decomposition," *Management Science,* Vol. 23, No. 9, May 1977.

Trinedi, V. M., and D. M. Warner, "A Branch and Bound Algorithm for Optimum Allocation of Float Nurses," *Management Science,* Vol. 22, No. 9, May 1976.

Vora, J., "Heuristics and Optimizing Techniques Applied to Long Range Facility Planning for Hospital Ancillary Departments," *Management Science,* Vol. 21, No. 4, December 1974.

Westerberg, C. H., B. Bjorklund, and E. Hultman, "An Application of Mixed Integer Programming to a Swedish Steel Mill," *Interfaces,* Vol. 7, No. 2, February 1977.

CHAPTER 10

Optimization Models
for Inventory Management

The first optimization model used by managers was an inventory model developed by F. W. Harris in 1915. Harris derived a formula for the Economic Order Quantity (*EOQ*), the optimum quantity of materials or items to purchase at one time.

Since World War II a great deal of research has been focused on inventory problems. We will begin with a general discussion of inventories and their functions in managerial systems, and the relevant costs associated with inventories. We will then formulate an optimization model for the quantity of an item to purchase at one time, the economic order quantity (EOQ). Given this conceptual framework, we develop extensions that take account of some complicating factors, such as stock shortages, quantity discounts, and further extensions that consider risk.

FUNCTIONS OF INVENTORIES

Inventories are necessary in many managerial systems in order to provide "off the shelf" service for stock items in retailing and wholesaling operations, and these needs are reflected back into the manufacturing and raw material supply functions. In systems that produce a service instead of a physical product, the proper functioning of that service is usually partially dependent on supply items—paper and forms in governmental and other offices, medical supplies in hospitals, repair parts in a maintenance operation, and so on.

Throughout the supply-manufacturing-distribution system, inventories are the "shock absorbers" that absorb the normal variations in demand and in supply lead time at each stock point. As such, they perform a decoupling function that makes it possible to carry on activities relatively independently and efficiently. Without inventories, such systems could not function effectively, and when inventories fall to dangerously low levels, we need virtually perfect coordination and scheduling to compensate. Unfortunately, this perfection is not normally attainable. When such enterprises are forced into a hand-to-mouth supply situation by strikes or other choking of supply lines the inventories are depleted, and the smoothly functioning machine breaks down. The vital nature of inventories is seen by examining the kinds of inventories that exist in a supply system.

Pipeline inventories

To illustrate the function of pipeline inventories, assume a production-distribution system with one product for which there is an average demand of 200 units per week

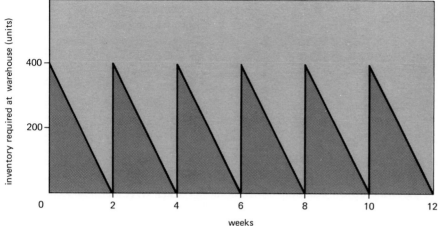

FIGURE 10-1
Idealized graph of inventories required at the warehouse to cover trucking time from the factory. The average transit inventory component of pipeline inventory is the product of truck time and demand rate, or 2×200 $= 400$ units. Average inventory for the transit function is $400/2 = 200$ units.

at the warehouse. Let us assume that normal warehousing procedures are to prepare a procurement order to the factory when the warehouse inventory falls to a critical level called the *reorder point.* It takes one week to prepare the order, get it approved, and have it received by the factory. Once the order is received at the factory, it takes two weeks for loading, trucking, and unloading at the warehouse.

The warehouse must carry enough stock on hand to meet demand during the transit time. Figure 10-1 shows an idealized graph of the inventories required at the warehouse just to cover trucking time from the factory. The average transit inventory is the product of the truck time and the demand rate, or $2 \times 200 = 400$ units. At all times, 400 units are in motion from the factory to the warehouse or, in an equivalent sense, the warehouse must maintain an inventory that takes account of this fact. The order time delay of one week has the same effect as a transit time, since the warehouse must also carry inventories to cover this delay. In general then, every lag in the system generates the need for inventory to fill the pipeline. These are the in-process inventories in production systems; however, the concept is completely general.

Lot size or "cycle" inventories

The number of items included in each order, or shipment, is called the *lot size.* To examine lot size inventories, let us continue with our simple example. Since the truck must make the trip from the factory to the warehouse, how many items should be moved at one time? Most of the trucking costs are fixed regardless of lot size, so hand-to-mouth supply would be prohibitively expensive. Let us assume that orders are placed for a truckload of 800 units, equivalent to a four-week supply. Figure 10-2 shows an idealized graph of inventories required at the warehouse when orders are placed for a truckload. Warehouse inventories must therefore be increased to take account of the fact that materials are trucked 800 at a time to gain transportation cost advantages.

Buffer inventories

At times, inventories must provide a buffer against variations. Figure 10-2 assumes that demand rate, truck time, and order time are all constant. We know, however, that these factors are not ordinarily constant, so we must have some way to protect against unpredictable variations in demand and in supply time. Figure 10-3 shows the contrast in inventory levels at the warehouse that might occur if the maximum demand* of 300 units per week occurred during the supply time of three weeks. In order to ensure that we do not run out of stock, a buffer inventory of 300 units is

FIGURE 10-2
Inventories required at the warehouse when orders are placed for a truckload of 800 units. Average inventory for this component is 800/2 = 400 units. Transit inventories are unchanged.

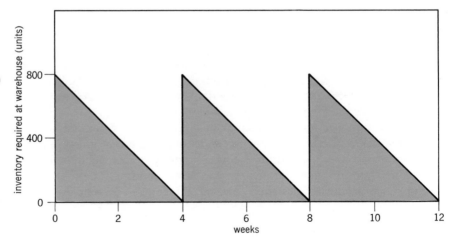

* The maximum demand is a point on the demand distribution curve that would not be exceeded more than a preset percentage of time. It is established by considering the cost of running out of stock.

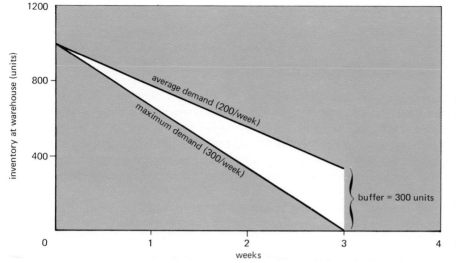

FIGURE 10-3
Buffer inventory required to avoid shortages. Difference between idealized average and maximum demand rates over the supply lead time represents a minimum or buffer stock required to protect against the occurrence of shortages resulting from random fluctuations in demand.

required [the difference in the maximum and average demand rates during the three-week supply time: $(300 - 200) \times 3 = 300$ units]. Techniques for taking account of these risk factors are very important in inventory models, and are discussed later in the chapter.

Seasonal inventories

Many products have a fairly predictable but seasonal pattern through the year. Where this is true, management has the choice of changing production rates over the year to absorb the fluctuation in demand or of absorbing some or all of the fluctuation in demand with inventories. If we attempt to follow the demand curve through the seasonal variations by changing production rates, the capital investment for the system must provide for the peak capacity, and we must absorb costs for overtime, hiring, training, and separating labor.

The discussion to this point has indicated the vital nature of inventories and the advantages gained by recognizing their functions. The question, however, is not one-sided. Inventories cost money and a knowledge of the behavior of inventory-related costs will be important to building inventory models and to the formulation of managerial objectives and an evaluation model.

Costs and management objectives

The following types of cost items are often relevant to inventory models: costs that depend on the number of orders, price or production costs, handling and storage costs, shortage costs, and capital costs.

Costs depending on the number of orders In deciding on purchase order quantities, there are certain clerical costs of preparing orders. These costs are the same regardless of the quantity ordered. They are important in the models with which we deal; however, our interest is in the true incremental cost of order preparation (or its equivalent). The average ordering cost derived by dividing the total cost of the purchasing operation by the average number of orders processed is not appropriate, since a large segment of the total costs are fixed. Our interest is in the variable cost component.

The parallel cost in production systems is the cost to prepare production orders, set up machines, and control the flow of orders through the plant.

Price or production costs When quantity discounts must be taken into account, unit price becomes relevant in determining purchase order quantities. *Quantity discounts* are unit price reductions that are allowed for relatively large orders. Comparably, production cost is relevant to determining the size of production lots.

Costs of handling and storing inventory There are certain costs associated with the level of inventories, represented by the costs of handling material in and out of inventory and the storage costs. The storage costs are made up of components such as insurance, taxes, rent, obsolescence, spoilage, and capital costs. These costs are commonly in proportion to inventory levels.

Capital costs As alluded to in the preceding paragraph, part of the storage cost is the opportunity cost of capital invested in inventory. The cost figure itself is the product of inventory value per unit, the time that the unit is in inventory, and the appropriate interest rate. In general, the appropriate interest rate should reflect the opportunities for the investment of comparable funds within the organization, and it should not be lower than the cost of borrowed money. Since the funds are tied up in inventories, they cannot be used for the purchase of other profit-producing investments, and an opportunity cost must be imputed.

Cost of shortages An extremely important cost that never appears on accounting records is the cost of running out of stock. Such costs appear in several ways. In profit-making concerns, sales may actually be lost as a result of stockouts or there may be additional costs resulting from back ordering. In production systems, a part shortage may cause idle labor on a production line or subsequent incremental labor cost to perform operations out of sequence, usually at higher than normal cost. Alternately, there may be costs of avoiding shortages. In nonprofit organizations, similar costs may be involved if the quality of the services is affected.

Management objectives The overall objective of management is to design policies and decision rules that view inventories in a "systems" context so that the broadly construed set of costs discussed are generally minimized. In addition, however, the existence of a cost of shortages raises a question concerning the appropriate service level. (Service level may be defined as the percentage of orders that can be filled from stock.) When shortage costs can be accurately estimated, the most economical service level can be determined by balancing buffer inventory costs against shortage costs. More commonly, however, shortage costs cannot be accurately determined, and the manager must reflect subjective tradeoffs for service versus buffer inventory costs in establishing service level policies.

FORMULATION OF A PURCHASE ORDER QUANTITY MODEL

Let us organize our knowledge about the functions of inventories, and inventory-related costs, with the objective of determining managerial policies concerning the number of units of an item to order at one time. We establish the following notation:

C = total incremental cost

C_0 = total incremental cost of an optimal solution

Q = order quantity

Q_0 = Economic Order Quantity (EOQ)

R = annual requirements in units

c_H = inventory holding costs per unit per year

c_P = preparation costs per order

c_S = shortage costs per unit per year

P = reorder point

The decision variable under managerial control is the order quantity Q, and we assume that we have a forecasting model to provide an estimate of the annual requirements R. Our initial objective is to develop a model to determine the order quantity Q_0 that minimizes the relevant incremental costs.

When an optimizing model is used, rather than identifying a specific alternative, managers can define the *set of all feasible alternatives*. That is, they can describe the characteristics of alternatives that will be acceptable solutions to the problem. In our inventory management problem the set of feasible alternatives consists of all of the possible order sizes, $Q = 1, 2, 3, \ldots n$, where n may be an upper bound reflecting warehouse capacity, or some other constraint. The optimizing model must search through this entire set of alternatives to identify Q_0.

With the set of feasible alternatives defined we can develop a model that relates system inputs to outputs. For the purchase order quantity system, given a specific order quantity, Q, the outcome of interest to the decision maker is the total incremental cost C with which it is associated. We must determine a logical relationship between the order quantity and these incremental costs. (We are assuming no price discounts and no shortages, since deterministic usage rate and precise timing of order receipt are a part of the model.)

Figure 10-4 describes the idealized functioning of the inventory system. When the inventory level of our item falls to the reorder point P, an order for Q units is placed.

FIGURE 10-4
Graphic model of inventory levels when the number purchased at one time is Q units. The time between the receipt of orders is t.

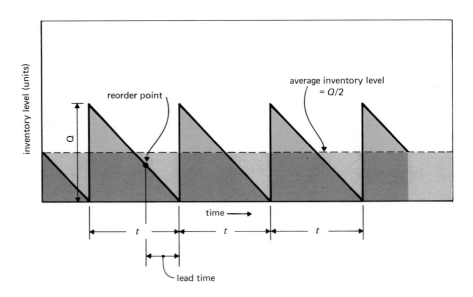

The reorder point P is set so that inventory is reduced to zero by normal usage at the rate determined by R precisely when the order for Q units is received. The inventory is then increased immediately by Q units and the cycle repeats as shown in Figure 10-4. The average inventory level is simply $Q/2$.

The total incremental costs C for this simple system are the costs of holding inventory and the costs associated with the procurement of an order of size Q. Therefore, the logical relationship for the costs is

$C =$ inventory holding costs $+$ preparation costs

We can see from Figure 10-4 that if Q is increased, the average inventory level $Q/2$ will increase proportionately. If the inventory holding cost per unit per year is c_H, the annual incremental costs associated with holding inventories are

$c_H \, (Q/2)$

If the cost to hold a unit of inventory for a specific product was $c_H = \$0.10$, we could express the inventory holding cost function as $0.10 \, Q/2 = 0.05Q$, a simple linear function. The inventory holding cost function is plotted in Figure 10-5 as curve (a).

Similarly, the annual preparation costs depend on the number of times orders are placed per year and the cost to place an order. The number of orders required for an annual requirement of R will vary with the lot size Q of each order; that is, the number of orders equals R/Q. If it costs c_P to place an order, the annual preparation costs are

$c_P \, (R/Q)$

If, for example, $R = 1600$ units per year, and $c_P = \$5$, we could express the annual preparation costs as $(5 \times 1600/Q) = 8000/Q$. This preparation cost function is plotted for different values of Q in Figure 10-5, curve (b).

The total incremental costs C are represented by the sum of the two cost components

$$C = c_H \, (Q/2) + c_P \, (R/Q) \tag{1}$$

Equation (1) is a model that will predict costs, given the parameters, and the values of R and Q. For the specific values of the parameters given, equation (1) becomes

$$C = 0.05Q + 8000/Q \tag{2}$$

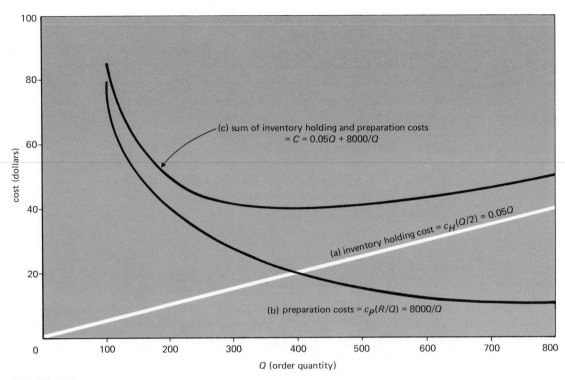

FIGURE 10-5
Graphic representation of inventory costs. $R = 1600$ units per year, $c_p = \$5.00$, $c_H = \$0.10$.

Curve (c) in Figure 10-5 shows this total cost function plotted for different values of Q. Note that curve (c) declines to a minimum as order size increases and then increases again as inventory holding costs become dominant. We can now use equation (2) to evaluate different order quantity policies.

Given equation (2) as a model that predicts inventory costs, we must now evaluate the outcomes it produces. The simple inventory problem we have described involves a single criterion, total incremental costs, and complete certainty. That is, we have assumed that there is no uncertainty regarding demand, inventory holding costs, preparation costs, the supply lead time, or other elements of the problem. These assumptions may or may not be appropriate in a specific real-world application. Later, we will see how additional detail can be added to this simple model, so that more realistic models may be obtained.

Since the criterion in this case is total incremental costs C, obviously we would like to minimize C. This could be accomplished by trial and error calculations using different alternate values of Q in equation (2), or by creating graphs such as Figure 10-5. However, an optimization model exists that simplifies this search for Q_0, the economic order quantity.

Optimization model

By inspecting Figure 10-5, we can see that the form of the total incremental cost curve is such that the minimum cost occurs when the slope of the curve is zero. We have placed all the elements of the optimization model in the flow chart shown in Figure 10-6.

We can use an iterative procedure as in Figure 10-6 and start with a value of Q and evaluate it by equation (1) and determine the direction of the slope in order to get the next value of Q. In fact, we will not actually use this iterative procedure, we will simply use a visual examination of the total cost curve of Figure 10-5 as our test. Let us start with $Q_1 = 100$ units and use increments of 100 units for sample calculations. Using equation (2) for the specific parameters of our example,

$$C = 0.05Q + 8000/Q$$
$$= 0.05 \times 100 + 8000/100 = \$85$$

Table 10-1 summarizes the successive calculations for $Q_2 = 200$, $Q_3 = 300$, $Q_4 = 400$, and $Q_5 = 500$ units, indicating the visual check for the direction of slope. In this instance we have actually gone past the zero slope point in calculating for Q_5 to indicate that the slope changes from negative to positive and that the value of C increases beyond the minimum at $Q_0 = 400$ units.

The power of the optimization model is not in the iterative procedure we have just used to demonstrate conceptually what happens as we converge on the optimum solution, but in using mathematical methods to derive a *general solution* for the entire class of order quantity problems. Using appropriate mathematical methods we can determine the general form of the slope of equation (1):

$$\text{Slope} = c_H/2 - c_P(R/Q^2) \tag{3}$$

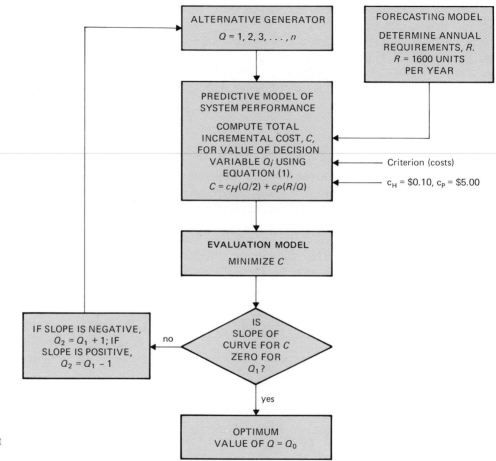

FIGURE 10-6
Flow chart for an optimizing inventory model that combines a forecasting model, an alternative generator, a predictive model, an evaluation model, a test for optimality, and a mechanism to direct changes in Q based on the test for optimality.

The value of equation (3) is, in fact, the slope of the line tangent to the total incremental cost curve. We wish to know the value of Q when this slope is zero. Therefore, we set equation (3) equal to zero and solve for Q_0:

$$0 = c_H/2 - c_P R/Q_0^2$$

$$Q_0^2 = 2\ c_P R/c_H$$

Computation of Costs C for Five Successive Values of Q_i TABLE 10-1

Order Quantity (Q_i)	Inventory Holding Costs (0.05 Q_i)	Preparation Costs (8000/Q_i)	Total Incremental Costs* (C)	Visual Check of Slope of C for Value of Q_i
100	5.0	80.0	85.0	—
200	10.0	40.0	50.0	—
300	15.0	26.7	41.7	—
400 = Q_0	20.0	20.0	40.0	0
500	25.0	16.0	41.0	+

Note: $R = 1600$ units per year, $c_H = \$0.10$, and $c_P = \$5$.

* The sum of the second and third columns of the table.

and

$$Q_0 = \sqrt{2c_PR/c_H} \qquad (4)$$

Equation (4) is a general solution for the optimum order quantity Q_0 and may be used for any values of requirements R and the cost parameters c_P and c_H. The cost of an optimal solution may be derived by substituting the value of Q_0 determined by equation (4) in equation (1).

$$C_0 = c_HQ_0/2 + c_PR/Q_0$$

This reduces to

$$C_0 = \sqrt{2c_Pc_HR} \qquad (5)$$

Now that we have equations (4) and (5), we may substitute the values for R, c_P, and c_H used in our example to obtain

$$Q_0 = \sqrt{2 \times 5 \times 1600/0.10} = \sqrt{160,000} = 400 \text{ units}$$

and

$$C_0 = \sqrt{2 \times 5 \times 0.10 \times 1600} = \sqrt{1600} = \$40$$

The basic *EOQ* model involves quite restricted assumptions. For example, no shortages or back orders are allowed (the timing of the receipt of orders is assumed to be perfect), there are no price discounts, and all aspects of the model are deterministic (demand is assumed to be known and constant, as is supply lead time). Given the basic model, we can successfully relax some of these assumptions and approach reality. In Chapter 2 we called this process of beginning with a simple model and then adding detail "bootstrapping."

Inventory model that allows shortages

If the assumption that shortages and back orders are zero is relaxed, we have the graphical structure of Figure 10-7. The problem is now to determine the minimum cost order quantity when shortages are allowed at a cost of c_S. The inventory level rises to only I_{max} on the receipt of Q because the difference $(Q - I_{max})$ is assumed to meet back orders instantaneously.

When shortage costs are accounted for, the basic *EOQ* model becomes slightly more general and the optimization model represented by equation (4) becomes a special case. The rationale for the derivation parallels the basic model, but it is somewhat more complex mathematically. Derivations may be found in Buffa and Miller [1979], and the resulting formulas are

$$Q_0 = \sqrt{2c_P R/c_H} \times \sqrt{(c_H + c_S)/c_S} \tag{6}$$

$$C_0 = \sqrt{2c_P c_H R} \times \sqrt{c_S/(c_H + c_S)} \tag{7}$$

$$I_{max_0} = \sqrt{2c_P R/c_H} \times \sqrt{c_S/(c_H + c_S)} \tag{8}$$

Note that when comparing equations (6) and (7) with equations (4) and (5), Q_0 is increased by the factor $\sqrt{(c_H + c_S)/c_S}$, and C_0 is decreased by the factor $\sqrt{c_S/(c_H + c_S)}$. The influence of shortages is consequently dependent on the relative size of c_H and c_S. If c_H is large relative to c_S, the effect of shortages on Q_0 and C_0 is considerable; that is, Q_0 will be increased and C_0 decreased compared to equations (4) and (5). If, on the other hand, c_H is small relative to c_S, minor changes in Q_0 and C_0 will result.

The net effect of shortage costs on Q_0 and C_0 may at first seem to be strange. Recognize, however, that when the model permits shortages, average holding costs are reduced because of smaller average inventory balances. This reduction will result in a larger Q_0. For the shortage case, C_0 is smaller than when shortages are not

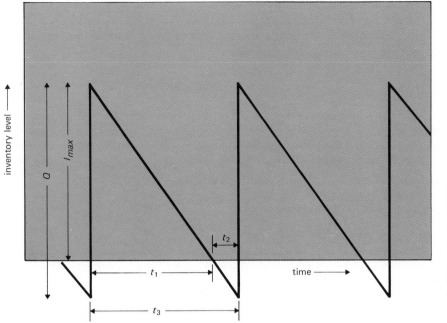

FIGURE 10-7
Idealized structure of inventory levels with back orders of $Q - I_{\max}$ allowed; $t_1 =$ time during which there are inventory balances on hand; $t_2 =$ time during which there is an inventory shortage; $t_3 =$ cycle time.

included because both holding costs and annual preparation costs are somewhat lower. If we consider shortages in the previous example where $R = 1600$ per year, $c_P = \$5$ per order, $c_H = \$0.10$ per unit per year, and in addition, $c_S = \$0.50$ per unit per year, we have the following results:

$$Q_0 = \sqrt{(2 \times 5 \times 1600)/0.10} \times \sqrt{(0.10 + 0.50)/0.50}$$

$$= 400\sqrt{1.2} = 400 \times 1.095 = 438 \text{ units}$$

$$C_0 = \sqrt{2 \times 5 \times 0.10 \times 1600} \times \sqrt{0.50/(0.10 + 0.50)}$$

$$= 40\sqrt{0.833} = 40 \times 0.913 = \$36.51$$

The limiting values of c_S provide valuable insight. As c_S becomes infinitely large, the factor in equation (6), $\sqrt{(c_H + c_S)/c_S}$, becomes 1 in the limit and we have the basic inventory model of equation (4). This corresponds to a policy of no shortages permitted. On the other hand, if c_S is set at zero, then $\sqrt{(c_H + c_S)/c_S}$ and Q_0 become infinity. This corresponds to a policy of infinite back ordering, hand-to-mouth supply, or supply only on the basis of special order.

The effect of quantity discounts

The basic *EOQ* model assumes a fixed price; therefore, the total cost equation (1) does not include the price of the item, since it is not a relevant cost in the basic model. Let us now consider a model that includes the value of the item as a factor in order to take account of price discounts. The total incremental cost associated with such a system is then:

$$C = \text{(annual cost of placing orders)}$$
$$+ \text{(annual purchase cost of } R \text{ items)} \tag{9}$$
$$+ \text{(annual holding cost for inventory)}$$
$$= c_P (R/Q) + kR + kF_H(Q/2)$$

where $k =$ cost or price per unit, and $F_H = $ *fraction* of inventory value representing inventory holding cost on an annual basis ($kF_H = c_H$). For example, if $k = \$1$ and $F_H = 0.25$, then $c_H = \$0.25$ per unit per year.

Following the rationale developed previously, we seek the value of Q, Q_0, that minimizes this total incremental cost equation. This leads to

$$Q_0 = \sqrt{2c_P R/kF_H} \tag{10}$$

$$C_0 = \sqrt{2c_P kF_H R} + kR \tag{11}$$

The derivations of equations (10) and (11) parallel the derivations for the previous *EOQ* formulas.

We may now use equations (10) and (11) in the analysis of inventory systems that involve a price break. For comparison let us assume the previous example data of $R = 1600$ units per year, $c_P = \$5$ per order, and $F_H = 10$ percent per year. Recall that Q_0 was 400 units without price discounts. Now let us assume in addition that the purchase prices are quoted as $1 per unit in quantities below 800 and $0.98 per unit in quantities above 800. If we buy in lots of 800, we save $1600 \times \$0.02 = \$32$ per

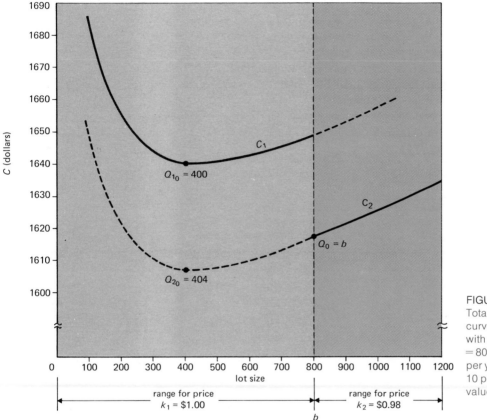

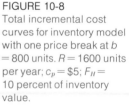

FIGURE 10-8
Total incremental cost curves for inventory model with one price break at $b = 800$ units. $R = 1600$ units per year; $c_p = \$5$; $F_H = 10$ percent of inventory value.

year on the purchase price plus $10 on order costs, since only two orders need to be placed per year to satisfy annual needs. This saving of $42 per year must be greater than the additional inventory costs that would be incurred if the price discount is to be attractive.

Referring to Figure 10-8, we see that there are two ranges of lot sizes where in fact two different total cost curves are effective. For the price $k_1 = \$1$, order sizes in the range of 0 to 799 are effective. For the discounted price of $k_2 = \$0.98$, order sizes greater than or equal to the price break order size of $b = 800$ are effective.

The logic of our analysis is first to note that the total incremental cost curve C_2 will fall below the curve C_1. This configuration is shown in Figure 10-8. The logical thing to do is to calculate Q_{2_0} to see if it falls within the range where the price $k_2 = \$0.98$ applies. Performing this calculation using equation (10), we find that $Q_{2_0} = 404$ units, which is less than the break point $b = 800$ units (below the effective range for C_2). Since 404 units corresponds to the minimum point on the C_2 curve, we know that the lowest possible cost of C_2 *within the range where the price k_2 applies* is at the order size $b = 800$ units.

If it had happened that Q_{2_0} was in the range for price k_2, this would have determined immediately that the *EOQ* for the system was the value calculated as Q_{2_0}. Since

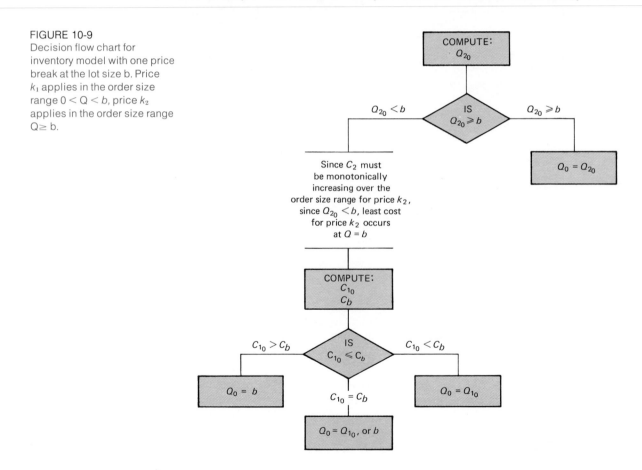

FIGURE 10-9
Decision flow chart for inventory model with one price break at the lot size b. Price k_1 applies in the order size range $0 < Q < b$, price k_2 applies in the order size range $Q \geq b$.

this is not the case, however, we must continue our analysis to see if the minimum point on the curve C_1 is below C_2 (which we now know is at the order size $b = 800$ units). We may calculate the cost associated with Q_{1_0} (C_{1_0}) from equation (11), and its value is $1640. Also, we may calculate the costs associated with the lot size $b = 800$ units (C_b) using equation (9), and we find this to be $1617. The decision is now clear; $Q_0 = b = 800$ units, since the total incremental costs at order size b are less than C_{1_0}.

The results can be seen from the graph of Figure 10-8; however, constructing the curves for each case would be laborious compared to the simple computations required to come to a decision. Figure 10-9 shows a decision flow chart for the inventory model with one price break, indicating the flow of computations and resulting decisions. In some instances, the final result is obtained with one calculation, as when Q_{2_0} falls in the order size range where the price k_2 is valid. Where this is not the case, simple calculations for comparative total incremental cost yield a final result.

The flow chart in Figure 10-9 is a series of steps that must be followed to solve the optimization inventory model. Recall that the steps needed to solve an optimization model are called an *algorithm*. Using the same general rationale, we can develop decision processes for inventory models with two or more price breaks. Also, models can be constructed for quantity discount situations that also take account of other factors such as shortage costs.

ASSESSING RISKS IN INVENTORY MODELS

In the basic *EOQ* model and in the simple extensions that we developed, we assumed that both demand and supply lead time were constant; that is, we assumed a deterministic model. Yet, variability of demand and supply lead time are elements of reality that can be of great importance because they impose risks, and the risks are commonly two-sided.

We can cushion the effects of demand and supply lead time variation, absorbing risks by carrying larger inventories, called buffer or safety stocks. The larger we make these buffer stocks, the greater the risk associated with the funds tied up in inventories, the possibility of obsolescence, and so on. But large buffer stocks minimize the risk of running out of stock. On the other hand, the inventory risk can be minimized by reducing buffer inventories, but the risks associated with poor inventory service increase, including the costs of back ordering, lost sales, disruptions of production, and so on. Our objective then will be to find a rational model for balancing these risks.

Service levels and buffer stocks with constant lead time

Figure 10-10 shows the general structure of inventory balance with a reordering system similar to the one we developed previously. When inventory falls to a preset reorder point P, an order for the quantity Q is placed. The reorder point P is set to take account of the supply lead time L, so that if we experience normal usage rates during L, inventory would be reduced to minimum levels when the order for Q units is received.

Note, however, that demand may not be at a constant rate. Inventories may decline to the reorder point P earlier or later than expected. But, what is more important, if demand during lead time is greater than expected values, inventory levels may decline below the minimum or planned buffer stock level. In the limiting situation, if we experienced maximum demand during lead time as shown in Figure 10-10, inventory levels would decline to zero by the time the order for Q units was received. The size of needed buffer stocks is then B, the difference between the expected or average demand $\overline{D}$ and $D_{\max}$, the maximum demand during the supply lead time, or $B = D_{\max} - \overline{D}$. The issue then must focus on how we define $D_{\max}$.

Defining maximum demand Maximum demand, $D_{\max}$, is not a fixed number that we can simply abstract from a distribution of demand, but depends on an analysis of the risks. Take as an example the record for the distribution of demand during lead time

FIGURE 10-10
Structure of inventory balance for a fixed reorder quantity system, with safety stocks to absorb fluctuations in demand and in supply time. The buffer stock level is set so that a reasonable figure for maximum usages would draw down the inventory to zero during the lead time. Q is a fixed quantity ordered each cycle.

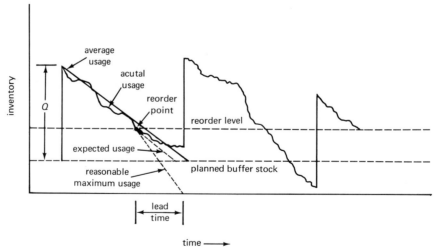

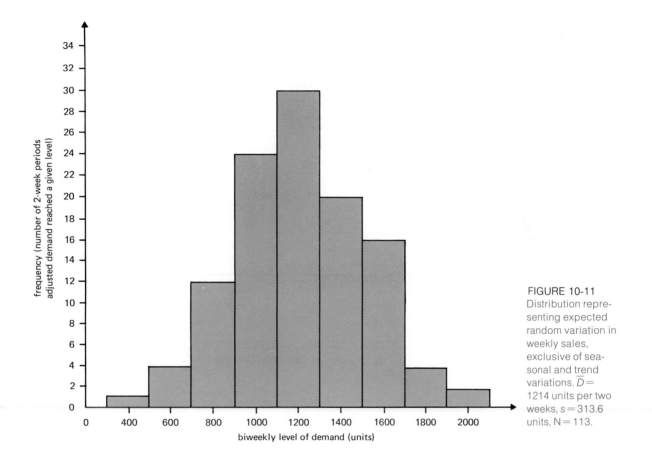

FIGURE 10-11
Distribution repre-
senting expected
random variation in
weekly sales,
exclusive of sea-
sonal and trend
variations. $\overline{D} =$
1214 units per two
weeks, s = 313.6
units, N = 113.

for an item shown in Figure 10-11. This figure represents just the random variations, and, if there were other effects such as trend and seasonal demand patterns, they have been removed by standard statistical techniques. We note that for the sample of $N = 113$, average biweekly demand was $\overline{D} = 1214$ units and the standard deviation was $s = 313.6$ units. The maximum *recorded* demand in the sample was 2000 units, which occurred twice in the distribution.

Let us convert Figure 10-11 to the form shown in Figure 10-12, so we can conveniently estimate the probability of various demand rates. Figure 10-12 was

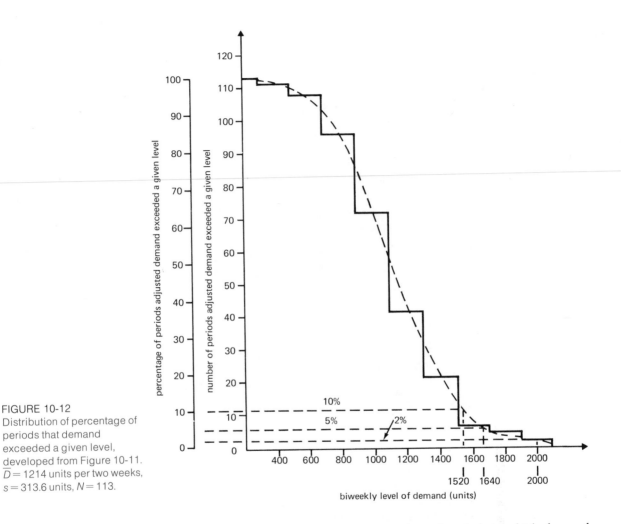

FIGURE 10-12
Distribution of percentage of periods that demand exceeded a given level, developed from Figure 10-11. $\overline{D} = 1214$ units per two weeks, $s = 313.6$ units, $N = 113$.

constructed from Figure 10-11 by plotting the number of periods in which demand exceeded a given level. We then established a percentage scale to estimate the probability of various levels of demand. Since the average two-week usage rate is 1214 units, if we assume a normal lead time of $L = 2$ weeks, we could be 90 percent sure of not running out of stock by having 1520 units on hand when the replenishment order is placed (see Figure 10-12 for the demand rate for 10 percent). The buffer stock required for this 90 percent service level is then $B = 1520 - 1214 = 306$ units.

Cost of Providing Three Levels of Service (from Figure 10-12) When the Item Is Valued at $50 Each and Inventory Holding Costs Are 20 Percent			TABLE 10-2
	Service Level (percent)		
	90	95	98
D_{max}, expected maximum usage for 2-week replenishment time	1,520	1,640	2,000
Buffer stock required $(B = D_{max} - 1214)$	306	426	786
Value of buffer stock $(50\ B)$	'15,300	$21,300	$39,300
Inventory holding cost at 20 percent	$ 3,060	$ 4,260	$ 7,860

Similarly, if we wish to be 95 percent sure of not running out of stock, then $B = 1640 - 1214 = 426$ units. For a 98 percent service level (2 percent risk of stockout) the buffer stock level must be increased to 786 units.

From the shape of the demand curve, it is clear that required buffer stock goes up rapidly as we increase service level, and therefore the cost of providing this assurance goes up. These effects are shown by the calculations in Table 10-2 where we have assumed the demand curve of Figure 10-12, assigning a value of $50 to the item and inventory holding costs of 20 percent of inventory value. The average inventory required to cover expected maximum usage rates during the two-week lead time is calculated for the three service levels shown. To offer service at the 95 percent level instead of the 90 percent level requires an incremental $1200 per year, but to move to the 98 percent level of service from the 95 percent level requires an additional $3600 in inventory cost.

Management could define any of the three levels of demand as D_{max} by setting a service level policy. Given the service level policy, the buffer stock required to implement that policy is simply $B = D_{max} - \overline{D}$.

Practical methods for determining buffer stocks

The general methodology for setting buffer stocks that we have discussed here is too cumbersome for practical use in systems where large numbers of items may be involved. Computations are simplified considerably if we can justify the assumption that the demand distribution follows some particular mathematical function, such as the normal, Poisson, or negative exponential distribution.

First recall the general statement for buffer stocks,

$$B = D_{max} - \overline{D} \tag{12}$$

Note, however, that $D_{max} = \overline{D} + n\sigma_D$, that is, the defined reasonable maximum demand is the average demand $\overline{D}$ plus some number of standard deviation units n that is associated with the probability of occurrence of that demand (n is now defined as the safety factor). Substituting this statement of D_{max} in the general definition of B, equation (12), we have

$$B = D_{max} - \overline{D} = (\overline{D} + n\sigma_D) - \overline{D}$$

or

$$B = n\sigma_D \tag{13}$$

This simple statement allows us to determine buffer stocks that meet risk requirements when we know the mathematical form of the demand distribution. The procedure is as follows:

1. Determine whether the normal, Poisson, or negative exponential distribution approximately describes demand during lead time for the case under consideration. This determination is critically important, involving well-known statistical methodology.

2. Set a service level based on managerial policy, an assessment of the balance of incremental inventory and stockout costs, or when stockout costs are not known, an assessment of the manager's tradeoff between service level and inventory cost.

3. Using the service level, define D_{max} during lead time in terms of the appropriate distribution.

4. Compute the required buffer stock from equation (13) where n is termed the safety factor and σ_D is the standard deviation for the demand distribution during lead time.

Buffer stocks for the normal distribution The normal distribution has been found to describe many demand functions adequately, particularly at the factory level of the supply-production-distribution system [Buchan and Koenigsberg, 1963]. Given the assumption of normality and a service level of perhaps 95 percent, we can determine B by reference to the normal distribution tables. A small part of these tables has been reproduced as Table 10-3.

The normal distribution is a two parameter distribution that is completely described by its mean value $\overline{D}$ and the standard deviation σ_D. To implement a service level of

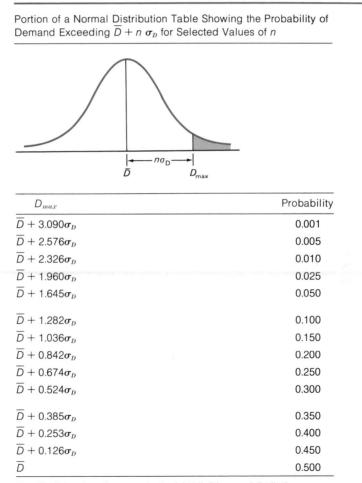

Portion of a Normal Distribution Table Showing the Probability of Demand Exceeding $\overline{D} + n\,\sigma_D$ for Selected Values of n TABLE 10-3

D_{max}	Probability
$\overline{D} + 3.090\sigma_D$	0.001
$\overline{D} + 2.576\sigma_D$	0.005
$\overline{D} + 2.326\sigma_D$	0.010
$\overline{D} + 1.960\sigma_D$	0.025
$\overline{D} + 1.645\sigma_D$	0.050
$\overline{D} + 1.282\sigma_D$	0.100
$\overline{D} + 1.036\sigma_D$	0.150
$\overline{D} + 0.842\sigma_D$	0.200
$\overline{D} + 0.674\sigma_D$	0.250
$\overline{D} + 0.524\sigma_D$	0.300
$\overline{D} + 0.385\sigma_D$	0.350
$\overline{D} + 0.253\sigma_D$	0.400
$\overline{D} + 0.126\sigma_D$	0.450
$\overline{D}$	0.500

Note: The figure shows the area under the right tail of the normal distribution.

95 percent means that we are willing to accept a 5 percent risk of running out of stock. From Table 10-3, demand exceeds $\overline{D} + n\sigma_D$ with a probability of 0.05 or 5 percent of the time when $n = 1.645$; therefore, this policy is implemented when $B = 1.645\sigma_D$. Using Figure 10-11 as an example, and assuming that it is drawn from a normal distribution, we find that a buffer stock to implement a 95 percent service level would be $B = 1.645 \times 313.6 = 516$ units. Such a policy would protect against the occurrence of demands up to $D_{max} = 1214 + 516 = 1730$ units per two weeks. Obviously any other service level policy could be implemented in a similar way.

Buffer stocks for the Poisson distribution   The Poisson distribution has been found to be applicable to retail sales in many situations [Buchan and Koenigsberg, 1963]. Buffer stock determination for the Poisson distribution is very simple because it is a single parameter distribution, since $\sigma_D = \sqrt{\overline{D}}$. Thus, a knowledge of the average demand, $\overline{D}$, is sufficient to completely describe the demand distribution. Using equation (13) then, $B = n\sigma_D = n\sqrt{\overline{D}}$.

Table 10-4 shows a small portion of the right tail of the Poisson distribution for selected values of $\overline{D}$ between 12 and 20. The Poisson distribution is not commonly applicable to distributions with mean values above 20. Since the risk values vary slightly for a given multiple of σ_D for different values of $\overline{D}$ in the Poisson distribution, the most satisfactory way of maintaining a preset risk level is by reference to the tables. For example, if average demand is $\overline{D} = 14$ per week, and we wish to hold the risk of stockout to about 4 percent, then from Table 10-4, $D_{max} = 20$ per week and $B = 20 - 14 = 6$ units, if L is one week. (From Table 10-4, the probability of D being greater than 20 is 0.048, or approximately 5 percent.)

Buffer stocks for the negative exponential distribution   The negative exponential distribution has been found to describe demand in some retail and wholesale situations [Buchan and Koenigsberg, 1963]. As with the Poisson distribution, the negative exponential distribution is a single parameter distribution described completely by its mean value ($\sigma_D = \overline{D}$). Therefore, $D_{max} = \overline{D} + n\sigma_D = \overline{D} + n\overline{D} = (n + 1)\overline{D}$.

Table 10-5 shows data on the unitized negative exponential distribution that is useful in implementing a given risk level. The ratio $D_{max}/\overline{D}$ is used to determine the probability that the stated D_{max} will be exceeded. For example, if $\overline{D} = 5$ units per week and we wished to hold the risk of stockout to 5 percent, then from Table 10-5 for a probability of 0.050, $D_{max}/\overline{D} = 3$. Therefore, $D_{max} = 3 \times 5 = 15$ units per week, and $B = 15 - 5 = 10$ units.

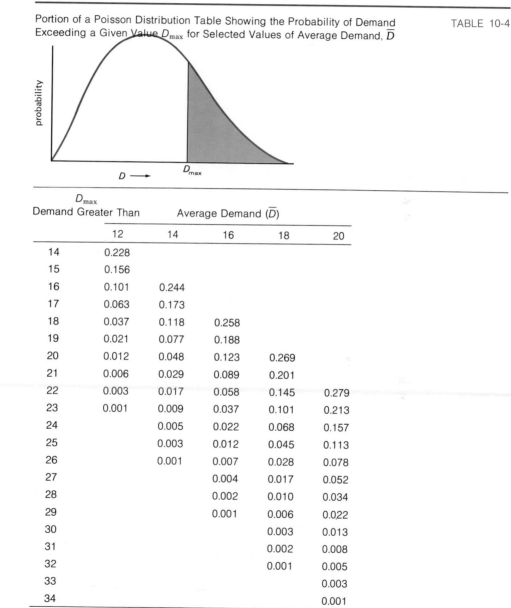

Portion of a Poisson Distribution Table Showing the Probability of Demand Exceeding a Given Value D_{max} for Selected Values of Average Demand, $\overline{D}$ TABLE 10-4

D_{max} Demand Greater Than	Average Demand ($\overline{D}$)				
	12	14	16	18	20
14	0.228				
15	0.156				
16	0.101	0.244			
17	0.063	0.173			
18	0.037	0.118	0.258		
19	0.021	0.077	0.188		
20	0.012	0.048	0.123	0.269	
21	0.006	0.029	0.089	0.201	
22	0.003	0.017	0.058	0.145	0.279
23	0.001	0.009	0.037	0.101	0.213
24		0.005	0.022	0.068	0.157
25		0.003	0.012	0.045	0.113
26		0.001	0.007	0.028	0.078
27			0.004	0.017	0.052
28			0.002	0.010	0.034
29			0.001	0.006	0.022
30				0.003	0.013
31				0.002	0.008
32				0.001	0.005
33					0.003
34					0.001

TABLE 10-5	Unit Negative Exponential Distribution Showing the Probability of Given Demands Being Exceeded

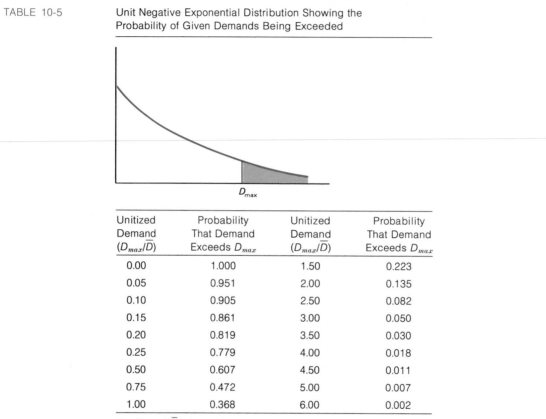

Unitized Demand $(D_{max}/\overline{D})$	Probability That Demand Exceeds D_{max}	Unitized Demand $(D_{max}/\overline{D})$	Probability That Demand Exceeds D_{max}
0.00	1.000	1.50	0.223
0.05	0.951	2.00	0.135
0.10	0.905	2.50	0.082
0.15	0.861	3.00	0.050
0.20	0.819	3.50	0.030
0.25	0.779	4.00	0.018
0.50	0.607	4.50	0.011
0.75	0.472	5.00	0.007
1.00	0.368	6.00	0.002

Note: Demand, $\overline{D} = 1$; $\sigma_D = 1$.

Buffer stocks with variable demand and lead time The problem of determining buffer stocks when both demand and lead time vary is somewhat more complex. When lead times also vary, we are faced with an interaction between the fluctuating demand and the fluctuating lead times similar to the situation shown in Figure 10-13.

In such situations, buffer stocks may be determined by a Monte Carlo simulation through a straightforward application of the methods presented in Chapter 12. To carry out the simulation, we need data describing both the demand and lead time distributions. With these distribution data, we can simulate demand during lead time

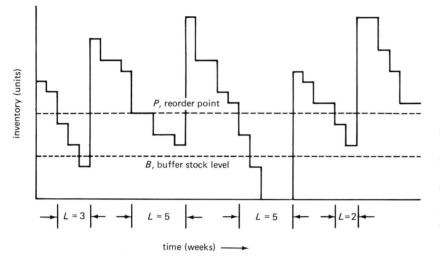

FIGURE 10-13
Inventory balance when both demand and lead time vary. When inventory falls to the reorder point *P*, the quantity *Q* is ordered. Inventory falls below the buffer stock level *B* twice, and a stockout occurs during the third cycle.

and finally develop buffer stock requirements for the various risk levels of stockout. We can then implement whatever risk level we choose by selecting the corresponding buffer stock. The methodology and computed examples are developed in Buffa and Miller [1979].

DETERMINING SERVICE LEVELS

The service level states the probability that all orders can be filled directly from inventory during a reorder cycle and, as we have stated, the buffer inventory designed to provide for the risk of stockout is $B = n\sigma_D$. Assuming a normal distribution and a safety factor of $n = 1.645$, then the chance of a stockout is 0.05 from Table 10-3, and the service level is 95 percent.

Now let us examine more closely the meaning of a service level statement of policy. The 95 percent service level means that there is one chance in twenty that demand during lead time will exceed the buffer stock *when there is exposure to risk*. It does not mean that 5 percent of the demand is unsatisfied. It means that demand during lead time can be expected to exceed buffer stock for 5 percent of the replenishment orders, or that the chance that demand will exceed the buffer stock for any given replenishment order is 5 percent.

Effect of order size

With this interpretation of service level, we see immediately that the expected quantity short over a period of time is proportional to the number of times we order, for we are exposed to shortages only once for each reordering cycle. For our example, if we ordered Q units twenty times per year we would expect shortages to occur an average of only once per year. If we ordered in quantities of $2Q$ only ten times per year, we would expect stockouts to occur only once every other year on the average. Larger orders provide exposure to risk less often and will result in lower annual expected quantities short for the same service level.

Expected quantities short

For a given safety factor and distribution of demand during lead time, we can compute the expected quantity short for service levels of 80, 90, 95, and 99 percent. From Table 10-3, the safety factors and computed buffer stocks are

$$B_1 = 0.842 \times 10 = 8.4, \quad \text{or} \quad 9 \text{ units} \qquad B_3 = 1.645 \times 10 = 16.45, \text{ or } 17 \text{ units}$$

$$B_2 = 1.282 \times 10 = 12.8, \quad \text{or } 13 \text{ units} \qquad B_4 = 2.326 \times 10 = 23.26, \text{ or } 24 \text{ units}$$

The values of B approximate the stated service levels, giving slightly better service because of rounding upwards to integer units.

The expected quantity short per order is the product of σ_D and $E(k)$, where $E(k)$ is the expected value of demands beyond some specified level. Brown [1967] developed tables of partial expectations for the normal distribution, and selected values of $E(k)$ for associated safety factors or service levels are reproduced in Table 10-6. Estimates of the expected quantity short per order can be obtained from Table 10-6 for a given safety factor, which in turn is associated with a given service level. From Table 10-6, the expected quantities short per order for our example and the four service levels are as follows:

Service Level (percent)	Expected Quantity Short per Order (units)
80	$0.112 \times 10 = 1.12$
90	$0.047 \times 10 = 0.47$
95	$0.021 \times 10 = 0.21$
99	$0.004 \times 10 = 0.04$

Expected Quantity Short per Order for Values of the Safety Factor n TABLE 10-6

Pr

Pr = 0.95   Pr = 0.05

Expected value of occurances above $1.645\,\sigma_D = 0.02089$

μ $+1.645\,\sigma_D$

Safety Factor (n)	Service Level (percent)	$E(k)$, Expected Quantity Short/σ_D
3.090	99.9	0.00028
2.576	99.5	0.00158
2.236	99.0	0.00441
1.960	97.5	0.00945
1.645	95.0	0.02089
1.282	90.0	0.04730
1.036	85.0	0.07776
0.842	80.0	0.11156
0.674	75.0	0.14928
0.524	70.0	0.19050
0.385	65.0	0.23565
0.253	60.0	0.28515
0.126	55.0	0.33911
0.000	50.0	0.39894

Source. R. G. Brown, *Decision Rules for Inventory Management*. Holt, Rinehart & Winston, New York, 1967

For each of the service levels indicated, the expected quantity short for each order is as given, and these expected shortages are startingly small. Thus, the effect of a given service policy may be misleading unless it is translated into its equivalent expected quantity short per order. While a 90-percent service policy may seem relatively loose, it holds fairly tight control in terms of the expected shortages on each ordering cycle.

Optimal service levels with shortage costs known

Now that we have methods for estimating the expected quantity short per order, we can determine the optimal service level if we know the relevant costs. Let us amplify slightly the example we have been using. Suppose that annual requirements for the example item are $R = 3000$ units per year, inventory holding costs are $c_H = \$20$ per unit per year, ordering costs are $c_P = \$25$ per order, and shortage costs are $c_S = \$100$ per unit short. If the order quantity were $Q = 500$ units, six orders per year would be required.

Let us examine the annual buffer inventory and shortage costs for the four different service levels. We computed the buffer inventory and expected quantities short per order previously. Since there are six orders per year, the *annual* expected quantity short is $6 \times \sigma_D E(k)$. These values and the relevant costs are summarized in Table 10-7. The service policy that minimizes relevant costs for these data is the 95 percent policy that involves maintaining a buffer of $B = 17$ units and results in an annual expected quantity short of $6 \times 0.21 = 1.26$ units and a minimum total relevant

TABLE 10-7 | Annual Buffer Inventory and Shortage Costs for Four Service Levels

	Approximate Service Level (percent)			
	80	90	95	99
Buffer inventory[a] $B = n\,\sigma_D = 10 \times n$	9	13	17	24
Expected quantity short per order[b] $\sigma_D\,E(k) = 10 \times E(k)$	1.12	0.47	0.21	0.04
Buffer inventory cost $c_H B = 20 \times B$	$180	$260	$340	$480
Shortage cost $c_S\,(R/Q) \times$ (expected quantity short per order) $= 100 \times 6 \times$ (expected quantity short per order)	$672	$282	$126	$ 24
Total incremental costs	$852	$542	$466	$504

Note: $\overline{D} = 50$ units during lead time, $\sigma_D = 10$ units, $c_H = \$20$ per unit per year, $c_S = \$100$ per unit short, $R = 3000$ units per year, and $Q = 500$ units per order.

[a] Values of n from Table 10-3 for given service level. Values of B rounded to next highest integer.

[b] $E(k)$ from Table 10-6.

cost of $466 per year. What would be the optimal service policy if the cost of shortages was only $c_S = \$40$?

Previously, we alluded to the fact that the annual expected quantity short depended on the quantity ordered at one time. Of course, this fact could affect the decision on service policy. You should now compare costs for order sizes of $Q = 500$ and 1000 for the different service levels. What are the relevant costs?

Optimal service levels with shortage costs unknown

It is perhaps most often true that we do not know the value of shortage costs, c_S, with any degree of confidence. There are many factors in a given situation that may affect the true cost of shortages. Some of these factors may be reasonably objective, but difficult to measure. For example, we know that part shortages in assembly processes cause disruptions and delays that are costly, but measuring these costs is quite complex. When shortages occur, it may be necessary to place the parts on back order, or they may be expedited with special handling and extra costs. These incremental costs are real, but they are not segregated in cost records, so making realistic estimates of their value would in itself be costly, and these costs could exceed the value of the information. If a shortage definitely causes a lost sale, we could impute a shortage cost equal to the lost contribution to profit and overhead. But is the sale lost with certainty or must we estimate the probability of a lost sale? Furthermore, the loss may be intangible, such as the loss of goodwill of a valued customer who receives poor service.

For all the preceding reasons, we may not be able to estimate values of c_S with sufficient precision to justify an analysis similar to that given in Table 10-7 as a basis for selecting an optimum service level policy.

Nevertheless, in the absence of known shortage costs, we still have valuable data from Table 10-7. We have objective annual buffer inventory costs for various service level policies, and we also have the expected annual quantities short that would result from each service level policy. The graphic relationship between buffer inventory cost and quantities short is shown in Figure 10-14. These data provide the manager with the basis for a tradeoff analysis between buffer inventory costs and the manager's willingness to be out of stock.

Thus, the problem of determining the optimal service level may be viewed as a problem involving multiple criteria under certainty (where the uncertain demand fluctuations are taken into account by the expected annual quantity of units short). The alternatives are the service levels. Although there are actually an infinite number

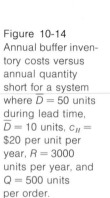

Figure 10-14
Annual buffer inventory costs versus annual quantity short for a system where $\bar{D} = 50$ units during lead time, $\bar{D} = 10$ units, $c_H = \$20$ per unit per year, $R = 3000$ units per year, and $Q = 500$ units per order.

of possible service levels, we can simplify the problem by considering service level policies of 80 percent (alternative A_1), 90 percent (A_2), 95 percent (A_3), and 99 percent (A_4). The criteria are simply the annual cost of the buffer inventory and the annual quantity of units short. From Table 10-7 we see that the outcome associated with the 80 percent service level policy (A_1) is an annual buffer inventory cost of \$180 and an expected number of units short of 6.72, since we expected to be short 1.12 units per order, and to order six times per year ($6 \times 1.12 = 6.72$). Table 10-8 summarizes these outcomes for the four alternatives.

TABLE 10-8   Annual Buffer Inventory Costs and Expected Annual Shortages for Four Service Levels

	Service Level (percent)			
	80 (A_1)	90 (A_2)	95 (A_3)	99 (A_4)
Annual buffer cost	\$180	\$260	\$340	\$480
Expected annual shortages (units)	6.72	2.82	1.26	0.24

We now ask the manager to determine the preferred service level subjectively by trading off buffer inventory costs against shortages. We might say: "For an annual cost of $180, you expect to be short of inventory a total of 6.72 units during the six reorder periods. Suppose you could reduce this total annual shortage to 2.82 units, a difference of 6.72 − 2.82 = 3.90 units. How much more would you be willing to pay? Consider both tangible and intangible costs in determining your answer."

The manager might estimate that the tangible costs of back ordering and expediting special orders are approximately $20 per unit. Therefore, the manager would be willing to pay at least $20 × 3.90 = $78.00 for this reduction, but how much more? To aid the manager with the question, we might say the following: "You would pay at least $78 more to reduce the annual shortage from 6.72 to 2.82 units. Would eliminating the uncertain costs of lost sales and the intangible costs of lost goodwill associated with the extra 3.90 units of inventory shortage be worth *at least* $80 − 78 = $2?" Suppose the answer is "yes" to this question.

To improve service to the 90 percent level would cost $260 − 180 = $80, the difference between the annual buffer inventory costs for the two service levels. Since the savings of tangible costs of $78 plus the uncertain and intangible costs of at least $2 are greater than or equal to $80, then the 90 percent service level (A_2) is preferred to the 80 percent service level (A_1).

Continuing in the same manner, we might ask if the manager would be willing to pay an additional $80 (difference in annual buffer inventory costs between the 95 and 90 percent service levels) to reduce the annual shortages from 2.82 units to approximately 1.26 units (2.82 units − 1.26 units = 1.56 unit reduction). This time, the savings in tangible costs would be $20 × 1.56 = $31.20. Would the uncertain and intangible costs be worth an additional $80 − 31.20 = $48.80? Suppose this time that the manager says "No." The optimal service level would then be approximately 90 percent.

MANAGERIAL CONTROL SYSTEMS

Let us now summarize the results of optimizing inventory models for managerial use. What are the variables under managerial control and how can they be incorporated in useful control systems? The basic control variables are the quantity ordered at one time, the service level, and the particular way these elements are combined in a control system.

The elements of inventory models that are normally outside managerial control are the costs c_H, c_P, c_S, and the supply lead time. These are parameters that managers cannot change at will, though they may try to reduce or control them in the longer term. The annual requirement, R, is dependent on external market factors and, again, the manager can try to influence R through marketing techniques, but cannot decide what it will be.

We will summarize two basic kinds of control systems that are widely used, recognizing that there are many variations in practice.

The fixed reorder quantity system

The fixed reorder quantity system is the one we have used for illustrative purposes in developing optimization inventory models. Its structure is best illustrated by Figure 10-10, in which a reorder level has been set by the point P, which allows the inventory level to be drawn down to the buffer stock level within the lead time if average usage rates are experienced. Replenishment orders are placed in a fixed predetermined amount (in practice, not necessarily the minimum cost quantity, Q_0) timed to be received at the end of the supply lead time. The maximum inventory level becomes the order quantity Q plus the buffer stock B. The average inventory is then $B + Q/2$.

Usage rates are reviewed periodically in an attempt to react to seasonal or long-term trends in requirements. At the time of the periodic reviews, the order quantities and buffer stock levels may be changed to reflect the new conditions. Buffer stock levels are set, based on determinations of the appropriate service level policy, which in turn reflects the balancing of buffer inventory costs and shortage costs, or the manager's tradeoff between buffer inventory cost and the expected quantity short.

One of the simplest methods for maintaining this close watch on inventory level is the use of the "two bin" system. In this system, the inventory is physically (or conceptually) separated into two bins, one of which contains an amount equal to the reorder inventory level. The balance of the stock is placed in the other bin, and day-to-day needs are drawn from it until it is empty. At that point it is obvious that the reorder level has been reached and a stock requisition is issued. From that point on, stock is drawn from the second bin, which contains an amount equal to the average use over the lead time plus a buffer stock. When the stock is replenished by the receipt of the order, the physical segregation into two bins is made again and the cycle is repeated. Fixed reorder quantity systems are common where a perpetual inventory record is kept, or where the inventory level is under rather continuous surveillance so that notice can be given when the reorder point has been reached. They are also common with low-valued items such as nuts and bolts.

Periodic reorder systems

In periodic reorder systems, control is maintained by ordering regularly on some fixed cycle, perhaps each week or each month. In its simplest form, the amount ordered is the quantity needed to replenish inventory to I_{max}, a preset level. This reorder quantity Q is variable and is equal to the amount used during the current period plus the expected usage during the supply lead time, as shown in Figure 10-15. The service level policies and resulting buffer stock requirements are based on the same general concepts and methods as before.

The managerial control variable is now the length of the reorder cycle, commonly called the review period, since inventory status is reviewed to determine replenishment requirements during the period. Optimal review periods can be derived with this system — periods that are equivalent to the optimum order quantity Q_0 in the fixed reorder quantity system. The optimal review period can be approximated by Q_0/R, where Q_0 is computed from equation (4). However, the optimal review period is seldom used, because other criteria tend to dominate in reorder cycle selection.

Periodic reorder systems are prominent with higher valued items and with a large number of items that are regularly ordered from the same vendor. Thus, one of the significant advantages of the periodic system is that freight cost advantages can often be gained by grouping these orders together for shipment. Also, the regular review of all items for replenishment ordering on the same basic cycle has procedural ad-

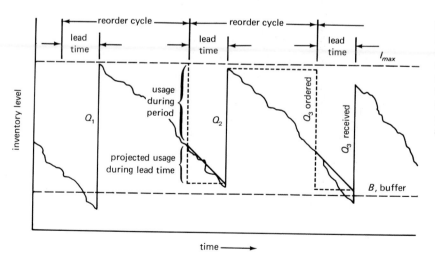

FIGURE 10-15
Fixed reorder cycle system of control. An order is placed at regular intervals. Stock is replenished by an order of variable size Q, which is the sum of usage during the immediate past period plus projected usage during the supply lead time.

vantages and provides close surveillance over inventory levels for all items. Thus, while it is possible to determine optimal review periods for each item — periods that depend on the cost parameters of the optimization model — review periods are actually set on the basis of all the considerations discussed, including individual optimal review periods.

Combination systems exist in which stock levels are reviewed periodically but orders are placed only when inventories have fallen to a predetermined reorder point. When an order is placed, its size is sufficient to replenish inventories, as in the periodic system. Periodic reviews of current usage rates may result in changes in I_{max}, P, and B. The combination systems have the advantages of close control associated with the periodic system, but since replenishment orders are placed only when the reorder point has been reached, fewer orders are placed on the average, so that annual ordering costs are comparable to those associated with the fixed quantity systems.

The inventory models in this chapter are for situations where demand for the item follows some statistical distribution that is independent from the demand for other items. In manufacturing systems, the demand for an item may be dependent on the production schedule for a final product. *Material Requirements Planning (MRP)* systems are designed to control inventories in these situations [see Buffa, 1980, Chapters 7 and 9].

WHAT SHOULD THE MANAGER KNOW?

Depending on the nature of the enterprise, inventories can be of extreme importance. It is not uncommon for inventories to account for 15 to 40 percent of assets. Especially in high volume operations, a changing demand pattern can have an enormous effect on inventories. For example, during the second quarter of 1979 there was a fantastic large-car inventory buildup in the automobile industry because of the energy crisis. The decrease in demand and resulting inventory buildup caused a virtual shutdown of the production operations, especially for Chrysler.

Interpretation of the results of inventory models

In order to manage inventories effectively, managers must know how they behave in relation to demand changes. The several components of system inventories behave differently in relation to average demand. First, the pipeline inventories vary directly with system volume. If the system is geared up for a higher volume, pipeline inventories must increase in direct proportion. Conversely, if volume declines, the pipeline inventory necessary to sustain the system declines and management must take action to ensure that inventories are reduced to reflect the change.

Note, however, that required cycle and buffer stocks may be a source of economy of scale in operations. If demand increases, the average cycle stock need increase only as the square root of demand [see equation (4)]. Thus, if demand doubles, cycle stock need increase by a factor of only $\sqrt{2} = 1.4$. There is a definite economy in larger scale operations. There may also be a similar economy of scale in relation to the size of buffer stocks needed to absorb the fluctuations in demand and supply time.

Another dimension in the interpretation of the results of inventory models has to do with the sensitivity of relevant costs to changes in order size from optimal levels. Note in equation (5) that relevant costs are proportional to the square root of demand, and the other relevant factors. Thus, near the optimum, costs do not change markedly as we deviate from optimality. We can note this effect in Figure 10-5; that is, the total incremental cost curve is "shallow" near the optimum. This fact of relative insensitivity of costs provides managers with flexibility. They can take account of factors not included in the model that may call for deviations from optimal order sizes, realizing that costs will not be affected greatly unless the deviation is quite large. It is important to be operating in the optimal range, but strict adherence to the results of order size models is of little importance.

Information requirements

Good inventory control systems are dependent on good forecasting and up-to-date inventory records. When this kind of information is available, inventory reordering decisions can be programmed in computing systems and become virtually automatic. In addition, however, the cost parameters need to be maintained up to date and the system parameters such as reorder points need to be examined periodically to ensure that the system remains appropriate to current conditions.

CHECK YOUR UNDERSTANDING

1. Explain the decoupling function of inventories.
2. An auto manufacturer produces at the rate of 2000 cars per day, seven days per week. The autos are driven off the assembly line to a temporary storage lot where

they await shipment for an average of two days. They are then loaded on trains or trucks and are moved to distribution points. The transit time averages five days. The cars remain in storage at distributors for an average of three days and are then shipped to dealers by truck, requiring an average of two days. They are unloaded at the dealers' lots and remain there for an average of two days until sold.
a. Compute the transit inventory.
b. Compute the finished goods pipeline inventory.
c. What is the investment tied up in finished goods inventory if the average value of a car is $2500?

3. Define the following terms:
a. cycle inventory
b. buffer inventory
c. seasonal inventory

4. List and define the cost components that are relevant to the control of inventories. Relate the costs to managerial objectives.

5. Define the following terms:
a. order quantity
b. Economic Order Quantity (EOQ)
c. inventory holding costs
d. preparation costs
e. shortage costs
f. reorder point
g. lead time

6. What are the assumptions involved in equation (4)? Which assumptions are relaxed in the shortage model? In the model that allows price discounts?

7. If c_H is $100 \times c_S$, what is the effect on EOQ compared to the basic model of equation (4)? What is the effect on incremental costs compared to the basic model of equation (5)? Explain why this effect should be true in terms of the relative values placed on inventories and shortages.

8. In the model that allows for shortages summarized by equations (6), (7), and (8), how is Q_0 affected if managerial policy is determined by the following statements:
a. We simply cannot run out of stock, our customers' needs must be satisfied.
b. We have a monopoly and they (customers) must come to us. Why should we go to the extra cost of warehousing the stuff? Let them wait.
c. We have a situation requiring a delicate balance. Inventory carrying costs are high, $50 per unit per year, but we have a standard product and the customer

can get it in a dozen places within 20 minutes of here. Don't forget, if we lose a sale we lose a $100 contribution to profit and overhead.

9. If the cost of holding inventory is $c_H = \$0.25$ per unit per year, the cost of writing orders is $c_P = \$10$ per order, and the annual requirements are $R = 10,000$ units,
   a. What is EOQ?
   b. What are the annual costs of ordering in EOQ lots?
   c. If $c_S = \$25$ per unit, what is EOQ? What are the annual costs of ordering in EOQ lots? What is the maximum inventory level?
   d. If $c_S = \$1.00$ per unit, what is EOQ? What are the annual costs of ordering in EOQ lots? What is the maximum inventory level?

10. In the text example concerning price discount models, the computed EOQ for the discounted price of $k_2 = \$0.98$ per unit was 404 units. The cost of a lot size of 404 units by equation (11) would be $1608, yet we chose the lot size of 800 units at a cost of $1617 as being more economical. Explain why.

11. If demand changes, perhaps an increase or decline of 50 percent, how do the following components of inventory change?
   a. buffer inventory
   b. cycle inventory
   c. transit inventory
   d. pipeline inventory
   e. decoupling inventory

12. If the EOQ for an item is 500 units, but there is a price advantage in ordering 550 units, how concerned should the manager be about deviating from the computed EOQ?

13. Define the following terms:
   a. buffer stock
   b. maximum demand
   c. safety factor
   d. expected quantity short
   e. optimal service level

14. If average demand is $\overline{D} = 52$ units during the supply lead time, and management designed a system where the buffer stock is set at $B = 23$ units, what is management's definition of maximum demand for this situation?

15. Using the demand distribution described by Figures 10-11 and 10-12 as an example, if the service level is set at 85 percent, estimate D_{max} and B.

16. Suppose on a statistical analysis of the demand for an item we isolate trend, seasonal, and random components of demand variation. Can we construct a meaningful buffer inventory for the item? How?

17. Explain why the cost of providing service goes up rapidly as the service level increases.

18. Give the mathematical statement defining buffer stock if the distribution of demand during lead time is:
    a. normal
    b. Poisson
    c. negative exponential

19. For the normal distribution, if the service level is set at 10 percent and the standard deviation is estimated to be $s = 50.3$ units, compute the buffer stock B. What is the value of the safety factor n?

20. For the Poisson distribution with an average demand of $\overline{D} = 18$ units during lead time, and a service level of 99 percent, what is the value of D_{max}? B? What is the implied safety factor n?

21. For the negative exponential distribution, if the service level is 97 percent and the standard deviation is estimated to be $s = 9$ units, compute the values of D_{max} and B. What is the implied value of n?

22. Explain the importance of "exposure to risk" in the concept of service levels. What is the effect of order size on actual service levels?

23. Average demand is $\overline{D} = 100$ units during lead time, and the standard deviation is $s = 24.3$ units (normal distribution). Which of the following service levels is most economical if the organization uses an EOQ ordering policy and shortages cost $100 per unit: 90, 95, or 99 percent?

24. Assume a situation where annual requirements are $R = 10,000$ units, $c_P = 20 per order, and $c_H = 10 per unit per year. Average demand during the supply lead time is $\overline{D} = 385$ units with a standard deviation of $s = 75$ units (normal distribution). Which of the following service levels is most economical if the organization uses EOQ ordering policy and shortages cost $100 per unit: 90, 95, or 99 percent?

25. Given the data generated in producing your answer to Exercise 24, suppose you had no reasonable estimate of an objective shortage cost. Outline how you could develop a service level policy. Plot a curve similar to Figure 10-14 as a basis for a manager's tradeoff analysis.

26. A manufacturing company produces a line of small one-cylinder engines used in lawn mowers, portable compressors, portable pumps, and so on. The parts for the engines are produced in lots and stored as manufactured parts for later use in assembly as needed. The costs of preparing manufacturing orders and controlling them through the shop are estimated as $50 per manufacturing order. The cost of holding in-process inventory is estimated as 25 percent of inventory value.

   The cylinder block for one of the engines has a usage rate of 25,000 per year and the value of the completed block including all labor, materials, and overhead is $10 per unit.

   How many manufacturing runs should be scheduled per year if incremental costs are to be minimized?

27. The Jensen Manufacturing Company has organized its inventory system into three main categories depending on urgency and the ordinary amount of follow-up required. It therefore wishes to simplify its use of equation (4) for use by ordering clerks. For class 1, 2, and 3 items ordering costs are respectively $5, $15, and $40.

   a. Derive simplified formulas for the three classes of items.

   b. Further examination shows that inventory carrying cost is virtually constant at 18 percent of cost value for all items. Derive further simplified formulas for the three classes of items.

28. The Jensen Manufacturing Company converted its entire ordering procedure to the EOQ basis described by Exercise 27. On examining one of the class 3 items ($c_P = \$40$), however, they noted very high annual freight costs under the new policy. Freight costs have been $200 per order under the EOQ policy and would cost only $400 for a carload lot of 500 units. $R = 5000$ units per year, and the average value of the item is $222.22. Should Jensen order in carload lots?

SHORT CASES

Dynaflap Company is a manufacturer of aircraft control surface systems, functioning as a major subcontractor in the aerospace industry. The purchasing function is of great importance in providing high quality materials, in the quantities needed, and in timely fashion so that disruptions in production do not occur. The Purchasing Department of Dynaflap is headed by an Assistant Vice President, with six purchasing agents who handle the purchasing of various kinds of materials and supplies. In addition, clerical personnel assist in the preparation of purchase

CASE 10-1

orders, correspondence, records, filing, and so on. The total annual purchasing department budget is $250,000. The volume of activity is measured in part by the placement of about 10,000 orders per year, with a total value of $50 million.

Other data concerning the inventory problem at Dynaflap are as follows:

Average value of an order	$5,000
Average time spent by a purchasing agent per order	1 hour
Average annual salary of purchasing agents	$25,000
Average cost to prepare orders (typing, forms, etc.)	$5
Average cost to follow up on and expedite orders (correspondence, telephone, etc.)	$5
Annual budget to operate Stores Dept., where inventory is maintained	$100,000
Internal rate of return (ROI) for Dynaflap	15 percent
Interest rate on borrowed capital available to Dynaflap	10 percent
Obsolescence of materials stored (percent of value of total inventory)	2 percent
Costs to handle material in and out of inventory, insurance, taxes, spoilage, rent for warehouse space (percent of total inventory value)	5 percent

The Assistant Vice President in charge of the Purchasing Department is considering the installation of EOQ ordering and is attempting to establish values for c_P, and F_H, the fraction of inventory value representing inventory holding cost. The appropriate values for these parameters has stirred considerable controversy among the staff. The Assistant Vice President has called you in as a consultant to advise him. What are your recommendations?

CASE 10-2   The pharmacy of a large hospital has established inventory-related costs to aid them in ordering and maintaining inventory levels of drugs for hospital use.

In establishing inventory holding costs, there was some controversy over the appropriate interest charge. The hospital was nonprofit, so an internal rate of return would be zero. Interest on borrowed money was 10 percent. The cost of storage, insurance, obsolescence, and pilferage averaged 15 percent of inventory value. The cost of storing some items such as narcotics, however, was 20 percent because of special precautions taken against theft. The cost of storing ordinary prescriptions was 15 percent, and of nonprescription items only 10 percent.

The cost to place an order seemed to vary considerably because some items—for example, narcotics—required special procedures to conform to control laws. At the other end of the spectrum were nonprescription items for which ordering was as simple as ordering any other common supply item. When aggregated, however, the average cost of preparing an order was $10, but the range seemed to be from $5 to $25.

Another problem in controlling inventories was the wide range of item value. The value of aspirin was as low as $2 per thousand, but some exotic drugs could have a value as high as $1000 per ounce.

Formulate an ordering policy for the pharmacy manager that takes account of her rather different supply items.

Suppose we are using an *EOQ* ordering policy on high valued items in *Case 10-2*, and ordering costs have been established as $c_P = \$25$ per order, and inventory holding costs as $c_H = \$100$ per unit per year. Average annual requirements are $R = 1000$ per year and, therefore, $Q_0 = 22.36$ for a typical item.   CASE 10-3

There is controversy over the appropriate ordering cost. Some think it should be only $20, but some state that the incremental costs are actually as high as $30. The inventory holding cost is also contested, with a high-low range of $c_H = \$80$ to $120. The controversy is not simply a matter of "feelings," but questions concerning which costs items should actually be included as incremental ordering and inventory costs.

Nevertheless, the manager is attempting to salvage what she thinks will be an improved ordering policy. She attempts to achieve agreement by saying, "The differences are small in terms of the resulting order sizes and costs, so why not use the original estimates of $c_P = \$25$ and $c_H = \$100$?" The individual holding out for the higher costs disagrees strongly. What should the manager do?

Suppose that the pharmacy manager in *Case 10-2* has decided to adopt an *EOQ* policy that recognizes three general categories of items. One of the problems was the lead time of supply from vendors. Each vendor was fairly reliable in meeting the stated supply time; however, there were variations between vendors. Therefore, the manager had set order points for each item that depended on the vendor, the average usage rate, and a safety stock.   CASE 10-4

Having installed the system, the manager now wishes to maintain it and adhere to the policy. Which parameters should she monitor most closely? Why

The pharmacy discussed in *Case 10-2* has some items for which a price discount is available. One such item is offered at $10 per unit in lots below 1000 and $9 per unit in lots above 1000. Annual requirements are 5000, $c_P = \$25$, and $F_H = 35$ percent of inventory value. Q_0 for the $10 price is 267 units and for the $9 price is 282 units. Is the price discount attractive? How should the pharmacy manager deal with this question?   CASE 10-5

CASE 10-6   HARDCO is a distributor of hardware to retail stores in a large metropolitan area. Retailers place their orders and can expect delivery within two to three days if the item is in stock, and almost immediate availability on an emergency basis. When an item is out of stock at HARDCO, it must be ordered from manufacturers, usually from regional distribution centers. The time to replenish supplies from manufacturers varies considerably, but is in the range of one to four weeks.

HARDCO has retained a consultant to help them review their service level policy which is currently set at only 85 percent. As a basis for analysis, the manager takes what he thinks is a typical item that has an average demand during the supply lead time of 100 units. The demand distribution is reasonably well described by the normal distribution with a standard deviation of 25 units. The value of the item is $2, and the inventory carrying cost is $c_H = \$0.50$ per unit per year. The item is ordered an average of 10 times per year.

When asked about the cost of a stockout, the manager responded that the lost contribution to profit and overhead would be $1 per unit. The consultant asked what would happen if they were out of stock: "Would a retailer order from another distributor, or what?" The manager said that retailers probably would not do that on specific items, but would backorder the item. We would probably retain their business unless they became really upset with us. Then they might drop us entirely except for items for which we are the only supplier in the area.

What should HARCO's service policy be? What buffer stock do you propose for the typical item?

GENERAL REFERENCES

Brown, R. G., *Decision Rules for Inventory Management,* Holt, Rinehart and Winston, New York, 1967.

Buchan, J., and E. Koenigsberg, *Scientific Inventory Management,* Prentice-Hall, Englewood Cliffs, N.J., 1963.

Buffa, E. S. *Modern Production/Operations Management,* sixth edition, John Wiley & Sons, New York, 1980.

Buffa, E. S., and J. G. Miller, *Production-Inventory Systems: Planning and Control,* third edition, Richard D. Irwin, Inc., Homewood, Ill., 1979.

Peterson, R., and E. A. Silver, *Decision Systems for Inventory Management and Production Planning,* John Wiley & Sons, New York, 1979.

Starr, M. K., and D. W. Miller, *Inventory Control: Theory and Practice,* Prentice-Hall, Englewood Cliffs, N.J., 1962.

APPLICATIONS REFERENCES

Austin, L. M., "Project EOQ: A Success Story in Implementing Academic Research," *Interfaces,* Vol. 7, No. 4, August 1977, pp. 1–12.

Cumming, P. D., K. E. Kendall, C. C. Pegels, J. P. Seagle, and J. F. Shubsda, "A Collections Planning Model for Regional Blood Suppliers: Description and Validation," *Management Science,* Vol. 22, No. 9, May 1976.

Flowers, A. D., and J. B. O'Neill, "An Application of Classical Inventory Analysis to a Spare Part Inventory," *Interfaces,* Vol. 8, No. 2, February 1978.

Jaikumar, R., and U. R. Rau, "An On-Line Integrated Materials Management System," *Interfaces,* Vol. 7, No. 1, Part 2, November 1976, pp. 19–30.

Lawrence, M. J., "An Integrated Inventory Control System," *Interfaces,* Vol. 7, No. 2, February 1977, pp. 55–62

Shapiro, A. C., "Incentive Systems and Implementation of Management Science: A Spare Parts Example." *Interfaces,* Vol. 7, No. 1, November 1976

Predicting the Effects of Risk

In our discussion of model building in Chapter 2 we stated that models that predicted system performance were in the input-transformation-output format of systems design, indicated by Figure 2-1. The variables in the systems modeled in that chapter were all deterministic with the exception of the last example; their values were assumed certain and constant. The parameters that specified alternatives were also assumed to be constants. Therefore, the logical relationships produced outputs or answers that were constants.

Now in Part III, we relax the assumption of deterministic parameters and variables. We do not do this because it is an attractive intellectual problem that is more challenging to mathematicians, but because there are managerial problems where the very essence of the real problem is expressed by the effects of variability and risk. Our first recognition of the effects of variability came in the previous chapter in dealing with the design of buffer inventories. We realized that demand during the supply lead time was really best represented by a demand probability distribution. Recognizing this fact made it possible to design inventory systems that balanced the *risks* of running out of stock against those of carrying excess inventory.

Sources of Risk

The sources of the risks that complicate a managerial problem may be from the external environment or from within the system itself. An example of the introduction of risk from the environment is a fluctuating pattern of demand for a service. An example from within the system is a random failure pattern for machines in a production process.

Suppose that you are the manager providing a service to the public in the form of a small post office. An important decision that you must make is the appropriate staffing level for the windows in the post office. The demand for service occurs when a customer joins the waiting line in front of the window. If the demand could be forecasted accurately, and if all the customers could be scheduled to arrive over the day at specific time intervals, it would be relatively simple to determine the appropriate number of windows to keep open.

Unfortunately, it is seldom possible to schedule or to predict accurately when customers will arrive for service. There may be several periods during each day when large numbers seem to converge on the post office all at once, and other periods when the post office is virtually vacant except for employees. These busy and slack periods may not occur with any regularity. Thus, the manager must make decisions in the face of an uncertain demand. At best, one can hope to describe the demand pattern probabilistically, perhaps in terms of an empirical probability distribution or perhaps in terms of some well-known probability distribution such as the normal distribution.

Why not simply compute the *mean* of the expected demand, and use this number as a basis for staffing decisions by treating it as though the mean were a known constant demand? There is an old saying that it is possible to drown in a lake that has a mean depth of only one foot. The problem, of course, is the variability in the depth of the water, and the problem for the manager is the variability in the level of demand. In order to understand and to *predict* how a system like the small post office will actually operate, it is necessary to use a mathematical model that explicitly incorporates a representation of the probabilistic demand pattern.

Why Not Optimization?

Suppose that we are convinced by this argument that some problems must be analyzed by mathematical models that explicitly include probabilistic descriptions of some key parameters, such as demand. It would still seem desirable to use an optimizing model to identify the optimal solution.

Unfortunately, the introduction of risk complicates the mathematical structure of most models to the degree that it is impossible or impractical to develop optimization algorithms to find the best solution. Instead, the manager must be satisfied with models that predict how the system will perform given some probabilistic descriptions of key parameters. Even the resulting prediction of the outcome will be probabilistic as well, since the uncertainty in the input parameters will be reflected in the output. For example, we might wish to predict how long the typical customer entering the small post office will have to wait in line before being served. If the arrival patterns of the customers are uncertain, then the waiting time will be uncertain as well. The evaluation of an outcome that can be described by another probability distribution may require a more sophisticated *evaluation model* than those normally associated with optimization models. *Evaluation models* for risky outcomes are discussed in Part IV.

Plan for Part III

All the models that we discuss in Part III are predictive, as indicated by the high-lighted area in our diagram of the relation between models, Figure III-1. In addition, we will restrict ourselves to predictive models involving the effects of risk.

FIGURE III-1
Predictive models in relation to alternatives and the evaluation of outcomes.

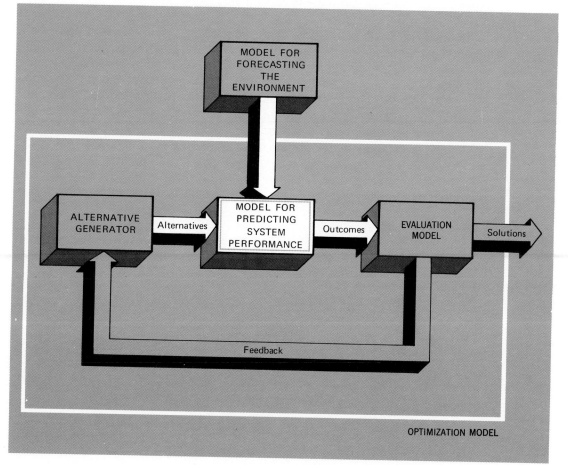

Chapter 11 deals with waiting lines, which occur in all kinds of service systems. Some(one) or some(thing) is placed in a waiting line to obtain service in post offices, banks, auto repair shops, and so on. The average length of the waiting line and the waiting time depend on the capacity of the system to process the units waiting for service, which is a managerial control variable. But demand on these kinds of systems is likely to be random, or at least quite variable. Therefore, managers are faced with the need to assess the risks of giving relatively poor service versus those of providing a larger service capacity at greater cost. Waiting line models can be very useful to managers in such situations.

Chapter 12 deals with Monte Carlo simulation, which makes it possible to introduce empirical statistical variation into analyses. It is useful in analyzing risky investments, risky decision processes, probabilistic networks, and waiting line structures where the distributions are best represented by empirical data instead of a known and tractable mathematical distribution. Monte Carlo is also useful in large complex managerial systems involving risk, where the only feasible mode of analysis is simulation.

Finally, the Markov chain models of Chapter 13 describe how elements of a system move from one state to another over time. In an important application of Markov chains, changes in consumer brand loyalty of a particular product are predicted over time.

CHAPTER 11

Waiting Line Models

Many systems and subsystems that occur throughout organized society can be conceptualized by waiting line models (also called *queuing* models). When you go to a bank you may have to wait in line for service. At the supermarket you line up at the checkout counter to have your purchases bagged and to pay the bill. To obtain service it seems that waiting in line is fairly typical. But waiting line systems are much more pervasive than the personal service situations. During the 1979 oil crisis an article in *Business Week* described the jam-up of ships in Jidda harbor in the Red Sea—they had to wait for dock space to be available. It was not tankers causing the problem, but the import boom in Saudi Arabia fueled by increasing petroleum wealth. Then too, while we never used to think of waiting lines in connection with filling our gas tanks, the 1974 oil embargo and the 1979 crisis have made gasoline waiting lines a stark reality.

All the preceding situations may be analyzed by waiting line models. They have inputs that may have to wait, a service to be performed, and an output. The input is composed of "arrivals," and arrival times are controlled by some probabilistic process. Similarly, the time required to process or service the input follows a probability distribution. The rate of output of such a system will depend on the interplay between the random arrivals and the variable service times. Predicting the output depends on this complex interplay, and queuing or waiting line theory is the basis for these pedictions. Table 11-1 shows the waiting line elements for a number of commonly known situations.

In this chapter we develop the concepts and methods of waiting line models and the mathematical solutions to relatively simple waiting line problems. However, when the mathematical analysis becomes too complex, we must resort to simulation. That approach to formulating and using waiting line models will be discussed in the next chapter.

NATURE OF SERVICE SYSTEMS

First, let us examine the characteristics of an emergency medical system. Such an example will help us to see how the concepts and methods described later in the chapter can be used. After we have discussed the assumptions and structure inherent in the models, the example will also help us to see the limitations of waiting line models. A study of the deployment of ambulance systems in Los Angeles forms the basis of the emergency medical system we shall discuss.

| Waiting Line Model Elements for Some Commonly Known Situations | | | TABLE 11-1 |

Situation	Unit Arriving	Processing Facility	Service or Process Being Performed
Ships entering a port	Ships	Docks	Unloading and loading
Maintenance and repair of machines	Machine breaks down	Repair crew	Repair machine
Assembly line, not mechanically paced	Parts to be assembled	Individual assembly operations or entire line	Assembly
Doctor's office	Patients	Doctor, the staff, and facilities	Medical care
Purchase of groceries at a supermarket	Customers with loaded grocery carts	Checkout counter	Tabulation of bill, receipt of payment, and bagging of groceries
Auto traffic at an intersection or bridge	Automobiles	Intersection of bridge with control points such as traffic lights or toll booths	Passage through intersection or bridge
Inventory of items in a warehouse	Order for withdrawal	Warehouse	Replenishment of inventory
Job shop	Job order	Work center	Processing

An emergency medical system

Figure 11-1 shows the essential activities of the ambulance and the patient in the emergency medical system. For the ambulance activities shown in Figure 11-1(a), ambulances are normally idle more than 70 percent of the time and the dispatch delay is usually less than one minute. Travel to the scene and the return trip to the hospital will be highly variable, depending on the ambulance deployment, the size of the area served, population density, traffic conditions, and so on. The one-way trip

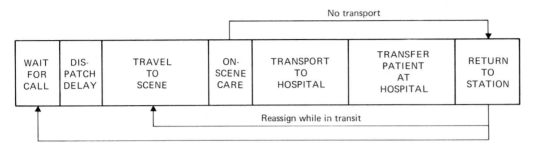

(a) AMBULANCE ACTIVITIES

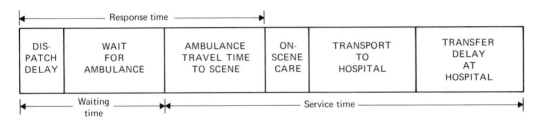

(b) PATIENT ACTIVITIES IN SYSTEM

FIGURE 11-1
Emergency medical system: (a) ambulance activities and (b) patient activities. From J. A. Fitzsimmons, "Emergency Medical Systems: A Simulation Study and Computerized Method for Deployment of Ambulances," Unpublished Ph.D. Dissertation, UCLA, 1970; used by permission.

in urban areas may be five to ten minutes, but it may be several times that figure for rural areas.

Figure 11-1(b) shows the service time as beginning with the trip to the scene and extending through the activities of on-scene care, transit to the hospital, and the transfer delay at the hospital. Waiting time is defined as the period between receipt of a "call" and the beginning of the ambulance trip. Response time, however, includes the travel time, and is the sensitive political and psychological variable.

Demand for service Part of the difficulty in providing emergency medical service is indicated in Figure 11-2. The incident or "call for service" rate is highly variable throughout the day. The load varies from a low of just over 0.5 calls per hour at 6 A.M. to a high of almost 3.3 per hour at 6 P.M. The peak load is more than six times the minimum load. Not only that, the mean values do not reflect the expected varia-

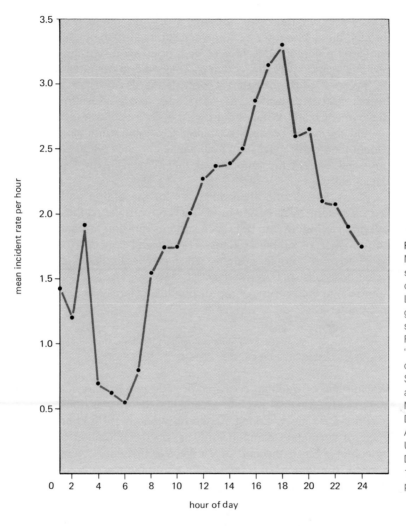

FIGURE 11-2
Mean "call for service" rate (incident rate) for the Los Angeles emergency medical system. From J. A. Fitzsimmons, "Emergency Medical Systems: A Simulation Study and Computerized Method for Deployment of Ambulances," Unpublished Ph.D. Dissertation, UCLA, 1970; used by permission.

tion in call rates. Previous research shows that call rates follow a Poisson distribution so that there is a 0.05 probability that the 6 P.M. call rate could be as high as approximately 7 per hour and a 0.05 probability that it could be as low as 1 per hour. (We will discuss the Poisson distribution as a forecast of arrival or call rates later in this chapter.)

System design and decision problems Note the highly variable demand patterns through the day and for each mean call rate, and the highly variable service times depending on deployment, area served, population density, and traffic conditions. It is obvious that the way the system is designed and operates will have a significant effect on measures of performance. Given standards of response time, what should be the overall system capacity? How does the needed system capacity interact with the deployment plan? What should be the size of service areas for a given ambulance? Should the areas be fixed or variable? Should ambulances have fixed locations or should they be mobile? If an ambulance in one location has already been dispatched on a call, should the ambulances that remain in the "available" inventory be redeployed?

These are all important decisions for the design and operation of this kind of service system. Waiting line models will not answer all these questions; however, they will provide insight into how such systems function and a methodology for predicting performance of simple systems. The general concepts of waiting line theory carry over into more complex systems, which can be simulated to provide a basis for making many decisions such as the ones listed above. The Monte Carlo computer simulation approach to the analysis of more complex systems involving waiting lines is discussed in Chapter 12.

WAITING LINE MODELS OF SERVICE SYSTEMS

Waiting line or queuing concepts provide insight into many problems in productive systems. The original work in waiting line theory was done by A. K. Erlang, a Danish telephone engineer. Erlang started his work in 1905 in an attempt to determine the effect of fluctuating demand (arrivals) on the utilization of automatic dial telephone equipment. Since the end of World War II, Erlang's work has been extended and applied to a variety of situations that are now recognized as being described by the general waiting line model.

Structure of waiting line models

There are four basic waiting line structures that describe the general conditions at the service facility. The simplest structure, shown in Figure 11-3(a), is our basic module. It is called the *single server case*. There are many examples of the simple module: the cashier at a restaurant, any single-window operation in a post office or bank, a one-chair barber shop.

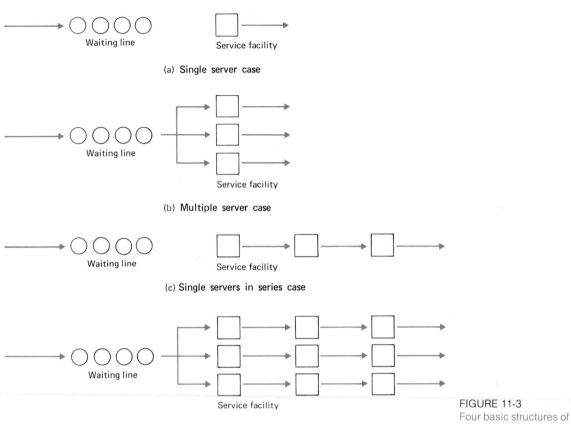

(a) Single server case

(b) Multiple server case

(c) Single servers in series case

(d) Multiple servers in series case

FIGURE 11-3
Four basic structures of
waiting line situations.

If the number of processing stations is increased but still draws on a single waiting line, we have the *multiple servers case* shown in Figure 11-3(b). A post office with several open windows but drawing on a single waiting line is a common example of a multiple server waiting line structure.

A simple assembly line or a cafeteria line has, in effect, a number of service facilities in series and is an example of the *single servers in series case* shown in Figure 11-3(c).

Finally, the *multiple servers in series case* can be illustrated by two or more parallel assembly lines as shown in Figure 11-3(d). Combinations of any or all of the basic four structures could also exist in networks in very complex systems.

The analytical methods for waiting lines divide into two main categories for any of the basic structures in Figure 11-3, depending on the size of the source population of the inputs. When the source population is very large, and in theory at least the length of the waiting line could grow without fixed limits, the applicable models are termed *infinite waiting line models*. On the other hand, when the arriving unit comes from a small fixed-size population, the applicable models are termed *finite waiting line models*. For example, if we are dealing with the maintenance of a bank of 20 machines and a machine breakdown represents an arrival, the maximum waiting line is 20 machines waiting for service, and a finite waiting line model is needed. On the other hand, if we operated an auto repair shop, the source population of breakdowns is very large and an infinite waiting line model would provide a good approximation. We will discuss both infinite and finite models.

There are other variations in waiting line structures that are important in certain applications. The "queue discipline" describes the order in which the units in the waiting line are selected for service. In Figure 11-3, we imply that the queue discipline is first-come first-served. Obviously there are many other possibilities involving priority systems. For example, in a medical clinic, emergencies and patients with appointments are taken ahead of walk-in patients. In production scheduling systems there has been a great deal of experimentation with alternate priority systems. Because of the mathematical complexity involved, Monte Carlo simulation has been the common mode of analysis for systems involving queue disciplines other than first-come first-served.

Finally, the nature of the distributions of arrivals and service is an important structural characteristic of waiting line models. Some mathematical analysis is available for distributions that follow the Poisson or the Erlang process (with some variations), or that have constant arrival rates or constant service times. If distributions are different from those mentioned or are taken from actual records, simulation is likely to be the necessary mode of analysis as we will describe in Chapter 12.

INFINITE WAITING LINE MODELS

We will not cover all possibilities of infinite waiting line models, but will restrict our discussion to situations involving the first-come first-served queue discipline and the Poisson distribution of arrivals. We will deal initially with the single server case (our basic service facility module), but later we will also discuss the multiple server case.

Our objective will be to develop predictions of some important measures of performance for waiting lines, such as the mean length of the waiting line, and the mean waiting time for an arriving unit.

Poisson arrivals

The Poisson distribution function has been shown to represent arrival rates in a large number of real-world situations. It is a discrete function dealing with whole units of arrivals, so that fractions of people, products, or machines do not have meaning, nor do negative values. The Poisson distribution function is given by

$$f(x) = \frac{\lambda^x e^{-\lambda}}{x!} \tag{1}$$

where

λ = the mean arrival rate

x = the number arriving in one unit of time

$x!$ = x factorial

(*Note:* $x!$ is simply $(x)(x-1) \ldots (3)(2)(1)$. For example, $4! = 4 \times 3 \times 2 \times 1 = 24$. $0! = 1$.) For example, if $\lambda = 4$ per hour, then the probability of $x = 6$ in one hour is

$$f(6) = \frac{4^6 e^{-4}}{6!} = \frac{4096 \times 0.0183}{720} = 0.104$$

The Poisson distribution for an average arrival rate of $\lambda = 4$ per hour (as well as for other values of λ) is shown in Figure 11-4. The Poisson distribution is typically skewed to the right. The distribution is simple in that its standard deviation is expressed solely in terms of the mean, $\sigma_\lambda = \sqrt{\lambda}$.

Evidence that the Poisson distribution in fact represents arrival patterns in many applications is indeed great. Many empirical studies have validated the Poisson arrival distribution in general industrial operations, traffic flow, and various service operations.

Arrival distributions are sometimes given in terms of the time between arrivals, or interarrival times. The distributions of the time between arrivals often follow the nega-

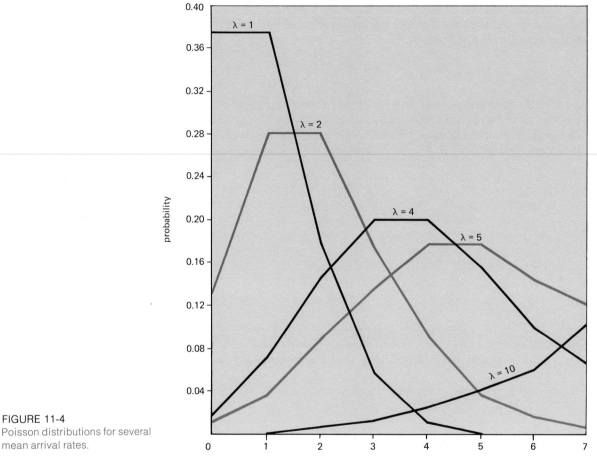

FIGURE 11-4
Poisson distributions for several
mean arrival rates.

tive exponential distribution. However, if the *number* of arrivals in a given interval is
Poisson distributed, then necessarily the times *between* arrivals have a negative
exponential distribution, and vice versa.

Although we cannot say that all distributions of arrivals per unit of time are adequately described by the Poisson distribution, we can say that it is usually worth
checking to see if it is true, for then a fairly simple analysis may be possible. It is logical

that arrivals may follow the Poisson distribution when many factors affect arrival time, since the Poisson distribution corresponds to completely random arrivals. This means that each arrival is independent of other arrivals as well as of any condition of the waiting line. The practical question is whether or not the Poisson distribution is a reasonable approximation to reality.

Poisson arrivals—service time distribution not specified

Since Poisson arrivals are common, a useful waiting line model is one that depends on Poisson arrivals but accepts any service time distribution. We assume that the mean service rate is greater than the mean arrival rate, otherwise the system would be unstable and the waiting line would become infinitely large. We also assume the single server case, first-come first-served queue discipline, and arrivals wait for service; that is, they neither fail to join the line nor leave it because it is too long. Under these conditions the expected length of the waiting line is

$$L_q = \frac{(\lambda\sigma)^2 + (\lambda/\mu)^2}{2(1 - \lambda/\mu)} \tag{2}$$

where

L_q = the expected length of the waiting line

λ = the mean arrival rate from a Poisson distribution

μ = the mean service rate

σ = the standard deviation of the distribution of service times

We define the average service facility utilization as $\rho = \lambda/M\mu$, where M is the number of servers in the waiting line system. In the single server case, $M = 1$ and ρ is simplified. Since λ is the mean arrival rate and μ is the mean service rate, then ρ may be interpreted as the proportion of time that at least one server is busy. For example, if $\lambda = 2$, $\mu = 4$, and $M = 1$, then on the average two units arrive per time unit and the single server has the capacity to process four units during the same time interval. Therefore, the server will be busy $\rho = \lambda/M\mu = 2/(1 \times 4) = 0.5$, or half the time. In the single server case, $\rho = \lambda/\mu$ represents the proportion of time that the service facility is in use and the expected number of units being served. Therefore, the probability that a unit will have to wait for service is $\rho_w = \lambda/\mu$. Also, $(1 - \rho)$ is the fraction of service facility idle time, or the fraction of time when no one is being served.

Since λ/μ is the expected number being served, the total number in the waiting line plus the expected number being served is the total number in the system, L,

$$L = L_q + \lambda/\mu \tag{3}$$

Similar simple logic leads to the formula for expected waiting time in line W_q, and time in the system including service W. The reciprocal of the mean arrival rate is the mean time between arrivals $(1/\lambda)$. For example, if $\lambda = 2$ units per hour on the average, then the expected time between arrivals of any two units is $1/2 = 0.5$ hours. The multiplication of the mean time between arrivals and the line length gives the waiting time

$$W_q = L_q/\lambda \tag{4}$$

If $\lambda = 2$ units per hour and $L_q = 3$, then one unit arrives in the system every 0.5 hours on the average, but the line is 3 units long. Therefore, units waiting in line must wait three times as long as the time between arrivals, or $3 \times 0.5 = 1.5$ hours, that is, $L_q/\lambda = 3/2 = 1.5$ hours.

Also, the multiplication of the mean time between arrivals and the mean total number in the system, L, gives the mean time in the system including service, that is,

$$W = L/\lambda = W_q + 1/\mu \tag{5}$$

The latter equality in equation (5) is true because the total time in the system must equal the waiting time plus the time for service. Equations (2), (3), (4), and (5) are useful relationships. The general procedure would be to compute L_q from (2), and compute the values of L, W_q, and W as needed, given the value of L_q. Note that equations (2) through (5) deal only with average or long-run equilibrium conditions.

An example Trucks arrive at the truck dock of a wholesale grocer at the rate of 8 per hour and the distribution of arrivals is Poisson. The loading and/or unloading time averages 5 minutes, but the estimate s of the standard deviation of service time is 6 minutes. Truckers are complaining that they must spend more time waiting than unloading and the following calculations verify their claim:

$$\lambda = 8/\text{hour}; \ \mu = 60/5 = 12/\text{hour}; \ s = 6/60 = 1/10 \text{ hours}$$

$$L_q = \frac{(8/10)^2 + (8/12)^2}{2(1 - 8/12)} = 1.63 \text{ trucks in line}$$

$L\ = 1.63 + 8/12 = 2.30$ trucks in the system

$W_q = 1.63/8 = 0.204$ hours, or 12.24 minutes in line waiting for service

$W\ = 2.30/8 = 0.288$ hours, or 17.28 minutes in the system

The calculations yield another verification of logic in that the average truck waits 12.24 minutes in line plus 5 minutes for service, or 17.28 minutes in the system. Thus, $W = W_q + 1/\mu$ as indicated in equation (5).

Let us pause for a moment to reflect on this model. Which are the decision variables and which are the uncontrollable parameters? The service-related variables can be altered by the manager if there is a willingness to invest capital in new capacity or if new procedures can be devised that can reduce the variability of service time. On the other hand, the arrival rate of trucks is presumably not under managerial control, and thus is a parameter.

The grocer knows, of course, that the problem could probably be solved by expanding the truck dock so that two trucks could be handled simultaneously. This solution, however, would require a large capital expenditure and disruption of operations during construction. Instead, the grocer notes the very large standard deviation of service time, and on investigation finds that some orders involve uncommon items that are not stored in a systematic manner. Locating these items takes a great deal of search time.

The grocer revamps the storage system so that all items can be easily located. As a result, the standard deviation is reduced to 3 minutes. Assuming that mean service time is not affected, we have an indication of the sensitivity of the system to changes in the variability of service time. The new values are $L_q = 0.91$, $L = 1.57$, $W_q = 6.8$ minutes, and $W = 11.8$ minutes. Waiting time has been almost cut in half. The truckers are happier, and the grocer has improved the system without a large capital expenditure.

SERVICE TIME DISTRIBUTIONS

While there is considerable evidence that arrival processes tend to follow the Poisson distributions as has been indicated, service time distributions seem to be much more varied in their nature. It is for this reason that the previous model involving Poisson arrivals and an unspecified service time distribution is so valuable. With equation (2), one can compute the waiting line statistics, knowing only the mean service rate and the standard deviation of service time.

The negative exponential distribution has been one of the prominent models for service time, and there is evidence that in some instances the assumption is valid. However, Nelson's study [1959] of distributions of arrivals and service times in a Los Angeles machine shop did *not* indicate that the exponential model fit the actual service time distributions adequately for all of the machine centers.

Figure 11-5 shows the service time distributions at a university outpatient clinic. The distributions for "walk-in" and "appointment" patients are definitely not negative exponential, while the "second-service" distribution is reasonably close to being represented by a negative exponential distribution. Second-service patients are those who have been seen by a physician, have been routed for tests or some other medical procedure, and are returning to complete the consultation with a physician.

Other evidence indicates that in some cases the negative exponential distribution fits. Figure 11-6, for example, shows that the service time at a tool crib was nearly negative exponentially distributed. The distribution of local telephone calls not made from a pay station has also been shown to be negative exponential.

Model for Poisson input and negative exponential service times

The negative exponential distribution is completely described by its mean value, since its standard deviation is equal to its mean. We can describe this model as a special case of equation (2). If the service times are adequately described by a negative exponential distribution, then the mean of the distribution is the reciprocal of the mean service rate, that is, $1/\mu$. Therefore, $1/\mu$ is also the standard deviation of the distribution of service times when the distribution is the negative exponential. Equation (6) can easily be derived from equation (2) when $1/\mu$ is substituted for σ (verify this derivation yourself):

$$L_q = \frac{\lambda^2}{\mu(\mu - \lambda)} \tag{6}$$

Also, the probability of n units in the system at any point in time is

$$P_n = \left(\frac{\lambda}{\mu}\right)^n \left(1 - \frac{\lambda}{\mu}\right) \tag{7}$$

The other relationships between L_q, L, W_q, and W, expressed by equations (3), (4), and (5), hold for the negative exponential service time distributions as well as for the

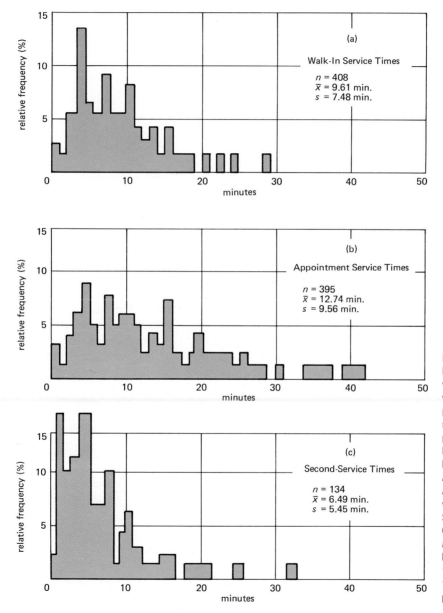

FIGURE 11-5
Histograms of service time for (a) walk-in, (b) appointment, and (c) second-service patients.
From E. J. Rising, R. Baron, and B. Averill, "A Systems Analysis of a University-Health-Service Outpatient Clinic," *Operations Research,* Vol. 21, No. 5, Sept.–Oct. 1973, pp. 1030–1047; used by permission.

FIGURE 11-6
Service time at a
tool crib.
From G. Brigham,
"On a Congestion
Problem in an
Aircraft Factory,"
*Operations Re-
search*, Vol. 3,
No. 4, 1955, pp.
412–28; used by
permission.

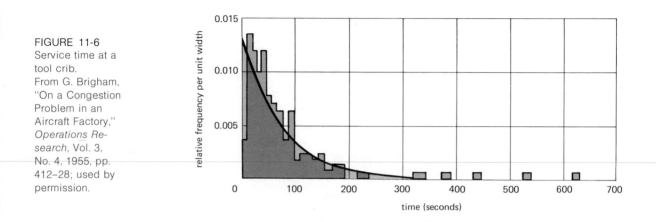

case where no service time distribution is specified. For the sake of simplicity, many individuals prefer to use equation (2), using the appropriate value of σ to reflect the special case.

We can now check to see the effect of exponential service times on waiting line statistics for the truck dock problem. If we assume that the service time in that situation was represented by a negative exponential distribution, then $\sigma = 1/\mu = 1/12$, and the value of L_q from equation (2) is 1.33. The other waiting line model statistics are $L = 2$, $W_q = 10$ minutes, and $W = 15$ minutes. The values are intermediate between the previous two calculations for the grocer's problem, since the value of σ is between the two previous values.

Model for Poisson input and constant service times

While constant service times are not usual in actual practice, they may be reasonable assumptions in cases where a machine processes arriving items by a fixed-time cycle. Also, constant service times represent a boundary or lower limit on the value of σ in equation (2). As such, a constant service time is also a special case of equation (2). The resulting equation for constant service times is

$$L_q = \frac{\lambda^2}{2\mu(\mu - \lambda)} \tag{8}$$

You should derive equation (8) from equation (2) by substituting $\sigma = 0$ in equation (2).

Again, for comparison, and to gain insight into what happens in waiting lines, let us see what the result would have been if the grocer could have made service time constant at 5 minutes, that is, reduced the standard deviation to zero. Substituting in equation (8), we have $L_q = 0.67$, $L = 1.33$, $W_q = 5$ minutes, and $W = 10$ minutes. Again, the other relationships between L_q, L, W_q, and W expressed by equations (3), (4), and (5) hold for the constant service time distribution as well as for the case where no service time distribution is specified.

Then, we can consider equation (2) as a fairly general model with service time distributions described by the negative exponential, or constant service times as special cases. Figure 11-7 shows a graph of L_q for various values of the standard deviation, including the values for the negative exponential distribution and for constant service times. Values of the standard deviation greater than that for the negative exponential distribution occur and are termed hyperexponential distributions. The extreme values of standard deviation are not representative of values found in practice; however, the tail of the curve in Figure 11-7 is shown to indicate how rapidly L_q increases with variability in the service time distribution.

Relationship of queue length to utilization

Recall that $\rho = \lambda/M\mu$ represents the service facility utilization. If $\lambda = \mu$, then $\rho = 1$ for the single server case where $M = 1$, and theoretically the service facility is used 100 percent of the time. But let us see what happens to the length of the queue as ρ varies from zero to one. Figure 11-8 summarizes the result for Poisson input and exponential service times for a single server. As ρ approaches unity, the number waiting in line increases rapidly and approaches infinity. We can see that this must be true by examining equations (2), (6), and (8) for L_q. In all cases, the denominator goes to zero as ρ approaches unity and the value of L_q becomes infinitely large.

We see now that one of the requirements of any practical system is that $\mu > \lambda$; otherwise we cannot have a stable system. If units are arriving faster on the average than they can be processed, the waiting line and waiting time will increase continuously and no steady state can be achieved. This simple fact also indicates that there is a value to be placed on idle time in the service facility. *We must trade off the value of rapid service against service facility costs that may include substantial service facility idle time.*

Multiple servers

In the multiple servers case we assume the conditions of Poisson arrivals, exponential service times, first-come first-served queue discipline, and all servers drawing on a

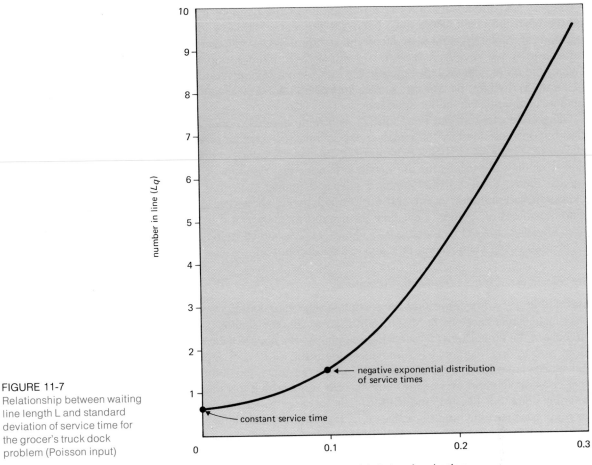

FIGURE 11-7

Relationship between waiting line length L and standard deviation of service time for the grocer's truck dock problem (Poisson input)

single waiting line. The effective service rate $M\mu$ must be greater than the arrival rate λ, where M is the number of servers. The facility utilization factor is $\rho = \lambda/M\mu$, and we define $r = \lambda/\mu$. First, it is necessary to calculate L_q, the mean number in the waiting line. The formula for L_q becomes relatively complex in the multiple server case, so we have computed L_q for various values of M (the number of servers) and $r = \lambda/\mu$ in Table C-2 of Appendix C.

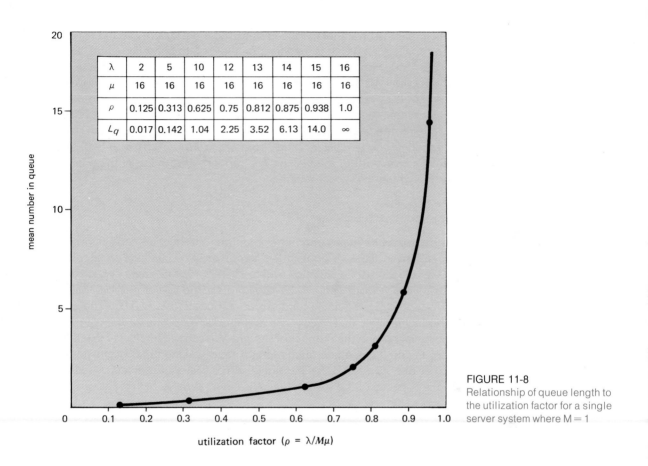

FIGURE 11-8
Relationship of queue length to the utilization factor for a single server system where M = 1

Given the value of L_q, then L, W_q, and W are easily computed from equations (3), (4), and (5). The probability that all servers are busy (the probability that there will be a wait), P_w, can be computed using the values of L_q in Table C-2 as:

$$P_w = \frac{L_q(M - r)}{r} \tag{9}$$

As an example, assume that the wholesale grocer decides to expand facilities and add a second truck dock. What is the effect on average truck waiting time? Recall the basic data: $\lambda = 8$ per hour, $\mu = 12$ per hour, but now $M = 2$. From Table C-2, for $M = 2$ and $r = \lambda/\mu = 8/12 = 0.67$, we find, by interpolating, that $L_q = 0.085$ trucks in line. Then $W_q = L_q/\lambda = 0.085/8 = 0.0106$ hours or 0.64 minutes. Compare these results with the single server solution for exponential service time of $W_q = 10$ minutes. Obviously, adding the second dock eliminates the truck waiting problem. Note that overall utilization of the facilities declines from $\rho = \lambda/M\mu = 0.67$ to $\rho = 0.34$. Table 11-2 provides a summary of the waiting line model statistics for all the models constructed for the wholesale grocer example.

The effect of pooling facilities

Sometimes managers have the option of organizing the needed capacity into two or more independent facilities or pooling the resources into one large facility. If for example, we were faced with a situation where $r = 0.9$ for the single server case, then L_q is approximately 8 from Table C-2. Adding a second server reduces the average line length to $L_q = 0.23$. Adding a third server reduces it to $L_q = 0.03$. The effects on L_q are surprisingly large; that is, we can obtain disproportionate gains in reducing waiting time by increasing the number of servers. We can see intuitively that this might be true from Figure 11-8, since queue length (and waiting time) begins to increase very rapidly at about $\rho = 0.8$, for the single server case represented. A rather small increase in the capacity of the system (decrease in ρ) at these high loads can produce

TABLE 11-2   Summary of Waiting Line Model Statistics for the Wholesale Grocer
Example. $\lambda = 8$/hour, $\mu = 12$/hour

	Single Dock, $M = 1$				Two Docks, $M = 2$, Negative Exponential Service Time
	$s = 6$ min.	$s = 3$ min.	Negative Exponential Service Time, $s = 1/\mu = 5$ min.	Constant Service Time, $s = 0$	
L_q, trucks in line	1.63	0.91	1.33	0.67	0.085
L, trucks in system	2.30	1.57	2.00	1.33	0.752
W_q, minutes	12.24	6.80	10.00	5.00	0.64
W, minutes	17.28	11.80	15.00	10.00	5.64

a large decrease in waiting line length and waiting time.

When we design a system with waiting lines, we can increase its service level by increasing the speed of a server, adding another server at the same physical location that draws on the same waiting line, or adding another server at a different physical location. Intuitively, we might expect these alternatives to produce essentially identical results. To investigate this issue, let us compare the doubling of capacity within the same service facility by doubling the service rate, doubling capacity by adding a second server within the same facility, and doubling capacity through parallel service facilities. Assume that $\lambda = 8$, $\mu = 10$, and $r = \lambda/\mu = 0.8$ for the base case with a single server. From Table C-2 and the equations, the mean number waiting is $L_q = 3.2$, the mean number in the system is $L = 4$, the mean waiting time is $W_q = 0.4$ hours or 24 minutes, and the mean time in the system is $W = 0.5$ hours, or 30 minutes. These data are summarized in Table 11-3.

If we double capacity by doubling the service rate within the same facility, all the waiting line model statistics improve dramatically as shown in Table 11-3. If we double capacity by adding a second server, service improves, but not as dramatically.

Now, however, suppose that we double capacity by establishing a second service facility in another location so that there must be two independent waiting lines. The arrivals are divided equally between the two facilities and $\lambda = 4$, $\mu = 10$, and $r = 0.4$. The information for comparison is given by the right-hand column in Table 11-3. Each service facility will provide the service indicated.

Now look at just the two alternatives of providing the same capacity with one large facility, either by doubling service rate or by adding a second server (the third and fourth columns of Table 11-3). Comparing them with two equivalent small facilities in the right-hand column, it is clear that either of the alternatives involving an enlarged single facility gives better service. One large facility definitely provides better service than two equivalent smaller facilities. Looking just at the two alternate ways of doubling capacity within the existing facility, doubling service rate is superior. While doubling service rate results in a larger waiting line ($L_q = 0.27$ versus 0.15, since sometimes two are being served simultaneously in the $M = 2$ case) and waiting time is proportionately greater, this condition is compensated for by faster service, and the mean number in the system as well as the *total* time in the system are smaller for the system with the higher service rate.

An example A large manufacturing concern with a 100-acre plant had a well-established medical facility, which was located at the plant offices at the eastern edge of the property. The plant had grown over the years from east to west and currently travel

TABLE 11-3

Effects of Doubling Capacity Within the Same Service Facility
by Doubling Service Rate Versus Adding a Second Server

	Base Case $(M = 1, r = 0.8)$	Capacity Doubled		
		Within Same Facility $(M = 1, r = 0.4)$	By Adding Second Server $(M = 2, r = 0.8)$	Second Facility, each $(M = 1, r = 0.4)$
$L_q{}^*$	3.2000	0.2666	0.1533	0.2666
$L = L_q + \lambda/\mu$	4.0000	0.6666	0.9533	0.6666
$W_q = L_q/\lambda$	0.4000 hr	0.0333 hr	0.0192 hr	0.0667 hr
$W = L/\lambda$	0.5000 hr	0.0833 hr	0.1192 hr	0.1667 hr
	or	or	or	or
	30.0 min	5.0 min	7.15 min	10.0 min

* Values from Table C-2 of Appendix C.

time to the medical facility was so great that management was considering dividing the facility. The second unit was to be established near the center of the west end of the plant. A study had been made of weighted travel times for the present single facility and for the proposed two-facility system. The result indicated that average travel time for the present large medical facility was 15 minutes. The volume averaged 1000 visits per week, or 250 worker hours for travel time. The two-facility plan would reduce the average travel time to 8 minutes, or 133 worker hours per week.

The question now was: what would happen to waiting time in the waiting rooms? For the one large facility, $\lambda = 25$ per hour, and average service time was 20 minutes, or a service rate of $\mu = 3$ per hour, and $r = 25/3 = 8.33$. There were 10 physicians who handled the load. Interpolating in Table C-2, $L_q = 2.45$, and $W_q = 2.45 \times 60/25 = 5.88$ minutes per person or 98 worker hours per week. Therefore, the travel time plus the waiting time was $250 + 98 = 348$ worker-hours per week.

The plan was to divide the medical staff for the two facilities, and it was assumed that the load would divide equally, so comparable data for the divided facilities are $\lambda = 12.5$ per hour per facility, $\mu = 3$ per hour, $M = 5$, and $r = 4.2$. From Table C-2 of Appendix C, $L_q = 3.3269$ and $W_q = 16$ minutes per person or 267 worker hours per week. The travel plus waiting time for the dual facility plan was therefore $133 + 267 = 400$ worker hours per week, compared to 348 for the single large facility. Other alternatives could be computed, probably involving an increased medical staff.

The waiting time for the single large facility was 5.88 minutes per person compared to 16.0 minutes per person for the two-facility plan. The large facility gives better service than the two smaller facilities. If we visualize the two decentralized facilities functioning side by side, we can see intuitively why waiting time increases. If facility *one* were busy and had patients waiting while at the same time facility *two* happened to be idle, someone from the facility *one* waiting room could be serviced immediately by facility *two*, thereby reducing average waiting time. In this situation the two facilities are drawing from one waiting line. When they are physically decentralized, the facilities must draw on two independent waiting lines and *the idle capacity of one cannot be used by the waiting patients of the other.*

Costs and capacity in waiting line models

While many decisions concerning service systems may turn on physical factors of line length, waiting time, and the service facility utilization, very often system designs will depend on comparative costs for alternatives. The costs involved are commonly the costs of providing the service *versus* the waiting time costs. In some instances the waiting time costs are objective, as when the enterprise is employing both the servers and those waiting. The company medical facility just discussed is such a case. The company absorbed all the travel time and waiting time costs, as well as the cost of providing the service. In such an instance, a direct cost-minimizing approach can be taken balancing the waiting costs, or the time-in-system costs, against the costs of providing the service.

When the arriving units are customers, clients, or patients, the cost of making them wait is less obvious. If they are customers, excessive waiting may cause irritation and loss of goodwill and eventually sales. Placing a value on goodwill, however, is not a straightforward exercise. In public service operations and other monopoly situations, the valuation of waiting cost may be even more tenuous because the individual cannot make alternate choices. In these situations where objective costs cannot be balanced, it may be necessary to set a standard for waiting time; for example, to adjust capacity to keep average waiting time at or below a given number of minutes at supermarket checkout counters.

Example one Let us refer to the data for the company internal medical facility. Recall that there were 10 physicians, whom we will assume are paid $3000 per month, or about $6928 per week for the 10 physicians. We also assume that the average hourly wage of employees coming to the medical facility is $5. Computations for the single

TABLE 11-4   Utilization, Waiting Time, and Costs for Different Levels of
                  Medical Service

	Number of Physicians		
	9	10	11
Utilization ($\rho = \lambda/M\mu$)	0.93	0.83	0.76
Mean waiting time (min)	23.4	5.88	2.26
Weekly waiting time (hr)	390	98	38
Cost of waiting time/week	$1950	$ 490	$ 190
Physicians' cost/week	6235	6928	7620
Total affected cost	$8185	$7418	$7810

central facility yield a travel time cost of $250 \times 5 = \$1250$ per week, and a waiting time cost of $98 \times 5 = \$490$ per week. The total weekly cost is then $8668, including physician's salaries. First, with the central facility only, how many physicians will minimize affected costs? Using Table C-2, we can determine average waiting time for 9, 10, and 11 physicians, and the resulting weekly costs. The results are shown in Table 11-4. Consequently, the present policy of having 10 physicians is a little less costly than having either 9 or 11.

Now, let us consider the dual facility concept, where travel cost is also affected. The travel, waiting, and physicians' cost for the central facility was $5(250 + 98) + \$6928 = \$8668$ per week. The comparable figures for the dual facilities were $5(133 + 267) + \$6928 = \$8928$ per week. Would increased capacity in either or both of the dual facilities improve affected costs? The answer is no. The weekly travel and waiting costs and service costs for 5 physicians in each facility, 5 in one and 6 in the other, and 6 in each are $8928, $9109, and $9292.

Now an important observation concerning the company medical facility is that the unit cost of providing the service is very large and tends to dominate, compared to unit waiting time costs. The physician is paid $3000 per month while the average employee waiting is paid only about $866 per month. If the unit costs change relative to each other, the best solution may be different.

Example two The manager of a large bank has the problem of providing teller service for customer demand, which varies somewhat during the business day from 10:00

A.M. to 4:00 P.M. She has a total capacity of six windows and can assign unneeded tellers to other useful work. She also wishes to give excellent service, however, which she defines in terms of customer waiting time as $W_q \leq 1$ minute. In order to give the best service for any situation, she has arranged the layout so that customers form one waiting line from which the customer at the head of the line goes to the first available teller.

The arrival pattern is as follows:

	Customers per Minute (λ)
10:00 A.M. –11:30 A.M.	1.8
11:30 A.M. – 1:30 P.M.	4.8
1:30 P.M. – 3:00 P.M.	3.8
3:00 P.M. – 4:00 P.M.	4.6

and each arrival pattern follows the Poisson distribution. The mean value of arrivals varies, but is always from a Poisson distribution. The mean service time is one minute and the distribution of service times is negative exponential. The service rate is $\mu = 1/1 = 1$ per minute.

The bank manager can make plans to adjust teller capacity to daily demand patterns very easily, maintaining the waiting time standard. The basic data comes from Table C-2 and is tabulated here in Table 11-5. We see there that to maintain the one-minute standard for W_q, the number of windows open must be:

	No. of Windows Open
10:00 A.M. –11:30 A.M.	3
11:30 A.M. – 1:30 P.M.	6
1:30 P.M. – 3:00 P.M.	5
3:00 P.M. – 4:00 P.M.	6

TABLE 11-5	Waiting Time for Different Numbers of Teller Windows Open at Different Times of Day		
No. of Windows Open (M)		Length of Waiting Line (L_q)	Waiting Time in Minutes (W_q)
	10:00 A.M. –11:30 A.M.	$r = \lambda/\mu = 1.8$	
2		7.67	4.26
3		0.53	0.29
	11:30 A.M. –1:30 P.M.	$r = \lambda/\mu = 4.8$	
5		21.64	4.50
6		2.07	0.43
	1:30 P.M. –3:00 P.M.	$r = \lambda/\mu = 3.8$	
4		16.94	4.45
5		1.52	0.40
	3:00 P.M. –4:00 P.M.	$r = \lambda/\mu = 4.6$	
5		9.29	2.01
6		1.49	0.32

FINITE WAITING LINE MODELS

Many practical waiting line problems that occur have the characteristics of finite waiting line models. This is true whenever the population of machines, people, or items that may arrive for service is limited to a relatively small finite number. The result is that we must express arrivals in terms of a unit of the population rather than as an average rate. In the infinite waiting line case the average length of the waiting line is effectively independent of the number in the arriving population, but in the finite case the number in the waiting line may represent a significant proportion of the arriving population, and therefore the probabilities associated with arrivals are affected.

The resulting mathematical formulations are somewhat more difficult computationally than those for the infinite waiting line case. Fortunately, however, finite queuing tables [Peck and Hazelwood, 1958] are available that make problem solution very simple. Although there is no definite number that we can point to as a dividing line between finite and infinite applications, the finite queuing tables have data for populations from 4 up to 250, and these data may be taken as a general guide. We have reproduced these tables for populations of 5, 10, 20, and 30 in Table C-3 of Appendix C, to illustrate their use in the solution of finite waiting line problems. The tables are based on a finite model for negative exponential times between arrivals and negative exponential service times, and a first-come first-served queue discipline.

Use of the finite queuing tables

The tables are indexed first by N, the size of the population. For each population size, data are classified by X, the service factor (comparable to the utilization factor in infinite waiting line models), and by M, the number of parallel servers. The service factor X is computed from the following formula:

$$X = \text{service factor} = \frac{\lambda}{\lambda + \mu}$$

where μ is the service rate as before, but λ is the mean arrival rate *per population unit.* For example, if our time unit is hours and each *population unit* arrives for service every four hours on the average, then $\lambda = 1/4 = 0.25$ per hour.

For a given N, X, and M, three factors are listed in the tables: D (the probability of a delay; that is, if a unit calls for service, the probability that it will have to wait), F (an efficiency factor, used to calculate other important data), and L_q (the mean number in the waiting line). To summarize, we define the following factors:

W_q $= \text{mean waiting time} = \dfrac{1}{\mu X} \dfrac{(1 - F)}{(F)}$

L $= \text{mean number waiting plus being served} = L_q + FNX$

W $= \text{mean time in system} = W_q + 1/\mu$

H $= \text{mean number of units being serviced} = FNX = L - L_q$

J $= \text{mean number of units not being served} = FN(1 - X)$

$M - H = \text{mean number of servers idle}$

The procedure for a given case is as follows:

1. Determine the mean service rate μ and the mean arrival rate λ per population unit, based on data or measurements of the system being analyzed.
2. Compute the service factor $X = \lambda/(\lambda + \mu)$.
3. Locate the section of the tables listing data for the population size N.
4. Locate the service factor calculated in (2) above, for the given population.
5. Read the values of D, F, and L_q for the number of servers M, interpolating between values of X when necessary.
6. Compute values for W_q, H, and J as required by the nature of the problem.

Example A hospital ward has thirty beds in one section, and the problem centers on the appropriate level of nursing care. The hospital management believes that patients should have immediate response to a call at least 80 percent of the time because of possible emergencies. The mean time between calls is 95 minutes *per patient*, for the thirty patients. The service time is approximated by a negative exponential distribution and mean service time is 5 minutes.

The hospital manager wishes to staff the ward to give service so that 80 percent of the time there will be no delay. Nurses are paid $5 per hour, and the cost of idle time at this level of service must be considered. Also, the manager wishes to know how much more patients will have to pay for the 80 percent criterion compared to a 50 percent service level for immediate response, which is the current policy.

The *solutions* to the problems posed by the hospital manager are developed through a finite waiting line model. The situation requires a finite model because the maximum possible queue is 30 patients waiting for nursing care.

In terms of the finite waiting line model for this situation, the mean service time is 5 minutes ($\mu = 0.2$/min., or 12/hr.), the mean time between calls is 95 minutes *per patient* ($\lambda = 0.0105$/min., or 0.632/hr.), and therefore the service factor is $X = \lambda/(\lambda + \mu) = 0.632/12.632 = 0.05$.

Scanning the finite queuing tables (Table C-3) under Population $N = 30$, and $X = 0.05$, we seek data for the probability of a delay of $D = 0.20$, since we wish to establish service such that there will be no delay 80 percent of the time. The closest we can come to providing this level of service is with $M = 3$ nurses and corresponding data (see Table C-3) of $D = 0.208$, $F = 0.994$, and $L_q = 0.18$. Note that we must select an integer number of servers (nurses).

The cost of this level of service is the cost of employing 3 nurses or $5 \times 3 = \$15$

per hour, or $360 per day, assuming day and night care. The average number of calls waiting to be serviced will be $L_q = 0.18$ and the mean waiting time will be

$$W_q = \frac{1}{\mu X}\left(\frac{1-F}{F}\right) = \frac{1}{0.2 \times 0.05}\left(\frac{1-0.994}{0.994}\right) = 0.6 \text{ minutes}$$

The waiting time due to waiting line effects is, of course, negligible, which is intended.

The average number of patients being served will be $H = FNX = 0.994 \times 30 \times 0.05 = 1.49$, and the average number of nurses idle will be $3 - 1.49 = 1.51$. The equivalent value of this idleness is $1.51 \times 5 \times 24 = \$181.20$ per day.

Finally, the number of nurses needed to provide immediate service 50 percent of the time is $M = 2$ from Table C-3 ($D = 0.571$, $F = 0.963$, and $L_q = 1.11$). The average waiting time under this policy is $W_q = 3.84$ minutes. The average cost to patients of having the one additional nurse to provide the higher level of service is $5 per hour or $120 per day. Divided among 30 patients, the cost is $4 per patient per day.

WHAT SHOULD THE MANAGER KNOW?

The waiting line models we have discussed have particular value in providing us with an insight into what happens in service systems. These models show why lines form and why waiting is probably necessary or at least costly to eliminate. They also indicate the effects of increased capacity, pooling of facilities, and variability in the service time distribution. Nevertheless, waiting line models themselves are useful only for fairly simple situations. For example, the emergency medical system problem is focused in location and deployment, and although waiting line aspects are important, they are only part of the problem. In such situations we resort to simulation where both the probabilistic nature of the problem and its complexity can be handled effectively. We will deal with the emergency medical system again in the next chapter.

Thus, for the manager, waiting line models can provide a better understanding of how service systems function. For example, with variable arrival rates and service times, it becomes immediately obvious that good facility utilization and good service are at odds. Indeed, there is a positive value to idle time for the service facility if we hope to provide rapid response in medical, fire protection, police protection, machine maintenance, and a variety of other services.

With a knowledge of waiting line models, a manager knows that adding parallel servers causes more than a proportional effect. Line length and waiting time drop dramatically with the addition of capacity through parallel servers. Also, the effect of pooling facilities is clear. If we wish to give good service, we can do it better with one large facility than with a number of smaller ones offering equivalent capacity. Furthermore, the pooling effect is not one of economy of scale in the traditional sense, but results from the unique interplay between arrivals and service that allows the use of what would be idle time in decentralized smaller facilities.

Through an examination of waiting line models we noted that variation in the service time can have a very important effect on line length and waiting time. In the Poisson input, exponential service time case, half of the queuing or congestion is in the service time variation. We see this by comparing equations (6) and (8). The other half of the congestion is due to the variable arrival process. Thus, managers who understand the source of the congestion can possibly make important improvements in service by *not* assuming that the arrival process is a given factor and out of their control. It may be possible to schedule arrivals or resort to other techniques to reduce variation in the arrival process. Indeed, a manager would wish to smooth demand, as has been commonly practiced in manufacturing systems.

In some instances we may be able to get the customer, patient, or client to do something productive while waiting. If we can transfer some of the service activity to the one being serviced, cost may be reduced, and this approach may be one of the few strategies available for managers in improving productivity in service activities. The acceptance of the idea of the customer doing part of the work has become quite widespread in self-service markets, gas stations, cafeterias, and other facilities.

CHECK YOUR UNDERSTANDING

(See Table 11-6 for a summary of waiting line models.)

1. Discuss the nature of service systems. What characteristics of these systems make them candidates for study as waiting line systems?
2. Classify the following in terms of the four basic waiting line structures shown in Figure 11-3:
   a. assembly line
   b. large bank—six tellers (one waiting line for each)
   c. cashier at a restaurant
   d. one-chair barbershop

   e. cafeteria line

   f. general hospital

   g. post office — four windows drawing from one waiting line

3. Identify the unit being processed, the server or service facility, and the waiting line structure for each of the following:

   a. car wash

   b. fire station

   c. toll bridge

   d. shipping dock

   e. appliance repair shop

   f. TV repairman

   g. supermarket

   h. large department store

Summary of Waiting Line Models; Poisson Arrivals and First-Come First-Served Queue Discipline   TABLE 11-6

Infinite Models				Finite Model, Negative Exponential Service Time, $N = 4 - 250$, Multiple Servers
Single Server Models			Multiple Server Model, Negative Exponential Service Time	
Service Time Distribution Not Specified	Negative Exponential Service Time	Constant Service Time		
$L_q = \dfrac{(\lambda\sigma)^2 + (\lambda/\mu)^2}{2(1 - \lambda/\mu)}$	$L_q = \dfrac{\lambda^2}{\mu(\mu - \lambda)},$ or use Table C-2 for $M = 1$	$L_q = \dfrac{\lambda^2}{2\mu(\mu - \lambda)}$	Compute $r = \lambda/\mu$. Use Table C-2 to find L_q for a given value of M	Compute $X = \dfrac{\lambda}{\lambda + \mu}$. Use Table C-3 to find values of L_q, D, and F for value of M wanted.
$W_q = L_q/\lambda$	$W_q = L_q/\lambda$	$W_q = L_q/\lambda$	$W_q = L_q/\lambda$	$W_q = \dfrac{1}{\mu X}\dfrac{(1 - F)}{(F)}$
$L = L_q + \lambda/\mu$	$L = L_q + \lambda/\mu$	$L = L_q + \lambda/\mu$	$L = L_q + \lambda/\mu$	$L = L_q + FNX$
$W = W_q + 1/\mu = L/\lambda$	$W = W_q + 1/\mu = L/\lambda$	$W = W_q + 1/\mu = L/\lambda$	$W = W_q + 1/\mu = L/\lambda$	$W = W_q + 1/\mu$
$\rho = \lambda/M\mu$	$\rho = \lambda/M\mu$	$\rho = \lambda/M\mu$	$\rho = \lambda/M\mu$	$H = FNX = L - L_q =$ mean number being served
	$P_w = \lambda/\mu =$ probability an arrival must wait		$P_w = L_q(M - r)/r =$ probability an arrival must wait	$J = FN(1 - X) =$ mean number not being served
	$P_n = (\lambda/\mu)^n(1 - \lambda/\mu)$			
	$P_0 = 1 - \lambda/\mu$		$P_0 = \dfrac{L_q(M - 1)!(M - r)^2}{(r)^{M+1}}$	$M - H =$ servers idle

4. Given a Poisson distribution of arrivals with mean of $\lambda = 5$ per hour, what is the probability of an arrival of $x = 4$ within an hour? What is the probability of the occurrence of 15 minutes between arrivals?

5. A barber decides that she would like to close an hour early to shop for an anniversary gift for her husband. She has just remembered the anniversary and can soothe injured feelings for not having mentioned the event at breakfast.

   The mean rate of customer arrival for haircuts is four per hour by a Poisson process. The haircut price is $6.

   a. What is the probability that the following numbers of customers will arrive during the hour?
      (1) none
      (2) one
      (3) four
      (4) six
      (5) more than six
   b. What is the barber's expected total cost if she plans to pay $100 for the gift?

6. A community is served by a single ambulance based at the hospital. During peak periods the call rate averages 3 per hour (Poisson distribution) and the average service time is 15 minutes with a standard deviation of 5 minutes.
   a. Compute the average number of emergencies waiting during peak demand.
   b. Compute the average waiting time and the average system idle time. Which is most relevant as a criterion in this system?

7. A machine in a processing line is designed to perform its function automatically in a constant time of one minute. Items to be processed are fed from the operation upstream, which is manual. The arrival rate to the machine is Poisson distributed and averages 50 units per hour. In spite of the fact that the machine is faster than the preceding manual operation, the supervisor is perturbed because there is an in-process inventory piled up in front of the machine and at the same time, the machine utilization is only 83 percent.

   Explain how the system functions. What is the average in-process inventory in front of the machine? Verify the machine utilization figure. How can the supervisor improve the machine utilization?

8. A taxi cab company has four cabs that operate out of a given taxi stand. Customer arrival rates and service rates are described by the Poisson distribution. The average arrival rate is 12 per hour and the average service time is 17.5 minutes. The service time follows a negative exponential distribution.

a. Calculate the utilization factor.
b. From Table C-2 of Appendix C, determine the mean number of customers waiting.
c. Determine the mean number of customers in the system.
d. Calculate the mean waiting time.
e. Calculate the mean time in the system.
f. What would be the utilization factor if the number of taxi cabs were increased from four to five?
g. What would be the effect of the increase in the number of cabs from four to five on the mean number in the waiting line?
h. What would be the effect of reducing the number of taxi cabs from four to three on the mean number in the waiting line?

9. A secretary serves five faculty members, performing a variety of stenographic and other clerical duties. On the average, faculty members bring three jobs per hour and the average job takes 10 minutes. Assume that once a faculty member has assigned a job that faculty member will not bring another job until the first is completed. Both arrival and service processes are adequately represented by the Poisson distribution.
a. Compute the mean number of faculty members waiting to be served.
b. Compute the mean waiting time.
c. Compute the mean time a faculty member must wait from the time work is given to the secretary until receiving the completed work.
d. What percent of the time is the secretary idle?
e. What is the probability that a faculty member bringing work to the secretary will find her busy?

10. Explain the benefits that accrue from pooling facilities.

SHORT CASES

Hank Gashog, the town mayor, said, "Victorville is a microcosm of the USA. What happens   CASE 11-1 here and the way it happens is a good forecast for how the whole country is affected." When the 1979 "gas crunch" hit, Hank moaned that his statement was more true than he wished it were.

Victorville was a good sized town with six gas stations. As gas shortages began to occur, the first visible effect was that stations began to close on weekends and to have shorter hours during the week. Hank had a survey made to help inform citizens and found that at any one time an average of only four stations were open. The average station has two lanes for pumping gas, and only one car can be served at a time in each lane.

a. Which waiting line model is appropriate to analyze Victorville's problem?

b. The average station before the crunch had a car arriving for service every 10 minutes, on the average. The stations were all "full service" stations and the average service time was five minutes. Being the analytical type, Hank had his staff analyze the arrival and service data. Their report was that both were adequately described by a Poisson process. What are the waiting line model statistics before and after the station closings?

c. When Hank got the full picture in mind he felt that it was his duty to report fully to his constituents. So he went on local TV and explained as best he could what was happening. Because he was a politician Hank dramatized the situation a bit, telling about how long people were waiting in line for gas, expressing sympathy for their plight. He also told how he had gone to the state capitol to try to get a larger gas allocation for Victorville. He said that the allocation formula in use did not allow for the tremendous population and economic growth that Victorville had experienced in the last five years, that the governor promised nothing and that the situation was likely to get worse before it got better. One citizen stated that Hank seemed to be saying, "What are you doing watching TV? You should be in a gas line!"

Gas station waiting lines continued to grow. It was a field day for the news media, which gave minute by minute bulletins on the progress of the advancing shortage with speculations on when it would end, if it would end, and the likelihood that it would get worse. Station owners reported that their average sale had dropped from 10 to 5 gallons. People were "topping off" their tanks, coming to fill up twice as often. With the smaller sale the service time was shortened to three minutes; not half as short because the fixed time to give full service had not changed. Tempers were flaring at the stations and owners eliminated one lane of service to control the situation.

What are the waiting line model statistics for the new situation and how do they compare with the previous statistics?

d. Citizens were up in arms because they were spending so much time in gas lines. Complaints to Hank's office were so frequent that he had to hire temporary help to receive the calls and open and answer the poison pen letters. "Do something" was the main theme of the more rational complaints. So Hank consulted his staff and then proposed to a committee of gas station owners that full service had to go and that each customer should not be served unless their gas gages showed half a tank or less. He figured that this policy should result in an average sale of 10 gallons again. Hank said that both actions would help, and the standard deviation of service time should become nearly constant at three minutes.

What are the waiting line model statistics for Hank's proposal and how do they compare with those in part c? What is your evaluation of Hank's proposals? What do you recommend?

If you want to sit in your car while you wait in line, here is another way. The California Motor Vehicles Department established auto inspection facilities to measure the smog emissions of cars. These inspections used to be performed by licensed garages, but the DMV took it over, perhaps to ensure uniform standards and to make the system efficient.

CASE 11-2

A typical test center has four parallel service channels. You simply pay the $11 fee, drive up and get in line. In effect, the four parallel service channels draw on a single waiting line. When you arrive, it is a natural desire to estimate the arrival rate, since there are quite a few cars in line. You estimate the arrival rate to be $\lambda = 22.8$ cars per hour.

After waiting your turn you are directed to one of the four service facilities. The data concerning your auto is taken, checked in catalog sources, and a physical inspection is made to see if the required smog control equipment is installed in your car. Then data pertinent to your car is typed into a computer terminal. A "hook-up" is made, you start your engine, and the test is made automatically, with the results printed out on a computer terminal. If you pass, you are given the test results and a certificate. If you fail, you are told what modifications or procedures you must follow to pass. With all pertinent activities completed, you drive away, having spent an average of 10 minutes for the services rendered.

a. Assuming that the arrival and service processes are Poisson, what is the mean waiting line length, waiting time, and total time in the system?
b. Additional parallel service channels could be installed, but each new facility requires an additional crew of two workers plus the sophisticated computer controlled analyzers. These crews and facilities would not serve more cars, but would enable the system to give better service. It is estimated that for each additional parallel service facility added, the price would go up by $3 to cover the variable and fixed costs.

   Compute the waiting line model statistics for situations involving five and six parallel service facilities and compare them with the results in a.
c. Considering the waiting time, time in system, and the price that would be charged, which of the three alternate systems would you prefer? Why?

Dynaflo, Inc. faces a decision of how to allocate its repair crew to various maintenance jobs. They have three journeymen mechanics who are paid $10 per hour, and four apprentices who are paid $3 per hour.

CASE 11-3

Dynaflo has a bank of ten identical machines that are subjected to severe conditions of temperature and dust, resulting in parts wearing out rapidly. The machines are operated 24 hours per day seven days per week. Downtime results in idle labor and lost contribution valued at $10 per hour. Maintenance records show that the average breakdown rate per machine is $\lambda = 0.1$ per hour. The average repair time is 1.9 hours for journeymen and 3.7 hours for apprentices. Both arrival and service distributions are representative of a Poisson process.

Should Dynaflo use journeymen or apprentices for the repair job? Why?

Joe Bettman is manager of a Pep Boys Supermarket and is reconsidering his policies regarding service. He currently has six checkers working during the busy period when customers arrive

CASE 11-4

at the rate of $\lambda = 60$ per hour but feels that he should be able to get by with only five. The average service time to total the bill, obtain payment that often requires check cashing, and bag the groceries is $1/\mu = 5$ minutes. Both arrival rates and service times follow a Poisson process.

Joe has received a directive from corporate headquarters to staff the checkstands so that the average time for a customer to get through the system is seven minutes or less.

    a. How many checkers should Joe schedule?

    b. If Joe provides a bagger in combination with a checker, the service time can be reduced to $1/\mu = 3$ minutes. Checkers are paid $6 per hour and baggers $2.75 per hour. Is it worthwhile to use baggers?

    c. From the point of view of service, would it be better for Joe to simply add another checker as the union is urging, that is, over and above the number determined in (a), thereby reducing waiting time, or should he use checker-bagger teams, thereby reducing service time?

CASE 11-5   Pep Boys Supermarket maintains a central warehouse from which they supply all of their markets. In general, each store places orders and obtains daily shipments from the warehouse.

The general routine is that order pickers assemble orders placed by stores and load them on one of the five company trucks waiting at the single truck dock. Trucks and their drivers wait in line to obtain their loads on a first-come first-served basis. They then proceed to the store for which the order is destined, unload and return for another order. Because of the many different routes and distances, and traffic problems at different times of the day, the time between arrivals of the trucks at the dock is random, averaging 30 minutes. The loading time follows a negative exponential distribution and averages 15 minutes.

Truck drivers are paid $10 per hour and the crew of two loaders are each paid $4 per hour. Truckers have complained about the long waiting, so a sample was taken showing that truckers did indeed wait an average of 32 minutes. The warehouse manager knows that a second truck dock would probably solve the problem, but the large capital expenditure plus the disruption of operations during construction are deterrents to this solution.

Tests are made with different crew patterns and it is found that a crew of three can be used to advantage, reducing the loading time to 10 minutes.

    a. Is the crew of three loaders more economical than the crew of two?

    b. What is the probability that an arriving truck will find at least one truck already in the system?

    c. How much of the time is the crew idle? What does the idleness cost?

CASE 11-6   The Wash-M-Clean Car Wash manager has problems in staffing the operation because of the fluctuating demand for car wash service. The crew is deployed to the gas pumps, vacuum cleaning and drive on the system, and the wipe and dry operations.

He can work with three different crew configurations, an eight, seven, and six worker crew. With an eight-worker crew, three work the gas pumps, collect fees and vacuum clean; one drives the car on the machine and stays in it, driving it to the wipe and dry area, running back to repeat the process; and four wipe and dry. With a crew of seven, the worker who drives and rides through the machine is dropped, and workers in the gas and vacuum area drive the cars on the system, letting someone in the wipe and dry area drive it off. Finally, with a crew of six, one of the wiper-driers is dropped from the crew.

The mean service times and standard deviations of service times for each of the crew sizes is as follows:

Crew Size	Service Time (minutes)	Standard Deviation (minutes)
8	6	4
7	7	5
6	8	9

The manager runs what is euphemistically called a 10-minute car wash, but when asked what service he would like to maintain, he said that he would be happy if he could get most people through the system in 25 minutes overall. "The problem is the variability in the number of people who want a wash at any one time." Data were gathered and on a typical Friday-Saturday, the cars arriving for service by a Poisson distribution were as follows:

8:30 A.M. –10:00 A.M., 6 cars per hour

10:00 A.M. – 3:00 P.M., 8 cars per hour

3:00 P.M. – 5:30 P.M., 5 cars per hour

How should the manager deploy the different crew sizes?

CASE 11-7

Present day universities have become complex systems of scholars where a value must be placed on communication, both within systems that are now multicampus giants and between systems throughout the nation. It is not surprising then that WATS (wide area telephone service) should be considered to allow faculty members and administrators to make unlimited toll-free long-distance calls.

Data gathered for one of these systems yielded the following information:

(1) The frequency of calls was estimated to be 10.4 per hour, based on present use of long-distance service plus an estimate of increased use if WATS were available (Poisson distribution).

(2) The length of calls was estimated to be 15 minutes (negative exponential distribution).

(3) The current long-distance telephone bill average was $10,000 per month.

(4) After much haggling, average faculty-administrator time was valued at $10 per hour.

(5) A WATS line costs $2000 per month.

Assume an average of 173 hours per month. The central issue finally resolved into the number of WATS lines that would be justified.

    a. Formulate the problem as a decision to determine the number of WATS lines to install. What cost components are involved and how do the costs vary with the number of lines installed?

    b. Determine the number of WATS lines to install. What criteria have you used?

    c. What should the university administration do? Why?

CASE 11-8   A supermarket chain has 30 stores in a large metropolitan area and supplies its stores from a central warehouse. The general routine is to supply each store every day on the basis of the store order list. Store managers compile these lists daily and transmit them to the warehouse. After receiving an order, the store manager may generate another order, even on the same day.

At the warehouse, store orders are taken in sequence as they arrive and "order picker" crews assemble the order in designated staging areas using a hand truck system for smaller items and dispatching fork truck operators to fill skid load items. When a store order is complete, it awaits transportation.

A fleet of five large closed trucks transports the orders. Trucks are loaded at the truck dock that can accommodate three trucks simultaneously. A special crew of loaders is used to load trucks from the staging areas. While the trucks are being loaded, the driver obtains the documents that indicate the list of items shipped and the store destination.

After loading, the trucks are driven to the store destination, and the contents are unloaded at the store truck dock by store personnel. The driver then returns the truck to the warehouse. At the end of the day, the truck is returned to the maintenance area at the warehouse where it is washed, refueled, and serviced for general maintenance and repair.

Formulate the system as a sequence of waiting line problems by first developing a flow chart that identifies the arrival, service, and exit processes. Identify each waiting line situation in terms of its structure and the type of waiting line model that might apply. In order to analyze the system as a waiting line system, what information is needed?

CASE 11-9   The order picking crews for the warehouse described in *Case 11-8* work an eight-hour day, and each of the 30 store orders must be filled during the shift. Studies indicate that the time to fill an order averages 47.9 minutes, and the distribution of times is approximated by the negative exponential distribution. Orders come in from store managers throughout the day, and the time between these orders is also approximated by the negative exponential distribution. The warehouse manager wants to be sure that orders are not delayed too long and wants an order backlog (unfinished orders) of no more than an average of one, to ensure that trucks do not wait.

How many crews does the manager need to maintain this standard? The aggregate wage of a crew is $10 per hour. What fraction of the time are the crews idle? What does the manager's policy on order backlog cost in terms of crew idleness?

After tires have been assembled, they go to curing presses where the various layers of rubber and fiber are vulcanized into one homogeneous piece and the final shape is molded, including the tread. Different tires require somewhat different curing times, which may range up to 90 minutes or more. The press operator can unload and reload a press in 3 minutes, so that one operator would normally service a bank of curing presses. Each press may be molding tires of a different design, so that presses are "arriving" for service at nearly random times. The presses automatically open when the preset cure time is complete.

In servicing a bank of 30 presses, the operator is ranging over a wide area approximately 90 by 200 feet. Indicator lights flash on, signifying that the press is ready for service, and the operator walks to the open press, unloading and reloading it. Sometimes, of course, the position of the open press may be quite close to the operator so that the walk is fairly short. In rare instances the operator is at one end of the area and the press requiring service is at the other end, requiring a fairly long walk. Thus, the operator's tasks in rendering service are made up of walking plus unloading and reloading the presses. The average time for these tasks is 3 minutes and is approximated by the negative exponential distribution.

When a press is idle, waiting to be serviced, the only costs that continue are the services to the press, mainly heat supply. The cost of supplying this heat is $4 per hour per press. Operators are paid $3.50 per hour, and contribution per tire is $5.

If the average cure time of tires being produced is 80 minutes, determine the number of operators (number of servers) to be used when market demand is less than plant capacity; when market demand is above plant capacity.

CASE 11-10

In the manufacture of photographic film, there is a specialized process of perforating the edges of the 35-mm film used in movie and still cameras. A bank of 20 machines are required to meet production requirements. The severe service requirements cause breakdowns that need to be repaired quickly because of high downtime costs. Because of breakdown rates and downtime costs, management is considering the installation of a preventive maintenance program. (See Table 11-7 for three proposed levels of preventive maintenance.)

The present breakdown rate is 3 per hour per machine, or a time between breakdowns of

CASE 11-11

Expected Changes in Breakdown Rates, Service Time, and Cost of Repair Parts for Three Levels of Preventive Maintenance			
Level of Preventive Maintenance	Breakdown Rate (percent)	Service Time (percent)	Cost of Repair Parts (percent)
L_1	−30	+20	+ 50
L_2	−40	+35	+ 80
L_3	−50	+75	+120

TABLE 11-7

20 minutes. The average time for service is only 3 minutes. The breakdown rate follows a Poisson distribution, and the service times a negative exponential distribution. The crew simply repairs the machines in the sequence of breakdown. Machine downtime is estimated to cost $9 per hour, and present repair parts cost an average of $1 per breakdown. Maintenance mechanics are paid $6 per hour. The breakdown rates, service times, and repair parts costs are expected to change with different levels of preventive maintenance as indicated in Table 11-7.

What repair crew size and level of preventive maintenance should be adopted to minimize costs?

CASE 11-12   A university must maintain a large and complex physical plant, so that plant maintenance is an important support function. The plant maintenance department maintains a crew of 6 maintenance mechanics who respond to calls for service from department heads and other authorized personnel on the campus. They answer a wide variety of calls that range from simple adjustments of room thermostats to actual repair of plant and equipment. In some instances, extensive work involving specialized personnel may be required, and this is scheduled separately.

During the work day, there are 5 calls per hour, and the distribution of the call rate is approximated by a Poisson distribution. The average time for service is 60 minutes, including travel time both ways and the time to actually perform the required work and is approximated by the negative exponential distribution. The wage rate of the mechanics is $8 per hour.

One of the mechanics has just resigned for personal reasons, and the university business manager has refused to replace him because of the budget squeeze. The head of the plant maintenance department is furious and produces a file of complaints from department heads about the slow response to calls for service. The business manager implies that the slow service reflects inefficiency and that it is time for the plant maintenance department to "shape up."

How many maintenance mechanics are economically justified? What action do you feel should be taken?

CASE 11-13   Since hospital nursing requirements depend on individual patient needs as well as on the number of patients, a method of classifying patients by their relative nursing needs was developed by Flagle [1960]. Patients were classified into three groups in terms of nursing care needs: self-care, partial care, and total care. A sample survey then indicated that the distributions of care time were very different for the three categories. The distribution for self-care patients had a mean of one-half hour and a very small standard deviation. The distribution of partial-care patients had a mean of one hour and a somewhat larger standard deviation. Finally, the distribution for total-care patients had a mean of 2.5 hours and a very large standard deviation. Studies of the number of patients in the total-care category in four different wards varied significantly. However, there seemed to be no correlation in work load between the wards.

A similar study of load fluctuation in England also indicated no correlation in weekly load between wards. Figure 11-9 indicates these load variations for two wards separately on the

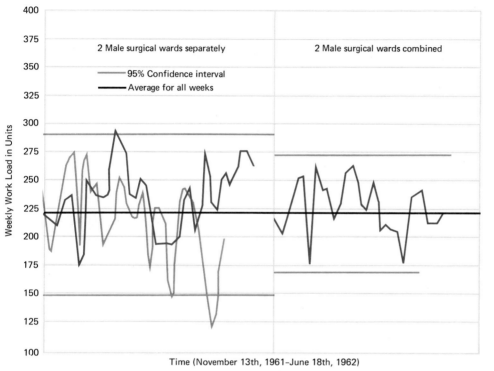

FIGURE 11-9
Effect of combin-
ing two wards on
fluctuation of work
load.

left and, when combined, on the right. The study indicated that the variance was reduced by about 30 percent when the two wards were combined.

What are the implications of this information concerning work loads when one views the wards as a waiting line system? If you were managing this system, what guidelines for staffing the wards might be indicated by the load information?

GENERAL REFERENCES

Cox, D. R., and W. L. Smith, *Queues,* John Wiley & Sons, New York, 1961.

Morse, P. M., *Queues, Inventories and Maintenance,* John Wiley & Sons, New York, 1957.

Nelson, R. T., "An Empirical Study of Arrival, Service Time, and Waiting Time Distributions of a Job Shop Production Process," Research Report No. 60, Management Sciences Research Project, University of California, Los Angeles, 1959.

Peck, L. G., and R. N. Hazelwood, *Finite Queuing Tables,* John Wiley & Sons, New York, 1958.

Prabhu, N. U., *Queues and Inventories,* John Wiley & Sons, New York, 1965.

Wagner, H. M., *Principles of Operations Research,* Prentice-Hall, Englewood Cliffs, N.J., 1969.

APPLICATIONS REFERENCES

Bleuel, W. H., "Management Science's Impact on Service Strategy," *Interfaces,* Vol. 6, No. 1, Part 2, November 1975, pp. 4–12.

Brigham, F., "On a Congestion Problem in an Aircraft Factory," *Operations Research,* Vol. 3, No. 4, 1955, pp. 412–428.

Cosmetatos, G. P., "The Value of Queueing Theory—A Case Study," *Interfaces,* Vol. 9, No. 3, May 1979, pp. 47–51.

Erikson, W. J., "Management Science and the Gas Shortage," *Interfaces,* Vol. 4, No. 4, August 1974, pp. 47–51.

Fitzsimmons, J. A., "Emergency Medical Systems: A Simulation Study and Computerized Method for Deployment of Ambulances," Ph.D. Dissertation, University of California, Los Angeles, 1970.

———, "A Methodology for Emergency Ambulance Deployment," *Management Science,* Vol. 19, No. 6, February 1973, pp. 627–36.

Foote, B. L., "A Queuing Case Study of Drive-In Banking," *Interfaces,* Vol. 6, No. 4, August 1976, pp. 31–37.

Gilliam, R. R., "An Application of Queueing Theory to Airport Passenger Security Screening," *Interfaces,* Vol. 9, No. 4, August 1979, pp. 117–123.

Kolesar, P., "A Quick and Dirty Response to the Quick and Dirty Crowd; Particularly to Jack Byrd's 'The Value of Queueing Theory'," *Interfaces,* Vol. 9, No. 2, Part 1, February 1979.

McKeown, P.G., "An Application of Queueing Analysis to the New York State Child Abuse and Maltreatment Register Telephone Reporting System," *Interfaces,* Vol. 9, No. 3, May 1979, pp. 20–25.

Paul, R. J., and R. E. Stevens, "Staffing Service Activities with Waiting Line Models," *Decision Sciences,* Vol. 2, April 1971, pp. 206–217.

Vogel, M. A. "Queueing Theory Applied to Machine Manning," *Interfaces,* Vol. 9, No. 4, August 1979, pp. 1–8.

CHAPTER 12

Monte Carlo Simulation

The complexity of many managerial systems, as well as the need to include empirical data, often makes the prediction of performance by analytical models either impossible or impractical. In such situations, simulation is the common methodology for predicting performance.

Simulation is a general term that means "imitation." In fact, the rigorous technique of simulation that has developed in management science and operations research does imitate the essential characteristics of processes, usually with the aid of a computer. Most of the simulation models we deal with in management science represent a problem by imitating what would happen in the real system. By keeping track of what happens in the model and recording results, we can build a representative record of what would probably happen if the policy, design, or system were actually installed. Simulation models are in a real sense management's laboratory.

Kinds of simulation models

Simulation models may be discrete or continuous, deterministic or stochastic. In continuous systems, the parameters that describe the system can take on any values within the ranges specified. Wind tunnel simulation of flight is an example of a continuous simulation system. Discrete systems take on only particular values within the possible ranges of parameters. These systems are characterized by the events that occur, and we keep track of the events, their timing, and other parameters that may describe them. In managerial systems we commonly deal with discrete simulation systems.

As noted, a system may also be deterministic or stochastic, depending on the nature of its input, process, and output. The output of a deterministic system is known exactly when the input is specified—there is no other cause of any variation in the output. In other words, the transformation function of the predictive model provides a completely determined output. The simple relationship in physics between force, mass, and acceleration is an example, $F = ma$. Given the mass m and the input state of the acceleration a, the force F is assumed to be determined exactly. Chapter 2 dealt with deterministic simulations.

Stochastic systems, however, respond to a given input with a range of possible outputs, following some distribution of values. For example, if in an emergency medical system there is a call for service, the time to perform the service is not a fixed time, as we noted in the discussion on waiting line models (Chapter 11). Service time will depend on many things that in themselves are not predictable, such as distance to the scene, traffic density, time of day, and availability of the ambulance. In addition, there may be random variation in service time that has no logical explanation.

Probably most processes in managerial systems are in fact stochastic; however, we often use deterministic relationships and average relationships when they reasonably represent what happens. They are simpler to handle and require less execution time in complex simulation models. On the other hand, many processes are only described adequately by probability distributions, such as those reflecting variable demand for services and products, and the queuing or waiting line models of Chapter 11. Special simulation techniques called Monte Carlo, or simulated sampling, are used to introduce statistical variations in simulation models. We will concentrate our discussion on these methods at a later point in this chapter.

Simulation models in managerial systems are usually of the discrete type and often a combination of deterministic and stochastic processes, especially in models representing a complex system.

THE SIMULATION PROCESS

Conceptually, the simulation process is a simple one, once we have a carefully specified model. The variables involved in the model are usually related in some way to the passage of time. There are in general two ways of organizing the simulation process: around the occurrence of discrete events and around updating events for discrete time periods.

Discrete event simulation

In the *discrete event* approach, the entire process follows the sequence of events or steps in the process, keeping track of what happens. Let us take a simple example, such as driving to the office each morning. Suppose the drive involves only two intersections as shown in Figure 12-1. A decision must be made at the first intersection: should the original or the alternate route by taken? The diagram of Figure 12-1 shows the alternate routes and gives a general description of how to get from home to office.

Suppose, however, that we are interested in choosing departure times for minimum driving time, or that we wish to predict driving time for different departure times. For these purposes, Figure 12-1 is inadequate. Although some of the factors that bear on driving time are implied in Figure 12-1, they are not explicit. The flow chart of Figure 12-2 adds detail, indicating that competing traffic will be a factor. There is a traffic light at the first intersection, and the driver joins a queue and may have to wait. Also, at the traffic light a decision between alternate routes must be

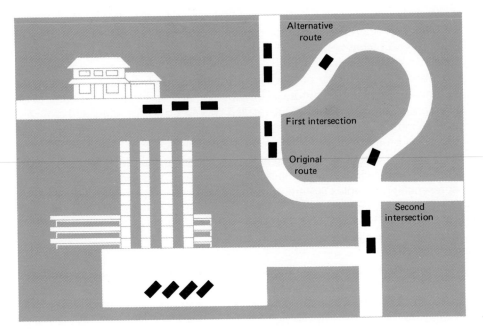

FIGURE 12-1
Pictorial representation of the drive to the office. *Source:* From J. Reitman, *Computer Simulation Applications.* John Wiley & Sons, New York, 1971, Figure 2.3, p. 41. Used by permission.

made. Competing traffic is a factor with either route, though it may not have an equivalent effect for both routes. Finally, both routes lead to a second queue at the second intersection and a continuation to the office.

While the flow chart of Figure 12-2 is still incomplete, it comes closer to describing the probabilistic nature of the time required to make the drive. If we are to predict driving time, obviously we need more information regarding speed in relation to competing traffic, waiting time at intersections, choice rules for the alternate routes, and the influence of abnormal events. We will not attempt prediction at this time, however.

If we attempted to simulate the drive to the office, we might logically follow the sequence of events shown in Figure 12-2 and record what happens at queues and intersections, and so on. Elapsed time between events would be recorded as the simulation progresses. Figure 12-3(a) is a simple flow chart describing the discrete event process.

In Figure 12-3(a), after reading in the input data and initializing all records, you

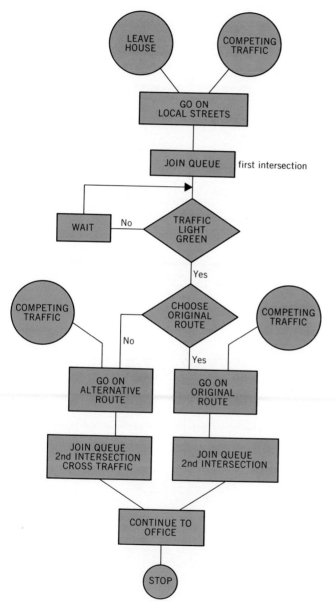

FIGURE 12-2
Course overview of the drive to the office. *Source:*
From J. Reitman, *Computer Simulation Applications,*
John Wiley & Sons, New York, 1971, Figure 2.1,
p. 32. Used by permission.

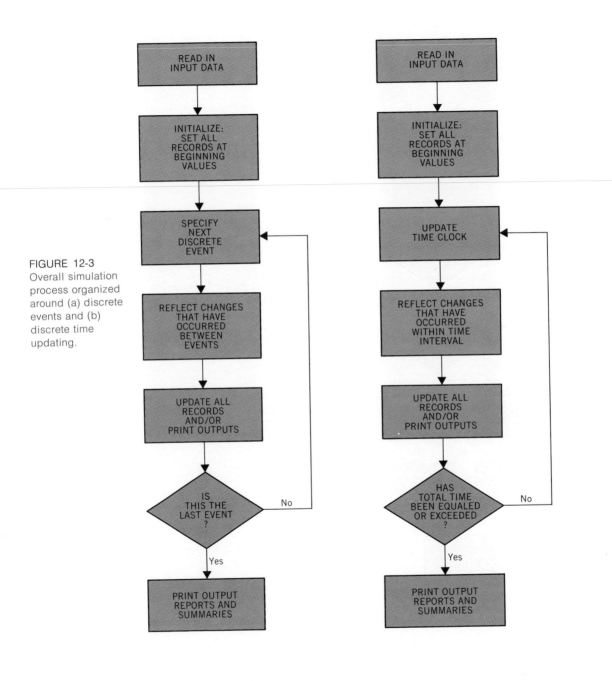

FIGURE 12-3
Overall simulation
process organized
around (a) discrete
events and (b)
discrete time
updating.

specify the next discrete event. For example, if you were simulating the arrival of people at a post office window, the next discrete event might be an arrival. In the next box of the flow chart you reflect all changes that have occurred since the last arrival. In the interval since the last arrival, perhaps the clerks have processed three customers. The records desired concerning this processing are recorded. In this instance, these records might reflect the waiting time of each customer and the time to service each. In the diamond box, the question ''Is this the last event?'' is asked. In other words, is the simulation completed? If the simulation was to include 100 trials and this is only the 99th, then the flow chart redirects the system back to the specification of the next event, and on the completion of that trial, the simulation is complete and the required reports and summaries are printed out.

Discrete time updating simulation

If we were to attempt to simulate the drive to the office by the *discrete time updating* approach, we would select a smallest time unit for the study and examine the state of the system in all its aspects at the end of each time interval, recording and updating the status of each element. The time interval might be 0.01 minute, 1 minute, 5 minutes, or 1 hour, as appropriate. When the total planned simulation time is equaled or exceeded, the process is stopped and the results printed out.

In the drive to the office example, perhaps the time interval would be set at 0.1 minute. At the end of the first 0.1 minute, we would determine where we were along the route, recording all relevant data at that time and reflecting all changes that might have occurred. These changes might be in the length of queues and traffic density. The time clock is then updated and the process repeated. Within some one of the time intervals, each of the events occurs, such as waiting for stop lights and the routing decisions. Figure 12-3(b) is a simple flow chart describing the discrete time updating simulation process.

In either the discrete event or discrete time updating simulation systems we could be dealing with stochastic processes or combinations of both deterministic and stochastic processes. Since dealing with stochastic processes as well as empirical data is so important in simulation, we now turn our attention to this subject.

MONTE CARLO—SIMULATED SAMPLING

Simulated sampling, generally known as Monte Carlo, makes it possible to introduce into a system data that have the statistical properties of some empirical distribution.

There are many types of applications in simulating complex financial models involving risk, simulating waiting line structures where the distributions do not fit the standard mathematical ones, simulating probabalistic network schedules, and other decision processes.

An example

Suppose you have an opportunity to invest $10,000 in an oil drilling venture. The drilling operator offers a deal where he will buy you out at the end of the year based on an independent geologist's report of the oil reserves found. You will receive 10 percent of the present value of the future reserves at present prices. Based on preliminary geological surveys and a knowledge of the performance of producing wells in the area you estimate that the probability of payoffs are as follows:

	Probability	Payoff
Pessimistic	0.40	0
Average	0.50	$4000
Optimistic	0.10	$9000

You are interested in the deal, but as a prudent investor you would like to know what return to expect. You know that for a given situation any of the possibilities could occur, but what would the return be on the average? So, you would like to perform a large number of experiments that reflect the probabilities to see how it would work out "on paper" before making the investment. Monte Carlo simulation can help provide the information you want.

In this case we can calculate what payoff to expect on the average. It is simply the probability weighted average of the payoffs, or $0.40 \times 0 + 0.50 \times 4000 + 0.10 \times 9000 = \$2900$. Being a very simple example for which we know the answer we use it to explain the Monte Carlo process.

STEP 1. *Determine the distribution that describes the statistical property of concern.* In the oil drilling situation, suppose we have access to records for the past performance of the operator. These records show the payoffs for $10,000 investments to be as indicated previously: 40 percent of the time the payoff has been

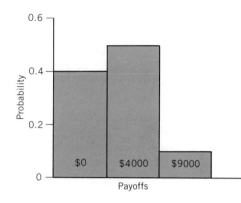

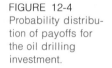

FIGURE 12-4
Probability distribu-
tion of payoffs for
the oil drilling
investment.

zero, 50 percent of the time $4000, and 10 percent of the time the payoff has been $9000. This data is plotted as a probability distribution in Figure 12-4.

STEP 2. *Convert the probability distribution to a cumulative probability distribu-tion.* Beginning with the lowest payoff of zero, the probability is 0.40. Then cumu-late the probabilities associated with payoffs. For example, there is a probability of $0.40 + 0.50 = 0.90$ that the payoff will be $4000 or less. Finally there is a probability of 1.00 that the payoff will be $9000 or less. The resulting cumulative probability distribution is plotted in Figure 12-5.

STEP 3. *Sample at random from the cumulative probability distribution to produce outcomes.* For the oil drilling process, this is the equivalent of repeating the process on paper a large number of times, that is, simulating the drilling process. First we allocate random numbers in proportion to the probability of occurrence in the cumulative probability distribution as follows (0 represents the random number 10, so that all our random numbers are a single digit):

Cumulative Probability	Random Numbers	Associated Payoff
0.40	1–4	0
0.90	5–9	$4000
1.00	0	$9000

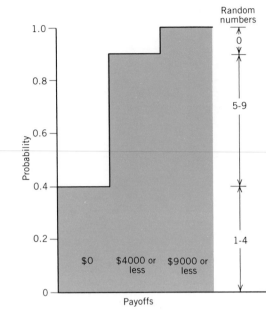

The preceding random numbers are also shown in relation to the cumulative probability distribution in Figure 12-5. Only one payoff can be associated with a given probability in the cumulative distribution. The random numbers could be selected by any random process, such as drawing numbered chips from a box. However, the easiest way to select random numbers manually is to use a table of random numbers such as Table C-4 in Appendix C. For example, select a starting point in the table at random and take one-digit numbers in sequence in that column for our example. If the probabilities are quoted for two places, for example, 0.45, take two-digit numbers in sequence.

By using random numbers to obtain payoffs in this way, we will obtain payoffs in proportion to their historical probabilities of occurrence as indicated in the distribution.

STEP 4. *Simulate the oil drilling process.* Associate payoffs with the random numbers drawn and average the results. Table 12-1 shows the results of a sample of 50 simulated drillings. The average payoff was $2800. There were 20 instances

Simulation of Oil Drilling ($n = 50$)			TABLE 12-1
Random Number	Payoff	Random Number	Payoff
8	4,000	9	4,000
0	9,000	4	0
5	4,000	5	4,000
9	4,000	4	0
3	0	9	4,000
2	0	6	4,000
7	4,000	8	4,000
3	0	3	0
8	4,000	4	0
0	9,000	7	4,000
9	4,000	1	0
8	4,000	5	4,000
3	0	5	4,000
3	0	8	4,000
2	0	3	0
8	4,000	4	0
9	4,000	9	4,000
3	0	2	0
3	0	0	9,000
3	0	2	0
5	4,000	5	4,000
6	4,000	8	4,000
7	4,000	0	9,000
7	4,000	3	0
3	0	6	4,000
			140,000

Average payoff = 140,000/50 = $2,800

of zero payoff, 26 of $4000, and 4 of $9000. The larger the sample taken, the more closely the average payoff will approach the computed expected value of $2900.

Simulation of a network schedule*

In Chapter 8 we studied network scheduling and the concepts of critical path. Recall that there are models applicable to both deterministic and probabilistic activity times. When the activity times are best described by a probability distribution, the network can be simulated and valuable information made available to the manager.

Let us use an example that was an exercise in Chapter 8: the production of a play. It has only eight activities and this simplicity will aid in explaining the simulation process. The eight activities, their sequence requirements, and times are:

Activity	Description	Immediate Predecessors	Time (Weeks)
a	Play selection	—	3
b	Casting	a	4
c	Costume design	a	3
d	Set design	a	2
e	Set construction	d	4
f	Rehearsals	b	3
g	Dress rehearsals	c, e, f	2
h	Printing tickets and programs	b	6

The simple network diagram is shown in Figure 12-6. The critical path can be determined by inspection since it is the longest time path through the network and there are only four paths. The four paths and their times are as follows:

a-b-h	13 weeks
a-b-f-g	12 weeks
a-c-g	8 weeks
a-d-e-g	11 weeks

The longest time path is a-b-h, requiring 13 weeks. The important activities to monitor in terms of their time requirements are then play selection, casting, and the printing of tickets and programs.

---

* This section assumes that the reader is familiar with network scheduling techniques covered in Chapter 8. It may be skipped without loss of continuity.

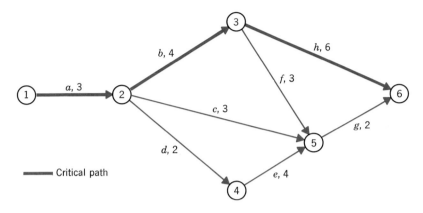

FIGURE 12-6
Network diagram
with deterministic
activity times for
the production
of a play.

In Chapter 8 we discussed how uncertainty about the activity times can be estimated by assuming that each activity time follows a Beta probability distribution. In
some cases this assumption may not be appropriate, and simulation can be used to
analyze the network using the empirical probability distributions. To illustrate this
idea, suppose we substitute probability distributions for the certain time estimates in
the play production example.

The probability distributions for each of the activities are shown superimposed on
the network diagram in Figure 12-7. We can simulate the execution of the network

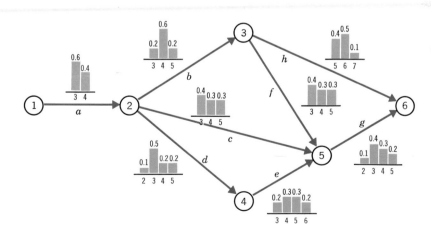

FIGURE 12-7
Network diagram
with activity times
represented as
probability distri-
butions.

schedule by using Monte Carlo sampling of activity times from each of the distributions. After having drawn a set of activity times at random we can determine the critical path for that set of activity times, noting the path and the project time. By repeating the simulation a large number of times, we can estimate the expected completion time and the probability of shorter or longer completion times.

Selection of random numbers All the distributions are quite simple and allocating random numbers to them is also simple. For activity a the probability of a time of 3 weeks is 0.6 so the random numbers 1 through 6 will result in the selection of an activity time of 3 weeks. The probability that activity a will require 4 weeks is 0.4 so the random numbers 7 through 0 result in the selection of an activity time of 4 weeks. Table 12-2 shows the random number equivalents for the distributions of all eight activities.

Network simulation To simulate the network we select at random sets of eight random numbers from Table C-4 (Appendix C). For example, a random number set and equivalent activity times are as follows:

Activity	a	b	c	d	e	f	g	h
Random number	0	3	6	8	9	3	3	0
Activity time	4	4	4	4	6	3	3	7

Figure 12-8 shows the network diagram with these activity times, indicating that the critical path would be a-d-e-g, requiring a project time of 17 weeks. The other three paths require times of only 11, 14, and 15 weeks; check this result yourself. Each

FIGURE 12-8
Network diagram with activity times determined by Monte Carlo sampling. The longest time path is a-d-e-g with a project completion time of 17 weeks.

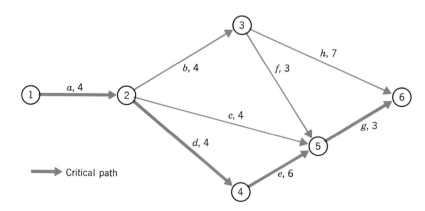

Random Number Equivalents for Eight Network Activities TABLE 12-2

Activity	These Random Numbers	Select These Activity Times
a	1–6	3
	7–0	4
b	1–2	3
	3–8	4
	9–0	5
c	1–4	3
	5–7	4
	8–0	5
d	1	2
	2–6	3
	7–8	4
	9–0	5
e	1–2	3
	3–5	4
	6–8	5
	9–0	6
f	1–4	3
	5–7	4
	8–0	5
g	1	2
	2–5	3
	6–8	4
	9–0	5
h	1–4	5
	5–9	6
	0	7

simulation run requires this process of selecting random numbers in sets of eight, determining the resulting activity times, critical path determination, and determination of project time.

Table 12-3 shows the results of 20 simulation runs with the critical activities, project completion times, and other computed data.

Interpretation of results The average project completion time is 15.75 weeks, ranging from 13 to 17 weeks. This information in itself is useful to a manager, but the bottom

TABLE 12-3   Simulation of 20 Trials for the Project Completion Time for Producing a Play

Simulation Number	Sampled Activity Times (* Indicates "On Critical Path")								Project Completion Time (Weeks)
	a	b	c	d	e	f	g	h	
1	4*	4	4	4*	6*	3	3*	7	17
2	3*	4	3	3*	5*	3	4*	5	15
3	3*	4*	3	3*	5*	4*	3*	7*	14
4	3*	3*	4	4*	4*	5*	3*	5	14
5	4*	4*	5	3	3	3*	5*	6	16
6	4*	4*	5	3	4	5*	4*	6	17
7	4*	4	4	3*	6*	4	4*	6	17
8	3*	5*	3	3	6	5*	3*	6	16
9	4*	5*	3	3	3	3*	3*	6*	15
10	4*	4*	3	4*	5*	5*	3*	6	16
11	3*	3	4	3*	6*	5	5*	6	17
12	4*	3*	5	3	3	4*	5*	6	16
13	4*	4*	5	3*	5*	4*	2*	5	14
14	3*	5*	4	3	4	4*	4*	6	16
15	3*	5*	4	3*	6*	4*	5*	6	17
16	4*	4*	4	5*	4*	5*	3*	6	16
17	4*	4	4	3*	5*	3	5*	6	17
18	3*	4*	3	3	3	3*	3*	6*	13
19	4*	5*	5	5	4	5*	3*	5	17
20	3*	4*	4	3*	4*	3*	5*	6	15
Number of times critical	$\overline{20}$	$\overline{15}$	$\overline{0}$	$\overline{12}$	$\overline{12}$	$\overline{15}$	$\overline{20}$	$\overline{3}$	$\overline{315}$
Critical ratio	1.00	0.75	0.0	0.60	0.60	0.75	1.00	0.15	
	Average project completion time = 315/20 = 15.75 weeks								

of Table 12-3 has additional information in the form of the number of times that each activity was critical, and the critical ratio.

The critical ratio is the proportion of runs during which each activity was critical, or the probability that the activity will be critical. Note, for example, that activity *h* has a critical ratio of only 0.15. On the other hand, activity *g* has a critical ratio of 1.0. Activity *c* was never on the critical path and has a ratio of 0.0. Of course, by the structure of the network, activity *a* is always on the critical path.

The critical ratios provide new and valuable information to the manager. Activities *a* and *g* should receive the most attention because they are likely to be critical in all instances. When activity *h* was critical it was always in combination with activity *g* because there were multiple critical paths in those instances. The next most important activities to monitor are *b* and *f,* and so on. A larger sample would refine these initial estimates of project completion time and critical ratios. With larger networks and the need for a large sample, network simulation requires the use of a computer.

COMPUTER SIMULATION

If a computer were programmed to simulate the emergency medical system, we would place the two cumulative distributions in the memory unit of the computer. Through a subroutine called a random number generator program, the computer would generate a random number and thereby select a call time. By comparing cumulative call time with cumulative ambulance time, the computer program could determine whether the ambulance was available, and, if it was available, whether or not it had to wait. The computations of patient waiting time, or ambulance idle time, would be routinely made and the program would direct the selection of another random number, thereby determining a service time. The necessary computations could then be made, with the resulting values held in memory. The cycle would then repeat as many times as desired, so that a large run could be made easily and with no more effort than a small run. *With the aid of a computer, a simulation model can become very realistic, reflecting all sorts of contingency situations that may be representative of the real problem.*

The investment and network scheduling examples are a demonstration of manual Monte Carlo simulation. Its value is in the close contact with the problem and the sequence of simulated sampling and resulting calculations. Often, however, the performance evaluation of large systems through simulation is complex so that manual methods are entirely impractical. In addition, even for simple problems similar to those two examples, the need for large samples to describe adequately the performance of stochastic elements of a system eliminates manual methods from consideration. Digital computer simulation is therefore almost synonymous with the term "simulation" insofar as management sicence is concerned.

Simulation languages

General purpose computer languages such as FORTRAN and PL/1 can be used to implement virtually any computing problem, and many simulation programs have been written in these languages. Because of some special common properties of simulation programs, however, simulation languages have been developed that increase programming efficiency and are very powerful. We will not attempt a thorough coverage of these languages, but we will discuss the basic nature of two of them, GPSS and SIMSCRIPT. (See Reitman [1971, Chapter 5] for a discussion of criteria and of the comparative advantages and disadvantages of various simulation languages.)

GPSS The fundamental structure of GPSS (General Purpose Simulation System) is conceptually different from the statement-oriented general purpose languages such as FORTRAN. GPSS defines four kinds of entities: dynamic, facility, statistical, and operational. Each has specific functions and calls forth automatically corollary functions commonly associated with simulation of systems. In so doing they provide a rational and efficient structure for simulation. We will discuss each briefly and then relate them to an example to illustrate their functions.

Blocks determine the flow logic of the system as well as the logic for the flow of transactions. There are about 40 to 60 blocks in GPSS, depending on which version is used, and these blocks are the heart of the simulation structure, since they control the way transactions interact with facilities, the transaction parameters, output, flow direction, and so on.

Dynamic entities are transactions of the system and may be created and destroyed as required. The nature of each transaction is defined by stating values for parameters associated with the transaction. For example, in the drive to the office, the transactions represent vehicles that must be moved through blocks.

The *facilities* used by the system are specified as entities and they service the transactions. Examples of facilities might be a toll booth, a road, a check-out counter, a machine processing center, and so on. GPSS automatically keeps track of utilization and other statistics on facilities, and these data are a part of the output of the simulation.

Statistical entities may be called on for analysis of results. An example is a queue entity that can automatically analyze the statistical properties of transactions that pile up for use by facilities.

A GPSS example[*] The drive to the office example discussed earlier in the chapter and described by Figures 12-1 and 12-2 serves as an example that illustrates the use of the various entities as well as being a good example of simulation.

First, in order to simulate the drive to the office, there are many assumptions that must be made explicit. Examples of these include the following:

1. The driver gets into the car every morning at the same time, 7:30 A.M.

2. The car leaves the driveway and merges into local street traffic without being delayed.

3. Average speed on local streets is 25 mph, unless subject to slowdown from traffic and abnormal conditions.

4. At the first major intersection there is a control signal and interaction with other traffic.

5. Competing cars will interact to provide degrees of traffic density. These cars come from separate sources. Their arrival rate at the intersection is variable and externally controlled.

6. At the first intersection there is a choice of two routes to the next major intersection. The choice is determined by traffic density, intersection delays, and abnormal conditions.

7. Average speed to the next intersection depends on the selection of route, either 35 mph for the original route or 55 mph on the alternate route. Both are subject to slowdown from traffic and abnormal conditions.

8. The second intersection is considered in a similar manner except that there is no route selection.

9. Average speed to the office parking lot, 15 mph, is also subject to slowdown and abnormal conditions.

These nine assumptions provide a framework for the specific input data, logical relationships, and analytical equations required to simulate the drive to the office.

[*] Summarized from J. Reitman, *Computer Simulation Applications*, John Wiley & Sons, New York, 1971, pp. 40–77; used by permission.

The major items of these inputs are:

1. The average levels of competing traffic during the various parts of the trip in the local traffic, over the original route, and on the alternate route must be specified exactly. Over the local segment there is a maximum of 10 vehicles generated every three minutes for a rate of 200 vehicles per hour. The amount of traffic generated during each three-minute interval from 7:00 to 9:30 A.M. is used as a basis for each day's traffic. The actual traffic for each day is derived from the value for the three-minute interval as modified by a random number.

2. The equations for the time to traverse each part of the trip are in the following form: time = (route distance/nominal speed) × slowdown factor caused by traffic density × abnormal condition factor, where either the slowdown or abnormal factor is 1.0 if there is no influence.

3. At each intersection, the rules are for the car to join the queue, if there is one. The queue discipline is first in, first out.

4. The rules for the route selection at the first intersection are either to continue on the original route or to take the alternate. The following factors control the choice:
   a. Signal condition at signal light—when the light is green or there is no queue, continue on the original route.
   b. Indication of traffic density—if there is light traffic, stay on original route.
   c. Abnormal conditions—when the weather is poor, rainy or snowy, or if there is an indication of an abnormal situation, take the alternate route.

We see that the simple problem of driving to the office becomes more complex if we hope to represent its crucial features in a simulation model.

As the oldest and most commonly used simulation language, GPSS offers great power and a logical structure to evaluate system performance by means of simulation. Details for users are available in the *GPSS V Users' Manual* [IBM Corporation, 1970], and in works by Maisel and Gnugnuoli [1972] and Reitman [1971].

Results Based on a GPSS simulation involving a 100-day sample, the range of times to drive to the office was 14 to 17 minutes, with an average of 14.669 minutes. The standard output also gave a variety of other statistics on the queues at the three intersections. In addition, graphic output was called for as shown in Figures 12-9 and 12-10. Figure 12-9 shows a histogram for drive duration, indicating that the most likely trip time was 14 minutes. Figure 12-10 shows the maximum queue size at each of the three intersections with the queue statistics output shown above the histogram. The average transfer time through the intersections is given in seconds.

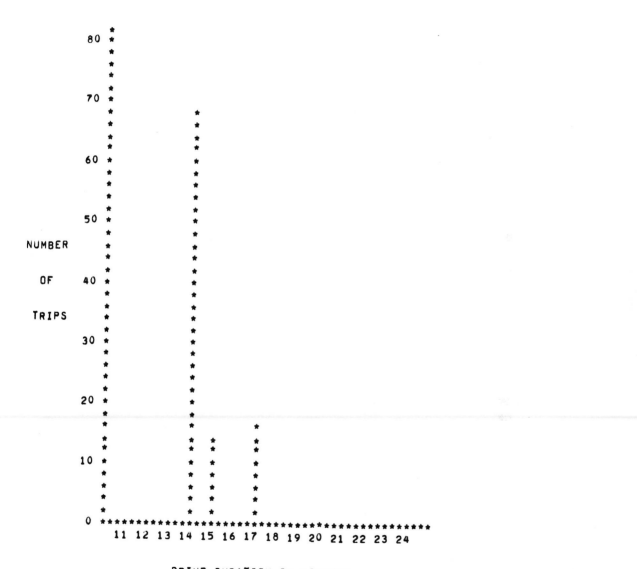

FIGURE 12-9
Graphic computer output of drive to the office duration. *Source:* From J. Retiman, *Computer Simulation Applications,* John Wiley & Sons, New York, 1971, Figure 2.14, p. 72. Used by permission.

QUEUE	MAXIMUM CONTENTS	AVERAGE CONTENTS	TOTAL ENTRIES	ZERO ENTRIES	PERCENT ZEROS	AVERAGE TIME/TRANS
INTS1	9	.063	27331		.0	20.058
INTS2	12	.012	36294	1	.0	24.283
INTS3	15	.137	61943	1	.0	19.100

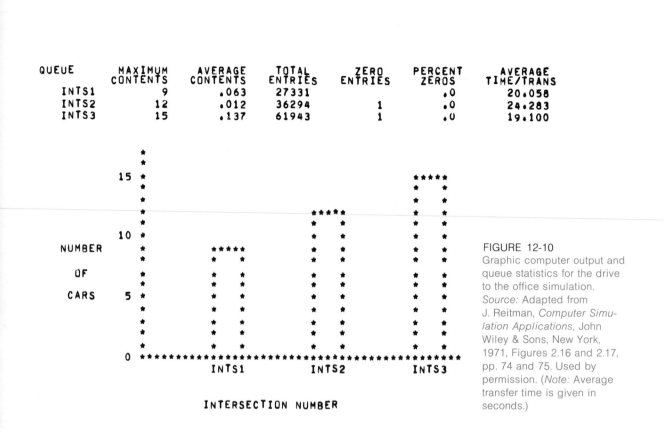

FIGURE 12-10
Graphic computer output and queue statistics for the drive to the office simulation. *Source:* Adapted from J. Reitman, *Computer Simulation Applications,* John Wiley & Sons, New York, 1971, Figures 2.16 and 2.17, pp. 74 and 75. Used by permission. (*Note:* Average transfer time is given in seconds.)

SIMSCRIPT Another very powerful computer language with special characteristics adapted to simulation is SIMSCRIPT. The conceptual framework is oriented around entities that can be assigned various attributes. For example, in the drive to the office problem, each intersection (an entity) has the attributes of a signal, a stated capacity, and a waiting line or queue.

The SIMSCRIPT user prepares the program following a prescribed format by naming and numbering temporary and permanent variables and sets, assigning attributes to each. To this description programs must be added to perform the required operations. With the system described in standard format, the SIMSCRIPT compiler regards the system description and programs as input data, preparing computer instructions for performing the system simulation. While the foregoing statement is true, it is not meant to convey the idea that the process is simple.

SIMSCRIPT is the second most commonly used simulation language and also offers great power and a logical structure to evaluate system performance by simulation. Time and effort to develop a program in SIMSCRIPT would be greater than for GPSS; however, many users feel that it has more flexibility. Details for users are available in works by Kiviat et al. [1969], Maisel and Gnugnuoli [1972], Reitman [1971], and Wyman [1970].

Validation of simulation models

Validation of all kinds of models is an important phase in their useful application. Given the model, how closely does it represent reality? Validation of complex simulation models has some extraordinary problems because their complexity raises some issues of validation that may be more important with simulation than with other kinds of models. Complexity puts a greater burden on verifying internal logic, including program debugging. Thus, in a first phase we must determine whether the simulation program actually represents what was intended in the program design by checking assumptions and reviewing the program with people familiar with the problem.

The second and crucial phase of validation requires us to determine in some satisfactory way whether the program represents the reality it was intended to simulate. If the simulation is meant to forecast the performance of a new system design, we are somewhat in the dark because there is no existing real system for comparative validation checks. In such situations, the nature of results can be reviewed by experts. Also, parts of a complex system may represent existing subsystems where direct validity checks can be made. Finally, statistical tests can be used to test hypotheses regarding general logic and validity.

Even though the final objective may be the design of a new system, we may develop simulation models to predict performance of an entire class of systems, a special case of which is an existing system. For example, in analyzing traffic flow, a simulator might be designed to take account of all the main variables such as traffic density, traffic light settings, number of lanes, rules for left and right turns, special left turn lanes, and so on. The simulator can be validated by predicting performance with the model for specified conditions, and comparing these results with actual field data.

Figure 12-11 represents just such a comparison in a traffic study. An intersection was selected within a network of five signalized intersections, and queue length predicted by the model (curved lines) was compared with measured queue length (vertical lines). The queue lengths are measured at 80-second intervals during the peak 15-minute period of the day. Eastbound traffic was 300 cars per 15 minutes over two through lanes and one left turn lane, and westbound traffic was 220 cars

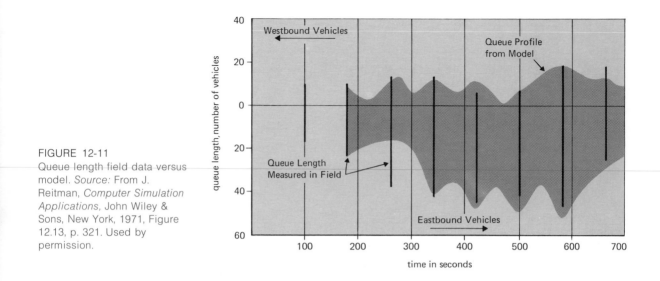

FIGURE 12-11
Queue length field data versus
model. *Source:* From J.
Reitman, *Computer Simulation
Applications,* John Wiley &
Sons, New York, 1971, Figure
12.13, p. 321. Used by
permission.

per 15 minutes. Average eastbound speed was measured as 7.3 mph compared to
6.3 mph predicted by the model, and westbound speed was measured as 10.2 mph
versus 9.0 mph for the model. The comparison was judged to be satisfactory validation for the model.

Validation studies may result in model changes that could be as drastic as re-
formulating the problem.

SIMULATION OF WAITING LINES

One of the most common situations calling for Monte Carlo simulation involves waiting lines. If the model involves the flow of orders according to the actual demand
distribution experienced, we can simulate the "arrival" of an order by Monte Carlo
sampling from the actual distribution, so that the timing and flow of activities in the
simulated system parallel the actual experience. If we are studying the breakdown of
a certain machine (perhaps an office copying machine) caused by bearing failure, we
can simulate typical breakdown times through simulated sampling from the distribution of bearing lives.

An example Suppose we are dealing with an emergency medical system, and we
wish to estimate the level of service that can be maintained by one ambulance. We

have available, or must obtain, data concerning the frequency of calls for service and the service time. As we noted in Chapter 11, if these empirical distributions are closely approximated by theoretical distributions, we could compute directly the results that we will determine here by simulation methods. However, the data summarized by Figures 12-12 and 12-13 are empirical data, and we will assume that they are not adequately described by any known mathematical model that we can solve. The procedure follows the steps described previously.

STEP 1. *Determine the distributions of the time between calls for service and service time.* If they were not available directly, we would have to make a study to determine these distributions, or use records of calls for service and service time, if available, from which the distributions might be constructed. Figures 12-12 and 12-13 show the distributions of the time between calls for service and the service times for 161 emergencies. These distributions will be the basis for the simulation.

FIGURE 12-12
Frequency distribution of the time between calls for 161 emergencies ($n = 161$, $\bar{x} = 17.5$ minutes).

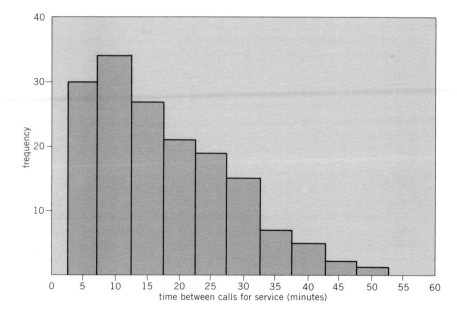

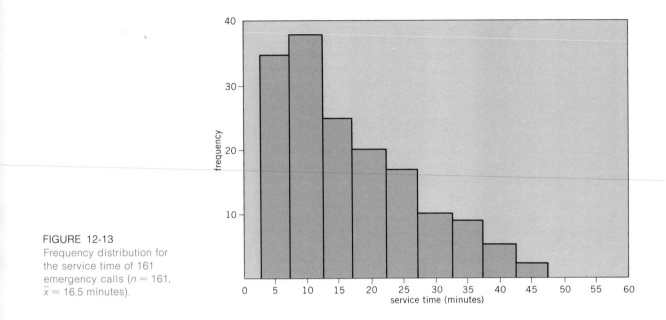

FIGURE 12-13
Frequency distribution for
the service time of 161
emergency calls ($n = 161$,
$\bar{x} = 16.5$ minutes).

STEP 2. *Convert the frequency distributions to cumulative probability distributions* (see Figures 12-14 and 12-15). This conversion is made by summing the frequencies that are less than or equal to each call or service time and plotting them. The cumulative frequencies are then converted to probabilities.

As an example, let us take Figure 12-12 and convert it to the cumulative distribution of Figure 12-14. Beginning at the lowest value for the time between calls, 5 minutes, there are 30 occurrences. For the call time 5 minutes, 30 is plotted on the cumulative chart. For the call time 10 minutes, there were 34 occurrences, but there were 64 occurrences of 10 minutes or less, so the value 64 is plotted for 10 minutes. For the call time 15 minutes, there were 27 occurrences recorded, but there were 91 occurrences of calls for 15 minute intervals or less.

Figure 12-14 was constructed from Figure 12-12 by proceeding in this way. When the cumulative frequency distribution was completed, a cumulative probability scale was constructed on the right of Figure 12-14 by assigning the number 1.0 to the maximum value, 161, and dividing the resulting scale into 10 equal parts. This process results in a cumulative empirical probability distribution. From

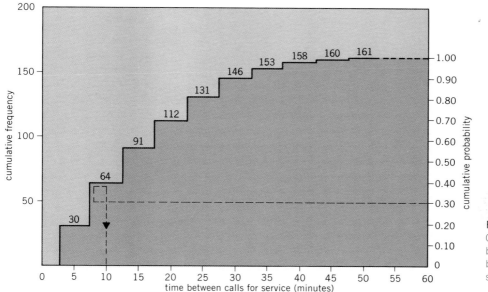

FIGURE 12-14
Cumulative distribution of the time between calls for service.

Figure 12-14 we can say that 100 percent of the call time values were 50 minutes or less; 99 percent were 45 minutes or less, and so on. Figure 12-15 was constructed from Figure 12-13 in a comparable way.

STEP 3. *Sample at random from the cumulative distributions to determine specific times between calls for service and service times; use these data in simulating the emergency medical operation.* This sampling is conducted by selecting numbers at random between 1 and 100 (00 represents 100).

The random numbers were used to enter the cumulative distributions to obtain time values in proportion to their occurrence in the distributions. An example is shown in Figure 12-14 where the random number 30 is shown to select a call time of 10 minutes.

By using random numbers to obtain call time values in this fashion from Figure 12-14, we will obtain call time values in proportion to the probability of occurrence indicated by the original frequency distribution. Of course, a table of random numbers that selects certain call and service times is simpler to use. For ex-

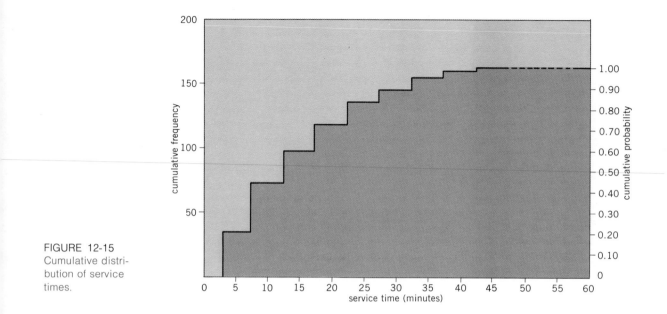

FIGURE 12-15
Cumulative distri-
bution of service
times.

ample, reading from Figure 12-14, the random numbers 1 through 19 give us a call time of 5 minutes, and so on. That is, 19 percent of the time we would obtain a call time of 5 minutes, $40 - 19 = 21$ percent of the time we would obtain a call time of 10 minutes, and so on. Table 12-4 shows the random number equivalents for Figures 12-14 and 12-15.

Sampling from Table 12-4 will now give call times and service times in proportion to the original distributions, just as if actual calls and services were happening. Table 12-5 gives a sample of 20 times between calls for service and service times, determined in this way.

STEP 4. *Simulate the actual operation of calls and services.* The structure of what we wish to do in simulating the emergency medical operation is shown by the flow chart of Figure 12-16. This operation involves selecting a call time, then determining whether or not the ambulance is available. If the ambulance is not available, the patient must wait until it is. If the ambulance is available, the question is, did the ambulance have to wait? If it did, we compute the ambulance idle time. If the ambulance did not have to wait, we select a service time and pro-

Random Numbers Used to Select Calls for Service and Service Times   TABLE 12-4

These Random Numbers	Select	These Call Times (min)	These Random Numbers	Select	These Service Times (min)
1–19		5	1–20		5
20–40		10	21–44		10
41–57		15	45–60		15
58–70		20	61–72		20
71–81		25	73–83		25
82–91		30	84–89		30
92–95		35	90–94		35
96–98		40	95–99		40
99		45	00		45
00		50			

Note: These data are in proportion to the occurrence probabilities of the original distribution.

ceed according to the flow chart, repeating the overall process as many times as desired, providing a mechanism for stopping the procedure when the desired number of cycles has been completed.

The simulation of the emergency medical operation for 20 calls for service is shown in Table 12-6. Here we have used the call times and service times selected by random numbers in Table 12-5. We assume that time begins *when the first call occurs,* and we accumulate call time from that point. The service time required for the first call was 20 minutes, and since this occurrence is the first in our record, neither the patient nor the ambulance had to wait. The second call occurred at 30 minutes, but the ambulance was available at the end of 20 minutes, so it waited 10 minutes for the next call to occur. Note that we are using the "discrete event" simulation process described by Figure 12-3(a).

We proceed in this fashion, making computations according to the requirements of the simulation model to obtain the record of Table 12-6. At the bottom of Table 12-6 we show that for the sample of 20 emergencies, total patient waiting time was 145 minutes, and total ambulance idle time was 70 minutes. Of course, to obtain a realistic picture we would have to use a much larger sample.

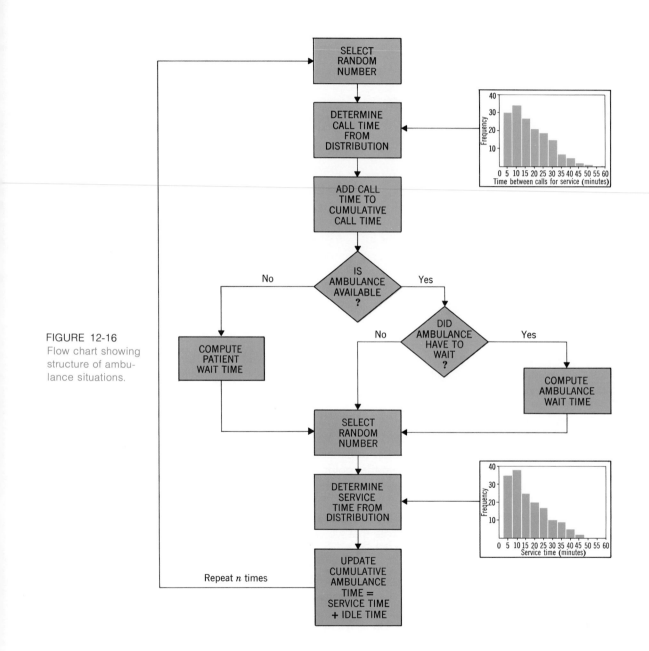

FIGURE 12-16
Flow chart showing
structure of ambu-
lance situations.

Simulated Sample of 20 Times Between Calls for Service   TABLE 12-5
and Service Times

Random Number	Call Time[a] (min)	Random Number	Service Time[b] (min)
27	10	71	20
89	30	43	10
27	10	16	5
51	15	64	20
96	40	75	25
54	15	28	10
13	5	54	15
53	15	11	5
14	5	12	5
87	30	86	30
54	15	92	35
63	20	06	5
00	50	49	15
13	5	03	5
28	10	63	20
15	5	41	10
83	30	09	5
29	10	72	20
49	15	14	5
01	5	83	25

[a] Data from Figure 12-14.
[b] Data from Figure 12-15.

Interpretation of results   Interpreting the results of the emergency medical system simulation is rather hazardous in view of the small sample; however, it would appear that the system is too heavily loaded for one ambulance to give really excellent service. Patient waiting time was required for 55 percent of the calls, while the ambulance was servicing another call. (Note, however, that response time for emergency medical systems, as defined in Figure 11-1 is somewhat longer, since response time includes waiting time plus ambulance travel time to the scene.)

TABLE 12-6

Simulated Ambulance Calls and Service

Time of Call for Service	Time Service Begins	Time Service Ends	Patient Waiting Time	Ambulance Idle Time
0	0	20	0	0
30	30	40	0	10
40	40	45	0	0
55	55	75	0	10
95	95	120	0	20
110	120	130	10	0
115	130	145	15	0
130	145	150	15	0
135	150	155	15	0
165	165	195	0	10
180	195	230	15	0
200	230	235	30	0
250	250	265	0	15
255	265	270	10	0
265	270	290	5	0
270	290	300	20	0
300	300	305	0	0
310	310	330	0	5
325	330	335	5	0
330	335	360	5	0
			145	70

The manager of such an emergency medical system would undoubtedly ask about the effect of doubling capacity by adding a second ambulance. We can, of course, predict the general effect from our knowledge of queuing systems — the patient waiting time will drop dramatically. In fact, using the same sample of call and service times from Table 12-5, but simulating for a system of two ambulances, a 5-minute patient waiting time is required in only one instance. The price paid for the improved service is the cost of a second ambulance and the added operating costs. The ambulance idle time increases from only about 20 percent to almost 60 percent for the small sample.

SIMULATION OF AN EMERGENCY MEDICAL SYSTEM

Given the preceding development of Monte Carlo simulation of ambulance service, we wish to place these inputs in context with an actual simulation study of the emergency medical system of the City of Los Angeles. The managerial objectives of the study were focused on the appropriate capacity and deployment of emergency medical facilities, and the results were an important input to the deployment decision.

The prediction of the performance of an emergency medical system is an ideal example of the need for a "systems" view because in such a system, performance cannot be inferred by examining the components separately. The demand for service, nature and location of medical need, ambulance availability, traffic problems, the location of hospitals, and so on, are all interacting parameters that define the system and have a bearing on the decision variables. The decision variables themselves are complex, involving deployment strategy, response time, system cost, and other factors.

The simulation methodology is an ideal vehicle for studying complex systems such as an emergency medical system, because it would not be feasible to perform the experiments on the real system in a controlled way. Since factors of known risk in the form of probability distributions enter the process, we can perform a large number of replications of the experiments to determine the expected values of measures of performance, and thus be able to make decisions based on the expected long-run conditions. In addition, with simulation we can assess the response of the system to peak loads. Indeed, in all kinds of emergency service systems such as police and fire protection, as well as medical systems, how the system performs when its capacity is stressed may be of the greatest importance.

The computer simulation model

Fitzsimmons [1970, 1973] programmed the emergency medical system in SIM-SCRIPT, driving the simulation process with an incident generator (call for service) that provided the forecasts of load.

The incident generator Based on studies of past actual loads for each hour of the day, the hourly pattern shown in Figure 12-17 was developed. Therefore, a specific mean hourly rate could be determined from Figure 12-17 in proportion to load experience through the day. Furthermore, previous statistical studies had shown that the Poisson distribution was a good description of call rates for the mean values of Figure 12-17. For each hourly mean call rate, the generator could determine a specific call rate

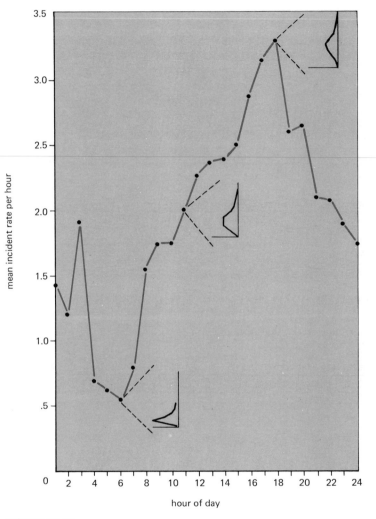

FIGURE 12-17
Mean call for service rate (incident rate) for the Los Angeles emergency medical systems. Three sample miniature Poisson distributions are shown for widely differing mean incident rates. *Source:* From J. A. Fitzsimmons, "Emergency Medical Systems: A Simulation Study and Computerized Method for Deployment of Ambulances." Unpublished Ph.D. Dissertation, UCLA, 1970. Used by permission.

based on Monte Carlo methods. Recall that the shape of the Poisson distribution varies with the mean; three sample distributions at different load levels are shown in Figure 12-17. Note that at low loads the Poisson distribution has a fairly sharp peak with a relatively high probability of arrival rates near the mean. At high loads, however, the variability is rather great and there is a reasonably high probability of call rates substantially lower and higher than the mean rate. Finally, an exact time for an incident was determined by sampling over the hour from a uniform distribution.

The simulator The main program of the simulator begins with an incident at a specific time, and the incident is processed according to the general logic of the flow chart shown in Figure 12-18. Travel time is computed as the sum of x and y distances converted to travel time, to correspond to the usual urban layout plan. Additional Monte Carlo sampling is required to compute the time required at the scene, the type of incident, and the delay at the hospital. Thus, the simulation contains both deterministic and stochastic elements.

While each vehicle has a home base, the simulator is designed to accommodate a mobile system (which can be dispatched en route) since vehicles can be reassigned in transit. The simulator includes capability for both ambulances and helicopters.

Model validation The model was validated both in terms of equivalent analytical models for simple cases and for a portion of the existing Los Angeles Ambulance System.

Fitzsimmons constructed single and multiple ambulance waiting line models using the basic definitions shown in Figure 11-1. The assumptions were first-come first-served queue discipline, Poisson input and exponential service time, and an infinite queuing system. On-scene care was assumed constant at seven minutes, all patients were transported to hospitals, and hospital transfer time was constant at three minutes in the validation studies. With these assumptions, waiting line lengths and times could be determined analytically for the complete model using the waiting line models of Chapter 11. Simulation runs included 10,800 and 3,240 calls for the single and multiple ambulance cases. Tests of significance of various queue statistics were made comparing analytical and simulation results, and all results indicated high conformance between the simulation and analytical models.

In validating the computer simulation model against the real-world Los Angeles Ambulance System, Fitzsimmons tested its ability to predict the behavior of the San Fernando Valley portion of the Los Angeles system. Actual data for 1967 were used in developing the model and historical verification was performed by comparing

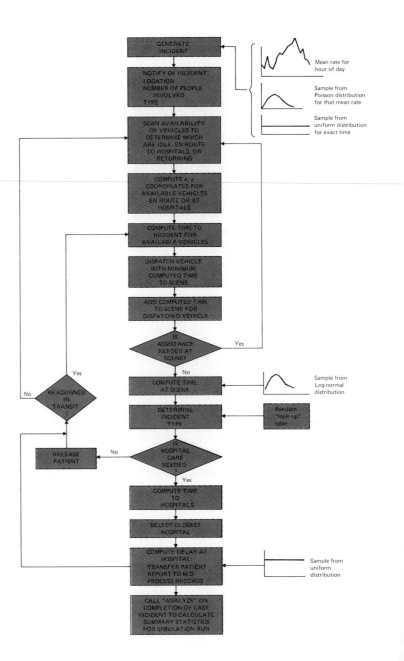

FIGURE 12-18
Summary flow chart for simulation of
emergency medical system.

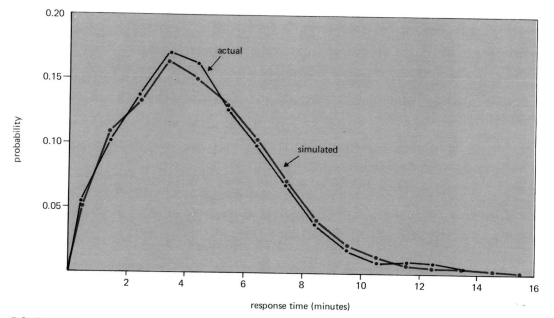

FIGURE 12-19

Distribution of response times for the San Fernando Valley Ambulance System. *Source:* J. A. Fitzsimmons, "Emergency Medical Systems: A Simulation Study and Computerized Method for Deployment of Ambulances." Unpublished Ph.D. Dissertation, UCLA, 1970. Used by permission.

records for 1967 with simulated results for the same period. (See Figure 12-19.) A number of statistical tests were performed. Again, statistical tests confirmed that the simulation system adequately duplicated reality.

Use of the emergency medical simulation model

Given the validated simulation model, we have an effective vehicle for the managerial evaluation of practical alternatives in the form of sensitivity analysis and the evaluation of alternate control policies. The alternatives were evaluated mainly in terms of response time.

Number and location of ambulances Fitzsimmons evaluated the effect on response time of having one to ten ambulances in the system for single and dispersed home

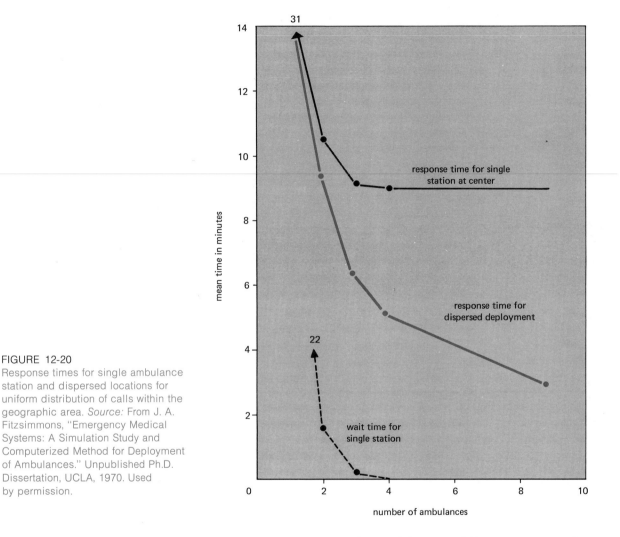

FIGURE 12-20
Response times for single ambulance station and dispersed locations for uniform distribution of calls within the geographic area. *Source:* From J. A. Fitzsimmons, "Emergency Medical Systems: A Simulation Study and Computerized Method for Deployment of Ambulances." Unpublished Ph.D. Dissertation, UCLA, 1970. Used by permission.

stations. The single home stations were at a hospital. In general, the response time for a single station leveled off at about three ambulances in the system, as shown in Figure 12-20; however, response time for dispersed deployment continued to decline. Waiting time for the single station fell to near zero with three ambulances in the system.

A series of 20 experimental runs evaluated hypotheses concerning location deployment patterns, and dispersed deployment dominated the single station alternative for all system performance criteria. Furthermore, optimal locations improved mean travel time to the scene by about 12 percent, compared to existing locations. Finally, it was found that optimal deployment was a function of incident or call rate.

Number and location of hospitals   A series of runs was made in which the number of hospitals was varied from one to four, using a single ambulance located centrally. Mean time to the hospital was reduced considerably with the addition of hospitals to the system, but response time and waiting time were only slightly reduced, and ambulance utilization declined about 2 percent, as shown in Figure 12-21. Mean

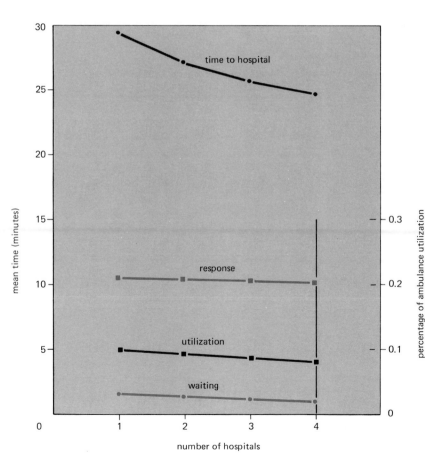

FIGURE 12-21
Effect of the number of hospitals in the system on response time. *Source:* From J. A. Fitzsimmons, "Emergency Medical Systems: A Simulation and Computerized Method for Deployment of Ambulances." Unpublished Ph.D. Dissertation, UCLA, 1970. Used by permission.

travel time to the scene actually increased slightly. Locating hospitals optimally reduced mean waiting time only slightly, because of reduced ambulance utilization.

Control policies Alternate dispatch policies were evaluated for no radio communication, radio dispatch without mobile transmitters on board ambulances, and two-way radio communication. These alternate policies were evaluated under loads varying from call rates of 15 to 45 per day. Simulated response time was reduced by 7 to 8 percent with radio dispatch; however, the two-way radio dispatch system was very little better than the basic system. Nevertheless, the two-way system was recommended since it effected some improvement.

Even when ambulance stations were physically dispersed, simulation experiments showed a definite advantage of pooling ambulances into one central dispatch command, as would be predicted from queuing theory.

Alternate ambulance deployment policies were also evaluated, indicating an advantage for an adaptive system that allows repositioning of vehicles as load builds up, rather than having each vehicle return to its home base at the end of an incident. Fitzsimmons [1973] developed a computer program named Computerized Ambulance Location Logic (CALL) to determine optimum ambulance deployment. Based on evaluations for particular ambulance locations, a computer search routine directs changes in the ambulance locations to progressively decrease the system's mean response time.

WHAT SHOULD THE MANAGER KNOW?

Computer simulation is a powerful tool, and simulated sampling is an extremely important component that makes it possible to assess the risk factors entering complex problems. The manager should have an understanding of the kinds of problems for which simulation might be useful. These problems are in general those that must reflect the complexities of systems—problems in which there are important interactions between components of the system. The emergency medical simulation is such a problem. The effectiveness of the emergency medical system depends on the demand for service, the number of vehicles available and their locations, the number and locations of hospitals, population and traffic densities and patterns, and the control and deployment policies used. Most organizations have some problems that require a systems approach in order to represent the problem adequately, and simulation has been used effectively in the analysis of industrial planning and control systems, hospital admissions systems, urban transportation systems, weapons systems, and other types of systems.

Model formulation

In deciding whether or not to place faith in the results of a simulation model, a manager must be involved in the initial phases of model formulation to be sure that the model will have the capability to examine the kinds of questions of interest. The manager's sense of the problems may be particularly important when risk factors need to be accounted for. While managers cannot be expected to know simulation languages and to program simulation problems, they need to be able to communicate effectively with the technical people who will implement the detailed formulation of the model. Thus, a manager should be able to make a flow chart of a problem, to indicate at least the major progressions involved in the system and the decision points that will be useful. In this process, the manager may also be defining basic data needs.

Problems for which simulation is particularly useful tend to be ones involving the evaluation of alternate policies and procedures. As such, they are commonly one-time studies. Thus, while managers need not know programming languages in detail, they may nevertheless find it worthwhile to know the general characteristics of languages. For example, simulation languages are efficient in terms of programming effort, but not necessarily efficient in terms of computer run time. Languages such as FORTRAN and PL/1 have the opposite characteristics. For a large-scale simulation program, it may be worthwhile to obtain capability in specialized simulation languages.

Interpretation of results

The validation process should be of great interest to managers in interpreting results. The managers should not use the results of a simulation model if they are not satisfied with the validation. With satisfactory validation, however, the sensitivity analysis should be of significant help to managers, for these studies can provide insight into how the real system functions, which variables are important and which are relatively unimportant, even though they may be under managerial control. Thus, the comments in Chapter 2 regarding validation and use of a model are especially significant for large-scale simulation models.

CHECK YOUR UNDERSTANDING

1. What are the essential differences between discrete event and discrete time updating simulations? Illustrate by indicating how the simulation of the activities of a single ambulance might be handled in each of the two simulation modes.

2. Outline the procedure for simulated sampling (Monte Carlo). What is the purpose of each step?

3. How does Monte Carlo sampling ensure that data enter the simulation in proportion to their occurrence in the original distribution? Can you envision a situation where the data entering the simulation might not be representative of the original distribution?

4. The manager of a small post office is concerned that her growing township is overloading the one-window service being offered. She decides to obtain sample data concerning 100 individuals who arrive for service. The data obtained are summarized in Table 12-7.
   a. Convert the distributions to cumulative probability distributions.
   b. Using a simulated sample of 20, estimate the average customer waiting time and the average percentage of idle time of the postal clerk.

TABLE 12-7

Arrival and Service Time Data for a One-Window Post Office

Time Between Arrivals (min)	Frequency	Service Time (min)	Frequency
0.5	2	0.5	12
1.0	6	1.0	21
1.5	10	1.5	36
2.0	25	2.0	19
2.5	20	2.5	7
3.0	14	3.0	5
3.5	10		100
4.0	7		
4.5	4		
5.0	2		
	100		

Arrival and Service Time Data for a Bank   TABLE 12-8

Time Between Arrivals (min)	Frequency	Service Time (min)	Frequency
0.0	10	0.0	0
1.0	35	1.0	5
2.0	25	2.0	20
3.0	15	3.0	40
4.0	10	4.0	35
5.0	5		100
	100		

5. The manager of a bank is attempting to determine how many tellers he needs during his peak load period. He wishes to offer service so that the average waiting time of a customer does not exceed two minutes. How many tellers does he need given the arrival and service distributions shown in Table 12-8? Customers form a single waiting line and are serviced by the next available teller. Simulate the system for alternate numbers of tellers with a sample of 20 arrivals in each instance.

6. Discuss the basic differences between the two computer simulation languages: GPSS and SIMSCRIPT.

7. You have carried through two simple simulations in connection with Exercises 4 and 5. How could you validate the results?

8. The discussion of the simulation of an emergency medical system is a report of how an extensive simulation was carried through, validated, and used. Place yourself in the position of the policy and decision maker responsible for the operation of the Los Angeles Emergency Medical System. Assume that a presentation has just been made to you similar to the report of the study given in the text. What questions would you ask the researcher? How would you satisfy yourself concerning the value of the study? What criteria would you use in making such decisions as the number of ambulances to use, the number of hospitals to establish for the system, and the type of radio communication to use?

SHORT CASES

CASE 12-1   A manufacturing company has a large machine containing three identical electronic components that are the major cause of downtime. The current practice is to replace the components as they fail. However, a proposal has been made to replace all three components whenever any one of them fails in order to reduce the frequency with which the machine must be shut down.

In the current situation, the machine must be shut down for one hour to replace one component or for 2.25 hours to replace all three.

a. What are the data requirements to analyze and compare the alternatives using simulation?

b. Formulate the problem in terms of a simulation system using the discrete event method. Prepare a flow chart of the simulation system similar to Figure 12-18 in the text.

CASE 12-2   Suppose we are dealing with the maintenance of a bank of 30 machines, and we wish to estimate the level of service that can be maintained by one mechanic. In order to make judgments about the effectiveness of the system, we need to have the simulation system generate data concerning the time that machines are down while waiting for service and being repaired. We also wish to know how well the mechanic is utilized in the system.

a. What are the data requirements necessary to construct a simulation of the system?

b. Formulate the problem in terms of a simulation system using the discrete time updating method. Prepare a flow chart of the simulation system similar to Figure 12-18.

CASE 12-3   A bank of 20 automatic machines is being maintained by a crew of six mechanics. Production forecasts indicate the need for two more machines to meet capacity needs. The question has been raised of whether the size of the repair crew should be enlarged.

There are two basic kinds of repair situations: the "run" call and the "downtime" call. A run call is one in which the mechanic can service the machine while it is still operating. On the average, 67 percent of the calls for service are of the run type. A downtime call for service normally comes from a more serious problem resulting in machine breakdown. In such situations, the mechanic completes the repair and the machine is put back in service. However, the mechanic spends additional time with the machine after it has started again, to make final adjustments and ensure that it is ready for service. This period is the mechanic's "run-in time."

a. What are the data requirements to develop a simulation of the repair system in order to analyze and compare the system for different numbers of machines in service and different numbers of mechanics?

b. Formulate the problem in terms of a simulation system using the discrete event method. Prepare a flow chart of the simulation system similar to Figure 12-18.

There are numerous full reports of simulations of complex systems, including those on the list   CASE 12-4
that follows:

a. Simulation of a district office of the United States Social Security System [Maisel and Gnugnuoli, 1972, pp. 343–94].
b. Simulation in business [Meier, Newell, and Pazer, 1969, Chapter 2].
c. Simulation in economic analysis (Meier, Newell, and Pazer, 1969, Chapter 4).
d. Prediction of passenger railroad system performance [Reitman, 1971, Chapter 8].
e. Performance of a computer system [Reitman, 1971, Chapter 11].
f. Auto traffic flow through a series of intersections [Reitman, 1971, Chapter 12].

    Read one of the simulation studies from the preceding list or from the Applications References at the end of this chapter. Prepare a report giving a brief summary and reviewing data requirements, methodology, and interpretation of results. If the report were presented to you as decision maker, what questions would you raise? What criteria other than those specifically included in the simulation do you think are pertinent in judging and deciding on the issues raised by the simulation study?

A professional football coach has six running backs on his squad. He wants to evaluate how   CASE 12-5
injuries might affect his stock of backs. A minor injury causes a player to be removed from the game and miss only the next game. A major injury puts the player out of action for the rest of the season. The probability of a major injury in a game is 0.05. There is at most one major injury per game. The probability distribution of minor injuries per game is:

Number of Injuries	Probability
0	0.2
1	0.5
2	0.22
3	0.05
4	0.025
5	0.005

Injuries seem to happen in a completely random manner, with no discernible pattern over the season. A season is ten games.

    Using random numbers given in Table C-4 of Appendix C, simulate the fluctuations in the coach's stock of running backs over the season. Assume that he hires no additional running backs during the season.

    The coach is fretting about the possibility that he could face the end of the season without enough running backs for post season games that can provide excellent returns. He has the opportunity to acquire an excellent running back from another team that has an excess, at a "reasonable price." What do you recommend?

CASE 12-6   A manufacturer of stereo systems uses a certain electronic component in all its models. The usage rate is quite variable, reflecting the many reasons for demand variability for the end products and their production schedules. In addition to the usage variability, the supplier of the item was not very reliable in meeting delivery schedules. As a result the production manager felt that she needed to carry extra inventories as a buffer to ensure that she would not be out of stock. She decided to carry a buffer stock that would give assurance of not stocking out 95 percent of the time.

An examination of inventory records revealed the following data on usage and supply lead time:

Weekly Usage	Probability	Weeks Lead Time	Probability
0	0.25	1	0.25
1	0.30	2	0.30
2	0.30	3	0.20
3	0.15	4	0.15
	1.00	5	0.10
			1.00

a. The production manager needs to develop the joint probability distribution of usage during the supply lead time in order to set an inventory level as a buffer. Note that if supply lead time were three weeks, the usage in week one might be 0, in week two it might be 3, and in week three usage might be 1. Therefore, usage during the three-week lead time would have been 4. The joint probability distribution would reflect the probability of occurrence of all such combinations of lead time and usage. Develop the joint probability distribution of usage during the supply lead time using Monte Carlo simulation. Use a sample of 30 supply cycles.

b. Based on the probability distribution developed in a, what buffer inventory level should the production manager set to ensure that she will not stock out 95 percent of the time?

c. How can the manager use the resulting information to improve inventory control?

CASE 12-7   Tex Muldoon is a "wildcat" oil driller, looking for financial backing. You are a potential investor hoping to make a million dollars so you can retire in luxury. Muldoon's deal is that you put up $300,000 and he puts up $200,000 plus his experience and a track record, and you split the proceeds. Muldoon's track record is clear—he has drilled 100 wells with 25 producing wells and 75 dry holes.

Muldoon says that a producing well will result in an average of a $1 million profit, and a dry hole results in the loss of the $100,000 drilling cost. He will continue to drill until reaching the total investment goal or until the venture loses all its money.

a. Develop a flow chart for a simulation of the problem so you can assess the risks and the probability of running your $300,000 up to $1 million.

b. Perform a manual simulation of the investment problem with a $500,000 initial investment, based on 20 trials. A trial results in a "win" if you run the investment up to $2 million (so you realize your $1 million), and a "loss" if the capital falls to zero or below.

c. Based on the results in *b*, what is the probability of running the $500,000 investment up to $2 million?

d. Muldoon taunts you with, "If you are willing to risk a larger investment the probability of winning is increased." This is an intriguing idea. How would you change the simulation flow chart to determine the probability of running an original investment up to $2 million for various values of initial capital, and that Muldoon invests $300,000?

e. Perform a second manual simulation of 20 trials for a total initial capital of $750,000, and calculate the probability of winning. How does this probability compare with that calculated in *c*? Would you be willing to increase your investment to $450,000, assuming that you can raise the capital?

Remember the Hula Hoop? Here is another novelty item, and if it takes off in the market, the promoters stand to make good money if they can get their price of $10 each, and if they can control their costs.   CASE 12-8

Their best estimate of the market is for the sale of 100,000 units at an expected variable cost of $4 per unit. If these estimates hold they would make $100,000(10 - 4) = $600,000$. Because the item is new, however, there is considerable uncertainty in all the estimates. Having been through similar situations in the past, the promoters express the three crucial variables as probability distributions as follows:

Market Size	Probability	Price	Probability	Costs	Probability
60,000	0.15	$ 6	0.10	$2	0.10
80,000	0.30	8	0.30	4	0.60
100,000	0.40	10	0.50	6	0.30
120,000	0.10	12	0.10		1.00
140,000	0.05		1.00		
	1.00				

Simulate 20 trials of the novelty product. What is the expected profit? Profit is defined here as price minus variable cost. How can the promoters use the information generated? Do you recommend that they proceed with the promotion?

CASE 12-9   An architect has been awarded a contract to prepare plans and specifications for an urban renewal project. The activities required, their sequencing requirements, and estimated time requirements are as follows:

Activity	Description	Immediate Predecessors	Time (days)
a	Preliminary sketches	—	2
b	Outline of specifications	—	1
c	Prepare drawings	a	3
d	Write specifications	a, b	2
e	Run off prints	c, d	1
f	Have specifications printed	c, d	3
g	Assemble bid packages	e, f	1

Figure 12-22 is a network diagram for the performance of the project using the deterministic activity times given, showing the critical path as *a-c-f-g*. The critical path may be identified by inspecting the paths through the network and establishing the critical path as the longest time path or paths. (See Chapter 8 for details.)

The architect reexamines the estimated activity times, since he is concerned about the effect of unanticipated events, a common occurrence in his office. He comes up with three time estimates for each activity together with the estimated probabilities of their occurrences as follows:

Activity	Optimistic		Expected		Pessimistic	
	Time	Prob	Time	Prob	Time	Prob
a	1	0.1	2	0.6	4	0.3
b	0.5	0.1	1	0.5	2	0.4
c	2	0.2	3	0.6	5	0.2
d	1.5	0.1	2	0.6	3	0.3
e	0.5	0.1	1	0.8	1.5	0.1
f	2	0.3	3	0.4	4	0.3
g	0.5	0.1	1	0.7	1.5	0.2

a. Assign random numbers to the optimistic, expected, and pessimistic activity times in proportion to their probabilities of occurrence.

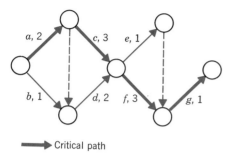

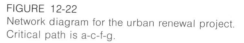

FIGURE 12-22
Network diagram for the urban renewal project.
Critical path is a-c-f-g.

b. Simulate 10 trials for the network, identifying activities on the critical path, and the project completion time for each trial. How does the average project completion time compare with the 9-day time resulting from the deterministic activity times?
c. What is the index of criticality for each activity?
d. The architect has agreed to finish the project in ten days, with a $500 per day penalty for each additional day. What advice would you give the architect?

GENERAL REFERENCES

Emshoff, J. R., and R. L. Sisson, *Design and Use of Computer Simulation Models,* The Macmillan Company, New York, 1970.

Evans, G. W., G. F. Wallace, and G. L. Sutherland, *Simulation Using Digital Computers,* Prentice-Hall, Englewood Cliffs, N.J., 1967.

IBM Corporation, *GPSS V Users' Manual,* Form No. SH20-0851-0, 1970.

Kiviat, P. J., R. Villanueva, and H. M. Markowitz, *The Simscript II Programming Language,* Prentice-Hall, Englewood Cliffs, N.J., 1969.

Maisel, H., and G. Gnugnuoli, *Simulation of Discrete Stochastic Systems,* Science Research Associates, Chicago, 1972.

Meier, R. W., T. Newell, and H. L. Pazer, *Simulation in Business and Economics,* Prentice-Hall, Englewood Cliffs, N.J., 1969.

Naylor, T. H., J. L. Balintfy, D. S. Burdick, and K. Chu, *Computer Simulation Techniques,* John Wiley & Sons, New York, 1966.

Schriber, T. J., *Simulation Using GPSS,* John Wiley & Sons, New York, 1971.

Wyman, F. P., *Simulation Modeling: A Guide to Using SIMSCRIPT,* John Wiley & Sons, New York, 1970.

APPLICATIONS REFERENCES

Cook, T. M., and R. A. Russell, "A Simulation and Statistical Analysis of Stochastic Vehicle Routing with Timing Constraints," *Decision Sciences,* Vol. 9, No. 4, October 1978.

Ferguson, C. E., Jr., J. B. Mason, and J. B. Wilkinson, "Simulating Food Shoppers Economic Losses as a Result of Supermarket Unavailability," *Decision Sciences,* Vol. 11, No. 3, July 1980, pp. 535–556.

Fetter, R. B., and J. D. Thompson, "The Simulation of Hospital Systems," *Operations Research,* 13(5), 1965, pp. 689–711.

Fitzsimmons, J. A., "Emergency Medical Systems: A Simulation Study and Computerized Method for the Deployment of Ambulances," unpublished Ph.D. Dissertation, University of California, Los Angeles, 1970.

———, "A Methodology for Emergency Ambulance Deployment," *Management Science,* Vol. 19, No. 6, February 1973, pp. 627–36.

Kwak, N. K. P., P. J. Kuzdrall, and H. H. Schmitz, "The GPSS Simulation of Scheduling Policies for Surgical Patients," *Management Science,* 22(9), May 1976, pp. 982–989.

Monarchi, D. E., T. E. Hendrick, and D. R. Plane, "Simulation for Fire Department Deployment Policy Analysis," *Decision Sciences,* Vol. 8, No. 1, January 1977.

Moore, L. J., and B. W. Taylor, III, "Experimental Investigation of Priority Scheduling in a Bank Check Processing Operation," *Decision Sciences,* Vol. 8, No. 4, October 1977.

Reitman, J., *Computer Simulation Applications,* John Wiley & Sons, New York, 1971.

Rising, E. J., R. Baron, and B. Averill, "A Systems Analysis of a University-Health-Service Outpatient Clinic," *Operations Research,* 21(5), September–October 1973, pp. 1030–1047.

CHAPTER 13

Markov Chains

Suppose a person enrolls as a freshman in a four-year college. What is the probability that he or she will be enrolled as a sophomore the next year? What is the probability that the person will actually graduate after four years? Suppose a person chooses brand X from three competitive products X, Y, and Z. What is the probability that she will purchase brand Y next time? Suppose a person is in a mental hospital in January. What is the probability that he will be in an outside home in May? Suppose a person has a job as a department head in a major corporation. What is the probability that she will be promoted to a corporate vice-president in five years?

In many real-world problems, it is convenient to classify individuals or items into distinct categories or *states*. We can then analyze the transitions of these individuals or items from one state to another over time. For example, if we are analyzing college enrollments, we may use the classifications of freshman, sophomore, junior, senior, graduated, and dropout as our states. We can then investigate the probability that a freshman will become a sophomore after one year, or a senior after three years. If we are concerned with analyzing alternate marketing strategies, we may use the classification of a purchaser of brand X, a purchaser of brand Y, or a purchaser of brand Z as our states. What would be the appropriate states to use in the analysis of a mental hospital or of job advancement in a major corporation?

Generally, we speak in terms of the probability that a person or an item will move from one state to another during time period n. Suppose the probability that a person moves from state i to state j during time period n depends only on the previous state i, and is independent of the time period n. Then the process can be analyzed using Markov chains. This approach will be illustrated through the use of several examples.

FORECASTING COLLEGE ENROLLMENTS

Accurate forecasts of college enrollments are extremely important for many decisions that relate to the management of higher education. The decision to expand the facilities at various campuses or to add a new campus may depend on enrollment forecasts. Questions that may be important include the following:

1. If 100 new students enroll as freshmen each year in a four-year college, what will the total increase in the enrollment be after four years?
2. If 100 new students enroll as freshmen each year, how many will actually graduate?

These questions can be answered by using the concepts of Markov chains.

Estimation of transition probabilities

The analysis of enrollments begins with the classification of students into mutually exclusive categories or states. The appropriate classification will depend on the particular problem that is being analyzed. For example, the states used to analyze enrollments in a major university might be lower division undergraduate, upper division undergraduate, master's level, and doctoral studies. For simplicity, we shall assume that we are analyzing enrollments in a four-year college with no graduate programs. The major student flows are illustrated in Figure 13-1.

Suppose we confine our interest to the states of dropout (*Do*), freshman (*Fr*), sophomore (*So*), junior (*Jr*), senior (*Sr*), and graduated (*Gr*). According to Figure 13-1, a freshman in one academic year either becomes a sophomore the next academic year or drops out. For simplicity in this example, we are ignoring the relatively small proportion of individuals who may drop out of college for a year or more and then return, and the individuals who make less than "normal" progress and do not move from one state to another after each academic year. However, these complicating factors could be incorporated into a similar, more detailed analysis.

Now we need the probability that a freshman will become a sophomore, and the probability that he or she will become a dropout. Actual data on the progress of students in the public four-year colleges of Texas from 1960 through 1967 are shown in Table 13-1. The number of sophomores as a percentage of freshmen is relatively constant with a mean value of 54.0 and a range of from 51.3 to 55.4. Thus, it would seem reasonable to use 0.54 as an estimate of the probability that a freshman will become a sophomore, and to assume that this probability does not depend on the particular academic year, since the figures show no notable trend or other systematic variation. It follows that $1.0 - 0.54 = 0.46$ is the probability that a freshman will drop out after one academic year, since this is the only other state possible according to the student flow diagram of Figure 13-1.

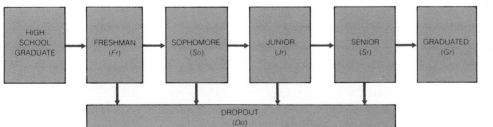

FIGURE 13-1
Major student flows in a four-year college.

TABLE 13-1   Progress of Entering Freshman Classes in the Public Four-Year Colleges of Texas

Fall Class Entered	No. of Freshmen	No. of Sophomores 1 Year Later	No. of Sophomores as Percentage of Freshmen	No. of Juniors 2 Years Later	No. of Juniors as Percentage of Sophomores	No. of Seniors 3 Years Later	No. of Seniors as Percentage of Juniors
1960	18,451	9,913	53.7	8,468	85.4	8,260	97.5
1961	20,687	11,473	55.4	9,235	80.5	9,350	101.2
1962	22,253	11,414	51.3	10,226	89.6	10,335	101.1
1963	23,611	12,695	53.8	11,446	90.2	11,373	99.4
1964	26,474	14,283	53.9	12,351	86.5	12,526	101.4
1965	30,484	16,652	54.6	14,685	88.2	—	—
1966	32,933	18,103	55.0	—	—	—	—
1967	33,411	—	—	—	—	—	—
Total	174,893	94,533	54.0	66,411	86.9	51,844	100.2

Source: Coordinating Board, Texas College and University System unpublished reports of enrollment. Fall 1960–Fall 1967.

Stated symbolically, we have the conditional probability that a freshman during academic year $n-1$ will become a sophomore the next academic year n, $P(So_n|Fr_{n-1})$ = 0.54. Similarly, $P(Do_n|Fr_{n-1}) = 0.46$, and $P(Jr_n|So_{n-1}) = 0.87$ and $P(Do_n|So_{n-1})$ = 0.13 from Table 13-1.

Notice that the number of seniors as a percentage of the number of juniors has a mean value of 100.2, indicating perhaps that there are individuals who remain classified as seniors for two or more academic years. For simplicity, we assume that $P(Sr_n|Jr_{n-1}) = 1.0$ and $P(Do_n|Jr_{n-1}) = 0.0$ are reasonable estimates. We also assume that *every* individual who becomes a senior will actually graduate, so $P(Gr_n|Sr_{n-1}) =$ 1.0 and $P(Do_n|Sr_{n-1}) = 0.0$.

These conditional probabilities can be conveniently summarized in tabular form as illustrated in Table 13-2. Each entry in Table 13-2 is the probability of moving from the state indicated by the corresponding row to the state indicated by the corresponding column. For example, the 0.87 entry indicates that the probability that a sophomore will become a junior after one academic year is 0.87.

Since the entries in Table 13-2 represent the probabilities of transition from one state to another, they are called *transition probabilities*. The table or matrix of probabilities is called the *transition matrix* for the problem.

TABLE 13-2

Probabilities of Transition from One State to Another

	To					
From	*Do*	*Fr*	*So*	*Jr*	*Sr*	*Gr*
Do	1.0	0.0	0.0	0.0	0.0	0.0
Fr	0.46	0.0	0.54	0.0	0.0	0.0
So	0.13	0.0	0.0	0.87	0.0	0.0
Jr	0.0	0.0	0.0	0.0	1.0	0.0
Sr	0.0	0.0	0.0	0.0	0.0	1.0
Gr	0.0	0.0	0.0	0.0	0.0	1.0

Use of transition probabilities

The transition probabilities in the transition matrix can be used to answer the questions posed initially regarding the impact of 100 new students enrolling as freshmen. Since $P(So_n|Fr_{n-1}) = 0.54$, there would be (100)(0.54) = 54 additional sophomores the following year, and since $P(Jr_n|So_{n-1}) = 0.87$, there would be $(54)(0.87) \cong 47$ new juniors two years hence.* Finally, since $P(Sr_n|Jr_{n-1}) = 1.0$, there would be 47 incremental seniors. The total increase in enrollment in the college after four years from an increase of 100 new students as freshmen each year would be 248, as calculated in Table 13-3. The number of additional persons who graduate each year would also be estimated as 47, since $P(Gr_n|Sr_{n-1}) = 1.0$.

This example has illustrated how transition probabilities can be obtained and used to analyze a problem of enrollment forecasting. Additional insights can be obtained

* The symbol $\cong$ is read "is approximately equal to."

TABLE 13-3

Total Increase in Enrollment After Four Years From an Additional 100 Freshmen Each Year

Increase in	
Freshmen	100
Sophomores	54
Juniors	47
Seniors	47
Total	248

when the transition matrix is actually used in the analysis. This process will be illustrated through a second example.

BRAND SWITCHING

An important application of transition matrices is in the analysis of *brand switching* among consumers. For example, suppose there are three major automobile manufacturers who dominate the automobile market. During the previous month, manufacturer X sold a total of 120,000 automobiles, manufacturer Y sold 203,000, and manufacturer Z sold 377,000. However, the sales totals do not tell the full story regarding customer preferences.

Customers do not always purchase a new automobile from the same producer that manufactured their previous automobile. This phenomenon, called *brand switching,* has important implications for marketing analysis and for planning advertising strategies. In order to analyze this phenomenon, data are needed on the manufacturer of the car previously owned by each of these purchasers.

Table 13-4 shows how these data might be displayed. From Table 13-4, we see that the market share of manufacturer Z has declined from $400/700 = 0.571$ to $377/700 = 0.539$, with most of the gain going to manufacturer X. Of the 120,000 new automobiles purchased from manufacturer X, 85,000 customers previously owned an automobile manufactured by X, 20,000 owned an automobile manufactured by Y, and 15,000 owned an automobile manufactured by Z. Of the 100,000 previous owners of automobiles manufactured by X, 8,000 purchased a new automobile from manufacturer Y, while only 7,000 purchased from Z. These data show not only the total sales and the market shares, but also indicate the relationship among the manufacturers in terms of customer brand loyalty and brand switching.

On the basis of these data, the following questions might be asked and analyzed:

1. Should the advertising campaign of manufacturer Z be directed toward attracting previous purchasers of automobiles manufactured by X or Y, or should it concentrate on retaining a larger proportion of the previous purchasers of automobiles manufactured by Z?

2. The purchaser of a new automobile keeps the car an average of three years. If this trend in brand switching continues, what will the market shares of the three companies be in three years? In six years?

3. If this trend in brand switching continues, will the market shares continue to fluctuate, or will an equilibrium eventually be reached?

Automobile Brand Switching					TABLE 13-4
Previously Owned Automobile Made by:	Purchased New Automobile Made by:			Total	Previous Market Share
	X	Y	Z		
X	85	8	7	100	0.143
Y	20	160	20	200	0.286
Z	15	35	350	400	0.571
Total	120	203	377	700	
New Market Share	0.171	0.290	0.539		

Note: Data given in thousands.

These questions can be analyzed by developing and using transition probabilities and the transition matrix.

The matrix of transition probabilities

Given the data in Table 13-4, it is a simple matter to compute the transition probabilities. The probability that a previous owner of an automobile manufactured by X will purchase a new automobile from Y is $8/100 = 0.08$, and from Z is $7/100 = 0.07$. The probability that X will retain a customer is $85/100 = 0.85$. Thus we simply divide each entry in Table 13-4 by the corresponding row total, as follows:

	X	Y	Z
X	$85/100 = 0.8500$	$8/100 = 0.0800$	$7/100 = 0.0700$
Y	$20/200 = 0.1000$	$160/200 = 0.8000$	$20/200 = 0.1000$
Z	$15/400 = 0.0375$	$35/400 = 0.0875$	$350/400 = 0.8750$

These calculations determine the transition matrix shown in Table 13-5.

Notice that the sum of the entries in each row in the transition matrix is 1.0. This is an important characteristic of a transition matrix. The columns of the transition matrix yield the following information:

1. X retains 85 percent of its customers, gains 10 percent of Y's customers, and gains 3.75 percent of Z's customers.

TABLE 13-5

Transition Matrix for Brand Switching

From	To: (1) X	(2) Y	(3) Z
X	0.8500	0.0800	0.0700
Y	0.1000	0.8000	0.1000
Z	0.0375	0.0875	0.8750

2. Y gains 8 percent of X's customers, retains 80 percent of its customers, and gains 8.75 percent of Z's customers.
3. Z gains 7 percent of X's customers, gains 10 percent of Y's customers, and retains 87.5 percent of its customers.

We will now consider how this matrix can be used to analyze marketing strategies.

An example of a Markov chain The matrix of transition probabilities can be used to study the dynamic behavior of consumer purchasing patterns if the following assumptions can be justified:

1. The probability that a customer will switch to another manufacturer or purchase again from the same manufacturer depends only on the brand of the automobile the person now owns. The brands of the automobiles owned previously are irrelevant.

2. The probability that a customer will switch to another manufacturer or purchase again from the same manufacturer is independent of how many previous purchases the person has made.

For example, suppose customer Jones owned an automobile manufactured by Z and then purchased an automobile from X, while customer Smith owned an automobile manufactured by X and purchased a new one from X. According to assumption 1, the probabilities that Jones and Smith will purchase their next cars from X, or switch to Y or Z, must be identical.

If these assumptions are reasonable, and in many real-world marketing analyses they are, then the series of purchases by consumers constitute a *Markov chain* of the first order. Under such conditions, the matrix of transition probabilities can be used to provide further insights into consumer purchasing patterns.

Prediction of market shares in future periods

The current market share for each of the manufacturers is 0.171 for manufacturer X, 0.290 for manufacturer Y, and 0.539 for manufacturer Z. These numbers appear in Table 13-4 and were obtained by dividing the number of automobiles sold by each manufacturer by the total number of automobiles sold by all three manufacturers.

The average length of time that a new automobile purchaser keeps an automobile is three years. If the brand switching behavior of the customers continues in the same manner as described in the transition matrix of Table 13-5, what will the market shares be in three years, when the customers purchase new automobiles again? We can write the current market shares as the column of numbers shown below:

	Market Share
X	0.171
Y	0.290
Z	0.539

where the numbers represent the proportion of the total new automobile sales attributable to each manufacturer.

By using the following procedure we can estimate the market share of manufacturer X in three years. From column (1) of Table 13-5, we know that X retains 85 percent of its customers, or 85 percent of its market share. Thus, we expect X to retain $(0.171)(0.85) = 0.145$ of its current market share. X also gains 10 percent of the customers of Y, or 10 percent of Y's market share. Therefore, X would gain $(0.290)(0.10) = 0.029$ of the market from Y. Likewise, X would gain 3.75 percent of the market of Z, or $(0.539)(0.0375) = 0.020$. Adding the proportion of the market share retained, 0.145, the proportion of the market gained from Y, 0.029, and the proportion of the market gained from Z, 0.020, gives

$$0.145 + 0.029 + 0.020 = 0.194$$

as the estimate of the market share of X in three years. This estimate represents a net gain of $0.194 - 0.171 = 0.023$, or 2.3 percent of the market.

Notice that these calculations are equivalent to simply multiplying the numbers in the market share column shown previously by the corresponding numbers in column (1) of the transition matrix (Table 13-5) and summing the results. That is, we have

Market Share Column		Column (1) of Transition Matrix		
0.171	×	0.8500	=	0.145
0.290	×	0.1000	=	0.029
0.539	×	0.0375	=	0.020
				0.194

To obtain the estimated market share for Y in three years, we can multiply the market share by the corresponding numbers in column (2) of the transition matrix as follows:

Market Share Column		Column (2) of Transition Matrix		
0.171	×	0.0800	=	0.014
0.290	×	0.8000	=	0.232
0.539	×	0.0875	=	0.047
				0.293

The net increase is 0.3 percent for the market share of Y. Verify that the estimate of the market share for Z in three years is 0.513.

Thus the estimated market share column in three years is

	Market Share
X	0.194
Y	0.293
Z	0.513

Now, to estimate the market shares of X, Y, and Z six years hence, when the typical customer will again purchase an automobile, we can multiply the new values in the column of market shares times the corresponding numbers in the columns of the transition matrix in Table 13-5. Thus the estimated market share of X in six years would be found as follows:

Market Share Column		Column (1) of Transition Matrix		
0.194	×	0.8500	=	0.165
0.293	×	0.1000	=	0.029
0.513	×	0.0375	=	0.019
				0.213

Again the market share of X has increased. If the estimated total sales six years hence is 900,000, then the estimated sales for manufacturer X would be (0.213)(900,000) = 191,700.

By continuing this process, we can find the estimated market shares for each manufacturer for any multiple of three years into the future. To find the estimated market shares nine years hence, simply take the estimated market shares in six years found as indicated above, and multiply them times the columns in the transition matrix. Using these estimates and the transition matrix, we can find the estimated market shares twelve years hence, etc. Naturally, this analysis assumes that the brand switching behavior of the customers as indicated in Table 13-5 remains constant (assumption 2).

In our analysis, the market shares of X and Y increased, while that of Z fell. If the brand switching behavior of the customers remains constant, will this shift of customers from Z to X and Y continue indefinitely, or will an equilibrium point be reached at which there are no more changes in the market shares?

Equilibrium

Suppose we assume that at some future time, an equilibrium point will be reached so that the market shares of X, Y, and Z do not change. At that point, the same proportion of customers would switch to each brand as switch from each brand over each purchase cycle of three years.

Let us assume that these equilibrium market shares are x for manufacturer X, y for manufacturer Y, and z for manufacturer Z. Thus the column of market shares at equilibrium is

	Equilibrium Market Share
X	x
Y	y
Z	z

To estimate the market shares of each manufacturer in another three years, we would simply multiply the numbers in this column times the corresponding numbers in the transition matrix columns (Table 13-5), and sum the results. However, we know the results will remain unchanged at the equilibrium point, so the sum for X will be the market share for X, which is simply x.

That is, to calculate the market share for X in three years *after* equilibrium has been reached, we would simply perform the following calculations:

Equilibrium Market Share Column		Column (1) of Transition Matrix		
x	$\times$	0.8500	=	0.8500x
y	$\times$	0.1000	=	0.1000y
z	$\times$	0.0375	=	0.0375z
		Equilibrium market share for X	=	x

But we know that the sum will simply be x, since the market share of X remains unchanged when equilibrium has been reached. We can rewrite this summation in the form of an equation,

$$0.8500x + 0.1000y + 0.0375z = x$$

which simplifies to

$$0.1500x - 0.1000y - 0.0375z = 0 \tag{1}$$

Performing similar calculations for the market share of Y gives

$$0.0800x + 0.8000y + 0.0875z = y$$

which simplifies to

$$0.0800x - 0.2000y + 0.0875z = 0 \tag{2}$$

Similarly, for Z we obtain

$$0.0700x + 0.1000y - 0.1250z = 0 \tag{3}$$

Since the market shares are proportions, we also know that

$$x + y + z = 1 \tag{4}$$

Thus, we have four equations and three unknowns. We may use equation (4) and any two of equations (1) through (3) and solve for the values of x, y, and z, using one of the methods for solving simultaneous equations. Substituting these values back into the fourth equation provides a check on our computations.

Suppose we choose equations (2), (3), and (4), and solve them by the method of substitution. We can eliminate y from (2) and (3) by multiplying (3) by 2 and adding it to (2) as follows:

$$
\begin{array}{llll}
0.1400x + 0.2000y - 0.2500z = 0 & \text{[(3) multiplied by 2]} \\
\underline{0.0800x - 0.2000y + 0.0875z = 0} & (2) \\
0.2200x \qquad\qquad\; - 0.1625z = 0 & & & (5)
\end{array}
$$

We can eliminate y from (3) and (4) by multiplying (3) by -10 and adding it to (4) as follows:

$$
\begin{array}{llll}
-0.70x - 1.00y + 1.25z = 0 & \text{[(3) multiplied by } -10] \\
\underline{\quad x + \quad y + \quad z = 1} & (4) \\
0.30x \qquad\qquad + 2.25z = 1 & & & (6)
\end{array}
$$

Finally, we can eliminate x from (5) and (6) by multiplying (5) by -0.3, multiplying (6) by 0.22, and adding the resulting equations:

$$
\begin{array}{ll}
-0.066x + 0.04875z = 0 & \text{[(5) multiplied by } -0.3] \\
\underline{0.066x + 0.49500z = 0.22} & \text{[(6) multiplied by 0.22]} \\
0.54375z = 0.22
\end{array}
$$

Therefore, $z = 0.22/0.54375 = 0.4046$. Substituting this value back into (6), we have

$$0.30x + (2.25)(0.4046) = 1$$

which simplifies to

$$0.30x = 0.0897$$

so that $x = 0.0897/0.30 = 0.2990$. Finally, we substitute these values of x and z into (4) to obtain

$$y = 1.0 - 0.2990 - 0.4046$$

or $y = 0.2964$.

We can check these results by substituting them into equation (1), which gives

$$(0.1500)(0.2990) - (0.1000)(0.2964) - (0.0375)(0.4046) = 0.0$$

as we expected. Note that these calculations are straightforward, but admittedly somewhat tedious, even for a problem with only three states. In real-world applications, there will generally be more than three states, but the calculations can be done efficiently on a computer in only a few seconds.

These results tell us that at equilibrium the market shares of manufacturers X, Y, and Z will be 0.30, 0.30, and 0.40 (rounding to two decimal places). This result assumes that the brand switching behavior of the consumers continues according to the pattern in Table 13-5. Thus we would expect X's market share to continue to grow from its current value of 0.17, but to stabilize at 0.30. The market share of Y will remain virtually unchanged, since its current value is 0.29. Manufacturer Z will continue to lose customers from its current share of 0.539, but will fall only to 0.40, and will still be the dominant manufacturer in the industry.

Use of the Markov chain analysis

The Markov chain analysis can be used to analyze the effects of various marketing strategies. Recall that the equilibrium market shares of 0.30, 0.30, and 0.40 were derived on the basis of the assumption that the brand switching behavior of the consumers as described in Table 13-5 remains unchanged. What if manufacturer X undertakes an aggressive marketing strategy designed to encourage more of the customers who previously purchased automobiles from manufacturer Z to switch to automobiles manufactured by X? Recall advertisements that you have seen in which one manufacturer focuses its marketing campaign on one competitor while ignoring others.

TABLE 13-6   New Transition Matrix for Brand Switching

From	To:		
	X	Y	Z
X	0.8500	0.0800	0.0700
Y	0.1000	0.8000	0.1000
Z	0.0750	0.0875	0.8375

Suppose the market analysts feel that such a campaign would increase the percentage of Z's customers who switch to automobiles manufactured by X from 3.75 to 7.5, so that the transition matrix for the automobile industry would become the one illustrated in Table 13-6. Verify that the new long-run (equilibrium) market shares of the three manufacturers based on this change would become 0.366 for X, 0.295 for Y, and 0.339 for Z. Thus, *a successful marketing campaign would make X the dominant force in the industry and relegate Z to second place.*

AN ANALYSIS OF A GERIATRIC WARD

Meredith [1973] presents an example of an analysis of a real-world problem using Markov chains. At the California Napa State Hospital, a resocialization program was instituted in 1964 to deinstitutionalize geriatric (elderly) patients so that they could be placed in boarding homes or their equivalent outside the hospital. The analysis was performed to determine the costs and the benefits of the program.

For the purposes of the analysis, it was convenient to classify current or former patients into the following states:

1. in the Geriatric Resocialization Program (GRP)
2. in one of the hospital wards
3. in a home but placed from GRP
4. in a home but placed directly from a ward
5. deceased

It seemed reasonable to assume that the movement of a patient from one state to another could be described by a Markov chain. This assumption implies that the probability of movement to the next state depends only on the patient's current state and not on the time period. The only concern was that for long-term projections, the probability of a patient's death would actually increase; however, since the probability of death is quite small, this effect was not considered significant, so the Markov chain assumption was made.

The probabilities of movement among the five states for a period of one month are given in Table 13-7. These probabilities were determined from actual hospital records in the same manner illustrated in the enrollment forecasting and in the brand switching examples. The cost of keeping a patient in each state for one month is shown in the right-hand column of Table 13-7.

TABLE 13-7   One-Month Transition Probabilities and Costs

			To:			
From	GRP	Ward	Home (from GRP)	Home (from Ward)	Deceased	Cost per Month ($)
GRP	0.854	0.028	0.112	0.000	0.006	682
Ward	0.013	0.978	0.000	0.003	0.006	655
Home (from GRP)	0.025	0.000	0.969	0.000	0.006	226
Home (from Ward)	0.000	0.025	0.000	0.969	0.006	226
Deceased	0.000	0.000	0.000	0.000	1.000	0

Source: J. Meredith, "A Markovian Analysis of a Geriatric Ward," *Management Science,* June 1972; used by permission.

Notice in Table 13-7 that the probability of moving to another state from *deceased* is 0.0, and the probability of remaining deceased is 1.0, as we would expect. What if we calculate the long-run, equilibrium probability of patients in each state? Once a patient reaches the state *deceased,* he or she can never leave it. In general terms, this is called an *absorbing state* in a transition matrix. In the enrollment forecasting example with the transition matrix shown in Table 13-2, the states *dropout* and *graduated* are absorbing states also. If an absorbing state exists in a transition matrix, all the persons or items will eventually move into the absorbing state (unless the transition matrix has other unusual characteristics that need not concern us here).

For the transition matrix in Table 13-7, the long-run proportion of patients in each state is obviously 0.0 in GRP, ward, home (from GRP), and home (from ward), and 1.0 in deceased. In other words, in the long run, all the patients are deceased. This analysis provides little useful information, so another type of long-run analysis is required when the transition matrix has absorbing states.

Using techniques slightly more involved than those presented here, Meredith computed the mean number of months a patient starting in each of the five non-absorbing states would stay in each of these states before entering the absorbing state *deceased.* He multiplied these results times the costs of being in each of these states for one month, and obtained the results shown in Table 13-8. For example, these figures indicate that a patient starting in the GRP can be expected to be in the program for a total of 26 months, in a ward for 38 months, in a home after placement from the GRP for 95 months, and in a home after direct placement from a ward for 4 months before dying.

The total cost to the state of treating this patient will be $64,950. Notice that a patient starting in a ward expects to spend much more time in the hospital ward and

Expected Stay Times (months) and Costs

TABLE 13-8

Initial State	GRP	Ward	Home (from GRP)	Home (from Ward)	Cost ($)
GRP	26	38	95	4	64,950
Ward	17	77	63	7	77,800
Home (from GRP)	21	31	109	3	59,900
Home (from Ward)	14	62	51	38	70,250

Source: J. Meredith, "A Markovian Analysis of a Geriatric Ward," *Management Science,* June 1972; used by permission.

Expected Stay Times (months) and Costs Without GRP

TABLE 13-9

Initial State	Ward	Home (from Ward)	Cost ($)
Ward	152	15	102,900
Home (from Ward)	123	44	90,400

Source: J. Meredith, "A Markovian Analysis of a Geriatric Ward," *Management Science,* June 1972, used by permission.

much less time in a home, since all patients are not selected for the GRP. Also notice that the expected total cost of treating a patient in the GRP is about $13,000 less than for one in the ward.

What if there were no GRP? A transition matrix similar to Table 13-7 was developed with only three states—ward, home (from ward), and deceased. The expected stay times for the average patient in each of the two states—ward and home (from ward)—before dying are shown in Table 13-9, along with the associated costs. The costs are significantly higher, about 30 percent. In addition, the average patient currently in the ward can now be expected to spend approximately 13 of his remaining 14 years in the ward (152 months in the ward and 15 months in a home after direct placement from a ward).

On the basis of this analysis Meredith was able to estimate that the GRP had resulted in a net savings to the state of some $15 million after only 5.5 years of operation. This amount corresponds to a savings of approximately $3 million per year.

WHAT SHOULD THE MANAGER KNOW?

Markov chains can be the basis for a predictive model for forecasting the future state of a person, a company, or an item. This predictive model is used when risk is involved in the form of probabilities of transition from one state to another. The approach is limited to problems with very special characteristics, but it does provide useful information to managers in those cases where it can be applied.

Problem characteristics

It must be possible to classify the items involved in the problem into unique states. For example, students were classified by academic level or by dropout or graduated status; the customers were classified according to the brands of automobiles they purchased; and patients were classified according to whether they were in a program, a home, a hospital ward, or deceased.

Next, it must be possible to determine the probability that a person or an item in each state will be in any other state in the next time period. This probability must

1. depend only on the current state, and
2. be independent of the particular time period.

These probabilities form a transition matrix.

Examples of real-world problems that often have these characteristics include enrollment forecasting, brand switching analysis, and health care system analysis. Trinkl [1974] presents an analysis of programs for the mentally retarded in Hawaii that is very similar to the analysis of Meredith [1973] in California. Pegels and Jelmert [1970] report the use of Markov chains to evaluate blood-inventory policies.

Several models for the evaluation of human resources and manpower planning also include Markov chains. For example, Flamholtz [1974] has used Markov chains to calculate the probabilities that individuals within an organization will occupy each of several jobs in the future. Charnes, Cooper, and Niehaus [1972] report that similar transition matrices have been developed for manpower planning in the U.S. Navy.

Formulation and data

The transition matrices are not particularly difficult to formulate. The manager should be involved in the identification of the relevant states. An attempt should be made to keep the number of states to a minimum. For example, in a brand switching analysis, it may be possible to ignore a large number of minor competitors or to group them into the single state *other*.

The required data are the transition probabilities. In such cases as the enrollment forecasting, mental retardation studies, and manpower planning studies, there may be sufficient historical data to determine proportions that can be converted into probabilities. However, the data must be carefully scrutinized. Adjustments may be required to compensate for recent trends or unusual patterns in the past that are not likely to repeat themselves. For example, data on college enrollments just before or just after a war should not be the basis for forecasts during peacetime. Similarly, brand switching data could be distorted by a strike in one of the companies during a particular year. The manager should be alert for such problems.

As a note of interest, the Market Research Corporation of America (MRCA) has established a sample of families who report their purchases of certain branded items to MRCA. These reports can be used as the basis for transition matrices in a brand switching analysis. Similar services are provided by other organizations.

When actual data are unavailable or of questionable validity for future projections, subjective probabilities can be used. Again, the manager should play an active role in the assessment of these subjective probabilities, as discussed in Chapter 14.

Computations

The computations are straightforward, but quickly become tedious. It is simple to develop or obtain computer programs that can perform the onerous arithmetic rapidly and present the results to the manager for interpretation.

Interpretation

There are three important results that can be obtained from the use of the transition matrices. First, forecasts of the proportion of individuals or items in each state can be attained for future time periods. These forecasts are obtained by multiplying a column of proportions (market shares in the brand switching example) times each column in the transition matrix, and summing the results. This information can be extremely useful for short-term forecasting of enrollments or sales.

Second, the long-run or equilibrium proportions can be developed for some transition matrices. The equilibrium state was illustrated for the brand switching problem. In the long run, these results indicate that the proportion of customers in each state will reach equilibrium values and remain unchanged. The sensitivity of these equilibrium values to changes in the probabilities in the transition matrices can be used as the basis for choosing among alternate marketing strategies.

Third, in some transition matrices, it is impossible to leave a state once it has been reached. Such a state is called an absorbing state. When absorbing states occur, the equilibrium analysis must take another form. The most relevant information is usually the expected number of time periods spent in each of the other states by an individual (or an item) before being absorbed. An example of this form of analysis was used in the study of the Geriatric Resocialization Program by Meredith [1973]. Although the mathematical details are straightforward, they are so tedious that they would be performed on a computer for any real-world application and have been omitted here. However, the manager should be aware of the use of this analysis. As illustrated, if the costs of being in each state are known, the results can be used in a cost analysis.

CHECK YOUR UNDERSTANDING

1. List the appropriate *states* to use in the analysis of the following:
   a. consumer credit policies
   b. a blood-inventory system
   c. the long-run ratio of tenured to nontenured professors in a university
2. Identify the two absorbing states in Table 13-2. Is it reasonable to assume that each of these are absorbing states? Why or why not?
3. Suppose that forecasts indicate that 34,000 students will enter the four-year colleges of Texas next year, 36,000 in two years, and 40,000 in three years. There are 30,000 enrolled in the current freshman class.
   a. Using the transition probabilities in Table 13-2, compute the expected total enrollment in the four-year colleges in three years.
   b. Suppose the average variable cost per student in the four-year colleges of Texas is estimated to be $800 for a freshman, $900 for a sophomore, $1100 for a junior, and $1400 for a senior. What should the variable portion of the state budget for higher education in the four-year colleges be in three years time?
4. Suppose that the *proportions* of students in each of the states in the four-year colleges of Texas are as follows:

State	Proportion
Do	0.00
Fr	0.40
So	0.25
Jr	0.20
Sr	0.15
Gr	0.00

    a. Using the data in Table 13-2, what will the proportions in each state be next year if just enough freshmen are admitted to maintain the *same* total enrollment?

    b. If the total current enrollment is 100,000 students, how many freshmen should be admitted next year to allow the total enrollment to increase to 105,000?

5. Discuss the assumptions that must be justified in order to use a Markov chain analysis in the enrollment forecasting problem, the brand switching problem, and the analysis of the geriatric ward.

    a. Are the assumptions met in each case?

    b. If not, would you expect the potential error to be so large that the results would be in question?

6. Determine the following, using the transition matrix for brand switching (Table 13-5):

    a. the market share of Z in three years

    b. the estimated sales for manufacturers Y and Z in six years if the estimated total sales is 900,000 automobiles

    c. the equilibrium market shares for X, Y, and Z using equations (1), (3), and (4).

7. Verify that the long-run (equilibrium) market shares of the three manufacturers based on Table 13-6 are 0.366 for X, 0.295 for Y, and 0.339 for Z.

8. Suppose there are 100 geriatric patients in the Napa State Hospital in January. There are 20 in GRP, 60 in one of the hospital wards, 15 in a home but placed from GRP, and 5 in a home but placed directly from a ward. Using the information in Table 13-7, determine the following:

    a. the cost of caring for the patients in January

    b. the expected number of patients in each state in February

    c. the expected number of patients in each state in March

    d. the expected cost of caring for the patients in March

SHORT CASES

Suppose that new razor blades were introduced on the market by three companies at the same time. When they were introduced, each company had an equal share of the market, but during the first year the following changes took place: CASE 13-1

(1) Company A retained 90 percent of its customers, lost 3 percent to B and 7 percent to C.

(2) Company B retained 70 percent of its customers, lost 10 percent to A, and 20 percent to C.

(3) Company C retained 80 percent of its customers, lost 10 percent to A, and 10 percent to B.

Assume that no changes in the buying habits of the consumers occur.

a. What are the market shares of the three companies at the end of the first year? Second year?

b. What are the long-run (equilibrium) market shares of the three companies?

CASE 13-2   The University of Lufkin employs nontenured and tenured professors to teach its classes. By obtaining a promotion, a nontenured professor may receive tenure (security of employment). Currently there are 100 nontenured and 50 tenured professors. On the basis of past records, 20 percent of the nontenured professors are promoted each year, and another 20 percent leave the university because of resignation or retirement. Similarly, 10 percent of the tenured professors leave the university each year. For every two faculty members who leave the university, one nontenured faculty member and one tenured faculty member are hired to replace them.

This situation may be summarized in the transition matrix shown in Table 13-10, where the state *outside* serves to indicate both resignations and new hires. (If the number of resignations did not equal the number of new hires, separate states would be required.) The mean salaries of tenured and nontenured faculty members are also shown. Assume that the number of faculty members initially classified as *outside* is 25.

a. Compute the current total annual cost of salaries at the University of Lufkin and the estimated total annual cost of salaries next year.

b. What are the long-run (equilibrium) proportions of nontenured and tenured faculty members? What total annual salary cost would be associated with these proportions, assuming that the total number of faculty members remains at 150?

c. Suppose a new policy is adopted so that every faculty member who leaves the university must be replaced by a nontenured faculty member (i.e., no one can be hired with tenure). What are the resulting long-run (equilibrium) proportions of tenured and nontenured faculty members? What total annual cost would be associated with these proportions assuming that the total number of faculty members remains at 150?

TABLE 13-10   Transition Probabilities and Mean Salaries for Faculty Members at the University of Lufkin

From	Nontenured	Tenured	Outside	Mean Salary
Nontenured	0.60	0.20	0.20	$14,000
Tenured	0.00	0.90	0.10	$20,000
Outside	0.50	0.50	0.00	—

One-Month Transition Probabilities and Costs for the   TABLE 13-11
Simplified GRP Analysis

From	To: GRP	To: Ward	To: Home	Cost per Month ($)
GRP	0.859	0.028	0.113	682
Ward	0.013	0.984	0.003	655
Home	0.012	0.012	0.976	226

Suppose we assume that approximately the same number of patients enter the geriatric program of the Napa State Hospital each month as the number who leave the system (die). Thus,
we could ignore the absorbing state *deceased* in Table 13-7. By combining the states of *home*
(*from GRP*) and *home* (*from ward*), we obtain the simplified data in Table 13-11.

a. In January, there are 20 persons in GRP, 70 persons in a ward, and 10 persons in a home.
   What is the cost of caring for these patients?

b. How many patients are expected to be in each state in February? In March? What are the
   expected costs in each month?

c. What are the long-run (equilibrium) proportions of patients in each state? What would be
   the cost of caring for 100 patients after equilibrium has been reached?

To compare the long-run costs of treating patients without GRP, we assume "that only those
patients who would have been placed directly from the ward will now be placed at all, since the
patients who actually *were* selected for GRP had been in the hospital for over five years already
without being placed and no reason exists to assume things would change suddenly."
[Meredith, 1973] The resulting transition matrix is shown in Table 13-12.

a. What are the long-run (equilibrium) proportions of patients in each state?

b. What would be the cost of caring for 100 patients after equilibrium has been reached?

c. Does this analysis provide sufficient justification for the GRP program? What weaknesses do
   you see in the analysis? What other considerations might influence a decision?

Finally, suppose a program is being contemplated that would double the number of placements
from GRP. Then the probability of going from GRP to home in Table 13-11 would increase to
0.226, and the probability of staying in GRP would fall to 0.746.

a. What are the long-run (equilibrium) proportions of patients in each state?

b. What would be the cost of caring for 100 patients after equilibrium has been reached?

c. What other noncost issues might be influential in a final decision regarding this new program? If you were the decision maker, what other information would you want?

TABLE 13-12

Modified Transition Probabilities and Costs Without GRP

From	To: Ward	To: Home	Cost per Month ($)
Ward	0.997	0.003	655
Home	0.024	0.976	226

CASE 13-4   A major travel and entertainment credit card company analyzed its credit history file to determine the transition probability matrix shown in Table 13-13.* For example, 6.4 percent of all current accounts (0 to 29 days past due) age to 30 to 59 days past due. The costs are based on estimates of the rate of return that the firm could obtain on investments if the money were not tied up in accounts receivable.

a. What are the long-run (equilibrium) proportions of accounts in each state?

b. Suppose the company estimates that sending a letter to all account holders in the 30 to 59 days past due state would result in the modified transition matrix of Table 13-14. What would be the effect on the long-run (equilibrium) proportion of accounts in each state? Suppose that the incremental cost of sending 100 letters is $25. Would this strategy be justified on an economic basis?

TABLE 13-13

Transition Probability Matrix and Costs for Credit Card Receivables

Days Past Due at Month t	Days Past Due at Month $t+1$ 0–29	30–59	60+	Costs ($)
0–29	0.94	0.06	0.00	1
30–59	0.70	0.10	0.20	2
60+	0.65	0.10	0.25	4

TABLE 13-14

Modified Transition Matrix for Credit Card Receivables

Days Past Due at Month t	Days Past Due at Month $t+1$ 0–29	30–59	60+	Costs ($)
0–29	0.94	0.06	0.00	1
30–59	0.85	0.10	0.05	2
60+	0.60	0.10	0.30	4

* Adapted from L. H. Liebman, "A Markov Decision Model for Selecting Optimal Credit Control Policies," *Management Science,* Vol. 18, No. 10, June 1972.

GENERAL REFERENCES

Freedman, D., *Markov Chains,* Academic Press, Inc., N.Y., 1970.

Kemeny, J. G., A. Schleifer, Jr., J. L. Snell, and G. L. Thompson, *Finite Mathematics with Business Applications,* second edition, Prentice-Hall, Inc., Englewood Cliffs, N.J., 1972.

Martin, J. J., *Bayesian Decision Problems and Markov Chains,* John Wiley & Sons, Inc., New York, 1967.

APPLICATIONS REFERENCES

Bessent, W. E., and A. M. Bessent, "Student Flow in a University Department: Results of a Markov Analysis," *Interfaces,* Vol. 10, No. 2, April 1980.

Brodheim, E., and G. P. Prastacos, "The Long Island Blood Distribution System as a Prototype for Regional Planning," *Interfaces,* Vol. 9, No. 5, November 1979, pp. 3–20.

Charnes, A., W. Cooper, and R. Niehaus, *Studies in Manpower Planning,* U.S. Navy Office of Civilian Manpower Management, Washington, D.C., 1972.

Dyer, J., "Cost-Effectiveness Analysis for a Public System of Higher Education," Ph.D. dissertation, The College of Business Administration, The University of Texas at Austin, May 1969.

Flamholtz, E., *Human Resource Accounting,* Dickenson Publishing Co., Encino, California, 1974.

Liebman, L. H., "A Markov Decision Model for Selecting Optimal Credit Control Policies," *Management Science,* Vol. 18, No. 10, June 1972.

Meredith, J., "A Markovian Analysis of a Geriatric Ward," *Management Science,* Vol. 19, No. 6, February 1973.

Pegels, C., and A. Jelmert, "An Evaluation of Blood-Inventory Policies: A Markov Chain Application," *Operations Research,* Vol. 18, 1970, pp. 1087–98.

Trinkl, F., "A Stochastic Analysis of Programs for the Mentally Retarded," *Operations Research,* Vol. 22, No. 6, November–December 1974.

Evaluation Models

In Part IV we will assume that we know how things work, subject perhaps to factors in the environment beyond our control. However, even in those situations where the environment is not known with certainty, we assume that we can list each of the possible states of the environment and provide probability estimates of their occurrence. Consider the decision of whether or not to take an umbrella to work. If we take the umbrella and it does not rain, we have unnecessarily burdened ourselves with the trouble of carrying it. We may not know with complete certainty whether it will rain. However, in Part IV we assume that we *can* estimate the probability of rain. Given this information, we can use the concepts of decision theory to develop an *evaluation model* that aids in making decisions.

Thus, in Part IV we will be concerned primarily with the evaluation models of management science as shown in Figure IV-1. The outcomes that we evaluate

FIGURE IV-1
The models of management science

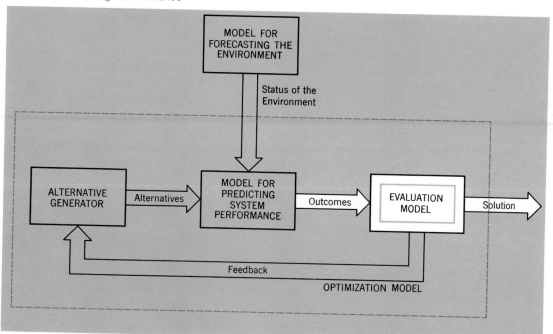

could have been generated by one of the optimizing models described in Part II or by one of the models that predict the effects of risk discussed in Part III.

The purpose of an evaluation model is to reflect the subjective judgments of the decision maker regarding the desirability of an outcome resulting from a decision. The choice of the appropriate evaluation model will depend on the circumstances under which the decision is actually being made. One of the important considerations is whether the outcome is known with certainty or only in terms of probability statements. For example, suppose we have $100 to invest. If we place it in a federally insured savings account paying 7 percent interest, we will receive $107 in return at the end of one year. We know this result with certainty. Naturally, we are ignoring such events as a political revolution, a world war, or other catastrophes that might prevent the bank from meeting its obligations. (In most real-world situations, we also ignore these "surprise" events that could happen but are sufficiently unlikely.) For practical purposes, we can say that the outcome of the decision to place $100 in a federally insured savings account is known with certainty.

The outcomes of most decisions, however, are not known with certainty. For example, we might consider an alternate investment of our $100. Suppose we pool our money with several other investors and finance the drilling of a wildcat oil well. If oil is actually found, we would receive $150 in return at the end of the year, but if no oil is found, we would receive $0 in return. This is clearly a *risky* investment, and our evaluation of its desirability will depend in part on the probability that we assign to finding oil. As we will see, an investor's personal attitude toward taking risks may also influence the evaluation of an alternative.

Another important consideration in defining the appropriate evaluation model is the number of different criteria that are relevant for evaluating the desirability of an action. For example, if we are trying to invest $100, the only important criterion may be the amount of money we receive in return. Thus, we would say that there is only a single criterion to be considered. In other cases, there may be multiple goals involved, and therefore *multiple criteria* must be considered. In purchasing an automobile, we consider not only cost but also such criteria as appearance and performance.

In order to be useful, the evaluation model must reflect the manager's concept of what ought to be. This concept requires a subjective judgment on the part of the manager. Thus, the evaluation model can be considered right or wrong only on the basis of how well it reflects these subjective judgments. In this sense, the evaluation model is also subjective. Some individuals make the mistake of interpreting this to mean that the evaluation model is arbitrary, since it is not objective. *However, there is a significant difference between a subjective model and an arbitrary model.* An evaluation model is a good one if it reflects the subjective judgments of the manager. It cannot be arbitrary, since if it were it might not reflect these judgments properly. This point is important, and we will return to it as we proceed through this section.

Since the purpose of an evaluation model is merely to reflect subjective judgments, it would be natural to question the model's practical usefulness. After all, the decision maker should simply be able to look at the different outcomes and state which one he or she prefers. However, in truly complicated situations involving risk and multiple criteria, this may be a difficult task. The development of an evaluation model can proceed on a step-by-step basis, so that the decision maker is not overwhelmed with the complexity of the total problem.

An Example: A Single Criterion Under Certainty

The simplest case from the standpoint of evaluation models involves a single criterion under conditions of certainty. To illustrate this case, let us return to our bank example. Suppose we have $100 to invest. For simplicity, assume that there are only two alternate investments available to us. The first, A_1, is a bank deposit paying 7 percent per year, while the second alternative, A_2, is another bank deposit paying 5 percent per year. Both accounts are fully insured and alike in every respect except for the interest rate.

Certainly this example seems trivial. No doubt you have already noted that the outcome O_1 from the first alternative A_1 is $107, while the outcome O_2 from alternative A_2 is only $105. Thus, we have identified the alternatives A_1 and A_2 and predicted their associated outcomes with certainty. According to our diagram of the models of management science, we still need an evaluation model to make the decision. However, in this case, the correct decision A_1 seems obvious. Why?

The reason is deceptively simple. There is a single criterion: money. Further, at least in our culture, most persons would agree that more money is preferred to less. That is, most persons would prefer having $107 to having $105. Therefore, we have actually used an evaluation model in making our decision, but since we agree that more money is preferred to less, and since there is no risk involved to complicate matters, the choice of the evaluation model is not a critical issue.

An obvious evaluation model can be constructed by defining $U(O_i) = O_i$ for $i = 1$ or 2. That is, we simply define the evaluation function as the identity function, so that this function assigns the number 107 to the outcome \$107, and the number 105 to the outcome \$105, and we choose the alternative with the highest value. This accurately reflects the feelings of *most* persons in our culture. When we are dealing with a single criterion such as money, we can often let $U(O_i)$ equal O_i. Therefore, we can speak of maximizing profit (or minimizing cost) without making explicit our evaluation model. Nevertheless, the choice of such a model is implied.

The function $U(O_i) = O_i$ is not the only function that we could use. For example, $V(O_i) = (2)(O_i)$ would be acceptable. Since $V(\$107) = (2)(107) = 214$ and $V(\$105) = 210$, and 214 is greater than 210, this function also indicates bank deposit A_1 should be chosen. Try to think of other functions that preserve the same ordering of these two outcomes as the simple identity function $U(O_i) = O_i$.

It is clear that we have a wide choice of evaluation models that will lead to the same decision. We could easily agree on the correct decision for our problem, A_1, without much concern regarding the appropriate form of U. As we will see, this is not always the case when risk is introduced.

One should not conclude, however, that decision making under certainty is always simple. In many problems that have special interest to managers, the models required to generate the alternatives may be very complex, creating possibly thousands of alternatives. Given the explicit identification of an evaluation model as a basis for ranking alternatives, it may be possible to use an optimization model of management science, such as linear programming, as an aid in these more complex situations.

An Overview of Part IV

In Chapter 14 we will see how decision making with a single criterion becomes more complicated when risk is involved. We introduce decision trees as a technique for simplifying the complex relationships and the calculations associated with risky choices. In Chapter 15 we study how to deal with situations in which the expected value of the outcome is not an appropriate evaluation model. These situations often occur because the stakes are very high in a decision involving risk. In such situations, the concepts of utility theory may be used to determine the appropriate evaluation model. One of the critical issues related to risky decisions is the availability of additional information that might reduce or even eliminate the risk in a problem. In Chapter 16 we show how an explicit value for this information can be calculated.

CHAPTER 14

Expected Value
and Decision Trees

Many managerial decisions involve some risk. For example, the decision regarding how many items to stock in a retail store must consider risk in the form of different probabilities for different levels of demand. The decision to drill a wildcat oil well involves risk in the form of the probability that an underground pool of oil actually exists on the site. The decision to build a new hospital involves risk in the form of different probabilities for different levels of demand for service. The decision to market a new product involves risk in the form of different probabilities for different costs of the production process and the raw materials, different probabilities for the price level that will be appropriate for the product, and different probabilities for the demand for the product at each price level. Situations that can be analyzed using the predictive models described in Part III all involve risk in some form.

Thus, it is essential that the manager be comfortable with the basic concepts of probability theory that provide a language for thinking about risks, and have an understanding of the alternate evaluation models that may be applied to decisions involving risk. In this chapter we focus on the use of *expected value* as an evaluation model for decisions involving a single criterion under risk. Expected value is commonly used as a decision criterion even though it does have some limitations, as we will see.

We can use the concept of expected value as an evaluation model even in rather complex situations. However, the probability calculations required to compute expected value become tedious. What we really need is a tool to aid us in structuring and visualizing these complex relationships more easily and a means of simplifying the probability calculations. The decision tree is just such a tool. It is one of the most practical and useful quantitative managerial aids. Decision trees are now routinely used in the analysis of major capital budgeting decisions, major marketing strategies, competitive bidding policies, and other significant decisions involving risk.

OBTAINING PROBABILITIES

In order to use expected value as a means of evaluating risky alternatives, we must assign probabilities to the various outcomes that might result from these alternatives. A natural question that arises immediately is the following: Where do these probabilities come from?

Loosely speaking, a probability is a measure of how likely something is to occur. This something that either does or does not occur is called an *event*. For example, an event might be a coin landing on heads after it is flipped or it might be a second oil embargo by the major oil producing nations before 1985. In either case, a probability number can be assigned to each event to express the likelihood of its occurrence. These probability numbers range from 0.0, which means that an event cannot occur, to 1.0, which means that it definitely will occur.

In the case of the flip of an ordinary coin, most of us would agree that the probability number that should be assigned to the event *heads* is 0.5. One interpretation of this number is that 0.5 is the proportion of the times that the coin will land on heads if it is flipped many times. But what about the probability number that should be assigned to the oil embargo? Will we all agree on this number? Can we observe the world many times from the present to 1985 and note in what proportion of these alternate futures an oil embargo actually occurs? No, of course not.

Subjective versus objective probabilities

The concept of probability is often introduced in terms of the notion of a *relative frequency of occurrence.* In our coin flipping example, the more times we flip the coin, the closer we would expect the *relative frequency* of heads to approach 0.5, the probability of the coin landing on heads on a single toss. The definition of the probability of an event as the relative frequency of the occurrence of that event in a long series of trials is *objective,* since it relates to a phenomenon we can observe in the real world.

Some probabilities obtained as a guide to managerial decisions might be considered objective since they can be estimated from historical frequency data. For example, suppose a loan officer in a bank is evaluating an application for a large consumer loan. She would like to obtain an estimate of the probability that the loan will be repaid. Examining the application, she finds that the individual has held his current job for two years and owns his own home. The bank has a long history of consumer loans, and checking the files, she finds that 574 individuals with characteristics similar to those of the applicant have been granted consumer loans in the past. Of this number, 563 actually repaid their loans. Therefore, the *relative frequency* of repayment has been 563/574 = 0.98 for similar cases, so she uses 0.98 as an estimate of the probability that this individual will repay his loan. Since this estimate is based on a calculation of relative frequency from historical data, the loan officer considers 0.98 to be an *objective* probability estimate.

Suppose you are shown a coin and asked to state the probability that it will land on heads if it is tossed. You might assume that it is a fair coin (one with an equal probability of landing heads or tails) and state that this probability is 0.5. In doing so, you would say that this is an objective probability. Now suppose you are shown a thumb tack and asked to state the probability that it will land point up if it is tossed. More than likely you have never conducted a long series of experiments of tossing thumb tacks and observing the relative frequency of a *point up*. Moreover, you may not have any information regarding such experiments by others, and you probably do not have the information and skills necessary to develop a predictive model based on the laws of physics. Nevertheless, you are forced to respond. After some reflection, suppose you say, "Well, I feel that the thumb tack is more likely to fall point up than point down. In fact, based on my understanding of how physical bodies behave when they hit the ground, I would say it is about twice as likely to land point up. Therefore, given the toss of a thumb tack, I would estimate the probability of a *point up* at about 0.67."

Since this estimate is not based on any historical experience or rigorous analysis, we would call 0.67 a *subjective probability*. In decisions faced by managers, subjective probabilities generally play a much more important role than objective probabilities. Organizations and their environments are in a constant state of flux, making the development of actual data on the relative frequency of important events a difficult task. In some cases, predictive models can be used to provide objective probability estimates. However, in most cases, the assignment of a probability to an event will be based on some individual's personal experience and understanding of the event, and it will thus be *subjective*. Further, it is only natural that two persons might make different probability assignments to the same event, since their experiences and understandings of the event may differ. Thus, the probability assigned to the occurrence of a second oil embargo before 1985 would be a *subjective probability*.

The decision maker is the person who has the responsibility for the decision to be made. It follows that the decision should be based on *that person's* preferences and expectations regarding future events. But he or she may choose to designate other persons as experts when it comes to estimating the probability of occurrence of a particular event, since the expert may have a better information base.

In a practical application, experts will be drawn from different fields. Estimates of market variables, such as sales volume, are likely to come from the marketing department; production variables, such as manufacturing costs, will be provided by accountants and industrial engineers. Some variables may even require experts from outside the organization.

We may be able to simply ask these experts to "think hard," and give us these probability assessments. However, if an individual experiences difficulty in expressing feelings about the likelihood of an event in the form of a probability number, then some techniques that simplify the process of assessing subjective probabilities can be used. Two of these techniques are described in the appendix to this chapter. In the following discussion, we will assume that the relevant probabilities have been determined objectively or that they are subjective estimates from the appropriate experts.

A SINGLE CRITERION UNDER RISK

We can now use these probability estimates to investigate the problem of making a decision on the basis of a single criterion under conditions of risk. One of several different outcomes will result from a decision, and the probability of each outcome can be specified. The simplest examples of decisions involving a single criterion and some risk regarding the outcome are provided by several gambles. Suppose you are offered the possibility of playing one of two games. In either game, you will flip a fair coin. In the first game (A_1) you win \$10 if the coin lands on heads, but lose \$2 if it lands on tails. In the second game (A_2), you win \$2 if heads occurs, but lose \$1 if the coin falls on tails.

What are the outcomes O_1 and O_2 for the two games? In this case, the outcomes depend on an external event, heads or tails on the coin flip, as well as on our decision. Thus, we may call the payoffs for the gambles conditional outcomes; that is, they are conditional on the result of the coin flip. We also know the probability of receiving each conditional outcome, given the choice of either alternative. This information may be summarized in tabular form as shown in Table 14-1.

Study Table 14-1 carefully; this approach to summarizing the information for a decision involving risk can be very helpful. Notice that there is a column in the table corresponding to each alternate decision and a row corresponding to each future event or future state of the world. The *conditional outcomes* in the table represent

Representation of Alternatives Involving Risk in a Payoff Table   TABLE 14-1

| | Alternatives | |
Events	Game 1 (A_1)	Game 2 (A_2)
Heads ($p_1 = 0.5$)	\$10	\$2
Tails ($p_2 = 0.5$)	−\$2	−\$1

the result of choosing an alternative, given each of these future states. This format for summarizing information is known as a *payoff table.*

Several alternate strategies have been suggested for choosing an alternative from a payoff table, especially when the probabilities of the events are not known precisely. A very conservative strategy, known as the *maximin* strategy, is to choose the alternative with the best conditional outcome even if the worst possible event occurs. Following this strategy, we would choose the second game A_2 since the worst possible conditional outcome from A_2, losing \$1, is better than the worst possible conditional outcome from the first game A_1, losing \$2. The maximin strategy is conservative almost to the point of paranoia, however, since it implicitly assumes that no matter which alternative you choose, the worst possible thing will happen with probability 1.0. Therefore, this approach should not be followed as a guide to rational decision making.

Another strategy, *maximax,* would appeal to the eternal optimist rather than to the pessimist. It states that we should always choose the alternative with the best conditional outcome given that the best possible event occurs. An individual following this approach would choose the first game A_1 with its best possible return of \$10 rather than A_2 with a best possible return of only \$2. Again, this strategy cannot be recommended as a basis for rational choice since it totally ignores the other conditional outcomes associated with each alternative.

Intuitively, it seems that an appropriate evaluation model should be based on *all* the information provided in a payoff table; that is, it should be based on all the conditional outcomes and their respective probabilities of occurrence. The concept of *expected value* satisfies this requirement.

Expected value

The *expected value* of an alternative is simply the sum of the possible conditional outcomes weighted by their respective probabilities of occurrence. When these conditional outcomes are dollars, this result is called the *expected monetary value* of an alternative. For example, the expected monetary value of the first gamble A_1 is

$$(0.5)(\$10.00) + (0.5)(-\$2.00) = \$5.00 - \$1.00 = \$4.00$$

Similarly, for A_2 we have

$$(0.5)(\$2.00) + (0.5)(-\$1.00) = \$1.00 - \$0.50 = \$0.50$$

The expected monetary value of an outcome has an intuitively appealing interpretation. If we were to accept the first gamble A_1 many times, we would expect to win $10 half of the time, and to lose $2 the other half of the time. The net result would be equivalent to winning the expected value of the gamble, $4, on each coin flip. Thus, $4 is what we expect to gain per flip if the coin is flipped many times. However, it is important to emphasize that this expected value is not one of the actual outcomes of the coin flip, which will be either "win $10" or "lose $2."

Example The Pacific Oil Company (POCO) is concerned with determining the appropriate strategy for developing its oil shale leases in Colorado and Canada. Oil shales are actually mined, much like coal, but liquid petroleum products can be extracted from the oil shales through a heating process. Given the current state of the art, it is not economical to obtain oil in this manner even with the recent increases in the price of crude oil. However, as the world's reserves of crude are depleted, it is likely that this price will eventually rise even further. In addition, improvements in techniques for extracting the petroleum from oil shales would reduce the costs of obtaining this resource. Thus, it appears that oil shales may eventually be an economical source of petroleum.

POCO has identified three basic strategies for developing their oil shale leases over the near term (the next 10 to 15 years). The choice of a near-term strategy will have little effect on long-run profits after this 10- to 15-year time horizon. The *first strategy* would concentrate exclusively on research work related to oil shale processing. Such a strategy would place POCO in a position to exploit these resources eventually, but they would be unable to respond significantly to any opportunities for actually selling petroleum products from oil shales over the near term. These opportunities might occur because of higher crude prices or as a result of an oil embargo from the major oil-producing nations. An embargo would ensure higher crude prices coupled with a high demand for domestically produced oil.

The *second strategy* would be to combine a research program with some actual development of production capabilities. At the current world prices of crude, the output from this process would not quite break even, but the loss would not be great. However, the company would be in a position to actually profit from increases in crude oil prices or from the excess demand for domestic oil created by an embargo.

The *third strategy* would be a crash program aimed at developing the capability to produce petroleum products from oil shales in quantity as quickly as possible. Such a venture would lose money at the current crude oil prices and only break even at higher prices. However, POCO would be in a position to make considerable profits if another embargo occurred.

If crude oil prices were to fall in the near term due to significant new discoveries of additional reserves, all three strategies would result in losses. However, such an event is considered unlikely by POCO.

How can POCO go about making a decision in this case? First, the manager may recognize that some insights into this problem can be gained by viewing it as a decision involving a single criterion (money) under risk. There are three alternatives, and each has a different conditional outcome, depending on the future price of oil or the occurrence of an oil embargo. Thus, the manager may construct a payoff table to display the relevant alternatives and the events that affect the outcomes from selecting each alternative. Such a display is shown in Table 14-2.

The construction of this table is an important exercise, since the manager now has identified the primary alternatives for consideration as well as the events that will determine the outcomes from these alternatives. It will generally be advantageous for the manager to discuss the assumptions with others at this point using this table as the basis for the discussion. In such a discussion, additional alternatives or other important events might be identified. For the sake of simplicity, we have used the events of lower prices, current prices, higher prices, and embargo. In an actual study, a manager might consider many more events. For example, all possible crude oil prices from $25 to $45 per barrel in increments of $1 might be considered. This would lead to sixteen possible events regarding prices plus the additional event of an embargo. Even that event could be stated in more detail by specifying embargos of various lengths of time.

The next task would be to predict the conditional outcome associated with each alternative and event combination. Such a task will be simplified if the manager has access to explicit predictive models such as those described in Chapter 2 or in Part III of this book. Finally, the manager must provide an estimate of the probability of the occurrence of each event. For our example, we suppose that the manager has preformed these tasks and now has the information in Table 14-3.

TABLE 14-2	Identification of Alternatives and Events		
Events	Research Only	Combined Research and Development	Crash
Lower prices			
Current prices			
Higher prices			
Embargo			

| Identification of Conditional Outcomes and Probabilities | | | TABLE 14-3 |

Events	Research Only	Combined Research and Development	Crash
Lower prices $(p = 0.1)$	-50	-150	-500
Current prices $(p = 0.3)$	0	-50	-200
Higher prices $(p = 0.4)$	50	100	0
Embargo $(p = 0.2)$	55	150	500

Note: Conditional outcomes given in millions of dollars.

The manager must identify some evaluation model in order to choose an alternative. In many practical situations, once the analysis has come this far, the solution will be obvious. However, in other cases the use of an explicit evaluation model may be helpful in making the final decision. The manager of POCO may apply the expected value evaluation model to these data and obtain the following results:

Research only: $(0.1)(-50) + (0.3)(0) + (0.4)(50) + (0.2)(55) = \quad 26$

Research and development:
$$(0.1)(-150) + (0.3)(-50) + (0.4)(100) + (0.2)(150) = \quad 40$$

Crash development: $(0.1)(-500) + (0.3)(-200) + (0.4)(0) + (0.2)(500) = -10$

Thus, on the basis of the expected monetary value of the alternatives, the choice of a combined research and development strategy would be preferable.

However, it would be naive to think that a manager facing a decision with such important consequences would stop the analysis at this point. For example, the conditional outcomes and the probabilities of the events are only estimates and may contain some errors. Thus, the manager would want to test the sensitivity of the decision to small changes in these estimates. For example, if the probability of current prices had been 0.5, and of higher prices 0.2, then alternative 1 (research only) would have been preferred. (Check this yourself.)

In order to use expected value as the basis for evaluating alternatives in more complicated situations, it is helpful to have a tool that aids in organizing the necessary information and in simplifying the probability calculations. For example, we have created a table for POCO with all the possible future events, or states of the environment, that will affect their decisions. In complicated situations, it may be very difficult to identify these events and their associated probabilities of occurrence, especially since some events and decisions may be dependent on others.

As an example of dependent outcomes, let us introduce a third alternative gamble, A_3, for a comparison against our original two. Suppose this gamble has the rules that follow. If the fair coin lands on heads, you flip it again. On the second flip if it lands on heads, you win $20; but if it lands on tails, you lose $5. If the fair coin lands on tails on the first flip, you flip a second coin that is "unfair." This coin is weighted and has only a 0.4 chance of landing on heads and a 0.6 chance of landing on tails. Nevertheless, if it falls on heads, you will win $5; but if it lands on tails, you lose $10. Which alternative is preferred using the expected value evaluation model?

Alternative A_3 has four conditional outcomes. That is, you either win $20, win $5, lose $5, or lose $10. However, the probability of receiving each of these outcomes is not immediately clear, so we must do some additional analysis. This analysis can be simplified by the use of a *decision tree.*

The idea of the decision tree is delightfully simple. Instead of compressing all the information regarding a complex decision into a payoff table, one draws a schematic representation of the problem that displays the information in a more easily understood fashion. In addition, the probability computations can be simplified through the use of this tree.

Growing the tree How can we schematically represent the problem of choosing from among the three alternate gambles? Very simply by showing each alternative as one of three possible branches on a tree, as illustrated in Figure 14-1.

The next step is to show the events that could occur in a similar fashion, as branch points on the tree with each branch representing the occurrence of a particular event. In the case of alternative A_3, the second toss of each coin can be represented with additional branches in the tree. Finally, the outcomes can be written on the branches where they are realized. A careful study of Figure 14-2 should clarify these concepts.

In the decision tree in Figure 14-2, we have indicated a decision point by a box, and a chance point where events are realized by a circle. There is no hard and fast rule requiring that the tree be drawn in this way. However, in more complex trees it may be helpful to distinguish decision points from chance points in some manner such as this. Further, we have shown the decisions, then the events, and finally the

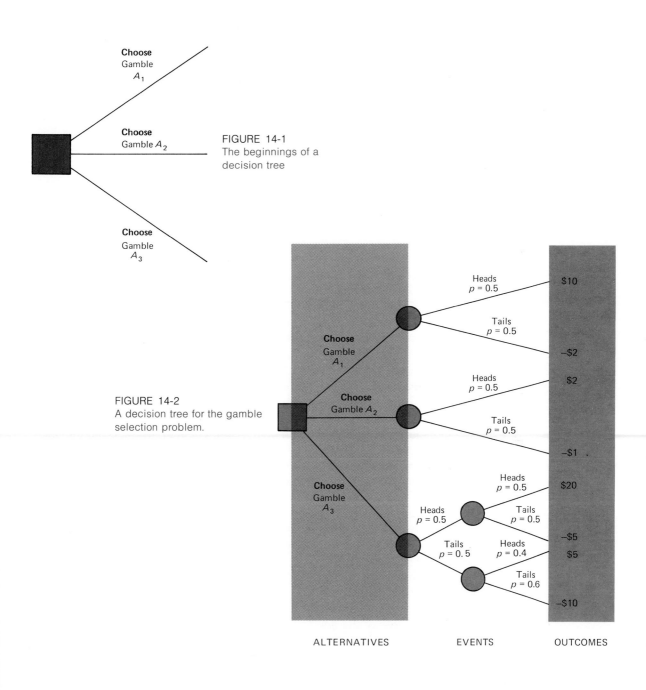

FIGURE 14-1
The beginnings of a
decision tree

FIGURE 14-2
A decision tree for the gamble
selection problem.

outcomes, in that order. In some practical situations, we will make an initial decision, and then have the opportunity to wait until some events have actually occurred before making another decision. This situation can also be represented in the decision tree format as we will see in a later example.

One important advantage of the decision tree is that a manager can quickly visualize the alternatives, the possible future events, and their outcomes. The logic and the assumptions that are the basis for a decision are laid out for easy scrutiny. Such trees can be useful in promoting a healthy discussion regarding the alternatives, the possible events, their probabilities, and the outcomes. In practical situations, a decision tree may be modified many times before general agreement can be reached that it accurately portrays the real problem. However, each revision of the tree will represent some additional learning about the nature of the problem.

Rolling back These advantages mean that merely drawing a decision tree can have a significant benefit for the manager. In addition, the calculation of the expected values associated with the alternate decisions can be simplified by studying each branch point, beginning at the tips of the branches. For example, let us begin by considering the one branch point for alternative A_1. We compute the expected value of this branch point by multiplying the probability on each branch by the outcome associated with the branch, and summing these results. For the branch point of A_1, we obtain $(0.5)(\$10) = \$5$ on the first branch, and $(0.5)(-\$2) = -\$1$ on the second branch. Summing these, we get \$4, and we replace the branch point on the tree by its expected value, as shown in Figure 14-3.

Since there was only one branch point for alternative A_1, the result is that the expected monetary value of the branch point is also equal to the expected monetary value of alternative A_1. A similar analysis would determine an expected monetary value of \$0.50 for alternative A_2.

Now consider alternative A_3, which includes a series of branches. Again, let us begin at the far right and compute the expected value of each chance branch. The first branch of alternative A_3 corresponds to the toss of the fair coin on the second trial and has an expected monetary value of $(0.5)(\$20) + (0.5)(-5) = \$7.50$. The other branch corresponds to the toss of the unfair coin and has an expected monetary value of $(0.4)(\$5) + (0.6)(-\$10) = -\$4$. Now—and this is important—we replace each of these two branches by their respective expected values. We then have the tree shown in Figure 14-4.

We now have only one chance branch point in the tree for alternative A_3, corresponding to the toss of the first coin. The two chance branch points corresponding to the toss of the second coin have been replaced by their respective expected values.

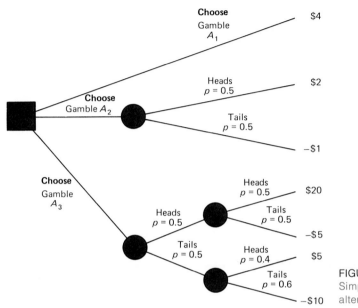

FIGURE 14-3
Simplifying the branch for
alternative A_1

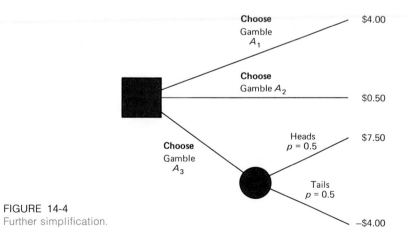

FIGURE 14-4
Further simplification.

FIGURE 14-5
The results of the
analysis; expected
monetary values for
three alternatives.

Finally, we compute the expected value of this remaining chance branch point in exactly the same manner as before, and obtain $(0.5)(\$7.50) + (0.5)(-\$4.00) = \$1.75$, the expected monetary value of alternative A_3. Thus, the use of the decision tree also simplifies the probability calculations that are required to obtain expected values.

This process of starting at the right and successively replacing each chance point by its associated expected value is referred to as *rolling back* the tree. Even when the tree gets very large and many different calculations are involved, they always remain simple in the sense that only expected values are calculated for each branch point. As a final result, the tree of Figure 14-2 has been reduced to Figure 14-5, and the desirability of alternative A_1, based on its expected monetary value, is apparent.

Rules for decision trees

The construction of a decision tree proceeds in a logical fashion, portraying decisions and events in chronological order. In a simple problem like the example of choosing among gambles, the task of drawing the tree is straightforward. As problems become more complex, and representative of those faced by managers in the real world, the task of drawing the tree may require some careful thought. The following rules may be helpful as a guide to the construction of more complicated decision trees:

1. *Determine a time horizon for the analysis.* The time horizon should be long enough so that the outcomes from all decisions will have been realized.

2. *Identify the immediate decision that must be made and the alternatives to be evaluated.* Remember that "do nothing," "delay," and "obtain more information" should always be considered to see if they are feasible alternatives.

3. *Identify all chance points whose events affect the outcome of the immediate decision.* In some decision trees chance points may actually precede the first decision, although they more commonly succeed it.

4. *Identify all future decisions that depend on the immediate decision and any intervening events.*

5. *Treating each future decision as the immediate decision, repeat rules 3 and 4 until all the chance points and decisions have been identified.*

All these rules must be implemented on the basis of good judgment and common sense. For example, the first rule says that we must choose a time horizon long enough so that all outcomes will have been realized. In many real-world situations, a decision made today may affect outcomes for many years into the future. Yet, for this approach to be a practical tool, we must choose an evaluation date so that we can total up the outcomes from the alternate decisions. Naturally, we wish to choose this time horizon so that all *significant* outcomes can be identified, and only overlook effects from the alternatives that are so inconsequential that they would not change our decision. Thus, implementing this rule may require careful thought by the individuals involved in the decision tree analysis.

In addition to these general rules, the logic of the decision tree requires that all alternatives at a decision point and all events at a chance point be *mutually exclusive* and *collectively exhaustive.* If the alternatives are mutually exclusive, then there is no overlap between them so only one will be chosen; if the events are mutually exclusive only one will occur. Collectively exhaustive means that all possible alternatives have been considered at each decision point, and that all possible events have been considered at each chance point. As a result of this requirement, exactly one alternative will be selected at each decision point and exactly one event will actually occur at each chance point.

These rules and concepts will now be illustrated in the context of a slightly more complex example.

A POCO example

Suppose we complicate the problem of the Pacific Oil Company (POCO) described earlier by recognizing the possibility of a breakthrough in oil shale processing technology resulting from the research efforts carried out either under the research-only strategy or under the combined research and development strategy. This breakthrough would significantly reduce the costs of extracting petroleum products from oil shales. POCO estimates the probability of such a breakthrough from following the research-only strategy at 0.4 and from following the combined research and development strategy at 0.3. Under the alternative of a crash development of production capabilities, the current state-of-the-art technology would be used.

If such a breakthrough occurred, POCO would have the option of changing strategies. If they had initially selected a research-only posture and a breakthrough occurred, they would begin either a combined research and development effort immediately or shift into the crash development program. If they were already in a combined research and development operating mode and the breakthrough occurred, they could continue in this mode or begin crash development. The conditional outcomes would depend on both the strategy selected after the breakthrough and the strategy the company selected initially. For example, the costs of shifting from a combined research and development strategy to a crash development program would be less than shifting from a research-only strategy to a crash development program. In addition, the news of the breakthrough in oil shale technology would reduce the probability of higher oil prices or an embargo, because the oil shales would provide additional supplies of petroleum products. The conditional outcomes for the different strategies and the probabilities of each event, *given* the occurrence of a breakthrough, are shown in Table 14-4.

TABLE 14-4   Conditional Outcomes and Probabilities, Given the Occurrence of a Breakthrough

| | Alternatives | | | |
Events	Change to Research and Development from Research Only	Change to Crash from Research Only	Continue Research and Development	Change to Crash from Research and Development
Lower prices ($p = 0.1$)	−100	−150	−50	−125
Current prices ($p = 0.5$)	0	−50	50	100
Higher prices ($p = 0.3$)	100	200	150	300
Embargo ($p = 0.1$)	120	300	200	500

Note: Conditional outcomes given in millions of dollars.

It would be difficult to organize all this information regarding POCO's options in a payoff table. However, the decision tree can be used to advantage here.

Growing the tree The time horizon for this analysis has been identified as the near term (the next 10 to 15 years). The conditional outcomes shown in Table 14-4 reflect net profits or losses that would be incurred over this time period.

The immediate decision to be made is the choice of an initial strategy—research only, a combined research and development activity, or a crash development program. We have assumed that one of these policies must be followed. The first set of branches in the decision tree will represent these three alternatives.

Next, we must identify the events that will affect the outcomes of the initial decision. In this problem, the occurrence of a breakthrough in oil shale processing technology is such an event, and it may be associated with either the research-only or the combined research and development strategies. There will be chance points on the tree representing the possibility of a breakthrough at the ends of the branches corresponding to the research-only and the combined research and development strategies.

Future decisions would follow a technological breakthrough, since it would be possible to change the initial oil shale development strategy. The outcomes from these future decisions would depend on the initial strategy and the occurrence of a breakthrough.

Finally, the outcomes of these future decisions would be affected by the price of crude oil or the occurrence of another oil embargo. Therefore, chance points with branches corresponding to three levels of prices and to an embargo will appear next in the tree.

Since we have not identified any additional decisions whose outcomes depend on these results, the construction of the tree can be terminated. The decision tree for this problem is shown in Figure 14-6. Notice that the alternatives at each decision point and the events at each chance point are mutually exclusive and collectively exhaustive. There are 28 different paths through the tree, and each leads to a distinct outcome.

Rolling back Now let us analyze this situation by rolling back the tree. First we replace the chance branch points at the far end of the tree by their respective expected values and obtain the tree shown in Figure 14-7. Notice that the results at the end of the no-breakthrough branches are the same expected monetary values that we computed previously for each strategy. At the end of the breakthrough branches, we

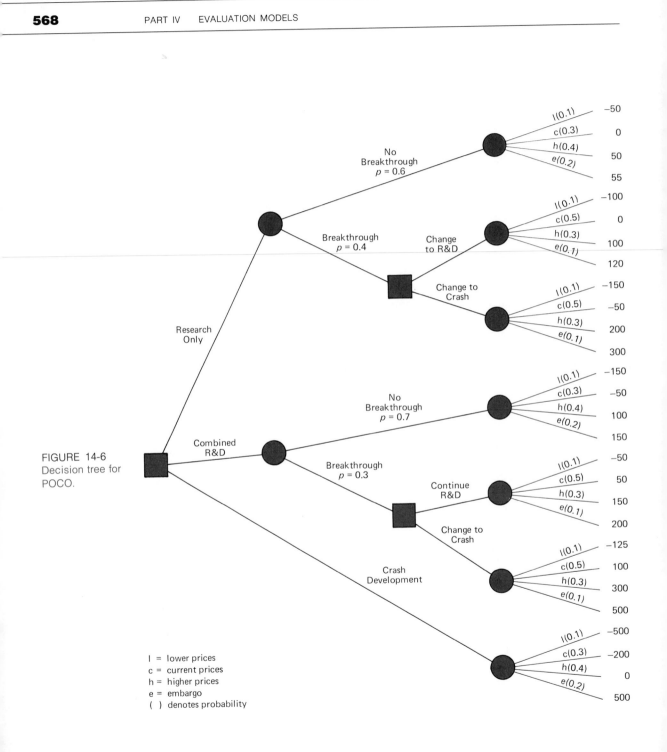

FIGURE 14-6
Decision tree for
POCO.

l = lower prices
c = current prices
h = higher prices
e = embargo
( ) denotes probability

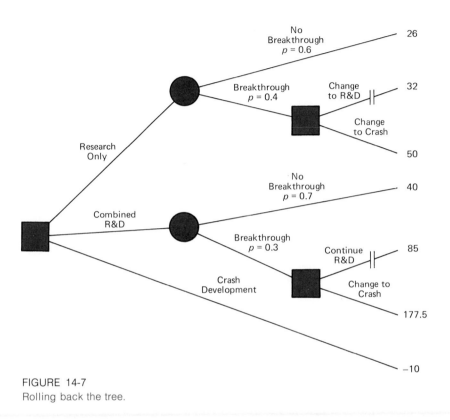

FIGURE 14-7
Rolling back the tree.

have the decision branches with an expected value for each strategy. On the basis of the expected value model, the best strategy in each case would be to begin a crash development program if a breakthrough occurs.

Branches broken by vertical parallel lines (see Figure 14-7) would be ignored if this decision point were reached. Thus, we can represent the decision point by the expected value of the best decision at that point, and continue to roll back the tree. That is, we would replace the decision point following the breakthrough from the research-only strategy by 50, the expected monetary value of the crash development strategy at that point. Similarly, the decision point following a breakthrough result-ing from an initial combined research and development effort would be replaced by the expected monetary value of the crash development effort, 177.5.

The expected monetary values of the initial research strategy and of the initial combined research and development strategy would be computed as

Research only: $(0.6)(26) + (0.4)(50) = 35.6$

Combined research and development: $(0.7)(40) + (0.3)(177.5) = 81.25$

Even allowing for the possibility of a breakthrough, the combined research and development strategy still remains the best alternative according to the expected value evaluation model. The tree reflecting these final calculations is shown in Figure 14-8.

At this point, there are several important observations to be made:

1. POCO does not expect to make $81.25 million from following an initial research and development strategy. They will actually receive one of eight different outcomes, which range from losing $150 million to making $500 million. *The expected value evaluation model provides a means of ranking alternatives under risky choice situations, but it does not give the actual result that will occur.*

2. Even though the problem was becoming complex because of the different strategies and events, the decision tree provided a useful means of organizing the relationships and the data.

3. The probability calculations at each step were straightforward and consisted of simple expected values.

As can be seen, a problem can become rather "messy" when there are several alternate strategies, some of which may depend on future events, and many different

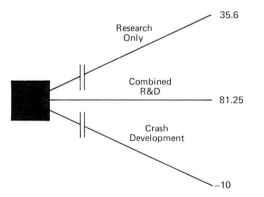

FIGURE 14-8
The results of the
analysis for POCO.

future events are possible. Nevertheless the decision tree can provide a practical, useful means of analyzing a problem.

WHAT SHOULD THE MANAGER KNOW?

The decision-making process with a single criterion under certainty is relatively straightforward. As long as all persons agree that more (or less) of the criterion is always better, the simple decision rule of finding the alternative that maximizes (or minimizes) this criterion obviously holds. Thus, the real task is in predicting the outcomes associated with each alternative.

However, when risk is involved in the problem, there is no longer a single outcome associated with each alternative. Instead, the "outcome" consists of several conditional outcomes, each with an associated probability of occurrence. In order to rank alternatives, some means of transforming these conditional outcomes and probabilities into a single number may be helpful. One evaluation model that performs this task is the expected monetary value model, which weights each conditional monetary outcome by its associated probability of occurrence.

The interpretation of the expected monetary value has an intuitive appeal. Basically, this value represents what the manager would receive, *on the average,* if the decision were made many times. But we continually emphasize that the expected monetary value does not represent the actual profit or loss that the company will obtain based on its decision. Rather, one of the conditional outcomes will actually occur (if all the predictions are accurate). This point is important and should not be overlooked by a manager. An alternative with a high expected monetary value may have some small probability of leading to a disastrous result, and *such a result could actually occur.* If it does, it does not mean that the original decision was bad, but merely that an unfortunate conditional outcome occurred. All that the manager can hope for in situations involving risk is to keep the odds in his favor. However, if the manager is really averse to making a decision involving even a small probability of an undesirable outcome, he or she can compensate with another evaluation model, as we will see in Chapter 15.

A key characteristic of problems that should be analyzed by using the expected value evaluation model is that the decisions are made repetitively. An example of such a problem would be the determination of the appropriate daily inventory level when probabilities can be assigned to various levels of demand. On any given day, the company might incur a relatively high cost from leaving too much or too little in inventory. But over a longer time horizon, the actual inventory costs will approximate their expected monetary value. Routine capital budgeting decisions that do not require a high proportion of the company's resources are also a natural area for the use of expected values as a guide to decision making.

The results from the calculation of expected values should always be subjected to an analysis of their sensitivity to the predictions of the conditional outcomes and the probabilities of the events. One approach is to deliberately bias the outcomes and probabilities against the best alternative from the initial analysis, then recompute the expected values. If this alternative remains the most desirable even when this deliberate bias is introduced, the manager's confidence should be improved that the best alternative has been identified. However, if the rankings of the alternatives are changed drastically by this second analysis, the manager may be well advised to spend more time and effort in obtaining better predictions. The value of additional information can be used as a guide in these efforts, as we demonstrate in Chapter 16.

As problems under risk become more complicated, it becomes difficult to organize the information and to maintain an understanding of the logical relationships among the possible decision alternatives and the chance events. One important aid in dealing with these problems is the decision tree.

The central issues related to the use of quantitative aids such as the decision tree are the following:

1. What are the characteristics of problems that should be analyzed with decision trees?
2. How should the decision tree be formulated?
3. What are the information requirements of the procedure?
4. How are the computations performed?
5. How should the results of the analysis be interpreted?

And, finally,

6. What are the advantages of using decision trees?
7. What are the possible problems and pitfalls that must be overcome in practice?

Let us briefly consider each of these issues.

Problem characteristics

Decision trees are especially helpful in analyzing decisions that involve risk and substantial costs or potential rewards. In problems of this type, simply identifying the alternate strategies and the possible events that may influence the outcomes, and gaining some appreciation of the probabilities of the occurrence of these events may be the most important part of the analysis. Certainly these are steps that successful managers must perform in any case, even if they have never heard of decision trees. However, the manager who has a knowledge of this technology has a means of organizing thoughts and improving the understanding of a complex problem.

Several examples of the actual use of decision trees have been reported. Notable examples are the following:

"Pillsbury switched from a box to a bag for one of its grocery products — and even scrapped plans to undertake an extensive market test — when the analysis indicated high expected profitability from this strategy. The switch was successful."

"General Electric decided to raise prices, rather than increase manufacturing capacity, for a mature industrial product. As part of the strategy, research and development expenditures were increased twenty fold, and the decision resulted in a highly profitable sales of some $20 million a year."

"Ford Tractor chose to introduce a new model into a regional market suffering from competitive inroads, rather than reduce prices. The strategy worked." (Raiffa, 1974)

Notice that these applications tend to be in the area of determining a marketing strategy for products. This fact is not surprising, since such situations often involve risk, and the potential for significant costs or profits.

Other areas that offer potential applications are decisions to expand production or service capacities, the determination of competitive bidding strategies, and the analysis of major government policies such as the decision to seed hurricanes (for an example see Howard, Matheson, and North [1972]). Thus, the manager should be sensitive to problems with these characteristics in order to take advantage of this useful decision-making aid.

Formulation

The issue of who should actually formulate the decision tree is an important one. In extremely complicated problems involving perhaps millions of dollars, the manager may wish to call on an analytic staff or on outside consultants for assistance. However, the *manager* should be involved in the formulation of the decision tree in order to ensure that he or she understands the assumptions made by the analysts and to ensure that the analysts actually understand the real problem. It is important that the manager have confidence in the analysis, which is unlikely to happen without personal involvement.

One approach would be for the manager to actually sketch out the first decision tree in gross terms. The major alternatives and events would be shown, perhaps with rough estimates of probabilities, in order to obtain some idea of the important aspects of the problem. Using only a crude analysis of this sort, that would be carried out "on the back of an envelope" in only an hour or so, the manager might be able to eliminate some alternatives as being undesirable, thus reducing the complexity of the problem. The rough tree consisting of the remaining alternatives could then be presented to the professional analysts as a takeoff point for a more detailed analysis.

Information requirements

The information requirements for a decision tree are basically the same as those for the manager who does not use the decision tree. That is, managers must obtain the following:

1. The alternate decisions and their relationships to possible future events.
2. The outcomes of selecting each alternative, given the occurrence of each future event.
3. The probabilities of the occurrence of each event.

In a complex, real-world problem, the decision tree could grow to enormous proportions and require many bits of information. However, a preliminary analysis can be used to eliminate some alternatives from a detailed consideration and to determine the sensitivity of the results to various future events, so that the number of chance branches can be held down. This process requires judgment on the part of the analyst, and it is another reason for encouraging the active participation of the manager in the initial formulation and analysis of the problem. The eventual information requirements can be reduced significantly by this process. The appendix to this chapter describes how estimates of the probabilities can be obtained.

Computations

Since the computation of expected values is a straightforward task, there is no reason why managers cannot perform their own analyses of decision trees that are of reasonable size. It would be especially desirable to do so in the initial phase of the analysis of a large, complex problem, or perhaps might be sufficient in the case of a problem where the potential losses or rewards do not justify a more elaborate analysis. Thus, the decision tree is one practical analytical aid for which the modern manager should actually be able to perform the required simple computations.

However, in larger, complex problems, the information regarding the decision tree can be input into specially programmed computer routines. Use of a computer would be especially helpful in checking the sensitivity of the solution to various estimates, since the results from changes in the information can be obtained instantly.

Interpretation of results

We continually emphasize that the expected monetary value does not represent the actual profit or loss that the company will obtain as a result of its decision. Instead, one of the conditional outcomes will actually occur (if all the predictions are accurate).

The expected value evaluation model is appropriate for repetitive decisions or for decisions in which the stakes are not high. For the nonrepetitive problems involving substantial costs or potential rewards, the expected value calculations may provide a means of discarding obviously inferior alternatives at an early stage in the analysis. However, it may be necessary to resort to an alternate evaluation model, expected utility, in order to make the final decision. As we shall see in Chapter 15, the decision tree format can also be used to simplify calculations with this alternate evaluation model.

Advantages of decision trees

The crucial question for the practicing manager is whether the use of a decision-making aid is really worth the effort. Will the actual decision be improved over the decision the manager would make based on his intuition? This question is difficult to answer, since the manager seldom has the opportunity to make the same decision both with and without a decision-making aid.

Certainly, we can point to numerous advantages of using decision trees. They force the manager to organize thoughts and to specify alternatives and the important events that will affect the outcomes of these alternatives. Further, the decision tree can be scrutinized by others and used as the basis for a discussion regarding the alternatives and the assumptions that have been made by the manager. This discussion can be carried on by managers and their advisers or by a committee. Without being overly dramatic, we can say that the decision tree structure provides a useful *language* for discussing complex problems among those who understand the technology. Even when the actual computation of expected values is not carried out, the construction of the decision tree with outcomes described in qualitative terms can be an extremely useful exercise.

Disadvantages of decision trees

The only objection to the use of decision trees is that problems in the real world are so complex that the tree expands beyond the limits of human comprehension. There are so many uncertain events and so many alternatives that the decision tree quickly becomes a "bushy mess." However, at this point the involvement of the manager in the preliminary analysis of the problem is required to quickly eliminate some alternatives and to aid in identifying the uncertain events that will have a major impact on the decision. There are no hard and fast rules for this pruning of the decision tree; it requires the judgment and, yes, perhaps the intuition of the manager. The final result of this combination of analysis and intuition would seem to provide the basis for improved decisions that the responsible manager is seeking.

APPENDIX TO CHAPTER 14
ASSESSING SUBJECTIVE PROBABILITIES

Reconsidering the problem of POCO offers a good context for discussing assessment of subjective probabilities. An important factor in determining POCO's final profit (or loss) for its oil shale development strategy is the near-term price of crude oil. Suppose an analyst wishes to obtain an estimate of this price. Further, we will assume that POCO has no formal predictive models to provide these estimates (although many oil companies actually do have such models). Therefore, the analyst identifies the person in the organization with the most knowledge in this area, perhaps the chief purchasing agent. Rather than simply asking for the probability of crude selling at different prices, the analyst tries to assist the purchasing agent in determining these estimates. First, the analyst ensures that there is no ambiguity in his questions. He might tell the purchasing agent that he is looking for the agent's estimate of the probability of the various prices of crude oil five years hence, for example, under the assumption that *there is no oil embargo*. Further, the purchasing agent is to assume that no breakthrough in oil shale processing technology will occur. Then the analyst begins a dialogue.

The analyst may wish to simply describe an event to the purchasing agent and ask for the estimate of a probability. He may ask, "What is the probability that crude oil prices will be $30 per barrel or lower five years from now, given that the current price is $31 per barrel?" The purchasing agent may find it difficult to respond to that question. He might say, for example, that the "chances are slim," but that he cannot be more precise.

The probability wheel

As an aid to the purchasing agent, the analyst might use a probability wheel — a disk with two sectors, one light and the other dark. A pointer is spun in the center of the disk and lands on either the light or the dark zone (see Figure 14-9). The dark zone can be adjusted to any size.

The analyst can begin with approximately one-half of the disk dark. He can ask the purchasing agent whether he would prefer to bet on the price of oil being $30 per barrel or below in five years, or on the spinner falling on the dark portion of the disk. Suppose the purchasing agent says he thinks the spinner is more likely to fall on the dark portion; the analyst then reduces the dark portion to one-fourth of the disk. Again the purchasing agent would prefer to bet on the spinner hitting the dark sector, so the analyst reduces it to one-eighth (0.125) of the disk. This time, suppose the purchasing agent wavers, and says, "Well, I would not really prefer betting on the spinner now. On the other hand, I would not really like to bet that prices will be $30 per barrel or lower. I guess I would be roughly indifferent between the two bets." Thus, the analyst would assign the probability of prices falling below $30 per barrel a value of 0.125. This dialogue is summarized in Table 14-5.

Next, suppose the analyst asks the purchasing agent about the probability that prices will be higher than $32, and finds that he is indifferent between bets immediately when one-half of the disk is dark. Thus, since the probability of prices falling below $30 is 0.125, and the probability of their rising above $32 is 0.5, the probability that they will be between $30 and $32 is $1.0 - (0.125 + 0.5) = 0.375$. As a check, the analyst should cover 0.375 of the disk with the dark sector and ask the purchasing agent if he would be indifferent between betting that prices are actually between $30

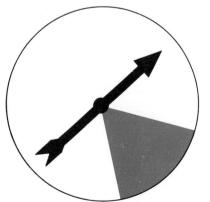

FIGURE 14-9
A probability
wheel.

TABLE 14-5

Summary of Elicitation of Subjective Probabilities with the
Probability Wheel

Situation: You may bet that the price of oil will be $30 or
less in five years or that the spinner will fall on the
dark portion of the probability wheel.

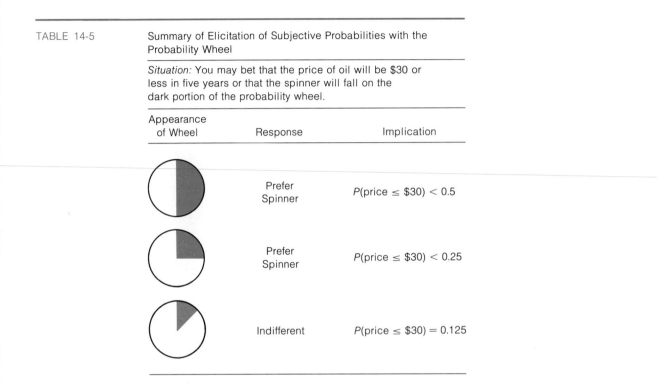

Appearance of Wheel	Response	Implication
	Prefer Spinner	$P(\text{price} \leq \$30) < 0.5$
	Prefer Spinner	$P(\text{price} \leq \$30) < 0.25$
	Indifferent	$P(\text{price} \leq \$30) = 0.125$

and $32 or that the spinner will fall on the dark sector. If the purchasing agent is not indifferent to this bet, the analyst should return to the first series of questions to discover the source of this inconsistency.

Now, in order to obtain additional detail, the analyst might continue this dialogue using the probability wheel as an aid and find the following estimates:

Price Range	Probability
$26.00–27.99	.010
28.00–29.99	.110
30.00–31.99	.375
32.00–33.99	.360
34.00–35.99	.135
36.00–37.99	.010
	1.000

If the initial set of probability estimates do not sum to 1.00, but they are "close" (say, within *plus or minus* 0.05), the analyst may wish to normalize them by simply dividing each estimate by the initial sum. Otherwise, he will have to interact further with the purchasing agent.

Successive subdivisions

As an alternative to the use of a probability wheel, the analyst may use the method of successive subdivisions to aid the purchasing agent in reaching his conclusion. He would say to the purchasing agent, "State the price of crude oil so that you would be indifferent between betting that the actual price will be higher than your stated price and betting that it will be lower." If the purchasing agent still finds it hard to respond, the analyst may suggest a price. He might ask if the purchasing agent would bet that prices will be higher than the current price of $30 per barrel. If so, he might increase the price to $32 per barrel and ask again. Suppose this time the purchasing agent is indifferent between betting that the actual price will be less than $32 or greater than $32. Then the probability of each is 0.5.

Now the analyst chooses a higher price, say $34, and asks if the purchasing agent would be willing to bet that the actual price will be between $32 and $34 or greater than $34. Suppose the purchasing agent says he would bet on the actual price being between $32 and $34. Next, the analyst asks a similar question regarding a price between $32 and $33 or greater than $33. This time, the purchasing agent would prefer betting on "greater than $33." This dialogue continues until the purchasing agent is indifferent between a bet on the actual price falling between $32 and $33.25 and the actual price being greater than $33.25. Since the probability that the price will be greater than $32 is 0.5, and since this indifference implies that the probability that the price will be between $32 and $33.25 is equal to the probability that the price will be greater than $33.25, the analyst estimates the probability of each of these latter two events at 0.5 divided by 2, which is 0.25.

Similarly, the analyst might find the probability that the price will be between $30.75 and $32 is 0.25, and the probability that it will be lower than $30.75 is also 0.25. Now, the analyst could use the same approach to subdivide each of these four intervals, if he desires.

When the probability wheel is used, the interval is specified and the objective is to determine the probability that the actual price will fall within this interval. The probability wheel helps the respondent to conceptualize the meaning of probabilities other than 0.0, 0.5, and 1.0. When such a device is unavailable, the respondent may find it very difficult to relate to probability statements. The method of successive subdivisions has the advantage of using only the probability 0.5, which most persons can conceptualize by relating it to the flip of a fair coin.

Use of probability estimates

The amount of detail required by the analyst will depend on how the results are to be used. In this example, suppose the analyst realizes that the results are to be used in a decision tree. He may choose to use only three price estimates to reduce the number of chance branches.

The first estimate might correspond roughly to the current price, $31 per barrel. The purchasing agent estimates that the probability of the actual price being between $30 and $32 in five years is 0.375. Thus, the analyst might take the current price of $31 as *representative* of this price range and calculate the profit (or loss) from each alternate oil shale development strategy at that price of crude oil. The probability of these outcomes, *given no embargo*, would be roughly 0.375.

Next, the analyst has the estimate that the probability that prices will be lower than $30 per barrel (lower prices) is 0.125. Again, he may choose a representative price, say $29 per barrel, and compute the outcome from each alternative. Finally, the probability of a price higher than $32 (higher prices) is 0.5, so he might compute the outcomes of the alternatives at a representative price such as $33.25.

These probabilities are based on the assumption that no oil embargo will occur. Now suppose the analyst consults with another "expert," perhaps an outside consultant, and obtains the estimate that the probability of an embargo is 0.2. He can then use the formula for a joint probability (see Appendix A) to modify his probability estimates for his prices as follows:

P(lower prices and no embargo) =
$\quad\quad P$(no embargo) $\times P$(lower prices|no embargo) $\quad = (0.8)(0.125) = 0.1$

P(current prices and no embargo) =
$\quad\quad P$(no embargo) $\times P$(current prices|no embargo) $= (0.8)(0.375) = 0.3$

P(higher prices and no embargo) =
$\quad\quad P$(no embargo) $\times P$(higher prices|no embargo) $\quad = (0.8)(0.5) \quad\quad = 0.4$

These are the probabilities used in the POCO example (see Table 14-3).

CHECK YOUR UNDERSTANDING*

(Exercises 1 through 3 are based on concepts presented in the Part IV introduction.)

1. When a decision is made on the basis of a single criterion under certainty, why is it often very easy to identify an acceptable evaluation model?

2. Give an example of a decision involving a single criterion under certainty for which it is *not* appropriate to simply maximize or minimize the criterion.

3. Suppose we have five alternatives under consideration that result in the following monetary returns with certainty:

Alternative	Outcome
A_1	$ 20
A_2	$100
A_3	$ 10
A_4	$ 50
A_5	$ 70

   a. Using the obvious evaluation model of maximizing returns $[U(O_i) = O_i]$, rank these alternatives.

   b. Rank these same alternatives using the following evaluation models:
      (1) $U(O_i) = (2)(O_i - 300)$
      (2) $U(O_i) = (3)(O_i^2)$
      (3) $U(O_i) = O_i - (0.1)(O_i^2)$
      (4) $U(O_i) = \$1000/O_i$

   c. Which of these evaluation models give the same rankings of the alternatives as $U(O_i) = O_i$?

   d. Would your answer to (c) change if a sixth alternative A_6 with a certain outcome of $-\$20$ (a loss) were introduced?

4. For each of the following probabilities, state whether it is objective or subjective. If it is objective, identify the data or basis for its determination. If it is subjective, identify the "expert" who should assess it.

   a. The probability of rain tomorrow.

   b. The probability of drawing an ace from a well-shuffled deck of playing cards.

---

* Exercises that require an understanding of the materials in the appendix are introduced with the notation (Appendix).

c. The probability that the demand for a company's product will increase by at least 5 percent next year.

d. The probability that the demand for a company's product will increase by at least 5 percent next year, given that it has increased by at least 5 percent in each of the past 10 years.

e. The probability that a light bulb will "burn out" after 100 hours of use.

5. Which of the following sets of events are mutually exclusive? Which are collectively exhaustive?

a. (1) an oil embargo before 1985; (2) an oil embargo before 1990; (3) an oil embargo before 2000.

b. (1) an oil embargo before 1985; (2) an oil embargo between 1985 and 1990; (3) an oil embargo after 1990.

c. (1) price rise of less than $0.05; (2) price rise of between $0.05 and $0.10; (3) price rise of between $0.10 and $0.20.

d. (1) price rise for product A of less than $0.05; (2) price rise for product A of $0.05 or more; (3) an increase in the demand for product A of 10 percent or more.

6. Explain the difference between a good decision and a good outcome. Should managers be evaluated on the basis of their decisions or on the basis of the outcomes that result from their decisions? Discuss.

7. What is the role of the manager in a decision tree analysis of a substantive, real-world problem?

8. Which of the three oil shale development strategies would be preferred for POCO if the probabilities in Table 14-3 were revised as follows:

	Lower Prices	Current Prices	Higher Prices	Embargo
a.	0.1	0.4	0.3	0.2
b.	0.0	0.3	0.4	0.3
c.	0.0	0.2	0.5	0.3

Calculate the expected monetary values of the alternatives using the data in Table 14-3 to determine your answers. What are the implications of this analysis?

9. (Appendix) Construct "pies" of different sizes from stiff paper that can be pinned to the center of a disk also made from stiff paper. By interchanging the pies, the disk can be used as a probability wheel. Obtain the cooperation of a friend. Using this crude probability wheel, determine his or her subjective probability

estimates of the retail price of one gallon of gasoline two years from now. Repeat the experiment using the approach of successive subdivisions. Which approach did your friend prefer?

10. (Appendix) Through self-interrogation, determine your own subjective probability estimates of the retail price of one gallon of gasoline in two years. Use a crude probability wheel, which may be constructed as described in Exercise 9. Repeat the experiment using the method of successive subdivisions. Which approach do you prefer?

SHORT CASES

A small grocery store must decide how many loaves of bread to stock each day. The store must pay $0.50 per loaf, and each loaf sells for $1 when it is fresh (deliveries are made each morning). However, if it is not sold on the day it is delivered, it must be sold for $0.25 per loaf as day-old bread. The demand for the bread varies between six and eight loaves per day. The probabilities for the different levels of demand are as follows: CASE 14-1

Level of Demand	Probability
6	0.25
7	0.60
8	0.15

a. Compute the profit if six loaves are stocked and all six are sold when fresh.
b. Compute the profit if eight loaves are stocked and only six are sold on the day they are delivered.
c. Construct a table similar to Table 14-3 for which the alternatives are "stock 6," "stock 7," and "stock 8," and the events are demands of 6, 7, and 8 loaves. Compute the conditional outcomes (see a and b above) and place them in the table.
d. What is the best decision according to the expected monetary value evaluation model? Discuss whether or not this evaluation model is appropriate for this decision.

POCO owns a lease that will allow it to explore for oil on the Aleutian Islands just west of Alaska. They have been offered $80 million for this lease by the Essex Oil Company. The three possible results of the exploration are shown as follows, along with their associated probabilities and monetary returns. The returns are based on the most recent estimates by the POCO engineers.   CASE 14-2

Result	Probability	Monetary Outcome (millions of $)
Dry well	0.4	−100
Discovery of oil reserves of moderate size	0.4	200
Discovery of oil reserves of major proportions	0.2	300

a. Draw a decision tree and compute the expected monetary value of the decision to explore the islands. Should POCO sell the lease to Essex?

b. Do you think that expected monetary value is an appropriate criterion for a decision such as this one? Would you use the results of this analysis if you were a manager at POCO? Discuss.

CASE 14-3   The objective of the U.S. Hurricane Modification Program is to determine whether any hurricane threatening the U.S. coast should be seeded with silver iodide crystals in an attempt to mitigate its destructive effects. To analyze this question, probability estimates were obtained concerning the likely impacts of seeding a hurricane on the maximum sustained surface wind speed. A predictive model was then developed to estimate the property damage that results from hurricanes with various wind speeds. As a result of the analysis, the following estimates were obtained for seeding and not seeding a hurricane.

Probability (Hurricane Seeded)	Probability (Hurricane Not Seeded)	Change in Maximum Sustained Wind (percent)	Property Damage Loss (millions of $)
0.038	0.054	+32	335.8
0.143	0.206	+16	191.1
0.392	0.480	0	100.0
0.255	0.206	−16	46.7
0.172	0.054	−34	16.3

The cost of seeding a hurricane is relatively inexpensive, only $0.25 million.

a. Compute the expected monetary values of the decisions to seed a hurricane and not to seed a hurricane.

b. As stated by Howard, Matheson, and North [1972], "The results of extensive sensitivity analysis may be summarized as follows: The expected loss in terms of property damage appears to be about 20 percent less if the hurricane is seeded. Varying the assumptions of the analysis causes this reduction to vary between 10 and 30 percent but does not change the preferred alternative."

Place yourself in the position of a government administrator responsible for making the hurricane seeding decision. Why might you recommend against seeding, despite the results of this analysis? In other words, what considerations may have been left out of the analysis? Discuss.

Assume that you are president of a company that manufactures electrical relays.* The position   CASE 14-4
in which you find yourself requires some interrelated decisions involving a labor dispute and bids on two government contracts.

The union has set a strike deadline of midnight tonight if you do not accept their demand for a 10 percent wage increase. You are certain that the union will carry out its threat and the resulting strike will cost you about $300,000. If you give in to the demand, the total cost per relay unit will increase to $4.05, compared to the present cost of $3.80 per unit. On the other hand, you feel certain that the union will be defeated if it strikes, and therefore your present costs will remain fixed for the coming year. You must decide whether to give the employees the wage increase and suffer the higher cost of production or to hold to the present wage scale and suffer the resulting strike loss.

The labor dispute is complicated by the fact that the government is letting a large contract for 10 million relay units within the next month and *you will not be in a position to bid on this contract if your employees go on strike.* However, even if you give in to the union demands and avert a strike, you still are not assured of getting the contract unless you can underbid your competitors. Possible bids and resulting probabilities of winning the contract are estimated as follows:

Bid (price per unit)	Probability of Getting Contract
$4.15	0.3
$4.12	0.5
$4.10	0.6
$4.07	0.8

Fortunately a second major government contract is anticipated in the latter part of the year if you do not receive the lucrative contract mentioned previously. (Because of production limitations it will not be possible for you to assume both contracts, should you receive the first contract.) To be in a position to bid on the second contract, it is necessary at this time for you to secure adequate financial backing to guarantee the government that you can provide certain expensive testing equipment.

* From J. B. Boulden, and E. S. Buffa, "The Strategy of Interdependent Decisions," *California Management Review,* Vol. I, No. 4, pp. 94–100, 1959.

The larger the test facilities you can provide, the more likely it is that you will be awarded the contract. The anticipated net profit for this second project is $3 million if your unit cost is $4.05 and $4 million if your unit cost is $3.80. These figures do not include the large investment in special test equipment that must be written off over the life of the contract. This investment is actually made only if you are awarded the contract. The investment costs and the probabilities of winning the second contract are shown below:

Investment	Probability of Winning Contract
$2,000,000	0.2
$2,400,000	0.4
$2,600,000	0.5
$2,900,000	0.6

a. Draw a decision tree for analyzing this problem.
b. On the basis of its expected monetary value, should you accept the union's demand for a 10 percent wage increase?
c. If your answer to b above was to grant the pay increase and avert the strike, what should you bid on the first contract?
d. How much should you invest in test facilities if you bid on the second contract?

CASE 14-5   Mid-Valley Manufacturers has the opportunity to bid on a government contract for 100,000 high pressure valves to be used in the hydraulic systems of aircraft. They estimate that these valves could be manufactured by their existing equipment at a cost of $12.50 per unit. However, one of their engineers has suggested a new process for manufacturing the valves.

The unit cost estimates for the new process are only $7.50 if all goes exceptionally well. If there are minor complications, the cost estimate is $9.50 per unit; but if major complications arise, the costs would be prohibitive, so they would have to return to the old process. The engineers estimate the probability of minor complications at 0.5, the probability of major complications at 0.2, and the probability of no complications at 0.3. The investment required for the new process is $100,000, which would not be recoverable even if the process is a failure.

The company must make its bid on the contract before the new process can be tested. The various bids under consideration and the estimated probability of obtaining the contract associated with each bid are shown below:

Bid	Probability of Receiving Contract
$17	0.2
14	0.6
12	0.9

Construct a decision tree to analyze this problem by calculating the expected monetary value of the alternatives. What should Mid-Valley bid? Which process should they use if they get the contract? Does the choice of the process depend on the bid price?

A chemical company must decide whether to build a small plant or a large one to manufacture a new product with an expected market life of 10 years.* If the company decides to build a small plant now, then finds demand high during the initial period, it can choose to expand its plant after two years.

CASE 14-6

Marketing estimates indicate a probability of 0.6 of a large market in the long run, and a 0.4 probability of a long-term low demand, developing initially as follows:

Demand Pattern	Probability
Initially high demand, sustained high	0.60
Initially high demand (yrs. 1–2), long-term low (yrs. 3–10)	0.10
Initially low demand, long-term low	0.30
Initially low demand, long-term high	0.0

Estimates of annual income are made under the assumptions of each alternative demand pattern.

(1) A large plant with high volume would yield $1,000,000 annually in cash flow.

(2) A large plant with low volume would yield only $100,000 because of high fixed costs and inefficiencies.

(3) A small plant with low demand would be economical and would yield annual cash income of $400,000.

(4) A small plant, during an initial period of high demand, would yield $450,000 per year, but this yield would drop to $300,000 yearly in the long run because of competition. (The market would be larger than under alternative 3, but would be divided up among more competitors.)

(5) If the small plant were expanded to meet sustained high demand, it would yield $700,000 cash flow annually (less efficient than a large plant built initially).

(6) If the small plant were expanded but high demand were not sustained, estimated annual cash flow would be $50,000.

* From J. F. Magee, "Decision Trees for Decision Making," *Harvard Business Review*, July–August 1964.

It is estimated further that a large plant would cost $3 million to put into operation, a small plant would cost $1.3 million, and the expansion of the small plant would cost an additional $2.2 million.

a. Draw a decision tree to structure the problem.

b. What should the initial decision of the company be on the basis of its expected monetary value?

c. If you were the manager of this company, what additional information would you wish to obtain before making your decision? Discuss.

CASE 14-7   A large manufacturer of heavy capital equipment operates on a multinational basis.* The firm's treasurer was concerned about a large, recently completed sale of equipment to a French firm. The balance on the terms of this sale was 25 million francs (about $5 million at the current exchange rate), which was receivable in a little less than 30 days. Recent events in France had shaken people's confidence in the franc. The current exchange rate for the franc was 0.2011 U.S. dollars, just above the lower rate of $0.2010 guaranteed by the French government. In addition, the franc could be bought or sold "forward" 30 days at only $0.2000, which reflected the possibility that it would be devalued.

If a devaluation did occur, the firm would lose a great deal of money. For example, a 20 percent devaluation would result in a loss of about $1 million.

The treasurer has two basic alternatives. He can hedge against devaluation by selling forward the 25 million francs for a sure return of $5 million. If he does *not* hedge, he must consider the risk associated with his decision. He estimates that there is only one chance in twenty that a new government will be formed within 30 days. If the old government remains in power, he is certain that the franc will *not* be devalued, and the return will be $5,025,000. However, if a new government is formed, he estimates that there is a 0.5 chance of an immediate devaluation.

Given a devaluation, the treasurer estimates that the possible range is from 5 to 20 percent, so he assigns returns of $4,750,000; $4,500,000; $4,250,000; and $4,000,000 equal probabilities of 0.25.

a. Construct a decision tree and analyze this problem. What is the better decision on the basis of its expected monetary value?

b. The argument has been made that a large company should *never* hedge against exchange devaluations because the market for currency futures is "efficient." Thus, it represents the expectations of persons involved in the market who obviously know more than a corporate treasurer (see Wheelwright [1975]). Would you support this argument or prefer the use of the decision tree? Discuss.

* From S. C. Wheelwright, "Applying Decision Theory to Improve Corporate Management of Currency-Exchange Risks," *California Management Review,* Summer 1975.

GENERAL REFERENCES

Brown, R. V., "Do Managers Find Decision Theory Useful?" *Harvard Business Review,* Vol. 48, 1970.

Holloway, C., *Decision Making Under Uncertainty,* Prentice-Hall, Inc., Englewood Cliffs, N.J., 1979.

Howard, R. A., "Social Decision Analysis," *Proceedings of the IEEE,* Vol. 63, No. 3, March 1975.

Howard, R. A. (ed.), "Special Issue on Decision Analysis," *IEEE Transactions on Systems Science and Cybernetics,* Vol. SSC-4, No. 3, September 1968.

Jones, J. M., *Statistical Decision Making,* Richard D. Irwin, Inc., Homewood, Ill., 1977.

Magee, J. F., "Decision Trees for Decision Making," *Harvard Business Review,* July–August 1964.

Raiffa, H., *Decision Analysis,* Addison-Wesley, Reading, Mass., 1968.

————, *Analysis for Decision Making* (an audiographic, self-instructional course), Encyclopedia Britannica Educational Corporation, Chicago, 1974.

Schlaifer, R., *Analysis of Decisions Under Uncertainty,* McGraw-Hill, New York, 1968.

Spetzler, C. S., and C. S. Stael von Holstein, "Probability Encoding in Decision Analysis," *Management Science,* Vol. 22, No. 3, November 1975.

APPLICATIONS REFERENCES

Gleason, J. M., and D. T. Barnum, "Effectiveness of OSHA Penalties: Myth or Reality?," *Interfaces,* Vol. 7, No. 1, November 1976.

Hax, A. C., and K. M. Wiig, "The Use of Decision Analysis in Capital Investment Problems," in D. Bell, R. Keeney and H. Raiffa (eds.), *Conflicting Objectives in Decisions,* John Wiley & Sons, New York, 1977.

Howard, R. A., J. E. Matheson, and D. W. North, "The Decision to Seed Hurricanes," *Science,* Vol. 176, June 17, 1972.

Magee, J. F. "How to Use Decision Trees in Capital Investment," *Harvard Business Review,* September–October 1964.

Hudson, R. G., J. C. Chambers, and R. G. Johnston, "New Product Planning Decisions Under Uncertainty," *Interfaces,* Vol. 8, No. 1, Part 2, November 1977.

Newman, J. W., *Management Applications of Decision Theory,* Harper and Row, Inc., New York, 1971.

Wheelwright, S. C., "Applying Decision Theory to Improve Corporate Management of Currency-Exchange Risks," *California Management Review,* Vol. 17, No. 4, Summer 1975.

CHAPTER 15

Evaluation Models Based on Utility Functions

We have seen that expected monetary value can be a useful guide to decisions involving risks, especially when the decisions are to be made over and over again as in many low- to middle-level company decisions. The expected monetary value represents the average return a manager expects to receive, given that the same (or similar) decision is made many times. Thus, a manager who makes many capital budgeting decisions under conditions of risk might be well advised to adopt the expected value evaluation model as a useful aid.

However, suppose you face a decision involving risks and you make the decision only once. For example, suppose you are offered the following choice and you have only one opportunity to accept it. You may receive $25 with certainty or you may accept the results of a gamble in which a fair coin will be tossed. If the coin falls on heads, you will win $150; but if the coin lands on tails, you will lose $50. Which do you prefer? Think hard about this. Many people, including perhaps yourself, would prefer taking the $25 even though the expected monetary value of the gamble is $50, *twice as much:* $[(0.5)(\$150) + (0.5)(-\$50) = \$50]$. Does this mean these people are irrational? No, they are simply expressing their feelings. They would prefer to accept the $25 rather than run the risk of losing $50, even though there is an equal chance of winning $150.

If the people who prefer the certain value of $25 are not irrational, then something must be wrong with the expected value evaluation model. This conclusion would also be incorrect. Expected monetary value is a useful evaluation model only so long as it adequately reflects the preferences of the decision makers. In situations involving similar choices that are repeated many times or that have relatively low stakes, decision makers may feel that their preferences are consistent with the simple expected value of the outcomes. However, in decisions made only once and involving relatively high stakes, they may wish to avoid the possibility of an unfortunate outcome, even though the odds are actually in their favor. If so, we would say they are risk averse.

Most persons are risk averse in their decision making, at least in some decision situations, although the degree of risk aversion varies greatly and is a personal matter. A few individuals, including some oil wildcatters, actually prefer to accept high risk situations. For example, they might prefer accepting the gamble we have posed to accepting, say, $60 with certainty because there is a good chance they could win $150. However, numerous experiments have shown that such individuals are in the minority.

A second complicating factor in many significant, real-world problems is the existence of several criteria of approximately equal importance. The strategy of using an evaluation model with a single criterion may not be particularly helpful in these instances. For example, the effects of an alternative on the share of the market, on prestige, or on labor relations might be considered roughly as important as the effect on profit or loss in some business decisions. In the context of educational decision making, the number of students actually enrolled at the undergraduate, Master's, and Ph.D. levels might be important criteria for some decisions. Similarly, the design of a rapid transit system must be evaluated not only on costs but also on such criteria as noise pollution, air pollution, appearance, safety, and the number of persons using the system.

The really important decisions that a manager makes generally represent unique opportunities and involve high stakes. Often there are multiple criteria. Since the expected monetary value may not be the appropriate criterion for such decisions, the manager should be aware of alternate evaluation models. As we will see, these alternate models have the disadvantage of requiring decision makers to reveal explicitly information about their preferences. Therefore, the information requirements are much more demanding than those of the simple expected monetary value models. Nevertheless, these evaluation models do help decision makers in dealing with perhaps the most important class of decisions that they must make—one-time, high-stake decisions.

UTILITY FUNCTIONS FOR A SINGLE CRITERION

The expected value of several conditional outcomes does not consider what each conditional outcome is actually worth to the decision maker. Thus, we need some means of transforming conditional outcomes into measures of worth or utility. Let us think about how this transformation might be made.

To understand this process, you should think about your own preferences when faced with choices involving risk. To facilitate your ability to relate to this discussion, we will again introduce the three simple gambles displayed in the decision tree (Figure 15-1), where the conditional outcomes are expressed in dollars. How can we transform the outcomes into measures of utility? The best and worst conditional outcomes are "win $20" and "lose $10," respectively. To get started, we might assign the conditional outcome "win $20" a utility of 1.0 and the conditional outcome "lose $10" a utility of 0.0. Then, we would assign each of the other conditional outcomes some utility between 1.0 and 0.0, depending on how the outcome compares with "win $20" and "lose $10." Thus, the utility number we assign to

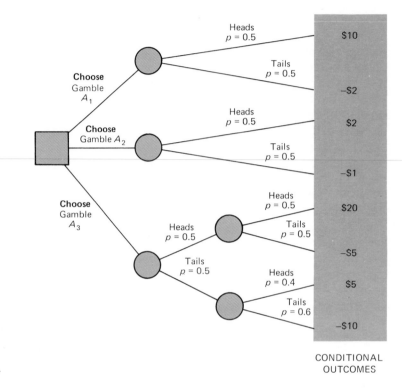

FIGURE 15-1
Decision tree for three alternate gambles.

CONDITIONAL
OUTCOMES

"win $10" will be larger than the one we assign to "win $2," since we would prefer the former to the latter.

We might assign these numbers on the basis of our personal reactions regarding what seems right. For example, you might think that winning $14 would make you almost as happy as winning $20, so you would assign the conditional outcome "win $14" a utility of perhaps 0.9. Similarly, you might think that you would be really happy if you won $20, but really sad if you lost $10. If you broke even, that would be about halfway between these two extremes *in terms of your feelings,* so you would give "win/lose $0" a utility of 0.5. You might continue assigning utility values and search your own mind until you felt comfortable with the responses. However, such a process does not force you to consider your attitude toward the *risk* associated with the alternatives.

Constructing the utility function

What we really want to do is generate values for these outcomes that can be used in risky situations. Therefore, we should introduce risk into a procedure for obtaining these values. Consider a simple gamble where you win $20 if a fair coin lands on heads, but you lose $10 if it lands on tails. The coin will be flipped only once and you either win or pay off immediately. As an alternative, you can take a fixed sum rather than play the game. Suppose you are offered the choice of taking the expected value of the game or having the coin flipped. The expected value of this game is $(0.5)(\$20) + (0.5)(-\$10) = \$5$. Which would you prefer? Think seriously about this.

To continue the example, suppose you responded after considerable thought that you would take $5. Instead of being paid, you are asked a similar question, except this time the payoff is only $2 for sure or the result of the coin flip. Again, suppose you prefer the certain payoff of $2 because you really do not like the 0.5 chance of losing $10. The next question, then, is would you *pay* $1 rather than have the coin flipped? Suppose you respond that you would accept the result from the gamble rather than pay to avoid it. After a few more questions of this sort, suppose you finally agree that if you are offered *any* certain winning, you would accept this certain payoff, but you would not *pay* to avoid the coin flip. Thus, at $0 for certain, you are indifferent about having the coin flipped. That is to say, you would just as soon walk away without winning or losing anything or you would accept the result of the coin flip. You just do not care at that point.

Thus, you are indifferent between receiving $0 for sure and the gamble shown in Figure 15-2. We would like to use this information to assign a utility number to the outcome of winning or losing $0 (breaking even) relative to the utility number 1.0 assigned earlier to winning $20 and the utility number 0.0 assigned to losing $10. These utility numbers are shown in parentheses in Figure 15-2.

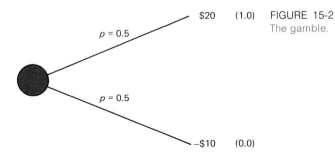

$20   (1.0)   FIGURE 15-2
The gamble.

$p = 0.5$

$p = 0.5$

-$10   (0.0)

TABLE 15-1   Summary of the Estimation of $u(\$0) = 0.5$

Question	Response	Implication
Do you prefer $5 for sure or the coin toss in Figure 15-2?	$5	utility of $5 is greater than 0.5
Do you prefer $2 for sure or the coin toss in Figure 15-2?	$2	utility of $2 is greater than 0.5
Do you prefer to pay $1 or to have the coin toss in Figure 15-2?	coin toss	utility of −$1 is less than 0.5
Do you prefer neither to gain nor lose any money for sure ($0), or to have the coin toss in Figure 15-2?	indifferent	utility of $0 is equal to 0.5

In our previous analysis, we used the expected value of the conditional outcomes of a chance point to replace the chance point in a decision tree. This time, let us compute the expected value of the *utility numbers* associated with the conditional outcomes of the chance point, obtaining $(0.5)(1.0) + (0.5)(0.0) = 0.5$. Much as before, we can let 0.5 be the utility number that we assign to this chance point. Since we were indifferent between breaking even ($0) and this risky situation, we will assign $0 a utility value of 0.5 also. This procedure is summarized in Table 15-1.

We can continue this procedure by creating 50–50 gambles between $0 and win $20 and between lose $10 and $0. For example, suppose you are asked to indicate the least amount you would take for certain rather than have a fair coin flipped with a $20 payoff on heads and a break-even payoff on tails. If you think hard about this question, you might say to yourself:

> *Well, I would certainly rather have $15 and I would also prefer $10. However, I would rather flip the coin than accept only $5 for sure, so it's somewhere between $5 and $10. Let's see, I would prefer flipping the coin if I were offered only $6, $7, or even $8. However, if I could get $9 for sure . . . well, I think I would take it. So, the least I would take is somewhere between $8 and $9, probably closer to $8, say $8.25.*

Thus, we assign $8.25 a utility number equal to the expected value of the utility numbers of the new gamble, which is $(0.5)(1.0) + (0.5)(0.5) = 0.75$.

Now, suppose we ask a similar question regarding a coin flip between losing $10 and breaking even. This time you say you would pay up to $5.85 to avoid facing this coin toss. Notice that you are willing to *pay more* than the expected monetary value of the coin flip to avoid the possibility of losing $10. The expected value of the utility number for this gamble is 0.25, which we assign to "lose $5.85."

We are obtaining values for some function that assigns utility numbers to conditional outcomes. We call such a function a utility function and denote it as $u(O_i)$ where O_i is a conditional outcome. For example, we have $u(+\$20) = 1.0$, $u(-\$10) = 0.0$, $u(\$0) = 0.5$, $u(\$8.25) = 0.75$, and $u(-\$5.85) = 0.25$. We could continue this process to obtain more utility numbers by creating hypothetical gambles between $20 and $8.25, between $8.25 and $0, between $0 and $-$5.85, and between $-$5.85 and $-$10.

As an alternative, we could ask the same type of question in another way. Suppose you are offered the choice of either $5 for sure or a gamble with payoffs of "win $20" or "lose $10." If the probability of winning $20 is 0.5 (and of losing $10 is $1.0 - 0.5 = 0.5$), you say you would prefer taking the $5. Now suppose there is a 0.9 chance of winning $20 but only a 0.1 chance of losing $10. Then, you might prefer the gamble. What we are looking for is the *probability* of winning the $20 that would make you indifferent between the $5 for certain and the gamble. To help you find this probability, questions such as those above might be asked explicitly. On the other hand, you might find it easier to ask such questions of yourself.

After much thought, suppose you say that if the odds favor the outcome of "win $20" by at least 2 to 1, you would take the gamble. Thus, the probability of winning $20 must be about 0.67 for you to be indifferent between the $5 for sure and the gamble, so we have $u(\$5) = 0.67$.

We can now plot these utility function values as shown in Figure 15-3 and sketch a smooth curve (the upper white line) that goes through these points. Notice that the curve is bowed slightly. This bow is a characteristic of utility functions that reflect risk averse preferences. Relatively more bow in the curve reflects relatively more risk aversion. Persons who are risk neutral would make choices based directly on the expected values of the conditional outcomes of a gamble, and their utility function would be a straight line (shown in Figure 15-3 for comparison). The utility curve of risk takers, persons who prefer high risk situations, would have an inverted bow as illustrated by the lower white line in Figure 15-3. It is also possible that persons might be risk takers for certain values of money and risk avoiders for others, so that they would have an S-shaped utility curve.

To summarize, we have described two methods of determining a utility function.

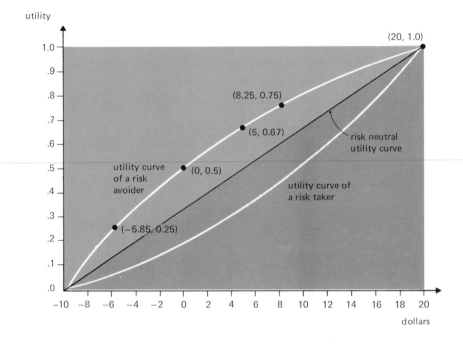

FIGURE 15-3
A utility function.

The steps of the first method are as follows:

1. Select the best conditional outcome O_i^* and the worst conditional outcome O_{i*}. Let $u(O_i^*) = 1.0$ and $u(O_{i*}) = 0.0$.

2. Ask the decision maker to identify some other outcome, $\bar{O}_i$, such that he or she would be indifferent between receiving $\bar{O}_i$ with certainty or accepting the results of the 50–50 gamble between the best and worst conditional outcomes, O_i^* and O_{i*}. Then, $u(\bar{O}_i) = (0.5)[u(O_i^*)] + (0.5)[u(O_{i*})]$, the expected value of the utility function values assigned to the conditional outcomes appearing in the gamble.

3. Continuing by constructing 50–50 gambles between O_i^* and $\bar{O}_i$ and between O_{i*} and $\bar{O}_i$. Repeat the procedure until enough points have been obtained to determine a curve as shown in Figure 15-3.

The second method is very similar to the first, except this time we specify O_i^*, O_{i*}, and $\bar{O}_i$ in advance. We ask the decision maker to specify the probability of getting

O_i^* in the gamble that will make him or her indifferent between receiving $\bar{O}_i$ with certainty or accepting the results of the gamble.

These two approaches for estimating utility functions are the most commonly used ones and have a sound theoretical basis. Other approaches have been suggested; these are reviewed by Fishburn [1967]. (For a more detailed discussion, see Keeney and Raiffa [1976, Chapter 4] and Holloway [1979, Part III]).

The utility function through the points can be drawn by hand in many cases. As an alternative, statistical curve-fitting techniques can be used. For theoretical reasons that are beyond the scope of this discussion, a utility function for a risk averse individual can often be approximated by a function of the form $u(O_i) = a + b \ln (O_i + c)$, where c is chosen to ensure $O_i + c > 0$. By introducing a new variable $z = \ln (O_i + c)$, this function becomes linear in z, and the curve can be fit using simple linear regression techniques with alternate values of c until the best fit is determined. The curve shown in Figure 15-3 corresponds to the utility function $u(O_i) = -1.66 + 0.721 \ln (O_i + 20)$.

The utility function as an evaluation model

The purpose of constructing a utility function for a decision maker is to use it in an evaluation model. When we use a decision tree to compute the expected monetary value of an alternative, we replace a chance point with conditional outcomes by the expected value of the conditional outcomes. Thus, we implicitly assume that the decision maker is indifferent between the chance point and the expected value of the conditional outcomes. As we have discussed, this assumption is only appropriate if the decision maker is risk neutral, but many persons are risk averse.

The assignment of the utility numbers was based on the following procedure. Consider a chance point or a gamble where the utility numbers of the conditional outcomes are known. Find a certain outcome such that the decision maker is indifferent between receiving that outcome and the chance point. This certain outcome is called the *certainty equivalent* of the chance point. Then, assign that certainty equivalent a utility number equal to the expected value of the *utility numbers* associated with the conditional outcomes of the chance point. The certainty equivalent may not be the expected value of the conditional outcomes. But, by our rules for constructing the utility function, *the utility number associated with the certainty equivalent will be the expected value of the utility numbers of the conditional outcomes.*

This result suggests that rather than using the expected value of the conditional outcomes to evaluate alternatives, we can use the expected value of the utility numbers associated with these outcomes. This evaluation model is identical to the simple expected value model, except for the introduction of the utility function u, which is unique to a particular decision maker. The practical disadvantage of the model is that it requires more information, since we must interact with the decision maker to obtain an estimate of u. Further, the result will be different for different decision makers, so there is no single answer.

Some persons would object to the use of this model on the grounds that it is not objective (as is the simple expected value model) because it incorporates subjective judgments. However, as we have stressed, the proper criterion for choosing an evaluation model is how well it captures the true preferences of the decision maker. Since the expected utility model explicitly incorporates these preferences, it is superior on this criterion. Notice that if the decision maker is actually risk neutral and is willing to act on the basis of the expected values of conditional outcomes, this attitude will also be reflected as a special case of the utility function, which is the straight line shown in Figure 15-3.

An example with gambles   Consider again the problem of choosing among three alternate gambles. The decision tree for analyzing the problem is shown in Figure 15-4. However, this time, the utility function values associated with the outcomes are shown in parentheses to the right of the outcomes. These values were obtained from the utility function we constructed earlier and are illustrated in Figure 15-5. For example, we find the conditional outcome of $10 on the horizontal axis. Following the dotted line up from $10 to the utility function and then across to its intersection with the vertical axis, we obtain the utility function value of approximately 0.79.

Now let us roll back this decision tree by calculating expected values at the chance points. However, rather than calculating the expected values of the conditional outcomes, we compute the expected values of the utility numbers associated with those outcomes. Performing these calculations, we have the results shown in Figure 15-6, with A_1 receiving an expected utility number of 0.605, A_2 of 0.515, and A_3 of 0.455. According to the expected utility evaluation model, the decision maker for whom we constructed this utility function should prefer A_1 to A_2 or A_3 and A_2 to A_3.

This result is the same for A_1, which was also preferred when we computed the expected monetary values of the alternatives. However, using the expected monetary values, A_3 with a value of $1.75 was preferred to A_2 with a value of $0.50. By the expected utility model, A_2 is preferred to A_3. Looking at the decision tree (Figure 15-4), we see that very little risk is involved in A_2. Although you can win only $2,

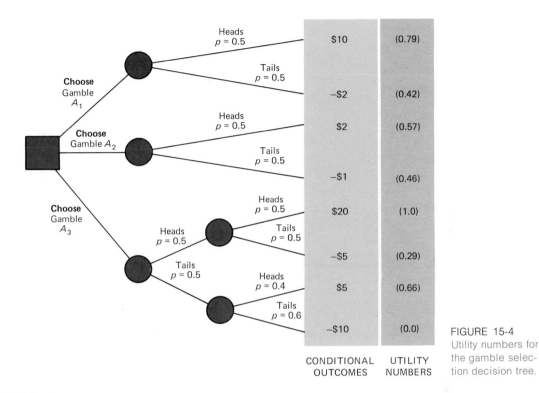

FIGURE 15-4
Utility numbers for the gamble selection decision tree.

you can lose only $1 at worst. However, A_3 includes the possibilities of losing either $5 or $10. These negative outcomes are penalized heavily by the utility function, so the safer alternative, A_2, is now preferred to A_3.

We can also transform these utility numbers associated with the alternatives back into dollars. These results represent the least amount the decision maker would accept for certain in each case rather than choose the gamble. For A_1, the monetary value corresponding to a utility number of 0.605 can also be read from the curve in Figure 15-5 as $3.23. Similarly, the dollar value corresponding to 0.515 or A_2 is $0.45; for A_3 it is −$1.21. Notice that each of these numbers is less than the expected monetary value of the conditional outcomes for the gambles because the decision maker is risk averse. Note also that this decision maker would actually be willing to *pay* up to $1.21 to avoid the third gamble, A_3, even though the expected monetary value is $1.75.

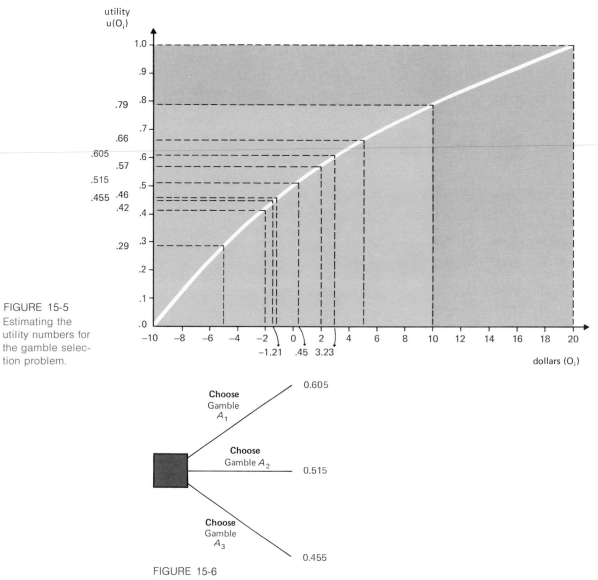

FIGURE 15-5
Estimating the utility numbers for the gamble selection problem.

FIGURE 15-6
The results of the analysis with utility numbers.

An example with POCO In Chapter 14 we introduced a strategic decision that was under consideration by the Pacific Oil Company (POCO). The issue was the appropriate strategy for the development of their oil shale leases. Three strategies were identified. The first strategy was a research-only effort to improve the oil shale processing technology. The second strategy was a combined research and development program that would result in some actual production capabilities. The third strategy was a crash development program aimed at developing the capability to produce significant quantities of crude oil from the oil shales by using the current state-of-the-art processing technologies. The problem was complicated by the possibility of a breakthrough in the oil shale processing technology that might result if either the research-only strategy or the combined research and development strategies were followed. The conditional outcomes associated with these strategies could vary over a wide range, from a possible gain of $500 million to a loss of $500 million.

Suppose we can find the decision maker in POCO who is responsible for this decision (perhaps not an easy task). He or she may say that for relatively small investment decisions, POCO is willing to make decisions based on expected monetary values. Since many such decisions are made, they actually expect to realize total returns roughly equivalent to the total of these expected values. However, for a major decision, such as the oil shale development strategy, the possibility of losing up to $500 million is a serious outcome. Therefore, the decision maker agrees to answer several questions involving 50–50 gambles, and we eventually construct the utility curve displayed in Figure 15-7.

You may question why we should use this decision maker's utility function. What we really want is a utility function for POCO, if such a thing exists. Perhaps so. However, we may assume that the decision maker is not reflecting *personal* risk aversion in his or her responses. Rather, the decision maker is reflecting the view of how POCO should respond in risky situations. If so, the responses may provide the basis for the best approximation to a utility function for POCO that we can hope to obtain. After all, POCO does not actually make decisions, this person makes the decisions. For an example of an attempt to determine such a utility function for a real company, see the account by Spetzler [1968].

Now, let us substitute the corresponding utility function values for the conditional outcomes in the decision tree for POCO shown in Figure 15-8. The utility function values shown to the right of their corresponding conditional outcomes were obtained from Figure 15-7. For example, the conditional outcome of a $300-million gain is found on the horizontal axis in Figure 15-7. Tracing up the dotted line and across to the vertical axis results in a utility function value of 0.898. This value appears just to the right of each $300-million conditional outcome in Figure 15-8.

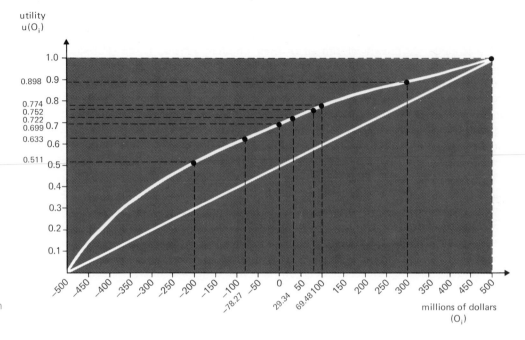

FIGURE 15-7
A utility function
for POCO.

Rolling back this decision tree, we now calculate the expected value of the utility numbers at each chance point rather than the expected value of the conditional outcomes. We obtain expected utility function values of 0.722 for the initial research-only strategy, 0.752 for the research and development strategy, and 0.633 for the crash development strategy. These results and the expected utility function values at the other chance branch points and decision points are shown in Figure 15-8. This compares with expected monetary values of $35.6 million for the research-only strategy, $81.25 million for the combined research and development strategy, and a loss of $10 million for the crash development strategy.

The relative ranking of these three strategies is the same when we compute the expected values of the utility function as when we compute their expected monetary values, although this will *not* be true in general. To correctly interpret results based on the utility function, we should translate the expected utility function values back into dollars. For example, the expected utility function value for the

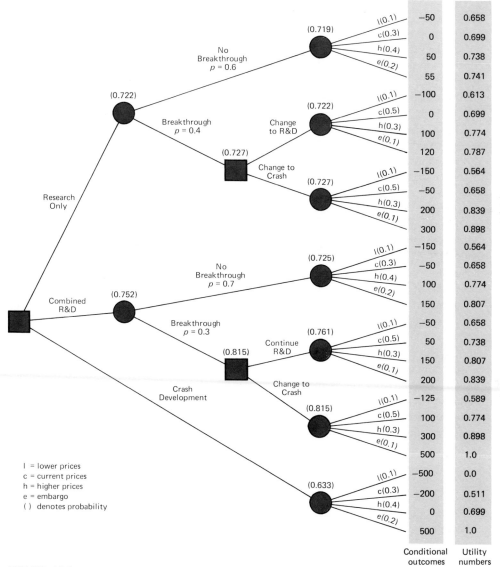

FIGURE 15-8
The decision tree for POCO with utility numbers.

research-only strategy is 0.722. Tracing along the appropriate dotted line in Figure 15-7, we find that the utility function value of 0.722 on the vertical axis corresponds to a monetary value of $29.34 million on the horizontal axis. This figure of $29.34 million is the certainty equivalent of the risky strategy of an initial research-only effort, even though this alternative has an expected monetary value of $35.6 million dollars. In a similar manner, we obtain the certainty equivalents of $69.48 million for the initial research and development strategy, and a loss of $78.27 million for the crash development strategy.

Using either the expected monetary value of the conditional outcomes or the expected value of the utility function, the best strategy for POCO is the initial research and development effort. Now suppose that Essex Oil Company contacts POCO and offers to lease their oil shale lands over the same time period considered in this analysis for a certain cash payment of $75 million. What should POCO do? On the basis of this analysis, the expected monetary value of pursuing the initial research and development effort is $81.25 million, which clearly exceeds the offer by Essex Oil. However, the certainty equivalent of this alternative using the utility function in Figure 15-7 is only $69.48 million. According to the logic that was used in assessing the utility function, this certainty equivalent is the best estimate of the actual monetary value of this risky alternative to POCO, since it incorporates both the monetary outcomes *and* POCO's attitude toward the risk involved in this decision. Therefore, POCO should lease the oil shale lands to Essex Oil.

An example with nonmonetary outcomes It is important to realize that utility functions can be constructed on outcomes other than money. For example, suppose an elementary school principal is trying to decide whether to continue his or her current reading program for third-graders or to adopt a new reading program based on a new approach to teaching reading.

The performance of students in a subject area, such as reading, can be measured by a standard test in terms of percentile scores. The principal feels certain that if the current program is continued, the third graders would score at the 50 percentile level on such a test. The new program has had a mixed record. Where it has truly been successful, the reading score of a class generally increases relative to conventional programs (such as the current one) by about 10 percentile points. However, in some cases it has little effect. Moreover, in a few situations, the results have been disastrous. The teachers have not been able to modify their methods to the new materials, and scores have actually fallen by as much as 15 percentile points.

Based on a knowledge of the students and teachers, this principal estimates the probabilities of the possible effects of the new program as follows:

Effect of Reading Program	Probability
Performance increased to 60th percentile	0.4
Performance unchanged (50th percentile)	0.4
Performance decreased to 35th percentile	0.2

Should the principal adopt this new program?

The answer to this question depends on how one values the different outcomes expressed in percentiles. If we calculate the expected value of the conditional outcomes of the decision to adopt the new program, we obtain $(0.4)(60) + (0.4)(50) + (0.2)(35) = 51$. Since this result is slightly higher than the outcome received with the current program, the new program should be introduced on the basis of the expected value evaluation model. However, this does not explicitly consider preferences regarding the relative value of these percentile scores, especially in risky choice situations such as this one.

Therefore, suppose we ask the principal a series of questions and obtain an estimate of his or her utility function for the performance of a class of students as measured in percentile scores. The results are shown in Figure 15-9. Calculating the expected utility of the conditional outcomes, we obtain $(0.4)(0.83) + (0.4)(0.78) + (0.2)(0.63) = 0.77$. The utility number 0.77 corresponds to a percentile score of 49, which the principal should be willing to accept for certain rather than choose this alternative involving risk. This is 1 percentile point lower than the score of 50 that pupils will score with the current program. Therefore, the principal should feel a slight preference for continuing this existing program. Notice that this result differs from the one based on the expected value of the conditional outcomes.

The utility curve in Figure 15-9 was actually obtained by interviewing 72 different elementary school principals and eliciting their preferences for percentile scores. Notice that this utility curve can be closely approximated by three linear segments over the following ranges of test performance: 0 to 15, 15 to 50, and 50 to 100. The difference in utility values between 0 and 15 is about equal to the difference in

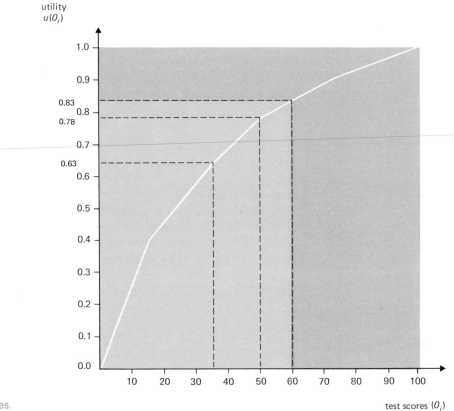

FIGURE 15-9
A utility function on test scores.

utility values between 15 and 50. This result indicates that elementary school principals associate great value with improving student performance from the worst possible score to the 15th percentile. Of nearly equal value, but involving a larger difference in student achievement, is improving student performance from the 15th to the 50th percentile. It is not surprising that the slope of the utility function changes abruptly at the 50th percentile, since this level is the "national average" and becomes a "target," or aspiration, level for the principals. A principal would probably experience less criticism if the school's performance is at least average than if the school's performance is below average. It is interesting that this utility curve exhibits the "bowed" appearance of a risk averse utility function that is commonly found when the criterion is money.

The information regarding elementary school principals' utility functions has been incorporated into a procedure for selecting educational subject areas for new programs. This procedure has been packaged in a "do-it-yourself" kit and has been made available to all elementary school principals (see Hoepfner et al. [1973]). The details of this study are described by Dyer, Farrell, and Bradley [1973].

The assumptions underlying utility functions

We have attempted to provide an intuitively appealing introduction to the subject of utility theory. However, there exists a formal body of knowledge that supports these ideas. The concept of a utility function is dependent on a set of assumptions regarding rational behavior. These assumptions are, loosely speaking, the following:

1. The decision maker can compare any two alternatives and consistently state a preference for one or state that he or she is indifferent between the two alternatives.

2. Suppose the decision maker prefers A_1 to A_2 and also prefers A_2 to A_3. Then, the decision maker must prefer A_1 to A_3. That is, the individual's preferences are transitive.

3. Suppose the decision maker prefers A_1 to A_2 and also prefers A_2 to A_3. Consequently, there must exist some probability (p) such that the decision maker is indifferent between A_2 and a gamble with a p chance of obtaining A_1 and a $(1 - p)$ chance of obtaining A_3.

4. Suppose the decision maker is indifferent between A_1 and A_2. Then, for any alternative A_3 and the probability p, the decision maker is indifferent between a gamble with a p chance of obtaining A_1 and a $(1 - p)$ chance of obtaining A_3, and a gamble with a p chance of obtaining A_2 and a $(1 - p)$ chance of obtaining A_3.

Most people are not perfectly consistent in their decisions at all times and may violate one or more of the above assumptions in some situations. However, these assumptions seem to provide a definition of behavior that agrees with the notion of rational decision making. Further, if one accepts these assumptions, it follows that maximizing expected utility function values is the appropriate evaluation model for use in risky choice situations.

UTILITY FUNCTIONS FOR MULTIPLE CRITERIA

Utility functions for multiple criteria have actually been assessed and applied in many real-world situations. This is because the introduction of multiple criteria, especially when combined with risk, makes the evaluation of alternatives extremely difficult, so that an explicit evaluation model is actually needed.

Previously, we assumed that there was only one outcome, or criterion, relevant for evaluating the alternatives. A more realistic interpretation would be that there is only one criterion of overriding importance, such as profit or loss. Other considerations (which could be thought of as secondary criteria) could be brought into play to choose among alternatives that were "close" on the primary criterion. Thus, the approaches we have described could be used to identify a smaller subset of alternatives that are roughly equivalent based on a criterion of overriding importance, such as profit (loss), but these approaches are inappropriate for explicitly dealing with multiple criteria.

Multiple criteria of approximately equal importance generally arise because the problem is complex. Major decisions involving a significant allocation of resources often exhibit this complexity. First, we will consider the initial issue in the case of a complex problem: the identification of the criteria. Next, an evaluation model for problems involving multiple criteria will be briefly described.

Identifying the criteria

An important issue that should be considered early in the problem-solving effort is the actual identification of the criteria that are relevant for comparing alternatives. These criteria (attributes, objectives, or goals) are simply the outcomes that are affected by the choice of an alternative and that affect the decision maker's preference for the alternative. The task of recognizing the aspects of the system that will be affected by the choice of an alternative may be the most difficult and the most important task in the analysis. The development of an evaluation and a predictive model may have to be accomplished simultaneously or iteratively, since the criteria may change as the decision maker learns more about the problem.

As an example, consider the imposition of a 55-mile-per-hour speed limit during the oil embargo in 1974. The stated objective of this law was to conserve fuel by forcing automobiles to travel slower. It also had the effect of communicating the seriousness of a situation to the general public. In addition, deaths and injuries from traffic accidents fell during this period. On the negative side, this law also touched off a nationwide strike by truckers and curtailed the demand at businesses depending on motorists and tourists. It is not clear that Congress or the President were aware of all these outcomes prior to the passage of the legislation.

Thus, the criteria may include outcomes, such as the probability of a strike by truckers, not directly related to the primary purpose of the alternative, conserving gasoline in this case. Nevertheless, these criteria must be included in the evaluation model if they affect the preference of the decision maker.

An additive evaluation model for multiple criteria

The most complex and important managerial decisions generally involve both multiple criteria and risk. Because of the importance of these decisions, the modern manager should know that evaluation models for dealing with them do exist. For example, suppose we are trying to decide which automobile to purchase and have narrowed our choice to two alternatives: a Starburst (A_1) or a Palomino (A_2). The Starburst and the Palomino are approximately the same in size and weight. Therefore, we have decided to base our decision on only two criteria: cost measured in dollars and performance measured in horsepower. We assume that the outcome of either decision is certain. If we purchase the Starburst (A_1), we obtain the outcome $O_1 = (\$3500, 140 \text{ hp})$ and if we purchase the Palomino (A_2), we obtain $O_2 = (\$3600, 170 \text{ hp})$. Now, which automobile should we choose?

The additive model Suppose we have only two criteria, and let (O^1, O^2) represent an outcome where O^1 and O^2 are the values of the two criteria. For example, O^1 might be the cost and O^2 might be a measure of performance, like horsepower. We would like to obtain a utility function $U(O^1, O^2)$ of the multiple outcomes. However, it would be difficult to interact with a decision maker to approximate such a function without some simplifying assumptions.

The simplest assumption is that $U(O^1, O^2)$ is additive. This means that it can be written,

$$U(O^1, O^2) = w_1 u_1(O^1) + w_2 u_2(O^2)$$

where u_1 and u_2 are single criterion utility functions scaled from 0 to 1 and w_1 and w_2 are scaling constants or weights. The practical implication is that we can apply the methods for estimating a single criterion utility function to obtain u_1 and then to obtain u_2. We next adjust for the relative importance of the two criteria by assessing w_1 and w_2.

For example, suppose we interact with a decision maker using the methods for

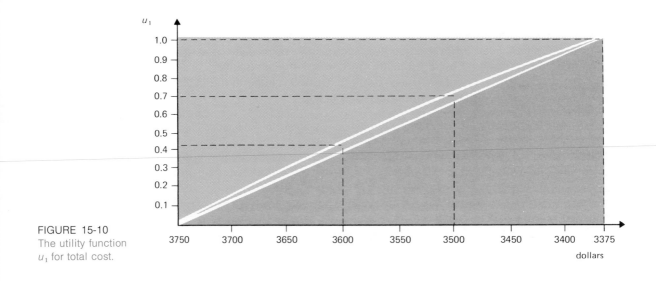

FIGURE 15-10
The utility function u_1 for total cost.

estimating a single criterion utility function over cost and obtain u_1, which is shown in Figure 15-10. Next, we assess a single criterion utility function for horsepower and obtain u_2 in Figure 15-11. Finally, suppose the decision maker estimates that a change in horsepower from 100 to 200 is about twice as important as a change in cost from \$3375 to \$3750; these changes are the ranges over which the utility functions are defined. Therefore, the weight w_2 for u_2 should be twice as large as the weight w_1.

We have estimated the additive utility function

$$U(O^1, O^2) = 1.0\ u_1(O^1) + 2.0\ u_2(O^2)$$

where u_1 and u_2 are shown in Figures 15-10 and 15-11. We now wish to evaluate the Starburst and the Palomino. The outcome for the Starburst is (\$3500, 140 hp). From Figure 15-10, we estimate $u_1(\$3500) = 0.7$ approximately; from Figure 15-9, we estimate $u_2(140\ hp) = 0.67$. Therefore, we have the total utility function value

$$U(\$3500, 140\ hp) = (1.0)(0.7) + (2.0)(0.67) = 2.04$$

for the Starburst.

In a similar manner, we obtain

$$U(\$3600, 170 \text{ hp}) = (1.0)(0.42) + (2.0)(0.87) = 2.16$$

for the Palomino. Since the result is larger for the Palomino, it should be preferred by the decision maker. It should also be noted that these same concepts can be applied in situations involving risk.

Unfortunately, it is not always true that the evaluation model over multiple criteria for a particular decision maker can be written in this additive form. That is, it may not be possible to determine the functions u_1 and u_2 nor the weights w_1 and w_2 so that the additive model accurately reflects the preferences of the decision maker. In such cases, alternate evaluation models can be used.

Additional details regarding evaluation models for multiple criteria are presented by Keeney and Raiffa [1976]. For real-world applications, these evaluation models are sufficiently complex to require the assistance of an analyst. However, the manager should recognize that such evaluation models do exist and that they can be constructed as a straightforward extension of the approach for a single criterion utility function.

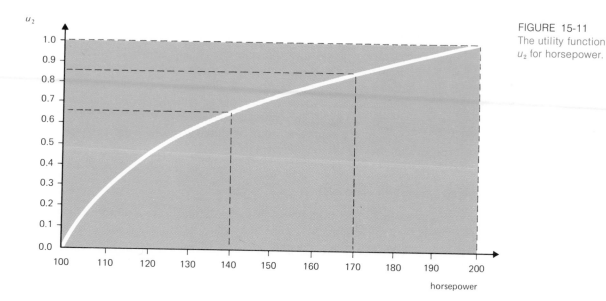

FIGURE 15-11
The utility function u_2 for horsepower.

WHAT SHOULD THE MANAGER KNOW?

The manager should know that the expected value of conditional outcomes is not the only available evaluation model for use in decision making when risk or multiple criteria are involved. The simple expected value model does not take into consideration the decision maker's feelings regarding risk nor does it deal with the problem of reconciling multiple criteria.

A utility function that reflects a decision maker's attitude toward risk can be constructed. In problems involving a single criterion and risk, the utility function values can be substituted for the corresponding conditional outcome values. The expected values of the utility numbers, which can be organized in tabular form or in a decision tree, can be computed and used to rank the alternatives. Most persons are risk averse, so the certainty equivalent associated with the expected utility function value of an alternative is generally smaller than the expected value of the conditional outcomes.

When multiple criteria are involved, an additive evaluation model can be used in some situations. Then, a single criterion utility function can be assessed on each of the criteria, and weights can be determined to compensate for the relative importance of the different criteria.

Problem characteristics

Utility functions involving single and multiple criteria are useful in analyzing nonrepetitive decisions involving risk and substantial costs and potential rewards. The nonrepetitive nature of the decision is especially important with the single criterion utility function. Otherwise, the expected value of the conditional outcomes would be an appropriate evaluation model. In addition, the potential rewards and costs must be substantial to justify the time and effort required to obtain the subjective estimates necessary to identify the utility function.

Obtaining subjective estimates

Modern managers may find themselves in the position of the decision maker from whom information is required to estimate a utility function for single or multiple criteria. It seems unlikely that managers will ever be interviewing others and trying to obtain subjective estimates from them. Why, then, did we present the methodology for eliciting this information in some detail?

If managers are questioned by analysts, they should recognize what the analysts are doing and cooperate with them. Perhaps more important, managers may be drawing a decision tree and performing the necessary calculations themselves. If so, they may find it helpful to carry on a structured dialogue *with themselves* to elicit the necessary information, that is, they may pose the questions involving gambles to themselves to crystallize their own thinking. Therefore, it is important that managers be aware of the basic approaches for eliciting judgmental responses.

Information requirements

The information requirements for utility functions for single or multiple criteria are relatively severe. Therefore, the manager may wish to ignore all but one criterion and perform a preliminary analysis with simple expected values based on this criterion. In many practical problems, the best alternative will be obvious from such an analysis. Recall that the decision for POCO was not changed by the introduction of utility function values. However, if two or more alternatives are "close" on the basis of an expected value model, an analysis using utility functions might then be performed.

No quantitative aid should be applied blindly. Why use a procedure requiring the gathering of expensive information when a simpler approach will work just as well? The manager should always trade off the benefit of using a quantitative aid against the cost of the required information.

Interpretation of results

The expected utility function values may be used to rank the alternatives. When there is only a single criterion, the outcome value corresponding to the expected utility value for an alternative can be estimated from the utility function. This estimate, called the certainty equivalent, is the least amount that the decision maker should actually be willing to accept for certain rather than choose the alternative. Again, we must emphasize that this certain value of the alternative will not actually occur. Instead, any one of the conditional outcomes of the alternative will be the result of the decision.

A sensitivity analysis should be performed to ensure that small errors in estimating the utility functions and/or in eliciting subjective probabilities will not affect the decision. It would be inappropriate to blindly follow the rankings resulting from these models, especially if several outcomes are relatively "close" according to the models.

These approaches do not relieve managers of the task of making a decision. They simply provide a systematic way of analyzing the alternatives. Often managers may wish to revise their utility functions and weights as they learn more about the problem. Such revisions are especially likely to occur in the public sector where inputs from citizens and public reactions to initial proposals may provide a basis for these revisions.

CHECK YOUR UNDERSTANDING

1. In the following situations, would the expected value of the outcomes or expected utility be a more appropriate evaluation model? Explain your reasoning.
   a. the determination of daily inventory policies
   b. the expansion of capacity by building a large plant
   c. the selection of a new product to market when approximately 20 new products are introduced by the firm each year
   d. the selection of a new product to market when a commitment of a high proportion of the firm's capital will be required
   e. the purchase of personal life insurance
   f. the decision to seed hurricanes

2. Distinguish between an outcome and the *worth* of the outcome to the decision maker.

3. Distinguish between a person who is risk averse and a risk taker. What professions might appeal to a risk taker?

4. Estimate the utility function values for each of the outcomes in the gamble selection decision tree of Figure 15-4 from the utility curve of a *risk taker* shown in Figure 15-3. Which gamble would the risk taker prefer?

5. Obtain the cooperation of a friend, a roommate, or your spouse. Using questions involving gambles, find at least five points on his or her utility function over the range of monetary values from −$10 (lose $10) to +$20 (win $20).
   a. Is the individual risk averse, risk neutral, or a risk taker?
   b. Plot these five points and draw in the corresponding utility curve. Using these results, analyze the gamble selection decision tree in Figure 15-4. Which gamble should he or she prefer?
   c. Describe the three alternate gambles to your friend. Ask her or him to choose one. Did this choice agree with your prediction in (b)?

6. By posing questions involving gambles to yourself, develop and plot your own utility curve over the range from $-\$10$ to $+\$20$.
   a. Are you risk averse, risk neutral, or a risk taker?
   b. Using your own personal utility function values, analyze the gamble selection decision tree in Figure 15-4. Which gamble should you prefer according to this analysis?
   c. Study the three alternate gambles carefully. Does your "gut reaction" agree with the analysis in (b)?

7. Review the assumptions of utility functions.
   a. Give an example of two alternatives where it would be difficult to state your preference consistently for one or indicate that you are indifferent between them. What seems to cause the difficulty?
   b. Try to think of an example of a problem where you prefer alternative A_1 to A_2, alternative A_2 to A_3, but where you prefer alternative A_3 to A_1.

8. List two or more criteria that might be considered of approximately equal importance for each of the following decision situations.
   a. the selection of a jet fighter from several alternate prototypes
   b. the design of an emergency medical system for a city
   c. the choice of a dam site on a river
   d. the creation of a new national park
   e. the purchase of a new computer system
   f. the selection of a particular product for further development and marketing
   g. the determination of the terms of a bargaining settlement in negotiating a labor contract

9. Suppose the decision maker wishes to apply the additive utility function with u_1 and u_2 shown in Figures 15-10 and 15-11 and with $w_1 = 1.0$ and $w_2 = 2.0$ to a new alternative, the Champion. The Champion is described as follows:

	Champion (A_3)
Cost	$3400
Horsepower	120 hp

Estimating the appropriate values of u_1 and u_2 from Figures 15-10 and 15-11, calculate the utility function value associated with the Champion from the additive utility function. Should it be preferred to the Palomino?

SHORT CASES

CASE 15-1   Consider the problem of POCO in determining whether to drill in the Aleutian Islands as described in Case 14-2 of Chapter 14.

a. Estimate the utility function values of POCO for $80 million, −$100 million, $200 million, and $300 million from Figure 15-7.

b. Repeat the analysis of Case 14-2 substituting the utility function values for the monetary outcomes. Does the decision change?

c. If you were a manager of POCO, would you feel more comfortable with the analysis based on expected monetary value or the one based on expected utility? Explain.

CASE 15-2   Consider the problem of a government decision maker who must decide if a particular hurricane is to be seeded. He finds the analysis of the hurricane seeding issue as described in Case 14-3 of Chapter 14 most interesting, but it omits an important consideration. Once a hurricane has been seeded, it is no longer an "act of God," but it becomes an "act of man." As a result, once a hurricane has been seeded, the government will be blamed for damages, even if they are smaller than they would have been otherwise. Hurricanes are unpredictable. If the surface windspeed should actually *increase* after the hurricane is seeded or if its direction of travel should shift into a heavily populated area, the public outcry would be tremendous.

Thus, the value of the outcome to the decision maker depends both on the property damage *and* on whether the hurricane was seeded. The best outcome would be the least damage, estimated at $16.3 million in Case 14-3, and no seeding. The worst outcome would be the highest property damage of $335.8 million after the hurricane was seeded. Suppose the decision maker assigns the best outcome a utility function value of 1.0, the worst outcome a utility function value of 0.0, and uses the approach involving gambles to assign utility function values to the remaining outcomes. The results and the probability estimates are as follows:

Property Damage Loss (millions of $)	Hurricane Seeded		Hurricane Not Seeded	
	Probability	Utility	Probability	Utility
$335.8	0.038	0.00	0.054	0.30
191.1	0.143	0.61	0.206	0.68
100.0	0.392	0.82	0.480	0.89
46.7	0.255	0.89	0.206	0.98
16.3	0.172	0.90	0.054	1.00

Notice that the decision maker is indifferent between a property damage loss of $46.7 million from a seeded hurricane and a loss of $100 million from an unseeded hurricane because of the difference in government responsibility in each case.

The utility function value assigned to the cost of seeding, only $0.25 million, is negligible and can be ignored.

a. Compute the expected utility associated with each of the two decisions. Which one should be preferred?

b. Does the preferred decision differ from the one that would be obtained using the expected monetary value model? Is this surprising?

c. As a practical matter, would you, in the role of the government decision maker, like these utility function values to be publicized? How would you defend the use of this procedure before a congressional committee?

Consider the problem of managing currency-exchange risks as described in Case 14-7 of   CASE 15-3
Chapter 14. Suppose we ask the treasurer a series of questions involving gambles and estimate the utility function for the firm shown in Figure 15-12.

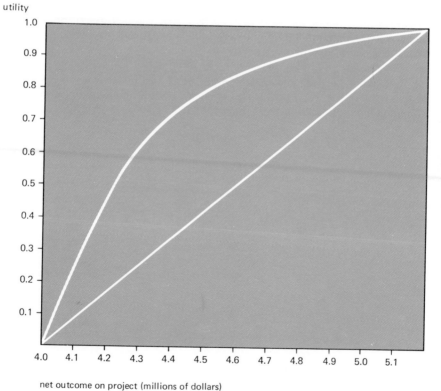

utility

net outcome on project (millions of dollars)

FIGURE 15-12
A preference curve
for the treasurer.
Source: (Adapted
from S. C. Wheel-
wright, "Applying
Decision Theory to
Improve Corporate
Management of
Currency-Exchange
Rates," *California
Management Re-
view,* Vol. 17, No. 4,
Summer 1975.)

a. Estimate the utility function values associated with the relevant outcomes and perform the decision tree analysis using the expected utility evaluation model. Do the results change?

b. It has been argued that we should *not* obtain the utility function from the treasurer. Since he will be blamed if an unfortunate outcome occurs, he will be too risk averse. Thus, his views are not in the best interests of the firm. Do you agree? If so, suggest a remedy for this problem.

CASE 15-4   Suppose you have just graduated and are trying to select your first job from several offers. You have decided to make your decision on the basis of the five criteria shown in the first column of Table 15-2. The criterion values associated with each alternative are also shown in Table 15-2.

Use the additive utility function to choose among the alternatives. Assess the single criterion utility function values for each criterion using the lottery approach. Also assess the weight for each criterion. Which job should you prefer?

CASE 15-5   Standard Oil of California proposes to construct a supertanker port and pipeline to supply its refinery at Richmond in the San Francisco Bay area. The port would consist of a single-point mooring two or three miles from shore to unload supertankers. Submarine pipelines would take the oil into a shore-based pumping station where it would enter the pipeline to the Richmond refinery.

There are several alternate sites on the west coast where a supertanker port could be located. On the basis of a preliminary screening, four sites were selected for a more detailed evaluation: Moss Landing, Estero Bay, Port Hueneme, and Oso Flaco Dunes. The major

TABLE 15-2	Alternate Jobs		
Criterion	Job 1	Job 2	Job 3
Salary	$16,000	$18,000	$22,000
Population of city	250,000	1 million	10 million
Climate	Hot, dry summers; mild winters	Hot, humid summers; mild winters	Pleasant summers; cold snowy winters
Daily commuting (one way)	0.25 hour	0.5 hour	1.0 hour
Nature of job	Much responsibility and opportunities for advancement	Routine work but opportunities for advancement	Routine work with few opportunities for advancement

Criteria Value Ranges and Weights   TABLE 15-3

Criterion	"Worst" Value for Each Criterion (lower limit = 0.0)	"Best" Value for Each Criterion (upper limit = 1.0)	Weights (w_k)
Facilities	No facilities to support super-tanker operations	All facilities completed for supertanker port operations	0.25
Port characteristics	Very rough seas and more than four miles from shore	Calm seas and one mile from shore	0.50
Location (Estero Bay as base)	Near Los Angeles with poor access to the San Joaquin Valley and Richmond	Between the Elk Hills oil field and San Francisco, but closer to Elk Hills with easy pipeline access to San Joaquin Valley	0.75
Initial cost (Estero Bay cost as base)	$60 million above base	$60 million below base	0.875
Annual cost (Estero Bay cost as base)	$5 million above base	$5 million below base	0.75
Possibilities for future development	No future development or expansion possible after initial part is completed	No limit on future growth or expansion of facilities	0.75
Attitude of local populace	Large, strong, vocal, and effective opposition	Small, weak, and ineffective opposition	0.50
Attitude of local politicians	Favorable vote unlikely	Favorable vote assured	1.00
Environmental impact from operation	Oil spill would seriously disrupt the community and harm wildlife; extreme danger due to proximity to military operations or other industry	Oil spill could be cleaned up relatively swiftly with no serious effect	0.50
Environmental impact from placement	Extreme blight on the area and interference with the natural environment	No major adverse effects from placement of facilities	0.25

criteria to be used in evaluating these alternatives are economics, the local political environment, and the environmental impacts. The three major criteria are refined into the 10 criteria listed in the left-hand column of Table 15-3. After some discussion, it was decided that the criteria were independent in terms of the preferences of decision makers at Standard Oil, so an additive utility function could be used.

TABLE 15-4   Characteristics of Alternatives

Criterion	Moss Landing	Estero Bay	Port Hueneme	Oso Flaco Dunes
Facilities	No	Yes	No	No
Post characteristics	Fair	Good	Excellent	Good
Location	Close to Richmond, farther from Elk Hills than base location	Central location	90 miles farther from Richmond than base location	Central location
Initial cost	$40 million less than Estero Bay	The cost-base location	$60 million more than Estero Bay	$5 million more than Estero Bay (estimate)
Annual cost	$2 million per year less than Estero Bay	Base location	$6 million more than Estero Bay	Near cost of base location
Possibilities for future development	Area already populated	Rolling terrain will hamper large expansion	Navy interference	Area available, subject to local politicians
Attitude of local populace	Possible opposition	Vocal opposition	Little effect on population	Little effect on population
Attitude of local politicians	Possibly opposed	Possibly favorable	Favorable	Possibly favorable
Environmental impact from operation	High impact—area is sandy to marshy, possibly difficult to clean up; possible long-term effects	High impact—tourism and fishing industry will be affected; marshy area and rocky coastline difficult to clean up; possible long-term damage to bird sanctuary and oyster beds	Minimal impact—area sandy; easy cleanup, area already industrialized	Minimal impact—area sandy; easy cleanup
Environmental impact from placement of facilities	Tank farm highly visible	Tank farm hidden, major restructure of existing creek	Tank farm visible (no nearby population)	Tank farm visible (no nearby population)

Utility Function Values for Alternate Locations

TABLE 15-5

| | Location | | | |
Criterion	Moss Landing	Estero Bay	Port Hueneme	Oso Flaco
Facilities	0.0	0.3	0.0	0.0
Port characteristics	0.3	0.6	0.7	0.5
Location	0.7	0.5	0.3	0.5
Initial cost	0.8	0.5	0.0	0.4
Annual cost	0.7	0.5	0.3	0.4
Possibilities for future development	0.1	0.6	0.1	0.6
Attitude of local populace	0.1	0.1	0.5	0.7
Attitude of local politicians	0.1	0.5	0.7	0.5
Environmental impact from operation	0.1	0.1	0.1	0.3
Environmental impact from placement of facilities	0.1	0.8	0.4	0.2

In order to determine the utility function for each criterion, it is necessary to specify a "worst" and a "best" outcome. The second column in Table 15-3 specifies the worst outcomes, which are assigned the value of 0.0; the third column contains the best values, which are assigned 1.0. Finally, the weights w_k for the criteria are in the fourth column.

The characteristics of each alternate site for each criterion are shown in Table 15-4. On the basis of these characteristics, the committee assigned the utility function scores shown in Table 15-5. For example, the utility function score for Estero Bay on the criterion "facilities" is 0.3, while it is 0.0 for Moss Landing, Oso Flaco, and Port Hueneme.*

a. On the basis of these weights and utility function values, which of the four alternatives should be preferred?
b. What if the weights on the two environmental criteria are increased to 1.0 for each one? Would the preferred alternative be different?

* From G. Hill, A. Kokin, and S. Nukes, "Standard Oil Supertanker Port Evaluation: Where Should They Put It?" unpublished report, Graduate School of Management, University of California, Los Angeles, June 1975. The alternatives, criteria, weights, and utility function values are only illustrative and do not represent the views of Standard Oil of California.

GENERAL REFERENCES

Brown, R. V. "Do Managers Find Decision Theory Useful?" *Harvard Business Review,* Vol. 48, 1970.

Fishburn, P., "Methods of Estimating Additive Utilities," *Management Science,* Vol. 13, No. 7, March 1967.

Hammond, J. C., "Better Decisions with Preference Theory," *Harvard Business Review,* November–December 1967.

Jones, J. M., *Statistical Decision Making,* Richard D. Irwin, Inc., Homewood, Ill., 1977.

Holloway, C. A., *Decision Making Under Uncertainty: Models and Choice,* Prentice-Hall, Englewood Cliffs, N.J., 1979.

Keeney, R., and H. Raiffa, *Decision Analysis with Multiple Objectives,* John Wiley & Sons, New York, 1976.

APPLICATIONS REFERENCES

Balke, W., K. Hammond, and G. Meyer, "An Alternative Approach to Labor-Management Negotiations," *Administrative Science Quarterly,* Vol. 13, 1973.

Dyer, J., "A Procedure for Selecting Educational Goal Areas for Emphasis," *Operations Research,* Vol. 21, No. 3, 1973.

Dyer, J., W. Farrell, and P. Bradley, "Utility Functions for Test Performance," *Management Science,* Vol. 20, No. 4, 1973.

Geoffrion, A., J. Dyer, and A. Feinberg, "An Interactive Approach for Multi-Criterion Optimization with an Application to the Operation of an Academic Department," *Management Science,* Vol. 19, No. 4, 1972.

Grayson, C. J., "Decisions Under Uncertainty: Drilling Decisions by Oil and Gas Operators," Division of Research, Harvard Business School, Boston, Mass., 1960.

Hill, G., A. Kokin, and S. Nukes, "Standard Oil Supertanker Port Evaluation: Where Should They Put It?" Unpublished report, Graduate School of Management, University of California, Los Angeles, June 1975.

Hoepfner, R., P. A. Bradley, S. P. Klein, and M. C. Alkin, *CSE Elementary School Evaluation Kit: Needs Assessment,* Allyn & Bacon, Boston, 1973.

Keeney, R., "A Decision Analysis with Multiple Objectives: The Mexico City Airport," *Bell Journal of Economics and Management,* Vol. 4, 1973.

———, "Utility Functions for Equity and Public Risk," *Management Science,* Vol. 26, No. 4, April 1980, pp. 345–353.

Klee, A., "The Role of Decision Models in the Evaluation of Competing Environmental Health Alternatives," *Management Science,* Vol. 18, No. 2, October 1971.

Pardee, F., T. Kirkwood, K. Kraemer, K. MacCrimmon, J. Miller, C. Phillips, J. Ranfti, K. Smith, and D. Whitcomb, "Measurement and Evaluation of Transportation System Effectiveness," RM-4869–DOT, The Rand Corporation, Santa Monica, California, September 1969.

Spetzler, C. S., "The Development of a Corporate Risk Policy for Capital Investment Decisions," *IEEE Transactions on Systems Science and Cybernetics,* Vol. SSC-4, No. 3, September 1968.

Stimson, D., "Utility Measurement in Public Health Decision Making," *Management Science,* Vol. 16, No. 2, October 1969.

Tversky, A., "On the Elicitation of Preferences: Descriptive and Prescriptive Considerations," in D. Bell, R. Keeney, and H. Raiffa, eds., *Conflicting Objectives in Decisions,* John Wiley & Sons, New York, 1977.

Wheelwright, S. C., "Applying Decision Theory to Improve Corporate Management of Currency-Exchange Risks," *California Management Review,* Vol. 17, No. 4, Summer 1975.

CHAPTER 16

The Value of Information

Most managers feel uneasy making a risky decision, even when the odds are in their favor. After all, there is always some chance that the *worst* conditional outcome associated with an alternative will actually occur. As a result, managers are often willing to invest time and money to reduce the risk associated with a decision, preferably turning a decision under risk into a decision under certainty. In some cases, it may not be possible to eliminate all of the risk associated with a decision, but it may be possible to obtain additional information that would reduce the risk. Since this information may be very costly, we should attempt to determine its value in improving our decision so that we can decide whether or not to pay the price of the additional information.

Additional information may come from several different sources. For example, a company may be trying to decide whether or not to market a new product. The success or failure of this venture will depend on the eventual demand for the product, which is uncertain. A better estimate of this demand might be obtained by a test market study prior to the nationwide distribution of the product. Unfortunately, the test market study would be expensive and would delay the introduction of the product by several months. This delay might even result in a similar product being marketed first by a competitor, which would reduce potential demand significantly. Would the reduction of the risk associated with the demand estimates be worth the costs of the marketing study?

Other sources of additional information include further research and development work on new products and new processes, engineering tests of land that may contain oil or other minerals, time delays that allow uncertainties to be resolved at the cost of lost sales or other opportunities, and expert opinions from professional consulting firms. Additional costs will be associated with these information sources as well.

Remarkably, the concepts of decision theory allow us to place a value on sources of additional information *before they are obtained*. This value may be used as the basis for deciding how much to pay for additional information from any source. In this chapter, we will use expected monetary value as the evaluation model. The value of any additional information can be determined by comparing the expected monetary value of making the decision *with* the information to the expected monetary value of making the decision *without* the information. Similar concepts can be applied to determine the value of additional information even when a utility function is used as an evaluation model.

PERFECT INFORMATION

In some risky situations, it may be possible to obtain additional information that will eliminate all risk from the problem so that the resulting decision can be made under certainty. We would call this *perfect information,* for obvious reasons. Even when it is not possible to obtain perfect information, an estimate of its value may serve as a useful upper bound on the level of expenditures that might be considered to resolve the risks inherent in a problem.

Example   Suppose you have inherited $100,000 and you have resolved to invest it in real estate. You place a call to your old friend Bubba Eledge who is in the real estate field.

Bubba reports that he is currently putting together two deals and you could invest in either one. The first alternative is to purchase 10 acres of undeveloped land for a price of $10,000 per acre, while the second alternative is to purchase an existing apartment house for $100,000. There is no way you can invest in both.

Bubba is reluctant to advise you regarding which one to choose, however, because of the risks involved. "The problem," he says, "is the city council election coming up early next year. There is almost an even split between the pro-growth and no-growth forces in this town."

"If the pro-growth forces win the election, the land investment will be a real winner. There is no question that you could subdivide that land into one-acre parcels and sell it for $18,000 per acre. It would be prime residential property. On the other hand, the value of the existing apartment would actually suffer since new apartments would be opening on the outskirts of town. It would be hard to keep it fully occupied, and you should probably take a loss and unload it at a price of $90,000, which I am sure you could get."

"If the no-growth slate wins, however, the apartment looks like a solid deal. With no new competition, you could keep it fully occupied and even raise the rents a bit. I am sure it would sell for $130,000 after the election. The land would really be hurt though. Without utilities and the right zoning decisions, it would be worth only about $5000 per acre."

"Those are my best estimates of the outcomes from those alternatives. You should base your decision on your own estimate of the probability that the no-growth forces will win the election."

Suppose you are uncertain about the likely winner of the election and assign each side a probability of winning of 0.5. To organize your thoughts you create the payoff table shown in Table 16-1.

TABLE 16-1   Payoff Table for the Investment Decision

	Alternatives	
Events	Land	Apartment
Pro-growth council ($p = 0.5$)	$80	−$10
No-growth council ($p = 0.5$)	−$50	$30

Note: Conditional outcomes are in thousands of dollars.

The expected monetary value associated with the land investment is (0.5)($80) + (0.5)(−$50) = $15 thousand, while the expected monetary value of the apartment investment is (0.5)(−$10) + (0.5)($30) = $10 thousand. Thus, on the basis of their expected monetary values, both decisions are attractive, but the land investment is preferred. However, you are uneasy with this result because you could *lose* $50 thousand from the land investment or *lose* $10 thousand from the apartment house. Clearly, you would like to resolve the risk associated with this problem.

Suppose we could poll *every* citizen in town and ask how he or she will vote in the forthcoming election. Assuming that they would be truthful, this poll would determine the election results and provide *perfect information*. How much would the poll be worth?

To determine this value, we need to identify the best alternative, *given that each possible event has occurred*. For example, if we know that a pro-growth city council will be elected, we would choose the land investment alternative and make $80 thousand. However, if we know that a no-growth city council will be elected, we would choose the apartment for an investment and make $30 thousand. Thus, we would have the following alternatives and outcomes:

Event	Alternative	Outcome
Pro-growth council	Land	$80 thousand
No-growth council	Apartment	$30 thousand

We have assigned a probability of 0.5 to the election of a pro-growth city council and 0.5 to the election of a no-growth council. Since the poll will be accurate, our estimate of the probability that it will predict the election of the pro-growth council is also 0.5, as is the probability that it will predict a no-growth council. This poll cannot control the future by changing the probability of an event, but its prediction will be correct.

If the poll predicts pro-growth, we will invest in land and make $80 thousand; if it predicts no-growth, we will invest in the apartment and make $30 thousand. Thus, given the prediction from the poll, we have a 0.5 chance of making $80 thousand and a 0.5 chance of making $30 thousand.

We can compute the *expected monetary value* of investing with perfect information. It is simply the probability of being told each event will occur multiplied by the outcome we would receive if we knew that event were going to occur. In this case, it would be

(0.5)($80) + (0.5)($30) = $55 thousand

However, the expected monetary value of choosing the land investment *without* perfect information was $15 thousand. Thus, the expected monetary value of investing after taking the poll (with perfect information) is $55 thousand, while the expected monetary value of investing without the poll and choosing the land investment is $15 thousand. So, the value of taking this poll (perfect information) in this case is $55,000 − $15,000 = $40,000. The value of perfect information is obtained by determining the expected value of the decision made with perfect information and subtracting the expected value of *the best alternative* without this information. This amount is an important upper limit or bound on what we should be willing to pay for the information.

It is important to recognize that the value of perfect information depends on both the outcomes *and* on the probabilities associated with the outcomes prior to obtaining the information. For example, suppose we had assigned the election of a pro-growth city council a probability of 0.9 rather than 0.5. Verify that the land investment would have an expected monetary value of $67 thousand in this case. Also verify that the expected monetary value of investing after taking the poll would be $75 thousand, so the value of perfect information with these new probabilities would be $75,000 − $67,000 = $8000 rather than $40,000 when the probabilities are 0.5 for each event. The higher probability of a pro-growth council reduces the value of additional information.

Why is the difference in the value of perfect information so great when the probabilities are changed? In the second case, we are almost sure (probability of 0.9) that a pro-growth city council will be elected anyway, so the value of additional information is relatively low since there is relatively little "risk" involved. When we think it is equally likely that either event will occur, however, we intuitively recognize that the uncertainty is extremely high, so information that will resolve this uncertainty is worth more.

Example The concept of perfect information can be applied even in more complex, real-world situations. The following example was taken from a presentation by Brock [1979] and represents a simplification of the actual analysis of a major strategic decision in a large international mining and metals corporation.

The company had to decide whether or not to proceed with a new venture that would commit it to the exploration, mining, and refining of a new type of ore. There was considerable uncertainty about the metallurgical properties of the ore as well as about the market price of the ore in the future.

The initial analysis of the problem was based on the decision tree shown in Figure 16-1. By rolling back the tree, verify that the expected monetary value of the new venture is $18.4 million. This venture was considered rather risky, however, since the outcomes indicate that it would actually be possible to lose $20 million, or even $40 million.

Because of these concerns, management decided to consider another alternative, postponing the go/no-go decision on the new venture and undertaking an applied research and development effort. The results of this study would eliminate the uncertainty about the metallurgical properties of the ore; that is, this strategy would actually provide *perfect information* regarding the metallurgical properties of the ore. The research and development effort would be costly, however, so the company wanted to estimate a value for the additional information.

In a more complex problem such as this one, the decision tree can be used ad-

FIGURE 16-1
Decision tree for
initial analysis of
new venture.

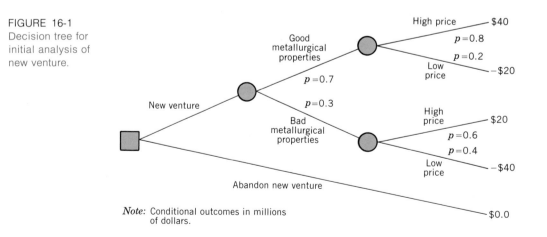

Note: Conditional outcomes in millions
of dollars.

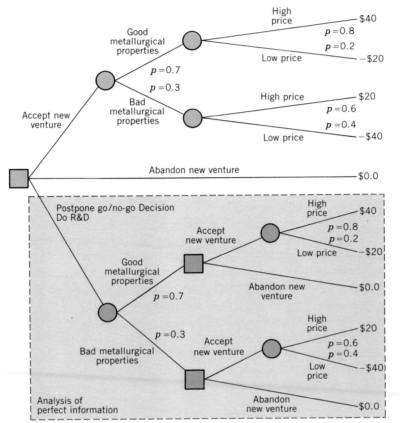

FIGURE 16-2
Expanded analysis to include R & D option providing perfect information.

vantageously again—this time as an aid in calculating the value of perfect information. The decision tree for the initial analysis of the problem shown in Figure 16-1 has been modified in Figure 16-2 to allow for the third alternative, obtaining perfect information regarding the metallurgical properties of the ore through a research and development effort.

Notice that the concept of perfect information does not mean that the chance point regarding the metallurgical properties of the ore can be removed from this new portion of the tree. Instead, it means that the resulting event will be known *prior* to the go/no-go decision, so that the chance branch point corresponding to the metallurgical properties appears *before* the go/no-go decision point in this new portion of the tree, not after the go/no-go decision shown in the portion of the tree used for the initial analysis.

Roll back the decision tree in Figure 16-2 and verify the following results:

1. If the metallurgical properties of the ore are determined to be "good," the company would accept the new venture with an expected monetary value of $28 million.

2. If the metallurgical properties of the ore are determined to be "bad," the company would abandon the new venture with an expected monetary value of $0.0 million.

3. The expected monetary value of the alternative of postponing the venture and doing research and development is $19.6 million, ignoring the cost of the research and development activity.

Since the expected monetary value of obtaining perfect information from research and development prior to the go/no-go decision is $19.6 million and the expected monetary value of the decision to accept the new venture without this information is $18.4 million, the value of perfect information regarding the metallurgical properties of the ore is $19.6 − $18.4 = $1.2 million. This figure represents the maximum amount of money that the company should be willing to spend for the research and development effort.

Notice that there is still uncertainty in the problem regarding the market price. What if the company could invest in a market survey to eliminate this uncertainty? Should the company be willing to pay more to eliminate the uncertainty about the metallurgical properties of the ore or about the market price? We will leave these questions to be answered as an exercise at the end of the chapter.

Also notice that the optimal strategy of the company based on the results shown in Figure 16-2 is now contingent on the results of the research and development activity. If the metallurgical properties of the ore are good, the company should proceed with the venture; if the properties are bad, the venture should be abandoned. Thus, the value of the research and development option results from allowing the company to *change* the decision it would otherwise make.

IMPERFECT INFORMATION

In many real-world problems, it is impossible to remove all the risk associated with an uncertain situation. It may be possible and practical, however, to obtain information that causes us to *revise* our initial probability estimates of some uncertain events. In the case of perfect information, we are able to revise these probabilities to 0.0 or 1.0. With imperfect information, the probabilities will be altered, but some risk will still remain in the problem. Nevertheless, there may be a value associated with this revision of the probabilities. This value can be computed in a similar manner to the approach used with perfect information.

The analysis of imperfect information requires an understanding of the basic concepts of probability theory (reviewed in Appendix A) and, especially, of the rules for revising probabilities.

Revision of probabilities

In many managerial problems, we may start with some probabilities of the occurrence of events, but we may be able to revise (improve) them as we obtain new information. For example, suppose we have a production process that is shown to produce products that are 95 percent good when it is set up properly. On the other hand, when it is improperly set up, only 20 percent of the products are acceptable. Previous data also indicate that 90 percent of the process settings were correct in the past. Suppose we set up the process and the first output is good. What is the probability that the process was properly set up?

We can compute the probability that the setup is correct, given the new information that the first output is good, through the use of the expression

$$P(A_i|B) = \frac{P(A_iB)}{P(B)} \tag{1}$$

which you may recognize as the formula for the *conditional probability* of the event A_i given that the event B has occurred. You should also recall that $P(B)$ is the *unconditional* or *marginal probability* that the event B will occur and that $P(A_iB)$ is the *joint probability* that both the events A_i and B will occur (see Appendix A). When this formula for conditional probabilities is used to revise probabilities, it is known as *Bayes rule.*

Now, what are the *events* in the production problem? First, there are two events associated with the setup of the process, "proper" or "improper." Next, there are two events associated with each unit produced, "good" or "bad." Suppose we define A_1 as the event *proper setup*, A_2 as the event *improper setup*, and B as the event *good product.* We will not need a symbol for the event *bad product* since the first unit of output was good.

From the problem description, we know that the probability of a proper setup, $P(A_1)$, is 0.9 prior to observing any output from the process. This is called the *prior probability* of the event A_1 since it is our best estimate of the probability of A_1 prior to obtaining additional information. Similarly, the prior probability of an improper setup, $P(A_2)$, is 0.1. Also, we know that the *conditional probability* of a good product given a proper setup, $P(B|A_1)$, is 0.95, while the conditional probability of a good product given a bad setup, $P(B|A_2)$, is 0.20.

According to our problem statement, we have a new setup and the first unit of output was good. Therefore, we would like to compute the conditional probability of a proper setup given a good product, $P(A_1|B)$, from the information given in the problem.

From Bayes rule (1) we see that

$$P(A_1|B) = \frac{P(A_1B)}{P(B)}$$

so our task is to compute $P(A_1B)$ and $P(B)$. The first step is easy, since

$$P(A_1B) = P(B|A_1) \times P(A_1) = (0.95)(0.9) = 0.855$$

Now, we need only find $P(B)$. We have the joint probability of A_1 and B, $P(A_1B)$. Since either A_1 or A_2 must occur (they are *collectively exhaustive*), we know that $P(B) = P(A_1B) + P(A_2B)$. Further, we can compute $P(A_2B)$ from

$$P(A_2B) = P(B|A_2) \times P(A_2) = (0.2)(0.1) = 0.02$$

which means that

$$P(B) = P(A_1B) + P(A_2B) = 0.855 + 0.02 = 0.875$$

We can now compute the probability that the process has a proper setup given the *additional information* that the first output of the process is good. Using Bayes rule (1), we obtain:

$$P(A_1|B) = \frac{P(A_1B)}{P(B)} = \frac{0.855}{0.875} = 0.977$$

Calculation of Revised Probabilities for Production Process   TABLE 16-2

Prior Probabilities[a]	Conditional Probabilities[b]	Joint Probabilities[c]	Revised Probabilities[d]
$P(A_1) = 0.9$	$P(B \mid A_1) = 0.95$	$P(A_1B) = 0.855$	$P(A_1 \mid B) = 0.977$
$P(A_2) = 0.1$	$P(B \mid A_2) = 0.20$	$P(A_2B) = 0.020$	$P(A_2 \mid B) = 0.023$
		$P(B) = 0.875$	

[a] Previous data indicate that 90 percent of process setting have been correct in the past.

[b] Production process has produced 95 percent good products when set up properly. If improperly set up, only 20 percent of products are acceptable.

[c] First two probabilities computed using Equation (1). The value of $P(B)$ computed from the relation $P(B) = P(A_1B) + P(A_2B)$.

[d] Computed from Equation (1).

which is the *revised prior* or *posterior probability* of A_1. Additional information regarding the output of the process could be used in an iterative fashion to continue to revise the probability of A_1.

The calculation of $P(A_1 \mid B)$ is straightforward but a bit tedious. It may be helpful to organize the necessary steps as shown in Table 16-2. The prior probabilities of the events of interest, in this case the settings of the production process, are written in column one. Next, the conditional probabilities of the event that provides information, a good product in this case, are in column two. The joint probabilities in column three are calculated by multiplying the prior probabilities in column one by the corresponding conditional probabilities in column two. The marginal probability of the event providing information is obtained by adding the joint probabilities in column three. Finally, the revised probabilities in column four are obtained by dividing each entry in column three by the sum of the entries in column three; that is, each joint probability is divided by the marginal probability of the event providing information.

An understanding of Bayes rule is important for managers since estimates of probabilities will be an important input to many real-world decisions. Studies have shown that individuals can actually do a reasonable job of estimating the prior probability of the occurrence of an event. However, they tend to be *much* too conservative in changing or revising these prior probabilities when confronted with new information. Notice that the information that only one good unit was produced should have revised our estimate of a proper setup of the process from 0.90 to 0.98. Most individuals would not expect such a significant change in this probability based only on one unit of production.

Value of imperfect information

Now, we will consider how to calculate the value of imperfect information. The rationale behind the approach is very similar to the rationale used to calculate the value of perfect information, but the calculations require the revision of probabilities.

Example   The National Motors Corporation is facing a critical decision. The smallest of the big five automobile producers is hoping to introduce a radical new car to increase its earnings and market share.

Two very different proposals have been submitted for the new car. The first has been developed under the code name Eagle and is a high price, high prestige sports car. The Eagle will have fully independent suspension, gull-wing doors, and a high performance engine. The company expects it to compare favorably in performance with the Corvette and Datsun sports cars, being priced in a similar range.

The second proposal has been code named Miser and is an economical automobile for suburban commuting. The company expects the Miser to be extremely efficient and average a minimum of 50 miles per gallon. This car will be produced exclusively with scotch plaid upholstery to promote its "miserly" image and should compete well against small cars by Volkswagen, Honda, and the major American manufacturers.

The problem is that National Motors has sufficient capital to tool up for the mass production of only one of these automobiles. Further, the unit sales and net profits from each car will depend on the status of the economy when it is introduced. Since there is a three-year lag between the decision to produce a new car and its introduction, this creates a risky decision for National Motors.

In a healthy economy, the Eagle will sell extremely well, while the Miser would actually lose money. In a mixed economy, neither car would be a great success, although the Miser would be a definite money marker. If the Miser were introduced during a recession, it should sell extremely well, despite tight money. Of course, the Eagle would be a disaster during a recession. The economists at National Motors have forecast a 0.3 chance of a healthy economy in three years, a 0.4 chance of a mixed economy, and a 0.3 chance of a recession. The specific estimates of the outcomes associated with these two alternatives are shown in the simple decision tree in Figure 16-3. Rolling back this decision tree, we find that the Eagle has an expected monetary value of $0.5 million, while the Miser has an expected monetary value of $1.4 million.

The president of National Motors is concerned, however, since the decision to produce the Miser would result in a $1-million loss if the economy is healthy, and

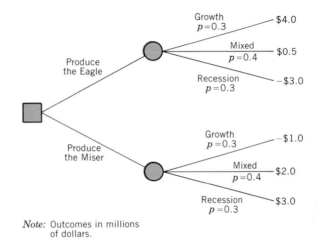

Growth
p=0.3 — $4.0

Mixed
p=0.4 — $0.5

Produce
the Eagle

Recession
p=0.3 — −$3.0

Growth
p=0.3 — −$1.0

Mixed
p=0.4 — $2.0

Produce
the Miser

Recession
p=0.3 — $3.0

Note: Outcomes in millions
of dollars.

FIGURE 16-3
Decision tree for
choosing between
the Eagle and
the Miser.

company economists' estimate the probability of this occurring as 0.3. He is considering hiring an economic forecasting company, Crystal Ball Associates, to advise him regarding the state of the economy in three years. Crystal Ball will offer only an assessment of whether the economic conditions in three years will be "favorable" or "unfavorable." Their record has not been perfect in predicting the state of the economy. The president has investigated their performance and has discovered that they have predicted a favorable economy 90 percent of the time that a healthy economy occurred, 60 percent of the time that a mixed economy occurred, and 20 percent of the time that a recession actually occurred. He is not sure whether their advice would be worth their handsome consulting fee.

Suppose we define H as the event "healthy economy," M as "mixed economy," and R as "recession." Also, F is a "favorable" assessment by Crystal Ball and U is "unfavorable." The economists have provided the prior probabilities $P(H) = 0.3$, $P(M) = 0.4$, and $P(R) = 0.3$. On the basis of Crystal Ball's record, the president estimates $P(F|H) = 0.9$, $P(F|M) = 0.6$, and $P(F|R) = 0.2$, so naturally $P(U|H) = 0.1$, $P(U|M) = 0.4$, and $P(U|R) = 0.8$ since each set of probabilities conditioned on the same event must sum to 1.0.

To find the value of the perfect information provided by Crystal Ball, we can use the decision tree in Figure 16-4. On the decision branch corresponding to the alternative "obtain information from Crystal Ball," the first chance point represents our uncertainty about their forecast. Thus, we need to calculate $P(F)$ and $P(U)$. Given a

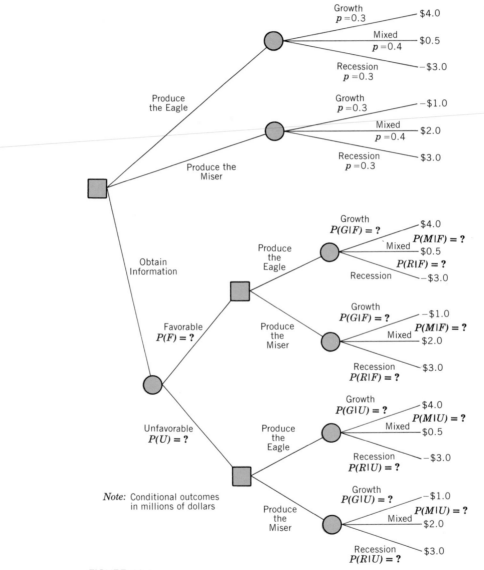

FIGURE 16-4
Structure of decision tree for calculation of value of imperfect information from Crystal Ball Associates.

Calculation of Revised Probabilities for National Motors				TABLE 16-3

Information Event *F*			
Prior Probabilities	Conditional Probabilities	Joint Probabilities	Revised Probabilities
$P(H) = 0.3$	$P(F|H) = 0.9$	$P(HF) = 0.27$	$P(H|F) = 0.47$
$P(M) = 0.4$	$P(F|M) = 0.6$	$P(MF) = 0.24$	$P(M|F) = 0.42$
$P(R) = 0.3$	$P(F|R) = 0.2$	$P(RF) = 0.06$	$P(R|F) = 0.11$
		$P(F) \quad = 0.57$	

Information Event *U*			
Prior Probabilities	Conditional Probabilities	Joint Probabilities	Revised Probabilities
$P(H) = 0.3$	$P(U|H) = 0.1$	$P(HU) = 0.03$	$P(H|U) = 0.07$
$P(M) = 0.4$	$P(U|M) = 0.4$	$P(MU) = 0.16$	$P(M|U) = 0.37$
$P(R) = 0.3$	$P(U|R) = 0.8$	$P(RU) = 0.24$	$P(R|U) = 0.56$
		$P(U) \quad = 0.43$	

forecast, we must decide whether to produce the Eagle or the Miser. These portions of the tree are exactly like the original decision tree in Figure 16-3, except that the probabilities associated with the states of the economy should be revised based on whether Crystal Ball predicted favorable or unfavorable conditions.

These new probabilities can be calculated using the same procedure that we illustrated for revising the probability of a proper process setup in Table 16-2. The analysis is shown in Table 16-3. Notice that we have one set of calculations corresponding to the information event favorable and another set corresponding to the information event unfavorable. *In general, there will be a similar set of calculations for each event that provides information.*

These revised probabilities have been substituted into the decision tree in Figure 16-5. The expected monetary value at each chance point and at each decision point is written near it. Notice that the expected monetary value of the decision to produce the Eagle is now $1.76 million *given* the favorable forecast by Crystal Ball, and would be preferable to the Miser in this case. With an unfavorable forecast, the Miser is the better choice.

The expected monetary value of the branch corresponding to seeking imperfect information from Crystal Ball is $2.01 million. Since the expected monetary value of producing the Miser without this information is $1.4 million, the president of

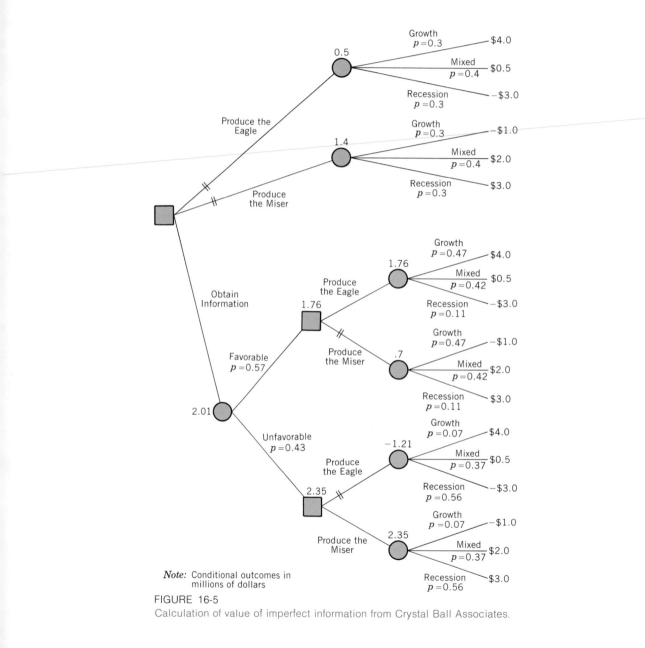

FIGURE 16-5
Calculation of value of imperfect information from Crystal Ball Associates.

National Motors should be willing to pay up to $2.01 − $1.4 = $0.61 million ($610,000) for the imperfect information provided by Crystal Ball.

Example Tex Gross, the production manager of POCO, is facing a major decision regarding a new wildcat oil well. A preliminary geological study of the underground structure at this oil lease in northern California indicates a "good chance" of oil. Based on a detailed analysis of similar sites, the geologists estimate a 0.2 probability that this new site will be extremely productive, or "wet," and a 0.3 probability that it will be marginally productive, or "moist." The chance of a "dry hole" is significant, with a probability of 0.5.

Tex's decision is complicated by the fact that if oil is discovered, it may be either "sweet" or "sour." Sweet crude is low in sulfur content and can be processed at a much lower cost than sour crude because expensive air pollution abatement equipment is not required. The geologists estimate that the probability that any oil discovered will be sweet crude is 0.4.

The potential profit from a productive oil well will depend on whether it is wet or moist and on whether it is sweet or sour. A wet well would return $4 million if the crude is sweet but only $3 million if it is sour. A moist well would return only $2 million if it is sweet and actually lose $0.5 million if it is sour. A dry hole would result in a loss of $1.0 million.

The decision tree for Tex's problem is shown in Figure 16-6. Rolling back, we find that the expected monetary value of the decision to drill is $0.52 million ($520,000).

Tex is considering the possibility of another seismic test at the site to provide additional information. This test will determine whether there is a dome, semi-dome, or no-dome structure in the underlying rock strata. Past history has shown that a dome structure occurs 50 percent of the time when a wet well is found, 60 percent of the time with a moist well, and only 30 percent of time with a dry hole. A semi-dome appears in 30 percent of the wet well, 30 percent of the moist well, and 40 percent of the dry hole discoveries. The remaining percentages are associated with no dome.

We define our events as W for a wet well, M for a moist well, and D for a dry hole. The initial probabilities are $P(W) = 0.2$, $P(M) = 0.3$, and $P(D) = 0.5$. The events providing information are defined as F for a favorable dome structure, S for a semi-dome, and N for no dome. Thus, the probability of a favorable dome structure given a wet well, $P(F|W)$, is 0.5 if we treat the historical percentages as our best estimate of their associated probabilities.

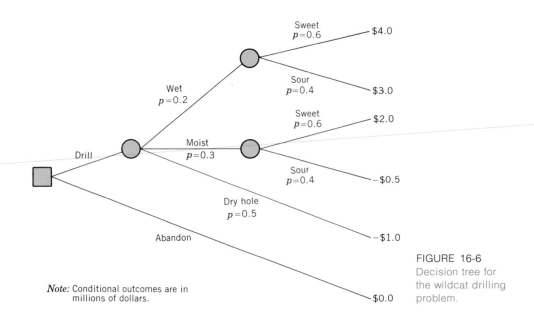

Sweet
$p=0.6$ — $4.0

Sour
$p=0.4$ — $3.0

Sweet
$p=0.6$ — $2.0

Wet
$p=0.2$

Drill

Moist
$p=0.3$

Sour
$p=0.4$ — −$0.5

Dry hole
$p=0.5$

Abandon — $1.0

Note: Conditional outcomes are in
millions of dollars.

$0.0

FIGURE 16-6
Decision tree for
the wildcat drilling
problem.

Once again, we must find the marginal probabilities of each event providing information and the revised probabilities of the events that determine the outcomes. Using the same approach as before, the necessary calculations are shown in Table 16-4.

The decision tree for analyzing the value of the imperfect information provided by this test is shown in Figure 16-7. The revised probabilities have been transferred to the tree from Table 16-4. For example, if the outcome of the test indicates the existence of a dome structure, then the probability of a dry hole, $P(D|F)$, is only 0.35. If the outcome of the test indicates no dome, then the probability of the dry hole, $P(D|N)$, increases to 0.68. The probabilities of sweet and sour crude are not affected by this new information. Once again, the expected monetary value at each chance point and at each decision point is written in a small circle. The decision to drill the wildcat well will result in an expected profit of $900,000 if the test indicates a dome structure, $300,000 if it indicates a semi-dome structure, and only $110,000 for a no-dome structure. Multiplying each of these expected monetary values by the marginal probabilities of their associated test results gives an expected monetary value of $0.52 million ($520,000) for the alternative of running the seismic test.

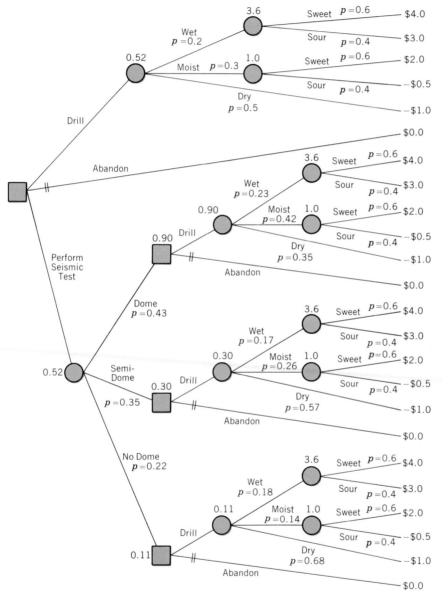

FIGURE 16-7
Calculation of expected
value of imperfect information
provided by seismic test.

TABLE 16-4   Calculation of Revised Probabilities for POCO

Information Event F (dome structure)

Prior Probabilities	Conditional Probabilities	Joint Probabilities	Revised Probabilities
$P(W) = 0.2$	$P(F|W) = 0.5$	$P(WF) = 0.10$	$P(W|F) = 0.23$
$P(M) = 0.3$	$P(F|M) = 0.6$	$P(MF) = 0.18$	$P(M|F) = 0.42$
$P(D) = 0.5$	$P(F|D) = 0.3$	$P(DF) = 0.15$	$P(D|F) = 0.35$
		$P(F) = 0.43$	

Information Event S (semi-dome structure)

Prior Probabilities	Conditional Probabilities	Joint Probabilities	Revised Probabilities
$P(W) = 0.2$	$P(S|W) = 0.3$	$P(WS) = 0.06$	$P(W|S) = 0.17$
$P(M) = 0.3$	$P(S|M) = 0.3$	$P(MS) = 0.09$	$P(M|S) = 0.26$
$P(D) = 0.5$	$P(S|D) = 0.4$	$P(DS) = 0.20$	$P(D|S) = 0.57$
		$P(S) = 0.35$	

Information Event N (no dome structure)

Prior Probabilities	Conditional Probabilities	Joint Probabilities	Revised Probabilities
$P(W) = 0.2$	$P(N|W) = 0.2$	$P(WN) = 0.04$	$P(W|N) = 0.18$
$P(M) = 0.3$	$P(N|M) = 0.1$	$P(MN) = 0.03$	$P(M|N) = 0.14$
$P(D) = 0.5$	$P(N|D) = 0.3$	$P(DN) = 0.15$	$P(D|N) = 0.68$
		$P(N) = 0.22$	

Notice, however, that the expected monetary value of the decision to drill *without* the test is also $520,000. Therefore, the value of the information provided by this seismic test is $520,000 − $520,000 = 0.

A close inspection of Figure 16-7 helps to understand this result. No matter which outcome results from the test, we still would drill for oil using the expected monetary value as the basis for the decision. Since this new information never affects the choice of the best decision, *it has no value.* Loosely speaking, the prior probabilities of the outcomes were not revised enough by the new information to make the expected monetary value of the decision to drill lower than the expected monetary value of the alternative to abandon the lease.

This example provides an important lesson for managers. It is *not* always better to collect more information. Information can be costly to collect, and it will be worthless to managers unless it has the potential actually to change the decision they would otherwise make.

WHAT SHOULD THE MANAGER KNOW?

A manager naturally seeks additional information that will reduce or eliminate the risk associated with a decision. Such information is costly, however. One of the most important advantages of a formal decision tree analysis of a risky problem is that this decision tree can be used as the basis for computing the value of perfect or imperfect information.

Perfect information will resolve the risk associated with some uncertain events so that the decision can be made with complete certainty regarding which event will occur. Imperfect information does not eliminate risk, but it revises the prior probabilities associated with a set of events. The value of perfect or imperfect information is calculated by computing the expected value of the decision *with* the additional information and subtracting the expected value of the best alternative without the information.

It is important to emphasize that the value of information depends on whether its availability *changes the decisions made by the manager*. If no change takes place, then the information will have no value, as illustrated by the POCO wildcat drilling example.

To obtain an intuitive feel for the value of information, you should recognize that its potential value depends on two factors. The first is the variation in the possible outcomes. For example, an alternative with an even chance (50-50) of making $15,000 or $5000 has the same expected value as an alternative with an even chance of making $120,000 or *losing* $100,000. However, the expected value of perfect or imperfect information is likely to be higher in problems involving such alternatives as the latter one.

The second factor is the prior probabilities. If we assign almost equal probabilities to all the possible outcomes from an alternative, then we are saying that we really do not know which outcome will occur. The value of additional information may be relatively high in these cases. However, if our prior estimate of the probability of one of the outcomes is close to 1.0, then we intuitively feel that there is less risk involved in the decision. This intuition will be confirmed by a relatively lower value of perfect or imperfect information if the outcomes are held constant.

To summarize, the value of additional information will be relatively high if there is considerable variation among the outcomes associated with the alternatives and almost an equal probability of the occurrence of any of these outcomes. The value of additional information will be relatively low when there is very little variation among the outcomes and when the probability of the occurrence of one of these out-comes is "close" to 1.0. Even if no formal analysis is performed, an understanding of these concepts may assist a manager in evaluating alternate sources of additional information.

CHECK YOUR UNDERSTANDING

1. What is meant by the term *perfect information?*
2. Comment on the following statement: "If information is imperfect, then it must be misleading. Therefore, it is worthless, at best."
3. Use the information presented in Table 16-1 for the investment decision to answer the following questions:
   a. Verify that if your *prior probability* of the election of a pro-growth city council is 0.9, then the value of perfect information is only $8000.
   b. Suppose your prior probability of the election of a pro-growth city council is 0.75. What is the value of perfect information?
   c. You realize that it would be impractical to poll every citizen in town regarding the forthcoming election. Many individuals would probably change their minds later anyway. However, you could take a telephone poll of 100 citizens. You estimate that if the pro-growth city council is actually going to win, then the probability that your poll will correctly predict this is 0.9. However, if the no-growth city council is going to win, you estimate that your poll would still predict a win by the pro-growth forces with a probability of 0.4. How much should you pay for this poll?
4. Consider the problem faced by the mining company illustrated in Figure 16-1.
   a. Suppose the estimate of the probability of good metallurgical properties had been 0.9 rather than 0.7. How much would the research and development effort be worth in this case?
   b. Instead of worrying about the metallurgical properties of the ore, suppose the company tries to obtain perfect information regarding the price of the ore. How much would this information be worth? Hint: the decision tree used to

analyze this problem will require moving *two* chance points prior to the decision regarding the new venture. The first chance point that will be resolved by perfect information concerns prices *if the metallurgical properties are good.* The second chance point occurring twice in this new tree at the branches of the previous chance point concerns prices *if the metallurgical properties are bad.*

c. Suppose the company can perform a "simple" research and development test for only $250,000. If the metallurgical properties of the ore are actually good, then the probability that this test will be "successful" is 0.95. If the metallurgical properties are bad, the probability that this test will be "successful" is only 0.25. Should they perform the test?

5. Recall the process discussed in this chapter that produces 95 percent good products when set up properly but only 20 percent acceptable products when improperly set up. In the past, some 90 percent of the setups have been correct.

a. Suppose we set up the process and the first output is bad. What is the probability that the process has been properly set up?

b. Suppose we set up the process and the first *two* units of output are good. What is the probability that the process has been properly set up?

   (1) Compute this probability by revising the probability of 0.977 that the process is set up properly. This is the result obtained after the first unit was found to be good, as described in the text.

   (2) Compute this probability directly by defining A_1 and A_2 as before and by defining the event B as *two good products.*

6. The National Motors Corporation wishes to perform some additional analysis of their automobile selection problem.

a. Suppose that National Motors could find a consulting firm with a *perfect* record of forecasting the economy. What is the maximum amount that they should be willing to pay for this advice?

b. The consulting fee charged by Crystal Ball Associates is $250,000. A second firm, Swami Sees, Inc., has approached National Motors with an offer to predict the future state of the economy for $400,000. They argue that their services are worth the additional cost since they will make one of *three* predictions, excellent (E), favorable (F), or unfavorable (U). They provide evidence which indicates that $P(E|H) = 0.9$, $P(E|M) = 0.4$, and $P(E|R) = 0.1$. Further, $P(F|H) = 0.05$, $P(F|M) = 0.5$, and $P(F|R) = 0.4$. Thus, $P(U|H) = 0.05$, $P(U|M) = 0.1$, and $P(U|R) = 0.5$. Should National Motors hire Crystal Ball or Swami Sees?

7. Suppose Tex Gross, the production manager of POCO, could obtain information from other sources to aid in making the decision diagrammed in Figure 16-6.

 a. A "whiff test" can be run for $100,000 to determine whether any oil that might be found will be sweet or sour. There still will be a 0.5 probability of a dry hole, however. Should Tex perform the whiff test?

 b. As a guide to assist Tex in the evaluation of additional information, what would be the value of *perfect information* regarding whether the result of drilling will be a wet well, a moist well, or a dry hole?

 c. Rather than a seismic test, Tex can drill a test hole for only $200,000. The result of this test will be success (S) or failure (F). Using W to represent the event wet well, M to represent moist, and D to represent dry as before, Tex knows that $P(S|W) = 0.9$, $P(S|M) = 0.7$, and $P(S|D) = 0.2$. Should he drill the test hole?

SHORT CASES

CASE 16-1   A company is considering the introduction of a new product. It is estimated that there is a 0.9 probability that the product will be successful if there is no competition within two years. However, there is only a 0.3 probability that it will be successful if competition does appear in the first two years. An independent estimate of the probability of competition within two years is 0.3. What is the probability that the product will be successful?

CASE 16-2   An analysis of the credit card data of POCO is focused on persons who avoided being classified as bad risks during the first year they held the card. Of these persons, 95 percent continue to be good customers, but 5 percent are classified as bad risks at some later point because of unpaid balances. The analysis reveals that 80 percent of the persons who continue to be good customers did not let their credit balance accumulate beyond $100 during the first year, but 70 percent of those who became bad risks did let their balances exceed $100 during the first year. Suppose that a new credit card customer lets his balance exceed $100 during the first year. What is the probability that he or she will become a bad risk?

CASE 16-3   The Pacific Oil Company has an interest in some offshore lands. They estimate the probability of finding oil on this land to be 0.3. Additional seismographic tests could be used to revise this probability. If there is oil on the land, there is a 0.95 probability that the test will be positive, but a 0.05 probability that it will be negative. If there is no oil, there is still a 0.1 probability of a positive test. If a positive test is obtained, what is the probability that the well will be a "dry hole" (no oil)?

CASE 16-4

Suppose we are faced with the two gambles shown in Table 16-5. Recall from Chapter 14 that the outcomes from these two gambles depend on the flip of a fair coin. Suppose someone tells us she is a clairvoyant; that is, she can predict the future, including the result of flipping a coin.

a. How much should we be willing to pay her for *perfect information* regarding this coin flip?

b. Suppose we find out that our friend does seem to have psychic powers, but she is not always correct. She can correctly predict the outcome of a coin flip 90 percent of the time. How much would this advice be worth?

c. Let us introduce alternative A_3 again. If we choose A_3, we flip a coin twice. The first flip is made with a fair coin. If it lands on heads, we flip the fair coin again. A second heads results in an outcome of $20, but tails means that we lose $5. If the first flip results in tails, we flip a weighted coin with only a 0.4 probability of heads. If heads occurs, we win $5, but, if tails occurs, we lose $10. The choice among the three gambles is illustrated in Figure 14-2 in Chapter 14.

(1) Suppose our clairvoyant friend can predict the outcome of the first coin flip with the fair coin in either gamble A_1, gamble A_2, or gamble A_3. If we choose A_3, we still will face the uncertainty of the second coin flip. How much would *perfect information* regarding the first flip be worth?

(2) Now suppose that our clairvoyant will predict the outcome of the first flip with only 0.9 percent accuracy. How much is this imperfect information worth?

TABLE 16-5

Alternate Gambles

Events	Game 1 (A_1)	Game 2 (A_2)
	Alternatives	
Heads ($p = 0.5$)	$10	$2
Tails ($p = 0.5$)	-$ 2	-$1

CASE 16-5

The problem faced by POCO in determining its oil shale development strategy was analyzed in Chapter 14 using the information provided on the decision tree shown in Figure 14-6. According to this analysis, the best strategy was a combined research and development effort with an expected monetary value of $81.25 million.

a. What if POCO could spend additional funds immediately and determine if a breakthrough in the processing technology could be made *from the initial research-only strategy?* The probability of a breakthrough from the initial strategy of a combined research and development effort would remain at 0.3. How much would this information be worth? Draw a decision tree appropriate for analyzing this question and perform the necessary roll-back calculations.

b. What if POCO could spend additional funds immediately and determine if a breakthrough in the processing technology could be made from *either the initial research-only strategy or the combined research and development strategy.* How much would this information be worth? Hint: the decision tree used to analyze this problem will have a chance node corresponding to the possibility of a breakthrough from research-only and chance nodes corresponding to a breakthrough from the combined research and development effort occurring *prior* to the decision point where the alternatives are chosen.

CASE 16-6   Case 14-5 in Chapter 14 describes a problem faced by Mid-Valley Manufacturers in trying to determine the appropriate bid on a government contract. Using the data in Case 14-5, answer the following questions.

a. What would be the value of resolving the risk regarding the proposed new process for manufacturing valves? That is, what would be the value of perfect information regarding this process?

b. For an investment of $20,000, the company can conduct a pilot test on the new process. Unfortunately, the results of the pilot test would not be conclusive. If the process will encounter no complications, then the engineers estimate that the probability that the test will be successful is 0.95. If it will encounter only minor complications, the probability of a successful test is 0.7. However, if the new production process will develop major complications, then the probability of a successful test is only 0.3. If they receive the contract, should Mid-Valley conduct this pilot test? Does your answer depend on the bid price? Why or why not?

CASE 16-7   The plant expansion problem described in Case 14-6 of Chapter 14 was complicated by the risk associated with the demand projections.

a. What would be the value of perfect information regarding the demand pattern? Draw the decision tree necessary to analyze this problem and roll it back.

b. Bettman and Lutz, Inc., a major West Coast marketing firm, has offered to do a market study for the chemical company. The results of this test will be either favorable or unfavorable. Bettman and Lutz admit that their test will not distinguish between a demand pattern that is sustained high and one that is initially high but long-term low. In either case, they estimate that the probability of a successful test result is 0.85. However, if the demand pattern will be initially low and long-term low, then the probability of a successful test result is only 0.2. What is the maximum fee that the company should be willing to pay for this market test?

CASE 16-8   An automobile dealer is trying to decide how many Pace Car editions of his manufacturer's sporty compact model he should order. The Pace Car edition was created to celebrate the use of this particular model as the official pace car in the famous Cleveland 450-mile race. The cars have a dealer's cost of $10,000 and would sell for a net profit of $2000 each *if* they are sold before the end of the model year, which is near. Any automobiles left over after the end of the model year will sell at a loss of $1000 each. The dealer also feels that an expected loss of $500 is incurred if an individual wishes to buy a Pace Car but none are available. On the basis of past experience, the dealer estimates the probability of demand for 0, 1, 2, or 3 of these Pace Car editions to be 0.1, 0.3, 0.4, and 0.2, respectively.

a. Compute a payoff table for this problem. How many of these Pace Car editions should the dealer order assuming the desire to maximize the expected monetary value of the decision?

b. What is the value of perfect information regarding the demand for these automobiles?

c. The Pace Car editions have already been delivered to dealers in the East. The dealer could call the East Coast and inquire about whether the sales have been "hot" or "cold." The following conditional probabilities are felt to be good estimates:

P (hot report|demand is 0) $= 0.3$

P (hot report|demand is 1) $= 0.4$

P (hot report|demand is 2) $= 0.5$

P (hot report|demand is 3) $= 0.6$

Should the dealer bother to make the call? Compute the expected value of this imperfect information.

GENERAL REFERENCES

Holloway, C., *Decision Making Under Uncertainty,* Prentice-Hall, Inc., Englewood Cliffs, N.J., 1979.

Jones, J. M., *Statistical Decision Making,* Richard D. Irwin, Inc., Homewood, Ill., 1977.

Raiffa, H., *Decision Analysis,* Addison-Wesley, Reading, Mass., 1968.

APPLICATIONS REFERENCES

Brock, H. W., "The Role of R and D Planning in Meaningful Strategic Decision-Making," Decision Analysis Group, SRI International, Palo Alto, Calif., 1979.

Green, P. E., "Bayesian Decision Theory in Pricing Strategy," *Journal of Marketing,* Vol. 27, No. 1, January 1963.

Newman, J. W., *Management Applications of Decision Theory,* Harper & Row, Inc., New York, 1971.

PART V

Synthesis

essential interrelationships among these categories. Continuing the analogy, the value of material in a textbook will be enhanced considerably if the reader understands the interrelationships among the materials within different chapters as well as the more specific details in each chapter.

As you have read each chapter, the title and the introduction have identified the nature of the problems and of the associated mathematical models and solution techniques to be discussed. In the real world there are no titles or introductory statements to tell you that a particular problem can best be modeled and analyzed using linear programming or any other technique of management science. An ability to recognize key problem characteristics that aid in identifying the appropriate form of the model must be developed. This ability can be of significant value in enhancing the problem-solving skills of a manager, even if a formal, mathematical analysis is not performed.

The later statement raises another important question: When should a formal, mathematical analysis of a problem be performed? There are no firm rules for selecting a particular model or for deciding whether to perform an analysis, but we will attempt to provide some guidance in Chapter 17.

In Chapter 1, we argued that a model simplifies a problem solver's view of a problem by leaving out much information and by creating categories. In a similar manner, an introductory textbook simplifies a complex body of knowledge by leaving out much information (recall our numerous comments that such details were primarily of interest to analysts) and by creating categories (called chapters). A useful model contains not only the important categories but also the

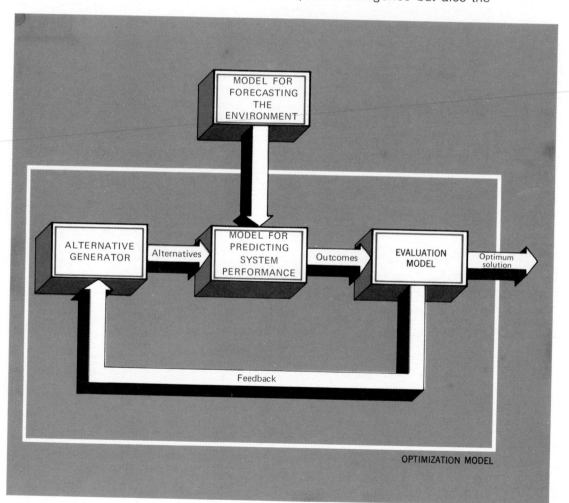

What Should the Manager Know?

CHAPTER 17

What should the manager know about the tools, techniques, and concepts of management science/operations research? At the end of each chapter, we have addressed this important question in terms of the specific materials included within the chapter. Now it is time to address this question by looking across the chapters to gain an appreciation for the total body of knowledge associated with the hybrid term, management science/operations research. In doing so, we will first consider whether a formal, mathematical analysis should be used to deal with a particular, real-world problem. Next, we will provide some summary guidelines for matching problems with models and solution techniques. These guidelines also serve as a means of summarizing and synthesizing the topics we have covered.

WHEN SHOULD MANAGEMENT SCIENCE/OPERATIONS RESEARCH BE USED?

We have presented numerous examples of ''successful'' applications of the models and tools of management science/operations research to real-world problems, but it is clear that not every real-world problem should be dealt with by formally applying these models and tools. How can an intelligent decision be made with regard to the use of these approaches? Perhaps some insights can be gained by considering what is meant by the term, ''successful application.''

Benefits versus cost

The use of a formal, mathematical model in the analysis of a problem is ''successful'' if the benefits exceed the costs. The costs include the time for model formulation, the time and cost of data collection, the time and cost of the development of necessary computer programs, and the cost of any computer runs required for the formal analysis.

These costs can be substantial and can easily exceed subjective estimates of the benefits that might result from an analysis. However, the continuing research and development in the fields of computer hardware design and information systems, and the development of efficient computer programs for performing the analyses guarantee that these costs will continue to decrease, so that, in the future, the potential benefits of applying formal mathematical models will exceed the costs in a growing number of problem areas. This relationship between the benefits and costs of analysis can be illustrated

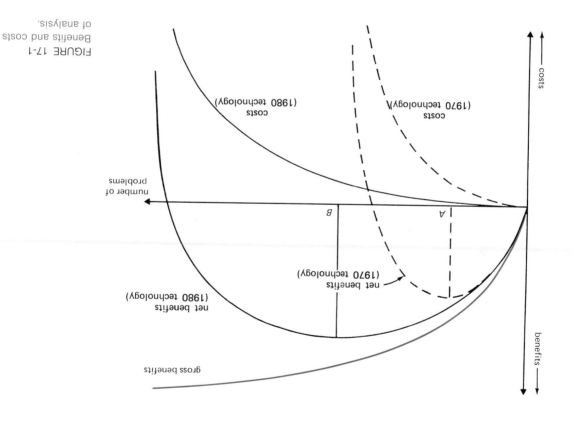

FIGURE 17-1
Benefits and costs
of analysis.

diagrammatically as shown in Figure 17-1. The gross benefits of applying formal mathematical models to problems within an organization increase rapidly as the problems with the highest payoff are analyzed first, and continue to increase but at a decreasing rate. The costs of applying the models are initially small, but increase at an increasing rate. However, the costs associated with 1970 technology, in terms of computers, information systems, and computer programs, increase much faster than the costs associated with 1980 technology. Therefore, the number of problems to which the formal analysis should be applied in order to maximize *net benefits* has increased from point A in 1970 to point B in 1980 (see Figure 17-1). It is likely that this increase will continue, making it even more important for the modern manager to have model-building skills in the future.

In any particular situation, a rough estimate of the potential benefits and costs will have to be made. For example, the expenses from the product transportation and distribution system of a large organization may run into millions of dollars annually. A large-scale formal analysis of the system could easily be justified, even if the costs of the analysis were several hundred thousand dollars.

In other situations, computer programs may be available that can analyze a problem by using readily accessible data. The costs of the analysis may be only a few hundred dollars, and these costs can easily be justified, even in small organizations dealing with relatively small problems.

Conceptual value

Suppose that you estimate that a formal mathematical model-building effort is not justified in a particular situation—perhaps because adequate data or the appropriate computer programs are not available and the cost or time required to develop them is prohibitive. Are the concepts of model building still of use in the problem-solving effort?

What you have learned may seem at first to be some detailed knowledge about linear optimization models, corporate planning models, network models, waiting-line models, decision trees, and so on. But it should have been more than that. Formal models should also teach us something about the basic structure of certain kinds of important problems.

For example, in studying linear optimization models, we learn not only the structure and application of this important model but also something fundamental about allocation problems in general. We learn to handle the effects of interacting and competing demands for limited resources and, perhaps more important, we learn the general nature of optimum solutions. Understanding these general concepts is important because they should carry over into situations for which the formal model is not applicable. In the practical operating situation, allocations of limited resources must often be made on an intuitive basis, either because there is not time for formal analysis or because the most important variables are not quantifiable. We believe that managers can exercise intuitive judgment most effectively if they understand the basic nature of a formal problem and the probable nature of good solutions.

Another excellent example is the general waiting-line model. The individual who understands formal waiting-line models should be able to make a good snap judgment about the level of service to provide in a practical situation by realizing the great value of idle time of the server. The value of idle time is a concept that runs contrary to our fundamental training to conserve time. Yet, in the design of many systems, provision of apparent overcapacity is the key to success.

Thus, one benefit of an understanding of formal mathematical model building is that it provides alternate ways of thinking about a problem: as a linear optimization model, a network model, or a waiting-line model. In each case, thinking about a model in these terms can also help determine the information that should be collected and the probable nature of the best solution. These benefits should accrue to a manager with model-building skills, even if no formal analysis is undertaken.

THE MANAGER AND MANAGEMENT SCIENCE

Throughout the book, we have focused on the manager, the use of management science and what the manager should know about each of the types of models. The entire thrust of the text has been on the presentation of management science for managerial use rather than for the technical specialist's use.

Management science models are most often developed around a current managerial problem and managers view management science as a decision support system, not as a decision system per se. The manager stands between the real system and the support system as indicated in Figure 17-2. The manager sees challenges and problems in the real system and has an extremely important role in formulating models that will be truly useful. Given a useful model in the managers' terms, pertinent questions may be asked and the model provides answers to at least some of these questions. The support system does not make decisions, however, the manager does, working interactively with the support system.

Why does the support system of management science not make decisions, thereby automating management's decision making role? After all, the entire thrust of Part II was on optimization models that give "best possible" answers. Also, many of the other types of analyses produce the best possible solution from among alternatives tested.

Managers who know how to use the management science support system appropriately also recognize its limitations. The answers given by models are always the best possible in relation to the model. But, there are many types of variables that are not represented in models but that are of great significance in the managers' attempt to attain a system-wide optimization.

Management science has an extremely important input to make in this system-wide optimization process, even though it cannot produce an answer (decision) that

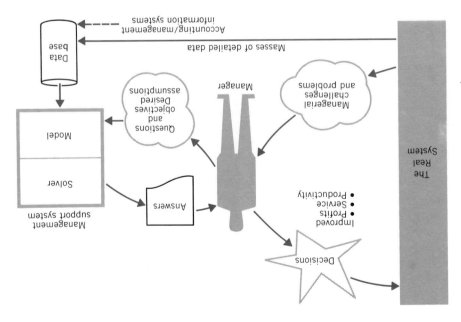

FIGURE 17-2
The role of a management support system. *Source:* A. M. Geoffrion and R. F. Powers, "Management Support Systems," working paper No. 287, *Western Management Science Institute, 1979.*

is optimum for the system as a whole. The contribution of management science is the reduction of the quantifiable part of the problem. This contribution plays an important role in the managers' trade-off process between objective and subjective factors as well as a role in the development of the rational trade-off process itself.

CHOOSING A MODEL

Which model should be used in analyzing a specific problem, either formally or simply as a way of thinking about the problem? Perhaps this issue is not critical since there is often no one *correct way* of modeling a problem. Additional insights may be obtained by trying to conceptualize a problem in terms of different mathematical forms—as a linear optimization model or a network model, for example. However, some models do "match" better with a particular problem than others, and, thus, offer greater insights into the problem. Therefore, it is important to be able to recognize key characteristics of a problem that have implications for model selection.

One strategy is to look for the problem characteristics that can be related to the categories of models shown in the now familiar Figure 17-3. In thinking about a problem, we may ask ourselves about the nature of the problem environment. Can it be *forecast* with relative certainty or is risk a major factor to be considered in the decision? Some of the models we have studied are appropriate for problems in which important elements can only be described in terms of probability statements. Examples are the waiting-line models and the Monte Carlo simulation models. Other models assume that the environment is relatively certain. These include the important optimization models described in Part II and the computer-based corporate simulation models discussed in Chapter 2.

A second question relates to the nature of the relationships among the important elements in the problem. In effect, we are trying to identify the nature of the mathematical expressions that may exist in the *predictive* model. The corporate simulation models and the elementary inventory models use simple, algebraic relationships.

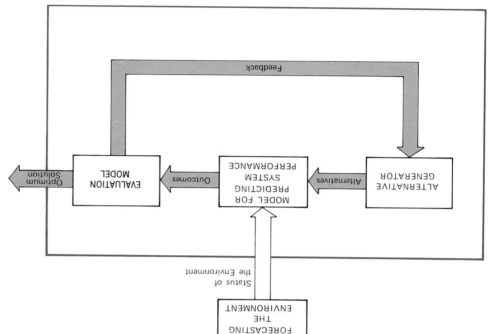

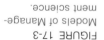

FIGURE 17-3
Models of Management science.

The relationships are required to be linear expressions in order to use the linear optimization models. If the relationships can be described with a network of arrows and circles, then one of the models in Chapter 7 or 8 might be appropriate. An important issue in a problem might be how the relationships among the problem elements change over time. If so, the Markov chain models might be helpful in analyzing the transition of problem elements from one state to another.

Finally, a third question relates to the purpose of the analysis. If we are seeking the *best* solution to a problem according to some clearly defined, quantifiable function of the decision variables (*evaluation model*), then we should look to the optimization models of Part II. If we wish to predict only the outcomes of selecting an alternative or the impact of changing one element of the problem on the other elements, then one of the predictive models of Chapter 2 or of Part III would be appropriate.

Table 17-1 provides a summary of the topics we have covered and a description of the assumptions regarding the nature of the environment, the predictive model, and the evaluation model for each topic. Like any other model, Table 17-1 omits some information in simplifying and summarizing these assumptions. As you gain experience with the techniques and tools of management science, you may recognize exceptions or quibble with some of the categories in Table 17-1. However, we hope that this summary will be helpful to the beginner in relating the materials.

Matching problem characteristics and models

Let us now illustrate how the summary in Table 17-1 might be used. Suppose we ask questions about the environment, the nature of the relationships among elements, and the purpose of the analysis of a specific problem. We identify the following problem characteristics:

1. A relatively certain environment
2. Simple algebraic relationships among the elements of the problem
3. No clearly defined quantifiable objective

Then from Table 17-1 the predictive models described in Chapter 2 seem most likely to provide a useful analysis.

As a second example, suppose we ask similar questions about a second problem and obtain the following conclusions:

1. A relatively risky environment

2. The logical relationships and/or the parameters change as a function of time
3. No clearly defined, quantifiable objective

Again from Table 17-1, the Markov chain models provide the appropriate "match." Finally, this questioning procedure might lead to the following set of problem characteristics in another study:

1. A relatively certain environment
2. Linear relationships among the elements of the problem
3. A clearly defined, quantifiable function of the decision variables to be maximized (minimized)

This time, a linear optimization model would be selected from Table 17-1.

Turn back through the book to any problem description, either in the text or in the problem section. Read it carefully, and then ask the following questions:

1. What is the nature of the environment (certain or risky)?
2. What is the nature of the relationships among the problem elements?
3. Is there a clearly defined, quantifiable function of the decision variables to be maximized (minimized)?

See if your answers to these questions for a problem in a particular chapter are consistent with the summary for that chapter shown in Table 17-1. If not, try to reconcile the differences.

Example: the cash management problem The cash balance of a firm normally fluctuates because of a lack of synchronization between cash inflows from accounts receivable, cash sales, and so forth, and cash outflows from payments on accounts and notes payable. The cash management problem is concerned with optimally financing these outflows with cash-on-hand, lines of credit, or sales of marketable securities, while investing net inflows in the appropriate marketable securities.

Suppose you were presented with the cash management problem of a large organization. How would you make your analysis? Are any of the models of management science appropriate for aiding this analysis? What questions should you ask and what additional information would you require?

First of all, let us take stock of what we know from this brief problem description. What is the nature of the environment? Can a firm accurately forecast its inflows and outflows of cash over a time horizon of several months? The answer depends on the

TABLE 17-1   Assumptions Regarding the Nature of the Environment, the Predictive Model, and the Evaluation Model

Chapter	Title	Environment	Relationships Among Elements	Objective
2	Mathematical model building	Certain	Simple, algebraic	Complex and/or not defined quantitatively
3	Linear optimization models	Certain	Linear expressions	Maximize (minimize) a quantifiable function of the decision variables
4	Applications of linear optimization models	Certain	Linear expressions	Maximize (minimize) a quantifiable function of the decision variables
5	Introduction to the Simplex method	Certain	Linear expressions	Maximize (minimize) a quantifiable function of the decision variables
6	Linear programming: special situations, sensitivity analysis, and duality	Certain	Linear expressions	Maximize (minimize) a quantifiable function of the decision variables
7	Network models: Transportation and transshipment	Certain	Network	Maximize (minimize) a quantifiable function of the decision variables
8	Network models: Shortest path and network scheduling	Certain	Network	Maximize (minimize) a quantifiable function of the decision variables
9	Optimization models with integer variables	Certain	Linear expressions with some variables restricted to integer values	Maximize (minimize) a quantifiable function of the decision variables
10	Optimization models for inventory management	Certain/ risky	Algebraic and statistical	Minimize costs or expected costs
11	Waiting-line models	Risky	Waiting lines and service facilities	Complex and/or not defined quantitatively

TABLE 17-1 Assumptions Regarding the Nature of the Environment, the Predictive Model, and the Evaluation Model

Chapter	Title	Environment	Relationships Among Elements	Objective
12	Monte Carlo simulation	Risky	May involve risky investments, PERT networks, waiting lines, decision processes, etc.	Complex and/or not defined quantitatively
13	Markov chains	Risky	Probability of transition from state to state over time	Complex and/or not defined quantitatively
14	Expected value and decision trees	Risky	Outcomes from predictive or optimization models, or subjective estimates	Maximize expected value
15	Evaluation models based on utility functions	Risky	Outcomes from predictive or optimization models, or subjective estimates	Maximize expected utility
16	The value of information	Risky	Outcomes from predictive or optimization models, or subjective estimates	Maximize expected value

nature of the organization and the stability of its market. It may also depend on the degree of detail that is required in the analysis. Very few firms can forecast cash inflows and outflows with *complete* certainty, but the assumption that they can may be a reasonable abstraction from reality for the purpose of analysis.

We shall consider the following three different conditions of the environment:

1. The outflow of cash is relatively constant over time.
2. The inflows and outflows of cash can be described only by probability statements.
3. Cash inflows and outflows vary, but these variations can be forecast with certainty.

Each of these conditions has implications for the choice of the appropriate model. Skipping to the last question in our list of three: Is there a clearly defined function of the decision variables to be maximized (minimized)? At first glance, the objective seems clear: maximize the returns (minimize the costs) from the cash management decisions. The returns are from the interest paid on marketable securities and from discounts commonly offered by creditors for early payments. The costs are from interest charges from the lines of credit, from losses on the sales of marketable securities that must be sold before maturity, and from the costs of the transactions.

But is the problem really this simple? Excess cash deposits improve a firm's credit rating and the banker's goodwill at the cost of earnings foregone from investments in securities. The determination of an appropriate "minimum" cash balance will require the consideration of issues other than short-term profits. However, it may still be appropriate to adopt the assumption of a single quantifiable objective function for the purpose of analysis, realizing that we are abstracting from and simplifying reality to gain the advantage of alternate ways of viewing this problem.

Now let us couple our assumption of a quantifiable objective function with each of the three different conditions of the environment. It is generally necessary to know the nature of the environment before we can identify the relationships among the problem elements. Suppose the outflow of cash is relatively constant over time. Given this condition in the environment, would it be possible to express the relationships among the problem elements in terms of simple, algebraic statements? Perhaps so.

We might view the cash management problem in the following manner. All cash outflows are to be made from a cash account. There is a cost associated with holding cash in this account since it could be earning interest in marketable securities. There is also a cost of adding cash to this account since marketable securities must be sold or lines of credit must be used. These latter transaction costs are similar to reordering costs in inventory management models. Thus, we have an analogy. We have a constant demand for cash, a holding cost, and a reordering (transaction) cost. The relationships among these elements can be expressed as simple, algebraic statements. The simple economic order quantity model of Chapter 10 could be employed to determine the maximum size of the cash account and frequency with which it should be replenished. Such an approach to cash management was suggested by Baumol [1952] in one of the first formal analyses of this problem.

Suppose the outflows of cash are not constant and can be described only by probability statements. It would be natural to adopt one of the inventory models described in Chapter 10 that account for risk. An example of such an extension is provided by Miller and Orr [1966].

The simple inventory models have been criticized on the grounds that they do not take into account all of the information that is actually available regarding cash inflows and outflows. The argument is that our third condition, that variations in cash inflows and outflows can be forecast with certainty, is actually correct. With these detailed forecasts, more complex models involving more detailed decision variables can be formulated.

Many firms *can* provide reasonable sales forecasts, and historical data can be used to relate sales to payments on accounts receivable. This information provides a reasonably certain forecast of cash inflows from sales. In addition, the firm may hold securities that can be sold before maturity to generate additional cash inflows if necessary, but these inflows result from controllable decisions by the cash manager. Similarly, production (or service activity) level forecasts can be used as the basis for estimating cash outflow requirements, and it may be possible to obtain reasonably certain estimates of these. Cash outflows for the purchase of securities also result from controllable decisions.

Given these certain forecasts, it is a straightforward task to formulate a linear programming model of the cash management problem. The relationships among the problem elements can be written as linear expressions involving the following decision variables:

1. Payment schedules for the predicted purchases in periods 1, 2, . . .

2. Transactions to be made on the securities held by the firm at the beginning of the planning period

3. The new investments to be made in securities in periods 1, 2, . . .

4. The use of the available lines of credit in periods 1, 2, . . .

An example of such a formulation is presented by Orgler [1969, 1970]. This model provides a detailed guide to cash management decisions. The only criticism of Orgler's model is that the level of detail may actually be too high. The complexity of the model may hinder its acceptance and use by managers (see the cash management example in Chapter 4).

Srinivasan [1974] took advantage of another analogy in constructing a different model of the cash management problem. Cash inflows and marketable securities are *sources of funds*, whereas accounts payable and the purchases of securities are *uses*. "Sources and uses" sounds like "supplies and demands." Recall the transportation and transshipment models of Chapter 7. Given the certain forecasts of cash inflows and outflows, Srinivasan realized that it would be possible to develop a *network model* of the cash management problem (see Case 7-3). The resulting transshipment formulation is shown in Figure 17-4. Suppose there

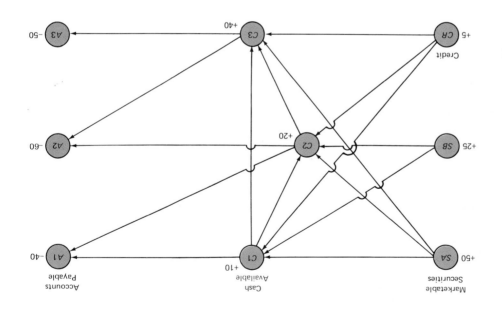

FIGURE 17-4
A transshipment model
formulation of the cash
management problem.

are only three time periods. The three nodes labeled C1, C2, and C3 denote cash availabilities in periods 1, 2, and 3 respectively. Notice that it is possible to "ship" excess cash from period 1 to periods 2 and 3 as well as from period 2 to period 3. Since this could be accomplished by investing in short-term securities that mature in periods 2 and 3, there would be a negative cost (a contribution) on each of these arcs.

The positive number by each cash node represents the forecast of the cash inflow in that period from payments on accounts receivable.

The nodes labeled A1, A2, and A3 represent the accounts payable by the firm in periods 1, 2, and 3 respectively. The forecasts of the amounts are shown as negative numbers written by the nodes. Cash available in period 1 may be used to pay accounts in period 1, as indicated by the arc from node C1 to node A1. Cash available in period 2 may be used to pay accounts in period 1 with an interest penalty (a cost on the arc from node C2 to node A1) or to pay accounts in period 2 (A2) at no charge. All accounts must be paid after a delay of no more than one period, so there is no arc from node C3 to node A1.

Nodes SA and SB represent marketable securities held by the firm. SA matures in period 3 at a face value of 50, so there is no cost on the arc from node SA to node C3. However, SA could be sold at a penalty to provide cash in periods 1 or 2. These penalty costs would be on the arcs from SA to C1 and to C2. Similarly, security SB matures in period 2, so there is no arc from SB to C3.

Node CR represents the line of credit of the firm, which could be used in any of the three periods to obtain additional cash. The costs on the arcs from CR would represent interest payments.

The advantages of this model are that it has the visual interpretation of Figure 17-4, and the relevant information can be summarized in a transportation table in a convenient, easy to understand format. Srinivasan [1974] estimates that the computer run time would be about 3 percent of that required for a linear programming model of the same cash management problem in a large organization. Since it is proposed that this model should be run each day, such considerations can become important.

The transshipment formulation does have some disadvantages since some details included in Orgler's linear optimization model must be omitted. Srinivasan [1974] presents a more complete discussion.

In summary, this example illustrates several important points. First, there is no one model that is "best" for analyzing a particular problem. We have seen that the cash management problem may be analyzed using a simple inventory model and an inventory model that allows probabilistic demand statements, a linear optimization model, or a network model. The choice of the appropriate model is dependent on the nature of the environment, the desired level of detail in the model, and the costs of computation. Such decisions should not be left entirely to a staff analyst but should involve the individual who will actually be using the model. For further discussion and some additional examples, see Mulvey [1979].

Second, the appropriate model can be identified by determining the nature of the environment, the nature of the relationships among the problem elements, and the objective of the analysis. This process is not automatic and requires judgment, but the manager can play an important and valuable role in it.

Adding complexity

Unfortunately, real-world problems are not always categorized as neatly as those we have presented here. It may actually be necessary to combine ideas from several types of models to analyze a complex problem. Moses [1975] describes the implementation of a corporate simulation model with an embedded linear optimization model that simply provides additional information to the simulation model.

Another example in which substantially different kinds of models have been coupled together is reported by Buffa [1972, pp. 690–704] concerning the firm of

Van Den Berghs & Jurgens, a subsidiary of Unilever. In general, a number of planning models of the type discussed in Chapter 2 are coupled together in a complex planning system: a raw material model, a distribution model, a packaging model, marketing models, brand models, a fixed expenses model, a cash flow model, an expense extraction model, a cost type model, and a divisional model. The company is a major producer of margarine and other fat products, and crude oil costs are of significance. Therefore, the formulation for each of the product groups is chosen on the basis of refined oil costs. The formulations themselves are generated by an off-line linear programming model and entered into the system as necessary by way of the formulations model. Thus, we have an optimizing model coupled with a set of predictive models.

Finally, an excellent example of the coupling of different kinds of models was developed by Hax and Meal [1975] and applied as a planning system in a process manufacturing firm described as being analogous to a chemical plant or steel mill. The example firm is a multiplant, multiproduct operation with three distinct seasonal patterns. There is a strong incentive to maintain a nearly level manufacturing rate for the following reasons:

1. The capital cost of equipment is very high compared with the cost of shift premium for labor, and the plants normally operate three shifts five days a week with occasional weekend work.

2. The labor union is very strong and exerts pressure to maintain constant production levels throughout the year for employment stabilization.

System structure   In structuring the system, levels of aggregation for the various items produced were developed first. The extent to which sets of decisions regarding production were interdependent was examined. If two sets of decisions were found to be independent, they were totally separated in the hierarchy of decisions. Beginning at the most detailed level, items sharing a major "setup" cost were grouped into "families." Thus, scheduling decisions for items in a family were very dependent, while the opposite was true for items in different families. It was also found that decisions for a family in one time period were strongly tied to decisions for the same family in other time periods. This time dependence resulted from the need to accumulate seasonal inventories in both product families. Product families were aggregated into "types" if they shared a common seasonal pattern and production rate. This process facilitated seasonal planning since only the aggregate for all families in the type needed to be considered in developing the plan.

The next step in the process was the development of a hierarchy of decisions based on the relationships developed in the aggregation process. The following steps were developed:

1. Assignment of families to plants
2. Seasonal planning
3. Scheduling of families
4. Scheduling of items

In addition to the preceding steps, basic inventory models were used to establish minimum production run lengths and overstock limits. The complete decision sequence is shown in Figure 17-5. A brief description of the several submodels and the nature of their interaction follows.

Plant product assignment subsystem (PAS) The PAS system determines the plant locations at which each family should be manufactured. The model balances the cost of interterritory transportation against the incremental capital investment cost required to manufacture the product family in question. The model is run annually to take account of new products and changes in variable manufacturing cost and demand patterns.

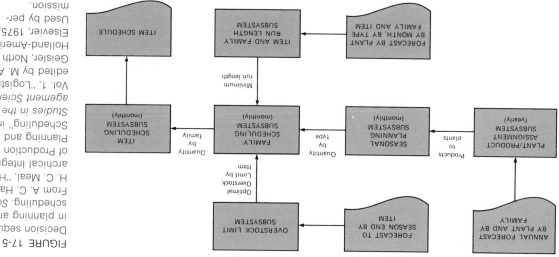

FIGURE 17-5
Decision sequence in planning and scheduling. *Source:* From A. C. Hax and H. C. Meal, "Hierarchical Integration of Production Planning and Scheduling" in *Studies in the Management Science, Vol. 1, "Logistics,"* edited by M. A. Geisler, North Holland-American Elsevier, 1975. Used by permission.

Seasonal planning subsystem (SPS) SPS, the aggregate planning subsystem, determines the production requirements and seasonal stock accumulations by product type for each plant. The objective is to minimize total regular and overtime production costs plus inventory holding costs, subject to constraints on available regular and overtime labor. Demand and safety stock requirements must also be met. Linear programming was used as the solution technique.

Family scheduling subsystem (FSS) The FSS subsystem is used to schedule enough production for the families in a product type to use the time allocated to the type by the SPS. This production includes the accumulation of the necessary seasonal stock.

Item scheduling subsystem (ISS) The ISS subsystem determines the production quantities for each item within the constraints of the family schedules determined by the FSS. As in FSS, overstock limits are observed and an attempt is made to maximize customer service. To carry out this task, Hax and Meal developed approaches that equalized the expected runout times for the items in the family.

Hax and Meal report a total development cost in the range of $150,000 to $200,000. Although exact benefits were not reported, cost reductions from smoother production, fewer emergency interruptions, and reduced inventory carrying cost were expected to be more than $200,000 per year in each plant.

Most of these more complex models generally result from a bootstrapping approach to model building as described in Chapter 2. A manager who has the basic knowledge of the models and solution techniques that we have studied should have no difficulty in participating in the development of more complex models, such as these, and in using their results.

WHAT SHOULD THE MANAGER KNOW?

We have come full circle. In the introduction, we argued that modern managers should have the following skills:

1. The ability to recognize situations in which management science might be used effectively.

2. The ability to conduct two-way communication with a technical specialist, that is, they must be able to

   a. explain the nature of their problem to a specialist in a meaningful way

   b. understand the specialist's product sufficiently well to verify its appropriateness and potential usefulness.

3. The ability to understand the results of management science studies so that they can obtain full value from the information available to them.

4. The ability to conceptualize a problem in terms of a particular model of management science, even if no formal analysis is performed.

5. The ability to formulate models appropriate for analyzing small, straightforward problems, utilize standard computer programs written by others to obtain solutions, and interpret the results.

If you have mastered these skills, you have added an important dimension to your managerial growth and abilities.

GENERAL REFERENCES

Baumol, W. J., "The Transactions Demand for Cash: An Inventory Theoretic Approach," *Quarterly Journal of Economics,* Vol. 66, 1952, pp. 454–456.

Buffa, E. S., *Operations Management: Problems and Models,* third edition, John Wiley & Sons, New York, 1972.

Eppen, G. D., and E. F. Fama, "Cash Balance and Simple Dynamic Portfolio Problems with Proportional Costs," *International Economic Review,* Vol. 10, 1969, pp. 119–133.

Hax, A. C., and H. C. Meal, "Hierarchical Integration of Production Planning and Scheduling," in *Studies in the Management Science, Vol. 1, Logistics,* edited by M. A. Geisler, North Holland-American Elsevier, 1975.

Miller, M. H., and D. J. Orr, "A Model of the Demand for Money by Firms," *Quarterly Journal of Economics,* Vol. 80, 1966, pp. 413–435.

Moses, M. A., "Implementation of Analytical Planning Systems," *Management Science,* Vol. 21, 1975, pp. 1133–1143.

Mulvey, J. M., "Strategies in Modeling: A Personnel Scheduling Example," *Interfaces,* Vol. 9, No. 3, May 1979, pp. 66–77.

Neave, E. H., "The Stochastic Cash Balance Problem with Fixed Costs for Increases and Decreases," *Management Science,* Vol. 16, 1970, pp. 472–490.

Orgler, Y., "An Unequal-Period Model for Cash Management Decisions," *Management Science,* Vol. 16, 1969, pp. B77–B92.

————, *Cash Management: Methods and Models,* Wadsworth Publishing Company, Belmont, Calif., 1970.

Srinivasan, V., "A Transshipment Model for Cash Management Decisions," *Management Science,* Vol. 20, June, 1974, pp. 1350–1363.

White, D. J., and J. M. Norman, "Control of Cash Reserves," *Operational Research Quarterly,* Vol. 16, 1965, pp. 309–328.

Review of Some
Probability Concepts

The following review of probability concepts is intended as a "prompter" or re-minder to those who have been exposed to comparable materials elsewhere. As with the other review materials in these appendixes, it is not intended as a substitute for a rigorous exposure to probability theory.

Probability concepts are important in many problems in management. These concepts enter the models associated with decisions under risk and uncertainty. Loosely speaking, a probability is a measure of how likely something is to occur. This something that either does or does not occur is called an *event*.

MUTUALLY EXCLUSIVE EVENTS

Events are called *mutually exclusive* if one and only one of them can occur. For example, on the flip of a coin, either "heads" or "tails" will be the event that occurs. Similarly, the events "a second oil embargo occurs before 1985" and "a second oil embargo does not occur before 1985" are mutually exclusive. On the other hand, the events "a second oil embargo occurs before 1985" and "a second oil embargo occurs before 1990" are not mutually exclusive since both events occur if the oil producing nations declare a second embargo between the present and 1984. If A and B are mutually exclusive events, then the probability that A or B occurs, written P(A or B), is equal to the probability of A, written P(A), plus the probability of B, written P(B). That is,

$$P(A \text{ or } B) = P(A) + P(B) \tag{1}$$

For example, if H represents the event of a coin landing on heads and T the event of its landing on tails, then

$$P(H \text{ or } T) = P(H) + P(T)$$
$$= 0.5 + 0.5 = 1.0$$

Since either heads or tails must occur, the probability of heads or tails must equal 1.0, the result we obtained. When exactly one event from a list of events must occur, we say the list of events is *collectively exhaustive*. That is, the list contains all of the future events that could possibly happen that relate to a given phenomenon. If a list of events is collectively exhaustive and the events are mutually exclusive, then the sum of the probabilities assigned to the events must equal to 1.0. This summing of probabilities provides a means of checking the logical consistency of subjective probability estimates.

Example The Pacific Oil Company (POCO) is engaged in a study that requires an estimate of the price of a barrel of crude oil in five years. Suppose the analyst identifies the purchasing agent of the company as the appropriate expert for questions involving crude oil prices and asks him to estimate the probability that the price will be lower than $40, between $40 and $50, and more than $50, assuming that there is no oil *embargo* during the period.

Suppose the purchasing agent responds with the following estimates:

Price Range	Probability
less than $40	0.125
$40–$50	0.375
more than $50	0.500
	1.000

Notice that these events are mutually exclusive and collectively exhaustive since exactly one of them must occur. Therefore, the sum of the probabilities must equal 1.00. If the initial set of probability estimates had not summed to 1.00, but it was "close" (say within ± 0.05), the analyst might have normalized them by simply dividing each estimate by the initial sum. Otherwise, he would have to interact further with the purchasing agent.

INDEPENDENT EVENTS

Two or more events are independent (or statistically independent) if the occurrence of one has no effect on the probability of the occurrence of the others. If the events A and B are independent, then the probability of both A and B occurring, written $P(AB)$, is equal to the product of their individual probabilities. That is,

$$P(AB) = P(A) \times P(B) \tag{2}$$

where $P(AB)$ is called the *joint probability* of A and B.

Example Suppose we flip a fair coin twice so that the probability of heads on each flip equals the probability of tails, which equals 0.5. Let H_1 denote the event of heads on the first toss of the coin, and let H_2 denote heads on the second toss. Similarly, T_1 and T_2 denote tails on the first and second tosses of the coin, respectively. Now, the occurrence of heads (or tails) on the first flip of the coin has no effect on the probability of heads or of tails on the second flip and vice versa. Therefore, H_1H_2, H_1T_2, T_1H_2, and T_1T_2 are pairs of independent events. We can compute the joint probability of heads on both tosses of the coin from:

$$P(H_1H_2) = P(H_1) \times P(H_2)$$
$$= (0.5)(0.5) = 0.25$$

Thus, the probability of two heads in a row is 0.25.

DEPENDENT EVENTS

Two events are dependent (or statistically dependent) if the occurrence of one does *affect* the probability of the occurrence of the other. Suppose we know that event A has occurred and we wish to compute the probability that B will now occur. If B is dependent on A, we write $P(B|A)$ to indicate the probability of B, given that A has occurred. The probability $P(B|A)$ is called a *conditional probability* since it depends, or is conditional on, the event A.

The conditional probability $P(B|A)$ can be computed from the expression

$$P(B|A) = \frac{P(AB)}{P(A)} \tag{3}$$

as long as $P(A) \neq 0$. Thus, the conditional probability of B, given that A has occurred, is equal to the joint probability of A and B divided by the probability of A.

Notice that the probability of A in equation (3) is *not* a conditional probability. To distinguish $P(A)$ from a conditional probability, we call it an unconditional or *marginal* probability. The reason for the term *marginal* will become clear momentarily.

We can rearrange equation (3) by multiplying both sides by $P(A)$, and obtain

$$P(AB) = P(B|A) \times P(A) \tag{4}$$

This equation provides a means of calculating the joint probability of A and B from the product of the conditional probability of B and the unconditional probability of A.

Notice that a second expression for $P(AB)$ can be obtained from

$$P(AB) = P(A|B) \times P(B)$$

since the designation of the events A and B is arbitrary.

The relationship between independent and dependent events can be seen if the expression for the joint probability of independent events in (2) is substituted for $P(AB)$ in equation (3). We obtain

$$P(B|A) = \frac{P(A) \times P(B)}{P(A)} = P(B)$$

If B is independent of A, then the conditional probability of B, given that A has occurred, is not affected and can be written simply as $P(B)$, the unconditional probability of B.

A simple example Let us consider a simple example to clarify the relationships among conditional, unconditional, and joint probabilities. Suppose we have two boxes; box 1 contains three balls (two red and one white), and box 2 contains four balls (two red and two white). We first select one of the two boxes at random so that each box has a probability of 0.5 of being chosen. Then we choose one ball from the box we have selected, again, so that each ball in the box has an equal probability of being selected. Figure A-1 shows a tree diagram of the sequential process indicating all of the possible outcomes. Taking the upper branch, the probability of selecting box 1, $P(1)$, is 1/2. Given that box 1 has been selected, the conditional probability of drawing a red ball is $P(R|1) = 2/3$ since there are two red balls in the box of three. Similarly, the probability of drawing a white ball, given that box 1 was selected, is $P(W|1) = 1/3$. Now, the joint probability of drawing box 1 and a red ball is

$$P(R1) = P(R|1) \times P(1)$$
$$= (2/3) \, (1/2) = 1/3$$

and of drawing box 1 and a white ball is

$$P(W1) = P(W|1) \times P(1)$$
$$= (1/3) \, (1/2) = 1/6$$

The other main branch probabilities are calculated in a similar way. Notice that the joint probabilities at the right-hand side of the tree enumerate all of the possible outcomes. Thus, the events are mutually exclusive and collectively exhaustive, so the probabilities must sum to 1.0.

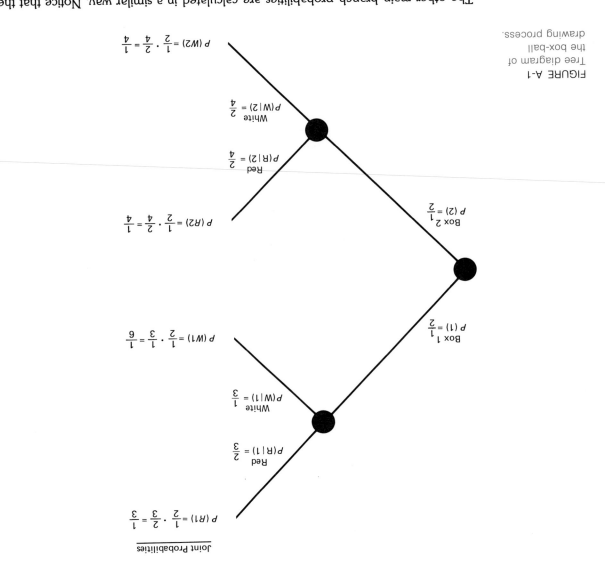

FIGURE A-1
Tree diagram of the box-ball drawing process.

TABLE A-1

Joint and Marginal Probabilities for the Box-Ball Drawing Process

Second Draw: Which Ball? / First Draw: Which Box?	Joint Probabilities		Marginal (Unconditional) Probabilities of Outcomes on First Draw
	Red Ball	White Ball	
Box 1	$P(R1) = \dfrac{1}{3}$	$P(W1) = \dfrac{1}{6}$	$\dfrac{1}{3} + \dfrac{1}{6} = \dfrac{1}{2}$
Box 2	$P(R2) = \dfrac{1}{4}$	$P(W2) = \dfrac{1}{4}$	$\dfrac{1}{4} + \dfrac{1}{4} = \dfrac{1}{2}$
Marginal (Unconditional) Probabilities of Outcomes on Second Draw	$\dfrac{1}{3} + \dfrac{1}{4} = \dfrac{7}{12}$	$\dfrac{1}{6} + \dfrac{1}{4} = \dfrac{5}{12}$	1.00

Let us now assemble the joint probability data from Figure A-1 in the form of Table A-1. The *unconditional* probabilities associated with selecting box 1 or box 2 are the sums of the two joint probabilities of $P(R1)$ and $P(W1)$ for box 1 and $P(R2)$ and $P(W2)$ for box 2, shown as the marginal probabilities in the right-hand column. Similarly, the unconditional probabilities associated with selecting red or white balls are the sums of the two joint probabilities in the bottom row. These probabilities are called *marginal* simply because they occur in the margins of the table. Their significance is that they are the probabilities of the ending events without stated conditions—that is, they are unconditional.

Review of Some Concepts of Statistics

The following review of statistical concepts is intended as a "prompter" or reminder to those who have been exposed to comparable materials elsewhere. As with the other review materials in these appendixes, it is not intended as a substitute for a rigorous course in statistics.

UNIVERSE AND SAMPLE

A sample is drawn from a *universe or population* and is therefore a subset of a universe or population.

A *finite universe* might be a lot of 1000 parts produced on a lathe. Any of the dimensions produced might in themselves be considered a finite universe.

An *infinite universe* might be represented by the time required for a worker to perform the lathe operation.

If we selected 100 parts from the 1000 and measured their diameters, we would have a sample distribution of diameters. If we let the selection of the sample of 100 parts be based strictly on chance, we would have a *random sample*.

It is often true that the entire universe data are difficult and expensive to obtain, or impossible in the case of an infinite universe. Therefore, one of the important objectives of statistics is to infer from a sample the characteristics of the universe distribution.

Parameters are designated as the characteristics of the universe, such as the mean, variance, and range (these terms will be defined later).

Statistics are designated as characteristics of a sample drawn from a universe and are intended to infer the characteristics of the universe.

Notation

It is of some importance to retain the distinction between *parameters* and *statistics*, and we will attempt to do this through a system of notation. In general, when we are referring to the parameters of a universe, we will use one set of symbols, and when we are referring to the statistics of a sample, we will use another set. In most instances, we will be dealing with statistics rather than parameters. The notation is as follows:

μ = the population mean (parameter)

$\bar{x}$ = the mean of a sample drawn from the population (statistic)

σ^2 = the population variance (parameter)

s^2 = the variance of a sample drawn from the population (statistic)

DESCRIPTIVE STATISTICS

One major area of the study of statistics has to do with the precise and efficient ways of describing what would otherwise be a mass of data that would communicate very little worthwhile information. Table B-1 illustrates this point. It lists measurements of the diameters of a sample of 50 shafts from a production lot of 10,000. By scanning the table we can pick out the maximum reading, 1.0043 inches, and the minimum reading, 0.9954 inches, but any generalization about the diameters of the 50 shafts is difficult. Similarly, inferences about the entire lot of 10,000 shafts are difficult.

Frequency distributions

The situation is improved by grouping the data into a frequency distribution. This process involves tabulating the number of shaft measurements that fall into certain class intervals, as in Table B-2. Immediately, we observe some characteristics of the data that were difficult to see before. For example, we see that the high and low readings represent a small minority of the cases and that a large percentage of the shafts measured somewhere between 0.9982 inch and 1.0018 inch, with the largest number occurring around 1.0000 inch. When the data are plotted in a histogram (see Figure B-1), the general relationships show up clearly. We see that we have a fairly symmetrical bell-shaped distribution of the measurements, centering on 1.0000 inch.

The normal distribution   The smooth bell-shaped curve that has been superimposed on the histogram of Figure B-1 is called the normal or Gaussian distribution. We see

TABLE B-1

Diameters of 50 Shafts

1.0039	0.9956	1.0026	1.0004	1.0005
1.0014	0.9996	0.9994	0.9977	1.0023
0.9980	1.0025	1.0043	1.0004	0.9989
1.0000	1.0028	0.9954	0.9974	0.9992
0.9973	0.9994	1.0000	1.0033	1.0005
0.9996	0.9998	1.0026	1.0031	1.0034
1.0010	0.9955	0.9976	1.0009	0.9991
0.9999	0.9979	0.9983	0.9972	0.9998
1.0003	0.9968	1.0013	1.0007	1.0041
1.0037	1.0012	0.9985	1.0018	0.9987

TABLE B-2 Frequency Distribution of the Data in Table B-1

Class Limits (in.)	Frequency (no. of shafts)
0.9946–0.9955	1
0.9956–0.9965	1
0.9966–0.9975	4
0.9976–0.9985	6
0.9986–0.9995	7
0.9996–1.0005	11
1.0006–1.0015	7
1.0016–1.0025	3
1.0026–1.0035	6
1.0036–1.0045	4
	50

that the distribution of diameter measurements fairly well approximates the normal distribution. The term *normal distribution* does not imply that distributions that do not approximate it are abnormal. The curve for the normal distribution has a specific mathematical function, so that for a distribution to approximate normality, the occurrence frequencies must follow closely the general pattern indicated in Figure B-1. There are statistical tests that can be used to determine how closely a distribution approximates normality. If there is anything "normal" about the normal distribution, it may be that a great number of actual distributions in industry, science, and nature can be closely approximated by it. Thus, a large part of statistical method is based on the normal distribution. Table C-1 in Appendix C gives areas under a standardized normal curve.

Other distributions There are a number of other important distributions that are useful in management science. For example, the Poisson and the negative exponential distributions are used in waiting line theory and are useful in determining buffer inventory levels.

Techniques parallel to those discussed here for the normal distribution have been developed for these other distributions as well as for situations in which no specific distribution is implied. We will review general statistical methods for the normal distribution and will not attempt to review the details of analysis for the other distributions.

Measures of a distribution

Several characteristics of distributions can be used to describe or specify them. In Figure B-1, we note that, first, the measurements tend to group around some central value; second, there is variability, that is, no one value represents the whole; third, the distribution is symmetric; and fourth, there is one peak or mode. To describe a distribution, we need measures of central value, variability, and symmetry as well as an observation of the number of modes. Note that if a distribution can be assumed

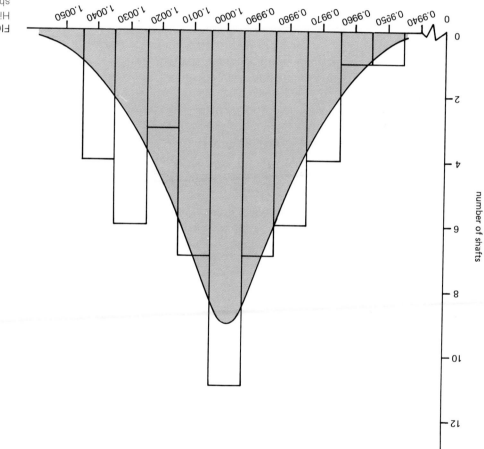

FIGURE B-1
Histogram of 50 shaft diameter measurements.

to be normal, only the first two measures will specify it since a normal distribution is unimodal and symmetric. Therefore, we will discuss measures of central value and of variability.

Measures of central value A measure of central value in the population is often made from a random sample drawn from the population. Suppose that the values for n individual items in a random sample are represented by $x_1, x_2, x_3, \cdots, x_n$. Then the arithmetic mean $\bar{x}$ of the sample can be computed by

$$\bar{x} = \frac{\sum\limits_{i=1}^{n} x_i}{n} = \frac{x_n + x_{n-1} + \cdots + x_3 + x_2 + x_1}{n}$$

The Greek letter Σ means "sum of," and the x_i are the individual observations, which are numbered from 1 to n, where n is the total number of observations.* Therefore, for our shaft diameter example, we calculate $\bar{x}$ from Table B-1 as follows:

$$\bar{x} = \frac{1.0039 + 1.0014 + 0.9980 + \cdots + 0.9987}{50} = 1.0002$$

The result, $\bar{x}$, is the estimate of the population mean of the parent distribution. There are two other measures of the center of a distribution, the median and the mode. *The median* is that point on the horizontal scale that divides the area under the histogram into two equal parts.

The mode is the most frequently occurring value. On a histogram, it is the midpoint of the class interval that has the largest frequency of occurrence. For the data of Table B-2, represented by the histogram of Figure B-1, the mode is 1.0000. Note then, that for a symmetrical distribution, the mean, the median, and the mode will all be equal.

Measures of variability or dispersion *The range,* which is the simplest and most easily determined measure of variability, is the difference between the highest and lowest values in the distribution. For the data of Table B-1, the range is $1.0043 - 0.9954 = 0.0089$ inch. It is not as stable a measure as the variance since it is based on only two values instead of the entire set of data.

The variance is the most commonly used measure of variability in statistics be-

* There is a shortcut method for calculating the mean based on the grouped data of Table B-2.

cause of its stability as a measure and because of other valuable properties we will discuss. The sample variance is defined by,

$$s^2 = \frac{\sum_{i=1}^{n} (x_i - \bar{x})^2}{n - 1}$$

It is simply the sum of the squares of the differences between the individual observations and the mean of a distribution, divided by $n - 1$. For the data of Table B-1, where we have already computed $\bar{x} = 1.0002$, the variance 0.0000494 is calculated as follows:

$$s^2 = \frac{(1.0039 - 1.0002)^2 + (1.0014 - 1.0002)^2 + (0.9980 - 1.0002)^2 + \cdots + (0.9987 - 1.0002)^2}{49}$$

$$= 0.0000494,$$

It is the estimate of the actual population variance of the parent distribution.

The standard deviation is the square root of the variance and is commonly denoted by s. For the data of Table B-1,

$$s = \sqrt{s^2} = \sqrt{0.0000494} = 0.00222$$

The standard deviation has special properties that are useful to us. If we consider a normal distribution with mean, μ, and standard deviation, σ, it is true that 68.27 percent of the area under the curve (equivalent to the frequency of occurrence in the histogram) is included within the limits of $\mu \pm \sigma$; 95.45 percent is included within the limits $\mu \pm 2\sigma$; and 99.73 percent is included within the limits $\mu \pm 3\sigma$ (see Figure B-2).

The significance of Figure B-2 is that we can now make a probability statement about values that we presume come from the universe or population from which the sample distribution is drawn. Using the shaft diameter example, which had an $\bar{x} = 1.0002$ inch and $s = 0.00222$ inch, we can say that there is a 0.9545 probability that shafts coming from the lot or universe from which the sample was drawn will have outside diameters measuring between 0.99546 and 1.00464 inches and that there is only a 0.0455 probability that shafts will measure outside these limits. Simi-

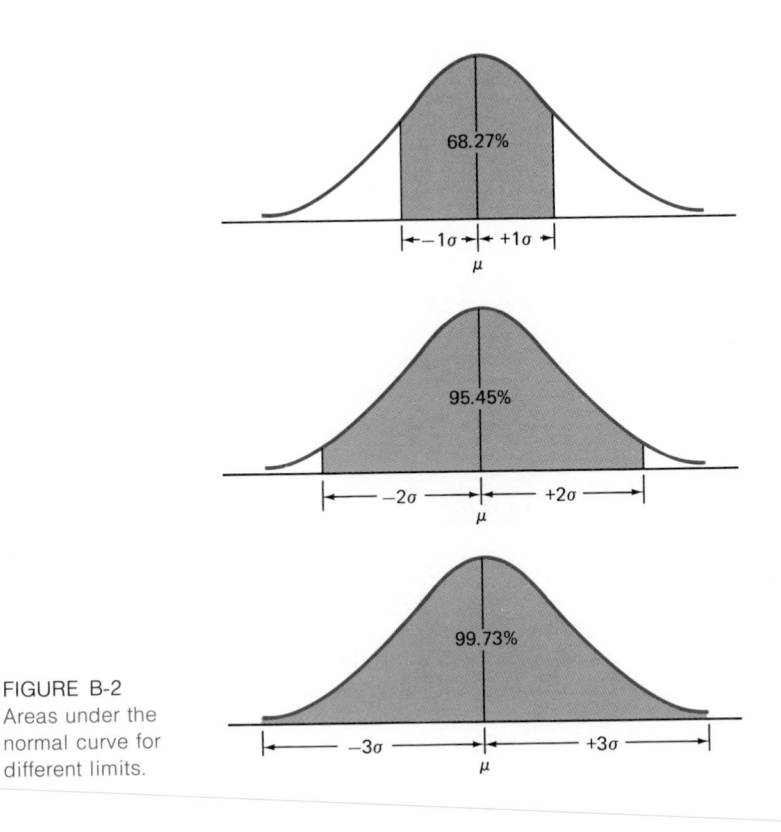

FIGURE B-2
Areas under the
normal curve for
different limits.

larly, virtually all shafts will measure between 0.99354 and 1.00686 inches, and there is only a 0.0027 probability that any shafts will measure outside these limits.

TABLE C-1 Areas Under the Normal Curve

Areas under the normal curve to the left of x for decimal units of σ' from the mean, x'

x	Area	x	Area	x	Area	x	Area
x' − 3.0σ'	0.0013	x' − 1.5σ'	0.0668	x' + 0.1σ'	0.5398	x' + 1.6σ'	0.9452
x' − 2.9σ'	0.0019	x' − 1.4σ'	0.0808	x' + 0.2σ'	0.5793	x' + 1.7σ'	0.9554
x' − 2.8σ'	0.0026	x' − 1.3σ'	0.0968	x' + 0.3σ'	0.6179	x' + 1.8σ'	0.9641
x' − 2.7σ'	0.0035	x' − 1.2σ'	0.1151	x' + 0.4σ'	0.6554	x' + 1.9σ'	0.9713
x' − 2.6σ'	0.0047	x' − 1.1σ'	0.1357	x' + 0.5σ'	0.6915	x' + 2.0σ'	0.9772
x' − 2.5σ'	0.0062	x' − 1.0σ'	0.1587	x' + 0.6σ'	0.7257	x' + 2.1σ'	0.9821
x' − 2.4σ'	0.0082	x' − 0.9σ'	0.1841	x' + 0.7σ'	0.7580	x' + 2.2σ'	0.9861
x' − 2.3σ'	0.0107	x' − 0.8σ'	0.2119	x' + 0.8σ'	0.7881	x' + 2.3σ'	0.9893
x' − 2.2σ'	0.0139	x' − 0.7σ'	0.2420	x' + 0.9σ'	0.8159	x' + 2.4σ'	0.9918
x' − 2.1σ'	0.0179	x' − 0.6σ'	0.2741	x' + 1.0σ'	0.8413	x' + 2.5σ'	0.9938
x' − 2.0σ'	0.0228	x' − 0.5σ'	0.3085	x' + 1.1σ'	0.8643	x' + 2.6σ'	0.9953
x' − 1.9σ'	0.0287	x' − 0.4σ'	0.3446	x' + 1.2σ'	0.8849	x' + 2.7σ'	0.9965
x' − 1.8σ'	0.0359	x' − 0.3σ'	0.3821	x' + 1.3σ'	0.9032	x' + 2.8σ'	0.9974
x' − 1.7σ'	0.0446	x' − 0.2σ'	0.4207	x' + 1.4σ'	0.9192	x' + 2.9σ'	0.9981
x' − 1.6σ'	0.0548	x' − 0.1σ'	0.4602	x' + 1.5σ'	0.9332	x' + 3.0σ'	0.9987
		x'	0.5000				

σ' units from the mean, x', associated with
given values of the area under the
normal curve to the left of x

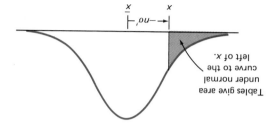

Tables give area under normal curve to the left of x.

x	Area	x	Area
x' − 3.090σ'	0.001	x' + 3.090σ'	0.999
x' − 2.576σ'	0.005	x' + 2.576σ'	0.995
x' − 2.326σ'	0.010	x' + 2.326σ'	0.990
x' − 1.960σ'	0.025	x' + 1.960σ'	0.975
x' − 1.645σ'	0.050	x' + 1.645σ'	0.950
x' − 1.282σ'	0.100	x' + 1.282σ'	0.900
x' − 1.036σ'	0.150	x' + 1.036σ'	0.850
x' − 0.842σ'	0.200	x' + 0.842σ'	0.800
x' − 0.674σ'	0.250	x' + 0.674σ'	0.750
x' − 0.524σ'	0.300	x' + 0.524σ'	0.700
x' − 0.385σ'	0.350	x' + 0.385σ'	0.650
x' − 0.253σ'	0.400	x' + 0.253σ'	0.600
x' − 0.126σ'	0.450	x' + 0.126σ'	0.550
x'	0.500		

TABLE C-2 Values of L_q for $M = 1 - 15$, and Various Values of $r = \lambda/\mu$. Poisson Arrivals, Negative Exponential Service Times

r						Number of Servers (M)									
	1	2	3	4	5	6	7	8	9	10	11	12	13	14	15
0.10	0.0111														
0.15	0.0264	0.0008													
0.20	0.0500	0.0020													
0.25	0.0833	0.0039													
0.30	0.1285	0.0069													
0.35	0.1884	0.0110													
0.40	0.2666	0.0166													
0.45	0.3681	0.0239	0.0019												
0.50	0.5000	0.0333	0.0030												
0.55	0.6722	0.0449	0.0043												
0.60	0.9000	0.0593	0.0061												
0.65	1.2071	0.0767	0.0084												
0.70	1.6333	0.0976	0.0112												
0.75	2.2500	0.1227	0.0147												
0.80	3.2000	0.1523	0.0189												
0.85	4.8166	0.1873	0.0239	0.0031											
0.90	8.1000	0.2285	0.0300	0.0041											
0.95	18.0500	0.2767	0.0371	0.0053											
1.0		0.3333	0.0454	0.0067											
1.2		0.6748	0.0904	0.0158											
1.4		1.3449	0.1778	0.0324	0.0059										
1.6		2.8444	0.3128	0.0604	0.0121										
1.8		7.6734	0.5320	0.1051	0.0227	0.0047									
2.0			0.8888	0.1739	0.0398	0.0090									
2.2			1.4907	0.2770	0.0659	0.0158									
2.4			2.1261	0.4305	0.1047	0.0266	0.0065								
2.6			4.9322	0.6581	0.1609	0.0426	0.0110								
2.8			12.2724	1.0000	0.2411	0.0659	0.0180								

TABLE C-2 (Continued)

3.0	1.5282	0.3541	0.0991	0.0282	0.0077							
3.2	2.3856	0.5128	0.1452	0.0427	0.0122							
3.4	3.9060	0.7365	0.2085	0.0631	0.0189							
3.6	7.0893	1.0550	0.2947	0.0912	0.0283	0.0084						
3.8	16.9366	1.5184	0.4114	0.1292	0.0412	0.0127						
4.0		2.2164	0.5694	0.1801	0.0590	0.0189						
4.2		3.3269	0.7837	0.2475	0.0827	0.0273	0.0087					
4.4		5.2675	1.0777	0.3364	0.1142	0.0389	0.0128					
4.6		9.2885	1.4867	0.4532	0.1555	0.0541	0.0184					
4.8		21.6384	2.0708	0.6071	0.2092	0.0742	0.0260					
5.0			2.9375	0.8102	0.2786	0.1006	0.0361	0.0125				
5.2			4.3004	1.0804	0.3680	0.1345	0.0492	0.0175				
5.4			6.6609	1.4441	0.4871	0.1779	0.0663	0.0243	0.0085			
5.6			11.5178	1.9436	0.6313	0.2330	0.0883	0.0330	0.0119			
5.8			26.3726	2.6481	0.8225	0.3032	0.1164	0.0443	0.0164			
6.0				3.6828	1.0707	0.3918	0.1518	0.0590	0.0224			
6.2				5.2979	1.3967	0.5037	0.1964	0.0775	0.0300	0.0113		
6.4				8.0768	1.8040	0.6454	0.2524	0.1008	0.0398	0.0153		
6.6				13.7692	2.4198	0.8247	0.3222	0.1302	0.0523	0.0205		
6.8				31.1270	3.2441	1.0533	0.4090	0.1666	0.0679	0.0271	0.0105	
7.0					4.4471	1.3471	0.5172	0.2119	0.0876	0.0357	0.0141	
7.2					6.3135	1.7288	0.6521	0.2677	0.1119	0.0463	0.0187	
7.4					9.5102	2.2324	0.8202	0.3364	0.1420	0.0595	0.0245	
7.6					16.0379	2.9113	1.0310	0.4211	0.1789	0.0761	0.0318	0.0129
7.8					35.8956	3.8558	1.2972	0.5250	0.2243	0.0966	0.0410	0.0168
8.0						5.2264	1.6364	0.6530	0.2796	0.1214	0.0522	0.0220
8.2						7.3441	2.0736	0.8109	0.3469	0.1520	0.0663	0.0283
8.4						10.9592	2.6470	1.0060	0.4288	0.1891	0.0834	0.0361
8.6						18.3223	3.4160	1.2484	0.5286	0.2341	0.1043	0.0459
8.8						40.6824	4.4806	1.5524	0.6501	0.2885	0.1298	0.0577
9.0							6.0183	1.9368	0.7980	0.3543	0.1603	0.0723
9.2							8.3869	2.4298	0.9788	0.4333	0.1974	0.0899
9.4							12.4189	3.0732	1.2010	0.5287	0.2419	0.1111
9.6							20.6160	3.9318	1.4752	0.6437	0.2952	0.1367
9.8							45.4769	5.1156	1.8165	0.7827	0.3588	0.1673
10.0								6.8210	2.2465	0.9506	0.4352	0.2040

TABLE C-3 Finite Queuing Tables

POPULATION 5

X	M	D	F	L_q
0.012	1	0.048	0.999	0.005
0.019	1	0.076	0.998	0.010
0.025	1	0.100	0.997	0.015
0.030	1	0.120	0.996	0.020
0.034	1	0.135	0.995	0.025
0.036	1	0.143	0.994	0.030
0.040	1	0.159	0.993	0.035
0.042	1	0.167	0.992	0.045
0.044	1	0.175	0.991	0.045
0.046	1	0.183	0.990	0.050
0.050	1	0.198	0.989	0.055
0.052	1	0.206	0.988	0.060
0.054	1	0.214	0.987	0.065
0.056	1	0.222	0.985	0.075
	2	0.018	0.999	0.005
0.058	1	0.229	0.984	0.080
	2	0.019	0.999	0.005
0.060	1	0.237	0.983	0.085
	2	0.020	0.999	0.005
0.062	1	0.245	0.982	0.090
	2	0.022	0.999	0.005
0.064	1	0.253	0.981	0.095
	2	0.023	0.999	0.005
0.066	1	0.260	0.979	0.105
	2	0.024	0.999	0.005
0.068	1	0.268	0.978	0.110
	2	0.026	0.999	0.005
0.070	1	0.275	0.977	0.115
	2	0.027	0.999	0.005
0.075	1	0.294	0.973	0.135
	2	0.031	0.999	0.005
0.080	1	0.313	0.969	0.155
	2	0.035	0.998	0.010
0.085	1	0.332	0.965	0.175
	2	0.040	0.998	0.010
0.090	1	0.350	0.960	0.200
	2	0.044	0.998	0.010
0.095	1	0.368	0.955	0.225
	2	0.049	0.997	0.015
0.100	1	0.386	0.950	0.250
	2	0.054	0.997	0.015
0.105	2	0.059	0.997	0.015

X	M	D	F	L_q
0.110	1	0.404	0.945	0.275
	2	0.065	0.996	0.020
0.115	1	0.421	0.939	0.305
	2	0.071	0.995	0.025
0.120	1	0.439	0.933	0.335
	2	0.076	0.995	0.025
0.125	1	0.456	0.927	0.365
	2	0.082	0.994	0.030
0.130	1	0.473	0.920	0.400
	2	0.089	0.993	0.035
0.135	1	0.489	0.914	0.430
	2	0.096	0.993	0.035
0.140	1	0.505	0.907	0.465
	2	0.102	0.992	0.040
0.145	1	0.521	0.900	0.500
	2	0.109	0.991	0.045
	3	0.011	0.999	0.005
0.150	1	0.537	0.892	0.540
	2	0.115	0.990	0.050
	3	0.012	0.999	0.005
0.155	1	0.553	0.885	0.575
	2	0.123	0.989	0.055
	3	0.013	0.999	0.005
0.160	1	0.568	0.877	0.615
	2	0.130	0.988	0.060
	3	0.015	0.999	0.005
0.165	1	0.582	0.869	0.655
	2	0.137	0.987	0.065
	3	0.016	0.999	0.005
0.170	1	0.597	0.861	0.695
	2	0.145	0.985	0.075
	3	0.017	0.999	0.005
0.180	1	0.611	0.853	0.735
	2	0.161	0.983	0.085
	3	0.021	0.999	0.005
0.190	1	0.638	0.836	0.820
	2	0.177	0.980	0.100
	3	0.024	0.998	0.010
0.200	1	0.665	0.819	0.905
	2	0.194	0.976	0.120
	3	0.028	0.998	0.010
0.210	1	0.689	0.801	0.995
	2	0.211	0.973	0.135
	3	0.032	0.998	0.010

X	M	D	F	L_q
0.220	1	0.713	0.783	1.085
	2	0.229	0.969	0.155
	3	0.036	0.997	0.015
0.230	1	0.735	0.765	1.175
	2	0.247	0.965	0.175
	3	0.041	0.997	0.015
0.240	1	0.756	0.747	1.265
	2	0.265	0.960	0.200
	3	0.046	0.996	0.020
0.250	1	0.775	0.730	1.350
	2	0.284	0.955	0.225
	3	0.052	0.995	0.025
0.260	1	0.794	0.712	1.440
	2	0.303	0.950	0.250
	3	0.058	0.994	0.030
0.270	1	0.811	0.695	1.525
	2	0.323	0.944	0.280
	3	0.064	0.994	0.030
0.280	1	0.827	0.677	1.615
	2	0.342	0.938	0.310
	3	0.071	0.993	0.035
0.290	1	0.842	0.661	1.695
	2	0.362	0.932	0.340
	3	0.079	0.992	0.040
	4	0.007	0.999	0.005
0.300	1	0.856	0.644	1.780
	2	0.382	0.926	0.370
	3	0.086	0.990	0.050
	4	0.008	0.999	0.005
0.310	1	0.869	0.628	1.860
	2	0.402	0.919	0.405
	3	0.094	0.989	0.055
	4	0.009	0.999	0.005
0.320	1	0.881	0.613	1.935
	2	0.422	0.912	0.440
	3	0.103	0.988	0.060
	4	0.010	0.999	0.005
0.330	1	0.892	0.597	2.015
	2	0.442	0.904	0.480
	3	0.112	0.986	0.070
	4	0.012	0.999	0.005
0.340	1	0.902	0.583	2.085
	2	0.462	0.895	0.515
	3	0.121	0.985	0.075
	4	0.013	0.999	0.005

TABLE C-3 (*Continued*)

X	M	D	F	L_q	X	M	D	F	L_q	X	M	D	F	L_q
POPULATION 5, Cont.														
	2	0.462	0.896	0.520		2	0.831	0.689	1.555		1	0.285	0.988	0.12
	1	0.911	0.569	2.155		1	0.993	0.357	3.215	0.034	2	0.037	0.999	0.01
0.360	4	0.017	0.998	0.010	0.580	4	0.113	0.984	0.080		1	0.302	0.986	0.14
	3	0.141	0.981	0.060		3	0.461	0.895	0.525	0.036	2	0.041	0.999	0.01
	2	0.501	0.880	0.600		2	0.854	0.670	1.650		1	0.320	0.984	0.16
	1	0.927	0.542	2.290		1	0.994	0.345	3.275	0.038	2	0.046	0.999	0.01
0.380	4	0.021	0.998	0.010	0.600	4	0.130	0.981	0.095		1	0.337	0.982	0.18
	3	0.163	0.976	0.120		3	0.497	0.883	0.585	0.040	2	0.050	0.999	0.01
	2	0.540	0.863	0.685		2	0.875	0.652	1.740		1	0.354	0.980	0.20
	1	0.941	0.516	2.420		1	0.996	0.333	3.335	0.042	2	0.055	0.999	0.01
0.400	4	0.026	0.997	0.015	0.650	4	0.179	0.972	0.140		1	0.371	0.978	0.22
	3	0.186	0.972	0.140		3	0.588	0.850	0.750	0.044	2	0.060	0.998	0.02
	2	0.579	0.845	0.775		2	0.918	0.608	1.960		1	0.388	0.975	0.25
	1	0.952	0.493	2.535		1	0.998	0.308	3.460	0.046	2	0.065	0.998	0.02
0.420	4	0.031	0.997	0.015	0.700	4	0.240	0.960	0.200		1	0.404	0.973	0.27
	3	0.211	0.966	0.170		3	0.678	0.815	0.925	0.048	2	0.071	0.998	0.02
	2	0.616	0.826	0.870		2	0.950	0.568	2.160		1	0.421	0.970	0.30
	1	0.961	0.471	2.645		1	0.999	0.286	3.570	0.050	2	0.076	0.998	0.02
0.440	4	0.037	0.996	0.020	0.750	4	0.316	0.944	0.280		1	0.437	0.967	0.33
	3	0.238	0.960	0.200		3	0.763	0.777	1.115	0.052	2	0.082	0.997	0.03
	2	0.652	0.807	0.965		2	0.972	0.532	2.340		1	0.454	0.963	0.37
	1	0.969	0.451	2.745	0.800	4	0.410	0.924	0.380	0.054	2	0.088	0.997	0.03
0.460	4	0.045	0.995	0.025		3	0.841	0.739	1.305		1	0.470	0.960	0.40
	3	0.266	0.953	0.235		2	0.987	0.500	2.500	0.056	2	0.094	0.997	0.03
	2	0.686	0.787	1.065	0.850	4	0.522	0.900	0.500		1	0.486	0.956	0.44
	1	0.975	0.432	2.840		3	0.907	0.702	1.490	0.058	2	0.100	0.996	0.04
0.480	4	0.053	0.994	0.030		2	0.995	0.470	2.650		1	0.501	0.953	0.47
	3	0.296	0.945	0.275	0.900	4	0.656	0.871	0.645	0.060	2	0.106	0.996	0.04
	2	0.719	0.767	1.165		3	0.957	0.666	1.670		1	0.517	0.949	0.51
	1	0.980	0.415	2.925		2	0.998	0.444	2.780	0.062	2	0.113	0.996	0.04
0.500	4	0.063	0.992	0.040	0.950	4	0.815	0.838	0.810		1	0.532	0.945	0.55
	3	0.327	0.936	0.320		3	0.989	0.631	1.845	0.064	2	0.119	0.995	0.05
	2	0.750	0.748	1.260							1	0.547	0.940	0.60
	1	0.985	0.399	3.005	POPULATION 10					0.066	2	0.126	0.995	0.05
0.520	4	0.073	0.991	0.045							1	0.562	0.936	0.64
	3	0.359	0.927	0.365	0.016	1	0.144	0.997	0.03	0.068	3	0.020	0.999	0.01
	2	0.779	0.728	1.360	0.019	1	0.170	0.996	0.04		2	0.133	0.994	0.06
	1	0.988	0.384	3.080	0.021	1	0.188	0.995	0.05		1	0.577	0.931	0.69
0.540	4	0.085	0.989	0.055	0.023	1	0.206	0.994	0.06	0.070	3	0.022	0.999	0.01
	3	0.392	0.917	0.415	0.025	1	0.224	0.993	0.07		2	0.140	0.994	0.06
	2	0.806	0.708	1.460	0.026	1	0.232	0.992	0.08		1	0.591	0.926	0.74
	1	0.991	0.370	3.150	0.028	1	0.250	0.991	0.09	0.075	3	0.026	0.999	0.01
0.560	4	0.098	0.986	0.070	0.030	1	0.268	0.990	0.10		2	0.158	0.992	0.08
	3	0.426	0.906	0.470	0.032	2	0.033	0.999	0.01		1	0.627	0.913	0.87

TABLE C-3 (*Continued*)

POPULATION 10, Cont.

X	M	D	F	L_q	X	M	D	F	L_q	X	M	D	F	L_q
0.080	3	0.031	0.999	0.01	0.145	4	0.032	0.999	0.01	0.220	5	0.030	0.998	0.02
	2	0.177	0.990	0.10		3	0.144	0.990	0.10		4	0.124	0.990	0.10
	1	0.660	0.899	1.01		2	0.460	0.941	0.59		3	0.366	0.954	0.46
0.085	3	0.037	0.999	0.01		1	0.929	0.662	3.38		2	0.761	0.815	1.85
	2	0.196	0.988	0.12	0.150	4	0.036	0.998	0.02		1	0.993	0.453	5.47
	1	0.692	0.883	1.17		3	0.156	0.989	0.11	0.230	5	0.037	0.998	0.02
0.090	3	0.043	0.998	0.02		2	0.483	0.935	0.65		4	0.142	0.988	0.12
	2	0.216	0.986	0.14		1	0.939	0.644	3.56		3	0.400	0.947	0.53
	1	0.722	0.867	1.33	0.155	4	0.040	0.998	0.02		2	0.791	0.794	2.06
0.095	3	0.049	0.998	0.02		3	0.169	0.987	0.13		1	0.995	0.434	5.66
	2	0.237	0.984	0.16		2	0.505	0.928	0.72	0.240	5	0.044	0.997	0.03
	1	0.750	0.850	1.50		1	0.947	0.627	3.73		4	0.162	0.986	0.14
0.100	3	0.056	0.998	0.02	0.160	4	0.044	0.998	0.02		3	0.434	0.938	0.62
	2	0.258	0.981	0.19		3	0.182	0.986	0.14		2	0.819	0.774	2.26
	1	0.776	0.832	1.68		2	0.528	0.921	0.79		1	0.996	0.416	5.84
0.105	3	0.064	0.997	0.03		1	0.954	0.610	3.90	0.250	6	0.010	0.999	0.01
	2	0.279	0.978	0.22	0.165	4	0.049	0.997	0.03		5	0.052	0.997	0.03
	1	0.800	0.814	1.86		3	0.195	0.984	0.16		4	0.183	0.983	0.17
0.110	3	0.072	0.997	0.03		2	0.550	0.914	0.86		3	0.469	0.929	0.71
	2	0.301	0.974	0.26		1	0.961	0.594	4.06		2	0.844	0.753	2.47
	1	0.822	0.795	2.05	0.170	4	0.054	0.997	0.03		1	0.997	0.400	6.00
0.115	3	0.081	0.996	0.04		3	0.209	0.982	0.18	0.260	6	0.013	0.999	0.01
	2	0.324	0.971	0.29		2	0.571	0.906	0.94		5	0.060	0.996	0.04
	1	0.843	0.776	2.24		1	0.966	0.579	4.21		4	0.205	0.980	0.20
0.120	4	0.016	0.999	0.01	0.180	5	0.013	0.999	0.01		3	0.503	0.919	0.81
	3	0.090	0.995	0.05		4	0.066	0.996	0.04		2	0.866	0.732	2.68
	2	0.346	0.967	0.33		3	0.238	0.978	0.22		1	0.998	0.384	6.16
	1	0.861	0.756	2.44		2	0.614	0.890	1.10	0.270	6	0.015	0.999	0.01
0.125	4	0.019	0.999	0.01		1	0.975	0.549	4.51		5	0.070	0.995	0.05
	3	0.100	0.994	0.06	0.190	5	0.016	0.999	0.01		4	0.228	0.976	0.24
	2	0.369	0.962	0.38		4	0.078	0.995	0.05		3	0.537	0.908	0.92
	1	0.878	0.737	2.63		3	0.269	0.973	0.27		2	0.886	0.712	2.88
0.130	4	0.022	0.999	0.01		2	0.654	0.873	1.27		1	0.999	0.370	6.30
	3	0.110	0.994	0.06		1	0.982	0.522	4.78	0.280	6	0.018	0.999	0.01
	2	0.392	0.958	0.42	0.200	5	0.020	0.999	0.01		5	0.081	0.994	0.06
	1	0.893	0.718	2.82		4	0.092	0.994	0.06		4	0.252	0.972	0.28
0.135	4	0.025	0.999	0.01		3	0.300	0.968	0.32		3	0.571	0.896	1.04
	3	0.121	0.993	0.07		2	0.692	0.854	1.46		2	0.903	0.692	3.08
	2	0.415	0.952	0.48		1	0.987	0.497	5.03		1	0.999	0.357	6.43
	1	0.907	0.699	3.01	0.210	5	0.025	0.999	0.01	0.290	6	0.022	0.999	0.01
0.140	4	0.028	0.999	0.01		4	0.108	0.992	0.08		5	0.093	0.993	0.07
	3	0.132	0.991	0.09		3	0.333	0.961	0.39		4	0.278	0.968	0.32
	2	0.437	0.947	0.53		2	0.728	0.835	1.65		3	0.603	0.884	1.16
	1	0.919	0.680	3.20		1	0.990	0.474	5.26		2	0.918	0.672	3.28

TABLE C-3 (*Continued*)

X	M	D	F	L_q	X	M	D	F	L_q	X	M	D	F	L_q
POPULATION 10, Cont.														
	1	0.999	0.345	6.55		3	0.875	0.728	2.72		6	0.363	0.949	0.51
0.300	6	0.026	0.998	0.02		2	0.991	0.499	5.01		5	0.658	0.867	1.33
	5	0.106	0.991	0.09	0.420	7	0.034	0.993	0.07		4	0.893	0.729	2.71
	4	0.304	0.963	0.37		6	0.130	0.987	0.13		3	0.986	0.555	4.45
	3	0.635	0.872	1.28		5	0.341	0.954	0.46	0.560	8	0.044	0.996	0.04
	2	0.932	0.653	3.47		4	0.646	0.866	1.34		7	0.171	0.982	0.18
	1	0.999	0.333	6.67		3	0.905	0.700	3.00		6	0.413	0.939	0.61
0.310	6	0.031	0.998	0.02		2	0.994	0.476	5.24		5	0.707	0.848	1.52
	5	0.120	0.990	0.10	0.440	7	0.045	0.997	0.03		4	0.917	0.706	2.94
	4	0.331	0.957	0.43		6	0.160	0.984	0.16		3	0.991	0.535	4.65
	3	0.666	0.858	1.42		5	0.392	0.943	0.57	0.580	8	0.057	0.995	0.05
	2	0.943	0.635	3.65		4	0.698	0.845	1.55		7	0.204	0.977	0.23
0.320	6	0.036	0.998	0.02		3	0.928	0.672	3.28		6	0.465	0.927	0.73
	5	0.135	0.988	0.12		2	0.996	0.454	5.46		5	0.753	0.829	1.71
	4	0.359	0.952	0.48	0.460	8	0.011	0.999	0.01		4	0.937	0.684	3.16
	3	0.695	0.845	1.55		7	0.058	0.995	0.05		3	0.994	0.517	4.83
	2	0.952	0.617	3.83		6	0.193	0.979	0.21		9	0.010	0.999	0.01
0.330	6	0.042	0.997	0.03		5	0.445	0.930	0.70		8	0.072	0.994	0.06
	5	0.151	0.986	0.14		4	0.747	0.822	1.78		7	0.242	0.972	0.28
	4	0.387	0.945	0.55		3	0.947	0.646	3.54	0.600	6	0.518	0.915	0.85
	3	0.723	0.831	1.69		2	0.998	0.435	5.65		5	0.795	0.809	1.91
	2	0.961	0.600	4.00	0.480	8	0.015	0.999	0.01		4	0.953	0.663	3.37
0.340	7	0.010	0.999	0.01		7	0.074	0.994	0.06		3	0.996	0.500	5.00
	6	0.049	0.997	0.03		6	0.230	0.973	0.27	0.650	9	0.021	0.999	0.01
	5	0.168	0.983	0.17		5	0.499	0.916	0.84		8	0.123	0.988	0.12
	4	0.416	0.938	0.62		4	0.791	0.799	2.01		7	0.353	0.954	0.46
	3	0.750	0.816	1.84		3	0.961	0.621	3.79		6	0.651	0.878	1.22
	2	0.968	0.584	4.16		2	0.998	0.417	5.83		5	0.882	0.759	2.41
0.360	7	0.014	0.999	0.01	0.500	8	0.020	0.999	0.01		4	0.980	0.614	3.86
	6	0.064	0.995	0.05		7	0.093	0.992	0.08		3	0.999	0.461	5.39
	5	0.205	0.978	0.22		6	0.271	0.966	0.34	0.700	9	0.040	0.997	0.03
	4	0.474	0.923	0.77		5	0.553	0.901	0.99		8	0.200	0.979	0.21
	3	0.798	0.787	2.13		4	0.830	0.775	2.25		7	0.484	0.929	0.71
	2	0.978	0.553	4.47		3	0.972	0.598	4.02		6	0.772	0.836	1.64
0.380	7	0.019	0.999	0.01		2	0.999	0.400	6.00		5	0.940	0.711	2.89
	6	0.083	0.993	0.07	0.520	8	0.026	0.998	0.02		4	0.992	0.571	4.29
	5	0.247	0.971	0.29		7	0.115	0.989	0.11	0.750	9	0.075	0.994	0.06
	4	0.533	0.906	0.94		6	0.316	0.958	0.42		8	0.307	0.965	0.35
	3	0.840	0.758	2.42		5	0.606	0.884	1.16		7	0.626	0.897	1.03
	2	0.986	0.525	4.75		4	0.864	0.752	2.48		6	0.870	0.792	2.08
0.400	7	0.026	0.998	0.02		3	0.980	0.575	4.25		5	0.975	0.666	3.34
	6	0.105	0.991	0.09		2	0.999	0.385	6.15		4	0.998	0.533	4.67
	5	0.292	0.963	0.37	0.540	8	0.034	0.997	0.03	0.800	9	0.134	0.988	0.12
	4	0.591	0.887	1.13		7	0.141	0.986	0.14		8	0.446	0.944	0.56

TABLE C-3 (*Continued*)

X	M	D	F	L_q	X	M	D	F	L_q	X	M	D	F	L_q
POPULATION 10, Cont.														
	7	0.763	0.859	1.41		1	0.484	0.978	0.44	0.060	4	0.026	0.999	0.02
	6	0.939	0.747	2.53	0.028	2	0.108	0.998	0.04		3	0.115	0.997	0.06
	5	0.991	0.625	3.75		1	0.519	0.973	0.54		2	0.392	0.978	0.44
	4	0.999	0.500	5.00	0.030	2	0.122	0.998	0.04		1	0.922	0.785	4.30
0.850	9	0.232	0.979	0.21		1	0.553	0.968	0.64	0.062	4	0.029	0.999	0.02
	8	0.611	0.916	0.84	0.032	2	0.137	0.997	0.06		3	0.124	0.996	0.08
	7	0.879	0.818	1.82		1	0.587	0.962	0.76		2	0.413	0.975	0.50
	6	0.978	0.705	2.95	0.034	2	0.152	0.996	0.08		1	0.934	0.768	4.64
	5	0.998	0.588	4.12		1	0.620	0.955	0.90	0.064	4	0.032	0.999	0.02
0.900	9	0.387	0.963	0.37	0.036	2	0.168	0.996	0.08		3	0.134	0.996	0.08
	8	0.785	0.881	1.19		1	0.651	0.947	1.06		2	0.433	0.972	0.56
	7	0.957	0.777	2.23	0.038	3	0.036	0.999	0.02		1	0.944	0.751	4.98
	6	0.995	0.667	3.33		2	0.185	0.995	0.10	0.066	4	0.036	0.999	0.02
0.950	9	0.630	0.938	0.62		1	0.682	0.938	1.24		3	0.144	0.995	0.10
	8	0.934	0.841	1.59	0.040	3	0.041	0.999	0.02		2	0.454	0.969	0.62
	7	0.994	0.737	2.63		2	0.202	0.994	0.12		1	0.953	0.733	5.34
						1	0.712	0.929	1.42	0.068	4	0.039	0.999	0.02
POPULATION 20					0.042	3	0.047	0.999	0.02		3	0.155	0.995	0.10
						2	0.219	0.993	0.14		2	0.474	0.966	0.68
0.005	1	0.095	0.999	0.02		1	0.740	0.918	1.64		1	0.961	0.716	5.68
0.009	1	0.171	0.998	0.04	0.044	3	0.053	0.999	0.02	0.070	4	0.043	0.999	0.02
0.011	1	0.208	0.997	0.06		2	0.237	0.992	0.16		3	0.165	0.994	0.12
0.013	1	0.246	0.996	0.08		1	0.767	0.906	1.88		2	0.495	0.962	0.76
0.014	1	0.265	0.995	0.10	0.046	3	0.059	0.999	0.02		1	0.967	0.699	6.02
0.015	1	0.283	0.994	0.12		2	0.255	0.991	0.18	0.075	4	0.054	0.999	0.02
0.016	1	0.302	0.993	0.14		1	0.792	0.894	2.12		3	0.194	0.992	0.16
0.017	1	0.321	0.992	0.16	0.048	3	0.066	0.999	0.02		2	0.545	0.953	0.94
0.018	2	0.048	0.999	0.02		2	0.274	0.989	0.22		1	0.980	0.659	6.82
	1	0.339	0.991	0.18		1	0.815	0.881	2.38	0.080	4	0.066	0.998	0.04
0.019	2	0.053	0.999	0.02	0.050	3	0.073	0.998	0.04		3	0.225	0.990	0.20
	1	0.358	0.990	0.20		2	0.293	0.988	0.24		2	0.595	0.941	1.18
0.020	2	0.058	0.999	0.02		1	0.837	0.866	2.68		1	0.988	0.621	7.58
	1	0.376	0.989	0.22	0.052	3	0.080	0.998	0.04	0.085	4	0.080	0.997	0.06
0.021	2	0.064	0.999	0.02		2	0.312	0.986	0.28		3	0.257	0.987	0.26
	1	0.394	0.987	0.26		1	0.858	0.851	2.98		2	0.643	0.928	1.44
0.022	2	0.070	0.999	0.02	0.054	3	0.088	0.998	0.04		1	0.993	0.586	8.28
	1	0.412	0.986	0.28		2	0.332	0.984	0.32	0.090	5	0.025	0.999	0.02
0.023	2	0.075	0.999	0.02		1	0.876	0.835	3.30		4	0.095	0.997	0.06
	1	0.431	0.984	0.32	0.056	3	0.097	0.997	0.06		3	0.291	0.984	0.32
0.024	2	0.082	0.999	0.02		2	0.352	0.982	0.36		2	0.689	0.913	1.74
	1	0.449	0.982	0.36		1	0.893	0.819	3.62		1	0.996	0.554	8.92
0.025	2	0.088	0.999	0.02	0.058	3	0.105	0.997	0.06	0.095	5	0.031	0.999	0.02
	1	0.466	0.980	0.40		2	0.372	0.980	0.40		4	0.112	0.996	0.08
0.026	2	0.094	0.998	0.04		1	0.908	0.802	3.96		3	0.326	0.980	0.40

TABLE C-3 (Continued)

POPULATION 20, Cont.

X	M	D	F	L_q	X	M	D	F	L_q	X	M	D	F	L_q
	2	0.733	0.896	2.08		2	0.960	0.703	5.94		6	0.154	0.991	0.18
	1	0.998	0.526	9.48	0.145	6	0.051	0.998	0.04		5	0.345	0.971	0.58
0.100	5	0.038	0.999	0.02		5	0.148	0.993	0.14		4	0.636	0.914	1.72
	4	0.131	0.995	0.10		4	0.358	0.972	0.56		3	0.913	0.768	4.64
	3	0.363	0.975	0.50		3	0.695	0.900	2.00		2	0.998	0.526	9.48
	2	0.773	0.878	2.44		2	0.969	0.682	6.36	0.200	8	0.025	0.999	0.02
	1	0.999	0.500	10.00	0.150	7	0.017	0.999	0.02		7	0.074	0.997	0.06
0.105	5	0.046	0.999	0.02		6	0.059	0.998	0.04		6	0.187	0.988	0.24
	4	0.151	0.993	0.14		5	0.166	0.991	0.18		5	0.397	0.963	0.74
	3	0.400	0.970	0.60		4	0.388	0.968	0.64		4	0.693	0.895	2.10
	2	0.809	0.858	2.84		3	0.728	0.887	2.26		3	0.938	0.736	5.28
	1	0.999	0.476	10.48		2	0.976	0.661	6.78		2	0.999	0.500	10.00
0.110	5	0.055	0.998	0.04	0.155	7	0.021	0.999	0.02	0.210	8	0.033	0.999	0.02
	4	0.172	0.992	0.16		6	0.068	0.997	0.06		7	0.093	0.995	0.10
	3	0.438	0.964	0.72		5	0.185	0.990	0.20		6	0.223	0.985	0.30
	2	0.842	0.837	3.26		4	0.419	0.963	0.74		5	0.451	0.954	0.92
0.115	5	0.065	0.998	0.04		3	0.758	0.874	2.52		4	0.745	0.874	2.52
	4	0.195	0.990	0.20		2	0.982	0.641	7.18		3	0.958	0.706	5.88
	3	0.476	0.958	0.84	0.160	7	0.024	0.999	0.02		2	0.999	0.476	10.48
	2	0.870	0.816	3.68		6	0.077	0.997	0.06	0.220	8	0.043	0.998	0.04
0.120	6	0.022	0.999	0.02		5	0.205	0.988	0.24		7	0.115	0.994	0.12
	5	0.076	0.997	0.06		4	0.450	0.957	0.86		6	0.263	0.980	0.40
	4	0.219	0.988	0.24		3	0.787	0.860	2.80		5	0.505	0.943	1.14
	3	0.514	0.950	1.00		2	0.987	0.622	7.56		4	0.793	0.852	2.96
	2	0.895	0.793	4.14	0.165	7	0.029	0.999	0.02		3	0.971	0.677	6.46
0.125	6	0.026	0.999	0.02		6	0.088	0.996	0.08	0.230	9	0.018	0.999	0.02
	5	0.088	0.997	0.06		5	0.226	0.986	0.28		8	0.054	0.998	0.04
	4	0.245	0.986	0.28		4	0.482	0.951	0.98		7	0.140	0.992	0.16
	3	0.552	0.942	1.16		3	0.813	0.845	3.10		6	0.306	0.975	0.50
	2	0.916	0.770	4.60		2	0.990	0.604	7.92		5	0.560	0.931	1.38
0.130	6	0.031	0.999	0.02	0.170	7	0.033	0.999	0.02		4	0.834	0.828	3.44
	5	0.101	0.996	0.08		6	0.099	0.995	0.10		3	0.981	0.649	7.02
	4	0.271	0.983	0.34		5	0.248	0.983	0.34	0.240	9	0.024	0.999	0.02
	3	0.589	0.933	1.34		4	0.513	0.945	1.10		8	0.068	0.997	0.06
	2	0.934	0.748	5.04		3	0.838	0.830	3.40		7	0.168	0.989	0.22
0.135	6	0.037	0.999	0.02		2	0.993	0.587	8.26		6	0.351	0.969	0.62
	5	0.116	0.995	0.10	0.180	7	0.044	0.998	0.04		5	0.613	0.917	1.66
	4	0.299	0.980	0.40		6	0.125	0.994	0.12		4	0.870	0.804	3.92
	3	0.626	0.923	1.54		5	0.295	0.978	0.44		3	0.988	0.623	7.54
	2	0.948	0.725	5.50		4	0.575	0.930	1.40	0.250	9	0.031	0.999	0.02
0.140	6	0.043	0.998	0.04		3	0.879	0.799	4.02		8	0.085	0.996	0.08
	5	0.131	0.994	0.12		2	0.996	0.555	8.90		7	0.199	0.986	0.28
	4	0.328	0.976	0.48	0.190	8	0.018	0.999	0.02		6	0.398	0.961	0.78
	3	0.661	0.912	1.76		7	0.058	0.998	0.04		5	0.664	0.901	1.98

TABLE C-3 (*Continued*)

POPULATION 20, Cont.

X	M	D	F	L_q	X	M	D	F	L_q	X	M	D	F	L_q
	4	0.900	0.780	4.40		8	0.237	0.981	0.38		6	0.909	0.777	4.46
	3	0.992	0.599	8.02		7	0.438	0.953	0.94		5	0.984	0.656	6.88
0.260	9	0.039	0.998	0.04		6	0.684	0.893	2.14		4	0.999	0.526	9.48
	8	0.104	0.994	0.12		5	0.892	0.788	4.24	0.400	13	0.012	0.999	0.02
	7	0.233	0.983	0.34		4	0.985	0.643	7.14		12	0.037	0.998	0.04
	6	0.446	0.953	0.94	0.320	11	0.018	0.999	0.02		11	0.095	0.994	0.12
	5	0.712	0.884	2.32		10	0.053	0.997	0.06		10	0.205	0.984	0.32
	4	0.924	0.755	4.90		9	0.130	0.992	0.16		9	0.379	0.962	0.76
	3	0.995	0.576	8.48		8	0.272	0.977	0.46		8	0.598	0.918	1.64
0.270	10	0.016	0.999	0.02		7	0.483	0.944	1.12		7	0.807	0.845	3.10
	9	0.049	0.998	0.04		6	0.727	0.878	2.44		6	0.942	0.744	5.12
	8	0.125	0.992	0.16		5	0.915	0.768	4.64		5	0.992	0.624	7.52
	7	0.270	0.978	0.44		4	0.989	0.624	7.52	0.420	13	0.019	0.999	0.02
	6	0.495	0.943	1.14	0.330	11	0.023	0.999	0.02		12	0.055	0.997	0.06
	5	0.757	0.867	2.66		10	0.065	0.997	0.06		11	0.131	0.991	0.18
	4	0.943	0.731	5.38		9	0.154	0.990	0.20		10	0.265	0.977	0.46
	3	0.997	0.555	8.90		8	0.309	0.973	0.54		9	0.458	0.949	1.02
0.280	10	0.021	0.999	0.02		7	0.529	0.935	1.30		8	0.678	0.896	2.08
	9	0.061	0.997	0.06		6	0.766	0.862	2.76		7	0.863	0.815	3.70
	8	0.149	0.990	0.20		5	0.933	0.748	5.04		6	0.965	0.711	5.78
	7	0.309	0.973	0.54		4	0.993	0.605	7.90		5	0.996	0.595	8.10
	6	0.544	0.932	1.36	0.340	11	0.029	0.999	0.02	0.440	13	0.029	0.999	0.02
	5	0.797	0.848	3.04		10	0.079	0.996	0.08		12	0.078	0.995	0.10
	4	0.958	0.708	5.84		9	0.179	0.987	0.26		11	0.175	0.987	0.26
	3	0.998	0.536	9.28		8	0.347	0.967	0.66		10	0.333	0.969	0.62
0.290	10	0.027	0.999	0.02		7	0.573	0.924	1.52		9	0.540	0.933	1.34
	9	0.075	0.996	0.08		6	0.802	0.846	3.08		8	0.751	0.872	2.56
	8	0.176	0.988	0.24		5	0.949	0.729	5.42		7	0.907	0.785	4.30
	7	0.351	0.967	0.66		4	0.995	0.588	8.24		6	0.980	0.680	6.40
	6	0.592	0.920	1.60	0.360	12	0.015	0.999	0.02		5	0.998	0.568	8.64
	5	0.833	0.828	3.44		11	0.045	0.998	0.04	0.460	14	0.014	0.999	0.02
	4	0.970	0.685	6.30		10	0.112	0.993	0.14		13	0.043	0.998	0.04
	3	0.999	0.517	9.66		9	0.237	0.981	0.38		12	0.109	0.993	0.14
0.300	10	0.034	0.998	0.04		8	0.429	0.954	0.92		11	0.228	0.982	0.36
	9	0.091	0.995	0.10		7	0.660	0.901	1.98		10	0.407	0.958	0.84
	8	0.205	0.985	0.30		6	0.863	0.812	3.76		9	0.620	0.914	1.72
	7	0.394	0.961	0.78		5	0.971	0.691	6.18		8	0.815	0.846	3.08
	6	0.639	0.907	1.86		4	0.998	0.555	8.90		7	0.939	0.755	4.90
	5	0.865	0.808	3.84	0.380	12	0.024	0.999	0.02		6	0.989	0.651	6.98
	4	0.978	0.664	6.72		11	0.067	0.996	0.08		5	0.999	0.543	9.14
	3	0.999	0.500	10.00		10	0.154	0.989	0.22	0.480	14	0.022	0.999	0.02
0.310	11	0.014	0.999	0.02		9	0.305	0.973	0.54		13	0.063	0.996	0.08
	10	0.043	0.998	0.04		8	0.513	0.938	1.24		12	0.147	0.990	0.20
	9	0.110	0.993	0.14		7	0.739	0.874	2.52		11	0.289	0.974	0.52

TABLE C-3 (*Continued*)

POPULATION 20, Cont.

X	M	D	F	L_q
	10	0.484	0.944	1.12
	9	0.695	0.893	2.14
	8	0.867	0.819	3.62
	7	0.962	0.726	5.48
	6	0.994	0.625	7.50
0.500	14	0.033	0.998	0.04
	13	0.088	0.995	0.10
	12	0.194	0.985	0.30
	11	0.358	0.965	0.70
	10	0.563	0.929	1.42
	9	0.764	0.870	2.60
	8	0.908	0.791	4.18
	7	0.977	0.698	6.04
	6	0.997	0.600	8.00
0.520	15	0.015	0.999	0.02
	14	0.048	0.997	0.06
	13	0.120	0.992	0.16
	12	0.248	0.979	0.42
	11	0.432	0.954	0.92
	10	0.641	0.911	1.78
	9	0.824	0.846	3.08
	8	0.939	0.764	4.72
	7	0.987	0.672	6.56
	6	0.998	0.577	8.46
0.540	15	0.023	0.999	0.02
	14	0.069	0.996	0.08
	13	0.161	0.988	0.24
	12	0.311	0.972	0.56
	11	0.509	0.941	1.18
	10	0.713	0.891	2.18
	9	0.873	0.821	3.58
	8	0.961	0.738	5.24
	7	0.993	0.648	7.04
	6	0.999	0.556	8.88
0.560	15	0.035	0.998	0.04
	14	0.095	0.994	0.12
	13	0.209	0.984	0.32
	12	0.381	0.963	0.74
	11	0.586	0.926	1.48
	10	0.778	0.869	2.62
	9	0.912	0.796	4.08
	8	0.976	0.713	5.74
	7	0.996	0.625	7.50
0.580	16	0.015	0.999	0.02

X	M	D	F	L_q
	15	0.051	0.997	0.06
	14	0.129	0.991	0.18
	13	0.266	0.978	0.44
	12	0.455	0.952	0.96
	11	0.662	0.908	1.84
	10	0.835	0.847	3.06
	9	0.941	0.772	4.56
	8	0.986	0.689	6.22
	7	0.998	0.603	7.94
0.600	16	0.023	0.999	0.02
	15	0.072	0.996	0.08
	14	0.171	0.988	0.24
	13	0.331	0.970	0.60
	12	0.532	0.938	1.24
	11	0.732	0.889	2.22
	10	0.882	0.824	3.52
	9	0.962	0.748	5.04
	8	0.992	0.666	6.68
	7	0.999	0.583	8.34
0.650	17	0.017	0.999	0.02
	16	0.061	0.997	0.06
	15	0.156	0.989	0.22
	14	0.314	0.973	0.54
	13	0.518	0.943	1.14
	12	0.720	0.898	2.04
	11	0.872	0.837	3.26
	10	0.957	0.767	4.66
	9	0.990	0.692	6.16
	8	0.998	0.615	7.70
0.700	17	0.047	0.998	0.04
	16	0.137	0.991	0.18
	15	0.295	0.976	0.48
	14	0.503	0.948	1.04
	13	0.710	0.905	1.90
	12	0.866	0.849	3.02
	11	0.953	0.783	4.34
	10	0.988	0.714	5.72
	9	0.998	0.643	7.14
0.750	18	0.031	0.999	0.02
	17	0.113	0.993	0.14
	16	0.272	0.980	0.40
	15	0.487	0.954	0.92
	14	0.703	0.913	1.74
	13	0.864	0.859	2.82

X	M	D	F	L_q
	12	0.952	0.798	4.04
	11	0.988	0.733	5.34
	10	0.998	0.667	6.66
0.800	19	0.014	0.999	0.02
	18	0.084	0.996	0.08
	17	0.242	0.984	0.32
	16	0.470	0.959	0.82
	15	0.700	0.920	1.60
	14	0.867	0.869	2.62
	13	0.955	0.811	3.78
	12	0.989	0.750	5.00
	11	0.998	0.687	6.26
0.850	19	0.046	0.998	0.04
	18	0.201	0.988	0.24
	17	0.451	0.965	0.70
	16	0.703	0.927	1.46
	15	0.877	0.878	2.44
	14	0.962	0.823	3.54
	13	0.991	0.765	4.70
	12	0.998	0.706	5.88
0.900	19	0.135	0.994	0.12
	18	0.425	0.972	0.56
	17	0.717	0.935	1.30
	16	0.898	0.886	2.28
	15	0.973	0.833	3.34
	14	0.995	0.778	4.44
	13	0.999	0.722	5.56
0.950	19	0.377	0.981	0.38
	18	0.760	0.943	1.14
	17	0.939	0.894	2.12
	16	0.989	0.842	3.16
	15	0.999	0.789	4.22

POPULATION 30

X	M	D	F	L_q
0.004	1	0.116	0.999	0.03
0.007	1	0.203	0.998	0.06
0.009	1	0.260	0.997	0.09
0.010	1	0.289	0.996	0.12
0.011	1	0.317	0.995	0.15
0.012	1	0.346	0.994	0.18
0.013	1	0.374	0.993	0.21
0.014	2	0.067	0.999	0.03
	1	0.403	0.991	0.27
0.015	2	0.076	0.999	0.03

TABLE C-3 (*Continued*)

POPULATION 30, Cont.

X	M	D	F	L_q	X	M	D	F	L_q	X	M	D	F	L_q
	1	0.431	0.989	0.33	0.042	3	0.138	0.997	0.09	0.064	5	0.038	0.999	0.03
0.016	2	0.085	0.999	0.03		2	0.442	0.980	0.60		4	0.128	0.997	0.09
	1	0.458	0.987	0.39		1	0.963	0.772	6.84		3	0.355	0.984	0.48
0.017	2	0.095	0.999	0.03	0.044	4	0.040	0.999	0.03		2	0.777	0.908	2.76
	1	0.486	0.985	0.45		3	0.154	0.996	0.12	0.066	5	0.043	0.999	0.03
0.018	2	0.105	0.999	0.03		2	0.474	0.977	0.69		4	0.140	0.996	0.12
	1	0.513	0.983	0.51		1	0.974	0.744	7.68		3	0.378	0.982	0.54
0.019	2	0.116	0.999	0.03	0.046	4	0.046	0.999	0.03		2	0.802	0.897	3.09
	1	0.541	0.980	0.60		3	0.171	0.996	0.12	0.068	5	0.048	0.999	0.03
0.020	2	0.127	0.998	0.06		2	0.506	0.972	0.84		4	0.153	0.995	0.15
	1	0.567	0.976	0.72		1	0.982	0.716	8.52		3	0.402	0.979	0.63
0.021	2	0.139	0.998	0.06	0.048	4	0.053	0.999	0.03		2	0.825	0.885	3.45
	1	0.594	0.973	0.81		3	0.189	0.995	0.15	0.070	5	0.054	0.999	0.03
0.022	2	0.151	0.998	0.06		2	0.539	0.968	0.96		4	0.166	0.995	0.15
	1	0.620	0.969	0.93		1	0.988	0.689	9.33		3	0.426	0.976	0.72
0.023	2	0.163	0.997	0.09	0.050	4	0.060	0.999	0.03		2	0.847	0.873	3.81
	1	0.645	0.965	1.05		3	0.208	0.994	0.18	0.075	5	0.069	0.998	0.06
0.024	2	0.175	0.997	0.09		2	0.571	0.963	1.11		4	0.201	0.993	0.21
	1	0.670	0.960	1.20		1	0.992	0.663	10.11		3	0.486	0.969	0.93
0.025	2	0.188	0.996	0.12	0.052	4	0.068	0.999	0.03		2	0.893	0.840	4.80
	1	0.694	0.954	1.38		3	0.227	0.993	0.21	0.080	6	0.027	0.999	0.03
0.026	2	0.201	0.996	0.12		2	0.603	0.957	1.29		5	0.088	0.998	0.06
	1	0.718	0.948	1.56		1	0.995	0.639	10.83		4	0.240	0.990	0.30
0.028	3	0.051	0.999	0.03	0.054	4	0.077	0.998	0.06		3	0.547	0.959	1.23
	2	0.229	0.995	0.15		3	0.247	0.992	0.24		2	0.929	0.805	5.85
	1	0.763	0.935	1.95		2	0.634	0.951	1.47	0.085	6	0.036	0.999	0.03
0.030	3	0.060	0.999	0.03		1	0.997	0.616	11.52		5	0.108	0.997	0.09
	2	0.257	0.994	0.18	0.056	4	0.086	0.998	0.06		4	0.282	0.987	0.39
	1	0.805	0.918	2.46		3	0.267	0.991	0.27		3	0.607	0.948	1.56
0.032	3	0.071	0.999	0.03		2	0.665	0.944	1.68		2	0.955	0.768	6.96
	2	0.286	0.992	0.24		1	0.998	0.595	12.15	0.090	6	0.046	0.999	0.03
	1	0.843	0.899	3.03	0.058	4	0.096	0.998	0.06		5	0.132	0.996	0.12
0.034	3	0.083	0.999	0.03		3	0.288	0.989	0.33		4	0.326	0.984	0.48
	2	0.316	0.990	0.30		2	0.695	0.936	1.92		3	0.665	0.934	1.98
	1	0.876	0.877	3.69		1	0.999	0.574	12.78		2	0.972	0.732	8.04
0.036	3	0.095	0.998	0.06	0.060	5	0.030	0.999	0.03	0.095	6	0.057	0.999	0.03
	2	0.347	0.988	0.36		4	0.106	0.997	0.09		5	0.158	0.994	0.18
	1	0.905	0.853	4.41		3	0.310	0.987	0.39		4	0.372	0.979	0.63
0.038	3	0.109	0.998	0.06		2	0.723	0.927	2.19		3	0.720	0.918	2.46
	2	0.378	0.986	0.42		1	0.999	0.555	13.35		2	0.984	0.697	9.09
	1	0.929	0.827	5.19	0.062	5	0.034	0.999	0.03	0.100	6	0.071	0.998	0.06
0.040	3	0.123	0.997	0.09		4	0.117	0.997	0.09		5	0.187	0.993	0.21
	2	0.410	0.983	0.51		3	0.332	0.986	0.42		4	0.421	0.973	0.81
	1	0.948	0.800	6.00		2	0.751	0.918	2.46		3	0.771	0.899	3.03

TABLE C-3 (*Continued*)

POPULATION 30, Cont.

X	M	D	F	L_q	X	M	D	F	L_q	X	M	D	F	L_q
	2	0.991	0.664	10.08		7	0.115	0.996	0.12		5	0.739	0.901	2.97
0.105	7	0.030	0.999	0.03		6	0.256	0.987	0.39		4	0.946	0.773	6.81
	6	0.087	0.997	0.09		5	0.494	0.960	1.20		3	0.998	0.588	12.36
	5	0.219	0.991	0.27		4	0.793	0.884	3.48	0.180	10	0.028	0.999	0.03
	4	0.470	0.967	0.99		3	0.979	0.710	8.70		9	0.070	0.997	0.09
	3	0.816	0.879	3.63	0.145	8	0.055	0.998	0.06		8	0.158	0.993	0.21
	2	0.995	0.634	10.98		7	0.134	0.995	0.15		7	0.313	0.980	0.60
0.110	7	0.038	0.999	0.03		6	0.288	0.984	0.48		6	0.546	0.948	1.56
	6	0.105	0.997	0.09		5	0.537	0.952	1.44		5	0.806	0.874	3.78
	5	0.253	0.988	0.36		4	0.828	0.867	3.99		4	0.969	0.735	7.95
	4	0.520	0.959	1.23		3	0.986	0.687	9.39		3	0.999	0.555	13.35
	3	0.856	0.857	4.29	0.150	9	0.024	0.999	0.03	0.190	10	0.039	0.999	0.03
	2	0.997	0.605	11.85		8	0.065	0.998	0.06		9	0.094	0.996	0.12
0.115	7	0.047	0.999	0.03		7	0.155	0.993	0.21		8	0.200	0.990	0.30
	6	0.125	0.996	0.12		6	0.322	0.980	0.60		7	0.378	0.973	0.81
	5	0.289	0.985	0.45		5	0.580	0.944	1.68		6	0.621	0.932	2.04
	4	0.570	0.950	1.50		4	0.860	0.849	4.53		5	0.862	0.845	4.65
	3	0.890	0.833	5.01		3	0.991	0.665	10.05		4	0.983	0.699	9.03
	2	0.998	0.579	12.63	0.155	9	0.029	0.999	0.03	0.200	11	0.021	0.999	0.03
0.120	7	0.057	0.998	0.06		8	0.077	0.997	0.09		10	0.054	0.998	0.06
	6	0.147	0.994	0.18		7	0.177	0.992	0.24		9	0.123	0.995	0.15
	5	0.327	0.981	0.57		6	0.357	0.976	0.72		8	0.249	0.985	0.45
	4	0.619	0.939	1.83		5	0.622	0.935	1.95		7	0.446	0.963	1.11
	3	0.918	0.808	5.76		4	0.887	0.830	5.10		6	0.693	0.913	2.61
	2	0.999	0.555	13.35		3	0.994	0.644	10.68		5	0.905	0.814	5.58
0.125	8	0.024	0.999	0.03	0.160	9	0.036	0.999	0.03		4	0.991	0.665	10.05
	7	0.069	0.998	0.06		8	0.090	0.997	0.09	0.210	11	0.030	0.999	0.03
	6	0.171	0.993	0.21		7	0.201	0.990	0.30		10	0.073	0.997	0.09
	5	0.367	0.977	0.69		6	0.394	0.972	0.84		9	0.157	0.992	0.24
	4	0.666	0.927	2.19		5	0.663	0.924	2.28		8	0.303	0.980	0.60
	3	0.940	0.783	6.51		4	0.910	0.811	5.67		7	0.515	0.952	1.44
0.130	8	0.030	0.999	0.03		3	0.996	0.624	11.28		6	0.758	0.892	3.24
	7	0.083	0.997	0.09	0.165	9	0.043	0.999	0.03		5	0.938	0.782	6.54
	6	0.197	0.991	0.27		8	0.105	0.996	0.12		4	0.995	0.634	10.98
	5	0.409	0.972	0.84		7	0.227	0.988	0.36	0.220	11	0.041	0.999	0.03
	4	0.712	0.914	2.58		6	0.431	0.967	0.99		10	0.095	0.996	0.12
	3	0.957	0.758	7.26		5	0.702	0.913	2.61		9	0.197	0.989	0.33
0.135	8	0.037	0.999	0.03		4	0.930	0.792	6.24		8	0.361	0.974	0.78
	7	0.098	0.997	0.09		3	0.997	0.606	11.82		7	0.585	0.938	1.86
	6	0.226	0.989	0.33	0.170	10	0.019	0.999	0.03		6	0.816	0.868	3.96
	5	0.451	0.966	1.02		9	0.051	0.998	0.06		5	0.961	0.751	7.47
	4	0.754	0.899	3.03		8	0.121	0.995	0.15		4	0.998	0.606	11.82
	3	0.970	0.734	7.98		7	0.254	0.986	0.42	0.230	12	0.023	0.999	0.03
0.140	8	0.045	0.999	0.03		6	0.469	0.961	1.17		11	0.056	0.998	0.06

TABLE C-3 (*Continued*)

X	M	D	F	L_q	X	M	D	F	L_q	X	M	D	F	L_q
POPULATION 30, Cont.														
	10	0.123	0.994	0.18		13	0.042	0.998	0.06		9	0.748	0.893	3.21
	9	0.242	0.985	0.45		12	0.093	0.996	0.12		8	0.901	0.820	5.40
	8	0.423	0.965	1.05		11	0.185	0.989	0.33		7	0.977	0.727	8.19
	7	0.652	0.923	2.31		10	0.329	0.976	0.72		6	0.997	0.625	11.25
	6	0.864	0.842	4.74		9	0.522	0.949	1.53	0.330	15	0.030	0.999	0.03
	5	0.976	0.721	8.37		8	0.733	0.898	3.06		14	0.068	0.997	0.09
	4	0.999	0.580	12.60		7	0.901	0.818	5.46		13	0.139	0.993	0.21
0.240	12	0.031	0.999	0.03		6	0.981	0.712	8.64		12	0.253	0.983	0.51
	11	0.074	0.997	0.09		5	0.999	0.595	12.15		11	0.414	0.965	1.05
	10	0.155	0.992	0.24	0.290	14	0.023	0.999	0.03		10	0.608	0.931	2.07
	9	0.291	0.981	0.57		13	0.055	0.998	0.06		9	0.795	0.876	3.72
	8	0.487	0.955	1.35		12	0.117	0.994	0.18		8	0.927	0.799	6.03
	7	0.715	0.905	2.85		11	0.223	0.986	0.42		7	0.985	0.706	8.82
	6	0.902	0.816	5.52		10	0.382	0.969	0.93		6	0.999	0.606	11.82
	5	0.986	0.693	9.21		9	0.582	0.937	1.89	0.340	16	0.016	0.999	0.03
	4	0.999	0.556	13.32		8	0.785	0.880	3.60		15	0.040	0.998	0.06
0.250	13	0.017	0.999	0.03		7	0.929	0.795	6.15		14	0.086	0.996	0.12
	12	0.042	0.998	0.06		6	0.988	0.688	9.36		13	0.169	0.990	0.30
	11	0.095	0.996	0.12		5	0.999	0.575	12.75		12	0.296	0.979	0.63
	10	0.192	0.989	0.33	0.300	14	0.031	0.999	0.03		11	0.468	0.957	1.29
	9	0.345	0.975	0.75		13	0.071	0.997	0.09		10	0.663	0.918	2.46
	8	0.552	0.944	1.68		12	0.145	0.992	0.24		9	0.836	0.858	4.26
	7	0.773	0.885	3.45		11	0.266	0.982	0.54		8	0.947	0.778	6.66
	6	0.932	0.789	6.33		10	0.437	0.962	1.14		7	0.990	0.685	9.45
	5	0.992	0.666	10.02		9	0.641	0.924	2.28		6	0.999	0.588	12.36
0.260	13	0.023	0.999	0.03		8	0.830	0.861	4.17	0.360	16	0.029	0.999	0.03
	12	0.056	0.998	0.06		7	0.950	0.771	6.87		15	0.065	0.997	0.09
	11	0.121	0.994	0.18		6	0.993	0.666	10.02		14	0.132	0.993	0.21
	10	0.233	0.986	0.42	0.310	15	0.017	0.999	0.03		13	0.240	0.984	0.48
	9	0.402	0.967	0.99		14	0.041	0.998	0.06		12	0.392	0.967	0.99
	8	0.616	0.930	2.10		13	0.090	0.996	0.12		11	0.578	0.937	1.89
	7	0.823	0.864	4.08		12	0.177	0.990	0.30		10	0.762	0.889	3.33
	6	0.954	0.763	7.11		11	0.312	0.977	0.69		9	0.902	0.821	5.37
	5	0.995	0.641	10.77		10	0.494	0.953	1.41		8	0.974	0.738	7.86
0.270	13	0.032	0.999	0.03		9	0.697	0.909	2.73		7	0.996	0.648	10.56
	12	0.073	0.997	0.09		8	0.869	0.840	4.80	0.380	17	0.020	0.999	0.03
	11	0.151	0.992	0.24		7	0.966	0.749	7.53		16	0.048	0.998	0.06
	10	0.279	0.981	0.57		6	0.996	0.645	10.65		15	0.101	0.995	0.15
	9	0.462	0.959	1.23	0.320	15	0.023	0.999	0.03		14	0.191	0.988	0.36
	8	0.676	0.915	2.55		14	0.054	0.998	0.06		13	0.324	0.975	0.75
	7	0.866	0.841	4.77		13	0.113	0.994	0.18		12	0.496	0.952	1.44
	6	0.970	0.737	7.89		12	0.213	0.987	0.39		11	0.682	0.914	2.58
	5	0.997	0.617	11.49		11	0.362	0.971	0.87		10	0.843	0.857	4.29
0.280	14	0.017	0.999	0.03		10	0.552	0.943	1.71		9	0.945	0.784	6.48

TABLE C-3 (*Continued*)

X	M	D	F	L_q	X	M	D	F	L_q	X	M	D	F	L_q
POPULATION 30, Cont.														
	8	0.988	0.701	8.97		10	0.985	0.724	8.28		14	0.874	0.854	4.38
	7	0.999	0.614	11.58		9	0.997	0.652	10.44		13	0.949	0.799	6.03
0.400	17	0.035	0.999	0.03	0.480	20	0.019	0.999	0.03		12	0.985	0.740	7.80
	16	0.076	0.996	0.12		19	0.046	0.998	0.06		11	0.997	0.679	9.63
	15	0.150	0.992	0.24		18	0.098	0.995	0.15		10	0.999	0.617	11.49
	14	0.264	0.982	0.54		17	0.184	0.989	0.33	0.560	22	0.023	0.999	0.03
	13	0.420	0.964	1.08		16	0.310	0.977	0.69		21	0.056	0.997	0.09
	12	0.601	0.933	2.01		15	0.470	0.957	1.29		20	0.117	0.994	0.18
	11	0.775	0.886	3.42		14	0.643	0.926	2.22		19	0.215	0.986	0.42
	10	0.903	0.823	5.31		13	0.799	0.881	3.57		18	0.352	0.973	0.81
	9	0.972	0.748	7.56		12	0.910	0.826	5.22		17	0.516	0.952	1.44
	8	0.995	0.666	10.02		11	0.970	0.762	7.14		16	0.683	0.920	2.40
0.420	18	0.024	0.999	0.03		10	0.993	0.694	9.18		15	0.824	0.878	3.66
	17	0.056	0.997	0.09		9	0.999	0.625	11.25		14	0.920	0.828	5.16
	16	0.116	0.994	0.18	0.500	20	0.032	0.999	0.03		13	0.972	0.772	6.84
	15	0.212	0.986	0.42		19	0.072	0.997	0.09		12	0.993	0.714	8.58
	14	0.350	0.972	0.84		18	0.143	0.992	0.24		11	0.999	0.655	10.35
	13	0.521	0.948	1.56		17	0.252	0.983	0.51	0.580	23	0.014	0.999	0.03
	12	0.700	0.910	2.70		16	0.398	0.967	0.99		22	0.038	0.998	0.06
	11	0.850	0.856	4.32		15	0.568	0.941	1.77		21	0.085	0.996	0.12
	10	0.945	0.789	6.33		14	0.733	0.904	2.88		20	0.167	0.990	0.30
	9	0.986	0.713	8.61		13	0.865	0.854	4.38		19	0.288	0.980	0.60
	8	0.998	0.635	10.95		12	0.947	0.796	6.12		18	0.443	0.963	1.11
0.440	19	0.017	0.999	0.03		11	0.985	0.732	8.04		17	0.612	0.936	1.92
	18	0.041	0.998	0.06		10	0.997	0.667	9.99		16	0.766	0.899	3.03
	17	0.087	0.996	0.12	0.520	21	0.021	0.999	0.03		15	0.883	0.854	4.38
	16	0.167	0.990	0.30		20	0.051	0.998	0.06		14	0.953	0.802	5.94
	15	0.288	0.979	0.63		19	0.108	0.994	0.18		13	0.985	0.746	7.62
	14	0.446	0.960	1.20		18	0.200	0.988	0.36		12	0.997	0.690	9.30
	13	0.623	0.929	2.13		17	0.331	0.975	0.75		11	0.999	0.632	11.04
	12	0.787	0.883	3.51		16	0.493	0.954	1.38	0.600	23	0.024	0.999	0.03
	11	0.906	0.824	5.28		15	0.633	0.923	2.31		22	0.059	0.997	0.09
	10	0.970	0.755	7.35		14	0.811	0.880	3.60		21	0.125	0.993	0.21
	9	0.994	0.681	9.57		13	0.915	0.827	5.19		20	0.230	0.986	0.42
	8	0.999	0.606	11.82		12	0.971	0.767	6.99		19	0.372	0.972	0.84
0.460	19	0.028	0.999	0.03		11	0.993	0.705	8.85		18	0.538	0.949	1.53
	18	0.064	0.997	0.09		10	0.999	0.641	10.77		17	0.702	0.918	2.46
	17	0.129	0.993	0.21	0.540	21	0.035	0.999	0.03		16	0.837	0.877	3.69
	16	0.232	0.985	0.45		20	0.079	0.996	0.12		15	0.927	0.829	5.13
	15	0.375	0.970	0.90		19	0.155	0.991	0.27		14	0.974	0.776	6.72
	14	0.545	0.944	1.68		18	0.270	0.981	0.57		13	0.993	0.722	8.34
	13	0.717	0.906	2.82		17	0.421	0.965	1.05		12	0.999	0.667	9.99
	12	0.857	0.855	4.35		16	0.590	0.938	1.86	0.650	24	0.031	0.999	0.03
	11	0.945	0.793	6.21		15	0.750	0.901	2.97		23	0.076	0.996	0.12

TABLE C-3 (*Continued*)

X	M	D	F	L_q	X	M	D	F	L_q	X	M	D	F	L_q
POPULATION 30, Cont.														
	22	0.158	0.991	0.27		24	0.240	0.986	0.42		24	0.760	0.932	2.04
	21	0.281	0.982	0.54		23	0.405	0.972	0.84		23	0.888	0.889	3.03
	20	0.439	0.965	1.05		22	0.587	0.950	1.50		22	0.957	0.862	4.14
	19	0.610	0.940	1.80		21	0.752	0.920	2.40		21	0.987	0.823	5.31
	18	0.764	0.906	2.82		20	0.873	0.883	3.51		20	0.997	0.784	6.48
	17	0.879	0.865	4.05		19	0.946	0.842	4.74		19	0.999	0.745	7.65
	16	0.949	0.818	5.46		18	0.981	0.799	6.03	0.900	29	0.047	0.999	0.03
	15	0.983	0.769	6.93		17	0.995	0.755	7.35		28	0.200	0.992	0.24
	14	0.996	0.718	8.46		16	0.999	0.711	8.67		27	0.441	0.977	0.69
	13	0.999	0.667	9.99	0.800	27	0.053	0.998	0.06		26	0.683	0.953	1.41
0.700	25	0.039	0.998	0.06		26	0.143	0.993	0.21		25	0.856	0.923	2.31
	24	0.096	0.995	0.15		25	0.292	0.984	0.48		24	0.947	0.888	3.36
	23	0.196	0.989	0.33		24	0.481	0.966	1.02		23	0.985	0.852	4.44
	22	0.339	0.977	0.69		23	0.670	0.941	1.77		22	0.996	0.815	5.55
	21	0.511	0.958	1.26		22	0.822	0.909	2.73		21	0.999	0.778	6.66
	20	0.681	0.930	2.10		21	0.919	0.872	3.84	0.950	29	0.226	0.993	0.21
	19	0.821	0.894	3.18		20	0.970	0.832	5.04		28	0.574	0.973	0.81
	18	0.916	0.853	4.41		19	0.991	0.791	6.27		27	0.831	0.945	1.65
	17	0.967	0.808	5.76		18	0.998	0.750	7.50		26	0.951	0.912	2.64
	16	0.990	0.762	7.14	0.850	28	0.055	0.998	0.06		25	0.989	0.877	3.69
	15	0.997	0.714	8.58		27	0.171	0.993	0.21		24	0.998	0.842	4.74
0.750	26	0.046	0.998	0.06		26	0.356	0.981	0.57					
	25	0.118	0.994	0.18		25	0.571	0.960	1.20					

TABLE C-4 Table of Random Digits

03689	33090	43465	96789	56688	32389	77206	06534	10558	14478
43367	46409	44751	73410	35138	24910	70748	57336	56043	68550
45357	52080	62670	73877	20604	40408	98060	96733	65094	80335
62683	03171	77109	92515	78041	27590	42651	00254	73179	10159
04841	40918	69047	68986	08150	87984	08887	76083	37702	28523
85963	06992	65321	43521	46393	40491	06028	43865	58190	28142
03720	78942	61990	90812	98452	74098	69738	83272	39212	42817
10159	85560	35619	58248	65498	77977	02896	45198	10655	13973
80162	35686	57877	19552	63931	44171	40879	94532	17828	31848
74388	92906	65829	24572	79417	38460	96294	79201	47755	90980
12660	09571	29743	45447	64063	46295	44191	53957	62393	42229
81852	60620	87757	72165	23875	87844	84038	04994	93466	27418
03068	61317	65305	64944	27319	55263	84514	38374	11657	67723
29623	58530	17274	16908	39253	37595	57497	74780	88624	93333
30520	50588	51231	83816	01075	33098	81308	59036	49152	86262
93694	02984	91350	33929	41724	32403	42566	14232	55085	65628
86736	40641	37958	25415	19922	65966	98044	39583	26828	50919
28141	15630	37675	52545	24813	22075	05142	15374	84533	12933
79804	05165	21620	98400	55290	71877	60052	46320	79055	45913
63763	49985	88853	70681	52762	17670	62337	12199	44123	37993
49618	47068	63331	62675	51788	58283	04295	72904	05378	98085
26502	68980	26545	14204	34304	50284	47730	57299	73966	02566
13549	86048	27912	56733	14987	09850	72817	85168	09538	92347
89221	78076	40306	34045	52557	52383	67796	41382	50490	30117
97809	34056	76778	60417	05153	83827	67369	08602	56163	28793
65668	44694	34151	51741	11484	13226	49516	17391	39956	34839
53653	59804	59051	95074	38307	99546	32962	26962	86252	50704
34922	95041	17398	32789	26860	55536	82415	82911	42208	62725
74880	65198	61357	90209	71543	71114	94868	05645	44154	72254
66036	48794	30021	92601	21615	16952	18433	44903	51322	90379
39044	99503	11442	81344	57068	74662	90382	59433	48440	38146
87756	71151	68543	08358	10183	06432	97482	90301	76114	83778
47117	45575	29524	02522	08041	70698	80260	73588	86415	72523
71572	02109	96722	21684	64331	71644	18933	32801	11644	12364
35609	58072	63209	48429	53108	59173	55337	22445	85940	43707
73703	70069	74981	12197	48426	77365	26769	65078	27849	41311
42979	88161	56531	46443	47148	42773	18601	38532	22594	12395
12279	42308	00380	17181	38757	09071	89804	15232	99007	39495